Managerial Economics

H. Craig Petersen
Utah State University

W. Cris Lewis
Utah State University

MANAGERIAL ECONOMICS

MACMILLAN PUBLISHING COMPANY
New York

COLLIER MACMILLAN PUBLISHERS
London

Macmillan Publishing Company
866 Third Avenue, New York, New York 10022

Collier Macmillan Canada, Inc.

Library of Congress Cataloging in Publication Data

Petersen, Harold Craig.
  Managerial economics.

  Includes index.
  1. Managerial economics.   I. Lewis, W. Cris.
II. Title.
HD30.22.P45 1986   338.5′024′658   85-5095
ISBN 0-02-394850-7

Printing: 1 2 3 4 5 6 7 8   Year: 6 7 8 9 0 1 2 3

ISBN 0-02-394850-7

Although managerial economics is an interesting and fundamental part of the business curriculum, it can be a very difficult course for some students. Mastering the subject requires a good understanding of how basic concepts of economics can be combined with tools of mathematics and statistics to analyze and make decisions involving scarce resources. But, in the process of studying managerial economics, students can get mired in the minutiae of data, graphs, equations, and definitions. One result is that they may fail to fully appreciate the value of economic principles as tools for decision making.

Part of the difficulty in teaching managerial economics can be explained by the limitations of existing textbooks. Some texts devote so much time to manipulating data, deriving equations, and explaining the subtleties of statistics that they leave students without a good grasp of basic economic principles. Others provide extensive discussions of these principles but are almost totally devoid of good examples which allow the student to see how these concepts can be applied.

Managerial Economics by Petersen and Lewis is written with two primary objectives in mind. First, it is intended that students will receive a complete and rigorous introduction to basic principles of microeconomics. Albert Einstein once commented that things should be made as simple as possible, but not more so. In this text we have tried to follow this counsel. Esoteric and peripheral points have been avoided in order to concentrate on fundamental economic principles. However, difficult concepts have been included when it was determined that they could provide important insights for decision making. Care has been taken to assure that the exposition of these concepts is as clear and uncomplicated as possible.

Our second objective in writing *Managerial Economics* is to demonstrate how applications of economic theory can improve decision making. This goal is realized by use of a concept/example format throughout the book. The approach involves first introducing basic concepts of managerial economics and then using these principles to analyze decisions faced by managers. In addition, numerous case studies and solved problems have been included in each chapter to illustrate important principles and to stimulate interest in related topics. The use of the concept/example format makes the text more readable and facilitates learning by allowing students to see how economic principles can be used in decision making.

A course in Managerial Economics taught at one university may be quite different than that offered at another school. Although it is impossible to provide a text that will meet the preferences of all instructors, *Managerial Economics* is designed to be suitable for many uses. For an undergraduate course, coverage of the first fourteen chapters provides a good understanding of basic economic principles and their application. For an MBA curriculum or a more comprehensive undergraduate course, additional topics can be selected from the remaining six chapters as time permits.

One of the most difficult choices we faced in writing *Managerial Economics* involved the level of mathematics to be used in the text. Some course instructors use calculus, while others prefer a graphical and algebraic presentation. For the most part, we have opted for the latter approach. However, there are some topics that are more easily understood using calculus. Accordingly, basic calculus is used to discuss selected concepts in some chapters. For those students who have not had calculus, the appendix to Chapter Two provides the necessary background to follow these presentations. For courses with greater emphasis on calculus, there are calculus footnotes and appendices. In addition, many chapters have supplementary problems that are clearly designated as requiring calculus for their solution.

Managerial Economics includes a number of special features to facilitate student learning. Each chapter has key concepts listed at the end of major sections. Together with the chapter outline and summary, these key concepts can aid in the review of material. Case studies interspersed throughout the chapters show how economic tools are relevant for decision makers. Solved problems included in the chapters are designed to provide guidance in working the problems found at the end of each chapter.

A unique feature of the instructional package is the computer software that is available as part of the instructor's manual. The multiple regression, linear programming, time value of money, input/output, benefit-cost, and investment analysis programs included will enable students to manipulate data and solve reasonably complex problems without tedious hand calculations.

We are indebted to those who reviewed the manuscript for *Managerial Economics*. Their incisive comments have changed and, we believe, significantly improved the final product. Specifically, we wish to express thanks to:

Andrew Buck	Kenneth Lyon
Thomas Cate	Michael Magura
Robert Crawford	John McKean
Clifford Dobitz	Louis Noyd
Thomas Edwards	John Peterson
Robert Greer	Michael Vaughan
George Hoffer	

We both appreciate and sympathize with our students who were subjected to the earlier versions of the end-of-chapter problems used in the text. Hopefully, others will benefit from their frustrations as they found the mistakes and ambiguities that always attend the initial versions of such work. We also acknowledge the help of Ruby Vasquez who typed drafts of much of the manuscript. Finally, our sincere thanks to our associates at Macmillan. Because of their efforts, our writing experience has been highly positive. In addition to meeting our requirements as textbook authors, Chip Price, Jack Repcheck, and John Travis at Macmillan have become good friends.

H. C. P.
W. C. L.

SECTION I: GETTING STARTED

Contents

SECTION II: DEMAND

SECTION III: PRODUCTION AND COST

SECTION VI: LIFE IN A MIXED ECONOMY

Managerial Economics

GETTING STARTED

Introduction to Managerial Economics

1

Preview

For most purposes, economics can be divided into two broad categories: microeconomics and macroeconomics. *Macroeconomics* is the study of the economic system as a whole. It includes techniques for determining the level and change in total output, total employment, the consumer price index, and the unemployment rate. Macroeconomics addresses questions about the effect of changes in investment, government spending, and tax-policy on exports, output, employment, and prices. Only aggregate levels of these variables are important. But concealed in the aggregate data are countless changes in the output levels of individual firms, the consumption decisions of individual consumers, and the prices of particular goods and services.

Although macroeconomic issues and policies command most of the attention in newspapers and on television, the microdimensions of the economy also are important and often are of more direct application to the day-to-day problems facing the manager. *Microeconomics* focuses on the behavior of the individual actors on the economic stage: firms and individuals and their interaction in markets.

Managerial economics is best defined as applied microeconomics. That is, managerial economics can be thought of as an application of that part of microeconomics focusing on those topics of greatest interest and importance to managers. These topics include demand, production, cost, pricing, market structure, and government regulation. A strong grasp of the principles that govern the economic behavior of firms and individuals is an important managerial talent.

In general, managerial economics can be used by the goal-oriented manager in two ways. First, given an existing economic environment, the principles of managerial economics provide a framework for evaluating whether resources are being allocated efficiently within a firm. For example, economics can help the manager determine if profit could be increased by reallocating labor from a marketing activity to the production line. Second, given changes in the economic environment such as an increase in the price of output or the development of a new production technology, the managerial economics framework can assist the manager to make the appropriate response. For example, an increase in the price of one input, say labor, may be a signal to substitute capital for labor in the production process.

The tools developed in the following chapters will increase the effectiveness of decision making by expanding and sharpening the analytical framework used by managers to make decisions. As such, managerial economics can increase the value of both the firm and the manager.

This chapter sets the stage for the development of managerial economic skills. The role of economics in decision making is covered first. Then the interrelationships among consumers, firms, and resource owners in a market economy are outlined. Finally, the nature and objective of the firm and the importance of profit as an incentive for firms to respond to consumer demands for output are discussed.

Economics and Decision Making

Where do the principles of microeconomics fit in the arena of managerial decision making? Nobel-prize-winning economist Herbert Simon (1960) identifies three primary activities in decision making:

1. Finding occasions for making decisions.
2. Identifying possible courses of action.
3. Choosing that one course of action that best meets the goal or objective of the firm.

Although economics may contribute to the first two activities, its primary role is in evaluating the implications of alternative courses of action and choosing the best course of action from among those several alternatives

Consider the following example of these activities. Suppose that a firm in the microcomputer industry learns that a major competitor will soon introduce a new desktop computer that is clearly superior to anything on the market. Clearly, this is an occasion for making decisions. Possible courses of action include (1) doing nothing, (2) implementing an entirely new marketing program for the current product line, (3) reducing the cost and price of the company's existing microcomputer, and (4) embarking on a crash program to develop a new microcomputer to compete with the competitor's new models. Each course of action will have an effect on the firm's revenue, costs, and, of course, profits. The evaluation of these effects for each alternative will rely heavily on the tools of managerial economics.

The Circular Flow of Economic Activity

Consider the roles played by individuals and firms in a market economy. Individuals own or control resources that have value to firms because they are necessary inputs in the production process. These resources are broadly classified as labor, capital, and natural resources. Of course, there are many types and grades of each resource. Labor specialties vary from brain surgeons to street sweepers; capital goods range from electronic computers to brooms. Most people have labor resources to sell, and many own capital and/or natural resources that are rented, loaned, or sold to firms to be used as inputs in the production process.

The interaction between individuals and firms occurs in two distinct arenas. First, there is a product market where goods and services are bought and sold. Second, there is a market for factors of production where labor, capital, and natural resources are traded. These interactions are depicted in Figure 1-1, which describes the circular flow of income, output, resources, and factor payments.

First, consider the product market. Individuals demand goods and services to

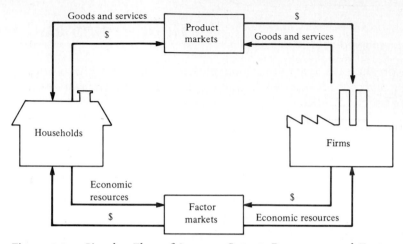

Figure 1-1.　*Circular Flow of Income, Output, Resources, and Factor Payments.*

satisfy their consumption desires.[1] They make these desires known by bidding in the product market for these goods and services. Firms, anxious to earn profits, respond to these demands by supplying goods and services to that market. The firm's production technology and input costs determine the supply conditions, while consumer preferences and income (i.e., the ability to pay) determine the demand conditions. The interaction of supply and demand determines the price and quantity sold. In the product market, purchasing power, usually in the form of money, flows from consumers to firms. At the same time, goods and services flow in the opposite direction—from firms to consumers.

The factor market is shown at the bottom of Figure 1-1. Here the flows are the reverse of those in the product market. Individuals are the suppliers in the factor market. They supply labor services, capital, and natural resources to firms that demand them to produce goods and services. Firms indicate the strength of their desire for these inputs by bidding for them in the market. The flow of money is from firms to individuals, and factors of production flow in the opposite direction. The prices of these productive factors are set in this market.

In the market economy depicted by this circular flow, individuals and firms are highly interdependent. Each participant needs the other participants. All participate willingly because they have something to gain by doing so. Firms earn profit, the consumption demands of individuals are satisfied, and resource owners receive wage, rent, and interest payments. If an individual does not benefit by buying and selling in these markets, he or she is not required to do so. Thus one can be sure that no individual is made worse off by voluntary trade in factor and product markets.

---

[1] It is necessary to distinguish between "wants" and "demand." Many individuals "want" goods and services but cannot afford to buy them. The term "demand" implies that both the desire to have the good and the ability to buy it exist.

KEY CONCEPTS

- The primary decision making role of managerial economics is in evaluating the consequences of alternative courses of an action.
- The interaction of individuals and firms in a market economy can be described as a circular flow of money, goods and services, and resources through product and factor markets.

The Nature of the Firm

In order to earn profits, the firm organizes the factors of production to produce goods and services that will meet the demands of individual consumers and other firms. The concept of the firm plays a central role in the theory and practice of managerial economics. A significant part of this text is focused on production, cost, and the organization of firms in the marketplace. These topics form the basis for what is known in economics as the theory of the firm. An understanding of the reason for the existence of firms, their specific role in the economy, and their objective provides a background for that theory.

The Rationale for the Firm[2]

In a free market economy, the organization and interaction of producers (i.e., firms) and consumers is accomplished through the price system. There is no need for any central direction by government, nor is such central control or planning thought to be desirable. Within the firm, however, transactions and the organization of productive factors generally are accomplished by the central control of one or more managers. For example, workers subject themselves almost completely to management during the work period. Thus there is an apparent dichotomy in the organization of production in a market economy. The price system guides the decentralized interaction among consumers and firms, while central planning and control tend to guide the interaction within firms. Why does not the price system completely guide the production system? That is, why do firms exist in a market economy?

CASE STUDY
ADAM SMITH AND THE INVISIBLE HAND

The 18th century philosopher Adam Smith is regarded as the father of modern economics. He apparently understood clearly how a decentralized market economy would function with little, if any, outside regulation required. In particular,

---

[2] This section draws heavily on the classic 1937 article by R. H. Coase, "The Nature of the Firm."

he saw that by seeking to maximize their own self-interest the individual participants in this economy would achieve socially desirable results. Indeed, the
coordinating mechanism in all of this, the price system, was described by Smith
as an "invisible hand" that guided private decisions in socially beneficial ways.
Smith described this system. In his book *An Inquiry into the Nature and Causes
of the Wealth of Nations.*

> Every individual necessarily labours to render the annual revenue of the society as
> great as he can. He generally, indeed, neither intends to promote the public interest,
> nor knows how much he is promoting it. By preferring the support of domestic to
> that of foreign industry, he intends only his own security; and by directing that
> industry in such a manner as its produce may be of the greatest value, he intends
> only his own gain, and he is in this, as in many other cases, led by an invisible hand
> to promote an end which was no part of his intention. Nor is it always the worse
> for the society that it was no part of it. By pursuing his own interest he frequently
> promotes that of the society more effectually than when he really intends to promote
> it. I have never known much good done by those who affected to trade for the public
> good. It is an affectation, indeed, not very common among merchants, and very few
> words need be employed in dissuading them from it.

Essentially, firms exist as organizations because the total cost of producing
any level of output is lower than if the firm did not exist. There are several reasons
why these costs are lower. First, there is a cost of using the price system to
organize production. The cost of obtaining information on prices and the cost
of negotiating and concluding separate contracts for each step of the production
process would be very burdensome. Firms often hire labor for long periods of
time under agreements that specify only that a wage rate per hour or day will
be paid for the workers doing what they are asked. That is, one general contract
covers what usually will be a large number of transactions between the entrepreneur and workers. The two parties do not have to negotiate a new contract
every time the worker is given a new assignment. The saving of the transactions
costs associated with such negotiations is advantageous to both parties and thus,
both voluntarily seek out such arrangements.

A secondary explanation for the existence of firms is that some government
interference in the marketplace applies to transactions among firms rather than
within firms. Sales taxes, price controls, and rationing usually apply only to
transactions between one firm and another. For example, in some states a construction company may have to pay sales tax on cabinets purchased from an
independent cabinetmaker. By hiring that person, this tax is avoided and the
cost of producing output is reduced. By internalizing some transactions within
the firm that would otherwise be subject to those interferences, production costs
are reduced. Because this is a secondary factor, firms would exist in the absence
of such interference, but it probably contributes to there being more and larger
firms.

Given that production costs are reduced by organizing production factors into
firms, why won't this process continue until there is just one large firm, such as
a giant General Motors or Exxon? There are two reasons. First, the cost of or-

ganizing transactions within the firm tends to rise as the firm gets larger. Logic dictates that the firm will internalize the lowest-cost transactions first and then the higher-cost transactions. At some point, these internal transactions costs will equal the costs of transacting in the market. At that point, the firm will cease to grow. For example, firms often need legal services. Usually, however, these services are not an integral part of the production process but are used sporadically. It would be too costly for many firms to have full-time lawyers whose services would not be needed on a continual basis. So, rather than having a full-time lawyer employed by the firm, legal services are contracted on a "when-needed" basis. The cost of such an arrangement for most firms is lower. In contrast, large firms that have a continual need for legal service frequently have an "in-house" legal staff.

A second factor constraining firm size is that an entrepreneur's organizational skill is limited. Resources within the company may not be efficiently allocated if the firm's size exceeds the manager's ability to control the operation. Stories about the use of highly skilled technicians in unskilled jobs in the Army are indicative of the problem. With several million employees, U.S. military leaders may have difficulty keeping all of them employed efficiently.

Both these reasons for a limit on the size of the firm fall under the heading of what economists have termed "diminishing returns to management." Stated another way, production costs per unit of output will tend to rise as firms grow larger because of limited managerial ability. It should be noted that many large firms recognize the problem of excessive size. As a result, they decentralize by establishing a number of separate divisions or profit centers that act as individual firms.

KEY CONCEPTS

- Firms exist because the costs of production are lower and returns to the owners of labor and capital are higher than if the firm did not exist.
- Limits are imposed on the size of firms because the cost of organizing transactions rises as the firm becomes larger and because managerial ability is limited.

The Objective of the Firm

This book approaches microeconomics from the perspective of efficient management of a business or other organization. To discuss efficient or optimal decision making requires that a goal or objective be established. For the firm, that goal is assumed to be profit maximization. That is, it is assumed that managers consistently make decisions in order to maximize profit. But profit in which period? This year? The next five years? Often, managers are observed making decisions that reduce current year profits in an effort to increase profits in future years. Expenditures for research and development, new capital equipment, and major marketing programs are but a few examples of activities that reduce profits initially but will significantly increase profits in later years.[3]

As both current and future profits are important, it is assumed that the goal is to maximize the present value of all future profits,[4] that is, to maximize the discounted value of all future profits. Formally stated, the goal or objective function for the firm is to

$$\text{maximize: } PV(\pi) = \sum_{t=1}^{\infty} \frac{\pi_t}{(1 + r)^t} \tag{1-1}$$

where π_t is profit in the time period and r is an appropriate discount rate used to reduce future profits to their present value. The Greek letter Σ means that the values for each of the periods are added together.

There is a controversy about management objectives. Advocates of alternative theories of the firm argue that the behavior of real-world managers is not always consistent with the profit-maximization goal. Other objectives are seen as being at least as important as profit maximization. Among the alternative objectives that have been identified are: maximizing total revenue; maximizing employment tenure and departmental budget; maximizing executive salaries; achieving "satisfactory" profit levels; and maximizing market shares subject to a satisfactory profit constraint. Indeed, an entire literature has developed on the subject of "satisficing" rather than "maximizing" management objectives (see, e.g., Cyert and March, 1963, and Simon, 1959).

Some critics of the profit-maximization assumption argue that it is unrealistic because managers must function in an environment characterized by inadequate information and uncertainty about the outcome of any strategy that might be adopted. Economist Fritz Machlup (1946) responded to this criticism by comparing managing a firm to driving a car. When deciding whether to pass another car on a two-lane highway, a driver must consider a variety of conditions. A few of these include the speed of his car, the car that is to be passed, and that of any on-coming vehicles; the road conditions; the existence of any curves or intersections that may be upcoming; and lighting conditions. To analyze the situation thoroughly prior to passing the car ahead might require the assistance of a physicist and several working days.

Clearly, however, the typical driver makes an intuitive evaluation of these conditions in a matter of a few seconds or less and makes a decision. Machlup contends that managers are seeking to maximize profit and simply react intuitively to a set of conditions characterized by incomplete information and uncertainty in the same manner as the automobile driver.

Although some managers may have other goals, most of the criticism leveled at the profit-maximization assumption may be irrelevant. Economics is less in-

---

[3] Some managers who must report profit performance monthly or quarterly claim that the pressure for increased short-term profits may cause them to make decisions that increase these profits at the expense of long-term profit.

[4] Many students will have already studied the concept of present value. For those who have not, the concept is developed more fully in Chapter 2.

terested in how managers really act than in understanding the economic environment in which managers must function and, more important, in developing a framework for predicting managerial responses to important changes in that environment.

To put this concept in perspective, consider two of the many decisions that managers face:

1. What change in output should be made in response to a significant decline in price?
2. What changes in the production process should be made when the price of energy increases relative to the prices of other inputs?

Now, suppose that there are two firms, *A* and *B*, identical except in one respect: the manager of *A* works sixteen hours, seven days a week, whereas the manager of *B* leaves the office shortly after lunch each day to play golf. Because of manager *A*'s commitment to work, it is probable that profits for firm *A* are greater than at firm *B*, but this difference in commitment to work and its effect on profit is not the issue. The fundamental question is: Will the two managers respond the same way to the kind of economic change described above? A rational manager, despite his work habits, ought to respond in predictable ways. Lower prices for output should result in both firms decreasing output. Similarly, higher energy prices should cause both managers to change production techniques in order to use less energy.

In another article, Machlup (1967) argues that it is fruitless to worry about how real-world business managers really behave and what their goals really are. The real question is: If we assume that firms attempt to maximize profit, will the principles of economics derived from that objective function explain the behavior of real-world firms? If the answer is yes, it really does not matter if the assumed goal is not entirely realistic. Most economists agree that the principles of managerial microeconomics do indeed allow accurate prediction of managerial decision making, and that profit maximization provides a useful assumption in that context. Indeed, no general theory has yet proven to predict more accurately than the models based on profit maximization. In this book as well, it will be assumed that the objective of the firm is to maximize profit.

The Concept of Economic Profit

Having assumed the goal of the firm to be profit maximization, it is necessary to define the term *profit*. The conventional notion of profit is relatively straightforward: Profit is defined as revenues minus costs. But the definition of cost is quite different for the economist than for the accountant. Consider an independent businessperson who has an MBA degree and $100,000 invested in a retail store.

There are no other employees. Her income statement for the year as prepared by an accountant is as shown:

Sales:		$90,000
Less: Cost of goods sold		40,000
Gross profit		$50,000
Less: Advertising	$10,000	
Depreciation	10,000	
Utilities	3,000	
Property tax	2,000	
Miscellaneous expenses	5,000	30,000
Net accounting profit		$20,000

This "accounting profit" is what is reported in publications such as the *Wall Street Journal* and in the quarterly and annual financial reports of businesses. It is a meaningful concept as far as it goes—it just does not go far enough.

The economist recognizes other costs, defined as implicit costs. These costs are not reflected in cash outlays by the firm, but are the costs associated with foregone opportunities. Such implicit costs are not included in the accounting statements but should be included in any decision-making framework. There are two major implicit costs in the example above. First, the owner has $100,000 invested in the business. Suppose the best alternative use for this money is a bank account paying a 10 percent interest rate. This riskless investment would return $10,000 annually. Thus $10,000 should be considered as the *implicit* or *opportunity cost* of having the $100,000 invested in the retail store.

The second implicit cost includes the manager's time and talent. The annual wage return on an MBA degree from a reasonably good business school may be $35,000 per year. This is the implicit cost of managing this business rather than working for someone else. Thus the income statement should be amended in the following way in order to determine economic profit:

Sales		$90,000
Less: Cost of goods sold		40,000
Gross profit		$50,000
Less: Explicit costs:		
Advertising	$10,000	
Depreciation	10,000	
Utilities	3,000	
Property tax	2,000	
Other expenses	5,000	30,000
Accounting profit (i.e., profit before implicit costs)		$20,000
Less: Implicit costs:		
Return on $100,000 of capital	10,000	
Forgone wages	35,000	45,000
Net "economic profit"		− $25,000

From this broader perspective, the business lost $25,000. The $20,000 accounting profit disappears when all "relevant" costs are included. Another way of looking at the problem is to assume that $100,000 had to be borrowed at, say, 10 percent interest and an MBA graduate hired at $35,00 per year to run the store. In this case, the implicit costs become explicit and the accounting profit is the same as the economic profit (i.e., −$25,000) because all costs have been made explicit.

Most decision makers are aware of this concept. The carpenter who works as an independent contractor rather than as an employee of another firm knows that his opportunity cost is the market wage rate for carpenters. The independent contractor's lament "I lost money on that job" may mean that his accounting profit was $80 per day when he could have made $100 per day working for someone else.

The important point of this discussion is that an entirely different signal may be given to management when the concept of economic profit is used. Sometimes, the operation of economically unprofitable businesses is continued because of a failure to understand and properly include implicit costs. Rational decision making requires that all relevant costs, both explicit and implicit, be recognized. The concept of economic profit accounts for all costs and therefore is a more useful management tool than the more normally defined concept of accounting profit. In the following chapters, the economic definition of profit will be used. Similarly, the term *cost* is defined to include all relevant costs, both explicit and implicit.

Profit in a Market System

Except for those who espouse the view that charity is the only virtue, contributors to output expect to be paid. Each workday, many people willingly spend about one-half of their waking hours in employment for which they are paid wages. Those who own land and structures will let others use those resources as long as rent is paid for their use. Owners of financial resources make their assets available in return for the payment of interest.

Of the total income generated in the U.S. economy each year, about 80 percent is in the form of wages. Rent accounts for 3 percent and interest accounts for about 7 percent. Profit, although representing only about 10 percent of national income, plays two primary roles in the functioning of the economic system. First, profit acts as a signal to producers to expand the rate of output or to enter or leave an industry. Second, profit is a reward that encourages entrepreneurs to organize factors of production and take risk.

High profits in an industry usually are a signal that buyers want more output from that industry. Those profits provide the incentive for firms to expand output and for new firms to enter the market. Conversely, low profits are a signal that less output is being demanded by consumers and/or that production methods are not efficient. When demand for output decreases, firms reduce production of that product, and resources are made available for the production of other goods and services for which demand has increased. If low profits are an indication of inefficiency in production rather than inadequate demand, management is signaled to reorganize the production process or otherwise reduce costs.

It seems clear that profit is the objective of most managers and entrepreneurs. Although sometimes characterized by greed, avarice, misrepresentation, and outright lawbreaking, the desire for profit drives the market economy. But the quest for profit is no more selfish than the quest for higher wages. Profit is a residual income after other participants in production have been paid. The sellers of labor inputs want their payments before the final goods are sold to consumers. They want no share of the risks. So, it is not surprising that entrepreneurs will not commit time and resources to risky activities unless there is the prospect of earning a profit. Profit is a reward for accepting the risk and uncertainty associated with virtually all business decisions. Virtually all of these decisions carry the risk that money will be lost. Clearly, if there is a chance of a loss, there must be the chance for a gain in the form of profit or such risks will not be taken.

Some critics of the capitalist system argue that profit is little more than a windfall gain that is randomly conferred on certain people. As such, they believe that it should be taxed away because it is "unearned." However, even if it is correct that profits are random windfalls, no one will "play the game" (i.e., make investments in business) if there is no chance of winning a prize in the form of profit. Furthermore, some workers also receive windfall gains when shifts in demand cause large increases in their wages.

CASE STUDY

STEVEN JOBS AND THE APPLE MONEY MACHINE

In 1976, 20-year-old Steven Jobs dropped out of Oregon's prestigious Reed College and went to work for the Atari Corporation as a video game programmer. In the evenings, Jobs and his friend Steve Wozniak worked on the prototype of a desktop computer that would revolutionize the electronics industry. They dubbed the machine the Apple. To raise capital for commercial production, Jobs sold his only important asset, a Volkswagen bus, for $1,000. With the help of an independent investor, the Apple Computer Company was launched and the rest is history.

In 1977, they sold $3 million worth of computers. By 1984, sales had increased to an annual rate of $1.4 billion and profits were $45 million. Clearly, this success was not lost on potential competition. In the early 1980s, new models of the "personal computer" were being introduced almost weekly by competitors. Among the most successful was the IBM-PC. In mid-1984, a personal computer magazine reported on seventy-five microcomputers that were vying for the market initially developed by the Apple.

The financial rewards to the founder of Apple Computer and others were great. By 1981, Steve Jobs' wealth was reported to be in the "hundreds of millions."

However, as a result of increased competition and some production and quality control problems in 1981, the per share value of Apple Computer stock plunged from a high of $49 in 1981 to $10 in 1982. When asked how it felt to have his personal wealth reduced by tens of millions in a matter of months, Jobs replied "it was very character building."

KEY CONCEPTS

- It is assumed that the objective of the firm is to maximize the present value of all future profits.
- Economic profit refers to revenues less all relevant costs, both explicit and implicit.
- Profit plays two roles in a market economy: (1) changes in profit signal producers to change the rate of production; and (2) profit is a reward to entrepreneurs for taking risks.

Summary

Managerial economics can be viewed as an application of that part of microeconomics that focuses on such topics as risk, demand, production, cost, pricing, and market structure. The approach to these topics emphasizes the decision-making perspective and sharpens the analytical framework that the manager brings to bear on managerial decisions.

A primary role of economics is in determining the optimal course of managerial action. In general, managerial economics will help managers to ensure that resources are allocated efficiently within the firm and that the firm makes appropriate reactions to changes in the economic environment.

Individuals and firms interact in both the product and the factor markets. Prices of outputs, and inputs are determined in these markets and guide the decisions of all market participants. The firm is an entity that organizes factors of production in order to produce goods and services to meet the demands of consumers and other firms. In a market system, the interplay of individuals and firms is not subject to central control. Price serves to guide this interaction. Within firms, however, activity is directed by managers. Central control within the firm is advantageous because transactions and information costs are reduced. The size of the firm is limited because transaction costs within the firm will rise as the firm grows and because management skill is limited.

It is assumed that the goal of the firm is to maximize the present value of all future profits defined as revenue less all costs, explicit and implicit. Opportunity costs such as the renumeration and interest that owners and managers have forgone on their labor and capital must be included as costs. Failure to account for these implicit costs may result in an inefficient allocation of resources. Profit plays two primary roles in the free-market system. First, it acts as a signal to producers to expand or contract the rate of output or to enter or leave an industry. Second, profit is a reward for entrepreneurial activity, especially risk taking.

Discussion Questions

1-1. Explain the way that firms and individuals participate and interact in the product market and in the factor market.

1-2. Explain the difference between the accounting and the economic concept of profit. How might accounting practices be changed to make financial statements and reports more useful for managerial decision making?

1-3. Explain how the principles of free market economics that guide interrelations among firms and individuals might guide pricing and resource allocation decisions within the large, multiplant firm.

1-4. Could the assumption that managers' objective is profit maximization be useful even if their real objective is maximizing market share or their salaries? Why is it important to state a managerial objective?

1-5. Explain the role of profit in a free-market economic system. How can such a small share of national income (less than 10 percent) be such an important determinant of resource allocation?

1-6. What might be the objective or objectives of each of the following nonprofit institutions:
       (a) The college of business at a major state university.
       (b) A municipal police department.
       (c) The emergency room of a hospital.
       (d) A museum.

1-7. Some argue that businesses need to be "socially responsible" (for example, reduce pollution, employ more minority workers, cease buying from and selling to countries that are not in political favor with the United States, sell at lower prices to low-income people, etc.). Evaluate the effects on the firm of being socially responsible in a competitive environment. Can one firm in a market afford to be socially responsible if its competitors are not? Explain. Would you invest in a company that devoted a significant part of its resources to be socially responsible? Why?

1-8. Milton Friedman has argued that the realism of a model is not as important as its predictive ability. That is, a model of economic behavior that appears to be unrealistic but predicts well is superior to a model that seems more realistic but does not predict well. Do you agree? Why or why not?

1-9. Suppose that the goal of a firm is revenue maximization. Explain how price and output decisions made in this environment might differ from those made if the goal were profit maximization.

1-10. In some large businesses, division managers must report profits monthly and, in some cases, more often. Some managers claim that the pressure to report favorable results continually on a month-to-month basis causes them to make decisions that will enhance short-term profit at the expense of profit in the long run. What actions might a manager take that would increase profit in the short run but that would reduce the present value of all future profits?

Problems

1-1. Lopez, a recent engineering graduate, turns down a job offer of $30,000 per year to start her own business. She invests $50,000 of her own money plus $100,000 that is borrowed at the market interest rate of 12 percent per year. Sales revenue during the first year was $107,000, while expenses were:

Advertising	$ 5,000
Rent	10,000
Taxes	5,000
Employees' salaries	40,000
Supplies	5,000

Prepare two income statements, one using the traditional accounting approach and one using the opportunity cost approach.

1-2. Tempo Electronics, Inc. has an inventory of 5,000 unique electronic chips originally purchased at $2.50 each; their market value is now $5 each. The production department has proposed to use these by putting each one together with $6 worth of labor and other materials to produce a wrist watch that would be sold for $10. Should that proposal be implemented? Explain.

References

Baumol, W. J. 1961. "What Can Economic Theory Contribute to Managerial Economics?" *American Economic Review* 51(May):142–146.

Beasley, W. H. 1981. "Can Managerial Economics Aid the Chief Executive Officer?" *Managerial and Decision Economics* 2(September):129–132.

Coase, R. H. 1937. "The Nature of the Firm." *Economica*, November, pp. 386–405.

Cyert, R. M., and Hedrick, C. L. 1972. "Theory of the Firm: Past, Present, and Future." *Journal of Economic Literature*, June, pp. 398–412.

Cyert, R. M., and March, J. G. 1963. *A Behavioral Theory of the Firm.* Englewood Cliffs, N.J.: Prentice-Hall.

Machlup, F. 1946. "Marginal Analysis and Empirical Research." *American Economic Review* 36(September):519–554.

Machlup, F. 1967. "Theories of the Firm: Marginalist, Behavioral, Managerial." *American Economic Review* 57(1):1–33.

Shubik, M. 1974. "A Curmudgeon's Guide to Microeconomics." *Journal of Economic Literature* 8(June):405–429.

Simon, H. A. 1959. "Theories of Decision-Making in Economics." *American Economic Review* 49(3):253–283.

Simon, H. A. 1960. "The Decision-Making Process." In *The Executive or Decision Maker: The New Science of Management Decisions.* New York: Harper & Row.

Smith, A. 1776. *An Inquiry into the Nature and Causes of the Wealth of Nations.* New York: George Rutledge & Sons, Ltd., 1890.

Solomons, D. 1961. "Economic and Accounting Concepts of Incomes." *The Accounting Review* 36(July):374–383.

Basic Training

2

Preview

Just as the skilled craftsman needs tools to build a new home, the manager needs tools to assist in making decisions that will maximize profit. Increasingly, these tools are of the quantitative sort. Algebra, calculus, statistics, and linear programming are widely used in all the functional areas of business today. This is especially true for decision makers in production and finance, but even those in marketing and business law increasingly find these tools of value.

The purpose of this chapter is to introduce the basic quantitative tools that are commonly used in managerial economics and to demonstrate their applications. The chapter presents four concepts essential to the study of managerial economics. Their use can make problem solving easier and more thorough. In the first section, functional relationships and economic models are discussed. Second, the concept of total, average, and marginal functions is developed and applied to several economics problems. Next, the least-squares regression technique is discussed. This is a statistical approach to estimating the numerical value of the parameters in an economic model. Finally, some of the basic principles of the time value of money are developed.

Functional Relationships and Economic Models

In mathematics, an equation of the form

$$y = f(x) \tag{2-1}$$

is read "y is a function of x." This means that the value of y depends on the value of x in a systematic way and that there is a unique value of y for each value of x. Usually, the variable on the left-hand side of the equation, y in this case, is called the *dependent variable*. The variable on the right-hand side is called the *independent variable*.

Of course, y may depend on two or more independent variables, such as

$$y = g(x, z) \tag{2-2}$$

or

$$y = h(x_1, x_2, \ldots, x_n) \tag{2-3}$$

The letters f, g, and h have no specific meaning other than to indicate that a functional relationship exists between y and the independent variable or variables.

In equation (2-3), y depends on an undefined number (n) of variables indicated by the subscripts $1, 2, \ldots, n$. Another way of writing equation (2-3) would be

$$y = f(x_i) \qquad i = 1, 2, \ldots, n$$

where the subscript i is an index that takes on the values 1, 2, through n.

Examples of specific equations that might be associated with each of these general functions are as follows:

General function   *Examples of specific functions*

$$y = f(x) \quad \begin{cases} y = 2x \\ y = 3x^2 + 10 \\ y = 9x^2 + 3x + \dfrac{1}{x} \end{cases}$$

$$y = g(x, z) \quad \begin{cases} y = 3x + 2z \\ y = 100x^2 z^3 \end{cases}$$

$$y = (x_1, x_2, \ldots, x_n) \quad \begin{cases} y = 3x_1 + 4x_2 + 5x_3 + \cdots + (n + 2)\, x_n \\ y = ax_1^2 + bx_2^2 + cx_3^2 + \cdots + zx_n^2 \end{cases}$$

In the aerospace industry, small model airplanes are flown in wind tunnels to test the flight characteristics of full-size planes having the same characteristics. In economics, graphs and/or equations are used to explain economic relationships and phenomena. Although such models are abstractions from reality and may even seem unrealistic, they are useful in studying the way an economic system works. Just as it is not sound practice to build a radically new jet aircraft before a model is used to test its flight characteristics, an economic decision should not be made without having analyzed its implications by using an economic model.

An economic model usually consists of several related functions. Recall the concepts of supply and demand from introductory economics. As shown in Figure 2-1, the demand curve (*DD*) slopes downward from left to right and shows the quantity of output that consumers are willing and able to buy at each price. The negative slope implies that a larger quantity is demanded at lower prices than at higher prices. The supply curve (*SS*) shows the amount that firms will

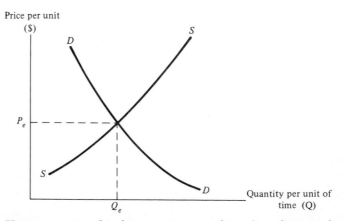

Figure 2-1.   *Graphical Representation of Supply and Demand Analysis.*

produce and offer for sale at each price. This curve has a positive slope because firms will supply a larger quantity at higher prices than at lower prices.[1]

Equilibrium in a market exists when the quantity demanded equals the quantity supplied. This is shown graphically as the intersection of the demand and supply functions in Figure 2-1. In this example, P_e and Q_e are the equilibrium price and quantity, respectively. In equilibrium there is no incentive for buyers or sellers to change price or the quantity. At point $\{P_e, Q_e\}$, buyers' demands are met exactly and suppliers are selling exactly the number of units they desire to sell at that price.

The foregoing is an economic model depicted by a graphical analysis. A simple algebraic model can be used to describe exactly the same economic phenomenon and do it more precisely. The quantity demanded (Q_d) and the quantity supplied (Q_s) are both functions of price. That is,

$$Q_d = f(P) \quad \text{and} \quad Q_s = g(P)$$

Suppose that the demand function is

$$Q_d = B + aP \quad \text{where } a < 0 \tag{2-4}$$

and the supply function is

$$Q_s = D + cP \quad \text{where } c > 0 \tag{2-5}$$

The constraints on the parameters (i.e., $a < 0$ and $c > 0$), simply mean that the demand curve must slope downward (i.e., have a negative slope) and that the supply curve must slope upward (i.e., have a positive slope). By adding an equilibrium condition that the quantity supplied equals the quantity demanded, that is,

$$Q_d = Q_s \tag{2-6}$$

the economic model, consisting of equations (2-4), (2-5), and (2-6), is complete.

By equating supply and demand, the equilibrium price (P_e) can be determined. Substituting equations (2-4) and (2-5) for Q_d and Q_s in (2-6) yields

$$B + aP = D + cP$$

Solving for P, the equilibrium price is

$$P_e = \frac{D - B}{a - c} \tag{2-7}$$

The equilibrium quantity is found by substituting the equilibrium price into either the supply or demand function and solving for quantity. Using the demand function, the equilibrium quantity is

$$Q_e = B + a\frac{D - B}{a - c}$$

If the values of the parameters a, B, c, and D are known, the actual values of P_e and Q_e can easily be calculated. In a later section of this chapter and in Chapter

---

[1] The principles of demand and supply are discussed in greater detail in Chapters 4 and 10.

5, some of the statistical methods used to estimate the numerical values of these parameters are reviewed.

EXAMPLE
DETERMINING EQUILIBRIUM PRICE AND QUANTITY

Suppose that the demand and supply equations have been estimated and that the demand and supply curves are given by

$$Q_d = 14 - 2P$$

and

$$Q_s = 2 + 4P$$

Determine the equilibrium price and quantity.

Solution

Note that the slopes of these functions meet the constraints specified above. That is, the demand function slopes downward and the supply curve slopes upward. Substituting the demand and supply functions above in the equilibrium condition, $Q_d = Q_s$ and solving for P_e yields

$$P_e = \frac{D - B}{a - c} = \frac{2 - 14}{-2 - 4} = 2$$

Substituting $P_e = 2$ into demand function yields the equilibrium quantity

$$Q_e = 14 - 2(2) = 10$$

Thus the price–quantity combination $\{P_e = 2, Q_e = 10\}$ results in equilibrium in this market. This combination corresponds to $\{P_e, Q_e\}$ in Figure 2-1.

Models of this type are used extensively in the study of economics. Indeed, one of the strengths of the discipline is that extremely important and powerful results can be derived from models that are quite simple. To be sure, some economic models in advanced books are very complex. However, a thorough grasp of most of the key principles of economics can be obtained by applying rather simple concepts and models to business and social problems. Indeed, an important reason for studying managerial economics is to develop a set of economic models that can be used to analyze the many resource allocation problems faced by managers.

KEY CONCEPTS

• The functional relationship

$$y = f(x_1, x_2, \ldots, x_n)$$

means that there is a systematic relationship between the dependent variable y and the independent variables $x_1, x_2, \ldots, x_n$ and that there is a unique value of y for any set of values of the independent variables.

• An economic model typically consists of one or more functional relationships. It is used to demonstrate an economic principle or to explain an economic phenomenon.

Total, Average, and Marginal Functions

In many economic models, a special set of functional relationships called total, average, and marginal functions is used. Such functions are used extensively in the theory of demand, cost, production, and market structure. A basic command of these concepts is essential to understanding the principles of managerial economics.

The following production example will help in understanding these relationships. Suppose that there is a small building containing four machines and a stock of raw materials ready to be processed. Ten equally skilled and diligent people are lined up outside ready to go to work in this factory. Unless the plant is completely automated, with no workers, output will be zero. As workers are added, output increases. The total amount of output associated with a particular input of labor working with those four machines is called the *total product of labor*. For example, the total product of one worker might be 2 units of output. For different rates of labor input, total output differs. An example of a total product schedule is shown in the first two columns of Table 2-1.

As indicated above, one person working alone in this factory produces 2 units of output. Adding a second person and organizing the production system so

Table 2-1. Total, Average, and Marginal Product of Labor Schedules

(1) Number of Workers (L)	(2) Total Product (Q)	(3) Average Product (AP)	(4) Marginal Product (MP)
0	0	—	
1	2	2.0	2
2	5	2.5	3
3	9	3.0	4
4	14	3.5	5
5	22	4.4	8
6	40	6.7	18
7	57	8.1	17
8	63	7.9	6
9	64	7.1	1
10	53	5.3	−9

that the workers complement each other results in total product increasing to 5 units. The first worker is associated with a 2 unit increase in output; having two workers instead of one will increase output by 3 units; three workers will increase output to 9 units; and so on. The incremental change in output associated with a 1-unit change in workers is called the *marginal product of labor*. Using the Greek capital letter delta (Δ) to indicate a change, the *marginal product function (MP)* can be defined as

$$MP = \frac{\Delta Q}{\Delta L}$$

(2-8)

where Q represents output and L represents the input of labor.[2]

Note in Table 2-1 that for the first six workers, the marginal product increases as the rate of labor input increases. However, marginal product declines thereafter. The sixth worker adds 18 units to output, but the seventh adds only 17. Finally, having ten workers actually causes output to decline. That is, the marginal product associated with the tenth worker is negative. The point has been reached where there are too many workers in this plant. Perhaps they are getting in each other's way; in any event, the presence of ten workers has thwarted the achievement of efficient production.[3]

The *average product of labor function (AP)* measures the average output per unit of labor used. Average product is found by dividing total product by labor input. That is,

$$AP = \frac{TP}{L}$$

The total product function is plotted in Figure 2-2a, and the average and marginal product functions are shown graphically[4] in Figure 2-2b. There are important relationships among the three functions that are true for all total, average, and marginal functions. First, the value of the average function at any point along that curve is equal to the slope of a ray drawn from the origin to the

---

[2] The marginal product function is the slope of the total product function. Slope can be defined as the change in the dependent variable divided by the change in the independent variable. Consider the function $y = 10 + 3x$. A 1-unit change in x, say from $x = 5$ to $x = 6$, is associated with a 3-unit change in y, from $y = 25$ to $y = 28$. Thus the change in y (i.e., Δy) is 3, and the change in x (i.e., Δx) is 1, so the slope is $\Delta y/\Delta x = 3/1 = 3$.

[3] That marginal product must ultimately decline as workers are added is clear in this example. The building has a finite amount of floor space. The change in output should be positive if one or two workers are added. But for some number of workers, output will be zero as workers fight for a place to stand rather than produce output. Therefore, beyond some rate of labor input, marginal product must decline.

[4] All three of the functions are drawn with graphs having the same units on both axes (i.e., output on the vertical axis and number of workers on the horizontal axis). Therefore, all three could have been included in the same graph. However, the range of the total product curve (0 to 64) is so much greater than the range of the average and marginal curves that it is more descriptive to use two graphs. Note that the height of each interval on the vertical axis in Figure 2-2b is considerably greater than in Figure 2-2a. This allows the relationships among all three functions to be seen more clearly than if they were all drawn in the same graph. Note also that the horizontal axis in both graphs is exactly the same. This allows comparison of points on one graph that correspond to points on the others.

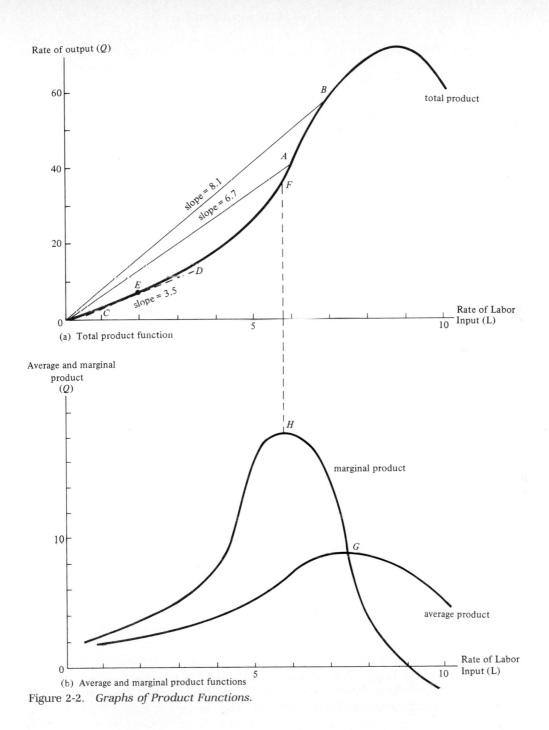

Rate of output (Q)

60

40

slope = 8.1
slope = 6.7

20

slope = 3.5

Rate of Labor
Input (L)

5   10

(a) Total product function

Average and marginal
product
(Q)

10

5   10

Rate of Labor
Input (L)

(b) Average and marginal product functions

Figure 2-2. *Graphs of Product Functions.*

total function at the corresponding point. For example, from Table 2-1 it is known that the average product of six workers is 6.7. The slope of a line (0A) drawn from the origin to point A on the total product function also has a slope of 6.7. Similarly, the average product of seven workers is 8.1; this is equal to the slope of a line drawn from the origin to point B on the total product function.

Another key relationship is that the value of the marginal function is equal to the slope of the line drawn tangent to the total function at a corresponding point. For example, the slope of line CD, which is drawn tangent to the total function at E, is about 3.5. The marginal product corresponding to this point (i.e., for 2 units of labor) is also 3.5.

Point F on the total function is called an *inflection point*. To the left of point F, the total function is increasing at an increasing rate; to the right of F, the total function is increasing but at a decreasing rate. Note that this inflection point, corresponding to six workers, occurs at the point where the marginal product function is at a maximum (i.e., point H).

If the marginal and average functions intersect, that point of intersection will be an extremum of the average function. An extremum refers to the minimum or maximum point on a function. In Figure 2-2b, the intersection occurs at point G, which is the maximum point of the average product function. The logic of this relationship is quite straightforward. Suppose that the average product for two workers is 2.5, and the marginal product of three workers is more than that average, say, 4. Thus the average product for three workers must increase to 3. If the additional output associated with hiring another worker is above the previous average product, the average product must be increasing.

Conversely, suppose that eight workers average 7.9 units of output per period, and that the marginal product of nine workers is only 1. This will cause average product to fall to 7.1. If an additional worker adds less to total output than the average product prior to that addition, average product must fall.

This logic leads to the following conclusion. For any set of average and marginal functions, if the marginal function is greater than the average function, the average must be rising. If marginal is below average, the average must be falling. This implies that the intersection of the two functions must occur where the average function is at a maximum or minimum. As will be shown in later chapters, this result is important in several managerial economics problems.

If the marginal function is positive, the total function must be rising. Note that it does not matter whether the marginal function is increasing or decreasing, as long as it is positive. Conversely, if the marginal function is negative, the total function must be declining. Again, it does not matter if marginal is rising or falling. If marginal is negative, the total function will be declining. For the data in Table 2-1 and Figure 2-2, the marginal product is positive for the first nine workers. It declines after the sixth worker but remains positive through the ninth. Note that total product increases until the tenth worker is added. The marginal product of ten workers is −9, and this negative marginal product is associated with a decline in total product.

Because the total function increases as long as the marginal function is positive and decreases when marginal is negative, it follows that total product is at a maximum (or minimum in other cases) when the marginal function is zero. In Figure 2-2 the maximum of the total product function occurs at nine workers. This point corresponds to the point where the marginal function intersects the horizontal axis, that is, where marginal changes from being positive to negative.

An understanding of total, average, and marginal relations is an important foundation for the effective study of managerial economics. Terms such as "average cost," "marginal product," and "total revenue" are integral parts of the manager's vocabulary, and the associated principles are some of the manager's most powerful tools.

CASE STUDY
APPLYING MARGINAL ANALYSIS TO AUTOMOBILE SAFETY

Suppose an automobile model is so fraught with engineering defects that the risk of having an accident is greatly increased. Although the car is no longer being manufactured, vehicles already on the road are expected to cause ten deaths during the next year. For simplicity, it is assumed that the engineering defects are so severe that none of the cars will be running after one year. The number of deaths can be reduced if the manufacturer recalls the cars and corrects some or all of the defects. Clearly, the more defects that are corrected, the greater the reduction in the number of deaths.

As shown in the table, the marginal cost of reducing the number of deaths from ten to nine is $200,000, but marginal cost rises as the number of deaths decreases. For example, the marginal cost of going from one death to no deaths is $2,000,000. This cost rises because some of the defects are easily corrected, whereas others require a substantial modification of the vehicle.

Deaths	Marginal Cost of Death Prevention	Marginal Benefit of a Life Saved	Total Net Benefits
10	$ 0		
9	200,000	800,000	$ 600,000
8	400,000	800,000	1,000,000
7	600,000	800,000	1,200,000
6	800,000	800,000	1,200,000
5	1,000,000	800,000	1,000,000
4	1,200,000	800,000	600,000
3	1,400,000	800,000	0
2	1,600,000	800,000	− 800,000
1	1,800,000	800,000	−1,800,000
0	2,000,000	800,000	−3,000,000

Suppose that the National Highway Traffic Safety Administration, a federal agency responsible for regulating automobile safety, uses marginal principles to make recall decisions and that the agency has determined that each life saved is worth $800,000 to society. That is, $800,000 is the marginal benefit associated with saving a life.

The benefits and costs of a recall/repair program shown in the table can be compared to make a decision. The marginal cost of saving the first life is $200,000 and the marginal benefit is $800,000. Thus it is clear that the manufacturer should be required to take some action. However, it is equally clear that it would be inefficient to attempt to eliminate all defects. For example, the marginal cost of going from one death to zero deaths is $2,000,000 but the marginal benefit is only $800,000.

The recall program should be designed to reduce those defects (and associated deaths) to the point where marginal benefits equal marginal costs. In this example, that equality occurs at six deaths. Note that total net benefits (a *net benefit* is defined as marginal benefit less marginal cost) are maximized ($1,200,000) at 6 deaths. Total benefits are $3,200,000 (i.e., four lives saved multiplied by $800,000 per life) and total costs are $2,000,000. To require additional repairs to reduce the number of deaths below six is not socially efficient because the costs exceed the benefits.

KEY CONCEPTS

- For any total function (e.g., total product, total revenue, etc.) there is an associated marginal function and average function.
- The key relationships among the total, average, and marginal functions are:
  1. The value of the average function at any point is the slope of a ray drawn from the origin to the total function.
  2. The value of the marginal function is the slope of a line drawn tangent to the total function.
  3. The marginal function will intersect the average function at either a minimum or a maximum point of the average function.
  4. If the marginal function is positive, the total function will be increasing. If the marginal function is negative, the total function will be decreasing.
  5. The total function reaches a maximum or minimum when the marginal function equals zero.

Estimation by Least-Squares Regression

It is clear that understanding the general relationships among variables in an economic model is an essential part of the study of managerial economics. However, actual decision making often requires that the quantitative magnitude of that relationship be known. For example, in the demand equation

$$Q_d = a + bP$$

the parameter b is hypothesized to be negative. For making decisions about price or the rate of output, this qualitative estimate of the slope (i.e., $b < 0$) may not be adequate. An estimate of the numerical value of b may be required.

Probably the most widely used technique for estimating the parameters of functions in economics and in other sciences is the least-squares regression method. The basic elements of this technique are developed in this section.

Parameter Estimation

Consider a firm with a fixed capital stock that has been rented under a long-term lease for $100 per production period. The other input into the firm's production process is labor. The rate of labor input can be increased or decreased quickly depending on the firm's needs. In this case, the cost of the capital input ($100) is fixed and the cost of labor is variable. The manager of the firm wants to know the relationship between output and cost, that is, the total cost function. Specifically, the manager is interested in estimating the parameters a and b of the function

$$Y = a + bX$$

where the dependent variable Y is total cost and the independent variable X is total output. The parameter a is the vertical intercept (i.e., where the function intersects the vertical axis) and b is the slope of the function. Recall that the slope of a total function is the marginal function. As $Y = a + bX$ is the total cost function, the slope, b, is marginal cost or the change in total cost per unit change in output.

Data on cost and output have been collected for each of seven production periods and are reported in Table 2-2. Note that there is a cost of $100 associated with an output level of zero. This represents the fixed cost of the capital input, which must be paid regardless of the rate of output. These data are shown as points in Figure 2-3. They suggest a definite upward trend but that they do not trace out a straight line. The problem is to determine the line that best represents the overall relationship between Y and X. One approach would be to simply "eyeball" a line through these data in a way that the data points were about equally spaced on both sides of the line. The parameter a would be found by extending that line to the vertical axis and reading the Y-coordinate at that point.

Table 2-2. Hypothetical Data on Total Cost and Total Output

Production Period	Total Cost (Y_i)	Total Output (X_i)
1	$100	0
2	150	5
3	160	8
4	240	10
5	230	15
6	370	23
7	410	25

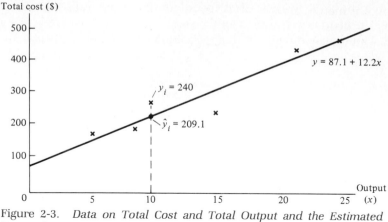

Figure 2-3. *Data on Total Cost and Total Output and the Estimated Regression Equation.*

The slope, *b*, would be found by taking any two points on the line, $\{X_1, Y_1\}$ and $\{X_2, Y_2\}$ and using the formula

$$b = \frac{Y_2 - Y_1}{X_2 - X_1}$$

Although this informal approach is used, the method is quite imprecise and can be used only when there is one independent variable. What if production cost depends on both the rate of output and the size of the plant? To plot the data for these three variables (total cost, output, and plant size) would require a three-dimensional diagram; it would be nearly impossible to "eyeball" the relationship in this case. The addition of another independent variable, say average skill levels of the employees, would place the data set in the fourth dimension, where any graphic approach is hopeless.

There is a better way. Statisticians have demonstrated that the best estimate of the parameters of a linear function is to fit the line through the data points such that the sum of squared vertical distances from each point to the line is minimized. This technique is called *least-squares regression estimation.*

Based on the output and cost data in Table 2-2, the least-squares regression equation will be shown to be

$$\hat{Y} = 87.1 + 12.2X$$

This equation is plotted in Figure 2-3. Note that the data points fall about equally on both sides of the line.

Consider an output rate of 10. As shown in Table 2-2, the actual cost associated with this output level is 240. The value predicted by the regression equation, referred to as $\hat{Y}$, is 209.1. That is, $\hat{Y} = 87.1 + 12.2(10) = 209.1$. The deviation of the actual *Y* value from the predicted value (i.e., the vertical distance of the point from the line), $Y_i - \hat{Y}$, is referred to as the *residual* or *error term.*

There are many values that might be selected as estimators of a and b, but only one of those sets defines a line that minimizes the sum of squared deviations [i.e., that minimizes $\Sigma(Y_i - \hat{Y}_i)^2$]. The equations for computing the least-squares estimators a and b are

$$\hat{b} = \frac{\Sigma(X_i - \bar{X})(Y_i - \bar{Y})}{\Sigma(X_i - \bar{X})^2} \tag{2-9}$$

and

$$\hat{a} = \bar{Y} - \hat{b}\bar{X} \tag{2-10}$$

where $\bar{Y}$ and $\bar{X}$ are the means of the Y and X variables.

Using the cost and output data from the example, the relevant data and computations are outlined in Table 2-3. Substituting the appropriate data into equations (2-9) and (2-10), the estimates of $\hat{b}$ and $\hat{a}$ are computed to be

$$\hat{b} = \frac{\Sigma(X_i - \bar{X})(Y_i - \bar{Y})}{\Sigma(X_i - \bar{X})^2} - \frac{6{,}245.8}{511.5} = \boxed{12.2}$$

$$\hat{a} = \bar{Y} - \hat{b}\bar{X} = 237.1 - 12.2(12.3) = \boxed{87.1}$$

Thus the estimated equation for the total cost function is

$$\hat{Y} = 87.1 + 12.2X$$

The estimate of the parameter a is 87.1. This is the vertical intercept of the estimated line. In the context of this example, $\hat{a} = 87.1$ is an estimate of fixed cost. Note that this estimate is subject to error because it is known that the actual fixed cost is $100. The value of $\hat{b}$ is an estimate of the change in total cost for a 1-unit change in output (i.e., marginal cost). The value of $\hat{b}$ $12.2, means that, on average, a 1-unit change in output results in a $12.20 change in total cost. Thus, $\hat{b}$ is an estimate of marginal cost.

Table 2-3. Data Manipulation for Computing the Estimates $\hat{a}$ and $\hat{b}$

Cost (Y_i)	Output (X_i)	$Y_i - \bar{Y}$	$X_i - \bar{X}$	$(X_i - \bar{X})^2$	$(X_i - \bar{X})(Y_i - \bar{Y})$
100	0	−137	−12	150.9	1,684.9
150	5	−87	−7	53.1	634.9
160	8	−77	−4	18.4	330.6
240	10	3	−2	5.2	−6.5
230	15	−7	3	7.4	−19.4
370	23	133	11	114.8	1,423.5
410	25	173	13	161.7	2,197.8
$\bar{Y} = 237.1$	$\bar{X} = 12.3$			$\Sigma(X_i - \bar{X})^2 =$ 511.5	$\Sigma(X_i - \bar{X})(Y_i - \bar{Y}) =$ 6,245.8

KEY CONCEPTS

- The least-squares regression technique is used to estimate the parameters of a function by fitting a line through the data such that the sum of squared deviations [i.e., $\Sigma(Y_i - \hat{Y}_i)^2$] is minimized.
- Estimates of the parameters of the function $Y = a + bx$ are given by the equations

$$\hat{b} = \frac{\Sigma(X_i - \overline{X})(Y_i - \overline{Y})}{\Sigma(X_i - \overline{X})^2} \quad \text{and} \quad \hat{a} = \overline{Y} - \hat{b}\overline{X}$$

- The value of a estimates the vertical intercept or the estimated value of Y when $X = 0$. The value of b estimates the change in Y for a 1-unit change in X.

Testing the Regression Estimates

Once the parameters have been estimated, the strength of the relationship between the dependent variable and the independent variable can be measured in two ways. Although a variety of statistics are used for this purpose, only the two most widely used tests are outlined here. The first uses a measure called the coefficient of determination, denoted as R^2, to measure how well the overall equation explains changes in the dependent variable. The second measure uses the t-statistic to test the strength of the relationship between the independent variable and the dependent variable.

Testing Overall Explanatory Power.   Define the squared deviation of any Y_i from the mean of Y [i.e., $(Y_i - \overline{Y})^2$] as the variation in Y. The total variation is found by summing these deviations for all values of the dependent variable. That is,

$$\text{total variation} = \sum(Y_i - \overline{Y})^2 \tag{2-11}$$

Total variation can be separated into two components: explained variation and unexplained variation. These concepts are explained below. For each X_i value, compute the predicted value of Y_i (denoted as $\hat{Y}_i$) by substituting X_i in the estimated regression equation:

$$\hat{Y}_i = \hat{a} + \hat{b}X_i$$

The squared difference between the predicted value $\hat{Y}_i$ and the mean value $\overline{Y}$ [i.e., $(\hat{Y}_i - \overline{Y})^2$] is defined as *explained variation*. The word "explained" means that the deviation of Y from its average value $\overline{Y}$ is the result of (i.e., is explained by) changes in X. For example, in the data on total output and cost used above, one important reason the cost values are higher or lower than $\overline{Y}$ is because output rates (X_i) are higher or lower than the average output rate.

Total explained variation is found by summing these squared deviations, that is,

$$\text{total explained variation} = \sum(\hat{Y}_i - \overline{Y})^2 \tag{2-12}$$

Unexplained variation is the difference between Y_i and $\hat{Y}_i$. That is, part of the deviation of Y_i from the average value $(\overline{Y})$ is "explained" by the independent variable, X. The remaining deviation, $Y_i - \hat{Y}_i$, is said to be unexplained. Summing the squares of these differences yields

$$\text{total unexplained variation} = \sum (Y_i - \hat{Y}_i)^2 \qquad (2\text{-}13)$$

The three sources of variation are shown in Figure 2-4.

The *coefficient of determination* (R^2) measures the proportion of total variation in the dependent variable that is "explained" by the regression equation. That is,

$$R^2 = \frac{\text{total explained variation}}{\text{total variation}} = \frac{\Sigma(\hat{Y}_i - \overline{Y}_i)^2}{(Y_i - \overline{Y})^2} \qquad (2\text{-}14)$$

The value of R^2 ranges from zero to 1. If the regression equation explains none of the variation in Y (i.e., there is no relationship between the independent variables and the dependent variable), R^2 will be zero. If the equation explains all the variation (i.e., total explained variation = total variation), the coefficient of determination will be 1. In general, the higher the value of R^2, the "better" the regression equation. The term *fit* is often used to describe the explanatory power of the estimated equation. When R^2 is high, the equation is said to fit the data well. A low R^2 would be indicative of a rather poor fit.

How high must the coefficient of determination be in order that a regression equation be said to fit well? There is no precise answer to this question. For some relationships, such as that between consumption and income over time, one might expect R^2 to be at least 0.95. In other cases, such as estimating the relationship between output and average cost for fifty different producers during one production period, an R^2 of 0.40 or 0.50 might be regarded as quite good.

Based on the estimated regression equation for total cost and output, that is,

$$\hat{Y}_i = 87.1 + 12.2X_i$$

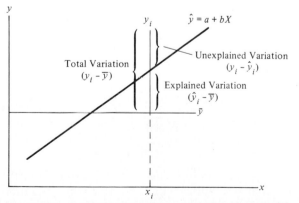

Figure 2-4. *Sources of Variation in a Regression Model.*

Table 2-4. Computing the Sources of Variation in a Regression Model

Y_i	Total Variation $(Y_i - \bar{Y})^2$	$\hat{Y}_i$	Explained Variation $(\hat{Y}_i - \bar{Y})^2$	Unexplained Variation $(Y_i - \hat{Y})^2$
100	18,808	87.1	22,511	166.3
150	7,594	148.2	7,917	3.4
160	5,951	184.8	2,739	615.2
240	8	209.2	779	946.9
230	51	270.3	1,099	1,623.2
370	17,651	368.0	17,120	4.1
410	29,880	392.4	24,108	309.4
	$\Sigma(Y - \bar{Y})^2 =$ 79,942		$\Sigma(\hat{Y}_i - \bar{Y})^2 =$ 76,273	$\Sigma(Y_i - \hat{Y})^2 =$ 3,668.4

the coefficient of determination can be computed using the data on sources of variation outlined in Table 2-4.

$$R^2 = \frac{\text{explained variation}}{\text{total variation}} = \frac{76,273}{79,942} = 0.954$$

The value of R^2, 0.954, means that more than 95 percent of the variation in total cost is explained by changes in output levels. Thus the equation would appear to fit the data quite well.

Evaluating the Explanatory Power of Individual Independent Variables. The *t-test* is used to determine if there is a significant relationship between the dependent variable and each of the independent variables. This test requires that the standard deviation (or standard error) of the estimated regression coefficient be computed. Because the relationship between any dependent variable and independent variable combination is not fixed but will vary somewhat for different periods, the estimate of b will vary for different data samples. The standard error of $\hat{b}$ from one of these regression equations provides an estimate of the amount of variability in $\hat{b}$. The equation for this standard error is

$$S_{\hat{b}} = \sqrt{\frac{\Sigma(Y_i - \hat{Y}_i)/(n - 2)}{\Sigma(X_i - \bar{X})^2}}$$

For the production cost example used above, the standard error of $\hat{b}$ would be

$$S_{\hat{b}} = \sqrt{\frac{3,668.4/5}{511.5}} = 1.19$$

The least-squares estimate of $\hat{b}$ is said to be a point estimate of the parameter b. But it is known that $\hat{b}$ is subject to error and thus will differ from the true value of the parameter b. That is why $\hat{b}$ is called an estimate. Using principles of statistics, a 95 percent confidence interval estimate for b is given by the equation

$$\hat{b} \pm t_{n-k-1}S_{\hat{b}}$$

where t_{n-k-1} represents the value of a particular probability distribution known as *Student's t distribution*. The subscript $(n - k - 1)$ refers to the number of degrees of freedom, where n is the number of observations or data points and k is the number of independent variables in the equation. A table of t-values for use in estimating 95 percent confidence intervals is included as Table V at the back of the book. In the example being discussed here, $n = 7$ and $k = 1$, so there are 5 (i.e., $7 - 1 - 1$) degrees of freedom, and the value of t in the table is 2.571. Thus in repeated estimations of the production–cost relationship, it is expected that about 95 percent of the time, the true value of parameter b will lie in this interval. For the production–cost data, the 95 percent confidence interval estimate would be

$$12.2 \pm 2.57(1.19)$$

or from 9.14 to 15.26. This means that the probability that the true marginal relationship between cost and output (i.e., the value of b) is within this region is 0.95.

If there is no relationship between the dependent and independent variables, parameter b would be zero. A standard statistical test for the strength of the relationship between Y and X is to check whether the 95 percent confidence interval includes the value zero. If it does not, the relationship between X and Y as measured by $\hat{b}$ is said to be statistically *significant*. If that interval does include zero, then $\hat{b}$ is said to be *nonsignificant*, meaning that there does not appear to be a strong relationship between the two variables. The confidence interval for $\hat{b}$ in the production–cost example did not include zero, and thus it is said that $\hat{b}$, an estimate of marginal cost, is statistically significant or that there is a strong relationship between cost and rate of output.

Another way to make the same test is to divide the estimated coefficient ($\hat{b}$) by its standard error. The probability distribution of this ratio is the same as Student's t distribution; thus this ratio is called a t-value. If the absolute value of this ratio is equal to or greater than the tabled value of t for $n - k - 1$ degrees of freedom, $\hat{b}$ is said to be statistically significant. Again, using the production–cost data, the t-value would be

$$t = \left|\frac{\hat{b}}{S_{\hat{b}}}\right| = \left|\frac{12.2}{1.19}\right| = 10.25$$

As the ratio is greater than 2.57, it is concluded that there is a statistically significant relationship between cost and output. In general, if the absolute value of the ratio $\hat{b}/S_{\hat{b}}$ is greater than t_{n-k-1}, the coefficient $\hat{b}$ is said to be statistically significant.

KEY CONCEPTS

- The coefficient of determination, R^2, is a measure of the proportion of total variation in the dependent variable that is "explained" by the regression equation.
- A 95 percent confidence interval estimate of the parameter b is given by $\hat{b} \pm t_{n-k-1}S_{\hat{b}}$. If this interval does not include zero, $\hat{b}$ is said to be statistically significant, meaning that there is a strong relationship between the dependent and independent variables.
- The ratio of an estimated regression coefficient to its standard deviation (the t-statistic) can also be used to test the statistical significance of an independent variable.

Prediction Using the Regression Equation

The regression equation can be used to predict or estimate the value of the dependent variable given the value of the independent variable.

The total cost function estimated above,

$$\hat{Y} = 87.1 + 12.2X$$

can be used to make a point estimate of the cost of a particular rate of output, say 20, by substituting $X = 20$ and solving for $\hat{Y}$. Thus

$$\hat{Y} = 87.1 + 12.2(20) = \boxed{331.1}$$

This means that the predicted cost of producing 20 units of output is \$331.10.

Recall from Figure 2-3 that the actual output–cost data points did not lie on the regression line but were dispersed above and below that line. This means that a value predicted by the regression equation will be subject to error. That is, one would not expect the predicted values to be 100 percent accurate. The standard error of the estimate (S_e) is a measure of the probable error in the predicted values. The formula for this standard error is

$$S_e = \sqrt{\frac{\Sigma(Y - \bar{Y})^2 - \hat{b} \, \Sigma \, (X - \bar{X})(Y - \bar{Y})}{n - 2}} \tag{2-15}$$

The predicted value $\hat{Y}$ is called a *point estimate* of the value of the dependent variable to distinguish that estimate from a confidence interval estimate. The latter is a range of Y values that are expected to include the actual Y value 95 percent of the time. The standard error of the estimate is a fundamental part of the confidence interval estimate. For example, for a given predicted value of the dependent variable, $\hat{Y}$, a 95 percent confidence interval estimate is given by

$$\hat{Y} \pm t_{n-k}S_e$$

This means that 95 percent of the time the actual value of Y will fall within that range.

For example, management may be considering a production run of 22 units of output and wants to know the estimated cost. Substituting 22 for X in the regression equation yields the point estimate:

$$\hat{Y} = 87.1 + 12.2(22) = \$355.5$$

Using equation (2-15) and data from Tables 2-3 and 2-4, the standard error of the estimate is computed as

$$S_e = \sqrt{\frac{79,942 - (12.2)6,245.8}{5}} = 27.4$$

Thus a 95 percent confidence interval estimate for the cost of producing 22 units of output is

$$\hat{Y} \pm 2.57 S_e \qquad \text{or} \qquad 355.5 \pm (2.57)(27.4)$$

Management would estimate that 95 percent of the time the actual cost of producing 22 units of output would be in the range of \$285 to \$426.

Multiple Regression

Estimation of the parameters of an equation where there is more than one independent variable is called *multiple regression*. Although in principle the concept of estimation in multiple regression is essentially the same as in simple linear regression, the computations are complicated. For this reason, virtually all multiple-regression estimations are made using a computer.

Because most economic relationships involve more than a simple relationship between a dependent and one independent variable, multiple-regression techniques are widely used in economics. For example, the demand for a product may depend on the price of that product, income, the prices of other goods, and possibly other variables. Thus a simple regression equation between only quantity and price would be incomplete and probably would result in an incorrect estimation of the relationship between quantity and price. This is because the effect of the other variables omitted from the equation is not be taken into account. The following example will help to explain the importance of including the correct independent variables in a regression equation.

Suppose it is hypothesized that the salary (S_i) of major league baseball players depends on the number of times the player strikes out (K_i) during the season. The more times a player strikes out, the lower his salary would be. Hence the sign of the estimated regression coefficient is expected to be negative.

Based on hypothesized data for 150 players, the following regression equation is estimated for annual salary (measured in thousands) and strikeouts in a season (K) with the following result:

$$S = -242.2 + 7.72K \qquad R^2 = 0.44$$
$$S_K = 3.07$$
$$t = 2.52$$

Note that the coefficient on strikeouts (7.72) is positive and statistically significant because the t-statistic, 2.52, is greater than 1.96, the value of Student's t for more than 120 degrees of freedom. But this suggests the nonsensical conclusion that players are paid more if they strike out more often! Because salary is measured in thousands of dollars, the coefficient 7.72 means that each additional strikeout is associated with an additional $7,720 in annual salary.

The problem is that a *misspecified* equation has resulted in a meaningless and misleading estimate of the relationship between strikeouts and salary. A better but probably still incomplete specification would have salary dependent on strikeouts and home runs (*H*). Using the same data on salaries and strikeouts but adding data on home runs results in the following multiple-regression equation:

$$S = 231.4 - \quad 1.64K \quad + \quad 8.57H \qquad R^2 = 0.92$$
$$(s_K = 1.93 \qquad (s_H = 1.33)$$
$$(t = -0.85) \qquad (t = 6.40)$$

By including information on the number of home runs, the estimated relationship between strikeouts and salary changes dramatically. That relationship now is negative (as hypothesized), although the coefficient is not significantly different from zero. However, there is a very strong relationship between salary and home runs. The estimated coefficient (8.57) suggests that each home run is associated with an additional $8,750 in salary. Furthermore, this coefficient is statistically significant because the *t*-statistic is greater than 1.96.

Changing the specification of the equation resulted in an entirely different set of conclusions about how salary is related to performance. By including data on home runs it is seen that the number of strikeouts is inversely related to salary. More important, the multiple-regression equation shows that salary is determined primarily by the number of home runs hit. Furthermore, in the first equation, R^2 is only 0.44—less than one-half the variation in the salary variable is explained. By including data on both strikeouts and home runs, R^2 increased to 0.92. The multiple-regression equation that includes both strikeouts and home runs fits the data much better.

The first equation failed to consider the number of home runs. By omitting this most important information, the strange result was obtained that suggested strikeouts result in higher salaries. This erroneous conclusion resulted because many home-run hitters tend to strike out quite often. Obviously, their high salaries are tied to home-run production, not strikeouts. But by estimating the relationship between salary and strikeouts, it appeared that baseball players receive higher salaries for striking out more often.

The more complete analysis suggests that the number of strikeouts is relatively unimportant when the effect of home runs is considered. This suggests one of the advantages of the multiple-regression approach over simple regression. In multiple regression, the regression coefficient measures the net or partial effect of each independent variable while holding the effect of the other independent variables constant. Often, in multiple-regression analysis, the estimated coefficients $\hat{b}_i$ are referred to as *partial regression coefficients* to emphasize this relationship. In the example, the coefficient on home runs is 8.57, which means while holding the effect of strikeouts constant, each additional home run is associated with an additional $8,570 in salary. The coefficient on strikeouts is −1.64. This means that after adjusting for the number of home runs, each additional strikeout is associated with $1,640 fewer dollars of salary.

KEY CONCEPTS

- A regression equation can be used to predict the value of the dependent variable for given values of the independent variable.
- In a multiple-regression equation there are two or more independent variables. The estimated coefficient for each independent variable measures the net relationship between that variable and the dependent variable, holding constant the influence of the other independent variables.
- If the wrong independent variables are included in the equation and/or if important independent variables are not included, the regression equation is said to be misspecified.

Time Value of Money

Many transactions involve making or receiving cash payments at various future dates. A home buyer trades a promise to make monthly payments for thirty years for a large amount of cash now to pay for a home. A person injured in an automobile accident accepts an insurance company's settlement of $1,000 per month for life in trade for a release of any additional liability. High-priced professional athletes offer their skills for multiyear, no-cut contracts. In all these cases, the concepts of the time value of money are required to make sound decisions. This section outlines the approach to analyzing problems that involve payment and/or receipt of money at one or more points in time.

Consider the choice of having $100 immediately or $100 in five years. Surely the $100 now is preferred. One may have a pressing need for goods and services. If not, the money could be deposited in a bank account, where interest would accrue each year, making the amount available in five years substantially more than $100. The key point is that dollar values in different time periods are not comparable. Decision making requires that these flows or payments made at different times be reduced to a common denominator so that they can be compared.

Understanding the following terms is essential to applying time-value of money principles:

Annuity: a series of equal payments per period for a specified length of time. For example, the repayment of a loan by making forty-eight monthly payments of $200 each is a form of annuity.

Amount: a specific number of dollars to be paid or received on a specified date.

Present value: the value today of an amount or an annuity, taking into consideration that interest can be earned.

Future value: the value of an amount or an annuity at a specified future date, taking into consideration that interest can be earned.

In this section the approach to solving the four basic time-value-of-money problems are outlined: (1) the future value of an amount, (2) the present value of an amount, (3) the present value of an annuity, and (4) the future value of an annuity.

Future Value of an Amount

Suppose that an amount of $100 is deposited in an account that earns 10 percent interest. In five years that amount would have grown to $161. Thus, it is said that at an interest rate of 10 percent, $161 is the future value of $100 in five years. Conversely, $100 is said to be the present value of $161 in five years if the interest rate is 10 percent.

How does $100 grow into $161 in five years? At the end of the first year the account would have increased to $110, that is,

$$FV_1 = 100(1 + 0.10) = 110$$

where FV_1 refers to the (future) value of the account at the end of one year. After two years, the account would have increased to $121:

$$FV_2 = FV_1(1.10) = 100(1.10)(1.10) = 100(1.10)^2 = \$121$$

Continuing this process for five years results in a balance of $161, computed as

$$FV_5 = 100(1.10)^5 = \$161$$

In general, the equation for the future value of any amount (S) for n periods at an interest rate of i is

$$FV_n = S(1 + i)^n \qquad (2\text{-}16)$$

Using electronic calculators, especially those with built-in financial functions, the computation of a future value is made easy. Alternatively, tables of various present and future value factors can be used. Consider the future value of a sum of $42,216 in ten years at 8 percent interest. The equation would be

$$FV = 42,216(1.08)^{10}$$

The term $(1.08)^{10}$ is the future value of $1 and is called the *future value interest factor* $(FVIF_{i,n})$, corresponding to an interest rate of 10 percent (i) for ten periods (n). By having a table of these factors for various periods of time and interest rates, the computation of the future value can be simplified considerably. First, take the factor from the table that corresponds to the specified interest rate and number of periods. Then multiply that factor by the amount in question.

A complete set of future value interest factors is included as Table I at the end of the book. Part of that table is shown in Table 2-5. By looking down the column

Table 2-5. Selected Future Value Interest Factors:
$FVIF_{i,n} = (1 + i)^n$

Periods	Interest Rate		
	8%	10%	12%
2	1.1664	1.2100	1.2544
4	1.3605	1.4641	1.5735
6	1.5869	1.7716	1.9738
8	1.8509	2.1436	2.4760
10	2.1589	2.5937	3.1058

labeled "8%" to the row that corresponds to ten periods ($n = 10$), the *FVIF* of 2.1589 is found. This number is the future value of $1 after ten periods at 8 percent interest per period. This means that $1 would have increased to about $2.16 during the ten-year period. By multiplying the *FVIF* by the amount $42,216, the future value is found, that is,

$$FV_n = 42{,}216 \times 2.159 = \$91{,}144$$

Present Value of an Amount

The basic equation for the future value of an amount S has been shown to be

$$FV = S(1 + i)^n$$

Because S refers to an amount of money today, it is also the present value. Thus substituting the symbol PV (present value) for S and solving for PV, the equation for the present value of sum is obtained:

$$PV = FV\left[\frac{1}{(1 + i)^n}\right] \tag{2-17}$$

The bracketed term,

$$\left[\frac{1}{(1 + i)^n}\right]$$

is the present value of $1 in n periods if the interest rate is i percent. It is called the *present value interest factor* ($PVIF_{i,n}$).

As an example, what is the present value of $91,144 in ten years if the discount rate is 8 percent per year?

The equation is

$$PV = \$91{,}144\left[\frac{1}{1.08}\right]^{10}$$

The present value interest factors ($PVIF_{i,n}$) for a range of interest rates and periods are found in Table II at the end of the book. Part of that table is reproduced as Table 2-6. Note that the present value factors decrease as the number of periods increases and as the interest rate increases. Because the interest rate is in the

Table 2-6. Selected Present Value Interest Factors:

$$PVIF_{i,n} = \left(\frac{1}{1+i}\right)^n$$

	Interest Rate		
Periods	8%	10%	12%
1	0.9259	0.9091	0.8929
2	0.8573	0.8264	0.7972
3	0.7938	0.7513	0.7118
4	0.7350	0.6830	0.6355
6	0.6302	0.5645	0.5066
8	0.5403	0.4665	0.4039
10	0.4632	0.3855	0.3220

denominator of the present value equation, there is an inverse relationship between the present value and the interest rate. Further, the longer the period of time before an amount is paid, the lower the present value of any amount.

By reading down the "8%" column in Table 2-6 to the row for $n = 10$ periods, the factor 0.4632 is found. This is the present value of $1 in ten years at 8 percent interest. Multiplying this factor by $91,144, we obtain

$$PV = 91,144(0.463) = \$42,200$$

which, except for rounding error, is the initial amount in the previous example. The two examples simply convert an amount, $42,216, to a future value and then convert it back to the original present value.

The process of reducing future values to their present values is often referred to as *discounting*. In this context, the interest rate used in present value problems is sometimes referred to as a *discount rate*.

CASE STUDY

THE $40 MILLION MAN

The period 1965–1985 was one of unprecedented escalation in the compensation paid to professional athletes. In the early part of that period, salaries for star football and basketball players of $100,000 to $200,000 per year made headlines. By the early 1980s, multiyear contracts valued at $2 million to $4 million were not uncommon for many athletes, including a few who were of something less than star caliber. In some cases, of course, the value of the contract was overstated as a publicity ploy, or part of the payment was in the form of a loan. Nevertheless, many athletes were being paid enormous amounts of money.

Despite being accustomed to routine reports of ever-higher salaries, the sports world was shaken by the announcement in early 1984 that Steve Young had signed a contract with the Los Angeles Express of the United States Football League (USFL) reportedly worth $40 million. Young had been an All-American quarterback at Brigham Young University for two seasons and was one of the most sought-after college players. Because the reported amount of the contract was so large (perhaps ten times what other star athletes were receiving), the news media subjected it to close scrutiny, and probably for the first time, reporters used time-value-of-money principles to evaluate the stream of payments.

The contract called for the following payments to be made in return for Young playing football for four years:

Bonus for signing: $2.5 million plus a $1.5 million interest-free loan.
Salary: 1984, $200,000; 1985, $280,000; 1986, $330,000; and 1987, $400,000.
Deferred payments: A total of $30 million in payments that begin in 1990 and are paid through the year 2027. Although the full details of these payments were not released, it is known that they escalate steadily, reaching $1 million in 2005 and $2.4 million in 2027.

In addition, Young signed an endorsement arrangement with a financial institution in Salt Lake City that would pay him $100,000 per year for four years.

Assuming the interest-free loan to be worth $150,000 a year for four years, and using a discount rate of 10 percent, the present value of the bonus, salary, and endorsement contract is about $4.3 million. Because the details of the deferred payments are not known, their present value cannot be determined precisely, but estimates of about $2 million have been made. (Note that the 1984 present value of $1 million in 2005 is $135,000 and the present value of $2.4 million in 2027 is $40,000.) Thus although the total payments are estimated to be about $40 million, their present value is probably "only" about $6 million.

Steve Young's contract had two major effects. First, it gave the fledgling USFL a tremendous amount of publicity; and second, it introduced the concept of the time value of money to the sports pages of most newspapers in the United States.

In early 1985, the Los Angeles Express ran into financial problems and the USFL made a lump-sum payment to Young to settle all the future annuity payments that were due. In addition, the Salt Lake City financial institution also experienced financial problems and was taken over by a larger savings and loan association.

The Present Value of an Annuity

An *annuity* has been defined as a series of periodic equal payments. Although the term is often thought of in terms of a retirement pension, there are many other examples of annuities. The repayment schedule for a mortgage loan is an annuity. A father's agreement to send his son $200 each month while he is in college is another example. Usually, the number of periods is specified but not always. Sometimes retirement benefits are paid monthly as long as a person is alive. In other cases, the annuity is paid forever and is called a *perpetuity*.

It must be emphasized that an annuity implies equal payments. A contract to make twenty annual payments, which increase each year by, say, 10 percent, would not be an annuity. As some financial arrangements provide for payments with periodic increases, care must be taken not to apply an annuity formula if the flow of payments is not an annuity.

The present value of an annuity can be thought of as the sum of the present values of each of several amounts. Consider an annuity of three $100 payments at the end of each of the next three years at 10 percent interest. The present value of each payment is

$$PV_1 = 100 \left(\frac{1}{1.10}\right)$$

$$PV_2 = 100 \left(\frac{1}{1.10}\right)^2$$

$$PV_3 = 100 \left(\frac{1}{1.10}\right)^3$$

and the sum of these would be

$$PV = 100 \left(\frac{1}{1.10}\right) + 100 \left(\frac{1}{1.10}\right)^2 + 100 \left(\frac{1}{1.10}\right)^3$$

Substituting the appropriate present value interest factors from Table 2-6 and multiplying yields the present value of this annuity:

$$PV = 100(0.909 + 0.826 + 0.751) = 100(2.486) = \$248.60$$

Although this approach works, it clearly would be cumbersome for annuities of more than a few periods. For example, consider using this method to find the present value of a monthly payment for forty years if the monthly interest rate is 1 percent per month. That would require evaluating the present value of each of 480 amounts!

In general, the formula for the present value of an annuity of A dollars per period, n periods, and a discount rate of i is

$$PV = A \left(\frac{1}{1 + i}\right)^1 + A \left(\frac{1}{1 + i}\right)^2 + \cdots + A \left(\frac{1}{1 + i}\right)^n$$

This can be written as

$$PV = \sum_{t=1}^{n} A \left[\left(\frac{1}{1 + i}\right)^t \right]$$

or

$$PV = A \left[\sum_{t=1}^{n} \left(\frac{1}{1 + i}\right)^t \right] \tag{2-18}$$

Equation (2-18) is the basic equation for the present value of an annuity. Recall that $\sum_{t=1}^{n}$ means the sum of n separate components, the first where $t = 1$, the second where $t = 2$, and so on, to $t = n$.

The term

$$\sum_{t=1}^{n} \left[\frac{1}{(1 + i)^t} \right]$$

Table 2-7. Selected Present Value Annuity Factors:

$$PVAF_{i,n} = \sum_{t=1}^{n} \frac{1}{(1 + i)^t}$$

Periods	Interest Rate		
	1%	2%	3%
12	11.2551	10.5753	9.9540
24	21.2434	18.9139	16.9355
30	25.8077	22.3965	19.6004

is called the *present value annuity factor* ($PVAF_{i,n}$). It is the present value of an annuity of $1 per period for n periods at a discount rate of i percent. Table III at the end of the book provides these factors. Part of that table is reproduced as Table 2-7.

Consider the present value of an annuity of $3,522 per month for thirty months with an interest rate of 1 percent per month. Note that this problem is different from the first two examples because it considers monthly (not annual) payments and a monthly discount rate. This should not be confusing. The general problem refers to n periods and a discount rate of i percent *per period*. As long as the length of period (i.e., month, year, etc.) and the interest rate for that period correspond, the approach is straightforward. For example, if the periods are years, the interest rate must be a yearly rate.

The equation for the present value of this annuity is

$$PV = 3,522 \left[\sum_{t=1}^{30} \left(\frac{1}{1.01} \right)^t \right]$$

The factor

$$\sum_{t=1}^{30} \frac{1}{(1.01)^t}$$

is the present value of an annuity of $1. From Table 2-7, that value is $25.81. Substituting that value and multiplying gives $PV = 3,522(25.81) = \$90,902$. This means that an amount of $90,902 invested at an interest rate of 1 percent per month would be just adequate to make thirty monthly payments of $3,522.

A similar problem might be stated in the following way. What is the present value of a series of 120 monthly payments of $150 if the discount rate is 15 percent per year? Note that the payments are monthly, but the discount rate is an annual rate. By dividing the annual discount rate by 12, the appropriate monthly rate is found (i.e., $15/12 = 1.25$). Thus the solution would be

$$PV = 150 \left[\sum_{t=1}^{120} \frac{1}{(1.0125)^t} \right] = 150(61.98) = \$9,297$$

CASE STUDY

ECONOMICS IN THE COURTROOM

Often when a person is injured or killed as a result of a wrongful act of another, a lawsuit is filed against the person committing that act. Usually, such a suit makes a claim for medical costs, pain and suffering, and economic damages. Economic damages include loss of income due to an inability to work and sometimes lost capacity to perform household services.

Consider the case of a worker who is injured and is expected to be disabled for five years. Assume that medical expenses will be $1,000 during the first year and $500 in each of the next four years. Furthermore, the worker would have earned $20,000 in the current year, and that salary would have increased by 7 percent each year. Thus the projected losses due to the accident are:

Year	Medical Expenses	Earnings	Total Economic Loss
1	$1,000	$20,000	$ 21,000
2	500	21,400	21,900
3	500	22,900	23,400
4	500	24,500	24,900
5	500	26,200	26,700
		Total	$122,000

An attorney might argue that the plaintiff (i.e., the injured party) claims $122,000 as the economic loss and that this amount should be paid now as compensation. Clearly, this is wrong, because $122,000 is not the present value of all future losses. The amount of $122,000 was determined by adding together dollar losses in each of the next five years, but these dollar values are not comparable and should not be added together because they have different present values.

To see that $122,000 is not the correct amount of the loss, assume that this amount was awarded and that the market interest rate is 10 percent. The money is invested and at the end of each year, interest is received and a disbursement made that is equal to the annual earnings loss and medical expenses projected for that year. The schedule of receipts and disbursements would be as follows:

Year	Fund Balance Beginning of Year	Plus: Interest	Less: Disbursement	Fund Balance End of Year
1	$122,000	$12,000	$21,000	$113,200
2	113,200	11,320	21,900	102,620
3	102,620	10,262	23,400	89,482
4	89,482	8,948	24,900	73,530
5	73,530	7,353	26,700	54,183

By investing that fund at the market rate of interest, each year an amount equivalent to the economic loss for that year could be paid and the plaintiff would still have more than $54,000 left at the end of five years. Clearly, an award of $122,000 would overcompensate the plaintiff for the losses sustained.

The problem is that the compensation should be the present value of the economic losses over the next five years. That is,

$$PV = \frac{21{,}000}{1.10} + \frac{21{,}900}{(1.10)^2} + \frac{23{,}400}{(1.10)^3} + \frac{24{,}900}{(1.10)^4} + \frac{26{,}700}{(1.10)^5} = \$88{,}356$$

This amount, invested at the market rate of interest, is exactly enough to meet the projected economic loss each year leaving a zero balance in the fund at the end of five years. The sum, $88,356, is the actual amount of the future economic loss in terms of present value and is the value that should be claimed by the plaintiff. The initial amount discussed, $122,000, was too high by $33,664.* In contrast, the payout schedule for the five-year period based on an initial fund of $88,356 would be as follows:

Year	Fund Balance Beginning of Year	Plus: Interest	Less: Disbursement	Fund Balance End of Year
1	$88,356	$8,836	$21,000	$76,192
2	76,192	7,619	21,900	61,911
3	61,911	6,191	23,400	44,702
4	44,702	4,470	24,900	24,272
5	24,272	2,427	26,700	0

Note that the last payment exactly exhausts the fund balance plus the interest earned in the fifth year, leaving nothing in the fund. Using the present value of the future appraised losses allows for payments to be made to the injured person that correspond exactly to those losses with no excess amount remaining at the end of the payout period.

---

* Note that this $33,644, invested at 10 percent interest for five years, will increase to $54,183, the amount left in the fund in the previous example.

Future Value of an Annuity

The last of the four time-value-of-money problems concerns the future value of annuity. A teenager saving $20 each month for college or a worker who contributes $15 weekly to a retirement fund are building up future values. Both will be interested in knowing how much money they will have at some future date.

Finding the future value of an annuity is equivalent to finding the future value of each of several amounts and then adding them together. For example, the future value of an annuity of $100 to be paid at the end of each of the next three years if the interest rate is 12 percent would be[5]

$$FV = 100(1.12)^2 + 100(1.12)^1 + 100(1.12)^0$$
$$= 100(1.25) + 100(1.12) + 100(1.00) = \$337$$

---

[5] Note that if each payment is made at the end of a year, over the three-year period the first payment would earn interest for two years (from the end of the first year to the end of the third); the second payment would earn interest for one year, and so on.

Table 2-8. Selected Future Value Annuity Factors:

$$FVAF_{i,n} = \sum_{t=1}^{n} (1 + i)^{t-1}$$

Periods	Interest Rate		
	8%	10%	12%
20	45.7620	57.2750	72.0524
30	113.2832	164.4940	241.3327
40	259.0565	442.5926	767.0914

In general, the equation for the future value of an annuity of A per period for n periods at i percent interest would be

$$FV = A(1 + i)^{n-1} + A(1 + i)^{n-2} + \cdots + A(1 + i)^0$$

which can be written

$$FV = \sum_{t=1}^{n} A(1 + i)^{t-1}$$

or   (2-19)

$$FV = A\left[\sum_{t=1}^{n} (1 + i)^{t-1}\right]$$

The bracketed term in equation (2-19) is the *future value annuity factor* ($FVAF_{i,n}$), which is the future value of an annuity of \$1 for n periods at i percent interest per period. These factors are reported for various interest rates and number of periods in Table IV. Part of that table is shown in Table 2-8.

For example, consider the entry 164.494 that corresponds to thirty periods and an interest rate of 10 percent per period. This means that if a dollar were deposited at the end of each period in an account that earned 10 percent interest, at the end of thirty periods there would be \$164.49 in that account.

KEY CONCEPT

- Given the interest rate per period (i), the number of periods (n), and the amount (S) or the annuity payment (A), there are four basic time-value-of-money problems.

Future value of an amount: $FV = S(1 + i)^n$

FV is the future value of an amount S invested at i percent per period for n periods. The term $(i + i)^n$ is the future value interest factor ($FVIF_{i,n}$).

Present value of an amount: $PV = S\left[\dfrac{1}{(1 + i)^n}\right]$

PV is the present value of an amount S to be received (or paid) in n periods if the interest rate is i percent per period. The term $(1/1 + i)^n$ is the present value interest factor ($PVIF_{i,n}$).

$$\text{Present value of an annuity: } PV = A \left[\sum_{t=1}^{n} \frac{1}{(1 + i)^t} \right]$$

Here PV is the present value of an annuity of A per period paid for n periods if the interest rate is i percent per period. The term $\sum_{t=1}^{n} [1/(1 + i)]^t$ is the present value annuity factor $PVAF_{i,n}$.

$$\text{Future value of an annuity: } FV = A \left[\sum_{t=1}^{n} (1 + i)^{t-1} \right]$$

FV is the future value of an annuity of A per period paid for n periods if the interest rate is i percent per period. The term $\sum_{t=1}^{n} (1 + i)^{t-1}$ is the future value annuity factor $FVAF_{i,n}$.

Summary

A functional relationship such as $y = f(x_1, x_2, \ldots, x_n)$ means that the value of the dependent variable y depends on the values of the independent variables x_1, $x_2, \ldots, x_n$ in a systematic way and that there is a unique value of y for any set of values for those independent variables. An economic model may consist of several related functions. Total, average, and marginal relationships are fundamental to understanding and using economics. The marginal function is the slope of the total function. The intersection of the marginal and average functions occurs at either the minimum or the maximum point of the average function.

The least-squares regression technique is used to estimate the parameters of a relationship between a dependent variable, Y, and one or more independent variables X_i. In simple regression there is one independent variable, whereas in multiple regression there are two or more independent variables. The coefficient of determination, R^2, is used to test the explanatory power of the entire regression equation. This statistic measures the proportion of total variation in the dependent variable that is explained by variation in the independent variable(s). The ratio of an individual coefficient to its standard deviation, called the t-statistic, is used to test the explanatory power of individual independent variables. If the absolute value of that ratio is greater than the tabled value from Student's t distribution for $n - k - 1$ degrees of freedom, the coefficient is said to be statistically significant. The regression equation can be used to make point and interval estimates of the predicted value of Y for any value of the independent variables. If the wrong variables are included in the equation and/or important variables are not included, the equation is said to be misspecified. If the equation is misspecified, the estimated coefficients may lead to incorrect conclusions about the relationship between the dependent and independent variables.

Time-value-of-money concepts are essential when analyzing dollar values associated with different times. The parameters of any time-value problems are the number of periods (n), the rate of interest (i), the amount (S) or annuity payment (A), and the present value (PV) or future value (FV). If any three of these four parameters are given, the fourth can be determined. The four basic time-value-of-money problems are as follows:

1. *Future value of an amount:* $FV = S(1 + i)^n$

2. *Present value of an amount:* $PV = S\left[\dfrac{1}{1+i}\right]^n$

3. *Present value of an annuity:* $PV = A\left[\displaystyle\sum_{t=1}^{n} \left(\dfrac{1}{1+i}\right)^t\right]$

4. *Future value of an annuity:* $FV = A\left[\displaystyle\sum_{t=1}^{n} (1 + i)^{t-1}\right]$

Discussion Questions

2-1. Explain the concept of an economic model. Why do economists and managers use such models as part of the decision-making process?

2-2. Economists are not the only scientists to use models in their work. Describe how other disciplines use models or similar abstractions from reality in their work.

2-3. Explain the relationship among the total, average, and marginal functions. Explain intuitively why any intersection of the average and the marginal function will occur at a maximum or a minimum point on the average function.

2-4. Sid Green is an assistant to the president but is untrained in the quantitative techniques of managerial economics. During a board meeting he complains that such techniques are of little value because they are always subject to error and therefore should not be part of the decision-making process. If the chairman asked for your opinion, what would be your response?

2-5. Explain how present value (or future value) depends on the amount or annuity payment, the number of payments, and the interest rate.

2-6. Is the statement "y is a function of x" equivalent to saying that "y is caused by x"? In this context, critically evaluate the following statement:
"The incidence of lung cancer is significantly higher for heavy smokers than for nonsmokers. Therefore, smoking causes cancer."

Problems

2-1. Given the following supply and demand equations

$$Q_D = 100 - 5P$$
$$Q_S = 10 + 5P$$

(a) Determine the equilibrium price and quantity.
(b) If the government sets a minimum price of $10 per unit, how many units would be supplied and how many would be demanded?
(c) If the government sets a maximum price of $5 per unit, how many units would be supplied and how many would be demanded?
(d) If demand increases to

$$Q_D' = 200 - 5P,$$

determine the new equilibrium price and quantity.

2-2. Given the following demand function

$$Q = 20 - 0.10P,$$

where P = price and Q = rate of output, complete the table below. (Note that total revenue is equal to price times quantity.)

Quantity	Price	Total Revenue	Average Revenue	Marginal Revenue
1				
2				
3				
4				
5				
6				
7				
8				
9				
10				
11				
12				

2-3. Given the total cost function

$$TC = 150Q - 3Q^2 + 0.25Q^3,$$

complete the following table by computing the total, average, and marginal costs associated with each output rate indicated.

Quantity	Total Cost	Average Cost	Marginal Cost
1			
2			
3			
4			
5			
6			
7			
8			
9			
10			
11			
12			

2-4. Using the data developed in Problems 2-2 and 2-3,

  (a) Plot the total, average, and marginal functions for both revenue and cost. [*Note:* Use a two-part graph similar to Figure 2-2 in the chapter that places the total functions in the upper part and the average and marginal functions in the lower half. Also, it is conventional to plot the marginal values at the midpoint between the quantity values to which they relate. For example, the marginal revenue associated with going from 2 units of output to 3 units is $50. This value should be plotted midway between the 2- and 3-unit marks on the quantity (i.e., horizontal) axis.]

  (b) What is true of the marginal revenue function at that level of output where total revenue is at a maximum?

  (c) Determine total profit by subtracting total cost from total profit at each rate of output. Plot this function in the upper part of your diagram.

  (d) By comparing the marginal revenue and marginal cost curves and relating them to the profit curve, can you think of a rule the firm might use to determine that output rate that would maximize profit?

2-5. The following regression equation estimates the relationship between the number of cups of hot chocolate sold (H) and number swimmers (S) at a beach:

$$H = 252.8 - 2.05S \qquad R^2 = 0.45$$
$$(2.06) \quad\; (-3.05)$$

(t-values are shown in parentheses).

  (a) Explain or interpret the regression coefficient, the t-value, and the coefficient of determination of this equation.

  (b) How is it possible that more hot chocolate is sold when there are fewer people at the beach? Does this relationship suggest anything about the specification of the equation?

2-6. Sid Gaston, mrketing vice president of United Feeds, Inc., has provided the following quarterly price–quantity data for UF Superb, a horsefeed additive. He has asked that the demand curve for this product be estimated.

	Quarter									
	1	2	3	4	5	6	7	8	9	10
Price	60	53	43	40	47	57	41	53	37	51
Quantity	83	93	100	108	97	80	105	86	110	90

  (a) Use the ordinary least-squares regression method to estimate this function. Compute all relevant statistics.

  (b) Gaston is considering a 30 percent price increase (from 51 to 66). Make a point and interval estimate of sales volume if this price increase is made.

  (c) Do you have any concerns about either part (a) or (b) of this assignment that you should communicate to Gaston?

2-7. Robert Ryan, general manager of the Chicago Stars professional football team, is currently negotiating a new contract with Ronnie Smith, the team's star running back. Under league rules, Smith is now a "free agent," which means that he is free to negotiate a contract with any other team in the league. Smith has presented Ryan with a final contract demand consisting of alternatives for a five-year contract. If

Ryan does not agree to one of these, Smith will sign with another team. The alternative contract demands are:

1. A $2,000,000 bonus payment immediately, a payment of $500,000 at the end of each of the next five years, and a deferred payment of $1,000,000 at the end of the fifth year of the contract.

2. A $500,000 bonus payment now, payments of $300,000 at the end of each of the next five years, and deferred payments of $200,000 each payable at the end of years 11 through 20.

Ryan has determined that Smith's value to the team over the next five years is about $3,000,000 (in terms of the present value of additional revenue from gate receipts and television discounted at 12 percent per year). Should Ryan accept one of Smith's contract demands, and if so, which one? Explain fully.

2-8. A rich uncle gives you the choice of one of the following legacies:

1. $15,000 each year for the next twelve years.

2. $13,000 each year for the next eighteen years.

3. $11,000 each year for the next twelve years plus a lump sum payment of $81,000 at the end of the eighteenth year.

Which would you take and why? Assume that the appropriate discount rate is 10 percent and all amounts would be received at the end of the year.

2-9. Rosemary Schwartz begins working on her twenty-fifth birthday and works for the next forty years. At the end of each year she pays $5,541 in social security taxes (the maximum combined employee-employer tax in 1985).

(a) If she had put this into a tax-deferred retirement account paying 10 percent interest, how much would be in that account when she retired?

(b) At 10 percent interest, how much interest could be paid each year without using any of the principal?

(c) If Schwartz makes one-time additions to this account of $20,000 on her thirty-fifth birthday and $30,000 on her forty-fifth birthday, how large will the fund be when she reaches age 65?

Problems Requiring Calculus

2-10. Given the following function that relates total revenue (*TR*) to output (*Q*),

$$TR = 20Q - 2Q^2,$$

determine:

(a) that rate of output that results in maximum total revenue;

(b) the marginal revenue function;

(c) the rate of output for which marginal revenue is zero. Is there any connection between your answers to parts a and c?

2-11. Given the total cost function

$$TC = 100Q - Q^2 + 0.3Q^3$$

where Q = rate of output and TC = total cost, determine:

(a) the marginal and average cost functions; and

(b) the rate of output that results in minimum average cost.

2-12. Given the firm's demand function is:

$$Q = 55 - 0.5P$$

where P = price and Q = rate of output; and the total cost function is

$$TC = 20 + Q + 0.2Q^2$$

where TC = total cost, determine:

(a) the total revenue function for the firm. (Hint: to find the total revenue function, solve the demand function for P and then multiply by Q.)

(b) the marginal revenue and marginal cost functions and find that rate of output for which marginal revenue equals marginal cost.

(c) an equation for profit by subtracting the total cost function from the total revenue function. Find that level of output that maximizes total profit. Compare your answer to that obtained in part (b). Is there any correspondence between these questions?

References

Chiang, A. C. 1983. *Fundamental Methods of Mathematical Economics*, 3rd ed. New York: McGraw-Hill.

Draper, N. R., and Smith, H. 1981. *Applied Regression Analysis*, 2nd ed. New York: Wiley.

Henderson, J, and Quandt, R. E. 1980. *Microeconomic Theory: A Mathematical Approach*, 3rd ed. New York: McGraw-Hill.

Intriligator, M. D. 1971. *Mathematical Optimization and Economic Theory*. Englewood Cliffs, N.J.: Prentice-Hall.

Johnston, J. 1984. *Econometric Methods*, 3rd ed. New York: McGraw-Hill.

Kelejian, H. H., and Oates, W. E. 1981. *Introduction to Econometrics*, 2nd ed. New York: Harper & Row.

Khoury, S. J., and Parsons, T. D. 1981. *Mathematical Methods in Finance and Economics*. New York: Elsevier/North-Holland.

Kmenta, J. 1971. *Elements of Econometrics*. New York: Macmillan.

McLagan, D. L. 1973. "A Noneconometrician's Guide to Econometrics." *Business Economics*, May, 38–45.

Samuelson, P. A. 1983. *Foundations of Economic Analysis*, enlarged ed. Cambridge, Mass.: Harvard University Press.

Appendix:
Calculus and Managerial
Economics

Many resource allocation decisions fall into the category of optimization problems. *Optimization* refers to finding the best way to allocate resources given an objective function. For example, a production manager may seek to maximize production for given inputs of capital and labor or to minimize the cost of producing a specified rate of output. In contrast, the president of the firm, who has a broader perspective, may want to organize the firm's labor and capital resources in order to maximize profit.

The terms *maximize* and *minimize* imply an optimization problem. Sometimes such problems can be solved graphically or by using algebra. In other cases, however, the solution requires the use of calculus. In many cases calculus can be used to solve optimization problems more easily and often with more insight into the economics underlying that solution.

Consider a firm whose total revenues from sales are given by the function

$$TR = 20Q - Q^2$$

where Q represents the rate of output. That is, the dollar amount of sales revenue for any output Q is given by substituting that value of Q into the equation. Assume that the total cost of producing any rate of output is given by the equation

$$TC = 50 + 4Q$$

Given the firm's objective of maximizing profits (i.e., total revenue minus total cost), how much output should be produced? One approach would be to graph both the total revenue and total cost functions. The vertical distance between the two functions is profit. By finding that point where this vertical distance is the largest, the profit-maximizing output is found. This is shown in Figure 2A-1, which shows profit is maximized by producing 8 units of output ($Q = 8$).

An alternative approach is to develop a table showing revenue, cost, and profit at each rate of output. Such data are shown in Table 2A-1. The tabular method has the advantage of being somewhat more precise. That is, at an output rate of 8, total revenue is 96, total cost is 82, and profit is 14. From the graph in Figure 2A-1, these values can only be approximated.

The problem is that both approaches are essentially trial-and-error processes. What if the profit-maximizing output level is 8,000 or 8,000,000 instead of 8? The answer could be found using either approach, but finding that answer would have taken considerable time. What if there had been two outputs (Q_1 and Q_2) and three inputs (land, labor, and capital)? In this case, there is no straightforward way to determine profit-maximizing output rates for Q_1 and Q_2 using this method.

Table 2A-1. Total Revenue, Total Cost, and Total Profit

Q	TR	TC	Profit (TR − TC)
0	0	50	− 50
1	19	54	− 35
2	36	58	− 22
3	51	62	− 11
4	64	66	− 2
5	75	70	5
6	84	74	10
7	91	78	13
8	96	82	14
9	99	86	13
10	100	90	10
11	99	94	5

A more powerful technique is needed so that the solution process can be both precise and straightforward. Elementary calculus is easily adapted to optimization problems in economics. Indeed, a few basic principles can be used in many different kinds of problems. The profit-maximization problem outlined above could have been solved using the most elementary calculus. In the following, some basic principles of calculus are outlined and their application to economic problems is demonstrated.

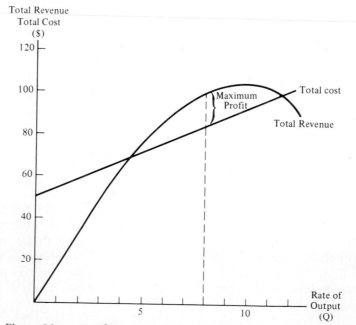

Figure 2A-1.   *Total Revenue and Total Cost.*

The Derivative of a Function

From algebra recall that for the function $y = f(x)$, the slope of that function is the change in y (denoted by Δy) divided by a change in x (i.e., Δx). The slope sometimes is referred to as the *rise* (the change in the variable measured on the vertical axis) over the *run* (the change in the variable measured on the horizontal axis). The slope is *positive* if the curve slopes upward from left to right and *negative* if the function slopes downward from left to right. A horizontal line has a *zero slope*, and a vertical line is said to have an *infinite slope*. For a positive change in x (i.e., $\Delta x > 0$), a positive slope implies that Δy is positive, and a negative slope implies that Δy is negative.

The function $y = 10 + x^2$ is graphed in Figure 2A-2. To determine the average slope of this function over the range $x = 1$ to $x = 2$, first find the corresponding y values. If $x_1 = 1$, then $y_1 = 11$, and if $x_2 = 2$, then $y_2 = 14$. Then the slope is found by using the formula

$$\text{slope} = \frac{\Delta y}{\Delta x} = \frac{y_2 - y_1}{x_2 - x_1} = \frac{14 - 11}{2 - 1} = 3$$

Actually, this method determines the slope of a straight line through the points a and b in Figure 2A-1. But the slope of $y = 10 + x^2$ is different at every point on that function. By making the interval smaller, a better estimate of the slope is determined. For example, consider the slope over the interval $x = 1$ to $x = 1.1$. If $x_1 = 1$, then $y_1 = 11$, and $x_2 = 1.1$ implies that $y_2 = 11.21$. Thus the slope is

$$\text{slope} = \frac{\Delta y}{\Delta x} = \frac{11.21 - 11}{1.1 - 1} = \frac{0.21}{0.10} = 2.1$$

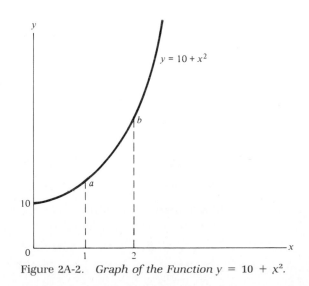

Figure 2A-2. *Graph of the Function* $y = 10 + x^2$.

By using calculus, the exact slope at any point on the function can be determined.

The first derivative of a function (denoted as dy/dx) is simply the slope of a function when the interval along the horizontal axis is infinitesimally small. Technically, the derivative is the limit of the ratio $\Delta y/\Delta x$ as Δx approaches zero, that is,

$$\frac{dy}{dx} = \lim_{\Delta x \to 0} \frac{\Delta y}{\Delta x}$$

Thus the calculus term dy/dx is analogous to $\Delta y/\Delta x$, but dy/dx is the precise slope at a point, whereas $\Delta y/\Delta x$ is the average slope over an interval of the function. The derivative can be thought of as the slope of a straight line drawn tangent to the function at that point. The derivative of $y = f(x)$ is sometimes written as $f'(x)$. For example, the slope of the function $y = 10 + x^2$ at point a in Figure 2B-2 is the slope of the straight line drawn tangent to that function at a.

What is the significance of this concept for managerial economics? Recall from the discussion of total and marginal relationships that the marginal function is simply the slope of the total function. Calculus offers an easy way to find the marginal function by taking the first derivative of the total function. Calculus also offers a set of rules for using these derivatives to make optimizing decisions such as minimizing cost or maximizing profit.

Standard calculus texts present numerous formulas for the derivative of various functions. In the hands of the skilled mathematician, these formulas allow the derivative of virtually any function to be found. Actually, only a few of these rules are necessary to solve most of the relevant problems in managerial economics. In this section each of these basic rules is explained and their use demonstrated.

The Derivative of a Constant.   The derivative of any constant is zero. When plotted, the equation of a constant (such as $y = 5$) is a horizontal line. For any Δx, the change in y is always zero. Thus for any equation $y = a$, where a is a constant,

$$\frac{dy}{dx} = 0 \qquad\qquad (2A\text{-}1)$$

The Derivative of an Identity.   The derivative of the identity function $y = x$ is 1; that is, if $y = x$,

$$\frac{dy}{dx} = 1 \qquad\qquad (2A\text{-}2)$$

The Derivative of a Constant Times a Function.   The derivative of a constant times a function is that constant times the derivative of the function. Thus the derivative of $y = af(x)$, where a is constant, is

$$\frac{dy}{dx} = af'(x) \qquad\qquad (2A\text{-}3)$$

For example, if $y = 3x$, the derivative is

$$\frac{dy}{dx} = 3f'(x) = 3(1) = 3$$

The Derivative of a Power Function.   For the general power function of the form $y = ax^b$, the derivative is

$$\frac{dy}{dx} = bax^{b-1} \tag{2A-4}$$

The function $y = x^2$ is a specific case of a power function where $a = 1$ and $b = 2$. Hence the derivative of this function is

$$\frac{dy}{dx} = 2x^{2-1} = 2x$$

The interpretation of this derivative is that the slope of the function $y = x^2$ at any point x is $2x$. For example, the slope at $x = 4$ would be found by substituting $x = 4$ into the derivative. That is

$$\left(\frac{dy}{dx}\right)_{x=4} = 2(4) = 8$$

Thus when $x = 4$, the change in y is 8 times a small change in x.

The function $y = x^2$ is shown in Figure 2A-3. Note that the slope changes continually. The slope at $x = 4$ is 8. As x increases, the slope becomes continually steeper. For negative values of x, the slope is negative. For example, if $x = -3$, the slope is -6.

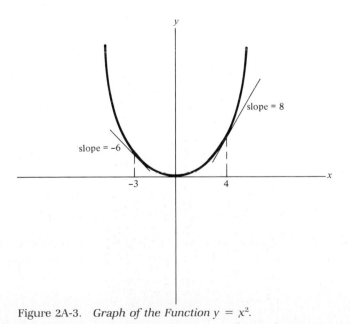

Figure 2A-3.   *Graph of the Function* $y = x^2$.

The Derivative of a Sum or Difference.   The derivative of a function that is a sum or difference of several terms is the sum (or difference) of the derivatives of each of the terms. That is, if $y = f(x) + g(x)$, then

$$\frac{dy}{dx} = f'(x) + g'(x) \tag{2A-5}$$

For example, the derivative of the function

$$y = 10 + 5x + 6x^2$$

is equal to the sum of the derivatives of each of the three terms on the right-hand side. Note that the rules for the derivative of a constant, a constant times a function, and a power function must be used. Thus

$$\frac{dy}{dx} = 0 + (1)5x^0 + (2)6x^1 = 5 + 12x$$

Consider a somewhat more complicated function:

$$y = 2x^3 - 6x^{-2} - 4x + 10$$

The derivative is

$$\frac{dy}{dx} = (3)2x^2 - (-2)6x^{-3} - 4 + 0$$
$$= 6x^2 + 12x^{-3} - 4$$

The Derivative of the Product of Two Functions.   Given a function of the form $y = f(x)\, g(x)$, the derivative dy/dx is given by

$$\frac{dy}{dx} = f'(x)g(x) + f(x)g'(x) \tag{2A-6}$$

That is, the derivative of the product of two functions is the derivative of the first function times the second function plus the first function times the derivative of the second.
   For example, the derivative of the function

$$y = (x^2 - 4)(x^3 + 2x + 2)$$

is

$$\frac{dy}{dx} = (2x)(x^3 + 2x + 2) + (x^2 - 4)(3x^2 + 2) = 5x^4 - 6x^2 + 4x - 8$$

The Derivative of a Quotient of Two Functions.   For a function of the form $y = f(x)/g(x)$, the derivative is

$$\frac{dy}{dx} = \frac{g(x)f'(x) - f(x)g'(x)}{[g(x)]^2} \tag{2A-7}$$

Given the function

$$y = \frac{x^2 - 3x}{x^2}$$

the first derivative would be

$$\frac{dy}{dx} = \frac{x^2(2x - 3) - (x^2 - 3x)(2x)}{(x^2)^2} = \frac{3x^2}{x^4} = 3x^{-2}$$

These seven rules of differentiation are sufficient to determine the derivatives of all the functions used in this book. However, sometimes two or more of the rules must be used at the same time.

EXAMPLE
FINDING THE MARGINAL FUNCTION

Given the total revenue function

$$TR = 50Q - 0.5Q^2$$

and the total cost function

$$TC = 2{,}000 + 200Q - 0.2Q^2 + 0.001Q^3$$

find the marginal revenue and marginal cost functions.

Solution:

Recall that a marginal function is simply the slope of the corresponding total function. For example, marginal revenue is the slope of total revenue. Thus, by finding the derivative of the total revenue function, the marginal revenue function will be obtained

$$MR = \frac{d(TR)}{dQ} = 50 - 2(0.5)Q^{2-1}$$

$$\boxed{MR = 50 - Q}$$

Similarly, the marginal cost function will be found by taking the first derivative of the total cost function:

$$MC = \frac{d(TC)}{dQ} = 0 + 200 - 2(0.2)Q^{2-1} + 3(0.001)Q^{3-1}$$

$$\boxed{MC = 200 - 0.4Q + 0.003Q^2}$$

KEY CONCEPTS

- The slope of a function $y = f(x)$ is the change in y (i.e., Δy) divided by the corresponding change in x (i.e., Δx).
- For a function $y = f(x)$, the derivative, written as dy/dx or $f'(x)$, is the slope

of the function at a particular point on the function. Equivalently, the derivative is the slope of a straight line drawn tangent to the function at that point.

- By using one or more of the seven formulas outlined in this appendix, the derivative of most functions encountered in managerial economics can be found.

Higher-Order Derivatives

The derivative of a function sometimes is called the *first derivative* as a way of indicating that there are higher-order derivatives. The *second derivative* of a function is simply the first derivative of the first derivative; it is written d^2y/dx^2. In the context of economics, the first derivative of a total function is the marginal function. The second derivative of the total function is the slope of the first derivative or the rate at which the marginal function is changing.

Higher-order derivatives are easy to find. One simply keeps taking the first derivative again. For example, given the function

$$y = 10x^3 + 3x^2 - 5x + 6$$

the first derivative is

$$\frac{dy}{dx} = 30x^2 + 6x - 5$$

and the higher order derivatives are:

$$\text{Second:} \quad \frac{d^2y}{dx^2} = 60x + 6$$

$$\text{Third:} \quad \frac{d^3y}{dx^3} = 60$$

$$\text{Fourth:} \quad \frac{d^4y}{dx^4} = 0$$

The second derivative has an important application in finding the maximum and/or minimum of a function. This application is explained in the following section.

Calculus and Optimization

Recall from the discussion of total and marginal relationships in the text that if the marginal function is positive, the total function must be increasing; if the marginal function is negative, the total function must be decreasing. It was shown that if the marginal function is zero, then the total function must be at either a maximum or a minimum. In Figure 2A-4, a total function and its associated marginal function are shown. At point *a*, which corresponds to $x = x_1$, the total

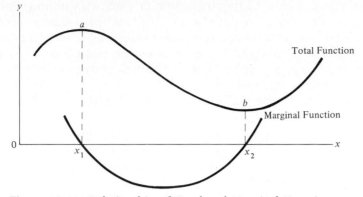

Figure 2A-4.   *Relationship of Total and Marginal Functions at Minimum and Maximum Points.*

function is at a maximum and the marginal function is zero. At point b, corresponding to $x = x_2$, the total function is minimized and the marginal function is again zero. Thus the marginal curve is zero at both x_1 and x_2. However, note the difference in the slope of the marginal function at these points. At x_1, the marginal curve has a negative slope, whereas at x_2, the slope is positive.

Because the total function is at a maximum or a minimum when its slope is zero, one way to find the value of x that results in a maximum or a minimum is to set the first derivative of the total function equal to zero and solve for x. This is a better approach than the trial-and-error method used earlier. In that example, a total revenue function,

$$TR = 20Q - Q^2$$

and a total cost function,

$$TC = 50 + 4Q$$

were given. The problem was to find the level of output, Q, that maximized profit.

The total profit function (π) is found by subtracting total cost from total revenue:

$$
\begin{aligned}
\pi &= TR - TC \\
&= 20Q - Q^2 - 50 - 4Q \\
&= -Q^2 + 16Q - 50
\end{aligned}
$$

The profit function will have a slope of zero where that function is at a maximum and also at its minimum point. To find the profit-maximizing output, take the first derivative of the profit function with respect to output, set that derivative equal to zero, and solve for output. That is, find the level (or levels) of output where the slope of the profit function is zero.

$$\frac{d\pi}{dQ} = -2Q + 16 = 0$$

$$2Q = 16$$

$$\boxed{Q = 8}$$

But is this output level a profit-maximum or profit-minimum point? Remember, setting the first derivative equal to zero and solving results in an extremum, but it could be a maximum or a minimum. But recall from Figure 2A-4 that if the total function is maximized, the marginal function has a negative slope. Conversely, a minimum point on a total function is associated with a positive slope of the marginal function.

Because the slope of the marginal function is the first derivative of that marginal function, a simple test to determine if a point is a maximum or minimum is suggested. Find the second derivative of the total function and evaluate it at the point where the slope of the total function is zero. If the second derivative is negative (i.e., the marginal function is decreasing), the total function is at a maximum. If the second derivative is positive at that point (i.e., the marginal function is increasing), the total function is at a minimum point.

In the profit-maximization problem above, the second derivative of the profit function is -2, which is negative. Therefore, profit is maximized at $Q = 8$.

When finding the extremum of any function, setting the first derivative equal to zero is called the *first-order condition*, meaning that this condition is necessary for an extremum but not sufficient to determine if the function is at a maximum or a minimum. The test for a maximum or a minimum using the second derivative is called the *second-order condition*. The first- and second-order conditions together are said to be sufficient to test for either a maximum or a minimum point. These conditions are summarized as follows:

	Maximum	Minimum
First-order condition	$\dfrac{dy}{dx} = 0$	$\dfrac{dy}{dx} = 0$
Second-order condition	$\dfrac{d^2y}{dx^2} < 0$	$\dfrac{d^2y}{dx^2} > 0$

In some problems there will be two or possibly more points where the first derivative is zero. In those cases, all those points will have to be evaluated using the second-order condition to test for a minimum or a maximum. As shown in Figure 2A-5, a function could have several points, such as *a*, *b*, *c*, and *d*, where the slope is zero. Points *a* and *c* are relative maxima and *b* and *d* are relative minima. The term *relative* means that the point is an extremum only for part of the function. For example, both points *a* and *c* in Figure 2A-5 are relative maxima. Point *a* is a maximum relative to other points on the function around it. It is not the maximum point for the entire function because the value of *y* at point *c* exceeds that at point *a*.

The Partial Derivative

Many economic phenomena are described by functions having two or more independent variables. Given a general function such as

$$y = f(x, z)$$

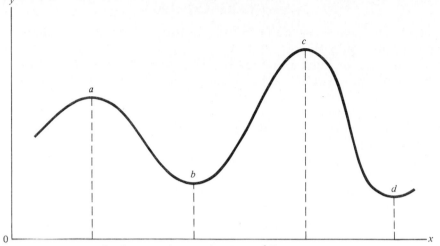

Figure 2A-5. *Graph of a Function Having Several Extrema.*

the first partial derivative of y with respect to x, denoted as $\frac{\partial y}{\partial x}$ or f_x, indicates the slope relationship between y and x when z is held constant. This partial derivative is found by considering z to be fixed and taking the derivative of y with respect to x in the usual way. Similarly, the partial derivative of y with respect to z $\left(\text{i.e., } \frac{\partial y}{\partial z} \text{ or } f_z \right)$ is found by considering x to be a constant and taking the first derivative of y with respect to z in the usual way.

For example, consider the function

$$y = x^2 + 3xz + z^2$$

To find the partial derivative $\frac{\partial y}{\partial x}$ or f_x, consider z as fixed and take the derivative. Thus

$$f_x = 2x^{2-1} + (3z) + 0 = \boxed{2x + 3z}$$

This partial derivative means that a small change in x is associated with y changing at the rate $2x + 3z$ when z is held constant at a specified level. For example, if $z = 2$, the slope between y and x is $2x + 3(2)$ or $2x + 6$. If $z = 5$, the slope between y and x would be $2x + 3(5)$, or $2x + 15$.

Similarly, the partial derivative of y with respect to z would be

$$f_z = 0 + 3x + 2z^{2-1} = \boxed{3x + 2z}$$

This means that a small change in z is associated with y changing at the rate $3x + 2z$ when x is held constant.

Although it has been possible to introduce only the basic elements of calculus and its applications, the problem-solving power of these tools should be clear. Furthermore, these basic principles are not difficult to learn and apply.

KEY CONCEPTS

- Higher-order derivatives are found by repeatedly taking the first derivative of each resultant derivative.
- The maximum or minimum point on a function $[y = f(x)]$ can be found by setting the first derivative of the function equal to zero and solving the value or values of x.
- When the first derivative of a function is zero, the function is at a maximum if the second derivative is negative or at a minimum if the second derivative is positive.
- For a function having two or more independent variables [e.g., $y = f(x, z)$], the partial derivative $\partial y / \partial x$ is the slope relationship between y and x, assuming z to be held constant.

Problems

2a-1. Determine the first and second derivatives of each of the following functions.

(a) $Y = 10$

(b) $Y = 3X^2 + 4X + 25$

(c) $Y = (X^2 - 4)(X^2 + 2X + 5)$

(d) $Y = \dfrac{X^2 + 3X + 4}{X^2 - 4}$

(e) $Q = 100 - 0.2P^2$

(f) $R = 500Q(1 - 5Q)$

(g) $Y = aX^2 + bX + c$

(h) $C = 2{,}000 - 200X^2 + 3X^3$

2a-2. Determine all the first-order partial derivatives for each of the following functions.

(a) $y = 3X^2 + 2XZ + Z^2$

(b) $Q = 10K^{0.5}L^{0.6}$

(c) $Q = 100P_1^{-1.2}P_2^{1.5}Y^{1.0}$

(d) $C = 200 + 10X_1^2 + 2X_1X_2 + 3X_2^2$

Risk and Decision Making

3

Preview

Before introducing new products, managers undertake consumer surveys, assess product lines of their competitors, and closely check estimated production costs. These actions are taken to increase the information base on which the decision will be made. Still, there are few sure things in the world of management. Many spectacular failures have occurred despite management having taken all possible steps to ensure success. It is simply not possible to predict consumer behavior or changes in production technology with complete accuracy. Every decision carries with it the prospect that something will go wrong and that instead of earning large profits as expected, losses may be incurred. Despite all of the modern techniques, learning to make decisions where there is risk and uncertainty is the essence of modern management.

Risk is said to exist when the outcomes associated with a decision and the probabilities of those outcomes occurring are known or can be estimated. In contrast, a manager faces *uncertainty* when the possible outcomes are known but the probabilities of those outcomes are unknown. An extreme form of uncertainty is where even the outcomes cannot be predicted. An example of risk would be where an established firm decides to introduce a new product. Market research is conducted that is used to estimate the probability of each of several sales volumes occurring. That is, the possible set of outcomes and their probabilities have been estimated. In contrast, the drilling of an oil well in an unproven field carries with it uncertainty. The decision maker may have no idea abut either the outcomes (i.e., the possible volumes of oil that might be produced) or their probabilities.

In this chapter, tools are developed for decision making under risk and uncertainty. First, basic principles of probability theory are presented and then integrated into a framework for decision making. Second, the concepts and methods for incorporating risk preferences into decisions are developed. Next, the concept of a decision tree and its use as a tool in making complex decisions are outlined. Finally, alternative decision criteria are considered for situations where the probabilities associated with the outcomes of a decision are unknown.

The Concept of Risk

The analysis of risk revolves around such terms as "strategy," "state of nature," "outcome," and "payoff matrix." A *strategy* refers to one of several alternative plans or courses of action that might be implemented in order to achieve a goal. For example, a manager might be considering three strategies designed to increase profits: (1) build a large plant, (2) build a small plant, or (3) not build a plant but increase advertising expenditures. A *state of nature* refers to some condition that may exist in the future that will have a significant effect on the success of any strategy. In making the decision about building a new plant, an important state of nature is the economic climate expected to prevail for the next few years. In this context, the possible states of nature might be (1) recession, (2) normal business conditions, or (3) economic "boom." An *outcome* specifies the gain or loss (usually measured in dollars) associated with a particular combination of strategy and state of nature. For instance, the outcomes associated with the decision to build a new plant might be the present value of all future net profits. Finally, a *payoff matrix* shows the outcome associated with each combination of strategy and state of nature.

Risk refers to the amount of variation in the outcomes associated with a particular strategy. Where there is only one probable outcome of a decision, there is said to be little risk; where there are many possible outcomes with substantially different dollar returns, there is said to be substantial risk. For example, a manager with $1 million to invest is faced with two alternatives. She could buy 91-day Treasury bills yielding 10 percent interest. At the end of 91 days, the $1 million investment will return $1,025,000. The only risk associated with this investment is that the federal government might be unable to pay its debts. This is so unlikely that there is essentially no risk associated with this investment (i.e., there is only one outcome). Indeed, Treasury bills are often referred to as a "riskless" investment.

The second alternative is drilling of an oil well in an unproven field. Suppose that it will take ninety-one days to complete. If oil is found, the well will immediately be worth $5 million, the present value of all net profits from selling this oil. If oil is not found, the well will be worth nothing. This is a risky investment because there is great variability in the range of possible outcomes. In general, the greater the variation in outcomes, the greater is the risk. Thus the definition of risk is based on the variation of the outcomes of a particular decision.

KEY CONCEPTS

- Risk exists when there is a range of possible outcomes associated with a decision and the probabilities of those outcomes occurring is known. If those probabilities are not known, the decision maker is said to face uncertainty.
- A strategy is a plan or course of action designed to achieve a management goal.
- A state of nature refers to a condition that may exist in the future that will have a significant effect on the success of a strategy.
- An outcome is the gain or loss associated with a particular combination of strategy and state of nature.
- A payoff matrix lists the outcomes associated with each strategy–state of nature combination.

Probability

To quantify risk, the concept of probability must be used. The *probability* of an event is the relative frequency of its occurrence in a large number of repeated trials. For example, in repeated tossing of a coin, a head will appear about one-half the time. That is, the relative frequency or probability of a head occurring is 0.50. In rolling a die, there are six possible outcomes, 1, 2, 3, 4, 5, 6. The relative frequency of any one of these outcomes is $\frac{1}{6}$, implying a probability of 0.167 for each outcome.

The probability of some events is known or can be computed with certainty. For example, the probabilities of most outcomes associated with rolling dice, drawing playing cards from a deck, and tossing coins are easily determined using standard principles of probability. Other probabilities are not easily determined mathematically but can be determined by repeating the process many times and observing how many times particular outcomes occur. For instance, there is no mathematical way to estimate the probability of winning a game of solitaire. But by playing the game many times and noting the number of times it is won, the probability of winning can be determined.

In other cases there is no accurate way to estimate probabilities except by using judgment. The weather forecaster's statement that "the probability of measurable precipitation tomorrow is 0.40" is based on an evaluation of how prevailing breezes, radar maps, and upper-air charts are associated with given weather conditions. Assessing the probability of a recession next year or a significant change in consumer preferences falls into the same category. Based on an analysis of current economic conditions, surveys of business capital-spending plans, and other information, a judgment can be made as to that probability. This judgment is necessarily subjective and may differ significantly among analysts, but predictions of this type are made daily by business managers, economists, and other decision makers.

Probability Distributions

For an experiment of some type with several possible outcomes, the probability of the ith outcome occurring is indicated by P_i, where

$$0 \leq P_i \leq 1 \qquad i = 1, 2, \ldots, n \tag{3-1}$$

That is, the probability must take on a value in the range 0 to 1. Negative probabilities and those in excess of unity have no meaning. For an event to have a probability of 1.25 would mean that it would occur more than 100 percent of the time!

Furthermore, the sum of the probabilities of all possible outcomes or events of an experiment must equal 1:

$$\sum_{i=1}^{n} P_i = 1 \tag{3-2}$$

Table 3-1. Probabilities For the Coin Tossing Experiment

Number of Heads (X_i)	Probability (P_i)
0	0.125
1	0.375
2	0.375
3	0.125

This means that when the experiment is conducted (i.e., the dice rolled, the coin tossed, or the investment made), one of the outcomes must occur. It follows that the probability that an event will *not* occur is 1 minus the probability that it will occur. For example, if the probability of a 6 occurring when rolling a die is $\frac{1}{6}$, this implies that the probability of not rolling a six is $1 - \frac{1}{6} = \frac{5}{6}$. This corollary is useful because it is sometimes easier to find the probability of an event not occurring than the probability that the event will occur.

A listing of each outcome of an experiment and its probability defines a *probability distribution*. For example, the probabilities of tossing 0, 1, 2, or 3 heads in three tosses of a coin are shown in Table 3-1. In this example, X_i is the number of heads observed in each experiment of three tosses. Note that each probability is between 0 and 1 and that the sum of the probabilities is equal to 1. Every time one uses a probability distribution, a check should be made that each probability is between 0 and 1 and that the sum of the probabilities for all outcomes is unity.

Understanding the laws of probability and applying them when making managerial plans and decisions can be very profitable. The financial success of gambling casinos in Las Vegas and Atlantic City is evidence of the truth of this statement. The managers of these firms use the principles of probability to structure the gambling games played in the casinos. The payoffs to the players are always set so that the "house" wins more than an equal share of the amounts wagered. The return on a gambling game is often referred to as the expected payoff. It is computed by multiplying the probability of winning by the amount to be won and adding the product of the probability of losing and the amount to be lost. A game is said to be fair if the expected payoff is zero. Consider a slot machine that costs $1 per play. The machine is programmed so that on average it pays off $8 once in every ten plays. The probability distribution is as follows:

Outcome	Probability	Payoff
Win	0.10	$8
Lose	0.90	−1

Because the expected payoff

$$\mu = 0.10(8) + 0.9(-1) = -0.10$$

is negative, this is not a fair game. The player expects to lose $0.10 (equivalently, the casino expects to win $0.10) every time the slot machine is played. Indeed the gambling games in casinos are never fair in a statistical sense.

Statistics of a Probability Distribution

Associated with any probability distribution is a set of measures that describe that distribution. Three of these measures, referred to as *statistics*, are the expected value, the standard deviation, and the coefficient of variation. They have a variety of uses in business, science, and engineering. In managerial economics they can be used to evaluate and compare the returns and risk associated with alternative strategies and thus help to make sound managerial decisions.

Expected Value.   The first of these statistics is the expected value or mean of the probability distribution. Effectively, it is a weighted average of the outcomes using the probabilities of those outcomes as weights. The expected value is referred to as a measure of *central tendency* because in repeated trials of an experiment, the values of most of the outcomes tend to be concentrated around this statistic. For example, the expected value of the distribution for rolling two dice is 7. The range of outcomes is 2 through 12, but the outcomes 6 through 8 occur much more often than the outcomes 2, 3, 11, or 12. This is because there are more combinations of the faces of the dice that yield 6, 7, or 8 than combinations that yield 2, 3, 11, or 12. There is only one combination $(1, 1)$ that yields 2, but there are six combinations $(1, 6)$, $(2, 5)$, $(3, 4)$, $(4, 3)$, $(5, 2)$, and $(6, 1)$ that yield 7.

The expected value of any probability distribution is computed by multiplying each outcome by its respective probability and then summing the products. Thus

$$\mu = P_1 X_1 + P_2 X_2 + \cdots + P_n X_n = \sum_{i=1}^{n} P_i X_i \tag{3-3}$$

Recall the probability distribution for the number of heads observed in three tosses of a coin.

Heads	Probability
0	0.125
1	0.375
2	0.375
3	0.125

The expected value of this distribution is computed to be

$$\mu = 0.125(0) + 0.375(1) + 0.375(2) + 0.125(3) = 1.50$$

This means that if this experiment were repeated many times and the number of heads observed for each trial recorded, the average number of heads would be 1.50. Obviously, it is not possible to toss 1.5 heads on any trial. The expected value is not a particular outcome but is merely an average of the outcomes for a large number or repetitions of the experiment.

Standard Deviation. The second statistic of interest measures the dispersion of possible outcomes around the expected value. This measure is called the standard deviation (σ) and is given by the equation

$$\sigma = \sqrt{\Sigma P_i (X_i - \mu)^2} \tag{3-4}$$

As indicated above, the standard deviation measures the variability of outcomes around the expected value of the distribution. If there is no variation in the outcomes, that is, if all $X_i = \mu$, then $\sigma = 0$. As the amount of variation about the expected value increases, the value of σ also increases.

The computation of σ for the probability distribution for tossing three coins is as follows:

$$\sigma = \sqrt{0.125(0 - 1.5)^2 + 0.375(1 - 1.5)^2 + 0.375(2 - 1.5)^2 + 0.125(3 - 1.5)^2}$$

$$\boxed{\sigma = 0.87}$$

Because the standard deviation provides information about the dispersion of the individual values or outcomes around the expected value, this measure of variation can be of use in decision making. Suppose that a person was planning to bet on the outcome of a football game. Initially, the only information available is that the average weight of both starting teams is 200 pounds. This is of no help in making the decision. But what if the standard deviation of the weights is 0 for team A and 100 for team B? This means that the team A players all weigh 200 pounds and that the weights of the team B players range from less than 100 pounds to more than 300 pounds. Knowing both the mean and the standard deviation in this case makes it clear that team A will probably win the game. Team B has players who are too small (a 100-pound player might be able to catch up with one weighing 200-pounds, but he will have trouble tackling him) and too big—with few exceptions, someone who weighs 300 pounds or more will have difficulty being an effective football player.

Coefficient of Variation. The third statistic is the coefficient of variation, which relates the variation of outcomes to the mean. It is given by the ratio of the standard deviation to the expected value:

$$\nu = \frac{\sigma}{\mu} \tag{3-5}$$

This statistic provides a useful way to compare the variation to the expected value of a probability distribution. It measures variation per unit of expected value. The use of the coefficient of variation can be illustrated by considering two other probability distributions, A and B, having the following statistics:

$$\mu_A = 100 \qquad \sigma_A = 50$$
$$\mu_B = 50 \qquad \sigma_B = 30$$

Both the mean and standard deviation for distribution A are greater than for distribution B. But the coefficient of variation is less for A than for B. That is,

$$\nu_A = \frac{50}{100} = 0.5 < \nu_B = \frac{30}{50} = 0.6$$

This means that distribution A has less dispersion relative to its mean than does distribution B.

KEY CONCEPTS

- A probability distribution lists the possible outcomes of an experiment and the probability associated with each outcome.
- The probability of any outcome must be in the range $0 \le P(X_1) \le 1.0$, and the sum of the probabilities for all outcomes must equal 1.
- The expected value of a probability distribution $(\mu = \Sigma P_i X_i)$ is a measure of the average outcome from repeated trials of an experiment.
- The standard deviation $[\sigma = \sqrt{\Sigma P_i (X_i - \mu)^2}]$ measures the dispersion of outcomes around the expected value.
- The coefficient of variation $(\nu = \sigma/\mu)$ is a measure of variation per unit of expected value.

Risk and Decision Making

The mean, standard deviation, and coefficient of variation have direct application in assessing the expected return and risk associated with managerial decisions and are referred to as *evaluation statistics*.

Suppose that two investments, C and D, are being considered. Both investments require an initial cash outlay of $100 and have a life of five years. The dollar returns on each depend on the rate of inflation over the five-year period. Of course, the inflation rate is not known with certainty, but suppose that the collective judgment of economists is that the probability of no inflation is 0.20, the probability of moderate inflation is 0.50, and the probability of rapid inflation is 0.30. The returns are defined as the present value of net profits for the next five years. These returns for each state of nature (i.e., rate of inflation) for each investment are shown in Table 3-2.

Analysis of these investments can be made by calculating and comparing the three evaluation statistics for each alternative. The expected value (μ) is an estimate of the expected dollar return for the investment. Because risk has been defined in terms of the variability in outcomes, the standard deviation (σ) is a measure of risk associated with the investment. The larger σ is, the greater the risk. Risk per dollar of expected return is measured by the coefficient of variation (ν).

**Table 3-2. Probability Distributions
for Two Investment Alternatives**

State of Nature	Probability (P_i)	Outcome (X_i)
Investment C		
No inflation	0.20	100
Moderate inflation	0.50	200
Rapid inflation	0.30	400
Investment D		
No inflation	0.20	150
Moderate inflation	0.50	200
Rapid inflation	0.30	250

The evaluation statistics for each investment alternative are computed as follows:

Investment C

$$\mu_C = \sum_{i=1}^{n} P_i X_i = 0.2(100) + 0.5(200) + 0.3(400) = \boxed{240}$$

$$\sigma_C = \sqrt{\sum_{i=1}^{n} P_i(X_i - \mu)^2} = \sqrt{0.2(100 - 240)^2 + 0.5(200 - 240)^2 + 0.3(400 - 240)^2}$$

$$= \boxed{111.3}$$

$$\nu_C = \frac{\sigma_C}{\mu_C} = \frac{111.3}{240} = \boxed{0.46}$$

Investment D

$$\mu_D = 0.2(150) + 0.5(200) + 0.3(250) = \boxed{205}$$

$$\sigma_D = \sqrt{0.2(150 - 205)^2 + 0.5(200 - 205)^2 + 0.3(250 - 205)^2} = \boxed{35}$$

$$\nu_D = \frac{35}{205} = \boxed{0.17}$$

The expected return for investment C of $240 is higher than for D ($205), but C is a riskier investment because $\sigma_C = 111.3$ compared to $\sigma_D = 35$. Also, the risk per dollar of expected returns for C ($\nu_C = 0.46$) is higher than for D ($\nu_D = 0.17$). Which is the better investment? The choice is not clear. It depends on the investor's attitude about taking risks. An entrepreneur may well prefer C whereas a person investing a few dollars in a retirement account where risk ought to be minimized might prefer D. The entrepreneur is in a better position to absorb a loss if it occurs and is probably accustomed to investing in risky ventures.

For the moment, one investment is said to be unequivocally preferred to another only if it has both a higher expected return and the risk per dollar of expected return is no greater than for the other investment. Unfortunately, higher returns are usually associated with higher risk. Indeed, the essence of economics is making choices where there is a trade-off. Virtually all investment choices require giving up expected returns for lower risk or accepting higher risk for a greater expected return. Clearly, attitudes about risk will play an important role in making managerial decisions. The next section describes how individual attitudes about risk affect decision making.

Risk Preference

Preference for risk differs substantially among individuals. Some investors are so averse to taking risk that they keep virtually all their assets in bank deposits that are insured by the federal government. Others are willing to risk all they own and can borrow to finance extremely risky ventures such as drilling oil wells or buying and selling contracts in the fast-moving commodities market.

Consider the following offer: "I will toss a coin ten times. If heads appear each time, you must pay me $1,000. If tails appear one or more times, I will pay you a dollar." Most people would reject this offer even though it is a fair game. That is, if the game were played many times, the amount lost would equal the amount won.

The probability distribution for the return or payoff for each outcome of the game is shown in Table 3-3. The probability of a head appearing on ten consecutive tosses of a coin is given by $(\frac{1}{2})^{10}$ or 0.001. The probability that there is at least one tail in ten tosses is 1 minus the probability that there would be ten heads or $(1.0 - 0.001 = 0.999)$.

To understand why most people would reject this kind of offer, one must understand the concept of preference for risk. It is assumed that individuals can associate satisfaction with money. More money usually means more satisfaction, although each additional dollar probably brings less satisfaction than the previous dollar did. Economists use the term *utility* as a measure of satisfaction. Although an individual's satisfaction is virtually impossible to measure, it will be assumed that this can be done for a hypothetical individual. This assumption will make it easier to develop several important concepts. One relationship between utility and money is shown in Figure 3-1a. The curve shows that relationship; that is, utility increases as money increases but at a continually decreasing rate. Equivalently, the function is concave to the horizontal axis. A person with this kind of utility function is said to be *risk averse*.

Suppose that this person has $10,000 and is offered the opportunity to bet $5,000 on the toss of a coin. She now faces the choice of having $10,000 with

Table 3-3. Probability Distribution and Expected Value for Coin-Tossing Example

Outcome	Probability	Payoff	Probability × Payoff
Ten heads	0.001	− $1,000	− $1.00
At least one tail	0.999	+ 1	+ 1.00
			Expected payoff = 0

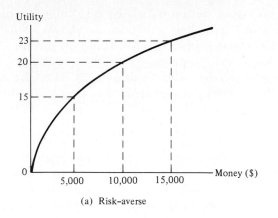

(a) Risk–averse

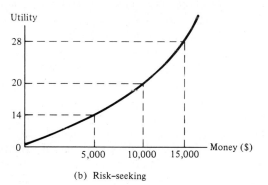

(b) Risk–seeking

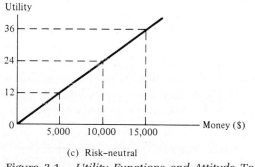

(c) Risk–neutral

Figure 3-1. *Utility Functions and Attitude To-ward Risk.*

certainty if she chooses not to bet (this option is called the *certain prospect*) or of having $15,000 with probability 0.5 or $5,000 with probability 0.5. The latter option is called the *uncertain prospect*. The expected monetary value of the uncertain prospect is $10,000, that is,

$$\mu = 0.5(\$5,000) + 0.5(\$15,000) = \$10,000$$

which is the same as the dollar value of the certain prospect.

The dollar payoff values can be translated into utility by using the function shown in Figure 3-1a. The certain prospect (i.e., having $10,000) is associated with a utility of 20. The expected value in utility of the uncertain prospect is determined as follows. A $5,000 payoff corresponds to a utility value of 15 and a $15,000 outcome is associated with a utility of 23. Thus, by substituting these utility values for the payoffs, the expected value in terms of utility is computed as

$$\mu = 0.5(15) + 0.5(23) = 19$$

which is less than the utility associated with certain prospect. Thus, this person prefers the certain prospect and chooses not to accept the wager.

This example suggests a formal definition of risk aversion. If the expected utility of a certain prospect is higher than the expected utility of an uncertain prospect when the two have an equal expected value in dollars, risk-aversion is said to exist.

Next, consider a utility function having a continually increasing slope as shown in Figure 3.1b. Here each additional dollar increases utility more than did the previous dollar. In this case, the expected value of utility for the gambling game described above is 21, i.e.,

$$\mu = 0.5(14) + 0.5(28) = 21$$

This expected value of utility is greater than the utility (20) associated with the certain prospect. Thus, this person would prefer the uncertain prospect. If the expected utility of an uncertain prospect is greater than that for a certain prospect when the expected dollar values of the prospects are equal, behavior is defined as risk-seeking.

Finally, in the risk-neutral case depicted in Figure 3.1c, the expected value of the utility associated with an uncertain prospect is equal to that of a certain prospect where both have equal expected dollar values. The utility associated with the certain prospect of $10,000 is 24. The expected utility associated with the uncertain prospect is also 24; that is, $0.5(12) + 0.5(36) = 24$. Thus an individual is said to be *risk neutral* if the expected values of the utility associated with both the certain and uncertain prospects are equal.

Risk Aversion and Insurance

Firms and individuals buy insurance to protect against the financial loss associated with a variety of risks, including fire, theft, floods, earthquakes, and death. The market for insurance exists because people are risk averse. Consider a manager who knows his firm will earn a net profit of $100,000 each year but also faces a probability of 0.5 that the plant will burn down. Assume that if the plant burns down, it will cost $80,000 to replace it. Now there are two possible outcomes: (1) the plant burns down, so net returns are $100,000 − $80,000 = $20,000; or (2) the plant does not burn down, so the net return is $100,000. Each outcome has a 0.5 probability of occurrence. The expected monetary value is $60,000, as outlined in Table 3-4.

Table 3-4. Probability Distribution and Expected Value of Net Profit

Event	Outcome	Probability	Outcome × Probability
Fire	$ 20,000	0.5	$10,000
No fire	100,000	0.5	50,000
			μ = $60,000

Suppose that manager's utility function is similar to that shown in Figure 3-2. Point *A* corresponds to the outcome associated with the plant burning down (i.e., a dollar payoff of $20,000 and utility = 100) and point *B* corresponds to the "no fire" outcome when the dollar payoff is $100,000 and the utility is 200. Thus the expected utility for this uncertain prospect is 150. That is,

$$\mu = 0.5(100) + 0.5(200) = 150$$

Now a certain prospect (i.e., an outcome that occurs with certainty or probability of 1) of $40,000 of income would also generate a utility of 150, as shown by point *C* in Figure 3-2. So the decision maker would be indifferent between a certain prospect of an income of $40,000 and the uncertain prospect described above having an expected dollar value of $60,000.

This suggests that the profit-maximizing (but risk-averse) manager would pay up to $60,000 for a fire insurance policy on the factory because having this policy would guarantee a certain outcome of $40,000 whether or not the plant burned down. That is, the manager would know that the firm would net $40,000 (i.e., $100,000 in profit less the $60,000 insurance premium). If there is a fire, the insurance company will rebuild the factory at no cost to the firm.

The expected payout by the insurance company is determined by multiplying the probability of a fire by the dollar loss, that is, 0.5 × $80,000 = $40,000. This

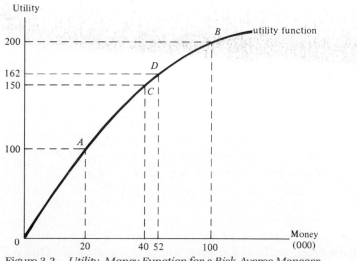

Figure 3-2. *Utility–Money Function for a Risk-Averse Manager.*

claim plus, say, 20 percent for operating expenses and profit suggests that a fire insurance policy for the plant could be offered for about $48,000. The result is that the manager could actually have a certain outcome of $52,000 ($100,000 profit less the $48,000 insurance premium). This outcome, shown as point D in Figure 3-2, has a utility level of 162 and is preferred to the utility level 150 that corresponds to the uncertain prospect. Thus, in this example, the manager can choose between the certain prospect of having a utility level of 162 or an uncertain prospect with an expected utility of 150. Clearly, the rational manager would opt for the certain prospect involving insurance.

Although utility is impossible to measure, the best evidence that most people are risk averse is the existence of a large number of insurance companies and the variety of risks that they insure against. For example, private firms have issued policies that insure pianists' hands, dancers' legs, and actresses' breasts. Ski resorts can buy insurance to protect against a lack of snow. In 1984, insurance companies paid more than $150 million in claims when rocket malfunctions sent two communications satellites into the oblivion of outer space.

CASE STUDY

PREFERENCE FOR RISK AMONG PHYSICIANS

Jury awards and out-of-court settlements of $1 million or more are not uncommon in malpractice suits against medical doctors. Because one mistake could mean financial ruin, virtually all doctors carry insurance against the risk of malpractice claims. Some in the so-called "high-risk" specialties, such as obstetrics and orthopedic surgery, face annual premiums in excess of $30,000 for malpractice coverage.

It is estimated that medical doctors pay $2 billion each year for insurnace protection against malpractice claims. Of this amount, only about 35 percent, or $700 million, is paid out to injured people. The remaining 65 percent ($1.3 billion) goes for insurance company operating expenses and profits. A large part of the expenses are legal fees to hire lawyers to defend doctors who are sued, and payments to the many expert witnesses (including economists) who testify in malpractice suits. Thus the average physician pays an insurance premium of $2 for every $0.70 of loss expected. This suggests risk-averse behavior on the part of physicians.

Consider a hypothetical surgeon whose income is $100,000 after all expenses except malpractice insurance. Assume that the award for any successful malpractice suit would be $100,000 and that the probability of that occurring is 0.10. Thus the expected loss in any one year is $10,000 (i.e., 0.10 × $100,000). Suppose that the cost of an insurance policy against the risk is $30,000.

If the doctor buys an insurance policy, risk has been eliminated and net income would be $70,000, that is, $100,000 less the $30,000 insurance premium. If insurance is not purchased, income will be (1) $100,000 with probability 0.9; or (2) zero, in the case where an injured patient wins a lawsuit, with probability 0.10. The expected value of the risky alternative is $90,000. That is.

$$\mu = 0.9(\$100,000) + 0.1(0) = \$90,000$$

If the decision were based solely on the expected value of dollar returns, the physician would not buy the insurance. But assume that the doctor is risk averse, as indicated by the utility function

$$U = 40I - 0.2I^2$$

where I is income in thousands. The utility $(u = 1,820)$ associated with the certain income of \$70,000 is higher than the expected utility (1,800) associated with not having insurance. That is,

$$\mu = 0.9(2,000) - 0.1(0) = 1,800$$

That virtually all doctors have malpractice insurance suggests that they are risk averse. However, there may be another explanation. Hospitals can be held responsible for a doctor's malpractice. As a result, almost all hospitals require that doctors have malpractice insurance before they are allowed to use the hospital. This reduces the risk of loss for the owners of the hospital. Because having hospital privileges is essential for most medical practices, one would find that even risk-seeking physicians would have insurance. Thus the high proportion of doctors who have malpractice insurance could be the result of risk-averse hospital administrators forcing their risk preferences on physicians.

Risk Seeking and Gambling

Consider a risk-seeking individual whose utility function is shown in Figure 3-3. This person has \$10, for which the measure of utility is 20. A wager of \$5 is

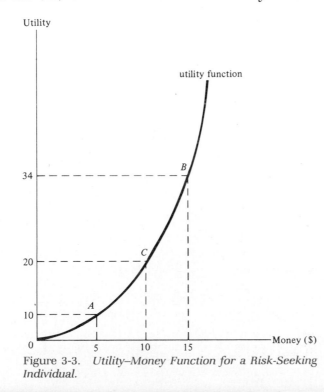

Figure 3-3.   *Utility–Money Function for a Risk-Seeking Individual.*

offered on the toss of a coin. By accepting this bet, the certain prospect of $10 (point C in the figure) is given up for the uncertain prospect of having $5 or $15 (points A and B in the figure), each occurring with probability 0.5. The expected values in dollars of the two prospects are equal, but the expected utility value of the uncertain prospect is 22, that is,

$$\mu = 0.5(10) + 0.5(34) = 22$$

This is higher than the utility associated with the certain prospect. Such a person would probably seek out opportunities to gamble or otherwise take risks. The existence of a variety of gambling games and establishments, including some operated by state governments, is a market response to the demands of risk-seeking individuals.

Gambling and Insuring: A Contradiction?

Individual behavior is either risk averse, risk neutral, or risk seeking. Thus one might expect to find risk-averse individuals spending their time reviewing their insurance coverage and to find risk-seeking persons in casinos in Las Vegas or Atlantic City. But if a survey were made, it probably would show that many people both buy insurance and engage in gambling games of one sort or another. For example, it is probably true that most people who engage in gambling in Las Vegas drove there in insured cars and live in insured homes. This appears to be a contradiction, as it suggests that people are risk seeking and risk averse at the same time. Actually, there is no contradiction, but a complete explanation is beyond the scope of this book. Suffice it to say that this behavior depends on the type of gambling games available and the nature and cost of insurance that can be purchased.

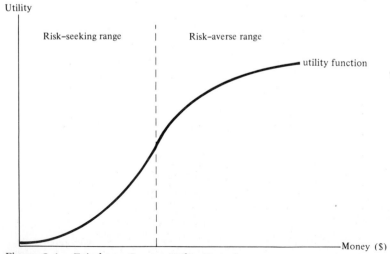

Figure 3-4.   *Friedman-Savage Utility Function.*

One rather simple explanation for this phenomenon is offered by Friedman and Savage (1948), who argue that the utility function may look as shown in Figure 3-4. It describes the person who is risk averse over part of that curve and risk seeking over another range. A person having a utility curve such as that shown in Figure 3-4 would engage in gambling games for relatively small amounts of money but would insure against large losses, such as those associated with a house fire or serious automobile accident. A utility function of this type is a sufficient condition for a rational person to gamble and have insurance at the same time.

EXAMPLE
RISK PREFERENCE AND DECISION MAKING

Consider the problem facing a manager who must choose between two investments, E and F, each having an initial cost of $10. The probability distributions for the payoffs for each investment are shown in the following table. Each payoff represents the present value of all future net profits.

E		F	
Probability (P_i)	Payoff (X_i)	Probability (P_i)	Payoff (X_i)
0.10	− $20	0.20	$10
0.50	20	0.40	20
0.40	50	0.40	30

The decision maker's utility function is $U = 100X - X^2$, where X is the dollar payoff.

1. Would you characterize this decision maker as risk seeking, risk neutral, or risk averse? Explain.
2. If the objective is to maximize expected net present value, which investment is the better choice? (For the moment, disregard risk.)
3. Evaluate the risk associated with the dollar returns for each investment.
4. If the objective is utility maximization, which investment should be chosen?

Solution:

1. Based on the utility function it is seen that the decision maker is risk averse. This can be shown in the following way. Select any two dollar payoffs, say, $20 and $40, and arbitrarily assign them probabilities of occurrence, say, 0.4 and 0.6, respectively. The expected value of these payoffs is

$$\mu(\text{dollars}) = 0.4(20) + 0.6(40) = \$32$$

From the utility function, the utility associated with $20 and $40 are 1,600 and 2,400, respectively. Thus the expected utility value is

$$\mu(\text{utility}) = 0.4(1,600) + 0.6(2,400) = 2,080$$

But if this person were offered \$32 with certainty (i.e., a certain prospect has the same value as the expected dollar value of the investments), the utility would be 2,176. Because the utility is higher for the certain prospect, the person is risk averse.

2. The expected returns for each investment are

$$\mu_E = 0.10(-20) + 0.50(20) + 0.40(50) = \boxed{28}$$
$$\mu_F = 0.20(10) + 0.40(20) + 0.40(30) = \boxed{22}$$

Thus E is the preferred choice because it has the highest expected value.

3. The evaluation statistics for risk and risk per dollar of expected return for both investments are:

Investment E:

$$\sigma_E = \sqrt{0.10(-20 - 28)^2 + 0.50(20 - 28)^2 + 0.40(50 - 28)^2} = \boxed{21.4}$$
$$\sigma_E = \frac{\sigma_E}{\mu_E} = \frac{21.4}{28} = \boxed{0.76}$$

Investment F:

$$\sigma_F = \sqrt{0.20(10 - 22)^2 + 0.40(20 - 22)^2 + 0.40(30 - 22)^2} = \boxed{7.5}$$
$$v_F = \frac{\sigma_F}{\mu_F} = \frac{7.5}{22} = \boxed{0.34}$$

The risk is greater for E ($\sigma_E = 21.4$ compared to $\sigma_F = 7.5$) and the risk per dollar of expected return is also greater for E ($v_E = 0.76$ compared to $v_F = 0.34$).

4. To make the decision assuming the goal is utility maximization, the payoffs must be transformed from dollars into utility using the utility function $U = 100X - X^2$. For example, the utility associated with a net payoff of -20 is

$$U = 100(-20) - 20^2 = -2,400$$

Repeating this for each outcome will yield two new probability distributions where the payoffs are in terms of utility.

Probability (P_i)	Payoff (U_i)	Probability (P_i)	Payoff (U_i)
0.10	$-2,400$	0.20	900
0.50	1,600	0.40	1,600
0.40	2,500	0.40	2,100

The expected utility returns are

$$\mu_E = 0.10(-2,400) + 0.50(1,600) + 0.40(2,500) = \boxed{1,560}$$
$$\mu_F = 0.20(900) + 0.40(1,600) + 0.40(2,100) = \boxed{1,660}$$

Hence, in terms of utility, investment F is the preferred alternative.

KEY CONCEPTS

- Behavior is said to be risk averse, risk neutral, or risk seeking, depending on whether the utility of a certain prospect is greater than, equal to, or less than the utility of an uncertain prospect that has the same expected dollar value as the certain prospect.
- The market for insurance exists because many people are risk averse. The market for gambling exists because some people are risk seekers.
- Some people exhibit risk-seeking behavior and risk-averse behavior at the same time. One explanation for this is that their utility functions first increase at an increasing rate, then increase at a decreasing rate.

Adjusting Business Decisions for Risk

Although there are several ways to incorporate risk into the decision process, the most common method is to use a risk adjusted discount rate in determining the present value of the future cash flows associated with an investment. Most investors are willing to accept greater risk only if there is the promise of greater returns when compared to an investment with less risk. For example, suppose that the typical return on an insured bank certificate of deposit is 10 percent per year. Clearly, no rational investor will invest in very risky ventures such as oil wells or gold mines unless the expected return is considerably higher than 10 percent per year.

Suppose that the line R in Figure 3-5 shows all combinations of risk and return for which a hypothetical investor is indifferent. That is, this function shows the willingness of this investor to trade off risk against return. Clearly, the shape of this function will vary for different individuals depending on their preference for risk. A very risk-averse person might have a trade-off function similar to the dashed line R'—any increase in risk must carry with it a significant increase in return. Conversely, a risk-seeking individual's trade-off function might be described by the crosshatched line R''. Here only a small increase in the rate of return is required for a rather large increase in risk.

Assume that the rate of return associated with a riskless investment is 10 percent. Recall that a riskless investment would have a standard deviation of zero. For the investor with trade-off function R, if the risk increases to, say, $\sigma = 1.0$, a 15 percent rate of return is required. The difference between this 15 percent return and the riskless rate of 10 percent is referred to as the risk premium. If $\sigma = 2.0$, the trade-off function R indicates that a 22 percent return is required. Thus the risk premium is 12 percentage points. In evaluating investments, these differential rates of return would be used to discount net cash flows for future periods. That is, net cash flows for a high risk investment would be discounted using a higher discount rate than would be used for a low-risk alternative.

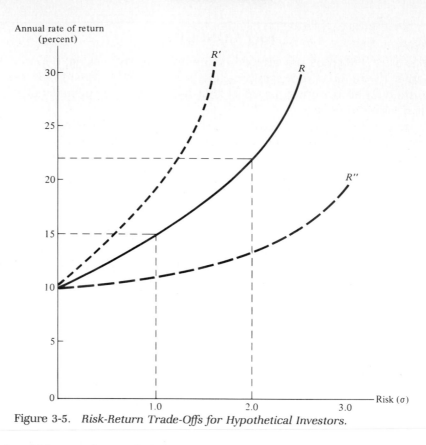

Figure 3-5.   *Risk-Return Trade-Offs for Hypothetical Investors.*

It should be emphasized that there is no equation or table that relates risk and the discount rate. Clearly, there is a positive relationship between these two factors, but the relationship between them is strictly judgmental and must be made by individual decision makers.

EXAMPLE
USING RISK ADJUSTED DISCOUNT RATES

Suppose that management at Showmax Theaters must decide whether to expand by building a few large theaters in large cities or building a number of minitheaters in small cities and towns. Each of the alternatives would require an initial investment of $2 million. Although the large theaters have a greater expected return, the option has greater risk because there is more competition in the larger cities. In contrast, there is less potential for profit in the small markets, but in many of them there is little or no competition. The expected values of the net cash flows in each of the next ten years is $600,000 per year in the large markets and $500,000 per year in the small markets.

The value of σ is estimated to be 1.5 in the large markets and 0.5 in the small cities. Management has a risk–return trade-off function similar to that shown by curve R in Figure 3-5. This means that a rate of about 17 percent would be used to discount cash flows in the large-city alternative and a rate of about 12 percent would be used to discount cash flows in the small-city alternative.

Solution

The net present value of an investment is determined by subtracting the initial cost of the investment from the present value of all future net cash flows. Note, that the appropriate risk-adjusted discount rate is used in each case.

Large-city alternative:

$$NPV = \sum_{t=1}^{10} \frac{600,000}{(1 + 0.17)^t} - \$2,000,000$$
$$= \$2,795,162 - \$2,000,000 = \$795,162$$

Small-city alternative:

$$NPV = \sum_{t=1}^{10} \frac{500,000}{(1 + 0.12)^t} - \$2,000,000$$
$$= \$2,825,112 - \$2,000,000 = \$825,112$$

Although the nondiscounted cash flows each year are greater for the large-city alternative, when adjusted for risk, the present value of the cash flows is greater for the small-city alternative. Thus building minitheaters in smaller cities is the preferred investment.

Decision Tree Analysis

The previous discussions of risk began with a set of outcomes for each investment and the probability of each outcome occurring. But some strategic decisions involve a sequence of decisions, alternative outcomes, and subsequent decisions. Given this complexity, how are the alternative strategies to be evaluated? One approach is to use a decision tree that traces the sequence of events and/or decisions that lead to each outcome. Such a diagram shows two or more "branches" at each point where a decision or event (i.e., a state of nature) leads to different outcomes. These branches are similar to those on a tree.

To illustrate the concept, consider the following gambling game. An initial bet of $10 is made. A card is drawn from an ordinary deck of playing cards and then a coin is tossed. If the player draws a heart and then tosses a head, he wins $30. If a heart is not drawn, but a head is tossed, the player is paid $15. For the other outcomes, the player wins nothing, that is, the player loses the initial $10 bet.

When drawing the card, the relevant probabilities are 0.25 that a heart is drawn (there are 13 hearts in a deck of 52 cards, so $\frac{13}{52} = 0.25$), and the probability that a spade, club, or diamond is drawn is 0.75. When tossing a coin, the probability of a head equals the probability of a tail, which is 0.5.

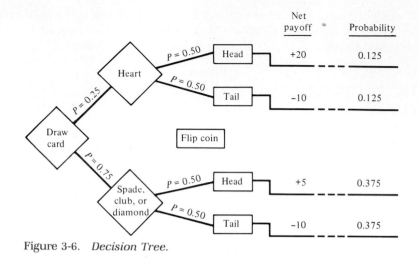

Figure 3-6.   *Decision Tree.*

The game is analyzed using the decision tree shown in Figure 3-6. The probability of the outcome at each step in the process is shown on the "branches" of the tree. The probability of each final outcome is equal to the product of the probabilities along the branches leading to that outcome. For example, the probability of drawing a heart and then tossing a head for a net payoff of $20 is 0.25 × 0.50 = 0.125. By repeating this for each path along the decision tree, the probability of each outcome is determined. By associating the net payoff for each outcome with its respective probability, the probability distribution is determined. Then the usual set of evaluation statistics that describe expected return, risk, and risk per dollar of expected return can be computed.

The decision tree approach can be directly applied to managerial decision making. Suppose that a firm is considering entering a new market. This entry would require building a large, medium, or small plant. The large plant would require a $10 million investment, the medium plant, a $6 million investment, and the small plant, a $4 million investment. This decision is shown in part I of Figure 3-7. A square is used to show decisions. Note that there are no probabilities associated with such decisions. A diamond is used to indicate branches associated with the various states of nature that may occur. A probability must be assigned to each of these branches.

There are two stochastic elements associated with each decision (the term *stochastic* refers to an outcome that is determined by chance): (1) the reaction of a major competitor in the business, and (2) the economic conditions that will prevail. Suppose it is learned that the competitor may respond to the new plant with a new national or regional advertising program or with no new advertising program. Assume that the probability of each occurring will depend on the size of plant built as shown in Table 3-5. The probabilities for each alternative competitive reaction are entered on the appropriate branches of part II of Figure 3-7. Note that the probabilities depend on the size of plant built. If a large plant is built, the probability is high that the competitor will respond with a major

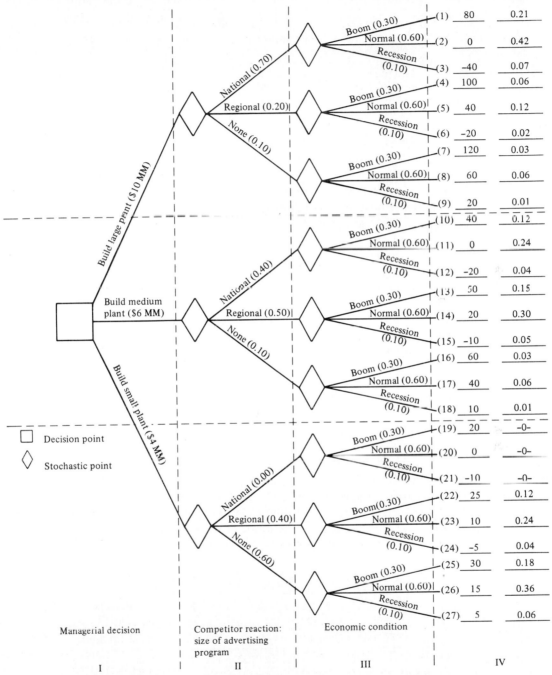

Outcome Probabilities

(1) 80	0.21	
(2) 0	0.42	
(3) −40	0.07	
(4) 100	0.06	
(5) 40	0.12	
(6) −20	0.02	
(7) 120	0.03	
(8) 60	0.06	
(9) 20	0.01	
(10) 40	0.12	
(11) 0	0.24	
(12) −20	0.04	
(13) 50	0.15	
(14) 20	0.30	
(15) −10	0.05	
(16) 60	0.03	
(17) 40	0.06	
(18) 10	0.01	
(19) 20	−0−	
(20) 0	−0−	
(21) −10	−0−	
(22) 25	0.12	
(23) 10	0.24	
(24) −5	0.04	
(25) 30	0.18	
(26) 15	0.36	
(27) 5	0.06	

Build large plant ($10 MM)

Build medium plant ($6 MM)

Build small plant ($4 MM)

National (0.70)
Regional (0.20)
None (0.10)

National (0.40)
Regional (0.50)
None (0.10)

National (0.00)
Regional (0.40)
None (0.60)

Boom (0.30)
Normal (0.60)
Recession (0.10)

☐ Decision point

◇ Stochastic point

Managerial decision

Competitor reaction:
size of advertising
program

Economic condition

I II III IV

Figure 3-7. *Decision Tree for New Plant Decision.*

89

Table 3-5. Probability of Alternative Responses by Competitor

	Probability That Competitor Responds with:		
Plant Size	National Program	Regional Program	No New Program
Large plant	0.70	0.20	0.10
Medium plant	0.40	0.50	0.10
Small plant	0.00	0.40	0.60

advertising program. Conversely, building a small plant would probably result in a regional program or none at all.

Suppose that the possible economic conditions and their probabilities are: recession (0.10), normal business conditions (0.60), and boom conditions (0.30). These states of nature and their respective probabilities are shown in part III of the decision tree. Finally, the present value of all future profits for each outcome has been determined by the firm.

Note that there is a payoff associated with each of the twenty-seven possible combinations of decisions and stochastic events. Each combination consists of a plant size, the competitor's reaction, and an economic condition. These payoffs have been listed in part IV of Figure 3-7 together with the probability of that sequence occurring. The probabilities are found by multiplying the probability along each of the branches leading to the outcome. For example, consider the top branch of the decision tree in Figure 3-7. The probability that the competitor responds with a national advertising program is 0.70 and the probability of an economic boom is 0.30. The product of these probabities is 0.21, and this is shown as the first entry in the probability distribution on the right-hand side of the figure.

There are three distinct probability distributions outlined in Figure 3-7. The first, consisting of the payoff–probability pairs (1) through (9), corresponds to the decision to build the large plant. Pairs (10) through (18) correspond to the decision to build the medium-size plant, and pairs (19) through (27) represent the probability distribution for the investment in the small plant.

Finally, based on these probability distributions, the evaluation statistics for each investment alternative are computed. These data are shown in Table 3-6. As usual, the decision will not be an easy one for management. The expected

Table 3-6. Evaluation Statistics for Each Plant-Size Alternative

	Alternative Plant Size		
	Large	Medium	Small
		(Dollar figures in millions)	
Expected return (μ)	$31.8	$21.3	$16.3
Expected net present value	21.8	15.3	12.3
Risk (σ)	33.9	19.6	8.9
Risk per million dollars of expected return (σ/μ)	1.07	0.92	0.55

return or expected net present value of all future profits increases with the scale of the plant, but so does risk, as measured by σ and v. For example, the expected net present value for the large plant, $21.8 million, is higher than the expected return for the other two plant sizes, but the risk per dollar of return (1.07) is also the highest of the three alternatives. The collective preference for risk of the managers may be the determining factor in making the decision.

Decision trees can easily become extremely complex. The total number of outcomes is equal to the product of the number of decisions or stochastic alternatives along each branch on the tree. For example, a decision to build a new plant might involve six different plant size alternatives, five different ways a competitor might react, and three different economic environments. Hence the number of outcomes in this case would be 90 (i.e., $6 \times 5 \times 3$). One could easily imagine decision trees with thousands of possible outcomes. Whereas a computer would have no problem computing the probabilities and evaluation statistics for each of a large number of intricate decision trees, the manager's capacity to evaluate the options would soon be exceeded.

Clearly, decision makers must keep the problem in proper perspective. One way is to include only those alternatives and outcomes that are relevant and significant in terms of both the probability of occurrence and the net payoff. Consider including the possibility of nuclear war as a possible state of nature when evaluating an investment decision. For military planners, this state of nature is both relevant and significant. However, for a business decision on a new plant or marketing program, such a possibility probably is not relevant, even though the payoff associated with that possibility might be a very large negative number. That is, the firm might incur huge losses in the event of a nuclear attack, but such an event probably is not relevant to most business decisions.

Decision Making Under Uncertainty

As suggested earlier, there is a subtle distinction between the concepts of risk and uncertainty. If for a set of strategies both the outcomes and probabilities of each outcome are known, the decision maker faces risk. In contrast, uncertainty exists when the outcomes are known but the probability of their occurrence is not. An extreme form of uncertainty exists when neither the outcomes nor their probabilities are known. Such cases might be found in basic research, such as genetic engineering, where researchers may have no idea what they might discover.

A complete lack of information on probabilities would be very unusual. Suppose it is known that the possible states of nature are S_1, S_2, S_3 and S_4, but the probability of their occurring is unknown. Even knowing that S_1 is more likely to occur than S_2 and that S_2 is more probable than S_3 is a major step in reducing uncertainty. However, occasions will arise where the probability distribution is unknown and cannot be estimated. In those cases, alternative decision criteria may have to be employed. One such approach to decision making under un-

Table 3-7. Hypothetical Payoff Matrix for Maximin Decision Rule

Strategies	S_1	S_2	S_3	S_4	Minimum Payoff
	State of Nature				
A	30	18	10	− 7	− 7
B	7	14	11	19	7
C	11	8	9	10	8

certainty, the *maximin decision method,* is outlined below. Consider the payoff matrix in Table 3-7. It consists of three strategies (A, B, and C) and four states of nature ($S_1, \ldots, S_4$). Assume the probabilities of these states are unknown.

The maximin decision approach is designed to identify that strategy that will result in the smallest undesirable outcome. The technique consists of two steps. First, determine the worst outcome or minimum payoff for each strategy. These are shown to the right of the payoff matrix. Second, select that strategy that has the highest of these minimum payoffs. That is, pick the strategy that *max*imizes the *min*imum payoff. In this case, strategy C is selected, as it has the highest of the minimum payoffs of the three strategies. The term "maximin" comes from this process of maximizing the minimum return.

Clearly, this is a very conservative approach to decision making. Only the most risk-averse manager would follow this approach strictly. This is demonstrated by using the maximin strategy for the payoff matrix in Table 3-8. This strategy will lead to selection of strategy B even though the difference in minimum payoffs is very small and the difference in maximum payoffs is very large. Certainly, most decision makers would choose A after reviewing the entire payoff matrix.

What would the probabilities for S_1 and S_2 have to be to make the expected payoffs equal for strategies A and B in Table 3-8? To determine those probabilities, first define P as the probability that S_1 occurs and $(1 - P)$ as the probability of S_2 occurring. Then equate the expected payoffs for strategies A and B. That is,

$$\mu_A = \mu_B$$
$$P(50) + [(1 - P)(-2)] = P(2) + [(1 - P)(0)]$$

Solving for P and $(1 - P)$ yields

$$50P - 2 + 2P = 2P$$
$$50P = 2$$
$$P = 0.04 \quad \text{and} \quad (1 - P) = 0.96$$

Table 3-8. Payoff Matrix

Strategy	S_1	S_2	Minimum Payoff
	State of Nature		
A	50	−2	−2
B	2	0	0

Unless it appeared that S_2 was almost sure to occur (a probability of 0.96 or higher), the expected payoff is higher for strategy A.

This example emphasizes the value of having even a highly subjective estimate of the probability distribution for the states of nature. Having those probabilities allows the decision maker to make use of superior decision-making tools, such as those described in earlier sections of the chapter.

KEY CONCEPTS

- A decision tree traces sequences of strategies and states of nature to arrive at a set of outcomes. The probability of any outcome is found by multiplying the probabilities on each branch leading to that outcome.
- The maximin decision rule is used for decision making under uncertainty (i.e., when the probabilities of the states of nature are unknown). Its use implies a risk-averse approach to decision making.

Summary

A decision maker faces risk when there are several outcomes associated with a decision and the probabilities of those outcomes are known. The greater the variation in those outcomes, the greater the risk. The set of outcomes and their associated probabilities comprise a probability distribution. If the probabilities of the outcomes are not known, the decision maker faces uncertainty.

The evaluation of an investment decision where risk is present is made by determining the mean (μ), the standard deviation (σ), and the coefficient of variation (ν) of the probability distribution for the investment. The mean estimates the expected return, the standard deviation measures risk, and the coefficient of variation measures risk per dollar of expected return. In general, decisions that promise higher expected returns also carry greater risk.

Behavior is said to be risk averse, risk neutral, or risk seeking, depending on whether the utility of a dollar amount with certainty is greater than, equal to, or less than the utility of an uncertain dollar amount that has the same expected dollar value as the certain prospect. The market for insurance exists because many people are risk averse. Gambling establishments serve risk-seeking individuals. Some people have insurance and also engage in gambling games. One explanation for this apparently contradictory behavior is that the utility function first increases at an increasing rate and then increases at a decreasing rate. The most common method for compensating for risk is to add a risk premium to the discount rate.

A decision tree traces the sequence of strategies and states of nature to arrive at the set of outcomes associated with a decision. The probability of any outcome is found by multiplying the probabilities on each branch leading to that outcome.

Alternative decision rules such as the maximin criterion can be used in decision making under uncertainty where the probabilities of the outcomes are unknown. However, these alternative approaches implicitly assume a risk-averse approach to decision making.

Discussion Questions

3-1. What is the difference between risk and uncertainty?

3-2. How can the principle of risk aversion be used to explain why the owner of a business would buy insurance on the life of a key employee?

3-3. Why does the maximin decision criterion imply extremely risk-averse behavior? Can you think of a situation where it would be impossible to even guess at the probabilities associated with the various states of nature?

3-4. What is the difference between the standard deviation of a probability distribution and the coefficient of variation?

3-5. Why do individuals who participate in gambling games (i.e., demonstrate risk-seeking behavior) also purchase insurance (i.e., demonstrate risk-verse behavior)?

3-6. How can decision trees help management evaluate the outcomes associated with several alternative investments?

3-7. Why do people willingly play gambling games when the expected dollar returns are negative?

Problems

3-1. Do each of the following distributions meet the requirements for a probability distribution? Why or why not?

(a)

P_i	X_i
0.10	10
−0.20	15
0.30	20
0.50	40
0.50	50

(b)

P_i	X_i
0.30	−40
0.30	−50
0.40	−200

(c)

P_i	X_i
0.20	4
0.40	8
0.30	0
0.15	12

3-2. For each of the following probability distributions, calculate the mean (μ), standard deviation (σ), and coefficient of variation (ν).

(a)

P_i	X_i
0.8	20
0.2	−5

(b)

P_i	Y_i
0.1	10
0.2	20
0.4	15
0.3	30

3-3. Janet Sills, a sales representative for the Rapid Vacuum Cleaner Company, knows from past experience that she will sell a vacuum cleaner in two of every five homes in which she gives a demonstration. In a typical day she will give demonstrations in ten homes. If it costs Janet $15 to give each demonstration (this includes all implicit and explicit costs) and if her commission is $60 for each cleaner sold, determine Janet's expected net profit per day.

3-4. The Lac DuFlambeau Corporation manufactures a broad line of fishing tackle and accessories. The firm has surplus cash and is considering the acquisition of a firm that manufactures flyrods. A broker identifies two firms. Flyrite and Perfect-Rod, that could be purchased for the same amount. The probability distributions for the present value of all future profits for each of these acquisition candidates are as follows:

Flyrite		Perfect-Rod	
Probability	Outcome	Probability	Outcome
0.40	—0—	0.20	100,000
0.20	200,000	0.50	200,000
0.40	500,000	0.30	250,000

(a) Make a complete investment analysis of each investment (i.e., compute the expected present value of all future profits; a measure of risk, and a measure of risk per dollar of expected returns).

(b) Which of the two firms should be acquired? Why?

3-5. For each of the following functions relating utility (U) and money (M), determine if the function implies risk-averse, risk-seeking, or risk-neutral behavior. Explain.

(a) $U = M + 0.25M^2$

(b) $U = 10M$

(c) $U = 500M - 2M^2$

3-6. United Steel, Inc. has experienced losses for several years. The production department has determined the only hope for reversing the negative trend in profits is to build a new plant outside the United States. Two alternative locations have been identified. Production in country A would be very efficient and low-cost, but the government is unstable. In the event of a revolution, United's assets might be appropriated. Country B has a much more stable government, but production costs are considerably higher than in A.

The following data show the probability distribution for the present value of all future profits for each alternative.

Country A		Country B	
Probability	Profits (mil)	Probability	Profits (mil)
0.40	0	0.40	10
0.20	20	0.40	20
0.40	60	0.20	30

(a) Make a complete investment analysis of both alternatives. Which alternative should be chosen? Why?

(b) If the collective utility function of the board of directors is:

$$U = 200X - X^2$$

where X is measured in millions of dollars of profit, which alternative should be selected? Explain.

3-7. Management at Unique Publishing has been paying an annual premium of $3,000 for fire insurance on their $100,000 plant. Net profit for Unique consistently is $100,000 per year after deducting the insurance premium. Any uninsured loss due to fire would be an expense in computing net income. A study has shown that the probability of fire during a year is only 0.004. (Assume that any fire would destroy the plant.) A consultant suggests that Unique cancel its fire insurance. Evaluate this recommendation for each of the following assumptions:

(a) The sole objective of management is to maximize profit (i.e., no consideration is given to risk).

(b) The sole management objective is maximizing utility and the relevant utility function is $U = 100\pi - 0.5\pi^2$, where π is net profit in thousands of dollars.

3-8. State University is considering an evening MBA program. Dean Smith determines that a minimum enrollment of 100 in a graduate program is necessary for a break-even operation. As the only MBA program in the state, enrollment probably would be 125 students. Southwestern, a private university, is the only other school in the area that offers graduate programs. The dean thinks the probability is about 0.67 that Southwestern would respond to the State program with their own MBA program. If it did, enrollment probably would only be 70 students in the State program. However, if State offered both MBA and MPA (Master of Public Administration) programs, Dean Smith thinks that enrollment would be 175 with no competition and 90 if Southwestern offers a program. Because of similarities in course requirements, Dean Smith thinks that the MBA and MPA programs could be run as one graduate program. The dean believes that offering both degrees would reduce the probability that Southwestern will enter the MBA degree market to about 0.2.

(a) Construct a decision tree that shows each possible outcome and the probability of it occurring.

(b) Determine the expected number of students in State's MBA program if offered by itself and in a combined MBA-MPA program, where both degrees would be offered.

3-9. Acme Manufacturing is considering three alternatives, A, B, and C, for a new plant. Cost data for each of these plants is shown below. The cost of shipping one unit of output to the market will vary because each plant would be at a different location.

	A	B	C
Annual fixed costs	$100,000	$200,000	$300,000
Production cost per unit	20	18	15
Shipping cost per unit	5	6	6

The quantity sold will depend on economic conditions for the next year as indicated below:

Economic Conditions	Probability	Quantity Sold
Normal	0.8	100,000
Recession	0.2	80,000

The per unit price of the product will depend entirely on the price set by Zenith Steel, the primary competitor in the market. It is thought that the probability of various prices being set will depend on the plant built by Acme as outlined below:

	Probability that Zenith Responds with a Price of:		
Acme Builds Plant	$20	$25	$30
A	.10	.40	.50
B	.30	.30	.40
C	.60	.20	.20

Because of Zenith's large size, whatever price it sets must be followed by Acme.
(a) Construct a decision tree showing the first year net profit for Acme for each combination of plant size, economic condition, and pricing reaction.
(b) Determine the expected first year profit for each plant alternative. Ignoring risk, which plant should be built?

3-10. Miramor Food Products is considering three alternative strategies, A, B, and C, for marketing a new food product. The only possible states of nature, N_1, N_2, and N_3, that will influence consumer acceptance have been identified. The present value of all future profits (in millions of dollars) for each strategy/state-of-nature combination is as follows:

	State of Nature		
Strategy	N_1	N_2	N_3
A	14	12	1
B	3	3	4
C	8	2	9

(a) Use the maximin criterion to select the best strategy.
(b) Based on an outside consultant's report, the probability of N_1 and N_2 occurring is 0.2 and 0.5, respectively. Based on this information, rank the strategies according to expected payoff. What does this answer suggest about the efficacy of maximin decision approach?

3-11. A manager must choose between strategies A and B having the following payoff matrix:

	State of Nature	
Strategy	N_1	N_2
A	50	1
B	2	2

(a) Use the maximin criterion to select the strategy.
(b) What would the probabilities for the states of nature have to be so that the expected payoffs for the two strategies would be equal?

3-12. Sharp Products, a major paper recycling firm, must replace its processing equipment. The only alternatives are the Century Processor, a very efficient but somewhat
unreliable machine, and the Sureshot Processor, a less efficient but almost repair
free piece of equipment. The two machines have equal initial costs and have a three
year life. Due to rapid technological change, the machines will have no significant
value at the end of that period. Sharp's engineering department has estimated the
expected net cash flows associated with each mchine over their three year lives.

Machine	Expected Net Cash Flows for Year		
	1	2	3
Century	300	400	400
Sureshot	250	350	450

The management at Sharp uses a 14 percent discount rate for most equipment
purchases. However, because of the unreliability of the Sureshot, a discount rate of
18 percent is appropriate for that machine. Which machine should be purchased?
Explain. (Assume that all cash flows occur at the end of each year.)

References

Blume, M. E. 1971. "On the Assessment of Risk." *Journal of Finance 26*(March):95–117.

Brunk, G. G. 1981. "A Test of the Friedman–Savage Gambling Model." *Quarterly Journal of Economics 96*(2):341–348.

Friedman, M., and Savage, L. J. 1948. "The Utility Analysis of Choices Involving Risk," *The Journal of Political Economy 56*(4):279–304. (Reprinted in Stephen Archer and Charles D'Ambrosio, eds., *The Theory of Business Finance: A Book of Readings*, 3rd ed. New York: Macmillan, 1983.)

Hertz, D. B. 1964. "Risk Analysis in Capital Investment." *Harvard Business Review 42*(January–February):95–106.

Hespos, R. F., and Strassman, P. A. 1965. "Stochastic Decision Trees for the Analysis of Investment Decisions." *Management Science 11*(August):244–259.

Magee, J. F. 1964. "Decision Trees for Decision-Making." *Harvard Business Review 42*(July–August):126–136.

Parsons, J. A. 1972. "Decision-Making Under Uncertainty." *Journal of Systems Management 23*(August):43–44.

Schlaifer, R. 1969. *Analysis of Decisions Under Uncertainty*. New York: McGraw-Hill. (Reprinted, 1978).

Schoemaker, P. J. H. 1982. "The Expected Utility Model: Its Variants, Purposes, Evidence and Limitations." *Journal of Economic Literature 20*(2):529–563.

INTEGRATING CASE PROBLEM I
BENTLEY ENTERPRISES, INC.

Bentley Enterprises is a manufacturer and nationwide distributor of specialty food products such as ice cream, candy, and bakery goods. The firm's strategic planning group has developed a proposal for locating a number of "shaved ice" retail outlets in the parking lots of shopping centers. The product consists of crushed ice in a paper cone that is mixed with one or more flavors. Management decides that the product can be sold for $0.80 each. Two alternatives have been proposed. In the first, called the "national" proposal, 500 stands would be located at shopping centers of various sizes across the United States. The second proposal, referred to as the "limited" plan, would place fewer stands (200) in the large malls of major urban areas.

The initial cost of the "igloo-like" structures, including the necessary equipment, is projected to be $55,000 each. Because of their specialized nature, the buildings will have no value at the end of the life of the project. The average payment of a four-year lease for each parking lot space would be $25,000. The entire lease payment would be paid at the beginning of the project. Thus, it is a one-time outlay that would pay for space for four years in advance.

At this time, the only competition in this field comes from a few "mom and pop" type operations scattered around the country. However, management at Bentley is concerned that Unique Foods, Inc., its major competitor, might respond to the Bentley plan with a similar program. Over the past twenty years, Unique has had a tendency to watch the actions of Bentley and then attempt to duplicate its new programs. In fact, for new products introduced on a national basis, Unique has responded with a similar program about 60 percent of the time. For programs developed on a more limited basis by Bentley, Unique has come up with an almost identical program in 30 percent of the cases.

Average daily volume for each unit for the first year of operation will depend on (1) whether the national or limited program is undertaken and (2) whether Unique responds with a similar program. Estimates of the volume under each combination of events are outlined below. The average volume is higher under the limited program because of the larger number of shoppers in the large malls. The stands would be open 365 days a year.

First Year Average Daily Volume (Units Sold)

Unique	Program	
	National	Limited
Responds	250	300
Doesn't respond	400	500

Although the per unit price of $0.80 is expected to remain constant, unit volume is expected to increase by 20 percent in the second year, an additional 20 percent in the third year from the level in the second year, and then to decline in the fourth year by 30 percent from the third year volume. Because of the novelty nature of the product, management is assuming a "worst case" scenario that there will be no demand for the product after the fourth year. Operating profit will increase and decrease in proportion to the change in revenue.

Although the profit associated with any one unit cannot be estimated with accuracy, management thinks that annual profit for the average unit can be determined based on the following operating profit data for eight experimental units that were in operation for one year at random locations throughout the country. The data do not include the cost of the structure or lease payments for parking lot space.

Unit No.	Annual Revenue (000)	Annual Operating Profit (000)
1	$ 80,000	$18,000
2	120,000	28,000
3	60,000	11,000
4	90,000	16,000
5	110,000	20,000
6	100,000	25,000
7	70,000	12,000
8	60,000	14,000

The management decision rule at Bentley for evaluating projects such as this is that a project should be implemented if the present value of all future operating profits exceeds the initial project cost. The only alternative for the firm would be to invest in a four-year certificate of deposit that would yield 10 percent interest. Management thinks that the risky nature of the "shaved-ice" stands implies a risk premium of 4 percentage points over the rate available on bank deposits. Management also insists on having a quantitative measure of the risk associated with each alternative. (Note: a rule of thumb at Bentley is to assume that all annual revenues are received and operating costs incurred on the last day of each year considered.)

Requirements

a. Prepare a report that justifies a course of action on this proposal.
b. Suppose that after finishing your report, a new president of the firm is appointed who insists that the "maximin" strategy be used to make all decisions of this type. Prepare an appendix to your original report documenting the use of the "maximin" decision rule in this problem.

DEMAND

Demand Theory and Analysis

4

Preview

Demand theory is a source of many useful insights for business decision making. Indeed, it is difficult to overstate the importance of understanding demand. Ultimately, the success or failure of a business depends primarily on its ability to generate revenues by satisfying the demands of consumers. Firms that are unable to attract the dollar votes of consumers are soon forced from the market.

The fundamental objective of demand theory is to identify and analyze the basic determinants of consumer demand. An understanding of the forces behind demand is a powerful tool for managers. Such knowledge provides the background needed to make pricing decisions, forecast sales, and formulate marketing strategies.

This chapter begins with a discussion of market demand and the demand faced by individual firms. The focus then shifts to a basic concern of managers—the total revenue earned by the firm. Finally, the concept of elasticity is introduced as a tool for measuring the responsiveness of quantity demanded to changes in prices and income. Three elasticity measures are discussed: price elasticity, income elasticity, and cross elasticity.

Market Demand

As used in the study of economics, the term *demand* denotes more than just a want. A demand for a good or service exists only if an individual has and is willing to use the purchasing power necessary to obtain the item. Although choices by individuals are the basis of the theory of demand, it is total or market demand that is of primary interest to managers.[1]

The market demand for a good or service is the sum of all individual demands. For example, consider a market that consists of only two buyers. The demand curves for these two consumers are depicted in Figure 4-1. Consumer 1's demand curve is shown in the first panel and that of consumer 2 in the second panel. At a price of $10, the individual quantities demanded are 5 and 8 units, respectively. Hence the total market demand (as shown in the third panel) is 13 units. The market demand at any price is the sum of the individual demands at that price.

Graphically, the market demand curve is the horizontal summation of the individual demand curves. That is, for any given price, the market demand curve is the sum of the horizontal distances from the vertical axis to each individual demand curve.

---

[1] Individual demands are the outcome of a complex decision process by the consumer. A discussion of the theory of consumer choice is included as an appendix to this chapter.

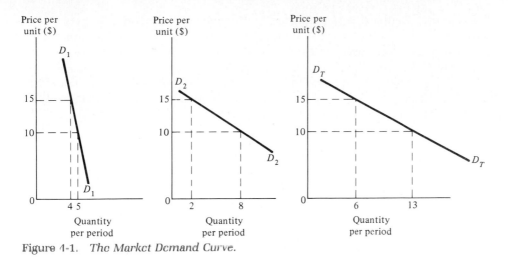

Figure 4-1. *The Market Demand Curve.*

Determinants of Market Demand

The demand curve shows the relationship between price and the quantity demanded of a good or service. The effect of changes in price are depicted as a movement from one point to another *along* a particular demand curve. For example, in Figure 4-1, as price increases from $10 to $15, moving along the market demand curve $D_T D_T$ depicts a decrease in quantity demanded from 13 to 6 units. Movements along the demand curve in response to changes in the price of a good or service are referred to as *changes in quantity demanded.*

The price of a good or service is not the only determinant of demand. However, in plotting a demand curve, it is assumed that other factors which affect demand are held constant. When these factors are allowed to vary, the demand curve may shift. Such shifts are referred to as *changes in demand.* A shift to the right is called an increase in demand, meaning that consumers demand more of the good or service at the same price than they did before. A leftward shift indicates a decrease in demand. That is, less is demanded at the same price than before.

In a market economy, firms must be responsive to consumer demands. Thus it is important that managers understand the determinants of demand. Among the most important are consumer preferences, income levels, and prices of other goods.

Consumer Preferences.   Obviously, an important determinant of demand is the preferences of consumers. These preferences can change rapidly in response to advertising, fads, and customs. There was a time when gloves were considered a must for the well-dressed woman. Today, gloves are usually worn only on special occasions. This change in preferences caused a decrease in the demand for gloves, meaning that fewer gloves are demanded at any given price. In contrast, pants for women have become more popular in recent years. In this case, the shift in preferences resulted in an increase in demand, with more women's pants now demanded at a given price.

Income.   Demand is also affected by the amount of income that consumers have available to spend. For most goods, an increase in consumer income would cause the demand curve for the product to shift to the right. For example, in the early 1980s, revenues from oil and gas leases left the state of Alaska awash with money. The state responded by providing a cash grant to every resident of the state. Alaskans used much of this extra income to buy additional goods and services. That is, the increased income resulted in an increase in demand for many goods and services.

Prices of Other Goods.   The demand for a good is often influenced by changes in the prices of other goods. The nature of the impact depends on whether the goods are substitutes or complements. *Substitutes* are goods that have essentially the same use. When the price of a good goes up, the demand for its substitutes is likely to increase. For example, 7-Up and Sprite are similar lemon-flavored soft drinks. An increase in the price of Sprite would cause people to purchase less of that beverage and consume more 7-Up. Thus the demand curve for 7-Up would shift to the right from *DD* to *D'D'*, as shown in Figure 4-2a. Note that more 7-Up is demanded at each price than before the shift.

Goods that are often used together are called *complements*. An increase in the price of one such good will cause the demand for its complement to decrease. Consider tennis rackets and balls. If the price of rackets increases, fewer people will take up tennis. With fewer people playing the sport, fewer tennis balls will be purchased. This outcome is illustrated by the leftward shift of the demand curve from *DD* to *D'D'* in Figure 4-2b.

The Market Demand Equation

The market demand can also be expressed mathematically. In that the primary determinants of demand are the price of the product, income, consumer pref-

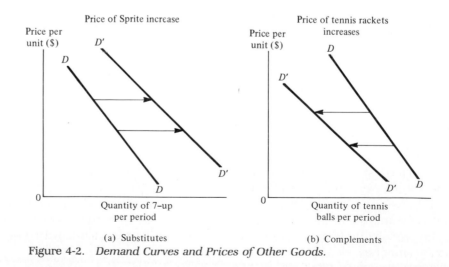

(a) Substitutes   (b) Complements

Figure 4-2.   *Demand Curves and Prices of Other Goods.*

erences, and the prices of other goods and services, the demand equation can be written as

$$Q_D = f(P, Y, P_o, T) \tag{4-1}$$

where P is the price of the good or service, Y is income, P_o is the prices of other goods, and T is a measure of consumer tastes and preferences. Equation (4-1) suggests that there is a correspondence between the quantity demanded and the variables on the right-hand side. However, the equation implies only that there are general relationships. It says nothing about their nature and magnitude. Depicting this information requires that a functional form be chosen to represent the equation for market demand. A linear form as shown in equation (4-2) is the simplest choice.

$$Q_D = a_pP + a_yY + a_oP_o + a_tT \tag{4-2}$$

The coefficients a_p, a_y, a_o, and a_t indicate the impact on quantity demanded of 1-unit changes in the associated variables. For example, a_p is the coefficient of price. Its interpretation is that, holding the other three variables constant, quantity demanded changes by a_p units for each 1-unit change in price. In most cases, a_p will be negative. For example, if $a_p = -2$ and price is measured in dollars, a \$1 increase in price would be associated with a 2-unit decrease in quantity demanded.

For many purposes it is useful to focus on the relationship between quantity demanded and the price of the good or service while holding the other variables constant. If Y, P_a, and T are not allowed to vary, then demand is a function only of P. Hence the linear form of the demand equation can be written as

$$Q_D = B + a_pP \tag{4-3}$$

where B represents the combined influence of all the other determinants of demand and $a_p \leq 0$. This simple demand equation is the basis for much of the analysis in the remainder of the chapter.

EXAMPLE
THE MARKET DEMAND FOR TESTS

Max, a graduating senior, has accumulated an impressive file of tests during his college career. But now he needs to sell his test collection to obtain money for his impending marriage. Three wealthy friends express interest in buying some of the tests. Max estimates that their individual demand equations are as follows:

$$Q_1 = 30.00 - 1.00P$$
$$Q_2 = 22.50 - 0.75P$$
$$Q_3 = 37.50 - 1.25P$$

where the quantity subscript denotes the three friends and price is measured in dollars per test.

What is the market demand equation for Max's tests, and how many more tests can he sell for each 1-dollar decrease in price? If he has a file of 60 tests, what price should he charge to sell his entire collection?

Solution

Market demand, Q_m, is the sum of the individual demands. Thus

$$Q_m = Q_1 + Q_2 + Q_3 = (30.00 - 1.00P) + (22.50 - 0.75P) + (37.50 - 1.25P)$$

Simplifying yields

$$Q_m = 90.00 - 3.00P$$

Because P is measured in dollars, a 1-dollar decrease in price will increase quantity demanded by three tests. To sell the entire 60-card collection, the price must be set such that

$$60 = 90 - 3.00P$$

Solving this equation gives $P = \$10.00$

Market Versus Firm Demand

Thus far, the discussion has focused on market demand curves. But from the perspective of managers, it is the demand curve facing the firm that is most relevant in pricing and output decisions.

Where a firm is the only seller in a market, the demand curve facing that firm is the market demand curve. As such, the firm will bear the entire impact of changes in incomes, consumer preferences, and prices of other goods. Similarly, the pricing policies of the firm will have a significant impact on purchasers of the firm's product. But few businesses have a market to themselves. In the vast majority of cases, a firm supplies only part of the total market. Consequently, the demand curve faced by the individual firm is not the same as the market demand curve.

One major difference between firm and market demand is that additional factors affect demand at the firm level. Perhaps the most important factor is decisions made by competitors. For example, a price cut by one firm probably would decrease sales of rival firms unless those firms also reduced price. Similarly, an effective advertising campaign can increase a firm's sales at the expense of its competitors.

Another difference between firm and market demand is the quantitative impact of changes in tastes, income, and prices of other goods. Consider beef and pork as examples of substitute goods. Suppose the market demand equation indicates that a 1-cent per pound increase in the price of beef would increase the market demand for pork by 1 million pounds per year. Now consider the demand equation for a small meatpacker with a 1 percent market share of pork sales. Because the firm's share is a small fraction of the total market, the impact on the firm's sales resulting from the change in beef prices will be much less than the total market change. That is, if the demand equation for the small firm was estimated, the coefficient showing the effect of changes in the price of beef would be much smaller than the coefficient for the market demand equation. Similarly, the coefficients showing the effects of changes in tastes and incomes would also be less than for the market demand equation.

For the remainder of the chapter the discussion will focus on the demand curve faced by the individual firm. However, most of the concepts discussed are equally applicable to market demand curves.

KEY CONCEPTS

- Changes in quantity demanded refer to movements along a particular demand curve caused by changes in the price of the good or service.
- Changes in demand are represented by shifts of the demand curve resulting from changes in consumer preferences, incomes, or prices of other goods.
- When the price of a good increases, demand for its substitutes also increases. If two goods are complements, a higher price for one will cause a decrease in the demand for the other.

Total and Marginal Revenue

One indication of a firm's success is the total revenue generated by the sale of its products. Rankings of firm size are usually made on the basis of total revenue. Similarly, growth is often expressed in terms of increases in total revenue. In that it reflects the ability of the firm to satisfy consumer demands, the use of total revenue as a measure of success has some merit.

Table 4-1 provides information on the demand faced by a firm. By multiplying price times quantity, the total revenue associated with each price–quantity pair is determined. These data are also shown in Table 4-1. Note that total revenue increases as price goes from $1 to $5 and then decreases for prices greater than

Table 4-1. Total and Marginal Revenue

Price	Quantity	Total Revenue	Marginal Revenue
$10	1	$10	
			$8
9	2	18	
			6
8	3	24	
			4
7	4	28	
			2
6	5	30	
			0
5	6	30	
			−2
4	7	28	
			−4
3	8	24	
			−6
2	9	18	
			−8
1	10	10	

$6. This suggests that sound pricing decisions require information about demand. In some cases higher prices may increase total revenue, whereas in other circumstances a price increase can have the opposite effect.

Table 4-1 also shows marginal revenue. Marginal revenue is defined as the change in revenues associated with the sale of 1 more unit of the product. For example, as quantity goes from 4 to 5, revenue increases from $28 to $30. Hence the marginal or extra revenue associated with the fifth unit is $2. Note that marginal revenue declines with increases in quantity. Beyond 6 units, marginal revenue is negative. The explanation stems from the inverse relationship between price and quantity. To sell extra units, the firm must reduce the price of all the units sold. Negative marginal revenue means that the dollars received from selling the extra unit are not sufficient to compensate for the dollars lost as a result of selling all other units at a lower price. Clearly, a firm should not increase output beyond the point where marginal revenue is zero.

The total and marginal revenue data of Table 4-1 can be plotted on a graph. If fractional units are allowed, the line has the appearance of a smooth curve, as shown in Figure 4-3. Note the relationship between the total and marginal revenue curves. As long as total revenue is increasing, marginal revenue is positive. At the maximum point on the total revenue curve marginal revenue is zero. But beyond that point, marginal revenue is negative.

Figure 4-3 also shows the relationship between the marginal revenue curve and the demand curve. Note that the two curves intercept the price axis at the same point. Using calculus it can easily be shown that for linear demand equations, the absolute value of the slope of the marginal revenue curve is twice the absolute value of the slope of the associated demand curve. Because the two curves have the same price intercept, this implies that the quantity intercept of the marginal revenue curve is exactly half that of the demand curve.

Suppose that the demand equation is given by $Q = B + a_pP$, where $a_p \leq 0$. Solving for price, the demand equation becomes

$$P = \frac{-B}{a_p} + \frac{Q}{a_p} \tag{4-4}$$

Multiplying by quantity gives

$$TR = PQ = -\frac{B}{a_p} Q + \frac{Q^2}{a_p} \tag{4-5}$$

Marginal revenue is the change in revenue per unit change in Q, or the derivative of TR with respect to Q. Thus

$$MR = \frac{d(PQ)}{dQ} = -\frac{B}{a_p} + \frac{2Q}{a_p} \tag{4-6}$$

Note that the marginal revenue equation has the same intercept $(-B/a_p)$ as the demand equation and that the absolute value of the slope of marginal revenue,

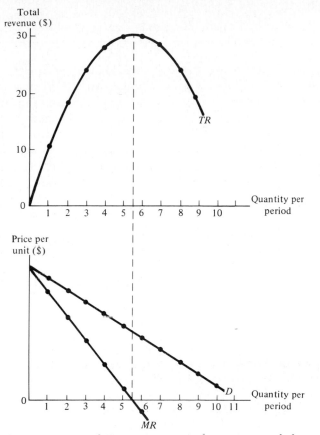

Figure 4-3. Total Revenue, Marginal Revenue, and the Demand Curve.

$2/a_p$, is twice the absolute value of the slope of the demand equation. Also note that $MR = 0$ at $Q = B/2$. This point corresponds to the maximum value of the total revenue function. For $Q < B/2$, marginal revenue is positive and total revenue is increasing. For $Q > B/2$, marginal revenue is negative and total revenue is decreasing.

KEY CONCEPTS

- Marginal revenue is the change in revenue associated with a 1 unit change in output.
- Marginal revenue is zero at the quantity that generates maximum total revenue and negative beyond that point.
- For a linear demand curve, the absolute value of the slope of the marginal revenue curve is twice that of the demand curve.

Price Elasticity

In the preceding section it was demonstrated that higher prices do not always result in greater total revenue. A price change can either increase or decrease total revenue, depending on the nature of the demand function. The uncertainty involved in pricing decisions could be reduced if managers had a method of measuring the probable effect of price changes on total revenue. One such measure is *price elasticity of demand,* which is defined as the percentage change in quantity demanded divided by the percentage change in price.[2] That is,

$$E_p = \frac{\%\,\Delta Q}{\%\,\Delta P} \tag{4-7}$$

where the symbol Δ is used to denote change. Thus, price elasticity indicates the percentage change in quantity demanded for a 1 percent change in price.

For example, suppose that a firm increases the price of its product by 2 percent and quantity demanded subsequently decreases by 3 percent. The price elasticity would be

$$E_p = \frac{-3\%}{2\%} = -1.5$$

Notice that E_p is negative. Except in rare and unimportant cases, price elasticities are always less than or equal to zero. The explanation is the *law of demand,* which states that price and quantity demanded are inversely related. Thus, when the price change is positive, the change in quantity demanded is negative, and vice versa.

Point Versus Arc Elasticity

There are two approaches to computing price elasticities. The choice between the two depends on the available data and the intended use. Arc elasticities are appropriate for analyzing the impact of discrete (i.e., measurable) changes in price. In actual practice, most elasticity computations involve the arc method. The other choice is point elasticity. This approach can be used to evaluate the effect of small price changes. Point elasticities are important in theoretical economics.

Arc Elasticity.   The percentage change in price is the change in price divided by price (i.e., $\Delta P/P$). Similarly, the percentage change in quantity demanded is

---

[2] In some texts, price elasticities are multiplied by -1 to make them positive. This convention is not adopted here because it obscures the inverse relationship between price and quantity demanded.

the change in quantity divided by quantity (i.e., $\Delta Q/Q$). Thus price elasticity can be expressed as

$$E_p = \frac{\Delta Q/Q}{\Delta P/P} \qquad (4\text{-}8)$$

By rearranging terms, equation (4-8) can be written as

$$E_p = \frac{\Delta Q}{\Delta P}\frac{P}{Q} \qquad (4\text{-}9)$$

Note that P and Q specify a particular point on the demand curve, while $\Delta Q/\Delta P$ is the reciprocal of the slope of the demand curve. Thus the price elasticity will vary depending on where the measurement is taken on the demand curve and also with the slope of the demand curve.

The price and quantity information presented earlier in the chapter can be used to demonstrate the calculation of arc price elasticities. Table 4-1 indicates that at a price of $6, quantity demanded is 5 units. The table also shows that if the price increases to $10, quantity demanded will be 1 unit. Thus for a $4 increase in price, the change in quantity demanded is -4 units. That is,

$$\frac{\Delta Q}{\Delta P} = \frac{-4}{4} = -1$$

Determining the value of P/Q poses a problem. Which should be used, the price–quantity data before the price change or the price–quantity values after the price increase? The choice makes a significant difference in the computed price elasticity. For example, if the initial data are used, then

$$E_p = \frac{\Delta Q}{\Delta P}\frac{P}{Q} = -1 \times \frac{6}{5} = -1.20$$

However, if the price–quantity data after the price change are selected, then

$$E_p = \frac{\Delta Q}{\Delta P}\frac{P}{Q} = -1 \times \frac{10}{1} = -10.00$$

In the first case, the price elasticity estimate indicates that a 1 percent increase in price results in a quantity decline of just over 1 percent. But the second estimate implies that the percentage impact on quantity demanded is 10 times that of the percentage price change.

The conventional approach used to calculate arc elasticities is to use average values for price and quantity. Thus arc price elasticity is defined as

$$E_p = \frac{Q_2 - Q_1}{(Q_2 + Q_1)/2} \bigg/ \frac{P_2 - P_1}{(P_2 + P_1)/2} \qquad (4\text{-}10)$$

where P_1 and Q_1 are the initial price–quantity pair and P_2 and Q_2 are the price–quantity values after the price change. Simplifying and rearranging terms, equation (4-10) can be written as

$$E_p = \frac{Q_2 - Q_1}{P_2 - P_1} \frac{P_2 + P_1}{Q_2 + Q_1} \qquad (4\text{-}11)$$

Now using the data from Table 4.1, the arc elasticity is computed to be

$$E_p = \frac{1 - 5}{10 - 6} \times \frac{10 + 6}{1 + 5} = -2.67$$

Thus as price increases from $6 to $10, the change in quantity demanded per 1 percent change in price averages -2.67 percent.

EXAMPLE

THE PRICE ELASTICITY OF DEMAND FOR PLAYING CARDS

Suppose the demand for playing cards is given by the equation

$$Q = 6{,}000{,}000 - 1{,}000{,}000P$$

where Q is the number of decks of cards demanded each year and P is the price in dollars. For a price increase from $2 to $3 per deck, what is the arc price elasticity?

Solution

Using the demand equation, quantity demanded can be computed to be 4,000,000 decks of cards at a price of $2. Similarly, it is known that the quantity demanded is 3,000,000 decks at a price of $3 per deck. The demand equation can also be used to determine $\Delta Q / \Delta P$. In that each $1 increase in price causes a 1,000,000 decrease in quantity demanded, it is known that $\Delta Q / \Delta P = -1{,}000{,}000$. Thus the arc price elasticity is

$$E_p = -1{,}000{,}000 \times \frac{2 + 3}{4{,}000{,}000 + 3{,}000{,}000} = -0.71$$

Point Elasticity.   Now consider extremely small changes in price. For ΔP approaching zero, the term $\Delta Q / \Delta P$ can be written as dQ/dP, where dQ/dP is the derivative of Q with respect to P. Basically, dQ/dP expresses the rate at which Q is changing for very small changes in P. For a linear demand curve, dQ/dP is constant and equal to the reciprocal of the slope. Thus the rate of change for a small price change is the same as for large changes.[3] Hence for linear demand curves, $dQ/dP = \Delta Q / \Delta P$.

---

[3] For nonlinear curves, the slope of the line changes from point to point along the curve. In such cases, the slope at each point is the slope of the tangent to the curve at that point. Thus dQ/dP is the reciprocal of the slope of the tangent and is constantly changing.

For small price changes, P_1 approaches P_2. Thus either P can be used in the calculation with no significant effect on the computed price elasticity. Thus the equation for point elasticity can be written as

$$E_p = \frac{dQ}{dP}\frac{P}{Q} \qquad (4\text{-}12)$$

Equation (4-12) is used to calculate price elasticities at a particular point on the demand curve. For example, consider the price–quantity data used earlier in this section. It has already been determined that $dQ/dP = -1$. If price is $6 and the quantity demanded is 5 units, the price elasticity is

$$E_p = \frac{dQ}{dP}\frac{P}{Q} = -1 \times \frac{6}{5} = -1.20$$

That is, for very small price changes above or below $6, the percentage change in quantity demanded is 1.20 times the percentage change in price. Again, the minus sign denotes that there is an inverse relationship between price and quantity.

Point elasticities can also be computed from a demand equation. Suppose that the demand equation is as follows:

$$Q_D = 100 - 4P$$

Because the relationship is linear, dQ/dP is constant and equal to the rate of change in Q_D for each 1-unit change in P. Note that quantity demanded changes by -4 units for each unit increase in P. Thus $dQ/dP = -4$.

Suppose that $P = \$10$. Substituting this value into the demand equation yields $Q_D = 60$. Thus the point elasticity at $P = \$10$ is

$$E_p = -4 \times \frac{10}{60} = -0.67$$

The interpretation is that a 1 percent increase in price causes a 0.67 percent reduction in quantity demanded.

Consider a second example using the same demand equation. Suppose that $P = \$20$, which implies that $Q = 20$. The equation is linear, so $dQ/dP = -4$, as before. Thus

$$E_p = -4 \times \frac{20}{20} = -4.0$$

That is, at $P = \$20$, a small change in price generates a percentage change in quantity demanded that is four times the magnitude of the price change.

Price Elasticity and Marginal Revenue

Table 4-2 reproduces the price, quantity, total revenue, and marginal revenue information from Table 4-1. It also shows the point price elasticity at each price.

Table 4-2. Price Elasticity, Total Revenue, and Marginal Revenue

Price	Quantity	Price Elasticity	Total Revenue	Marginal Revenue
$10	1	−10.00	$10	
9	2	−4.50	18	$8
8	3	−2.67	24	6
7	4	−1.75	28	4
6	5	−1.20	30	2
5	6	−0.83	30	0
4	7	−0.57	28	−2
3	8	−0.38	24	−4
2	9	−0.22	18	−6
1	10	−0.10	10	−8

Note that the absolute value of the elasticities becomes smaller as prices decrease. At $P = \$10$, the elasticity is -10.00, while at $P = \$1$, it is -0.10.

Often, it is useful to classify demand relationships on the basis of price elasticities. The following classification scheme is frequently used:

	If:	*Then Demand is said to be:*
$E_p < -1$		Elastic
$E_p = -1$		Unitary elastic
$-1 < E_p \leq 0$		Inelastic

Thus, based on the data in Table 4-2, at some price between $5 and $6, demand is unitary elastic because the price elasticity is equal to -1. For prices below this price, demand is inelastic. For prices above, demand is elastic.

Figure 4-4 shows the demand and marginal revenue curves for the price–quantity data of Table 4-2. The figure has been labeled to show where demand is elastic, unitary elastic, and inelastic. The figure indicates that demand becomes less elastic at lower prices. This is a characteristic of linear demand curves. Because the curve is linear, dQ/dP is a constant. Thus price elasticity is determined by the value of P/Q. But as price decreases, P/Q also decreases. Consequently, the absolute value of E_p gets smaller and demand becomes less elastic.

Figure 4-4 can be used to interpret the three elasticity categories. The figure shows that the point of unitary elasticity corresponds to the point where the marginal revenue crosses the quantity axis. That is, marginal revenue is zero where demand is unitary elastic. The explanation is not difficult. Unitary elasticity means that a 1 percent increase in price causes quantity demanded to decrease by 1 percent. But total revenue is computed by multiplying price times quantity. Thus, if demand is unitary elastic, the increase in price is exactly offset by the decrease in quantity demanded. As a result, there is no change in total revenue—marginal revenue is zero.

Figure 4-4 also shows that marginal revenue is positive where demand is elastic and negative when demand is inelastic. Although the demand curve in Figure 4-6 is linear, these relationships are also true for nonlinear demand curves. The

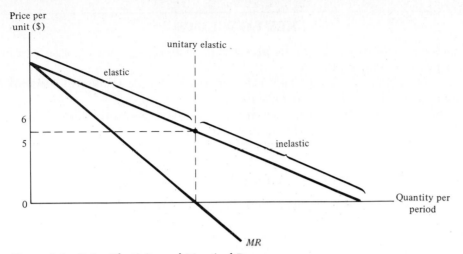

Figure 4-4. *Price Elasticity and Marginal Revenue.*

point where marginal revenue is zero always divides the elastic and inelastic regions of the demand curve.[4]

The choice of the terms "inelastic" and "elastic" is appropriate when viewed in light of the relationship between price elasticity and marginal revenue. The word "inelastic" carries the connotation of something that is not flexible or responsive. Consider a vertical demand curve. For such a curve, quantity demanded is not affected by changes in price. That is, $dQ/dP = 0$ and thus $E_p = 0$. Such curves are sometimes referred to as totally inelastic.

In contrast, for a horizontal demand curve quantity demanded is highly responsive to changes in prices. In fact, an arbitrarily small change in price causes an infinitely large change in quantity demanded. That is, $dQ/dP = -\infty$ and hence $E_p = -\infty$. Horizontal demand curves are said to be totally elastic. Although there are probably no goods or services for which market demand is totally elastic or totally inelastic, an understanding of these cases is useful in economic analysis. Also, individual producers may face demand curves that approach these extremes.

---

[4] However, it should be noted that there are some demand relationships for which marginal revenue is never zero. For example, consider a demand equation of the following form:

$$Q = P^a$$

Taking the derivative with respect to P yields

$$\frac{dQ}{dP} = aP^{a-1}$$

Thus the price elasticity is

$$E_p = (aP^{a-1})\frac{P}{Q} = \frac{aP^a}{Q}$$

But $P^a = Q$. Thus $E_p = a$. Because a is a constant, it follows that E_p is constant for all values of price and quantity. If $a < -1$, demand is elastic for all points on the curve. Thus marginal revenue is always positive. Conversely, demand is inelastic and marginal revenue negative if $a > -1$. If $a = -1$, marginal revenue is zero and demand is unitary elastic for all price–quantity combinations.

KEY CONCEPTS

- Price elasticity is defined as the percentage change in quantity demanded for a 1 percent change in price.
- Point elasticities are used where price changes are very small. Arc elasticities are appropriate for larger changes in price.
- Demand is said to be elastic where marginal revenue is positive, unitary elastic when marginal revenue is zero, and inelastic if marginal revenue is negative.

Determinants of Price Elasticity

Price elasticities have been estimated for many goods and services; Table 4-3 provides some examples. The short-run elasticities reflect periods of time during which the consumer has little opportunity to adjust to changes in prices. The long-run values refer to situations where consumers have had more time to adjust.

Note the variation in elasticities in Table 4-3. The long-run demand for motion pictures is elastic with $E_p = -3.69$. In contrast, the long-run demand for water is highly inelastic with $E_p = -0.14$. Electricity demand is inelastic in the short run, but elastic in the long run. Three factors determine the price elasticity of demand. They are (1) availability of substitutes, (2) proportion of income spent on the good or service, and (3) length of time.

Availability of Substitutes.   Products for which there are good substitutes tend to have higher price elasticities than products for which there are few adequate substitutes. Motion pictures are a good example. Movies are a form of recreation, but there are many alternative recreational activities. When ticket prices at the movie theater increase, these substitute activities are used more often. Thus the demand for motion pictures is relatively elastic, as shown in Table 4-3.

At the other extreme, consider the short-run demand for electricity. When the local utility increases prices, consumers have few options. The owner of an

Table 4-3. Estimates of Price Elasticity

Good or Service	Estimated Price Elasticity	
Electricity	−0.13	Short run
Electricity	−1.89	Long run
Water	−0.14	Long run
Motion Pictures	−3.69	Long run
Gasoline	−0.15	Short run
Gasoline	−0.78	Long run

Source: H. S. Houthhakker and L. D. Taylor, Consumer Demand in the United States; Analysis and Projections (Cambridge, Mass.: Harvard University Press, 1970), pp. 166–167; and J. L. Sweeney, "The Demand for Gasoline: A Vintage Capital Model," Department of Engineering Economics, Stanford University.

electrically heated home can turn down the thermostat, but the savings are limited by the desire to keep warm. The owner of an electric clothes dryer may try drying his or her clothes on an outside line, but this option will not be very successful during the winter or for the residents of some apartment buildings. Similarly, there are few short-run alternatives to using electricity for refrigeration and lighting. Hence the short-run demand for electricity is found to be very inelastic.

Proportion of Income Spent.   Demand tends to be inelastic for goods and services that account for only a small proportion of total expenditures. Consider the demand for salt. A 1-pound container of salt will meet the needs of the typical household for months and costs only a few cents. If the price of salt were to double, this change would not have a significant impact on the family's purchasing power. As a result, price changes have little effect on the household demand for salt.

Time Period.   Demand is usually more elastic in the long run than in the short run. The explanation is that, given more time, the consumer has more opportunities to adjust to changes in prices. Table 4-4 indicates that the long-run elasticity for electricity is more than ten times the short-run value. It has already been mentioned that in the short run, a person living in an electrically heated home has few options. But over a longer period, the person may switch to gas or improve the energy efficiency of the home. Similarly, higher electricity prices may ultimately cause consumers to use other energy sources for cooking and clothes drying.

CASE STUDY

THE SHORT RUN VERSUS LONG RUN DEMAND FOR GASOLINE

Gasoline prices increased dramatically from 1973 to 1981. At first, consumers had little choice but to use about the same amount of gasoline and pay the higher prices. Some vacation trips were canceled and there were those who started going to work in buses or car pools, but the options were limited. From 1973 to 1975 average fuel consumption per vehicle declined from 736 to 685 gallons per year. However, given more time to adjust, consumers were able to lessen the impact of higher gas prices. Smaller, fuel-efficient cars became popular. People changed jobs or moved closer to their places of work. The result was that fuel consumption per vehicle in the United States declined from 736 to 557 gallons per year between 1973 and 1981.

Price Elasticity and Decision Making

Information about price elasticities can be extremely useful to managers as they contemplate pricing decisions. If demand is inelastic at the current price, a price decrease will result in a decrease in total revenue. Alternatively, reducing the price of a product with elastic demand would cause revenue to increase.[5] The effect on total revenue would be the reverse for a price increase. However, if demand is unitary elastic, price changes will not change total revenues.

The relationship between elasticity and total revenue can be shown using simple calculus. Total revenue is price times quantity. Taking the derivative of total revenue with respect to quantity yields marginal revenue:

$$MR = \frac{d(TR)}{dQ} = \frac{d(PQ)}{dQ} = P + \frac{QdP}{dQ} \qquad (4\text{-}13)$$

This equation can be written

$$MR = P\left(1 + \frac{Q}{P}\frac{dP}{dQ}\right) \qquad (4\text{-}14)$$

But note that $(Q/P)\, dP/dQ = 1/E_p$. Thus

$$MR = P\left(1 + \frac{1}{E_p}\right) \qquad (4\text{-}15)$$

If demand is unitary elastic, $E_p = -1$ and

$$MR = P\left(1 + \frac{1}{-1}\right) = 0$$

Because marginal revenue is zero, the implication is that a price change would have no effect on total revenue. In contrast, if demand is elastic, $E_p < -1$ and $(1 + 1/E_p) > 0$. Hence, marginal revenue is positive which means that, by increasing quantity demanded, a price reduction would increase total revenue. Equation (4-15) also implies that if demand is inelastic, marginal revenue is negative indicating that a price reduction would decrease total revenue.

Some analysts question the usefulness of elasticity estimates. They argue that elasticities are redundant in that the data necessary for their determination could be used to determine total revenues directly. Thus managers could assess the effects of a change in price without knowledge of price elasticity. Although this is true, elasticity estimates are valuable in that they provide a quick way of evaluating pricing policies. For example, if demand is known to be elastic, it is also known that a price increase will reduce total revenues.

KEY CONCEPTS

• Demand tends to be less elastic if:

There are few good substitutes available.

Purchase of the good or service represents only a small proportion of total expenditures.

---

[5] However, a price reduction is not always the correct strategy when demand is elastic. The decision must also take into account the impact on the firm's costs and profits. More will be said about pricing strategy in later chapters.

Consumers have not yet had time to adjust fully to change in price.
- A price *increase* will have the following effects:
  Increase total revenues if demand is inelastic $(-1 < E_p \leq 0)$.
  Decrease total revenues if demand is elastic $(E_p < -1)$.
  Leave total revenues unchanged if demand is unitary elastic $(E_p = -1)$.

EXAMPLE

HOW MUCH TUITION FOR COLLEGE STUDENTS?

The Board of Regents of a leading state university is faced with a critical financial problem. At present tuition rates, the university is losing $5 million per year. The president of the university, a well-known biologist, urges that tuition be raised $500 over the present $2,000 rate—a 25 percent increase. Based on the 10,000 students now attending the school, he projects that this increase would cover the short-fall in revenues.

Student leaders protest that they cannot afford a tuition hike, but the president responds that the only alternative is to cut back significantly on programs and faculty. The faculty supports the tuition increase as a means of preserving their jobs.

The students quickly realize that any appeal which involves compassion for their plight is likely to fall on deaf ears. Their only hope is to demonstrate that the tuition hike is not in the best interest of the university. What can they do?

Solution

The university administration sees a tuition increase as a means of increasing total revenue. The Board of Regents is likely to reject the administration's proposal only if the students can demonstrate that it would not achieve this purpose.

As part of a term paper, an economics major discovers a journal article that discusses the price elasticity of demand for a college education. The author of the article estimates that the elasticity for enrollment at state universities is -1.3 with respect to tuition changes. That is, a 1 percent increase in tuition would decrease enrollments by 1.3 percent. The data are current and the paper was written by a highly respected scholar.

Based on the elasticity estimate from the paper, the students calculate that the proposed tuition hike of 25 percent would decrease enrollment by 32.5 percent, or nearly 3300 students. This would result in a decrease in total revenue from $20,000,000 at present to less than $17,000,000 after the tuition increase.

Faced with this startling information, the Board of Regents asks the university president if cost savings from fewer students would compensate for the revenue drop. The president replies that most of the university's costs are independent of enrollment and hence there would not be a significant cost saving. Without a dissenting vote, the Board of Regents rejects the tuition increase and orders the president to find some other way to meet the revenue deficiency.

Income Elasticity

Income elasticities are used to measure the responsiveness of demand to changes in income. When other factors are held constant, the *income elasticity* of a good or service is the percentage change in demand associated with a 1 percent change in income. Specifically, the income elasticity of a good or service is defined as

$$E_i = \frac{\%\Delta Q}{\%\Delta I} = \frac{\Delta Q}{Q} \Big/ \frac{\Delta I}{I} \qquad (4\text{-}16)$$

where I denotes income. Rearranging terms, equation (4-16) can be written

$$EI = \frac{\Delta Q}{\Delta I} \frac{I}{Q} \qquad (4\text{-}17)$$

As with price elasticity, income elasticity can be expressed in either arc or point terms. Arc income elasticity is used when relatively large changes in income are being considered, and is defined as

$$E_I = \frac{Q_2 - Q_1}{I_2 - I_1} \frac{I_2 + I_1}{Q_2 + Q_1} \qquad (4\text{-}18)$$

where Q_1 and I_1 represent the initial levels of demand and income, and Q_2 and I_2 are the values after a change in income.

For example, suppose that the demand for automobiles as a function of income per person is given by the equation

$$Q = 50,000 + 5I$$

What is the income elasticity as per capita income increases from \$10,000 to \$20,000? Substituting $I = $10,000$ into the equation, quantity demanded is 100,000 cars. Similarly, at $I = $20,000$, quantity demanded is computed to be 150,000 automobiles. Thus

$$E_I = \frac{150,000 - 100,000}{20,000 - 10,000} \times \frac{20,000 + 10,000}{150,000 + 100,000} = 0.60$$

The interpretation of this result is that over the income range \$10,000 to \$20,000, each 1 percent increase in income causes a six-tenths of 1 percent increase in quantity demanded.

If the change in income is small or if income elasticity at a particular income level is to be determined, a point elasticity is appropriate. In this case, $\Delta Q/\Delta I$ is expressed as dQ/dI. Thus

$$E_I = \frac{dQ}{dI} \frac{I}{Q} \qquad (4\text{-}19)$$

To illustrate, if $Q = 50,000 + 5I$ as before, each 1-unit increase in income is associated with a 5-unit increase in demand. Thus $dQ/dI = 5$. At $I = \$15,000$, demand is 125,000 units and the income elasticity is

$$E_I = 5 \times \frac{15,000}{125,000} = 0.60$$

Note that this value is identical to the arc elasticity between $10,000 and $20,000 of income. They are equal because demand is a linear function of income. Thus the rate of change in quantity does not vary as income increases. Hence the average rate of change between $10,000 and $20,000 is the same as the instantaneous rate of change at $15,000. However, for nonlinear demand equations, the arc and point elasticities at the midpoint of the arc are not necessarily equal.

Inferior Goods, Necessities, and Luxuries

Income elasticities can be either negative or positive. When they are negative, the interpretation is that increases in income are associated with decreases in the quantity demanded of the good or service. Cheap hot dogs might be an example. Those living on tight budgets may be unable to afford any other kind of meat. But as their real incomes increase, they abandon the hot dogs and switch to other types of meat, such as roasts and steaks. Thus the increase in income causes a decrease in demand for hot dogs. Goods with negative income elasticities are categorized as inferior goods.

Normal goods and services have positive income elasticities. They can be further classified by the magnitude of E_I. If $0 < E_I \leq 1$, the percentage change in demand is less than or equal to the percentage change in income. Such goods and services are referred to as necessities. That is, demand is relatively unaffected by changes in income. A good example is bread, a basic food item eaten by even the poorest families. As families become more affluent, more bread will be purchased, but the increase is usually not proportionate to the increase in income.

Finally, luxuries are goods and services for which $E_I > 1$. This means that the change in demand is proportionately greater than the change in income. For example, if $E_I = 4$, a 1 percent increase in income would cause a 4 percent increase in demand. Jewelry is an example of a luxury good. As individuals become wealthier, they have more disposable income. Thus purchases of necklaces, rings, and fine watches tend to represent a larger share of their incomes.

Income Elasticity and Decision Making

The income elasticity for a firm's product is an important determinant of the firm's success during fluctuations in economic activity. During prosperous times, when incomes are rising, firms selling luxury items such as gourmet foods and exotic vacations will find that the demand for their products will increase at a rate faster than the rate of income growth. However, during a recession, demand may decrease rapidly. Conversely, sellers of necessities such as fuel and basic food items will not benefit as much during periods of prosperity, but will also find that their markets are somewhat recession-proof.

Knowledge of income elasticities can be useful in targeting marketing efforts. Consider a firm specializing in expensive men's colognes. Because such goods are luxuries, those in high-income groups would be expected to be the prime customers. Thus the firm should concentrate its marketing efforts on media that reach the more wealthy segments of the population. For example, advertising dollars should be spent on space in *Esquire* and *Playboy* rather than in the *National Enquirer* and *Wrestling Today.*

CASE STUDY

ENGEL'S LAW AND THE PLIGHT OF THE FARMER

In the nineteenth century a German statistician, Ernst Engel, etched his name in economic history by proposing what has become known as *Engel's law.* Engel studied the consumption patterns of a large number of households and concluded that the percentage of income spent on food decreases as incomes increase. That is, he determined that food is a necessity. His finding has repeatedly been confirmed by later researchers.

One of the implications of Engel's law is that farmers may not prosper as much as those in other occupations during periods of economic prosperity. The reason is that if food expenditures do not keep pace with increases in gross national product, farm incomes may not increase as rapidly as incomes in general. Thus Engel's law is a possible explanation for the plight of the farmer in recent years. However, part of the problem has been offset by the rapid increase in farm productivity in recent years. In 1940, each U.S. farmer grew enough food to feed about 11 other people. Today, the typical farmworker produces enough to feed 75 people.

KEY CONCEPTS

- Income elasticity is the percentage change in demand per 1 percent change in income.
- Negative income elasticities denote inferior goods. Normal goods are those with positive income elasticities. If $0 < E_I \leq 1$, the product is a necessity. For luxuries, $E_I > 1$.

Cross Elasticity

Demand is also influenced by prices of other goods and services. The responsiveness of quantity demanded to changes in prices of other goods is measured by *cross elasticity* which is defined as the percentage change in quantity demanded of one good caused by a 1 percent change in the price of some other good. That is,

$$E_c = \frac{\% \Delta Q_x}{\% \Delta P_y}$$ (4-20)

where x and y represent the goods or services being considered.

For large changes in the price of y, are cross elasticities are appropriate. The arc elasticity is computed as

$$E_C = \frac{Q_{x,2} - Q_{x,1}}{P_{y,2} - P_{y,1}} \frac{P_{y,2} + P_{y,1}}{Q_{x,2} + Q_{x,1}}$$ (4-21)

where the subscript 1 refers to the initial prices and quantities and 2 to the final values. Suppose that demand for x in terms of the price of y is given by

$$Q_x = 100 + 0.5P_y$$

If P_y increases from \$50 to \$100, then, using the equation, it is known that Q_x increases from 125 to 150 units. Thus

$$E_C = \frac{150 - 125}{100 - 50} \times \frac{100 + 50}{150 + 125} = 0.27$$

The interpretation is that a 1 percent increase in the price of y causes a 0.27 percent increase in the quantity demanded of x.

Point cross elasticities are analogous to the point elasticities already discussed. For small changes in P_y,

$$E_C = \frac{dQ_x}{dP_y} \frac{P_y}{Q_x}$$ (4-22)

Based on the demand equation $Q_x = 100 + 0.5P_y$, it is known that $dQ_x/dP_y = 0.5$. At $P_y = \$20$, quantity demanded is 110 units. Hence the point cross elasticity is

$$E_C = 0.5 \times \frac{20}{110} = 0.09$$

Substitutes and Complements

Cross elasticities are used to classify the relationship between goods. If $E_C > 0$, an increase in the price of y causes an increase in the quantity demanded of x, and the two products are said to be *substitutes*. That is, one product can be used in place of (substituted for) the other. Suppose that the price of x increases. This means that the opportunity cost of x in terms of y has increased. The result is that consumers purchase less x and more of the relatively cheaper good y. Beef and pork are examples of substitutes. Higher beef prices usually have the effect of increasing the demand for pork, and vice versa.

When $E_C < 0$, the goods or services involved are classified as *complements* (goods that are used together). Increases in the price of x reduce the quantity demanded of that product. The diminished demand for x causes a reduced demand for y. Bread and butter, cars and tires, and computers and computer programs are examples of goods that are complements.

Cross elasticities are not always symmetrical. That is, the change in demand for good x caused by a change in the price of good y may not equal the change in demand for y generated by a change in the price of x. Consider the case of margarine and butter. One study (Wold, 1953) determined that a 1 percent increase in the price of butter caused a 0.81 percent increase in demand for margarine. However, a 1 percent increase in the price of margarine increased demand for butter by only 0.67 percent. Although the two elasticities are different, note that they are both positive, indicating that butter and margarine are substitutes.

Cross Elasticity and Decision Making

Many large corporations produce several related products. Gillette makes both razors and razor blades. Ford sells several competing makes of automobiles. Where a company's products are related, the pricing of one good can influence the demand for other products. Gillette probably will sell more razor blades if it lowers the price of its razors. In contrast, if the price of Fords is reduced, sales of Mercurys may decline. Information regarding cross elasticities can aid decision makers in assessing such impacts.

Cross elasticities are also useful in establishing boundaries between industries. Sometimes it is difficult to determine which products should be included in an industry. For example, should the manufacturing of cars and trucks be considered one industry or two? One way of answering such questions is to define industries based on cross elasticities. This approach defines an industry as including firms whose products exhibit a high positive cross elasticity. Goods and services with negative or small cross elasticities are considered to belong to other industries. The definition of an industry might seem to be an unimportant matter, but the choice can have important implications. For example, the outcomes of antitrust cases are sometimes determined primarily by the industry definition used by the judges assigned to the case. This concept is discussed in greater detail in Chapter 19.

EXAMPLE

USING ELASTICITIES IN DECISION MAKING

The R. J. Smith Corporation is a manufacturer and seller of romance novels—nothing exotic or erotic—just stories of common people falling in and out of love. The corporation hires an economist to determine the demand for its product. After months of hard work and submission of an exorbitant bill, the analyst tells the company that demand for the firm's novels (Q_x) is given by the following equation:

$$Q_x = 12,000 - 5,000P_x + 5I + 500P_p$$

where P_x is the price charged for the R. J. Smith novels, I is income per capita, and P_p is the price of pornographic books.

Using this information, the company's managers want to:

1. Determine what effect a price increase would have on total revenues.
2. Find out how sale of the novels would fare during a period of rising incomes.
3. Assess the probable impact if sellers of pornographic books raise their prices.

Assume that the initial values of P_x, I, and P_p are $5, $10,000, and $6, respectively.

Solution

1. The effect of a price increase can be assessed by computing the point price elasticity of demand. Substituting the initial values of I and P_p yields

$$Q_x = 12,000 + 5(10,000) + 500(6) - 5,000P_x$$

which is equivalent to

$$Q_x = 65,000 - 5,000P_x$$

Note that $dQ_x/dP_x = -5,000$. At $P_x = $5, quantity demanded is 40,000 books. Using these data, the point price elasticity is computed to be

$$E_p = -5,000 \times \frac{5}{40,000} = -0.625$$

In that demand is inelastic, raising the price of the novels would increase total revenue.

2. The income elasticity determines whether a product is a necessity or a luxury. It has already been determined that the initial level of demand at the given values of the price and income variables is 40,000. From the demand equation it is known that $dQ_x/dI = 5$. Thus the income elasticity is

$$E_I = 5 \times \frac{10,000}{40,000} = 1.25$$

Because $E_I > 1$, the novels are a luxury good. Thus as incomes increase, sales should increase more than proportionately.

3. The demand equation implies that $dQ_x/dP_p = 500$. Thus it is known that E_C is positive, meaning that romance novels and pornographic books are viewed by consumers as substitutes. Computing E_C yields

$$E_C = 500 \times \frac{6.00}{40,000} = 0.075$$

Hence, a 1 percent increase in the price of pornographic books results in a 0.075 percent increase in demand for romance novels.

KEY CONCEPTS

- Cross elasticity is the percentage change in quantity demanded of good x per 1 percent change in the price of good y.
- Cross elasticities are positive for substitutes and negative for complements.

Summary

Demand refers to the number of units of a good or service that consumers are willing and able to buy at various prices over a specified interval of time. Market demand is the sum of all individual demands. A movement along the demand curve is caused by changes in price and is referred to as a change in quantity demanded. A change in demand is represented by a shift of the demand curve. Changes in demand can be caused by changes in tastes and preferences, income, and prices of other goods and services.

Marginal revenue is the change in total revenue per 1-unit change in demand. Total revenue is increasing as long as marginal revenue is positive. Marginal revenue is zero at the point of maximum total revenue and total revenue is declining when marginal revenue is negative. For linear demand curves, the absolute value of the slope of the marginal revenue curve is twice that of the demand curve.

Elasticities measure the responsiveness of demand to various factors. Price elasticity is defined as the percentage change in quantity demanded per 1 percent change in price. Arc price elasticity is used to assess the impact of discrete changes in price. Point price elasticity is appropriate for very small price changes.

Demand is said to be elastic where $E_p < -1$ and inelastic for $-1 < E_p \leq 0$. Demand is unitary elastic if $E_p = -1$. Marginal revenue is positive where demand is elastic, zero at the point of unitary elasticity, and negative for inelastic demand. Demand tends to be more elastic when (1) there are many substitutes for a good or service, (2) a substantial proportion of total income is spent on the product, and (3) the time period is longer.

Income elasticity is the percentage change in quantity demanded per 1 percent change in income. Inferior goods have negative income elasticities, while normal goods are those with positive income elasticities. For necessities, $0 < E_I \leq 1$. Luxuries are goods and services with income elasticities greater than 1.

Cross elasticity is defined as the percentage change in quantity demanded of one good per 1 percent change in the price of some other good. Cross elasticities are positive for substitutes and negative for complements. Goods with high positive cross elasticities are considered to be in the same market.

Discussion Questions

4-1. Suppose that the possession of marijuana was legalized in all states. What would happen to the demand for marijuana? Explain.

4-2. Why is the market demand curve usually less elastic then demand curves faced by the individual firms in that market?

4-3. The income elasticity for liquor is estimated to be 1.00. As an executive of a liquor firm, how could this information be used in forecasting sales?

4-4. The profit-maximizing price will never be set where demand is inelastic. True or false? Explain.

4-5. If demand is unitary elastic, what action could a manager take to increase total revenue? Explain.

4-6. Why would demand for natural gas be more inelastic in the short run than in the long run?

4-7. Which of the following pairs of goods are substitutes and which are complements?
   (a) Insulation and heating oil.
   (b) Hot dogs and mustard.
   (c) Televisions and videocassette recorders.
   (d) Rice and potatoes.

4-8. In a world with just two goods where all income is spent on the two goods, both goods cannot be inferior. True or false? Explain.

4-9. In 1975, tuition at Commonwealth College was $4,000 per year and enrollment was 5,000 students. By 1985, tuition had increased to $8,000, but enrollment had increased to 5,500 students. Does this change imply an upward sloping demand curve? Explain.

Problems

4-1. It is known that quantity demanded decreases by 2 units for each $1 increase in price. At a price of $5, quantity demanded is 10 units.
   (a) What will be the quantity demanded if price is zero?
   (b) Write an equation for quantity demanded as a function of price.
   (c) Write an equation that expresses price as a function of quantity.
   (d) Write an equation for total revenue.

4-2. A market consists of two individuals. Their demand equations are $Q_1 = 16 - 4P$ and $Q_2 = 20 - 2P$, respectively.
   (a) What is the market demand equation?
   (b) At a price of $2, what is the point price elasticity for each person and for the market?

4-3. The demand equation faced by DuMont Electronics for its personal computers is given by $P = 10,000 - 4Q$.
   (a) Write the marginal revenue equation.
   (b) At what price and quantity will marginal revenue be zero?
   (c) At what price and quantity will total revenue be maximized?
   (d) If price is increased from $6,000 to $7,000, what will be the effect on total revenue? What does this imply about price elasticity?

4-4. Sailright Inc. manufactures and sells sailboards. Management believes that the price elasticity of demand is -3.0. Currently, boards are priced at $500 and the quantity demanded is 10,000 per year.
  (a) If the price is increased to $600, how many sailboards will the company be able to sell each year?
  (b) How much will total revenue change as a result of the price increase?

4-5. Demand for a managerial economics text is given by $Q = 20,000 - 300P$. The book is initially priced at $30.
  (a) Compute the point price elasticity of demand at $P = \$30$.
  (b) If the objective is to increase total revenue, should the price be increased or decreased? Explain.
  (c) Compute the arc price elasticity for a price decrease from $30 to $20.
  (d) Compute the arc price elasticity for a price decrease from $20 to $15.

4-6. Write a demand equation for which the price elasticity of demand is zero for all prices.

4-7. A consultant estimates the price–quantity relationship for New World Pizza to be $P = 50 - 5Q$.
  (a) At what output rate is demand unitary elastic?
  (b) Over what range of output is demand elastic?
  (c) At the current price, 8 units are demanded each period. If the objective is to increase total revenue, should the price be increased or decreased? Explain.

4-8. The price elasticity for rice is estimated to be -0.4 and the income elasticity is 0.8. At a price of $0.40 per pound and a per capita income of $20,000, the demand for rice is 50 million tons per year.
  (a) Is rice an inferior good, a necessity, or a luxury? Explain.
  (b) If per capita income increases to $20,500, approximately what will be the quantity demanded of rice? (Hint: Consider the income change as being very small.)
  (c) If the price of rice increases to $0.41 per pound, and per capita income is initially $20,000, about how much must per capita income change for the quantity demanded to remain at 50 million tons per year? (Hint: Consider the price change as being very small.)

4-9. Acme Tobacco is currently selling 5,000 pounds of pipe tobacco per year. Due to competitive pressures, the average price of a pipe declines from $15 to $12. As a result, the demand for Acme pipe tobacco increases to 6,000 pounds per year.
  (a) What is the cross elasticity of demand for pipes and pipe tobacco?
  (b) Assuming that the cross elasticity does not change, at what price of pipes would the demand for pipe tobacco be 3,000 pounds per year? Use $15 as the initial price.

4-10. The McNight company is a major producer of steel. Management estimates that the demand for the company's steel is given by the equation:

$$Q_s = 5,000 - 1,000P_s + 0.1I + 100P_a$$

where Q_s is steel demand in thousands of tons per year, P_s is the price of steel in dollars per pound, I is income per capita, and P_a is the price of aluminum in dollars per pound. Initially, the price of steel is $1 per pound, income per capita is $20,000, and the price of aluminum is $0.80 per pound.
  (a) How much steel will be demanded at the initial prices and income?
  (b) What is the point income elasticity at the initial values?
  (c) What is the point cross elasticity between steel and aluminum? Are steel and aluminum substitutes or complements?

(d) If the objective is to maintain the quantity of steel demanded as computed in part (a), what reduction in steel prices will be necessary to compensate for a $0.20 reduction in the price of aluminum?

4-11. The price of oil is $30 per barrel and the price elasticity is constant and equal to -0.5. An oil embargo reduces the quantity available by 20 percent. What will be the percentage increase in the price of oil?

Problems Requiring Calculus

4-12. The Inquiry Club at Jefferson University has compiled a book which exposes the sordid private lives of many of the professors on campus. Economics majors in the club estimate that total revenue from sales of the book is given by the equation:

$$TR = 120Q - 0.1Q^3$$

(a) Over what range of sales is demand elastic?

(b) Initially, the price is set at $71.60. To maximize total revenue, should the price be increased or decreased? Explain.

4-13. The demand equation for a product is given by:

$$P = 30 - 0.1Q^2$$

(a) Write an equation for the point elasticity as a function of quantity.

(b) At what price is demand unitary elastic?

References

Henderson, J. M., and Quandt, R. E. 1980. *Microeconomic Theory*. New York: McGraw-Hill.

Hicks, J. R. 1959. *A Review of Demand Theory*. London: Oxford University Press.

Hogarty, T. F. 1972. "The Demand for Beer." *The Review of Economics and Statistics* 54(May):195–198.

Houthakker, H. S., and Taylor, L. D. 1970. *Consumer Demand in the United States: Analyses and Projections*. Cambridge, Mass.: Harvard University Press.

Leibenstein, H. 1976. *Beyond Economic Man: A New Foundation for Microeconomics*. Cambridge, Mass.: Harvard University Press.

Mansfield, E. 1985. *Microeconomics: Theory and Applications*. New York: Norton.

Wold, H. 1953. *Demand Analysis*. New York: Wiley.

Appendix:
Behind the Demand Curve:
The Theory of Consumer Choice

The discussion of demand in Chapter 4 began by assuming that the relationship between price and quantity demanded was known. The purpose of this appendix is to go behind the demand function and develop a theory of consumer choice. This theory provides an understanding of the consumer decision-making process. It also serves as a guide for predicting consumer behavior under various conditions.

Consumer Preferences

Individuals make choices based on their personal tastes and preferences. Those who enjoy skiing may spend a large fraction of their income on ski equipment, whereas those who are inclined to less strenuous activities may use their income to buy books or records. Tastes and preferences are shaped by many factors. Some of the determinants are family environment, physical condition, age, sex, education, religion, and location. In the analysis that follows, tastes and preferences will be viewed as a given and the discussion will focus on how those tastes and preferences are transformed into consumption decisions.

In the well-established tradition of economics, four basic assumptions are made in developing the model of consumer choice. First, it is assumed that individuals can rank their preferences for alternative bundles of goods and services. Consider a world in which only two goods are available: deodorant and mouthwash. Suppose that a consumer is confronted with the following combinations of those two goods:

A	B	C
5 cans deodorant	2 cans deodorant	4 cans deodorant
2 bottles mouthwash	6 bottles mouthwash	4 bottles mouthwash

The ability to rank means that the individual can assess the relative amount of satisfaction that would result from each bundle of goods. For example, suppose that B is considered the most desirable bundle, and that C and A are viewed as providing equal but lesser amounts of satisfaction than B. Using the terminology

132

of the theory of consumer choice, it is said that *B* is preferred to both *C* and *A* and that the consumer is indifferent between *C* and *A*.

Nonsatiation is the second assumption. This means that individuals consider themselves better off if they have more of a good or service than if they have less. Consider a bundle *D* that consists of

D
3 cans deodorant
7 bottles mouthwash

The nonsatiation assumption implies that this bundle would be preferred to bundle *B* because it includes more deodorant *and* more mouthwash.

Transitivity is the third assumption. It can be thought of as requiring that preferences be consistent. Transitivity states that if bundle *D* is preferred to bundle *B* and if *B* is preferred to both *A* and *C*, bundle *D* must be preferred to bundles *A* and *C*.

Finally, it is assumed that in order to get additional units of one good, consumers are willing to give up successively fewer units of other goods. For example, a consumer may be willing to forgo the purchase of five cans of deodorant to obtain the first bottle of mouthwash. However, if the person already has three bottles of mouthwash, the value of another bottle in terms of deodorant is likely to be less than five cans.

KEY CONCEPT

- Four assumptions form the basis for the theory of consumer choice. They are:
  1. Individuals can rank their preferences.
  2. Nonsatiation—people prefer more to less.
  3. Transitivity—rankings are consistent.
  4. Individuals are willing to give up successively smaller amounts of one good in order to get additional units of other goods.

Indifference Curves

Recall that bundles *A* and *C* were viewed as being equally desirable. That is, an individual would be indifferent to having *A* rather than *C*. If asked to select one over the other, there would be no basis for choice. Now suppose that other bundles, designated as *E*, *F*, *G*, and *H*, are also considered equivalent to *A* and *C*. If these bundles are plotted on a graph as shown in Figure 4A-1, the points can be joined to form an *indifference curve* that represents all bundles of goods that provide an individual with equal levels of satisfaction.

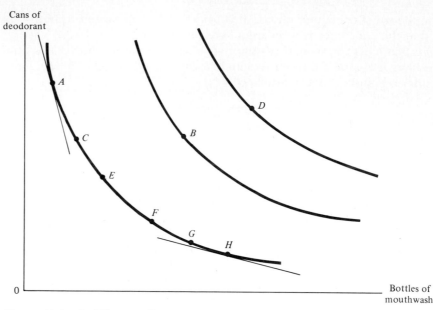

Figure 4A-1.   *Indifference Curves.*

Note that Figure 4A-1 depicts several indifference curves. All points passing through bundle *B* are considered equivalent to that bundle. Because *B* is preferred to *A*, the assumption of transitivity guarantees that all the points on the indifference curve passing through *B* are preferred to all the points on the curve associated with *A*. Similarly, since *D* provides more satisfaction than *B*, all points on the curve passing through *D* are preferred to those on the curves passing through *B* and *C*. In general, because of non-satiation, higher indifference curves denote increased levels of satisfaction.

The four assumptions stated earlier determine the basic characteristics of indifference curves. The assumption that individuals are capable of ranking their preferences implies that indifference curves exist. The assumption of nonsatiation assures that the curves will have a negative slope. This is easily shown by considering a curve with positive slope such as the curve passing through point 1 in Figure 4A-2. Pick any other point on the curve such as 2. Note that point 1 denotes a bundle with more of both mouthwash and deodorant than point 2. But because of the nonsatiation assumption, having more of both goods implies that 1 is preferred to 2. Thus the two points cannot be on the same indifference curve. Hence indifference curves must be downward sloping.

Transitivity and nonsatiation guarantee that two indifference curves will not intersect. This can also be seen from Figure 4A-2, which shows two indifference curves crossing at point 3. Consider points 4 and 5. The bundle denoted by 4 has more of both goods than 5 and hence must be preferred to 5. In that 3 and 5 are on the same indifference curve, transitivity requires that 4 be preferred to 3. But this is not true; 3 and 4 are on the same indifference curve. Thus the assumption of transitivity has been violated because preferences are not con-

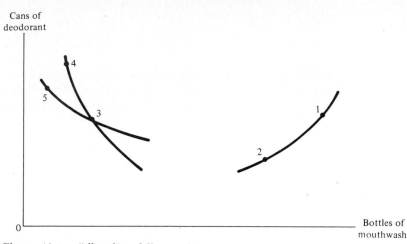

Figure 4A-2. "Illegal" Indifference Curves.

sistent. The assumption of transitivity is always violated when indifference curves intersect.

The assumption that consumers will be willing to give up successively fewer units of one good in order to get additional units of other goods assures that indifference curves will have the convex shape shown in Figure 4A-1. The slope of an indifference curve is the tangent to the line at any point. This slope represents the number of cans of deodorant that will be given up to get one more bottle of mouthwash, while still remaining on the same indifference curve. That is, it is the rate at which the individual is willing to trade deodorant for mouthwash. This trade-off is referred to as the *marginal rate of substitution (MRS)*. For example, in Figure 4A-1, if the slope of the tangent to the indifference curve at point A is −8, the individual will be willing to substitute eight cans of deodorant for one bottle of mouthwash.

To satisfy the fourth assumption, the absolute value of the MRS must decrease when moving down an indifference curve. Indifference curves that are convex to the origin have this property. Note that the absolute value of the slope of the curve in Figure 4A-1 decreases from point A to point H. If the slope of the tangent at point H is $\frac{1}{8}$, the individual is now willing to give up eight bottles of mouthwash to get a single can of deodorant. An indifference curve must be convex in order to depict this declining marginal rate of substitution.

KEY CONCEPTS

- Indifference curves are downward sloping, convex, and do not intersect. Higher indifference curves reflect greater levels of satisfaction.
- The slope of an indifference curve is called the marginal rate of substitution (MRS). It denotes the rate at which an individual is willing to trade two goods or services.
- Convex indifference curves depict a declining marginal rate of substitution.

Budget Constraints

Wants reflect individual tastes and preferences. But actual purchases are strongly influenced by income and prices. Let I be income and P_D and P_M be the prices of deodorant and mouthwash, respectively. In a two-good world, possible purchases are defined by the following expression:

$$I \geq P_D Q_D + P_M Q_M \tag{4A-1}$$

where Q_D and Q_M are the quantities of deodorant and mouthwash purchased. The interpretation of equation (4A-1) is straightforward. It states that the sum of money spent on deodorant plus the sum spent on mouthwash must be less than or equal to total income available.

If equation (4A-1) is treated as an equality, it denotes the possible bundles of deodorant and mouthwash that can be purchased if all the income is spent. Solving this equation for Q_D yields

$$Q_D = \frac{I}{P_D} - \frac{P_M}{P_D} Q_M \tag{4A-2}$$

which expresses possible purchases of deodorant in terms of income, prices, and the quantity of mouthwash purchased. Equation (4A-2) can be graphed as shown in Figure 4A-3.

The line in Figure 4A-3 is called a *budget constraint*. All the points to the left of the curve, such as point A, represent quantities of deodorant and mouthwash that can be purchased using less than all the available income. Points to the right of the budget constraint, such as point B, are bundles that cannot be purchased with the available income.

Note that the vertical intercept of the budget constraint is I/P_D. It represents

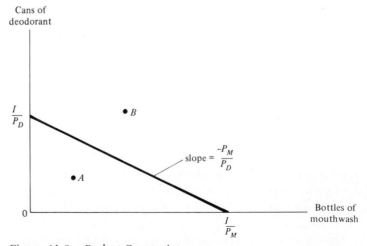

Figure 4A-3. *Budget Constraint.*

the number of cans of deodorant that could be purchased if all income was spent on that commodity. The horizontal intercept is I/P_M and has a similar interpretation. The slope of the budget constraint is $-P_M/P_D$. It represents the rate at which one good can be substituted for another in the marketplace. For example, if $P_M/P_D = \frac{1}{2}$, two bottles of mouthwash must be given up to get one more can of deodorant.

Utility Maximization

It is assumed that individuals strive to achieve the most satisfaction possible from their purchase choices. This objective is often referred to as *utility maximization.* It involves consideration of both indifference curves and the budget constraint. Suppose that a consumer is contemplating purchase of bundle X as shown in Figure 4A-4. Point X lies on the budget constraint, indicating that it is an affordable bundle. But X is not the bundle that will maximize the individual's utility. Note that Y is also on the budget constraint, but is on a higher indifference curve. Thus Y is preferred to X.

Point Y lies at the point of tangency between the budget constraint and the indifference curve. That is, point Y is the only point on the curve that touches the budget constraint. Note that points on any higher indifference curve would be above the budget constraint and hence are not affordable. Thus the bundle represented by point Y is the utility-maximizing point.

Given the individual's tastes and preferences, income, and the prices of the two goods, there is no other point that will provide the same level of utility or satisfaction as point Y. In that Y is the point of tangency between the indifference curve and the budget constraint, the slope of the two lines is equal at that point. Remember that the slope of an indifference curve is the marginal rate of substi-

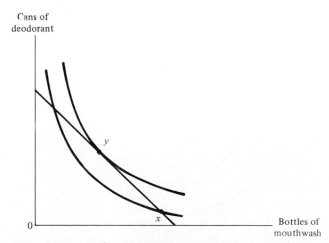

Figure 4A-4. *Utility Maximizing Point.*

tution and the slope of the budget constraint is the price ratio, $-P_M/P_D$. Hence the utility maximizing bundle is the point where

$$-\frac{P_M}{P_D} = MRS \qquad\qquad (4A\text{-}3)$$

Equation (4A-3) is easily interpreted. The price ratio represents the rate at which the market requires consumers to substitute the two goods. The MRS is the rate at which the individual desires to substitute the goods. Utility maximization occurs where the rate at which the consumer wants to substitute is just equal to the rate at which he or she must substitute. If these two rates are not equal, purchases can be rearranged in such a way as to increase satisfaction or utility.

KEY CONCEPTS

- The utility-maximizing point occurs where the highest indifference curve is tangent to the budget constraint.
- At the utility-maximizing point, the rate that products must be traded in the market is just equal to the rate at which the individual is willing to substitute one good for another.

Consumer Choice and the Demand Curve

The price–quantity combinations shown on an individual demand curve are the result of utility-maximizing decisions at various prices. This can easily be seen by considering the demand for mouthwash. Suppose that tastes and preferences, income, and the prices of deodorant and mouthwash generate indifference curves and budget constraints as shown in Figure 4A-5. If mouthwash costs $1 per

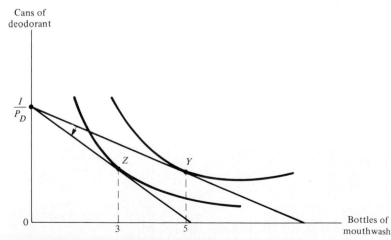

Figure 4A-5. *Price Changes and Utility Maximization.*

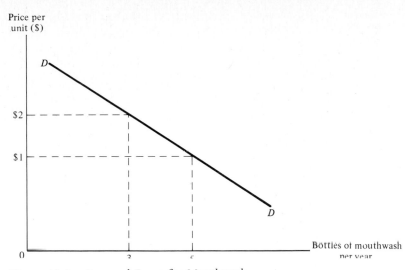

Figure 4A-6.   *Demand Curve for Mouthwash.*

bottle, let the utility-maximizing bundle be point Y which denotes five bottles of this good. That is, at $P = \$1$, quantity demanded is five bottles. Thus Y corresponds to one point on the demand curve for mouthwash.

If the price of mouthwash changes, Y will no longer be the utility-maximizing bundle. Suppose that P_M increases to $2. This change causes the budget constraint to rotate in a clockwise manner, as shown in Figure 4A-5. Note that the vertical intercept is the same as before (I/P_D). But the slope of the budget constraint is $-P_M/P_D$. Thus the increase in P_M causes the line to rotate clockwise.

With the new budget constraint, the point Y is no longer affordable. Hence the consumer must select a new utility-maximizing bundle. As before, this point is where the highest indifference curve is tangent to the budget constraint. In Figure 4A-5 the utility-maximizing point is Z. Note that Z is a bundle with less mouthwash (3 bottles compared to 5) than point Y. The higher price of mouthwash reduced purchasing power and increased the opportunity cost of mouthwash relative to deodorant.

Point Z represents another price–quantity point on the demand curve. It is the quantity demanded when $P_M = \$2$. As shown by Figure 4A-6, the individual demand curve is generated by plotting these quantities as a function of price. Additional points are obtained by changing the price of mouthwash and determining the utility-maximizing quantity of the product.

Consumer Choice and Changes in Demand

In the preceding section the theory of consumer choice was used to show how changes in quantity demanded (movements along the demand curve) occur. The theory can also be used to explain changes in demand (i.e., shifts of the demand

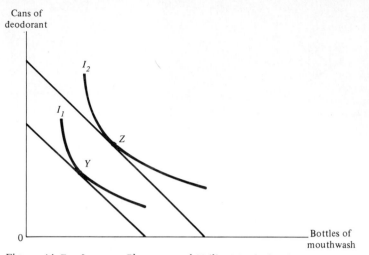

Figure 4A-7.   *Income Changes and Utility Maximization.*

curve). Such shifts result from a change in tastes and preferences, a change in income, or a change in the price of other goods. Consider the impact of an increase in income. When income increases, the budget constraint shifts outward, as shown in Figure 4A-7. Because the slope of the constraint is determined by prices and not by income, the new budget constraint is parallel to the initial budget constraint.

Initially, the utility-maximizing point was at Y where I_1 is tangent to the budget constraint, but the extra income allows movement to a higher indifference curve. The utility-maximizing point is now Z, where I_2 is tangent to the new budget constraint. Note that Z involves more mouthwash than did Y. At the same price of mouthwash, there is a greater demand for mouthwash than before. The result of this income change would appear as a rightward shift of the demand curve—more mouthwash would be demanded at each price.

The effect on demand of changes in tastes and preferences is shown by Figure 4A-8. Initially, let the utility-maximizing point be Y. Now suppose that concern about environmental impacts of aerosol cans causes the consumer to view deodorant less favorably. This is shown by a shift in the indifference curve from I_1 to I_2. Note that at the new utility-maximizing point, Z, less deodorant is selected than before the change in preferences. This would be represented on the demand curve as a leftward shift. That is, less deodorant would be demanded at any price of deodorant.

In a similar way, the theory of consumer choice can be used to show how changes in the prices of other goods cause the demand curve to shift. Point Y in Figure 4A-9 is the utility-maximizing bundle for given income, tastes and preferences, and prices of deodorant and mouthwash.

Now suppose that the price of mouthwash decreases. This is depicted in Figure 4A-9 by a counterclockwise rotation of the budget constraint. The new utility-maximizing bundle is point Z, where I_2 is tangent to the new budget

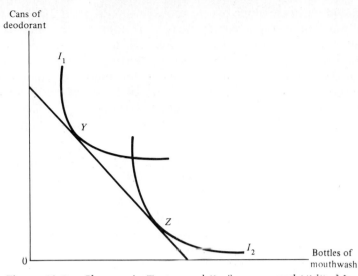

Figure 4A-8. *Changes in Tastes and Preferences and Utility Maximization.*

constraint. Note that this point specifies more mouthwash than was selected before the price reduction. This is because the opportunity cost of buying mouthwash has declined.

Note also that point Z involves less deodorant than did point Y. That is, the decrease in the price of mouthwash resulted in a decrease in the demand for deodorant. This change causes a shift in the demand curve for deodorant—less will be demanded at each price.

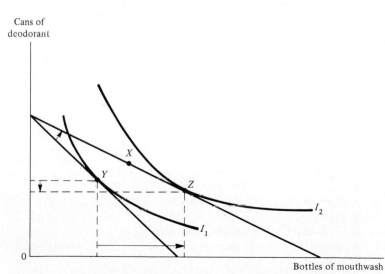

Figure 4A-9. *Changes in the Price of Other Goods and Utility Maximization.*

The impact of a price change of one good on the demand for the other good depends on the relationship between the two products. Apparently, mouthwash and deodorant were considered by the consumer to be substitutes. Thus a decrease in the price of mouthwash decreased the demand for deodorant. If the goods had been complements, analysis using the theory of consumer choice would have predicted an increase in the demand for deodorant. In this case, a decrease in the price of mouthwash would have resulted in a utility-maximizing point such as *X*, which specifies more deodorant than before the price change.

KEY CONCEPTS

- Changes in income are depicted as a parallel shift of the budget constraint. A change in the price of one good causes the budget constraint to rotate.
- At different prices, the quantities demanded shown by the demand curve correspond to the points of tangency between budget constraints and indifference curves.
- Shifts of the demand curve reflect changes in the budget constraint or indifference curves caused by changes in income, prices of other goods, or tastes and preferences.

Discussion Questions

4A-1. "The price ratio is the rate at which individuals must substitute goods in the marketplace." Explain this statement.

4A-2. How do changes in income affect the slope of the budget constraint? Explain.

4A-3. Suppose that bundle *A* is preferred to *B*, *C* is preferred to *D*, and *D* is preferred to *B*. What can be said about *C* in relation to *B*? What about *C* in relation to *A*? Are any of the assumptions of the theory of consumer choice violated by these preferences?

Problems

4A-1. Consider a world in which there are only two goods. An individual has an income of $9,000, the price of deodorant is $3 per bottle, and the price of mouthwash is $2 per bottle.
   (a) Expressing deodorant as the dependent variable, write the equation for the budget constraint.
   (b) What is the slope of the budget constraint?
   (c) If the price of mouthwash increases to $4, write the new equation for the budget constraint.

4A-2. Assume that the budget constraint is given by the equation $Q_1 = 1,000 - 5Q_2$, where Q_1 and Q_2 represent quantities of two goods. Normally, indifference curves are convex to the origin, but assume in this case that they are linear with a constant slope of -2.

    (a) Graph the budget constraint (with Q_1 on the vertical axis).

    (b) Draw in a set of indifference curves and label the utility-maximizing point.

    (c) Where would the utility-maximizing point have been if the indifference curves had a constant slope of -6?

References

Henderson, J. M., and Quandt, R. E. 1980. *Microeconomic Theory.* New York: McGraw-Hill.

Mansfield, E. 1985. *Microeconomics: Theory and Applications.* New York: Norton.

Demand Estimation and Forecasting

5

Preview

The vast majority of business decisions involve some degree of uncertainty—managers seldom know exactly what the outcomes of their choices will be. One approach to reducing the uncertainty associated with decision making is to devote resources to demand estimation and forecasting. Estimation involves determining how factors such as income and prices affect demand. Forecasting involves predicting future economic conditions and assessing their effect on the operations of the firm.

Frequently, the objective of forecasting is to predict demand. In some cases, managers are interested in the total demand for a product. For example, the decision by an office products firm to enter the home computer market may be determined by estimates of industry sales growth. In other circumstances, the projection may focus on the firm's probable market share. If a forecast suggests that sales growth by existing firms will make successful entry unlikely, the company may decide to look for other areas in which to expand.

Forecasts can also provide information on the proper product mix. For an automobile manufacturer such as General Motors, managers must determine the number of full-size versus compact cars to be produced. In the short run, this decision is largely constrained by the firm's existing production facilities for producing each kind of car. However, over a longer period, managers can build or modify production facilities. But such choices must be made long before the vehicles begin coming off the assembly line. Accurate forecasts can reduce the uncertainty caused by this long lead time. For example, if the price of gasoline is expected to increase, the demand for compact cars is also likely to increase. Conversely, a projection of stable or falling gasoline prices might stimulate demand for larger cars.

Forecasting is an important management activity. Major decisions in large businesses almost always are based on forecasts of some type. In some cases, the forecast may be little more than an intuitive assessment of the future by those involved in the decision. In other circumstances, the forecast may have required thousands of work hours and tens of thousands of dollars. It may have been generated by the firm's own economists, provided by consultants specializing in forecasting, or be based on information provided by government agencies.

This chapter focuses on basic techniques of demand estimation and forecasting. The first section considers various methods for collecting the necessary data. Next is a discussion of trend projection using time-series data. The third section considers statistical methods of demand estimation. The basic principles of input/output analysis are presented in the last section of the chapter.[1]

---

[1] In addition, a discussion of barometric forecasting is included as an appendix to the chapter.

Sources of Data

A forecast cannot be better than the data from which it is derived. Three important sources of data used in forecasting are expert opinion, surveys, and market experiments.

Expert Opinion

The collective judgment of knowledgable persons can be an important source of information. In fact, some forecasts are made almost entirely on the basis of personal insights of key decision makers. This process may involve managers conferring to develop projections based on their assessment of the economic conditions facing the firm. In other circumstances, the company's sales personnel may be asked to evaluate future prospects. In still other cases, consultants may be employed to develop forecasts based on their knowledge of the industry. Although predictions by experts are not always the product of "hard data," their usefulness should not be underestimated. Indeed, the insights of those closely connected with an industry can be of great value in forecasting.

Methods exist for enhancing the value of information elicited from experts. One of the most useful is the *Delphi technique.* Its use can be illustrated by a simple example. Suppose that a panel of six outside experts is asked to forecast a firm's sales for the next year. Working independently, two panel members forecast an 8 percent increase, three members predict a 5 percent increase, and one person predicts no increase in sales. Based on the responses of the other individuals, each expert is then asked to make a revised sales forecast. Some of those expecting rapid sales growth may, based on the judgments of their peers, present less optimistic forecasts in the second iteration. Conversely, some of those predicting slow growth may adjust their responses upward. However, there may also be some panel members who decide that no adjustment of their initial forecast is warranted.

Assume that a second set of predictions by the panel includes one estimate of a 2 percent sales increase, one of 5 percent, two of 6 percent, and two of 7 percent. The experts again are shown each other's responses and asked to consider their forecasts further. This process continues until a consensus is reached or until further iterations generate little or no change in sales estimates.

The value of the Delphi technique is that it aids individual panel members in assessing their forecasts. Implicitly, they are forced to consider why their judgment differs from that of other experts. Ideally, this evaluation process should generate more precise forecasts with each iteration.

One problem with the Delphi method is its expense. The usefulness of expert opinion depends on the skill and insight of the experts employed to make predictions. Frequently, the most knowledgable people in an industry are in a position to command large fees for their work as consultants. Another potential problem is that those who consider themselves experts may be unwilling to be influenced by the predictions of others on the panel. As a result, there may be few changes in subsequent rounds of forecasts.

Surveys

Surveys of managerial plans can be an important source of data for forecasting. The rationale for conducting such surveys is that plans are likely to be translated into future actions. For example, capital expenditure budgets for large corporations are usually planned well in advance. Thus a survey of investment plans by such corporations should provide a reasonably accurate forecast of future demand for capital goods.

Several private and government organizations conduct periodic surveys of plant and equipment expenditure plans. One of the most widely followed is sponsored by McGraw-Hill Inc. This survey is conducted twice yearly and includes corporations accounting for more than 50 percent of total investment in the U.S. economy. An even more comprehensive survey of capital expenditure plans is undertaken quarterly by the U.S. Department of Commerce. Results are reported in the Department's *Survey of Current Business.*

Useful data for forecasting can also be obtained from surveys of consumer plans. For example, the Survey Research Center at the University of Michigan polls consumers as to their intentions to purchase specific products such as household appliances, housing, and automobiles. The results are used to project consumer demand and also to measure the level of consumer confidence in the economy. The U.S. Bureau of the Census also conducts surveys of consumer intentions.

If data from other sources do not meet its specific needs, a firm may conduct its own survey. Perhaps the most common example involves companies that are considering a new product or making a substantial change in an existing product. But with new or modified products there are no data on which to base a forecast. One possibility is to survey households regarding their anticipated demand for the product. Typically, such surveys attempt to ascertain the demographic characteristics (e.g., age, education, and income) of those who are most likely to buy the product and how their decisions would be affected by different pricing policies.

Although surveys of consumer demand can provide useful data for forecasting, their value is highly dependent on the skills of their originators. Meaningful surveys require careful attention to each phase of the process. Questions must be precisely worded to avoid ambiguity. The sample must be properly selected so that responses will be representative of all consumers. Finally, the methods of survey administration should produce a high response rate and avoid biasing the answers of those surveyed.

Even the most carefully designed surveys do not always predict consumer demand with great accuracy. In some cases, respondents do not have enough information to determine if they would purchase a product. In other situations, those surveyed may be pressed for time and unwilling to devote much thought to their answers. Sometimes the response may reflect a desire (either conscious or unconscious) to put one's self in a favorable light or to gain approval from those conducting the survey. Because of these limitations, forecasts seldom rely entirely on results of consumer surveys. Rather, these data are considered supplemental sources of information for decision making.

CASE STUDY
THE ART OF SURVEY DESIGN

Recently, the manufacturer of LASECAL, an instrument used to calibrate lasers, wanted to determine the likely impact of price changes on the demand for this product. A consultant was hired to conduct a survey designed to generate this information. Recognizing that collection of such data is an extremely difficult task, the consultant developed a questionnaire which included several questions about demand. Each question required the respondent to think about the product in a slightly different way. The survey was mailed to a random sample of potential purchasers of the product. Abbreviated versions of two demand-related questions follow.

1. Listed below are three items of scientific equipment typical of those found in an electro-optical laboratory. Please compare the LASECAL with each of the three items below, and indicate whether the detector is of greater value, equal value, or lesser value than each scientific instrument listed. Retail prices for the three equipment items are provided to aid you in making comparisons. Place an "X" in one of the spaces provided for each of the three choices.

	LASECAL of Lesser Value	LASECAL of Equal Value	LASECAL of Greater Value
Multifunction voltmeter ($1,600)	_____	_____	_____
Laser power meter ($1,020)	_____	_____	_____
Quadrant detector ($1,795)	_____	_____	_____

2. Listed below are different dollar amounts. One randomly selected business responding to this survey will receive either a check for the amount circled or a free LASECAL. We will decide whether to award the money or the LASECAL. What sum would make you indifferent to having the money or the LASECAL? Circle one of the following amounts.

$600	$1,050	$1,500
$750	$1,200	$1,650
$900	$1,350	$1,800

Note that neither question specifically asks whether the product would be purchased for a specific price. The first question asks the respondent to compare the device to similar instruments with known price. This allows an indirect assessment of the value placed on the product. The second question is more direct. It requires the respondent to place a dollar value on the equipment. There was an incentive to give careful thought to this question, because the response was more than hypothetical—a LASECAL was actually awarded to a survey participant.

If the survey respondents can be considered a random sample of potential LASECAL buyers, the data can be used to estimate the quantity that would be demanded at different prices. In addition, by analyzing how responses to the survey questions vary by type of business, the most likely purchasers can be identified.

Market Experiments

A serious problem with survey data is that survey responses may not translate into actual consumer behavior. That is, consumers do not necessarily do what they say they are going to do. This weakness can be partially overcome by use of market experiments designed to generate data prior to the full-scale introduction of a product or implementation of a policy.

To set up a market experiment the firm first selects a test market. This market may consist of several cities, a region of the country, or a sample of consumers taken from a mailing list. Once the market has been selected, the experiment may incorporate a number of features. It may involve testing consumer acceptance of a new product in the test market. In other cases, different prices for an existing product might be set in various cities in order to determine demand elasticity. A third possibility would be a test of consumer reaction to a new advertising campaign.

Market experiments have an advantage over surveys in that they reflect actual consumer behavior, but they still have limitations. One problem is the risk involved. In test markets where prices are increased, consumers may switch to products of competitors. Once the experiment has ended, it may be difficult to recapture those customers. Another problem is that the firm cannot control all the factors that affect demand. The results of an experiment can be influenced by bad weather, changing economic conditions, or the tactics of competitors. Finally, because most experiments are of relatively short duration, consumers may not be completely aware of pricing or advertising changes. Thus their responses may understate the probable impact of those changes.

KEY CONCEPTS

- The Delphi technique is an iterative technique that can be used to enhance the value of expert opinion.
- Surveys of consumer intentions require careful attention to wording, sample selection, and administration.
- Market experiments provide actual data on consumer behavior. However, they are expensive, risky, and may be influenced by factors beyond the firm's control.

Trend Projection

One of the most commonly used forecasting techniques is trend projection. As the name implies, this approach is based on the assumption that the future can be predicted by identifying trends or patterns from historical data. These historical data are often referred to as a time series because they consist of data points at regular intervals over a period of time. The interval may be a week, month, quarter, or a year. For example, Table 5-1 is a time series of a firm's quarterly sales over a three-year time span.

Graphical Curve Fitting

Note that the data show generally increasing sales quarter by quarter. But a useful forecast usually requires greater precision than is implied by the statement "generally increasing sales." To be of value in forecasting, a numerical estimate of the increase in sales per quarter must be formulated. One way to make this estimate is to graphically fit a line to the data. This approach is called *curve fitting* and is shown in Figure 5-1. In the figure a straight line is drawn through the data points in such a way as to portray the trend of the data as accurately as possible.

The upward slope of the line reflects sales increases over time. By computing the slope of this trend line, it is possible to determine the average rate of increase per quarter. This value can be used to calculate sales in future periods. Alternatively, by extending the trend line beyond the last data point (i.e., the fourth quarter of 1986), the estimated sales can be read directly from the graph. Suppose that sales are to be forecasted for the third quarter of 1987. Based on an extrapolation of the data to that period, the graph indicates that sales will be about $480 million.

Table 5-1. Sample Time-Series Data

Period Number	Quarter	Sales (millions)
1	1984:I	$300
2	1984:II	305
3	1984:III	315
4	1984:IV	340
5	1985:I	346
6	1985:II	352
7	1985:III	364
8	1985:IV	390
9	1986:I	397
10	1986:II	404
11	1986:III	418
12	1986:IV	445

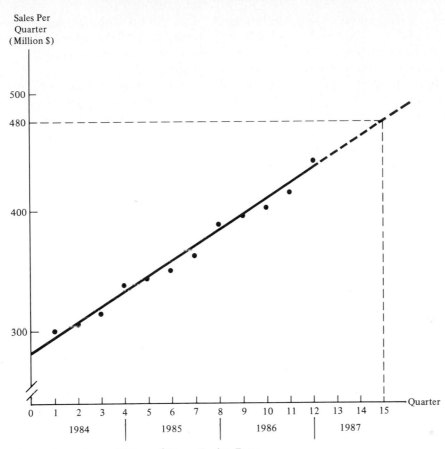

Figure 5-1.   *Curve Fitting of Time Series Data.*

Statistical Curve Fitting

One limitation of graphical curve fitting should be obvious—the quality of fore-cast depends on the analyst's ability to fit a curve to the data. A more sophisti-cated approach is to use mathematical methods to fit the data to an equation of specified functional form. Basically, this involves using the ordinary least-squares concept developed in Chapter 2 to estimate the parameters of the equation.

Constant Rate of Change.   Suppose that an analyst determines that a fore-cast will be made assuming that there will be a constant rate of change in sales from one period to the next. That is, the firm's sales will change by the same amount between two periods. The time-series data of Table 5-1 are to be used to estimate that rate of change. Statistically, this involves estimating the param-eters of the equation

$$S_t = S_0 + bt \qquad\qquad (5\text{-}1)$$

where S denotes sales and t indicates the time period. The two parameters to be estimated are S_0 and b. The value of S_0 corresponds to the sales (vertical) axis intercept of the line in Figure 5-1. The parameter b is the constant rate of change and corresponds to the slope of the line in Figure 5-1.

Many hand calculators can estimate the parameters of equation (5-1). Specific procedures vary from model to model, but usually the only requirement is that the user input the data and push one or two designated keys. The machine then returns the estimated parameters. For the data of Table 5-1, the quarters would have to be inputted as sequential numbers starting with 1. That is, 1984:I would be entered as 1, 1984:II would be entered as 2, and so forth. Based on the data from the table, equation (5-1) would be estimated as

$$S_t = 281.394 + 12.811t$$

The interpretation of the equation is that the estimated constant rate of increase in sales per quarter is \$12.811 million. A forecast of sales for any future quarter, S_t, can be obtained by substituting in the appropriate value for t. For example the third quarter of 1987 is 15 quarters from the beginning of the time series. Thus the estimated sales for that quarter would be $281.394 + 12.811(15)$, or \$473.56 million.

Constant Percentage Rate of Change.   Now suppose that the individual responsible for the forecast wants to estimate a percentage rate of change in sales. That is, it is assumed that

$$S_t = S_{t-1}(1 + g)$$

and

$$S_{t-1} = S_{t-2}(1 + g)$$

where g is the growth rate. These two equations imply that

$$S_t = S_{t-2}(1 + g)^2$$

and, in general,

$$S_t = S_0 (1 + g)^t \tag{5-2}$$

As shown, the parameters of equation (5-2) cannot be estimated using ordinary least squares. The problem is that the equation is not linear. However, there is a simple transformation of the equation that allows it to be estimated using ordinary least squares.

First, take the logarithm of equation (5-2). The result is

$$\log S_t = \log [S_0 (1 + g)^t]$$

But the log of a product is just the sum of the logs. Thus

$$\log S_t = \log S_0 + \log [(1 + g)^t]$$

The right-hand side of the equation can be further simplified by noting that

$$\log [(1 + g)^t] = t[\log (1 + g)]$$

Hence

$$\log S_t = \log S_0 + t[\log(1 + g)] \qquad (5\text{-}3)$$

Equation (5-3) is linear in form. This can be seen by making the following substitutions:

$$Y_t = \log S_t$$
$$Y_0 = \log S_0$$
$$b = \log (1 + g)$$

Thus the new equation is

$$Y_t = Y_0 + bt \qquad (5\text{-}4)$$

which is linear.

The parameters of equation (5-4) can easily be estimated using a hand calculator. The key is to recognize that the sales data have been translated into logarithms.[2] Thus, instead of S_t, it is $\log S_t$ that must be inputted. However, note that the t values have not been transformed. Hence for the first quarter of 1984, the data to be entered are $\log 300 = 5.704$ and 1; for the second quarter, $\log 305 = 5.720$ and 2; and so forth.

Using the ordinary least-squares method, the estimated parameters of the equation are

$$Y_t = 5.6623 + 0.0353t$$

But these parameters are based on the logs of the data. Thus, for interpretation in terms of the original data, they must be converted based on the relationships $\log S_0 = 5.6623$ and $\log (1 + g) = 0.0353$. Taking the antilogs yields $S_0 = 287.810$ and $1 + g = 1.0359$. Substituting these values for S_0 and $1 + g$ back into equation (5-2) gives

$$S_t = 287.810(1.0359)^t$$

where 287.810 is sales (in millions of dollars) in period 0 and the estimated growth rate is 0.0359 or 3.59 percent.

To forecast sales in a future quarter, the appropriate value of t is substituted into the equation. For example, predicted sales in the third quarter of 1987 (i.e., the fifteenth quarter) would be $287.810(1.0359)^{15}$, or \$488.51 million.

The logarithmic transformation of an equation is an important technique in statistical analysis. In addition to estimating the constant percentage rate of change, it is frequently put to other uses, such as estimating the parameters of demand and production functions. These applications will be discussed later.

---

[2] Either natural logs or logarithms to the base 10 can be used. In this section, natural logs are used for all computations.

Seasonal Variation in Time-Series Data

A close examination of the data in Table 5-1 indicates that the quarterly sales increases are not uniformly distributed over the year. The increases from the first quarter to the second, and from the fourth quarter to the first, tend to be small, while the fourth quarter increase is consistently larger than that of other quarters. That is, the data exhibit seasonal fluctuations as shown by the dashed line in Figure 5-2.

Seasonal fluctuations in time-series data are not uncommon. In particular, a large increase in sales for the fourth quarter is a characteristic of certain industries. Indeed, some retailing firms make nearly half of their total sales during the Christmas holiday period. Other business activities have their own seasonal sales patterns. Electric utilities serving hot, humid areas have distinct peak sales periods during the summer months, whereas those in colder regions have peaks in winter. Similarly, housing sales drop off during the winter, whereas the demand for accountant's services increases in the first quarter as income tax deadlines approach.

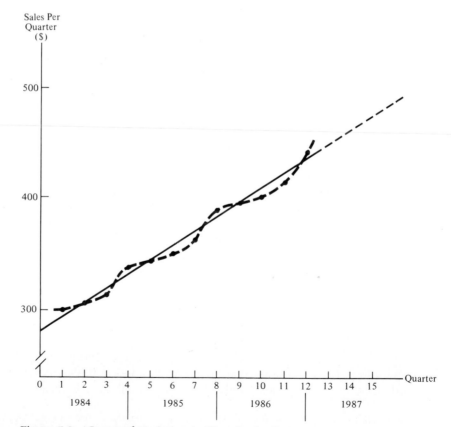

Figure 5-2. *Seasonal Variation in Time Series Data.*

Pronounced seasonal variation can cause serious errors in forecasts based on time-series data. For example, Table 5-1 indicates that actual sales for the fourth quarter of 1986 were $445 million. But if the estimated equation is used to predict sales for that period (using the constant rate of change model), the predicted total is $281.394 + 12.811(12)$, or $435.13 million. The large difference between actual and predicted sales occurs because the equation does not take into account the fourth-quarter sales jump. Rather, the predicted value from the equation represents an averaging of individual quarters. Thus sales will be underestimated for the strong fourth quarter. Conversely, the predicting equation may overestimate sales for the other quarters.

The accuracy of the forecast can be improved by seasonally adjusting the data. Probably the most common method of adjustment is the *ratio-to-trend* approach. Its use can be illustrated using the data from Table 5-1. Based on the predicting equation,

$$S_t = 281.394 + 12.811t$$

actual and calculated fourth-quarter sales are shown in Table 5-2. The final column of the table is the ratio of actual to predicted sales for the fourth quarter. This ratio is a measure of the error in the forecast.

For the three-year period, average actual sales for the fourth quarter were 2.0 percent greater than the average forecasted sales for that quarter. This factor can be used to adjust future fourth-quarter sales estimates. For example, if the objective is to predict sales for the fourth quarter of 1986, the predicting equation generates an estimate of $435.13 million. Multiplying this number by the 1.020 adjustment factor, the forecast is increased to $443.8 million. A similar technique could be used to make a downward adjustment for predicted sales in other quarters.

Seasonal adjustment can improve forecasts based on trend projection. However, trend projection still has some shortcomings. One is that it is limited primarily to short-term predictions. If the trend is extrapolated much beyond the last data point, the accuracy of the forecast diminishes rapidly. Another limitation is that factors such as changes in relative prices and fluctuations in economic growth are not considered. Rather, the trend projection approach assumes that historical relationships will not change.

Table 5-2. Seasonal Adjustment Using the Ratio-to-Trend Method

Year	Forecasted Fourth Quarter Sales	Actual Fourth Quarter Sales	Actual/Predicted Fourth Quarter Sales
1984	332.64	$340	1.022
1985	383.88	390	1.016
1986	435.13	445	1.023
			Average = 1.020

KEY CONCEPTS

- Forecasts based on the assumption of a constant rate of change can be made by fitting time-series data to an equation of the general form

$$S_t = S_0 + bt$$

- Forecasts assuming a constant percentage rate of change involve estimating the parameters of the equation

$$S_t = S_0 (1 + g)^t$$

- Forecast errors due to seasonal fluctuations can be reduced using the ratio-to-trend adjustment method.

Econometric Methods

The term *econometrics* means, literally, economic measurement. Econometric methods integrate statistics, mathematics, and economic theory in order to measure relationships among economic variables. Although frequently more complicated than trend projections, forecasts based on econometric methods have at least two advantages compared to other forecasting techniques. First, in addition to predicting values of important variables, they provide insights into the relationships between variables. These insights can be very useful to managers in evaluating the probable effects of alternative decisions. For example, an econometric study that estimates the impact of advertising on demand could be used to assess advertising strategies. Second, econometric methods estimate the magnitude of relationships between variables. In contrast, forecasts based on other approaches, such as survey data, frequently can do little more than indicate the general nature of those relationships.

Four steps are involved in the formulation of an econometric forecast: (1) development of a theoretical model, (2) data collection, (3) choice of functional form for the equation to be estimated, and (4) estimation and interpretation of results. Each of these steps is discussed below.

Development of a Theoretical Model

In using econometric methods, the analyst must first formulate a theoretical model of the economic relationships involved. This model should be based on sound economic theory and be expressed in mathematical terms. Fundamentally, the model-building process involves determining which variables should be included in the model and if there is a theoretical rationale for predicting the nature and magnitude of relationships between variables. For example, if the object is to forecast demand, the price–quantity relationship would be a logical theoretical foundation for the model. A simple mathematical expression of this relationship is

$$Q = f(P)$$

Economic theory predicts an inverse relationship between price and quantity demanded. As such, it would be expected that dQ/dP (the derivative of quantity with respect to price) would be negative. Should the data fail to support this hypothesis, the model or the data may need to be reexamined.

Considerable care must be exercised in developing a model. The choice of variables to be included is particularly important. A model that does not include all factors that have an important influence on the variable to be predicted can generate inaccurate or misleading forecasts and may lead to faulty conclusions about relationships between those variables that are included. The need for careful specification of a theoretical model can be illustrated using the simple $Q = f(P)$ demand relationship just discussed.

Suppose that three observations on price and quantity have been obtained from market experiments. A line drawn through those points is shown in Figure 5-3a. This curve is downward sloping, as expected for a demand relationship. If the line DD is interpreted as a demand curve, marginal revenues and elasticities at various points on the curve can be calculated to aid managers in making decisions. But does the curve in Figure 5-3a really indicate the true relationship between quantity demanded and price? There is reason to believe that it may not.

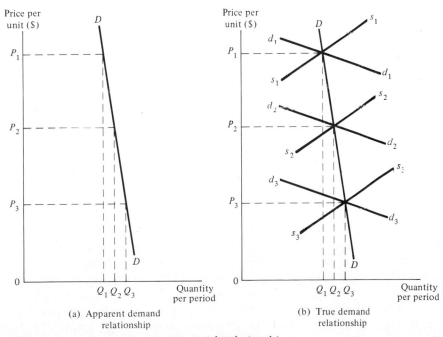

(a) Apparent demand relationship

(b) True demand relationship

Figure 5-3. *Apparent vs. True Demand Relationships.*

Prices and quantities in a market economy are the result of the interaction between supply and demand. The equilibrium levels occur at the point where quantity supplied equals quantity demanded. For a given supply and demand curve, only one price–quantity pair is consistent with equilibrium. This is shown in Figure 5-3b. The first price–quantity point, (P_1, Q_1), is determined by the intersection of the supply curve s_1s_1 and the demand curve d_1d_1. In order to observe a different equilibrium price and quantity, one or both of the two curves must shift. Thus, the second observation, (P_2, Q_2), might be generated by curves such as s_2s_2 and d_2d_2. Similarly, the third price–quantity point is the equilibrium for s_3s_3 and d_3d_3.

Thus DD in Figure 5-3a really is not a demand curve at all. Demand curves show relationships between price and the quantity demanded, assuming that factors which shift the demand curve are held constant. But as shown in Figure 5-3b, the line DD really is a series of equilibrium points for a series of shifting supply and demand curves. Thus it cannot properly be interpreted as a demand curve. To do so could result in erroneous decisions. For example, viewed as a demand curve, DD in Figure 5-3a would indicate that demand is relatively inelastic. In reality, the true curves such as d_1d_1 of Figure 5-3b indicate that demand is quite elastic.

The situation just discussed is referred to as the *identification problem* of demand estimation. It shows that using only price and quantity data, it may be impossible to separate the effect of price from the other factors that affect demand. That is, the impact of price cannot be uniquely identified.

The existence of an identification problem does not mean that econometric methods cannot be used to estimate demand equations. What is implied is that the theoretical model must be carefully selected to allow the effect of price changes to be isolated from the other determinants of demand. One approach is to include in the model other variables that are expected to significantly influence demand. Guidance as to the proper choice of variables can be obtained from demand theory. In Chapter 4 it was argued that demand is a function of the price of the good, income, the prices of other goods, and tastes and preferences. This suggests that a revised theoretical model might take the general form

$$Q = f(P, I, P_o, T) \tag{5-5}$$

where I is income, P_o represents prices of other goods, and T is a measure of tastes and preferences.

Use of this model reduces the magnitude of the identification problem by allowing the impact of factors that shift the demand curve to be taken into account. For example, in Figure 5-3b, let d_1d_1 be the actual demand curve for a particular time period. Suppose that consumer preferences and prices of other goods remain constant but there is a decrease in per capita income. For a normal good, the income change will cause a decrease in demand as shown by d_2d_2 in Figure 5-3b. But by including per capita income in the estimating equation, the effect of the income change can be identified. Similarly, the impact of changes in the prices of other goods and changes in consumer preferences can be identified. That is, those factors that shift the demand curve can be separated from price changes which cause movements along a particular demand curve. Hence the observed relationship between price and quantity demanded can be properly interpreted as a demand function.

CASE STUDY

A MODEL FOR ESTIMATING ELECTRICITY DEMAND

In addition to having a basis in economic theory, the model used for demand estimation must take into account the characteristics of the industry being studied. Forecasting the demand for electricity is a good example.

Demand for electricity by residential users is primarily a function of three factors: (1) The number of households in the market area, (2) The stock of electricity-using appliances in the typical household, and (3) Average electricity consumption per appliance. This suggests the following model for electricity demand:

$$Q - f(H, S_i, U_i), \quad i = 1, \cdots, n$$

where Q is quantity demanded per period, H is the number of households, S_i is the proportion of those households having the ith electricity-using appliance, and U_i is the average electricity consumption per period of the ith appliance. Assume that n electricity-using appliances are to be considered.

To predict residential demand, it is necessary to identify the determinants of H and of each S_i and U_i. The number of households is a function of total population in the market area. Thus

$$H = f(\text{population})$$

The proportion of households owning different types of electricity-using appliances is determined by factors such as income, past and present prices of the appliances, demographic characteristics of households (such as age and number of children), prices of electricity and other energy sources, and climate. Hence for each of the n appliances,

$$S_i = f(\text{income, appliance prices, demographics, energy prices, climate})$$

Factors such as income, prices, climate, and household demographics also determine average consumption per appliance. Let the general form of the equation explaining average electricity consumption for each appliance be:

$$U_i = f(\text{income, demographics, energy prices, climate})$$

When the equations for H, S_i, and U_i have been estimated, the results can be used to forecast total residential electricity demand. Specifically, demand is forecast based on the following relationship:

$$Q = U_1 S_1 H + U_2 S_2 H + \cdots + U_n S_n H$$

The equation implies that the electricity consumption of each of the n appliances is the product of the number of households, the proportion of households having the appliance, and average use of electricity by the appliance. Thus total consumption, Q, is just the sum of the electricity demands by each device.

For example, suppose that an electric range is the only electricity-using device and that there are 100,000 households in a firm's market area at a particular time. Further assume that 50 percent of households have electric ranges and that average annual electricity consumption is 900 kilowatt-hours per electric range. Thus total annual electricity demand would be:

$$Q = (900)(0.50)(100,000)$$

or 45 million kilowatt-hours.

Now suppose that the managers of the firm want to forecast future electricity demand. To do so, they must predict changes in the number of households, proportion of homes having each device, and consumption per device. This can be done based on the estimated relationships between the variables. Consider a simple example. Assume that the number of households is the only factor expected to change in the future and that the equation for estimating households indicates that one new household results from each four person increase in population. That is, $H = $ population$/4.0$.

If the population in the firm's market area is projected to increase by 60,000 during the next ten years, how much will electricity demand increase? The population change is estimated to produce 15,000 new households, an increase of 15 percent over the present number. Thus if consumption per electric range and the proportion of households having electric ranges remains constant, a 15 percent increase in electricity demand would be predicted.

In actual practice, forecasting the demand for electricity is a complicated undertaking. However, most forecasts are based on the procedure described here.

Data Collection

To estimate demand, data for each of the variables that influence demand first must be obtained. These data may be collected from surveys, market experiments, or existing sources such as historical records of the firm or government publications. Either time-series or cross-section data may be used. Time-series data were discussed in connection with trend projection. For use in estimating demand, time-series data would consist of period-by-period observations in a specific market for each of the variables that affect demand.

In contrast, cross-section data are based on a number of markets at a single point in time. For example, cross-section data might consist of quantity demanded, income, prices, and tastes and preferences for 100 different markets during a recent year. If the cross-section data exhibit variation from market to market, they can be used to estimate relationships between quantity demanded and the other variables.

KEY CONCEPTS

- The first step in econometric analysis is to formulate a model based on economic theory.
- In estimating the price–quantity relationship, an identification problem may occur if other factors that influence demand are not taken into account.
- Time series data consist of observations from a single market over a period of time. Cross-section data are based on information from a number of markets at a single point in time.

Choice of Functional Form

Equation (5-5) indicates a general relationship between quantity and the factors expected to influence demand. That is,

$$Q = f(P, I, P_0, T) \qquad (5\text{-}5)$$

However, estimation by econometric techniques of the relationships between quantity demanded and the independent variables in equation (5-5) requires the choice of a specific functional form for the equation. A linear equation is the simplest possible form. The linear equation corresponding to the general relationships of equation (5-5) is

$$Q = b + a_p P + a_I I + a_0 P_0 + a_T T \qquad (5\text{-}6)$$

The linear form has several advantages. First, it can be estimated without modification—no transformations of the data are necessary. Second, the coefficients of the variables have a simple interpretation. If values of the other independent variables remain unchanged, each coefficient represents the change in quantity per unit change in the associated independent variable. Furthermore, the estimated changes are constant for each independent variable and unaffected by values of the other variables. These properties make computations much easier. For example, it is a simple matter to forecast the impact on quantity demanded of changes in per capita income. If per capita income increases by $1,000 and $a_I = 0.05$, the increase in quantity demanded will be 0.05 × 1,000, or 50 units per period.

Various functional forms can be used for econometric analysis. Other than the linear equation, probably the most common is the multiplicative functional form. For estimating demand, the multiplicative equation is

$$Q = bP^{a_p} I^{a_I} P_o^{a_0} T^{a_T} \qquad (5\text{-}7)$$

As shown, this equation cannot be estimated using ordinary least squares because it is not linear. However, a transformation to a linear form can be made by taking logarithms of both sides

$$\log Q = \log b + a_p \log P + a_I \log I + a_o \log P_0 + a_T \log T \qquad (5\text{-}8)$$

Because this equation is linear in terms of the logarithms of the original variables, the coefficients can be estimated using the ordinary least-squares method. Note that the log transformation is similar to the method used to estimate the constant percentage rate of change in the discussion of trend projection.

The coefficients a_p, a_I, a_o, and a_T in equations (5-7) and (5-8) have an important interpretation. Using calculus, it can easily be shown that they are elasticities for the independent variables. Consider the price elasticity of demand. Taking the derivative of equation (5-7) with respect to price yields

$$\frac{dQ}{dP} = (a_p)\, bP^{a_p-1}I^{a_I}P_o^{a_o}T^{a_T}$$

Multiplying both sides of the equation by P/Q gives

$$E_p = \frac{dQ}{dP}\frac{P}{Q} = \frac{(a_p)bP^{a_p}I^{a_I}P_o^{a_o}T^{a_T}}{Q}$$

But

$$Q = bP^{a_p}I^{a_I}P_o^{a_o}T^{a_T}$$

Hence

$$E_p = a_p$$

Using an analogous approach, it can be shown that a_I is the income elasticity, a_o is the cross elasticity, and a_T is an elasticity measure for tastes and preferences. Thus, an advantage of the multiplicative form is that it yields estimates of elasticities. Note that these elasticities are constant—they are unaffected by changes in the independent variables.

Another feature of the multiplicative form is that the change in quantity demanded per unit change in an independent variable is not constant. Rather, it is determined not only by the associated variable, but also by the values of the other independent variables. This makes computations using multiplicative equations somewhat more difficult, but may be more realistic in depicting the relationship between the variables.

The choice of an appropriate functional form depends on the underlying theoretical model and the intended use of the results. If quantity demanded is believed to be a linear function of the independent variables and if ease of computation is important, a linear form would be appropriate. In contrast, the multiplicative form may be a better choice if the objective is to estimate elasticities.

CASE STUDY

THE POPE AND THE PRICE OF FISH

For over a thousand years the Catholic Church required that members abstain from eating meat on Fridays as an act of penance. Many Catholics responded by including fish as part of their Friday meals. The effect of this practice was to increase the demand for fish.

But in February, 1966, Pope Paul VI authorized local Bishops to end meatless Fridays. In December, 1966, church leaders in the United States stipulated that members could eat meat on non-Lent Fridays (usually 46 Fridays during the year). With abstinence no longer required on these days, it was expected that Catholics would consume less fish and more meat. As a result, the price of fish, at least in the short run, should have decreased.

This hypothesis was examined by economist F. W. Bell. Noting that New England is 45 percent Catholic, he collected data on fish prices in that region before and after the change. He also collected data on other factors that affect fish prices, such as personal income and prices of meat and poultry. Using multiple regression techniques to hold the effects of these other factors constant, Bell was able to assess the impact of the action by the Church. He estimated that there was an average decline in fish prices of 12.5 percent as a result of the decree. For some types of fish, the price effect was as much as 20 percent.

Source: Bell, Frederick W. 1968. "The Pope and the Price of Fish." *American Economic Review.* December pp 1346–1350.

Estimation and Interpretation of Results

The parameters of simple trend projection equations can be estimated using hand calculators, but econometric problems that involve more than one independent variable are usually estimated using computers. Many software packages are available for econometric analyses. Most require little more than that the analyst specify the form of the equation to be estimated and input the data. The computer then performs the necessary calculations and provides results in a format that is usually relatively easy to interpret. Table 5-3 shows sample output from a demand estimation problem. The equation to be estimated is

$$Q = b + a_p P + a_I I + a_o I'_o$$

and the price and income variables are measured in dollars.

The estimated coefficient of the constant term suggests the quantity demanded if values of the other variables are zero. However, this coefficient has little economic meaning in most demand estimation problems. The other coefficients estimate the change in quantity demanded per dollar change in the associated

Table 5-3. Sample Output from a Regression Problem

		Variable Name		
	Constant	Price	Income	Price of Other Good
Estimated Coefficient	50.7836	−4.9892	0.0034	−1.2801
Standard error	10.2189	1.3458	0.0045	0.5890
t-statistic	(4.97)	(−3.71)	(0.76)	(−2.17)
Number of observations = 182		$R^2 = 0.6837$		

independent variable. For example, the price coefficient is -4.9892. This estimate implies that if the other independent variables are held constant, a \$1 change in the price of the good will result in a change in quantity demanded of almost 5 units per period.

In evaluating regression results, the estimated relationships between the variables should be considered in terms of economic theory. Note that the coefficient of price is negative. This implies an inverse relationship between price and quantity demanded which is consistent with economic theory. Note also the coefficients of income and prices of other goods. The signs of these coefficients could not be predicted using economic theory, but theory does provide information regarding their interpretation. The coefficient of income is positive, indicating that the item is a normal good. The "price of other good" coefficient is negative. Hence the two goods must be complements.

The standard errors reported in Table 5-3 indicate the precision of the estimates. Dividing the estimated coefficients by their standard errors gives the t-statistics. These can be used for hypothesis testing. A common hypothesis is that a coefficient is not significantly different from zero. As discussed in Chapter 2, this hypothesis can be tested by comparing the computed t-statistics to the values shown for the t-distribution in Appendix V at the end of the book.

For samples with more than about 120 observations (such as in Table 5-3), 95 percent of the t-distribution lies between $+1.960$ and -1.960. Thus t-statistics greater than $+1.960$ or less than -1.960 imply that the hypothesis that an estimated coefficient is equal to zero can be rejected with only a 5 percent probability of error. That is, the probability of erroneously concluding that a coefficient is not equal to zero is 5 percent or less.

In Table 5-3, the t-statistics for the constant term, price, and the price of the other good all have absolute values greater than 1.960. Thus the traditional interpretation is that these coefficients are significant (i.e., the probability of erroneously rejecting the hypothesis that they are equal to zero is less than or equal to 5 percent). In contrast, the t-statistic for the income varible is 0.76, meaning that there is more than a 5 percent probability of erroneously rejecting the hypothesis that the coefficient is equal to zero. Consequently, the income coefficient is referred to as nonsignificant.

Finally, the value of the coefficient of determination or R^2 indicates the overall explanatory power of the model. As discussed in Chapter 2, this number represents the proportion of total variation in the dependent variable explained by changes in the independent variables. The R^2 value from Table 5-3 is 0.6837. Thus about two-thirds of the total variation in quantity demanded is explained by price, income, and the price of the other good.

KEY CONCEPTS

- The functional form of an equation to be estimated should be selected based on the underlying economic theory and the intended use of the estimates.
- The estimated parameters of a linear equation indicate the impacts of a change in each independent variable.

- Without additional computation, the estimated parameters of multiplicative equations can be interpreted as elasticities.
- The parameters of an equation are evaluated by examining their signs and magnitudes. The associated t-values are used to test hypotheses about statistical significance.
- The R^2 value indicates the proportion of variation in the dependent variable explained by the independent variables.

EXAMPLE

INTERPRETING AN ESTIMATED DEMAND EQUATION

A multiplicative demand function of the form

$$Q = hP^{a_p} I^{a_I} P_U^{a_O}$$

is estimated using cross-section data. The results are as follows:

	Constant	Price	Income	Variable Name Price of Other Good
Estimated Coefficient	0.02248	−0.2243	1.3458	0.1034
Standard Error	0.01885	0.0563	0.5012	0.8145
t-statistic	(1.19)	(−3.98)	(2.69)	(0.13)
Number of observations = 224	R^2 = 0.2515			

1. How should the coefficients and R^2 value be interpreted?
2. What will the quantity demanded be if the values of the independent variables are:
   a. Price = $10.
   b. Income per capita = $9,000.
   c. Price of the other good = $15.
3. How much would quantity demanded change if price were decreased to $8 and the values of the other variables held constant?

Solution

1. Because the functional form was multiplicative, the estimated coefficients represent elasticities. The price elasticity is −0.2243, indicating that demand is inelastic, and the income elasticity is 1.3458, suggesting that the good is a luxury. Both of these elasticity estimates are significantly different from zero. In contrast, the coefficient of the "other good" price is positive but not significant. The implication is that there is a weak substitute good relationship between the two products.

   The R^2 reported for this problem is 0.2515. This is a rather low value, even for cross-section data. It means that only about one-fourth of the variation in demand can be explained by the model. Thus forecasts generated by the estimated equation are unlikely to be very accurate. A possible explanation for the low R^2 is that important explanatory variables have been omitted from the model.

2. In multiplicative form, the estimated equation is

$$Q = 0.02248P^{-0.2243}I^{1.3458}P_o^{0.1034}$$

A forecast of demand can be obtained by substituting in the given values for the independent variables. Making these substitutions, the quantity demanded is estimated to be 3,722 units.

3. The impact of reducing price can be estimated by recomputing quantity demanded for $P = \$8$, while holding the other variables constant. The resulting Q is 3,913. Hence the $2 price decrease is estimated to increase quantity demanded by 191 units.

Input/Output Analysis

Econometric models can be used to forecast changes in demand in one sector, but such models seldom have the detail necessary to assess the impacts of those changes on other sectors. But modern economic systems are highly interrelated. Changes in demand in one sector of the economy can have significant impacts on demand in other sectors. Some of these impacts are immediate and obvious. For example, steel, rubber, glass, and plastics are all important inputs in the production of motor vehicles. Thus an increase in the demand for automobiles would cause an increase in the demand for those four products.

The direct impact that automobile sales have on the demand for steel, rubber, glass, and plastics is augmented by secondary effects generated in still other sectors. Consider the resulting increase in demand for steel. As steel output increases to meet the requirements for producing automobiles, steel industry managers will find it necessary to purchase additional inputs. These may include iron ore, coal, and electricity. If the increase in demand is expected to be permanent, management may also decide to expand the capacity of their production facility by acquiring additional capital goods such as blast furnaces.

In turn, these secondary impacts will affect other parts of the economy. Over time, the increase in automobile demand may be the cause of change in hundreds of different industries. To the casual observer many of these changes would seem unrelated to the production of automobiles.

Input/output analysis is a useful technique for sorting out and quantifying sector-by-sector impacts. This approach captures not only the direct effects but also related impacts in other parts of the economy. For example, an input/output matrix developed by the U.S. Department of Labor can estimate the impact of increased automobile sales on nearly 500 individual sectors in the U.S. economy.

Transactions Matrix

Input/output analysis is based on a table that indicates historic patterns of purchases and sales between industries. Data for this table are usually generated from surveying a sample of firms. A simple two-sector version of such a table is shown in Table 5-4. The two sectors identified in the table are manufacturing and agriculture. Within each sector are firms producing specific products. For example, the manufacturing sector might include firms making electronic components and also firms that produce television sets and computers. Similarly, the agriculture sector could include firms producing cotton and wool.

The rows of Table 5-4 show the disposition of each sector's output. Consider first the manufacturing sector which is depicted in the first row. If the numbers represent billions of dollars, the first element in the first row indicates that firms engaged in manufacturing sold $8 billion of their product to other manufacturing firms. An example of these "within-sector" transactions might be the sale of electronic components to a television manufacturer. The second element of the first row shows that $10 billion of manufactured goods were sold to firms in the agricultural sector. Together, these first two elements indicate total sales by manufacturing to other firms. Such sales are sometimes called *intermediate sales* because they represent output that is used as inputs for making products sold to consumers. The first two elements of the second row are interpreted in a similar manner. They show intermediate sales by the agriculture sector.

The third element of each row is designated as final demand and shows sales to ultimate consumers. Finally, the last element is total sales. This number is the sum of the intermediate sales and final demand and represents the total sales by the sector. Thus the $20 billion of total sales in manufacturing were made up of $18 billion in intermediate sales to other firms and $2 in sales to final consumers.

The columns of Table 5-4 indicate uses of revenues by each of the sectors. The elements in the first column show that firms in the manufacturing sector spent $8 billion to purchase intermediate goods from other manufacturing firms and $6 billion on goods from the agriculture sector. Subtracting that $14 billion amount from total sector sales of $20 billion leaves a residual of $6 billion. This amount is referred to as value added because it represents the difference between the

Table 5-4. Two-Sector Input/Output Table

	Sales to Manufacturing	+	Sales to Agriculture	+	Final Demand	=	Total Sales
Purchases from Manufacturing	8	+	10	+	2	=	20
+	+		+				
Purchases from Agriculture	6	+	12	+	12	=	30
+	+		+				
Value Added	6		8				
=	=		=				
Total Sales	20		30				

Table 5-5. Transactions Matrix

	Sales to Manufacturing	Sales to Agriculture
Purchases from Manufacturing	8	10
Purchases from Agriculture	6	12

value of inputs purchased and the product finally sold. Value added consists of payments to workers, owners of capital, and governments.

The elements of the table indicating intermediate sales and purchases are of particular interest for input/output analysis. Together, they make up the transactions matrix of the model. Based on the numbers in Table 5-4, the transactions matrix would be as shown in Table 5-5. In matrix notation, let this matrix be designated as X, where

$$X = \begin{bmatrix} 8 & 10 \\ 6 & 12 \end{bmatrix}$$

Direct Requirements Matrix

If each element in a column of the transactions matrix is divided by the total sales of that sector's product, the result is the direct requirements matrix of an input/output model. The elements of each column of the direct requirements matrix can be interpreted as indicating the immediate or direct change in revenue for a sector generated by a $1 change in demand for the product of the sector represented by the column. The direct requirements matrix for the sample problem is shown in Table 5-6.

Consider the elements of the manufacturing column. They were computed by dividing the first column of the transactions matrix by total sales in manufacturing—$20 billion. The first element indicates that for each dollar of manufacturing sales, $0.40 of intermediate sales to other firms in the manufacturing sector are initially generated. The second element shows that $0.30 in sales by agricultural firms will be the direct result of each dollar of sales in the manufacturing sector. The elements of the second column have a similar interpretation with respect to each dollar of sales by the agricultural sector. Let the direct requirements matrix be designated as A. Thus

$$A = \begin{bmatrix} 0.40 & 0.33 \\ 0.30 & 0.40 \end{bmatrix}$$

Table 5-6. Direct Requirements Matrix

	Manufacturing	Agriculture
Manufacturing Sales per Dollar	0.40	0.33
Agricultural Sales per Dollar	0.30	0.40

Direct and Indirect Requirements Matrix

The direct requirements matrix shows the immediate or direct impact of changes in demand in a sector. But the elements of this matrix do not incorporate secondary and other impacts. For example, Table 5-6 indicates that the direct result of a $1 increase in agricultural sales would be a $0.33 increase in the demand for manufactured goods. However, such an increase would require that manufacturing firms purchase additional goods from other firms in the manufacturing and agricultural sectors. These purchases would stimulate still other purchases by firms in the two sectors. Thus the ultimate impact would be greater than predicted by the coefficient of the direct requirements matrix.

To take into account secondary impacts of changes in demand, input/output analysis requires computation of a direct and indirect requirements matrix. The derivation and calculation of this matrix is beyond the scope of this book, but conventionally it is designated by the notation $(I - A)^{-1}$, where A is the direct requirements matrix, I is the identity matrix and the exponent denotes the inverse of a matrix.[2] For the example being considered, the direct and indirect requirements matrix is shown in Table 5-7.

The direct and indirect requirements matrix has a straightforward interpretation. The elements of each column indicate the change in total demand in each sector that would result from a $1 change in final demand for the sector designated by the column. For example, consider the first column. The first element shows that after all direct and secondary effects have been taken into account, a $1 change in final demand for manufactured goods will cause a $2.30 change in total demand in the manufacturing sector. The second element of the first column estimates the change in total demand in agriculture resulting from a $1 change in final demand for manufactured goods. In this case, the number is $1.15. Similarly, the elements of the second column show changes in total demand in each sector caused by a $1 change in final demand in the agricultural sector.

Forecasting with an Input/Output Model

The direct and indirect requirements matrix can be used to forecast sector-by-sector impacts of changes in final demand. For example, suppose that an in-

Table 5-7. Direct and Indirect Requirements Matrix

	Manufacturing	Agriculture
Change in total Demand in manufacturing	2.30	1.26
Change in total Demand in agriculture	1.15	2.30

[2] An identity matrix has "1s" on its main diagonal and "0s" for its other elements. It is analogous to the number "1" in arithmetic. The inverse of a matrix is a matrix which if multiplied by the original yields the identity matrix. The concept is analogous to the reciprocal in arithmetic. For a more detailed discussion of input/output theory, see Miernyk (1965).

crease in exports causes a $5 billion increase in final demand in the agricultural sector. After taking into account all the direct and secondary effects, what impact would this change have on total demand for manufactured and agricultural goods?

With respect to manufacturing, Table 5-7 shows that each $1 change in agricultural final demand causes a $1.26 change in the total demand for manufactured goods. Thus a $5 billion increase would increase total demand in manufacturing by $5 billion × 1.26, or $6.30 billion. Similarly, the increase in total demand in the agriculture sector would be $5 billion × 2.30, or $11.50 billion.

Input/output anaysis can also be used to forecast employment impacts. This is done by assuming a constant ratio of employment to total demand. To illustrate, assume that total demand in the manufacturing sector is $500 billion and the total number of workers in that sector is 5,000,000. Hence the employment ratio is 1 to $100,000. That is, one job exists for each $100,000 in total demand.

If this ratio is constant, one additional job in the manufacturing sector will be created for each $100,000 increase in total demand. Thus if a $5 billion increase in final demand for agricultural products causes a $6.3 billion increase in total demand in the manufacturing sector, the employment impact would be $6.3 billion divided by $100,000, or 63,000 new jobs. A similar computation could be made to estimate the employment increase in the agricultural sector.

EXAMPLE

AUTOMOBILE SALES AND THE DEMAND FOR GLASS

Assume that by 1990, automobile sales to consumers are forecast to be $10 billion greater than at present. A manufacturer of glass is contemplating a plant expansion and desires information regarding the probable effect of the increase in automobile demand on the total demand for glass. Union leaders in the industry want to know the employment impact.

	Direct and Indirect Requirements Matrix				
	Steel	Automobiles	Computers	Glass	Electricity
Steel	1.034	0.334	0.008	0.010	0.010
Automobiles	0.008	1.010	0.009	0.002	0.007
Computers	0.003	0.004	1.110	0.001	0.100
Glass	0.009	0.090	0.048	1.004	0.005
Electricity	0.142	0.045	0.010	0.086	1.009
	Employment Ratios				
	Steel	Automobiles	Computers	Glass	Electricity
Jobs per million $ of total sales	2.00	10.00	8.00	4.50	1.00

The forecasts are to be based on a five-sector input/output model that includes sectors for glass and automobiles. The direct and indirect requirements matrix is shown on page 170. The employment ratios are also shown. What will be the total demand and employment impacts in the glass industry of the projected increase in final demand for automobiles?

Solution

The elements in the second column of the direct and indirect requirements matrix indicate the change in total demand resulting from a $1 change in final demand for automobiles. For the glass industry, the coefficient is 0.090. Thus a $10 billion increase in final demand for automobiles is estimated to increase total sales of glass by 0.090 × $10 billion, or $900 million. For the glass industry, the employment ratio is 4.5 jobs per $1 million in total sales. Thus the $900 million increase in total sales of glass is estimated to create 4,050 new jobs.

The construction of input/output models is a very expensive and time-consuming task. It would rarely be feasible for a firm to develop its own tables. Fortunately, several large models have been developed by various governmental agencies. Perhaps the most important is a 460-sector model of the U.S. economy maintained by the Department of Labor. The department also publishes employment ratios. This information is used by government analysts to evaluate impacts of public policy. It is also available for use by firms in forecasting. In addition, there are state and regional input/output models that can be used for forecasting on a more localized basis.

The major value of input/output analysis is that it takes into account interrelationships between sectors. However, the approach has limitations in addition to its high cost. A fundamental problem is that input/output forecasts are based on ratios that are assumed to be fixed. This assumption may not be very realistic in situations where rapid technological change is occurring.

KEY CONCEPTS

- Input/output analysis can be used to forecast the direct and indirect impacts of changes in one sector on other sectors of the economy.
- The transactions matrix shows the pattern of sales and purchases between sectors. The direct requirements matrix indicates the proportion of revenues used to purchase goods and services from each sector.
- The elements of the direct and indirect requirements matrix show the impact that a $1 change in final demand would have on total demand in each of the sectors of the model.
- Input/output analysis can be used to predict sector-by-sector sales and employment impacts.

Summary

Additional data for use in forecasting can be obtained from expert opinion, surveys, and market experiments. Forecasts of experts can be refined by procedures such as the Delphi technique, which uses an iterative process to aid individuals in assessing their judgments. Surveys of plans and attitudes by consumers and managers can be useful in forecasting. However, considerable care must be exercised to assure that the responses reflect subsequent consumer choices. Market experiments have an advantage over surveys because they provide information on actual consumer behavior. Their limitations include the risk of losing customers, high cost, problems of making consumers aware of changes, and inability to control all factors.

Trend projections are based on time-series data. Basically, the technique involves estimating the coefficients that provide the best fit of data to a specified equation. The two most common equation forms estimate a constant rate of change and a constant percentage rate of change. Fitting the constant-percentage rate-of-change equation requires that the data be inputted in logarithmic form. Forecasts based on trend projection of time-series data can be improved by adjusting for seasonal variations.

In addition to forecasting, econometric methods are useful because they provide insights into the relationships between variables. The first step in developing an econometric forecast is to formulate a model based on economic theory. If important variables are omitted from the model, the results may be inaccurate or misleading. In particular, an identification problem may occur if the demand function is not carefully specified.

Econometric techniques may be applied to either time-series or cross-section data. If the equation whose parameters are to be estimated is linear, the coefficients represent the change in the dependent variable resulting from a 1-unit change in the associated independent variable. The coefficients of a multiplicative equation can be interpreted as elasticities.

The signs and magnitudes of estimated coefficients should be evaluated in relation to the economic theory on which the model is based. The t-statistics can be used to test hypothesis about statistical significance of individual coefficients. The R^2 value indicates the overall explanatory power of the model.

Input/output analysis can be used to forecast the direct and indirect impacts of final demand changes in one sector on total demand in other sectors of the economy. The technique relies on data that show patterns of sales and purchases between sectors. These patterns are summarized in a transactions matrix. The direct requirements matrix is computed by dividing the columns of the transactions matrix by sector total sales. It shows the proportions of total revenues used to make purchases from the other sectors.

The direct and indirect requirements matrix is the basic tool used for forecasting with input/output analysis. Its columns show the impact that a $1 change in final demand in one sector would have on total demand in each of the other sectors of the model. By assuming constant employment/total sales ratios, input/output analysis can also be used to estimate sector-by-sector employment impacts.

Discussion Questions

5-1. The manager of Harrison Toys assembles a panel of five experts to assist in formulating a sales forecast. The intent is to use the Delphi technique, but after examining the projections of the others, none of the experts are persuaded to make any changes in their initial forecasts. What insight might the manager obtain from the inability of the experts to agree on a projection?

5-2. A business surveys its customers to generate information about the demand for a proposed new product. Under what circumstances might the customers understate their true demand for the product? When might they overstate their true demand? Explain.

5-3. To test consumer response, on January 1 a soft-drink manufacturer introduces a new brand in the Chicago market area. Over a three-month period, sales are slow and the company concludes that the product is unlikely to be profitable in nationwide marketing. Should the firm base its decision entirely on this experiment? Why or why not?

5-4. Using trend projection, how should a manager decide whether to use the constant-rate-of-change model or the constant-percentage rate of change?

5-5. Quarterly data from the beginning of 1980 to the end of 1986 are used to estimate the coefficients of the equation $S_t = S_0 + bt$, where S_t is sales in the tth quarter. No seasonal adjustments are made. How accurate are each of the following forecasts likely to be? Explain.
   (a) Annual sales of a tire manufacturer for 1995.
   (b) Fourth-quarter sales for 1987 for a retail gift store.
   (c) Fourth-quarter sales for 1987 for a newspaper publisher.

5-6. A recently hired MBA uses data on average price and quantity over the last twelve months to plot a graph that he interprets as the firm's demand curve. As the manager of the company, how much confidence would you have in his interpretation? Explain.

5-7. A demand equation is estimated, but the coefficient of the income variable is not significant. In using the equation to forecast sales, should the income variable be omitted? Explain.

5-8. A district manager proposes that her division develop its own state-level input/output model for use in forecasting? Is this a good idea? Why or why not?

5-9. A 20-sector input/output model gives value added as a percent of sales. Can this estimate be used to rank relative profitability of the sectors? Why or why not?

5-10. Would input/output analysis be useful in forecasting sales in a rapidly changing industry such personal computers? Explain.

Problems

5-1. The management of Romano's decides to test market a new frozen pizza. As the person in charge of the market experiment, what considerations should affect your decisions with respect to:
   (a) The number and locations of cities in which the new pizza would be test marketed?

(b) The duration of the experiment?

(c) Pricing of the product?

5-2. Quarterly sales for Swarthmore Cycles are as follows:

Period	Sales	Period	Sales
1984 : I	100	1985 : I	130
1984 : II	110	1985 : II	135
1984 : III	115	1985 : III	145
1984 : IV	125	1985 : IV	150

(a) Plot the sales data and graphically fit a straight line to the points.

(b) In using the data for trend predictions, would the constant rate of change or the constant percentage change model be more appropriate? Explain.

(c) Using a hand calculator or the computation methods described on pages 28–31 of Chapter 2, use the data to estimate the coefficients of the equation $S_t = S_0 + bt$, where S_t are sales in the tth quarter.

5-3. Based on quarterly data from 1982 : I to 1985 : IV, Highland Foods estimates that potato chip sales can be projected using the equation

$$S_t = 5,000,000 + 100,000t$$

where 1982: I is period #1. Actual fourth-quarter sales were as follows:

1982	5,450,000
1983	5,860,000
1984	6,270,000
1985	6,680,000

(a) Project sales for the first three quarters of 1986.

(b) Without using a seasonal adjustment, project sales for 1986 : IV.

(c) Project seasonally adjusted sales for 1986 : IV.

5-4. Annual prices and beef consumption per capita in six cities are as follows:

City	Price per Pound	Consumption per Capita
1	$2.00	55
2	1.90	60
3	2.10	50
4	1.80	70
5	2.30	45
6	2.20	48

(a) If a demand equation is to be estimated using these data, would the linear form (i.e., $Q = b + aP$) or the multiplicative form (i.e., $Q = bP^a$) be more appropriate? Explain.

(b) Could the resulting equation be properly interpreted as a demand function? Explain.

5-5. The MacWend Drive-In has determined that demand for hamburgers is given by the following equation:

$$Q = 205.2 + 23.0A - 200.0P_M + 100.0P_C + 0.5Y$$
$$(1.85) \quad (2.64) \quad (-5.61) \quad (2.02) \quad (4.25)$$

where Q is the number of hamburgers sold per month (1,000), A is the advertising expenditures during the previous month ($1,000), P_M is the price of MacWend burgers (dollars), P_C is the price of hamburgers of the company's major competitor (dollars), and Y is income per capita in the surrounding community ($1,000). The t-statistic for each coefficient is shown in parentheses below each coefficient.
   (a) Are the signs of the individual coefficients consistent with predictions from economic theory? Explain.
   (b) If A = $5,000, P_M = $1, P_C = $1.20, and Y = $20,000, how many hamburgers will be demanded?
   (c) What is the advertising elasticity at A = $5,000?
   (d) If it costs $0.75 to make a hamburger, should advertising expenditures be increased or decreased? Explain.
5-6. Motorland Recreational Vehicles estimates the monthly demand (Q) for its product is given by the equation

$$\log Q = 1.00 - 1.50(\log P) + 3.00(\log Y) \qquad R^2 = 0.21$$
$$(1.20) \quad (-2.50) \quad (0.02)$$

where P is price and Y is income per capita in thousands. The t-statistics are shown in parentheses and natural logs were used to transform the equation.
   (a) Rewrite the expression as a multiplicative demand equation.
   (b) Based on the equation, is the product an inferior good, a necessity, or a luxury good? How much confidence do you have in your answer? Explain.
   (c) Is the equation likely to be useful in predicting demand for Motorland's product? Why or why not?
5-7. Each year, sector A purchases $5 million of goods from sector B and $10 million from sector C. Sector B makes annual purchases of $2 million from sector A and $8 million from sector C. Annual purchases of sector C are $3 million from sector A and $6 million from sector B. Within-sector purchases are $1 million for sector A, $4 million for sector B, and $5 million for sector C. Total sales in the sectors are $20 million, $20 million, and $30 million, respectively.
   (a) Write the transactions matrix for the three sectors.
   (b) How much is value added for sector A?
   (c) How much is final demand in sector A?
   (d) Write the direct requirements matrix for the model.
5-8. The Ohio Planning Commission has developed a four-sector regional input/output model with a direct and indirect requirements matrix as follows.

		Sector		
	1	2	3	4
Sector 1	1.20	0.45	0.90	0.60
Sector 2	0.20	1.50	0.80	0.75
Sector 3	0.89	0.63	1.10	0.10
Sector 4	0.24	0.80	0.43	1.24

(a) What is the interpretation of the element in the first row of the second column?

(b) If final demand decreases by $5 million in sector 3, what will be the effect on total sales in sector 1?

(c) The commission estimates that 1 ton of sulfur dioxide particles enters the atmosphere for each $10 million increase in total sales in sector 2. How much pollution will result from a $5 million increase in final demand in sector 1?

Problem Requiring Calculus

5-9. Economists on a skiing vacation in Aspen, Colorado decide to study the demand for lift tickets in the area. Using multiple regression analysis the demand equation is estimated to be:

$$\log Q_t = 7.00 - 2.0\log (P_t) + 0.5\log(S)$$

where Q_t is quantity demanded per day, P_t is the price of a full day lift ticket, and S is accumulated snow depth in inches at the lodges. Using calculus, show that for small changes, a one percent increase in accumulated snow depth will increase daily lift ticket demand by 0.5 percent.

References

Almon, C., Jr., et al. 1974. *1985 Interindustry Forecasts of the American Economy.* Lexington, Mass.: Lexington Books.

Bell, Frederick W. 1968. "The Pope and The Price of Fish." *American Economic Review.* December, pp. 1346–1350.

Butler, W. F., Kavesh, R. A., and Platt, R. B. 1974. *Methods and Techniques of Business Forecasting.* Englewood Cliffs, N.J.: Prentice-Hall.

Dillman, D. A. 1978. *Mail and Telephone Surveys: The Total Design Method.* New York: Wiley.

Granger, C. W. J., and Newbold, P. 1977. *Forecasting Economic Time Series.* New York: Academic Press.

Houthakker, H. S., and Taylor, L. D. 1970. *Consumer Demand in the United States, 1929–1970: Analysis and Projections,* 2nd ed. Cambridge, Mass.: Harvard University Press.

Manning, W. G., and Phelps, C. E. 1979. "The Demand for Dental Care." *The Bell Journal of Economics 10*(2): 503–525.

Miernyk, W. H. 1965. *The Elements of Input–Output Analysis.* New York: Random House.

Suits, D. B. 1979. "The Elasticity of Demand for Gambling." *Quarterly Journal of Economics,* February, pp. 155–162.

Wheelwright, S. C., and Makridakis, S. 1977. *Forecasting Methods for Management.* New York: Wiley.

Appendix:
Barometric Forecasting

Trend projection uses time-series data to predict the future based on past relationships. But if there is no clear pattern in a time series, the data are of little value for forecasting. An alternative approach is to find a second series of data that is correlated with the first. Hence, by observing changes in the second series, it may be possible to predict changes in the first. For example, suppose that a lumber company's sales exhibited large yearly fluctuations over the last decade—so large that any forecast based on trend projection is useless. But over the same period, it is also determined that the firm's sales were highly correlated with the number of housing starts. Thus if housing starts can be predicted, this information can be used to forecast lumber sales.

A time series that is correlated with another time series is sometimes called an *indicator* of the second series. Substantial time and effort have been expended searching for good indicators of economic trends. *Business Conditions Digest*, a monthly publication of the Department of Commerce, reports information on over 300 time-series.[1] These data are closely followed by economists, managers, and financial analysts.

Leading Indicators

If two time series of data frequently increase or decrease at the same time, one series may be regarded as a coincident indicator of the other. For example, in Figure 5A-1a, series 1 is a coincident indicator of series 2 because the two series have their peaks and troughs in the same periods.

If changes in one series consistently occur prior to changes in another, a leading indicator has been identified. In Figure 5A-1b, series 1 can be considered a leading indicator of series 2 because the peaks and troughs of series 1 consistently occur two periods before the corresponding peaks and troughs of series 2.

For purposes of forecasting, leading indicators are of primary interest. Much as a meteorologist uses changes in barometric pressure to predict the weather, leading indicators can be used to forecast changes in general economic conditions. Consequently, the use of such indicators is commonly referred to as *barometric forecasting*.

The value of a leading indicator depends on several factors. First, the indicator must be accurate. That is, its fluctuations must correlate closely with fluctuations

[1] Dept. of Commerce, *Business Conditions Digest.* monthly. (Washington, D.C.: U.S. Government Printing Office)

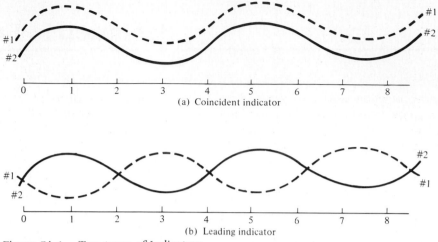

Figure 5A-1.   *Two types of Indicators.*

in the series that it is intended to predict. Second, the indicator must provide adequate lead time. Even if two series are highly correlated, an indicator will be of little use if the lead time is too short. For example, because of the time needed to put idle furnaces into operation, a series that predicts changes in steel demand by, say, one week, would not be a useful forecasting tool for managers in the steel industry. A third requirement is that the lead time be relatively constant. If a series leads another by six months on one occasion and by two years the next, the indicator will be of little use because it cannot provide useful forecasts.

Fourth, there should be a logical explanation as to why one series predicts another. If enough time-series are studied, it is likely that a correlation can be found between pairs of series. However, unless there is a causal relationship between the two series, the historical pattern may not be very useful in forecasting future events because there is no reason to expect the pattern to be repeated. Finally, an indicator's value is affected by the cost and time necessary for data collection. A time-series that can be maintained only at a very high cost may not be worth the expense. Similarly, if there is a long delay before the data are available, the effective lead time of the indicator may be too short to be useful.

Table 5A-1 lists selected leading indicators and an economic variable that each is used to predict. For some of the indicators, there is an obvious link between the two series. One example is new building permits and private housing starts. When a permit is issued, this indicates a strong commitment to build a new house. Thus changes in permits should be closely correlated to changes in housing starts. Clearly, housing permits represent a leading indicator because builders are legally required to have a permit before beginning construction. Similar arguments can be made to explain new orders as leading indicators of sales in the durable goods and capital equipment industries.

Table 5A-1. Selected Leading Indicators

Leading Indicator	Economic Variable Predicted by the Indicator
1 Average workweek	Manufacturing output
2. Average weekly initial unemployment claims	State unemployment insurance payments
3. New orders for durable goods	Sales of durable goods
4. New orders for capital goods	Sales of capital goods
5. New building permits	Private housing starts
6. Change in manufacturing and trade inventories	General economic conditions
7. Industrial material prices	Consumer prices
8. Common stock prices	General economic conditions

For some of the indicators, it is more difficult to explain the correlation between the two series. Consider stock prices as a predictor of general economic conditions. Historically, indices of common stock prices have been a relatively accurate predictor of cycles in business activity. One possible explanation is that stock prices reflect expectations and plans of managers and consumers which are implemented in future months.

Composite and Diffusion Indices

Although a time-series showing the changes in stock prices may be somewhat useful in predicting general economic conditions, no single leading indicator yet identified comes close to having a perfect forecasting record. In addition, even when an indicator correctly predicts variations in economic activity, the lead time often shows considerable fluctuation. The basic problem is that any time-series contains random fluctuations that do not conform to the general pattern of the data.

One way to improve barometric forecasting is by construction of an index. Such indices represent a single time-series made up of a number of individual leading indicators. The purpose of combining the data is to smooth out the random fluctuations in each individual series. Ideally, the resulting index should provide more accurate forecasts. The most commonly used barometric forecasting indices are composite indices and diffusion indices.

Composite Indices

A composite index is a weighted average of individual indicators. The weights are based on the predictive ability of each series. That is, a series that does a better job of predicting would be given greater weight than a less accurate series.

The index is interpreted in terms of percentage changes from period to period. For example, the most widely followed composite index is maintained by the U.S. Department of Commerce and is based on twelve leading indicators. This index is constructed to have a value of 100 for its base year of 1967.

Each month the department reports the change in the index. Monthly swings have little significance, but sustained increases for several months are interpreted as a sign that general economic conditions are likely to improve. Conversely, successive declines in the index suggest that the economy is weakening.

Diffusion Indices

The same twelve leading indicators are also used by the Department of Commerce to construct a diffusion index. This index is a measure of the proportion of the individual time series that increase from one month to the next. For example, if eight of the indicators increased from June to July, the diffusion index for July would be $\frac{8}{12}$ or 66.7 percent. When the index is over 50 percent for several months, the forecast is for improved economic conditions. As the index approaches 100 percent, the likelihood of improvement increases. Conversely, if less than 50 percent of the indicators exhibit an increase, a downturn is indicated.

The use of indices improves the accuracy of barometric forecasting. However, the prediction record of this technique is far from perfect. On several occasions the Department of Commerce indices have forecast recessions that failed to occur. Variability in lead time is another weakness. A third problem is that, while the barometric approach signals the likely direction of changes in economic conditions, it says little about the magnitude of such changes. As such, it provides only a qualitative forecast. Finally, although there has been much study on leading indicators of general economic conditions, the managers of individual firms may find it difficult to identify leading indicators that provide accurate forecasts for their specific needs.

KEY CONCEPTS

- The value of a leading indicator depends on the accuracy of prediction, length and stability of the lead time, and the cost and availability of data.
- Composite indices consist of a weighted average of several leading indicators.
- A diffusion index is calculated as the proportion of indicators that increase from one period to the next.

EXAMPLE
CALCULATING COMPOSITE AND DIFFUSION INDICES

Following are data for three leading indicators for a three-month period. The first month represents the base period and the three series are to be given equal weight. Construct a composite and a diffusion index from the data.

Month	Leading Indicator I	Leading Indicator II	Leading Indicator III
1	400	30	100
2	425	29	110
3	460	33	135

Solution

The diffusion index is generated by determining whether each series increased or decreased from month to month. For the second month, series I and III increased, but series II decreased. Hence the index is 66.7 for that month. During the third month, all of the series increased in comparison to month 2. Thus the index for that month is 100.

The composite index can be computed by first calculating the percentage changes (relative to the base month) for each series. Percentage changes during the second month were 6.25 percent for the first series, −3.33 percent for the second and 10 percent for the third. Giving each series equal weight, the average percentage change was 4.31 percent. The value of the composite index for the first month is arbitrarily set to 100, so the index for the second month is 104.31. For the third month, the changes from the base period are $60/400 = 15$ percent, $3/30 = 10$ percent, and $35/100 = 35$ percent, respectively. Thus the average change is 20.0 percent. Hence the index for that month is 120.0.

Values for the two indices for each month are shown in the following table. Both indices suggest that economic conditions should improve in future months.

Month	Diffusion Index	Composite Index
1	—	100.00
2	66.70	104.31
3	100.00	120.00

Discussion Questions

5A-1. A particular composite and a diffusion index are constructed based on the same three time series of data. In a given month, could the composite index increase while the diffusion index decreased? Use a simple example to explain your answer.

5A-2. Could the lead time necessary for an indicator to be useful in forecasting be longer in one industry than in another? Give an example.

5A-3. The average workweek is considered a leading indicator of general economic activity. Would longer workweeks predict an upturn or a downturn in economic activity? Explain.

Problem

5A-1. The demand for newsprint over a ten-year period is shown in the following table. Also shown are three time-series for the same time period.

	Year									
	1	2	3	4	5	6	7	8	9	10
Quantity of Newsprint	100	110	115	115	130	145	140	135	135	150
Series A	25	30	25	35	30	40	45	50	45	45
Series B	200	220	225	225	240	260	255	250	255	240
Series C	20	20	23	26	25	24	24	28	28	26

(a) Which of the time-series is a roughly coincident indicator of newsprint demand?

(b) Which series is a leading indicator of newsprint demand? For the leading indicator, what is the lead time?

(c) Based on the leading indicator, is newsprint demand likely to increase, decrease, or stay the same in period 11? Explain.

INTEGRATING CASE PROBLEM II
U.R. TURKEY

U.R. Turkey's production division operates ten turkey-producing facilities in Tennessee and Kentucky. The firm's marketing division sells frozen turkey and turkey products throughout the southeastern United States. U.R. has been in business since 1955 and currently has an 80 percent market share in the region. There are numerous other sellers, but they have little impact on U.R.'s operations. Quarterly sales data for the company (in thousands of pounds) for the past four years are shown in the following table.

	Sales (thousands)			
	I	II	III	IV
1982	10,000	10,500	10,500	14,000
1983	10,500	10,500	11,000	14,500
1984	11,000	11,500	11,500	15,000
1985	11,500	11,500	12,000	16,000

A concern of managers at U.R. is that they lack information about factors that affect demand for their product. In the past, some sales forecasts have been inaccurate because of fluctuations in prices of substitute goods or changes in general economic conditions. To obtain needed data, management approved a marketing experiment in 200 cities in the firm's market area. This experiment was conducted during the first six months of 1985 and involved charging different prices for turkey and then measuring the per capita consumption in each city. In addition, data were collected on income per capita and prices of chicken, beef, and pork for each of the 200 cities. Then multiple-regression techniques were used to estimate the following demand function for turkey:

$$Q = 7.00 - 0.100P_T + 0.020P_C + 0.010P_B + 0.005P_P + 0.500I$$

$$(4.29) \quad (-5.642) \quad (3.333) \quad (2.876) \quad (0.503) \quad (2.000)$$
$$R^2 = 0.75$$

where the t-statistics are in parentheses and

Q = annual turkey consumption per capita (pounds)
P_T = price of turkey (cents)
P_C = price of chicken (cents)
P_B = price of beef (cents)
P_P = price of pork (cents)
I = per capita income (thousands of dollars)

At the present time, the average selling price of U.R.'s turkey is $0.50 per pound. In the southeastern United States, the average prices of chicken, beef, and pork are $0.50, $1.50, and $1.50 per pound, respectively. Income per capita in that region is $12,000.

Questions

1. How much turkey will the firm sell in 1986 and 1987? Describe and justify your choice of a forecasting technique. Identify possible sources of error in your forecast.

2. At this time, the firm's production facilities are capable of producing 17,500,000 pounds of turkey every three months. However, management has tentative plans to expand capacity by constructing two new production facilities. These additions will be started in mid-1987 and be operational by June 1988. They will increase the firm's production capacity to 19,000,000 pounds per quarter. Should U.R.'s management proceed with its timetable for expanding capacity? Why or why not?

3. Historically, prices have been determined by using a markup over production cost. Is there reason to believe that the current price of $0.50 per pound is not optimal? Explain.

4. Does the management of U.R. have any information that would suggest how the demand for turkey is affected by general economic conditions? Explain. Be specific.

5. Government forecasts predict beef and chicken prices will be 10 percent higher in 1987, while pork prices will decline by 20 percent. Estimate the individual impacts of each of these changes on demand for turkey. How confident are you about your estimates? Explain.

PRODUCTION AND COST

Production Theory

6

Preview

The firm is an entity that combines and processes resources in order to produce output that will directly or indirectly satisfy consumer demand. The goal of the firm is to maximize the profit earned from this activity. Firms range in size from the person who bakes apple pies at home for sale to neighbors to the largest multinational conglomerate. However, when reduced to the basics, all firms do the same thing—they employ resources to produce output in order to earn profits.

The general production problem facing the firm is to determine how much output to produce and how much labor and capital to employ to produce that output most efficiently. Both engineering information in the form of a production function and economic information on prices of outputs and inputs are required to answer those questions.

In this chapter a framework for understanding the economics of production is presented and a set of conditions for efficient production developed. In the first section, the concept of a production function is outlined. In the following sections, techniques for determining cost-efficient production and input rates are determined. This is done first for the case of one variable input and then for two variable inputs. The concept of returns to scale is discussed in the last section of the chapter.

The Production Function

For simplicity, assume that all inputs can be grouped into two broad categories, labor (L) and capital (K). The general equation for the production function is

$$Q = f(K, L) \tag{6-1}$$

This function defines the maximum rate of output (Q) per unit of time obtainable from a given rate of capital and labor input. Output may be in physical units such as automobiles or microcomputers, or it may be intangible, as in the case of medical care, transportation, or education.

The production function is really an engineering concept that is devoid of economic content. That is, it simply relates output to input quantities. The production function does not yield information on the least-cost capital–labor combination for producing a given level of output, nor does it reveal that output rate that would yield maximum profit. The production function only shows the maximum output obtainable from any and all input combinations. Then economic principles can be used to determine which of the many possible input combinations is best given the firm's objective.

The definition of the production function as defining maximum output rates is important. Obviously, firms can fail to organize or manage resources efficiently and produce less than the maximum output for given input rates. However, in

Table 6-1. Production Table for the Production Function $Q = 100 \sqrt{KL}$

Rate of Capital Input (K)								
8	283	400	490	565	632	693	748	800
7	265	374	458	529	592	648	700	748
6	245	346	424	490	548	600	648	693
5	224	316	387	447	500	548	592	632
4	200	283	346	400	447	490	529	565
3	173	245	300	346	387	424	458	490
2	141	200	245	283	316	346	374	400
1	100	141	173	200	224	245	265	283
	1	2	3	4	5	6	7	8

Rate of Labor Input (L)

a competitive environment, such firms are not likely to survive because competitors using efficient production techniques will be able to sell at lower prices and ultimately drive inefficient producers out of the market. Thus only firms using the best production methods (i.e., maximizing production from any input combination) are considered in this chapter.[1]

There are many ways the production function can be written. Production functions of the multiplicative form

$$Q = AK^a L^b \qquad (6\text{-}2)$$

are widely used in economics. This specific functional form is referred to as a *Cobb–Douglas production function*. Because it has properties considered to be common to many production processes, it will be used as the basis for many of the examples in this chapter.

Consider a Cobb–Douglas production function with parameters $A = 100$, $a = 0.5$, and $b = 0.5$. That is,

$$Q = 100K^{0.5}L^{0.5}$$

which can also be written as

$$Q = 100 \sqrt{KL} \qquad (6\text{-}3)$$

A production table shows the rate of output associated with each of a number of input combinations. For example, given the production function (6-3), if 2 units of labor and 4 units of capital are used, maximum production is 283 units of output. Table 6-1 shows a production table for various input-rate combinations.

---

[1] Over time, improvements in production techniques, labor skills, and/or quality and type of capital equipment may result in an increase in the maximum level of output attainable from a given input rate combination. This phenomenon is referred to as technological change and is characteristic of production in most modern economies. During the post–World War II period, technological advance has resulted in an increase in output per unit of inputs averaging about 3 percent per year in the United States. However, in this chapter it will be assumed that the production period is sufficiently short that there is no technological change. This will allow attention to be focused on other more relevant principles.

There are three important relationships shown by the data in this production table. First, the table indicates that there are a variety of ways to produce a particular rate of output. For example, 245 units of output can be produced with any one of the following input combinations:

Combination	K	L
a	6	1
b	3	2
c	2	3
d	1	6

This implies that there is *substitutability* between the factors of production. The firm can use a capital-intensive production process characterized by combination *a*, a labor-intensive process such as *d*, or a process that uses a resource combination somewhere between these extremes, such as *b* or *c*.[2] The concept of substitution is important because it means that managers can change the mix of capital and labor in response to changes in the relative prices of these inputs.

Second, in Table 6-1, if input rates are doubled, the output rate also doubles. For example, maximum production with 1 unit of capital and 4 units of labor is 200. Doubling the input rates to $K = 2$, $L = 8$ results in the rate of output doubling to $Q = 400$. The relationship between output change and proportionate changes in both inputs is referred to as *returns to scale*. In Table 6-1, production is characterized by constant returns to scale. This means that if both input rates increase by the same factor (e.g., both input rates double), the rate of output also will double. In other production functions, output may increase more or less than in proportion to changes in inputs. Returns to scale have implications for the size of individual firms and the number of firms in an industry. For example, in producing a product, if output increases more than in proportion to increases in inputs, that industry is likely to have only a few large firms. The U.S. automobile industry is an example.

Finally, if the rate of one input is held constant while the other is increased, output increases but the successive increments become smaller. For example, from Table 6-1 it is seen that if the rate of capital input is held constant at 2 and labor is increased from $L = 1$ to $L = 6$, the successive increases in output are 59, 45, 38, 33, and 30. As discussed below, this relationship holds for virtually all production processes and is the basis for an important economic principle known as the law of diminishing marginal returns.

In Table 6-1, changes in output are shown only for discrete changes in the inputs. That is, only integer values of capital and labor are used. If the input rates of capital and labor can be varied continuously (i.e., any value of K and L such as $K = 6.24$ or $L = 3.15$ is possible), a production function traces a smooth continuous surface such as that shown in Figure 6-1. In this three-dimensional diagram, capital and labor are shown on the K,L axis and output is measured

[2] The term *capital-intensive* refers to a production system where the ratio of capital to labor is relatively high. In a *labor-intensive* case, the capital-to-labor ratio would be relatively low.

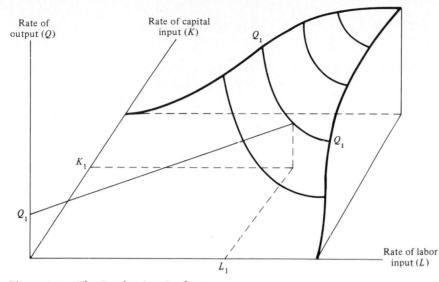

Figure 6-1. *The Production Surface.*

on the third axis, which is perpendicular to the K,L plane. The rate of output forthcoming from a given capital–labor combination is found by identifying the point representing an input combination (such as K_1 and L_1 in Figure 6-1) and drawing a perpendicular line up to the production surface. The height of this perpendicular line defines the rate of output Q_1 corresponding to the input combination K_1 and L_1. In general, any point on the production surface defines the maximum output possible from the input combination associated with that point.

Although the production table provides considerable information on production possibilities, it does not allow for the determination of the profit-maximizing rate of output or even the best way to produce some specified rate of output. For example, the production table shows four different combinations of capital and labor that will generate 245 units of output. Which is the best combination? Similarly, of the infinite number of possible output levels, which will result in maximum profit for the firm? The production function alone cannot answer these questions. As indicated previously, the production function is an engineering relationship and must be combined with data on the price of capital, labor, and output to determine optimal allocation of resources in the production process.

KEY CONCEPTS

- The production function is an engineering concept that defines the maximum rate of output forthcoming from specified input rates of capital and labor.
- The Cobb–Douglas or multiplicative form of the production function, $Q = AK^aL^b$, is widely used in economics.

Production with One Variable Input

The problem of optimal production will be approached in two ways. In this section it is assumed that the period of production is of such length that the rate of input of one factor of production is fixed. That is, the period is not long enough to change the input rate of that factor. The problem, then, is to determine the optimal rate of the variable input given the price of output and the price of the variable input. In the next section, both inputs will be allowed to vary, and the optimal rates of both variable inputs, capital, and labor, will be determined.

The period of time during which one of the inputs is fixed in amount is defined as the short run. In contrast, all inputs are variable in the long run. The period of time for the short run will vary among firms. For some firms, such as a child's lemonade stand, the short run may be just long enough to run home for another cardboard box to augment the capital stock. For an electric utility company, the short run may be a number of years—the period of time necessary to plan and build a new generation unit.

Generally, at any point in time, the firm is operating in the short run. That is, one or more factors are fixed in amount. But most firms are planning or considering changes in the entire scale of operation that would involve changes in all input rates. Thus it is said that the firm plans in the long run but operates in the short run. For example, an automobile manufacturer may have six plants with maximum production capacity of 1.5 million vehicles per year. To build a new plant may take several years. At any particular time, the firm operates the existing plants (i.e., makes short-run decisions), but based on current and projected demand conditions, plans to augment or reduce plant capacity in the future (i.e., a long-run decision).

The Product Functions

For a two-input production process, the total product of labor function (TP_L) is defined as the maximum rate of output forthcoming from combining varying rates of labor input with a fixed capital input. Denoting the fixed capital input as $\overline{K}$, the total product function is

$$TP_L = f(\overline{K}, L) \tag{6-4}$$

Similarly, the total product of capital function would be written as

$$TP_K = f(K, \overline{L}) \tag{6-5}$$

Two other product relations are relevant. First, marginal product (MP) is defined as the change in output per 1-unit change in the variable input. The marginal product of labor is

$$MP_L = \frac{\Delta Q}{\Delta L}$$

and the marginal product of capital is

$$MP_K = \frac{\Delta Q}{\Delta K}$$

For infinitesimally small changes in the variable input, the marginal product function is the first derivative of the production function with respect to the variable input. For the Cobb–Douglas production function,

$$Q = AK^a L^b$$

the marginal products are

$$MP_K = \frac{dQ}{dK} = aAK^{a-1}L^b$$

and

$$MP_L = \frac{dQ}{dL} = bAK^a L^{b-1}$$

Second, average product (AP) is total product per unit of the variable input, and is found by dividing the rate of output by the rate of the variable input, that is,

$$AP_L = \frac{TP_L}{L} \tag{6-6}$$

and

$$AP_K = \frac{TP_K}{K} \tag{6-7}$$

Consider a hypothetical production function. If capital is fixed at 2 units, the output forthcoming by combining various levels of labor with 2 units of capital (i.e., the total product of labor) is as shown in Table 6-2. The average and marginal product of labor are also shown in the table.

The total product function can be thought of as a cross section or vertical slice

Table 6-2. Total, Average, and Marginal Product of Labor for K = 2

Rate of Labor Input (L)	TP_L	AP_L	MP_L
0	0	—	
			20
1	20	20	
			30
2	50	25	
			40
3	90	30	
			30
4	120	30	
			20
5	140	28	
			10
6	150	25	
			5
7	155	22	
			−5
8	150	19	

of a three-dimension production surface such as that shown in Figure 6-1. Consider the production surface shown in Figure 6-2a, and suppose that the capital stock is fixed at K_1. The total product of labor function $f(K_1, L)$ is shown as the line starting at K_1 and extending through point a. Similarly, if the labor input is fixed at L_3, the total product of capital function is shown as the line beginning at L_3 and going through points a and b. Other total product functions are shown as the lines beginning at L_1, L_2, K_2, and K_3. If one of these cross sections was shown in a two-dimensional graph having output on the vertical axis and either labor or capital on the horizontal axis, it would appear as shown in Figure 6-2b.

Diminishing Marginal Returns

Consider a clothing manufacturer having a 5,000-square-foot building housing 100 sewing machines. Obviously, having only one or two workers in such a plant

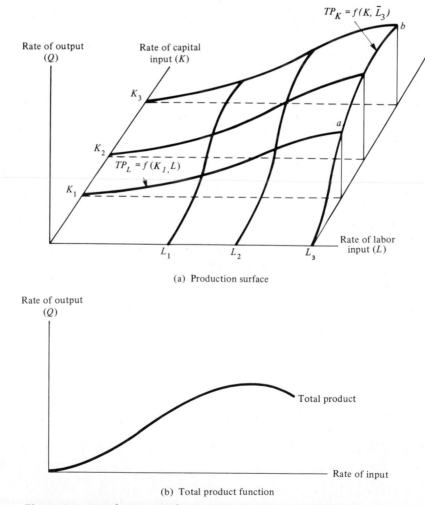

(a) Production surface

(b) Total product function

Figure 6-2. *Production Surface and Total Product Function.*

would be inefficient. As more labor is added, production should increase rapidly as more machines are placed in operation and better coordination achieved among workers and machines. As more labor is added, the efficiency gains will slow and output will increase but at a slower rate (i.e., marginal product will decline). Finally, a point may be reached where adding more labor will actually cause a reduction in total output, that is, where marginal product becomes negative. Because only so many workers can be put in a finite space, enough labor could be added so that the production process would come to a standstill, reducing output to zero.

This example illustrates an important economic principle known as the *law of diminishing marginal returns.* This law states that when increasing amounts of the variable input are combined with a fixed level of another input, a point will be reached where the marginal product of the variable input will decline. This law does not result from a theoretical argument but is based on actual observation of many production processes. Virtually all studies of production systems have verified the existence of diminishing marginal returns.

CASE STUDY

MARGINAL PRODUCT "DOWN" ON THE FARM

Many studies of production in agriculture have confirmed the law of diminishing marginal returns. One study investigated the marginal relationship between fertilizer application and production of corn. Based on a hypothesized production function for bushels of corn produced per acre (Q),

$$Q = f(\text{land, water, fertilizer})$$

the land and water inputs were held constant and fertilizer input varied on selected plots of land. As shown by the data in the following table, the marginal product of fertilizer increases for the first 2 units of fertilizer, then declines (but remains positive) for 3 through 6 units, and is negative after 7 units were applied. Thus diminishing marginal returns were observed beginning with the third unit of fertilizer.

Units of Fertilizer	Total Output (bushels of corn/acre)	Marginal Product
0	0	
1	32	32
2	73	41
3	110	37
4	129	19
5	136	7
6	140	4
7	137	−3
8	129	−8

Source: J. R. Webb, "Economics of Nitrogen Fertilizer in Corn," in *Selected Readings in Farm Management,* (Ames, Iowa: Iowa State University Press, 1975).

Relationships Among the Product Functions

A set of typical total, average, and marginal product functions for labor is shown in Figure 6-3. Total product begins at the origin, increases at an increasing rate over the range 0 to L_1, and then increases at a decreasing rate. Beyond L_3, total product actually declines. The explanation is as follows. Initially, the input proportions are inefficient—there is too much of the fixed factor, capital. As the labor input is increased from 0 to L_1, output rises more than in proportion to the increase in the labor input. That is, marginal product per unit of labor increases as a better balance of labor and capital inputs is achieved. As the labor input is increased beyond L_1, diminishing marginal returns set in and marginal product declines; the additional units of labor still result in an increase in output, but each increment to output is smaller. When the labor input has increased to L_3, total product reaches a maximum, and then, beyond L_3, the amount of labor has become excessive and slows the production process with the result that total product actually declines.

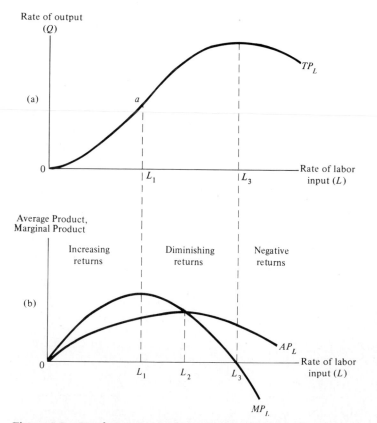

Figure 6-3. *Total, Average, and Marginal Product of Labor Curves.*

Several relationships among the total, average, and marginal product functions are important:

1. Marginal product reaches a maximum at L_1, which corresponds to an inflection point (a) on the total product function. At the inflection point, the total product function changes from increasing at an increasing rate to increasing at a decreasing rate.
2. Marginal product intersects average product at the maximum point on the average product curve. This occurs at labor input rate L_2. Whenever marginal product is above average product, the average is rising—it makes no difference whether marginal product is rising or falling. When marginal product is below average product, the average is falling. Therefore, the intersection must occur at the maximum point of average product in this case.
3. Marginal product becomes negative at labor input rate L_3. This corresponds to the point where the total product curve reaches a maximum.

KEY CONCEPTS

- The short run is that period of time for which the rate of input use of at least one factor of production is fixed. In the long run, the input rates of all factors are variable. The firm operates in the short run but plans in the long run.
- In the short run, total product is the set of outputs obtained by combining varying rates of one input with a fixed rate of the other input.
- Marginal product is the change in output associated with a 1-unit change in the variable input (i.e., $MP_L = \Delta Q/\Delta L$) or the first derivative of the production function with respect to the variable input (i.e., $MP_L = dQ/dL$).
- Average product is the rate of output produced per unit of the variable input employed (i.e., $AP_L = Q/L$).
- The law of diminishing marginal returns states that when increasing rates of a variable input are combined with a fixed rate of another input, a point will be reached where marginal product will decline.

Optimal Employment of a Productive Factor

The General Motors Corporation has a physical capital stock valued at about $20 billion. Consider this to be the fixed input for the firm. About 750,000 workers are employed to use this capital stock. What principles guide the decision about the level of employment? In general, to maximize profit, the firm should hire labor as long as the additional revenue associated with hiring another unit of labor exceeds the cost of employing that unit. For example, suppose that the marginal product of an additional worker would be 4 units of output and each unit of output is worth $10,000. Thus the additional revenue to the firm will be $40,000 if the worker is hired. If the additional cost of a worker (i.e., the wage rate) is $30,000, that worker should be hired because $10,000, the difference between additional revenue and additional cost, will be added to profit. However, if the wage rate is $45,000, the worker should not be hired because profit would be reduced by $5,000.

Formally stated, the basic principle is that additional units of the variable input should be hired until the marginal revenue product (MRP) of the last unit employed is equal to the cost of the input. The MRP is defined as marginal revenue times marginal product and represents the value of the extra unit of labor.[3] Thus labor is hired until MRP_L equals the wage rate (w):

$$MRP_L = w \qquad (6\text{-}8)$$

Similarly, additional units of capital should be hired until the MRP_K equals the price of capital (r). That is,

$$MRP_K = r \qquad (6\text{-}9)$$

Table 6-3 shows the total product, marginal product, total revenue, and marginal revenue product of labor for the production function $Q = 100\sqrt{KL}$. Recall that this production function was used to generate the production table shown as Table 6-1. Assume that the capital stock is fixed at 4 and the price of output is $2 per unit. In the example, MRP_L can be determined either by multiplying each MP_L entry by $2 (the output price per unit) or by finding the change in total revenue for each 1-unit increase in labor.

It is easily seen that the two methods are equivalent. Marginal revenue product is equal to marginal revenue multiplied by marginal product. That is,

$$MRP_L = MR \cdot MP_L$$

But

$$MR = \frac{\Delta TR}{\Delta Q}$$

Table 6-3. Total and Marginal Product, Total Revenue, and Marginal Revenue Product Functions for Labor for the Production Function $Q = 100\sqrt{KL}$ and $K = 4$

L	TP_L	MP_L	TR	MRP_L
0	0		0	
		200		$400
1	200		$ 400	
		83		166
2	283		566	
		63		126
3	346		692	
		54		108
4	400		800	
		47		94
5	447		894	
		43		86
6	490		980	
		39		78
7	529		1,058	
		36		72
8	565		1,130	

[3] In general, marginal revenue product is equal to $MR \cdot MP$. If price is constant, $P = MR$ and marginal revenue product is $P \cdot MP$.

and

$$MP_L = \frac{\Delta Q}{\Delta L}$$

Substituting, it is seen that

$$MRP_L = \frac{\Delta TR}{\Delta Q} \frac{\Delta Q}{\Delta L} = \frac{\Delta TR}{\Delta L}$$

Thus marginal revenue product can be written as the change in total revenue per 1-unit change in the rate of labor input.

The optimal rate of labor to be hired depends on the wage rate. If a unit of labor costs $108, then 4 units of labor are hired because the firm will hire labor only as long as MRP_L is greater than or equal to the wage rate. If the wage rate is lower, say $78 per unit of labor, 7 units will be hired. Clearly, if the wage rate is lower, more labor will be purchased.

The marginal revenue product is the labor demand function for the firm. That is, it indicates the amount of labor that will be hired at any wage rate. In graphing the labor demand curve, the vertical axis is measured in dollars, and the horizontal axis is measured as the rate of input use. The labor demand curve is downward sloping because of the law of diminishing marginal returns.

The MRP_L curve corresponding to Table 6-3 is shown in Figure 6-4. The horizontal line at $w = \$78$ in the figure can be thought of as the supply function for labor facing the firm. It implies that the firm can hire all the labor it wants at $78 per unit. The optimum quantity of labor is determined by finding the intersection of the demand and supply functions, that is, the point where $MRP_L = w$. The figure shows that 7 units of labor should be hired. If the wage rate increased to $108 (shown by the $w = 108$ line in Figure 6-4), the quantity of labor demanded by the firm would fall to 4 units. If the wage rate were lower than $78, more labor would be hired as the firm moved down the MRP_L curve.

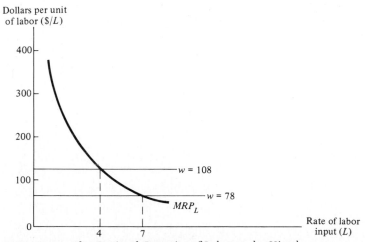

Figure 6-4. *The Optimal Quantity of Labor to be Hired.*

KEY CONCEPTS

- Marginal revenue product (MRP) is found by multiplying the marginal product function by marginal revenue (i.e., $MRP = MR \cdot MP$).
- The marginal revenue product function for a productive factor is the demand curve for that factor.
- Additional units of a productive factor should be hired until the value of the marginal product of that input is equal to the price of that input.

EXAMPLE

THE OPTIMAL LABOR INPUT

Suppose that a firm has the production function

$$Q = 2\sqrt{KL}$$

with marginal product functions for labor and capital given by

$$MP_L = \frac{dQ}{dL} = \sqrt{\frac{K}{L}}$$

and

$$MP_K = \frac{dQ}{dK} = \sqrt{\frac{L}{K}}$$

respectively. Assume that the capital stock is fixed at 9 units (i.e., $K = 9$). If the price of output (P) is \$6 per unit, and the wage rate (w) is \$2 per unit, determine the optimal or profit-maximizing rate of labor to be hired. What labor input rate is optimal if the wage rate increased to \$3 per unit?

Solution:

First, determine the MRP_L, assuming that K is fixed at 9 (note that $P = MR$):

$$MRP_L = P \cdot MP_L = P\sqrt{\frac{K}{L}} = 6\left(\sqrt{\frac{9}{L}}\right) = \frac{18}{\sqrt{L}}$$

Now, equate the MRP_L function and the wage rate and solve for L. That is,

$$MRP_L = w$$

but

$$MRP_L = \frac{18}{\sqrt{L}}$$

so

$$\frac{18}{\sqrt{L}} = 2$$

Thus

$$L = 81$$

Therefore, 81 units of labor should be employed.

If the wage rate increases to \$3 per unit of labor, the profit-maximizing condition $MRP_L = w$ would be

$$\frac{18}{\sqrt{L}} = 3$$

$$L = 36$$

This example shows that as the price of labor increases, the firm demands less labor. That is, the labor demand curve is downward sloping.

Production with Two Variable Inputs

If both capital and labor inputs are variable, a different set of analytical techniques must be applied to determine optimal input rates. There are three ways the firm may approach the problem of efficient resource allocation in production. They are: (1) maximize production for a given dollar outlay on labor and capital, (2) minimize the dollar outlay on labor and capital inputs necessary to produce a specified rate of output, or (3) produce that output rate that will maximize profit.

The first two problems are called *constrained optimization problems*. In problem 1 the constraint is a fixed dollar outlay for capital and labor. In problem 2 the constraint is a specified level of output that must be produced. However, in problem 3 the firm seeks that output level that will maximize profit; there is no constraint on either the budget available for production or the output level to be produced.

In this section the approach to solving each of these problems is presented. A standard managerial economics technique using the concept of production isoquants and production isocosts is used to determine efficient input rate combinations for given production rates.

The Production Isoquant

In Figure 6-5, the three-dimensional production surface for the production function $Q = 100\sqrt{KL}$ is shown. Think of an output rate, say, $Q_1 = 490$, being specified and a "horizontal slice" cut through the production surface at that height. By cutting through the surface horizontally, the rate of output is held constant. This slice, denoted as Q_1Q_1, is a smooth curve that defines all combinations of capital and labor that yield a maximum production rate of 490. Two points on that isoquant, a and b, are used to show how the capital and labor input combinations are determined. Starting at point a, draw a perpendicular line from a

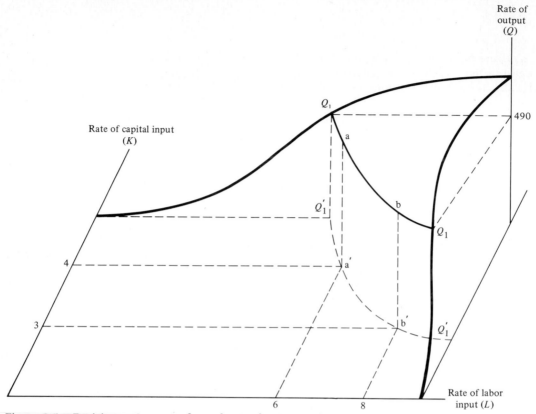

Figure 6-5. *Deriving an Isoquant from the Production Surface.*

to point a' on the capital–labor plane (i.e., the base of the diagram). Point a' denotes a capital input of 4 and labor input of 6. Repeating that process at b yields another capital–labor combination (3, 8) that also generates 490 units of output. If this process was repeated many times, it would trace out the smooth curve shown as the dashed curve $Q_1'Q_1'$ in the capital–labor plane. That curve is shown as the $Q = 490$ isoquant in the two-dimensional diagram in Figure 6-6.

Formally, an isoquant is the set of all combinations of capital and labor that yield a given output level. If fractional input units are allowed, there are an infinite number of points on any isoquant. Further, there is an isoquant through every point in the capital–labor space. Equivalently, there is an output rate corresponding to every combination of input rates. This implies that there are an infinite number of isoquants. For example, in addition to the isoquant for 490 units of output, isoquants for $Q = 200$ and $Q = 346$ are shown in Figure 6-6.

In general, isoquants are determined in the following way. First, a rate of output, say Q_o, is specified. Hence the production function can be written as

$$Q_o = f(K, L) \qquad (6\text{-}10)$$

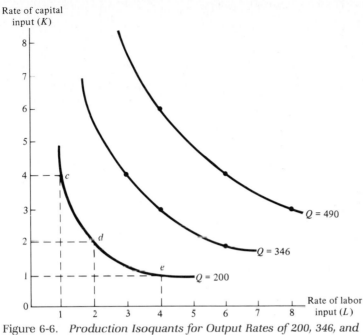

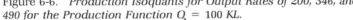

Figure 6-6. *Production Isoquants for Output Rates of 200, 346, and 490 for the Production Function Q = 100 KL.*

Those combinations of K and L that satisfy this equation define the isoquant for output rate Q_o.

The slope of the isoquant shows the rate at which one input can be substituted for the other such that the level of output remains constant. This slope is referred to as the *marginal rate of technical substitution* (*MRTS*). For example, consider points c, d, and e on the 200-unit isoquant in Figure 6-6. Moving from point c to d involves substituting 1 additional unit of labor for 2 units of capital. That is, the marginal rate of substitution of labor for capital averages 1 : 2 over the range c to d. From point d to point e, it takes 2 units of labor to replace 1 unit of capital in order to maintain output at the 200 level. Thus the marginal rate of substitution of labor for capital is 2 : 1 over the range d to e.

If the production process is such that the two inputs are perfect substitutes, the isoquant is a straight line, as shown in Figure 6-7a. That is, the rate of substitution is the same at all points on the isoquant. For example, there may be a production process where 2 units of labor will always substitute for 1 unit of capital (or vice versa). Examples of inputs that are perfectly substitutable might include natural gas, fuel oil, and electricity for firing boilers.

The L-shaped isoquant in Figure 6-7b describes a production process where there is no substitutability between inputs. In this example, the capital/labor input ratio is fixed at 1 : 2. Adding additional labor without adding more capital (or adding more capital to a fixed labor input) will neither increase nor decrease output. In such a production system the inputs are said to have zero substitut-

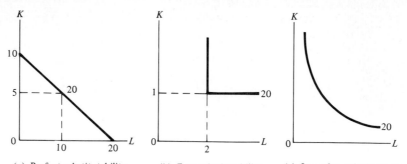

(a) Perfect substitutability   (b) Zero substitutability   (c) Imperfect substitutability

Figure 6-7.   *Production Isoquants With Differing Substitutability Between Inputs.*

ability. For example, the production of some drugs requires specific amounts of each ingredient. There is no way to substitute more of one for less of another. Similarly, in the manufacturing of automobiles, certain inputs are required in fixed amounts per car (e.g., one frame, one body, four wheels, etc.).

However, perfect and zero substitutability among inputs are unusual cases. For most production functions, the isoquant is a smooth curve that is convex to the origin as shown in Figure 6-7c. The shape of this isoquant implies that inputs are imperfectly substitutable, and the rate of substitution declines as one input is substituted for another. For example, consider a factory having many machines but few workers. Adding an additional worker and reducing the number of machines may result in a much more efficient production system—that is, a relatively large increase in output would be obtained by adding that worker. But as more labor is added and machines removed, those efficiency gains fall. Thus it takes more and more workers to replace fewer machines.

The slope of an isoquant (i.e., the *MRTS*) is equal to the negative of the ratio of the marginal products, that is,

$$MRTS = -\frac{MP_L}{MP_K} \qquad (6\text{-}11)$$

This relationship can be explained in the following way. Note that if the rate of labor input is varied by ΔL, the change in output (ΔQ_L) will equal the marginal product of labor times the change in labor (ΔL), or

$$\Delta Q_L = MP_L \, \Delta L$$

Similarly, if the rate of capital input is changed by ΔK, the rate of output will change by

$$\Delta Q_K = MP_K \, \Delta K$$

As movements along an isoquant involve changing capital and labor in such a way that output is unchanged, it must be that the increase in output associated with an increase in one input, say labor, is equal to the decrease in output associated with the decrease in the capital input. That is,

$$\Delta Q_L = -\Delta Q_K$$

and substituting $MP_L \, \Delta L$ for ΔQ_L and $MP_K \, \Delta K$ for ΔQK yields

$$MP_L \, \Delta L = -MP_K \, \Delta K$$

These terms can be rearranged to read

$$\frac{\Delta K}{\Delta L} = -\frac{MP_L}{MP_K}$$

But $\Delta K/\Delta L$ is the slope of the isoquant. Thus it is seen that the slope is the negative of the ratio of the marginal products. This principle will be useful in determining the optimal rates of capital and labor to be hired when both inputs are variable.

KEY CONCEPTS

- An isoquant shows all combinations of capital and labor input rates that will produce a specified rate of output.
- The slope of an isoquant is the marginal rate of technical substitution or the rate that one input can be substituted for another so that a given rate of output is maintained.
- In general, the marginal rate of substitution diminishes as more of one input and less of another are combined.
- The marginal rate of technical substitution is equal to the negative of the ratio of the marginal products of the two inputs. That is, $MRTS = -(MP_L/MP_K)$.

The Production Isocost

The isoquant is a physical relationship that denotes different ways to produce a given rate of output. The next step toward determining the optimal combination of capital and labor is to add information on the cost of those inputs. This cost information is introduced by a function called a production isocost.

Given the prices of capital (r) and labor (w), the total expenditure (C) on capital and labor inputs is

$$C = rK + wL \tag{6-12}$$

For example, if $r = 3$ and $w - 2$, the combination of 10 units of capital and 5 units of labor will cost \$40. That is,

$$40 = 3(10) + 2(5)$$

Now, for any given cost, C_0, the isocost defines all combinations of capital and labor inputs that can be purchased for C_0.

Rewrite equation (6-12) by solving for K as a function of L,

$$K = \frac{C_0}{r} - \frac{w}{r}L \qquad (6\text{-}13)$$

Equation (6-13) is an equation for a straight line where C_0/r is the vertical intercept and $-w/r$ is the slope. The ratio $-w/r$ is the rate that labor can be exchanged for capital in the market. For example, if $w = 2$ and $r = 3$, 1 unit of capital can be traded for 1.5 units of labor or 1 unit of labor can be traded for $\frac{2}{3}$ unit of capital.

Using the data from the above example ($w = 2, r = 3$, and $C = 40$), the isocost line becomes

$$40 = 3K + 2L$$

or

$$K = \frac{40}{3} - \frac{2}{3}L$$

$$= 13.33 - \frac{2}{3}L$$

This information is shown as the $40 isocost line in Figure 6-8. Note the intercept terms on both the capital and labor axis. If all of the $40 budget is spent on labor, 20 units can be purchased. Conversely, if the budget is spent entirely on capital, 13.3 units can be obtained.

If the budget constraint is increased to, say, $50, the equation for the isocost equation becomes

$$50 = 3K + 2L$$

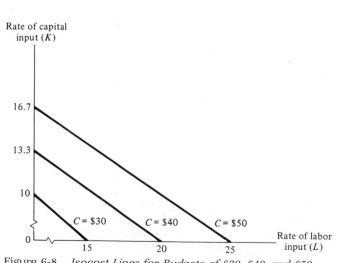

Figure 6-8.   *Isocost Lines for Budgets of $30, $40, and $50.*

or

$$K = \frac{50}{3} - \frac{2}{3}L$$

Note that the intercept term on the capital axis has increased but the slope $(-\frac{2}{3})$ remains the same because the input prices are unchanged. That is, the isocost has shifted outward but remains parallel to the $40 isocost. The capital and labor intercept (K, L) are now $(16.7, 0)$ and $(0, 25)$. Similarly, a decrease in the budget to, say, $30 causes a parallel shift in the function toward the origin. These three isocost lines ($30, $40, and $50) are shown in Figure 6-8.

Now, consider how the isocost function shifts if an input price changes instead of the budget amount. Initially, assume that $C_0 = 40$, $w = 5$, and that r is variable. Thus the equation for the isocost is

$$K = \frac{40}{r} - \frac{5}{r}L$$

If r increases from, say, 2 to 3, the equation for the isocost changes from

$$K = \frac{40}{2} - \frac{5}{2}L$$

to

$$K = \frac{40}{3} - \frac{5}{3}L$$

These isocosts are shown in Figure 6-9a. Note that both the vertical (capital) intercept and the slope of the isocost function have changed. But the horizontal or labor intercept is unchanged. That intercept is determined by the ratio C_0/w, which is not influenced by a change in the price of capital. Thus, as r changes, the isocost pivots about the point $(40/5, 0)$, which is the horizontal intercept.

Conversely, if the price of capital is held constant at 2 and the price of labor changes from, say, 3 to 5, the $40 isocost function will pivot about the point $(0, 20)$ on the vertical axis, as shown in Figure 6-9b.

KEY CONCEPTS

- The isocost function is the set of all combinations of capital and labor that can be purchased for a specified total cost.
- Changes in the budget amount, C_0, cause the isocost line to shift in a parallel manner. Changes in either the price of labor or capital cause both the slope and one intercept of the isocost function to change.

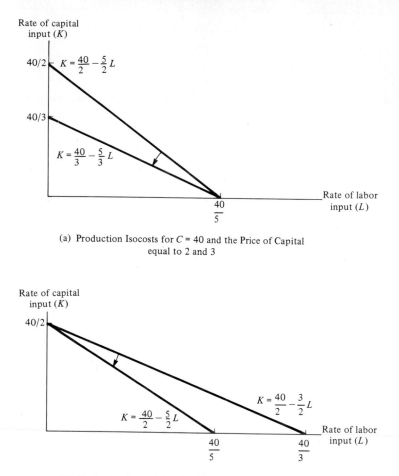

(a) Production Isocosts for $C = 40$ and the Price of Capital equal to 2 and 3

(b) Production Isocosts for $C = 40$ and the Price of Labor equal to 3 and 5

Figure 6-9. *Production Isocosts for $C = 40$ for Varying Prices of Capital and Labor.*

Optimal Employment of Two Inputs

When both capital and labor are variable, the determination of the optimal input rates of capital and labor requires that the technical information from the production function (i.e., the isoquants) be combined with the market data on input prices (i.e., the isocost functions).

Consider the problem of minimizing the cost of a given rate of output. Specifically, suppose that the firm's objective is to produce ten units of output at minimum cost. To help analyze this problem, two production isoquants are shown in Figure 6-10. The infinite number of capital–labor combinations that yield an output of 10 are indicated by the 10-unit isoquant. Three of these combinations are indicated by points *a, b,* and *c*. Points *a* and *c* are on the $150

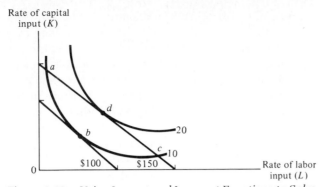

Figure 6-10. *Using Isocost and Isoquant Functions to Solve the Production Problem.*

isocost and *b* is on the $100 isocost. Of these, clearly *b* is the best of the three in the sense of being the lowest cost. In fact, *b* is the absolute minimum cost combination of capital and labor. At point *b*, the 10-unit isoquant is tangent to the $100 isocost line. Note that all other input combinations shown on the 10-unit isoquant would correspond to higher isocost curves and would cost more than $100. That is, any other capital–labor combination on the 10-unit isoquant will be on a higher isocost line.

At the tangency of the 10-unit isoquant and the $100 isocost, the slopes of the two functions are equal. Thus the marginal rate of technical substitution (i.e., the slope of the isoquant) equals the price of labor divided by the price of capital. That is,

$$MRTS = \frac{w}{r} \qquad (6\text{-}14)$$

Equation (6-14) is a necessary condition for efficient production. If this equality does not hold such as at points *a* and *c*, there is some other combination of capital and labor inputs that will reduce the cost of producing 10 units of output. Equivalently, there is a way to move along the 10-unit isoquant to a lower isocost.

Consider a different production problem. Suppose that the objective is to maximize output given a budget constraint of $150. Now the choice of input combinations is limited to points on the $150 isocost function. Three points are shown on that isocost line, *a*, *d*, and *c*. These all satisfy the budget constraint, but they are on different isoquants. For example, output at points *a* and *c* is 10 units, but at point *d* output is 20 units. Clearly, *d* is the preferred point among these three because a higher rate of output is produced. In fact, *d* is the best of all points on the $150 isocost. No other combination of capital and labor that costs $150 will yield as much output. Again, at that optimal point, the isoquant is tangent to the isocost. Hence the same efficiency condition ($MRTS = w/r$) applies. That is, the marginal rate of technical substitution in production must equal the rate of exchange of labor for capital in the market.

Regardless of the production objective, efficient production requires that the isoquant be tangent to the isocost function. If the problem is to maximize output subject to a given cost, the solution is found by moving along the specified isocost until the tangency is found. If the problem is to minimize cost subject to an output constraint, the solution is found by moving along the specified isoquant until the tangency is found. The same efficiency rule holds in both problems. For example, consider point d in Figure 6-10. That point can be thought of either as the minimum cost capital–labor combination for producing 20 units of output or as the point of maximum output obtainable on a $150 budget.

These principles can be used to test for efficient resource allocation in production. It has been shown that the slope of the isocost is the negative of the ratio of the wage rate and price of capital (i.e., $-w/r$) and that the slope of the isoquant is the negative of the ratio of the marginal product of labor to that of capital (i.e., $-MP_L/MP_K$). Further, it has been shown that at a point of tangency, the slopes of both the isocost and isoquant are equal. Thus

$$-\frac{MP_L}{MP_K} = -\frac{w}{r}$$

or

$$\frac{MP_L}{MP_K} = \frac{w}{r}$$

This condition must be met for efficient production.

Rewriting this efficiency condition as

$$\frac{MP_L}{w} = \frac{MP_K}{r} \tag{6-15}$$

suggests an important principle. For an input combination to be efficient, the marginal product per dollar of input cost must be the same for both inputs. For example, consider the following inefficient situation. Assume that both w and r are equal to 2 but that the marginal product of labor is 10 compared to 8 for capital. Thus we have

$$\frac{10}{2} > \frac{8}{2}$$

This cannot be an efficient input combination. The firm is getting more output per dollar for funds spent on labor than on capital. But because the input prices are the same, labor can be traded for capital on a one-to-one basis. If 1 unit of capital is sold to obtain 1 unit of labor, the reduction of capital by 1 unit causes output to fall by 8, but increasing the labor input by 1 unit will increase output by 10. Thus the substitution of labor for capital would result in a net increase of 2 units of output at no additional cost.

The inefficient combination corresponds to a point such as a in Figure 6-10. At that point the ratio of capital to labor is too high. The profit-maximizing firm will substitute labor for capital by moving down the isocost line. Conversely, at a point such as c in Figure 6-10, the reverse is true—there is too much labor, and the inequality,

$$\frac{MP_L}{w} < \frac{MP_K}{r}$$

will hold. That is, the firm generates more output per dollar spent on capital than from dollars spent on labor. Thus the firm should substitute capital for labor.

Suppose that the firm is producing at the inefficient point c in Figure 6-10. If the problem is to minimize the cost of producing a given rate of output, the firm would move from point c along the 10-unit isoquant to b, thereby reducing cost by $50 while maintaining the rate of production at 10 units. Alternatively, if the firm is maximizing output subject to a $150 cost constraint, it would move from c along the $150 isocost to point d, where that isocost is tangent to the 20-unit isoquant. Note that in the latter case, output would increase from 10 to 20 at no additional cost.

Profit Maximization

The efficiency condition is a necessary but not sufficient for profit maximization. There are many points of tangency between isocosts and isoquants. For example, both points b and d in Figure 6-10 are efficient resource combinations. However, profits probably will be different at each point. Thus the problem is to determine that one point among the many efficient points that results in the largest profit. That the efficiency condition is necessary for maximum profit is obvious. If the firm is not operating at an efficient point, there will be some way to reduce the cost of that level of output and thereby increase profit. Thus only the efficient points defined by the tangencies of isocost and isoquant functions need to be considered.

To maximize profit, inputs must be hired until the marginal revenue product equals the price of the input for both capital and labor. That is, the conditions for profit maximization are that

$$MRP_K = r \qquad \qquad (6\text{-}16)$$

and

$$MRP_L = w \qquad \qquad (6\text{-}17)$$

Marginal revenue product measures the additional dollars of revenue added by using 1 more unit of input. As long as MRP is greater than the cost of the input, profit can be increased by adding more of that input. That is, if an additional unit of an input adds more to revenue than that input cost, profits will increase, and those profits will increase until marginal revenue product equals the input price.

These conditions for a profit maximization imply that the condition for efficient production (i.e., $MP_L/P_L = MP_K/P_K$) will be met. That is,

$$MRP_K = r$$

and

$$MRP_L = w$$

can be rewritten as

$$P \cdot MP_L = w \qquad\qquad (6\text{-}18)$$

and

$$P \cdot MP_K = r \qquad\qquad (6\text{-}19)$$

Dividing equation (6-18) by (6-19) yields

$$\frac{MP_L}{MP_K} = \frac{w}{r}$$

and rewriting results in the efficiency condition

$$\frac{MP_L}{w} = \frac{MP_K}{r}$$

KEY CONCEPTS

• Efficient production requires that the isoquant function be tangent to the isocost function. At those points the marginal product per dollar of input cost is equal for both inputs. That is,

$$\frac{MP_L}{w} = \frac{MP_K}{r}$$

• If the condition for efficient production is not met, there is some way to substitute one input for the other that will result in an increase in production at no change in total cost.
• Profit maximization requires that inputs be hired until $MRP_K = r$ and $MRP_L = w$.

Changes in Input Prices

If the price of one input, say labor, increases, the firm will adjust the input mix by substituting capital for labor. If the price of labor declines, thus making labor relatively less expensive, labor will be substituted for capital. In general, if the relative prices of inputs change, managers will respond by substituting the input that has become relatively less expensive for the input that has become relatively more expensive.

The isoquant–isocost framework can be used to demonstrate this principle. Consider Figure 6-11. Suppose the firm currently is operating at point a where

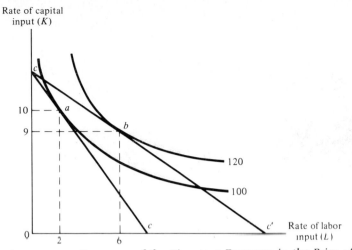

Figure 6-11. *Response of the Firm to a Decrease in the Price of Labor.*

100 units of output are produced using the resource combination (K = 10, L = 2). This is an efficient resource mix because the 100-unit isoquant is tangent to the isocost line cc. Assume that the firm's goal is to maximize production subject to a cost constraint (i.e., the firm is limited to resource combinations on a given isocost function).

Now, assume that the price of labor falls while the price of capital remains unchanged (i.e., labor has become relatively less expensive). The isocost pivots to the right from cc to the isocost cc'. The reduction in the price of labor means that the firm is able to increase the rate of production. Hence the firm moves from point a to point b, which is a new efficient resource combination. That is, the new isocost is tangent to the 120-unit isoquant at point b. Now 9 units of capital and 6 units of labor are employed. Note that at point a, the efficient ratio of capital to labor was 5 : 1. Now the efficient ratio of the two inputs is 3 : 2. The reduction in the price of labor has caused the firm to substitute that relatively less expensive input for capital.

CASE STUDY

INPUT SUBSTITUTION IN RESPONSE TO HIGHER ENERGY PRICES

The decade of the 1970s was one of rapidly rising prices for virtually all energy prices. The price of gasoline, fuel oil, and natural gas increased much more rapidly than the prices of most other products and services. For example, during the period 1971–1980, the real price (i.e., the price adjusted for overall inflation) of crude oil, natural gas, and coal increased 240 percent, 347 percent, and 113 percent, respectively.

Because energy is an important input in many production systems, principles of managerial economics would predict that firms would have substituted other

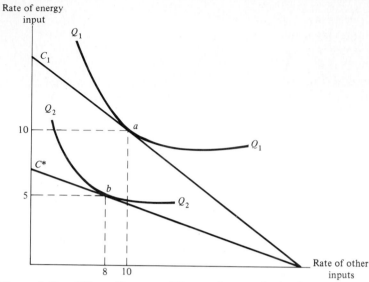

Figure 6-12.   *Effect of Increased Energy Cost on Optimal Input Rates.*

inputs for the relatively more expensive energy products. In Figure 6-12, the input of energy is measured on the vertical axis, and a composite measure of other inputs is measured on the horizontal axis. Assume that before the increase in energy prices, a hypothetical firm is producing at point a, where the Q_1 isoquant is tangent to the C_1 isocost. The optimal input ratio is 10 : 10, or 1 unit of energy for every unit of the "other input."

If the price of energy increased, the isocost would pivot downward from C_1 to C^*. The firm now will operate at point b, where the ratio of energy to other inputs is 5 : 8. Thus the firm has substituted other inputs for energy.

As shown in the following table, producers in the United States did reduce their dependence on energy by substituting other inputs for energy. As measured by energy consumption (thousand Btu) per dollar of value added, dependence on this input was reduced significantly. Even an energy-producing sector, petroleum refining, conserved on its use of energy by using relatively more of other inputs.

Energy Consumption per Dollar of Value Added in Selected Industries

Year	All Manufacturing	Paper	Organic Chemicals	Petroleum Refining	Steel	Aluminum
1971	52.5	316.2	277.9	631.4	314.7	418.5
1977	42.3	308.7	193.9	573.4	282.7	379.9
Percent change	−19.4	−2.4	−30.2	−9.2	−10.2	−9.2

Source: Bureau of the Census, U.S. Department of Commerce, *Statistical Abstract of the United States, 1981*, (Washington, D.C.: U.S. Government Printing Office, 1981).

The Expansion Path

Consider the system of isoquants and isocosts shown in Figure 6-13. Suppose that a firm is producing 20 units of output using 12 units of capital and 10 units of labor (i.e., point *a*) at a cost of $44. If output is to be increased, how much capital and labor will be hired? That is, how will the firm expand production? Clearly, it will move to point *b* if 30 units are to be produced and then to point *c* if 35 units of output are to be produced. In general, the firm expands by moving from one tangency or efficient production point to another. These efficient points represent the expansion path. An expansion path is formally defined as the set of combinations of capital and labor that meet the efficiency condition $MP_L/w = MP_K/r$. Because both inputs are variable, the expansion path is clearly a long-run concept.

An equation for the expansion path can be determined by first substituting the marginal product function and input prices into the efficiency condition, and then by solving for capital as a function of labor. For example, suppose that the production function is of the form $Q = 100\sqrt{KL}$. The corresponding marginal product functions are

$$MP_L = \frac{dQ}{dL} = 50\sqrt{\frac{K}{L}}$$

and

$$MP_K = \frac{dQ}{dK} = 50\sqrt{\frac{L}{K}}.$$

Substituting these marginal product equations in the efficiency condition $\left(\frac{MP_L}{MP_K} = \frac{w}{r}\right)$ yields

$$\frac{50\sqrt{K/L}}{50\sqrt{L/K}} = \frac{w}{r}.$$

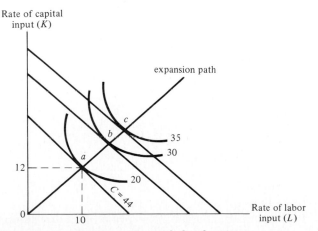

Figure 6-13. *The Expansion Path for the Firm.*

Solving for K gives:

$$K = (w/r)L. \qquad (6\text{-}20)$$

This expression is the equation for the expansion path for the production function $Q = 100\sqrt{KL}$. If w and r are known, equation (6-20) defines the efficient combination of capital and labor for producing any rate of output. That is, it is an equation for an expansion path such as that shown in Figure 6.13. For example, if $w = 2$ and $r = 1$, the expansion path defined by equation (6-20) would be

$$K = 2L.$$

If the expansion path is known, then knowing the isoquant-isocost system is not necessary to determine efficient production points. The firm will only produce at those points on the expansion path.

The expansion path indicates optimal input combinations, but it does not indicate the specific rate of output associated with that rate of input use. The output rate is determined by substituting the equation for the expansion path into the original production function. In the example, substituting the equation for the expansion path, $K = (w/r)L$, into the production function, $Q = 100\sqrt{KL}$, gives

$$Q = 100\sqrt{(w/r)L \cdot L},$$

or

$$Q = 100L\sqrt{w/r}. \qquad (6\text{-}21)$$

The two equations (6-20) and (6-21) have three unknowns: K, L, and Q. [Recall that the prices of labor (w) and capital (r) are assumed to be known.] If the value of K, L, or Q is given, the efficient rate of the other two variables can be calculated.

Consider the problem of determining the efficient input combination for producing 1,000 units of output if $w = 4$ and $r = 2$. The steps are as follows. First, substitute $Q = 1,000$ into equation (6-21) and solve for L. Thus

$$1,000 = 100L\sqrt{\frac{4}{2}}$$
$$\boxed{L = 7.07}$$

Then, substitute $L = 7.07$ into (6-20), the equation for the expansion path, to find K.

$$K = \left(\frac{4}{2}\right)7.07$$
$$\boxed{K = 14.14}$$

Thus the input combination ($K = 14.14$, $L = 7.07$) is the most efficient way to produce 1,000 units of output.

How would the input mix change if the price of capital increased to $r = 4$

and the firm still wanted to produce 1,000 units of output? Again, substitute $Q = 1,000$ into equation (6-21) and solve for L:

$$1,000 = 100L\sqrt{\frac{4}{4}}$$

$$\boxed{L = 10}$$

Now substitute $L = 10$ into equation (6-20) and solve for K:

$$K = \left(\frac{4}{4}\right)L$$

$$\boxed{K = 10}$$

The new efficient combination is $(K = 10, L = 10)$. The firm responded to the higher price of capital by substituting labor for capital.

KEY CONCEPTS

- If the price of one or both inputs change, the firm will respond by substituting the input that has become relatively less expensive for the other input.
- The firm expands production by moving from one efficient production point (where the isoquant and isocost functions are tangent) to another. These efficient points define the firm's expansion path.
- By using the production function and the production efficiency condition together, the optimal level of capital and labor to be used to produce a given level of output can be determined.

Returns to Scale

Empirical studies suggest that for a telephone company, a 1 percent increase in both the labor and capital inputs is associated with an output increase of about 2 percent (Eldor et al., 1981). That is, the percentage increase in output is about twice the percentage increase in the inputs. This relationship between a proportionate change in both inputs and the resultant change in output is the basis for an important principle of managerial economics.

A given rate of input of capital and labor defines the scale of production. Proportionate changes in both inputs result in a change in that scale. The term "returns to scale" refers to the magnitude of the change in the rate of output relative to the change in scale. For example, given the production function

$$Q = 100\sqrt{KL}$$

if both capital and labor are 10, output will be 1,000. A doubling of both inputs to 20 will result in a doubling of output to 2,000. This proportionate response of output to change in inputs is known as *constant returns to scale*.

In general, there is no reason to expect that output will always change in proportion to the change in inputs. As in the telephone company example above, output might increase more than in proportion (increasing returns to scale) or less than in proportion (decreasing returns to scale). Returns to scale are formally classified as follows. Given the general production function

$$Q = f(K, L) \qquad (6\text{-}22)$$

if both inputs are changed by some factor λ, output will change by a factor h. That is,

$$hQ = f(\lambda K, \lambda L) \qquad (6\text{-}23)$$

If $h = \lambda$, the production function is said to be characterized by constant returns to scale because the change in output is proportional to the change in both inputs. If $h < \lambda$, there are decreasing returns to scale, and if $h > \lambda$, returns to scale are increasing.

There is a simple way to test for constant, decreasing, or increasing returns to scale. Solve the production function (i.e., determine the rate of output) for one set of input values, double both inputs and again solve for output. If output doubled, the production function is characterized by constant returns to scale over that range of output. If output changed by less than twice the initial rate, decreasing returns to scale apply. Finally, if output more than doubled, the function exhibits increasing returns to scale.[4]

Returns to scale can also be depicted using the isoquant map. Figure 6-14 shows three sets of isoquants, each generated by different production functions. Figure 6-14a shows a proportionate change in both inputs resulting in an equi-proportionate change in output. For example, a doubling of the capital and labor input rates (K, L) from $(1, 1)$ to $(2, 2)$ results in output doubling from $Q = 10$ to $Q = 20$. Similarly, a 50 percent increase in inputs from $(2, 2)$ to $(3, 3)$ increases output by 50 percent from $Q = 20$ to $Q = 30$.

Now consider the isoquant system in Figure 6-14b. Each 10-unit increase in the rate of output requires a more-than-proportionate increase in inputs. The production function giving rise to these isoquants exhibits decreasing returns to scale. For example, the input combination (K, L) of $(1, 1)$ yields 10 units of output, whereas a tripling of both inputs to $(3, 3)$ results in the output rate only doubling to $Q = 20$. Thus returns to scale are decreasing. Note that the isoquants that represent equal 5-unit output changes become farther apart as output increases. This shows the more-than-proportionate increase in inputs required to produce a constant output change.

Finally, Figure 6-14c depicts an isoquant map for a production function characterized by increasing returns to scale. A doubling of the rate of both inputs from $(1, 1)$ to $(2, 2)$ results in a tripling of output from $Q = 10$ to $Q = 30$. Note that the isoquants represent equal (10-unit) changes in output but are progres-

---

[4] There are production functions that are characteried by increasing returns over part of the output range and decreasing returns over another part of the range. For these functions, this simple technique will test for the nature of returns to scale only for that part of the output range that is evaluated.

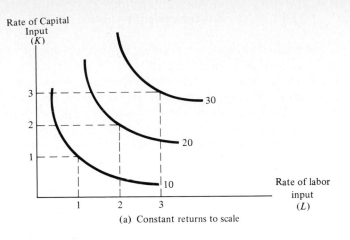

(a) Constant returns to scale

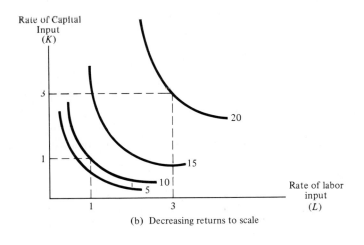

(b) Decreasing returns to scale

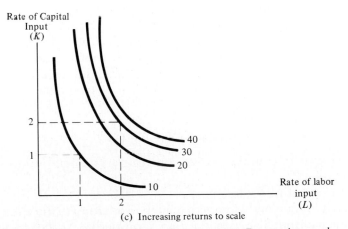

(c) Increasing returns to scale

Figure 6-14. *Isoquant Maps, For Constant, Decreasing, and Increasing Returns to Scale.*

sively closer together, showing that smaller input increments are needed to produce each additional 10 units of output.

There are several reasons why increasing returns to scale occur. First, technologies that are cost-effective at high levels of production may actually increase unit costs at lower levels of output. For example, the million-dollar machinery used for cutting and stamping auto bodies by General Motors would make little sense for the backyard car manufacturer. Geometric relations are another factor causing decreasing average costs. A gas company using 12-inch pipe has 3 cubic inches of pipe volume per square inch of pipe surface, while a firm with output sufficient to justify 24-inch pipe will have 6 cubic inches of volume per square inch of surface. The reduced cost per unit of pipe volume occurs because the materials requirement varies with the diameter of the pipe, while the volume varies with the square of the radius of the pipe. Thus the larger firm using bigger pipelines will have lower unit costs.

Two other causes of increasing returns are specialization of labor and inventory economies. As a firm becomes larger, the demand for employee expertise in specific areas grows. Instead of being generalists, workers can concentrate on learning all the aspects of particular segments of the production process. Size also affects unit costs, because larger firms may not have to increase inventories or replacement parts proportionately with size. For example, suppose that a small firm uses a machine that is critical to the firm's operations. Let the probability that the machine will break down during a month be 10 percent. If a replacement is not readily obtainable from a nearby supplier, the firm may be forced to keep a backup on the premises. Suppose that a larger firm uses five of the same machines, each with a 10 percent probability of malfunctioning. The probability that two of those machines will break down in a month is 0.1×0.1, or 1 percent. The likelihood that the five machines will become inoperative is 0.1^5, which is essentially zero. Thus whereas the small firm may be required to have one backup machine for each operating machine, the larger firm may have a high degree of reliability with a much lower ratio of backup to operating machines and hence a lower per unit cost.

Decreasing returns to scale may occur because the firm grows so large that management cannot effectively manage it. For example, the costs of gathering, organizing, and reviewing information on all aspects of a large firm may increase more rapidly than output. Further, managing large numbers of employees and coordinating the several divisions of a large firm may be difficult.

KEY CONCEPTS

- Returns to scale refer to the change in output when both inputs are changed proportionately.
- Returns to scale are said to be:
  Increasing if output increases more than in proportion to the change in inputs.
  Decreasing if output increases less than in proportion to the change in inputs.
  Constant if the change in output is proportionate to the change in inputs.

Summary

Firms buy capital and labor and transform them through the production process into output of goods and services to meet the demands of consumers and other firms. The production function is an engineering or technological concept that specifies the maximum rate of output obtainable with given rates of input of capital and labor. Decisions on optimal production rates and/or efficient input combinations require that data on input prices be combined with the information generated by the production function.

The short run is defined as the period during which the rate of input use of one factor of production is fixed. By varying the rate of input of the other factor, total, average, and marginal product functions are determined. The law of diminishing marginal returns states that as more of a variable input is combined with a fixed input, a point will be reached where marginal product declines. The marginal revenue product function (MRP), found by multiplying marginal product by marginal revenue, is the firm's demand curve for an input. The profit-maximizing firm will hire an input until MRP equals the price of the input.

An isoquant is derived from the production function and shows all combinations of labor and capital that will produce a given rate of output. The isocost line shows all combinations of capital and labor that can be purchased for a given cost. If one or both input prices change, the slope of the isocost line will change.

The firm faces one of three production problems: (1) maximize output subject to a cost constraint, (2) minimize cost subject to an output constraint, or (3) produce that output rate that will maximize profit. Regardless of the problem addressed, the optimal input combination is determined by the tangency of an isoquant and isocost curve. At that point the slope of the isoquant [the marginal rate of technical substitution (MRTS)] equals the ratio of the input prices. The firm's expansion path is defined as the locus of those points of tangency.

For production to be efficient, the marginal product per dollar of input cost must be the same for both inputs. If that condition is not met, there is some way to substitute one input for the other and increase output at no additional cost. In addition, profit maximization requires that inputs be hired until the marginal revenue product of each input equals the input's price.

The concept of returns to scale refers to the change in output associated with proportionate changes in all inputs. Such returns are increasing, decreasing, or constant, depending on whether output increases more than in proportion, less than in proportion, or proportionately with the input changes.

Discussion Questions

6-1. Explain the concept of a production function. Why is only having information about the production function inadequate for making decisions about efficient input combinations and the profit-maximizing rate of output?

6-2. Explain the law of diminishing marginal returns. Provide an example of decreasing marginal returns in higher education.

6-3. What is the difference between the short run and the long run? Provide an example of a firm where the short run would be quite "short" (e.g., a few days or weeks) and an example where it would be quite "long" (e.g., several months or a year or more). Explain.

6-4. What is meant by the statement that "firms operate in the short run and plan in the long run"?

6-5. Legislation in the United States requires that most firms pay workers at least a specified minimum wage per hour. Use principles of marginal productivity to explain how such laws might affect the quantity of labor employed.

6-6. What is an example of a production process where inputs are perfect substitutes, and what is an example where inputs have zero substitutability.

6-7. Explain why the isocost function will shift in a parallel fashion if the cost level changes, but the isocost will pivot about one of the intercepts if the price of either input changes.

6-8. Suppose wage rates at a firm are raised 10 percent. Use theoretical principles of production to show how the relative substitution of one input for another occurs as a result of the increased price of labor. Provide an example of how input substitution has been made in higher education.

6-9. It is always better to hire the best qualified, most productive workers regardless of the cost. True or False? Explain.

Problems

6-1. Use the production function

$$Q = 10K^{.5}L^{.6}$$

to complete the production table below.

Rate of Capital
Input (K)

	1	2	3	4	5	6
6	24.5			56.3		71.8
5						
4		30.3				
3					45.5	
2		27.3				
1	10.0					29.3

Rate of Labor Input (L)

(a) For this production system, are returns to scale decreasing, constant, or increasing? Explain.

(b) Suppose the wage rate is $28 and the price of capital is $56 per unit, and the firm currently is producing 30.3 units of output per period using four units of capital and two units of labor. Is this an efficient resource combination? Explain. What would be a more efficient (not necessarily the best) combination? Why?

6-2. Use the data from problem 6-1 to answer the following questions.

(a) If the rate of capital input is fixed at three, and if output sells for $5 per unit, determine the total, average and marginal product functions, and the marginal revenue product function for labor in the following table:

L	TP_L	AP_L	MP_L	MRP_L
0	_____	_____		
1	_____	_____	_____	_____
2	_____	_____	_____	_____
3	_____	_____	_____	_____
4	_____	_____	_____	_____
5	_____	_____	_____	_____
6	_____	_____	_____	_____

(b) Using the data from part (a), if the wage rate is $28 per unit, how much labor should be employed?

(c) If the rate of labor input is fixed at 5, determine the total, average and marginal product functions for capital, and the marginal revenue product of capital in the following table:

K	TP_K	AP_K	MP_K	MRP_K
0	_____	_____		
1	_____	_____	_____	_____
2	_____	_____	_____	_____
3	_____	_____	_____	_____
4	_____	_____	_____	_____
5	_____	_____	_____	_____
6	_____	_____	_____	_____

(d) Using the data from part (c), if the price of capital is $40 per unit, how many units of capital should be employed?

6-3. International Publishing has kept the following data on labor input and production of textbooks for each of eight production periods.

Production Period	Labor Input	Output of Books (Total Product)
1	4	260
2	3	190
3	6	310
4	8	240
5	2	110
6	7	290
7	5	300
8	1	50

(a) Use the data on labor input and total product to find the average and marginal product functions for labor input rates from one to eight. (Assume that a zero labor input would result in zero output.)

(b) Using two graphs similar to that of Figure 6.3 in the chapter, plot the total product function in the upper graph and average and marginal product functions in the lower graph. On the graph identify the rate of labor input: (1) where total output is at a maximum and the corresponding point where marginal product is zero; (2) where there is an inflection point on the total product function and the corresponding point where the marginal product function is at a maximum; and (3) where the slope of a line drawn through the origin to a point on the total product function would have maximum slope and the corresponding point where the average product curve is at a maximum.

(c) Given that the objective of the firm is to maximize profit, can you determine from these data how much output should be produced? If not, what additional information would you need? Can you think of any circumstance where the firm would use more than six units of labor per period in this production process?

6-4. The marginal product of labor function for Central Milling Inc. is given by the equation

$$MP_L = 10\left(\frac{K}{L}\right)^{.5}$$

Currently, the firm is using 100 units of capital and 121 units of labor. Given the very specialized nature of the capital equipment, it takes six to nine months to increase the capital stock, but the rate of labor input can be varied daily. If the price of labor is $10 per unit and the price of output is $2 per unit, is the firm operating efficiently in the short run? If not, explain why, and determine the optimal rate of labor input.

6-5. For each of the following production functions, determine whether returns to scale are decreasing, constant, or increasing:

(a) $Q = 2K + 3L + KL$
(b) $Q = 20K^{.6}L^{.5}$
(c) $Q = 100 + 3K + 2L$
(d) $Q = 5K^{a}L^{b}$, where $a + b = 1$
(e) $Q = K/L$

6-6. The revenue department of a state government employs certified public accountants (CPAs) to audit corporate tax returns and bookkeepers to audit individual returns. CPAs are paid $31,200 per year, while the annual salary of a bookkeeper is $18,200. Given the current staff of CPAs and bookkeepers, a study made by the department's economist shows that devoting one year of CPAs' time to auditing corporate returns results in an average additional tax collection of $52,000. In contrast, the bookkeepers only achieve additional tax collections of $41,600 per year of bookkeepers' time.

(a) If the department's objective is to maximize tax revenue collected, is the present mix of CPAs and bookkeepers optimal? Explain fully and be sure to make explicit any assumptions.

(b) If the present mix of CPAs and bookkeepers is not optimal, explain what reallocation should be made.

6-7. The production function for Superlite Sailboats, Inc. is

$$Q = 20K^{.5}L^{.5}$$

with marginal product functions

$$MP_K = 10(L/K)^{.5} \quad \text{and} \quad MP_L = 10(K/L)^{.5}.$$

If the price of capital is $5 per unit and the price of labor is $4 per unit:

(a) Determine the expansion path for Superlite.

(b) The firm currently is producing 200 units of output per period using input rates of $L = 4$ and $K = 25$. Is this an efficient input combination? Why or why not? If not, determine the efficient input combination for producing an output rate of 200.

6-8. For the production function

$$Q = 20K^{.5}L^{.5}$$

Determine four combinations of capital and labor that will produce 100- and 200-unit isoquants. Plot these points on a graph and use them to sketch the 100- and 200-unit isoquants.

6-9. Suppose the price of labor is 10 and the price of capital is 2.5.

(a) Use this information to determine the isocost equations corresponding to a total cost of $200 and $500.

(b) Plot these two isocost lines on a graph.

(c) If the price of labor falls from $10 per unit to $8 per unit determine the new $500 isocost and plot it on the same diagram used in part (b)

Problems Requiring Calculus

6-10. Squaretire, Inc., a small producer of automobile tires, has the following production function:

$$Q = 100K^{.5}L^{.5}$$

During the last production period, the firm operated efficiently and used input rates of 100 and 25 for capital and labor, respectively.

(a) What is the marginal product of capital and the marginal product of labor based on the input rates specified?

(b) If the price of capital was $20 per unit, what was the wage rate?

(c) For the next production period, the price per unit of capital is expected to increase to $25 while the wage rate and the labor input will remain unchanged under the terms of the labor contract with the United Rubber Workers Local No. 25. If the firm maintains efficient production, what input rate of capital will be used?

6-11. Given the production function

$$Q = 30K^{.7}L^{.5}$$

and input prices $r = 20$ and $w = 30$, determine the expansion path.

References

Douglas, P. H. 1948. "Are There Laws of Production?" *American Economic Review* 38(March):1–41.

Eldor, D., Sudit, E. F., and Vinod, H. D. 1981. "Economies of Scale in Telecommunications: A Further Reply." *Applied Economics* 13(2):255–256.

Ferguson, C. E. 1969. *The Neoclassical Theory of Production and Distribution.* Cambridge: Cambridge University Press, Chap. 5.

Heady, E. O., and Dillon, J. 1961. *Agricultural Production Functions.* Ames, Iowa: Iowa State University Press.

Henderson, J. M., and Quandt, R. E. 1980. *Microeconomic Theory,* 3rd ed. New York: McGraw-Hill.

Johnson, J. E., Flanigan, G. B., and Weisbart, S. N. 1981. "Returns to Scale in the Property and Liability Insurance Industry." *Journal of Risk and Insurance* 48(1):18–45.

Mansfield, E. 1982. *Microeconomics: Theory and Applications.* New York: W. W. Norton.

McBride, M. E. 1981. "The Nature and Source of Economies of Scale in Cement Production." *Southern Economic Journal* 48(1):105–115.

Minasian, J. R. 1969. "Research and Development, Production Functions, and Rates of Return." *The American Economic Review* 59(May):80–84.

Webb, J. R. 1975. "Economics of Nitrogen Fertilizer in Corn." In *Selected Readings in Farm Management.* Ames, Iowa: Iowa State University Press.

Appendix: Calculus and Production Theory

The tools of calculus can be used to demonstrate important principles of production theory. Two applications are discussed here. First, the relationships among the product functions are examined. Second, calculus is used to derive the conditions for profit-maximizing production.

Average and Marginal Product Functions

Given the production function

$$Q = f(K, L)$$

if capital is fixed at $K = \overline{K}$, the resultant relation is the total product of labor function. That is,

$$TP_L = f(\overline{K}, L) \tag{6A-1}$$

The associated average product function is

$$AP_L = \frac{f(\overline{K}, L)}{L} \tag{6A-2}$$

and the marginal product function is the first derivative of the total product function, or

$$MP_L = \frac{d[f(\overline{K}, L)]}{dL} \tag{6A-3}$$

It can be shown that marginal product equals average product at the maximum point of average product. The maximum point of average product is found by setting the first derivative of equation (6A-2) equal to zero. Using the formula for the derivative of the ratio of two functions,

$$\frac{d(AP_L)}{dL} = \frac{Lf_L - f(\overline{K}, L)}{L^2} = 0$$

where f_L is the partial derivative of the total product function with respect to labor. For this ratio to equal zero, the numerator must be zero. That is,

$$Lf_L - f(\overline{K}, L) = 0$$

Moving the term $-f(\overline{K}, L)$ to the right-hand side of the equation and dividing both sides by L yields

$$f_L = \frac{f(K, L)}{L} \tag{6A-4}$$

But the left-hand term of equation (6A-4) is the marginal product, while the right-hand term is average product. Thus the two functions are equal when average product is at a maximum.

The Cobb–Douglas production function can be used to illustrate this relationship. If the capital input is fixed at $\overline{K}$, the general form of the Cobb–Douglas production function becomes $Q = A\overline{K}^\alpha L^\beta$. The average and marginal product functions are

$$AP_L = \frac{(A\overline{K}^\alpha L^\beta)}{L} = A\overline{K}^\alpha L^{\beta - 1} \tag{6A-5}$$

and

$$MP_L = \frac{dQ}{dL} = \beta A\overline{K}^\alpha L^{\beta - 1} \tag{6A-6}$$

The maximum of average product is

$$\frac{d(AP_L)}{dL} = (\beta - 1)A\overline{K}^\alpha L^{\beta - 2} = 0 \tag{6A-7}$$

Note that equation (6A-7) can be written

$$\frac{(\beta - 1)A\overline{K}^\alpha L^{\beta - 1}}{L} = 0$$

and for the ratio on the left-hand side of this equation to equal zero, the numerator must equal zero. That is,

$$(\beta - 1)A\bar{K}^{\alpha}L^{\beta-1} = 0 \tag{6A-8}$$

Now equation (6A-8) can be written

$$\beta A\bar{K}^{\alpha}L^{\beta-1} - A\bar{K}^{\alpha}L^{\beta-1} = 0$$

Rewriting and arranging terms yields

$$\beta A\bar{K}^{\alpha}L^{\beta-1} = A\bar{K}^{\alpha}L^{\beta-1} \tag{6A-9}$$

Note that the left-hand term of equation (6A-5) is the marginal product of labor and the right-hand term is the average product of labor. Thus marginal intersects average at the maximum point of average product.

Production with Two Variable Inputs

Calculus can be used to determine that combination of capital and labor that will result in a profit-maximizing output level for the firm. Assume that product price is constant for all rates of output (i.e., price equals marginal revenue).

First, write the profit function as

$$\pi = TR - TC$$

Total revenue is given by price times quantity (i.e., PQ), and total cost is the sum of the input prices times input quantities (i.e., $TC = rK + wL$). Thus the profit function can be written as

$$\pi = PQ - rK - wL$$

Because $Q = f(K, L)$, the profit function can be rewritten as

$$\pi = Pf(K, L) - rK - wL \tag{6A-10}$$

If input prices r and w are given, profit is a function of two variables, capital and labor. To find maximum profit, take the first partial derivatives of profit with respect to K and L (i.e., f_K and f_L) and set them equal to zero, that is,

$$\frac{\partial \pi}{\partial K} = Pf_K - r = 0$$

$$\frac{\partial \pi}{\partial L} = Pf_L - w = 0$$

Rewriting these expressions yields

$$Pf_K = r \tag{6A-11}$$

and

$$Pf_L = w \tag{6A-12}$$

The terms Pf_K and Pf_L are the marginal revenue products for capital and labor, respectively. That is, f_K is the marginal product of capital, f_L is the marginal product of labor, and price equals marginal revenue. The product of marginal revenue and marginal product is marginal revenue product. Thus profit maximization requires that inputs be employed until marginal revenue product equals the input price for each input.

Dividing equation (6A-12) by (6A-11) gives

$$\frac{Pf_L}{Pf_K} = \frac{w}{r}$$

and rewriting the relationship implies

$$\frac{f_L}{w} = \frac{f_K}{r}$$

or

$$\frac{MP_L}{w} = \frac{MP_K}{r} \tag{6A-13}$$

Equation (6A-13) demonstrates that profit maximization requires that the ratio of marginal product to input price be equal for both inputs. That is, conditions (6A-11) and (6A-12) are sufficient for a profit maximum because they imply the general efficiency condition (6A-13).

Linear Programming

7

Preview

In Chapter 6, the concept of a constrained optimization problem was introduced. In general, such problems consist of an objective function and one or more constraints. For example, one problem addressed in Chapter 6 is to minimize cost (the objective) subject to meeting a specified level of production (the constraint). The essence of economics is efficient resource allocation when resources are scarce. Specifying one or more constraints is simply a way of identifying this scarcity.

Linear programming is a technique for solving a special set of constrained optimization problems where the objective function is linear and there are one or more linear constraints. It is a powerful decision-making technique that has found application in a variety of managerial problems. Not only does linear programming have value in decision making, it also helps in understanding the concepts of constrained optimization and opportunity cost.

In the first section of this chapter, examples of problems that lend themselves to linear programming analysis are suggested. In the next two sections, different types of programming problems are considered. For the first, the objective is profit maximization, whereas cost minimization is the goal in the problem discussed in the following section. In each case, both a graphical and an algebraic approach to the solution are presented. Actually, most real-world programming problems are solved by computers, but it is essential that the principles underlying the solutions be understood. In the fourth section, a set of special considerations relevant to linear programming problems is presented. Finally, the concept of primal and dual linear programs is discussed.

Linear Programming Applications and Assumptions

As all managers face constrained optimization problems, it should not be surprising that linear programming has found many uses in business. The earliest applications were in production-related problems. For example, managers in multiproduct firms sought the combination of output rates for each of several products that would maximize profit subject to a limited number of machine-hours and worker-days. An alternative production problem might have been to find that combination of output rates that could be produced at minimum cost while meeting a specified set of orders and inventory requirements.

In the marketing area, the problem may be to select the minimum-cost mix of radio, television, and magazine advertising that will meet constraints relative to the total number of people exposed to the advertising and the number in certain age, sex, and income classes. Financial managers have used linear programming models to determine the lowest-cost method of financing the firm given such constraints as bank borrowing limitations and a maximum ratio of debt to equity.

Many transportation problems can also be solved by linear programming. Consider an automobile producer with several manufacturing plants and numerous dealers throughout the country. How should shipments of cars be made from plants to dealers to minimize total transportation costs? A special transportation variant of linear programming has been developed to solve problems of this type.

Linear programming has been widely used in agriculture. For example, dairy farmers and beef cattle producers have used the technique to determine the lowest-cost combination of feeds that would meet minimum nutrition requirements for the animals. Agribusiness managers also have used linear programming to determine the profit-maximizing allocation of land to different crops subject to such constraints as fixed land area, differing soil characteristics, and limited water availability.

These are but a few of the many constrained optimization problems that face managers. Historically, some managers used intuition and guesswork to make the resource allocation decisions required. In the era of scientific management, however, better techniques are available and should be used if the firm is to compete successfully. Linear programming is among the most important of these techniques.

The Linearity Assumption

All the important relationships in a linear programming problem must be linear. These important relationships often include the production, total cost, total revenue, and profit functions. The assumption that these functions are linear also means that it is assumed that there are constant returns to scale in production, the price of output is constant for all output levels, and that input prices are constant regardless of the amount of input purchased. The combination of constant returns to scale and constant input prices means that production cost per unit of output is constant. Further, the combination of constant per unit cost and output price imply a constant rate of profit per unit of output.

Some critics of linear programming argue that the assumption of linearity is inconsistent with other aspects of economic theory that are based on U-shaped cost curves, production functions having other than constant returns to scale, and nonlinear profit functions. Although these critics have a point, cost and profit per unit may be constant over a limited range of output, and thus the assumptions underlying linear programming would be valid for that range. More important, the successful application of linear programming to many managerial problems suggests that the technique is a useful management tool. Even where the important relationships are not exactly linear, the programming approach still may be the best way to approximate optimal resource allocation.

KEY CONCEPTS

- Linear programming is a quantitative technique for solving constrained optimization problems where both the objective function and the constraints are linear.
- The linearity assumption means that there are constant output and input prices, constant returns to scale in production, and constant cost and profit per unit of output.

Constrained Profit Maximization

Many firms simultaneously produce several products in a plant. Management faces the problem of whether to produce more or less of one product (i.e., to allocate more or less resources to that product) relative to the others. That decision is based on a comparison of the profit earned on an additional unit of output relative to the opportunity cost of the resources devoted to producing that unit. Linear programming is well suited to solving problems of this type.

Structuring the Problem

Consider a firm that produces two products, A and B, that require processing on three different machines. During the production period, the number of hours available on each machine is limited. Assume that profit per unit of each output is constant for all relevant rates of output. The problem facing the firm is to determine the production rates of Q_A and Q_B that will maximize profit. Q_A and Q_B are referred to as *decision variables*.

The management's objective must be stated in the form of a function, hence, the term *objective function*. In this problem the objective function is

$$\pi = aQ_A + bQ_B \tag{7-1}$$

where π represents total profit and a and b are the profit per unit of A and B produced. Solving for Q_B yields

$$Q_B = \frac{\pi}{b} - \frac{a}{b}Q_A \tag{7-2}$$

Equation (7-2) describes a straight line where the vertical intercept is determined by the ratio of total profit to profit per unit of product B (i.e., π/b) and the slope is the negative of the ratio a/b, or the relative profitability of the two products. As both a and b are positive, the slope will be negative.

Suppose that profit per unit of output is $3 for product A and $1 for product B. The profit or objective function is then

$$\pi = 3Q_A + Q_B$$

which can be rewritten as

$$Q_B = \pi - 3Q_A \tag{7-3}$$

If the rate of profit, π, is specified, equation (7-3) defines all combinations of Q_A and Q_B that yield that rate of profit. Thus equation (7-3) can be considered an isoprofit equation. For example, if $\pi = 90$, some of the combinations of Q_A and Q_B which yield that profit rate are:

Q_A	Q_B
0	90
10	60
20	30
30	0

This $90 isoprofit line is shown in Figure 7-1 together with isoprofit lines for $\pi = 60$ and 120. The management problem is to attain the highest isoprofit line possible given the resource constraints facing the firm.

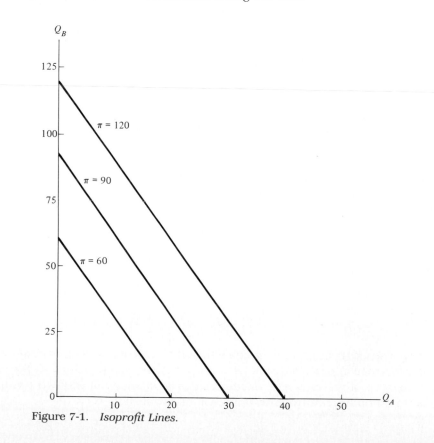

Figure 7-1.   *Isoprofit Lines.*

Table 7-1. Resource (Machine Time) Requirements per Unit of Output and Total Machine Time Available

Machine	Hours of Machine Time Required per Unit of Output for:		Total Hours of Machine Time Available
	Product A	Product B	
X	1	3	90
Y	2	2	80
Z	2	0	60

Recall that producing products A and B requires processing on three different machines. Let these machines be designated X, Y, and Z. Table 7-1 lists the hours of time per unit of output that are required on each machine and the hours of time available on each machine during the production period.

For example, on machine X each unit of product A requires one hour and each unit of B requires three hours. For any output rate, Q_A, the number of machine X hours required is Q_A; for any output rate, Q_B, the number of hours required on machine X is $3Q_B$. Thus the total hours of time on machine X is $Q_A + 3Q_B$, and Table 7-1 indicates that this total is limited to no more than ninety hours during the production period. Therefore, the constraint for machine X is written

$$Q_A + 3Q_B \leq 90 \tag{7-4}$$

Both products require two hours of time per unit of output on machine Y and the total time available is eighty hours. Thus the constraint for machine Y is

$$2Q_A + 2Q_B \leq 80 \tag{7-5}$$

Finally, product A requires two hours of time on machine Z per unit of output, but product B does not require the use of this machine, so the constraint is

$$2Q_A \leq 60 \tag{7-6}$$

In addition, a set of nonnegativity requirements is added to assure that the solution makes economic sense. These requirements specify that all relevant variables (e.g., output and machine time) be positive. Negative values for either output or hours of time would be meaningless, but without these nonnegativity constraints, the mathematical approach could easily result in one or more values of the decision variables being negative. For example, because profit per unit of output is higher for A than for B, if the nonnegativity requirements were not imposed, a solution might result in a very large positive value for Q_A and a negative value for Q_B.

Requiring that both Q_A and Q_B be nonnegative (i.e., $Q_A \geq 0$ and $Q_B \geq 0$) also ensures that the hours of machine time will also be nonnegative. The hours of time on each machine are specified by constraints (7-4), (7-5), and (7-6). The only way that negative machine hours could occur would be for there to be negative values for the output rates Q_A and Q_B.

Now the linear programming problem is complete and can be stated as follows:

$$\text{maximize: } \pi = 3Q_A + Q_B \quad \text{(objective function)}$$

$$\begin{aligned}
\text{subject to: } Q_A + 3Q_B &\leq 90 \quad \text{machine } X \text{ constraint} \\
2Q_A + 2Q_B &\leq 80 \quad \text{machine } Y \text{ constraint} \\
2Q_A &\leq 60 \quad \text{machine } Z \text{ constraint} \\
Q_A, Q_B &\geq 0 \quad \text{nonnegativity constraint}
\end{aligned}$$

The Feasible Region

The next step is to determine the output rates Q_A and Q_B that can be produced without violating the constraints. The five constraints are shown graphically in Figure 7-2. Consider the first constraint, $Q_A + 3Q_B \leq 90$, which is shown as the machine X constraint in the figure. To draw this constraint, consider the relation as an equality and solve for Q_B, that is,

$$Q_B = 30 - \frac{1}{3} Q_A$$

Now find two points on that line by setting $Q_A = 0$ and solving for $Q_B = 30$, yielding the point (0, 30), and then by setting $Q_B = 0$ and solving for $Q_A = 90$, thus yielding a second point (90, 0). These two points are sufficient to identify the line. Because it is a "less than or equal to" constraint, all values on or below

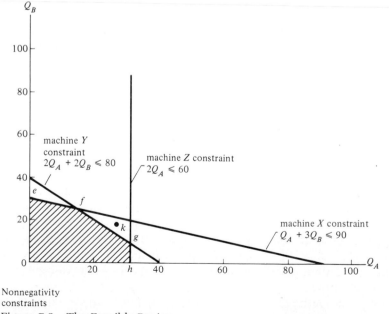

Figure 7-2   *The Feasible Region.*

this line meet the constraint. Similarly, all points on or below the line $2Q_A + 2Q_B \leq 80$ meet the machine Y constraint, and points to the left of $2Q_A \leq 60$ meet the constraint on hours available for machine Z. Finally, the nonnegativity requirements $Q_A, Q_B \geq 0$ restrict the allowable rates of the decision variables to the "northeast" quadrant, that is, where Q_A and Q_B are nonnegative.

In general, the feasible region consists of all values of the decision variables that satisfy all the constraints simultaneously. In this example, the feasible region of production is that set of combinations of the decision variables, Q_A and Q_B, that meet all five constraints. This set is shown as the shaded area in Figure 7-2. Any point on or within that boundary can be produced because all the constraints are satisfied. A point such as k is not in the feasible region because it does not satisfy the constraint for machine Y. The linear programming problem is to identify the one combination (Q_A, Q_B) within the feasible region that yields maximum profit.

Graphic Solution

Recall the problem of maximizing production subject to a budget constraint from Chapter 6. The budget constraint defined a feasible set of input combinations. The problem was to find the highest isoquant that touched that budget constraint. The linear programming problem discussed here is analogous to that production problem. Here the problem is to find the highest isoprofit line that still meets the constraints, that is, to find the highest isoprofit line that has at least one point in common with the feasible region.

In Figure 7-3, the feasible region is shown together with three isoprofit functions that are depicted as dashed lines. The highest profit line that satisfies the constraints is $\pi = 100$, which touches the feasible region at poing g. The coordinates of point g $(Q_A = 30, Q_B = 10)$ provide the solution to this profit-maximizing problem. Substituting these values into the profit function confirms that profit is $100 at this point:

$$\pi = 3(30) + (10) = 100$$

Any higher profit line, for example, that for $150 of profit, would have no point in common with the feasible region. There are feasible combinations of Q_A and Q_B on profit lines below the $100 isoprofit line, such as point j on the $60 isoprofit line, but they are suboptimal because higher profits could be obtained by using other output rates.

The machine time allocated to each product is determined by multiplying the solution values Q_A and Q_B by the machine time requirements specified in Table 7-2. For example, for machine X, the number of hours used is $30 + 3(10)$, or 60 hours. The number of hours of time on each machine allocated to each product is shown in Table 7-2. Note that the available hours for machines Y and Z are all used, but there are unused hours available for machine X. Producing 30 units of A requires 30 hours on machine X, and producing 10 units of B also requires 30 hours, for a total of 60 hours required. As there are 90 hours available, 30 hours remain unused. In the language of linear programming, it is said that the con-

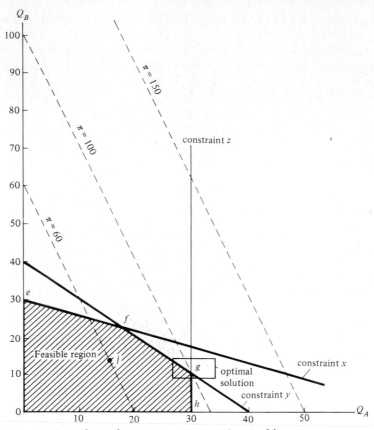

Figure 7-3   *Solving the Linear Programming Problem.*

straints for machines Y and Z are binding but there is slack in time for machine X. The constraint for X is said to be nonbinding. Note the optimal point (g) in Figure 7-3. That point lies on constraints Y and Z but is below the constraint for machine X. This also shows that all of the available hours on machines Y and Z are used but that there are unused hours on machine X.

The concept of binding and nonbinding constraints has implications for determining the opportunity cost of the limited resources. With regard to the specific problem, hours of time on machines Y and Z have an opportunity cost; if they were reallocated to some other use, total profit would be reduced. That is,

Table 7-2. Hours of Machine Time Allocated to Each Product

Machine	Hours of Time Allocated to: Product A	Product B	Hours Available	Slack Hours
X	30	30	90	30
Y	60	20	80	0
Z	60	0	60	0

reducing hours available on machine Y or Z would result in a reduction in the rate of one or both outputs Q_A and Q_B. The result of this reduced output would be a smaller profit. But there are thirty hours of time available on machine X that could be allocated to some other use without affecting profit. Thus those hours have zero opportunity cost as far as producing products A and B are concerned.

Also note in Figure 7-3 that the profit-maximizing solution occurred at a corner of the feasible region. Because both the objective function and the constraints are linear, the optimal solution always will occur at one of the corners.[1] By having to evaluate only the corner solutions, the number of computations is greatly reduced. For instance, in the example, points e, f, g, and h are the corners and therefore are the only points that need to be considered. In the computer programs written to solve linear programming problems, the approach is to pick one corner arbitrarily, evaluate the objective function at that point, and then systematically move to other corners that offer higher profits until no other corner yielding greater profit is found. This process greatly reduces the time necessary to determine the optimal solution.

In Figure 7-4, two different isoprofit lines, π_1, and π_2, are drawn. The optimal solution for the original profit equation,

$$\pi_1 = 3Q_A + Q_B$$

(labeled π_1 in the figure), is, of course, at point g. For the other objective function,

$$\pi_2 = Q_A + 2Q_B$$

The optimal solution is at corner point f. This demonstrates the effect of the slope of the objective function on the optimal solution.

Algebraic Solution

The graphic approach used above demonstrates the conceptual solution to linear programming problems and actually could be used to solve some problems. However, if there are more than two decision variables and/or if the number of constraints is large, the graphic approach cannot be used. Fortunately, there is an algebraic technique that can be used to solve linear programs of almost any size.

The problem considered in the preceding section involved an objective function, three inequalities denoting the resource constraints, and the nonnegativity requirements. That is,

$$\begin{aligned} \text{maximize:} \quad & \pi = 3Q_A + Q_B \\ \text{subject to:} \quad & Q_A + 3Q_B \leq 90 \\ & 2Q_A + 2Q_B \leq 80 \\ & 2Q_A \leq 60 \\ & Q_A, Q_B \geq 0 \end{aligned}$$

[1] It is possible that the highest isoprofit line will coincide with one of the sides of the feasible region, such as fg in Figure 7-3. In this case, points f, g, and all others in between are optimal in that they yield the same level of profit. Still a corner solution, f or g, will optimize the objective function. This possibility is discussed in detail later in the chapter.

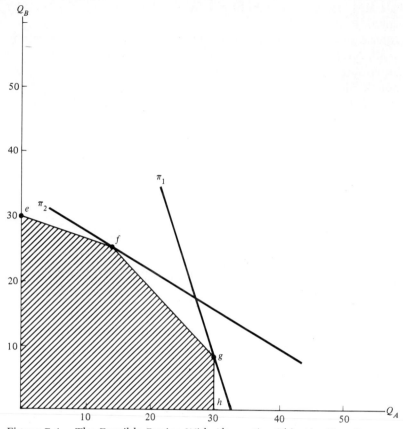

Figure 7-4.   *The Feasible Region With Alternative Objective Functions.*

The general approach to solving the problem is to identify corners of the feasible region and then evaluate profits at each corner. As the corners are defined by the intersection of the constraints, those corners can be identified by identifying which constraints combine to form that corner, and then solving those two constraint equations for the values of the decision variables Q_A and Q_B at that point of intersection.

Refer again to the feasible region shown in Figure 7-4. The only points that have to be evaluated are the corners e, f, g, and h. Technically, the origin, 0, is a corner of the feasible region, but it is obvious that profits cannot be maximized at that point. Also, point h can be dismissed as a possibility because point g yields the same output rate for A and a greater output rate for B; thus g is unequivocally better. Therefore, only points e, f, and g require consideration. Hence the linear programming problem can be solved by finding the values (Q_A, Q_B) at points e, f, and g, evaluating the profit rate at each, and selecting that combination that yields the greatest profit.

Point e is the intersection of constraint X with the vertical (Q_B) axis. Thus Q_B

is determined by substituting $Q_A = 0$ (the equation for the vertical axis) into the first constraint,

$$0 + 3Q_B = 90$$

and solving for Q_B, yielding

$$Q_B = 30$$

Thus, at point e, the values of the decision variables are $Q_A = 0$ and $Q_B = 30$.

Point f is the intersection of constraints X and Y. By writing these constraints as equalities and solving them simultaneously, the value of Q_A and Q_B can be determined. The two equations are

$$Q_A + 3Q_B = 90$$
$$2Q_A + 2Q_B = 80$$

To solve for the values of Q_A and Q_B, first multiply the first equation by -2 and add the two equations:

$$
\begin{array}{r}
-2Q_A - 6Q_B = -180 \\
\underline{2Q_A + 2Q_B = 80} \\
-4Q_B = -100
\end{array}
$$

Thus

$$Q_B = 25$$

Now, substitute $Q_B = 25$ into the first equation to find the value of Q_A. That is,

$$Q_A + 3(25) = 90$$

or

$$Q_A = 15$$

Thus, at point f, the values of the decision variables are $Q_A = 15$ and $Q_B = 25$.

Point g is the intersection of constraints Y and Z. The values of Q_A and Q_B are found by simultaneously solving the equations

$$2Q_A + 2Q_B = 80$$
$$2Q_A = 60$$

which yields the solution $Q_A = 30$ and $Q_B = 10$.

Now, by substituting the values (Q_A, Q_B) at each corner into the profit function

$$\pi = 3Q_A + Q_B$$

Table 7-3. Values of the Decision Variables and Profit at Each Corner Point

Corner Point	Decision Variables		Profit
	Q_A	Q_B	
0	0	0	0
e	0	30	30
f	15	25	70
g	30	10	100
h	30	0	90

the profit at each corner is determined. For example, at point f, Q_A = 15 and Q_B = 25. Therefore,

$$\pi = 3(15) + 1(25) = 70$$

The values of the decision variables and the associated profit rate at each corner are reported in Table 7-3. The values at the origin and point h have been included even though it is known that they cannot be profit-maximizing points.

Corner point g yields the highest profit (π = 100), and therefore the optimal solution for the firm is to produce 30 units of Q_A and 10 units of Q_B. Of course, this is the same solution obtained in the graphic approach.

As the linear programming problem becomes larger, the number of computations increases rapidy. For this reason, most solutions are found by using computers. It is not unusual for a problem to have ten, twenty, or more decision variables and literally dozens of constraints. It simply is not practical even to attempt to solve such problems without the aid of a computer. Numerous computer programs for solving linear programming problems are available and are easily used.

EXAMPLE

THE OPTIMAL OFFICE PARTY

Lopez, a recent MBA graduate, is asked to be in charge of beverage service for the firm's Christmas party. Because the firm is losing money, there is no money available to purchase additional liquor and related supplies, so Lopez must maximize the number of drinks that can be made from the existing private stock in the bottom drawer of the president's desk. An inventory shows the following supplies:

Vodka	30 ounces	Lemon juice	20 ounces
Whiskey	25 ounces	Gin	20 ounces
Vermouth	10 ounces	Orange juice	30 ounces

A secretary gives Lopez a list of the drinks preferred by the staff and their composition (in ounces):

Drink	Ingredient (ounces)					
	Vodka	Whiskey	Vermouth	Lemon Juice	Gin	Orange Juice
Manhattan (*MH*)		1.5	0.75			
Whiskey sour (*WS*)		1.5		1.0		
Martini (*MT*)			0.25		1.5	
Gimlet (*GT*)				0.5	1.5	
Bronx (*BX*)					1.0	0.5
Harvey wallbanger (*HW*)	1.5					3.0
Moscow mule (*MM*)	1.5			0.5		

Lopez is delighted with this assignment because for the first time since graduation he can use his MBA training in quantitative methods and the microcomputer that has been gathering dust on his desk. How many of each kind of drink should Lopez make?

Solution

This is a constrained optimization problem that can be solved using linear programming. The objective is to maximize the number of desired drinks (N), so the problem would be to maximize

$$N = MH + WS + MT + GT + BX + HW + MM$$

(where *MH* is the number of manhattans, *WS* is the number of whiskey sours, etc.), subject to the resource constraints

$$1.5HW + 1.5MM \leq 30 \quad \text{(Vodka)}$$
$$1.5\,MH + 1.5WS \leq 25 \quad \text{(Whiskey)}$$
$$0.75MH + 0.25MT \leq 10 \quad \text{(Vermouth)}$$
$$1.0WS + 0.5GT + 0.5MM \leq 20 \quad \text{(Lemon Juice)}$$
$$1.5\,MT + 1.5GT + 1.0BX \leq 20 \quad \text{(Gin)}$$
$$0.5BX + 3.0HW + \leq 30 \quad \text{(Orange Juice)}$$

and the nonnegativity constraints

$$MH,\ WS,\ MT,\ GT,\ BX,\ HW,\ MM \geq 0$$

The first resource constraint limits the amount of vodka in the Harvey wallbangers and the Moscow mules to the available supply of 30 ounces. The second constraint states that the amount of whiskey in the manhattans and whiskey sours cannot exceed 25 ounces, and so on.

After five minutes on his microcomputer, Lopez has the solution:

Drink	Number Made
Manhattan	13.3
Whiskey sour	3.3
Martini	0
Gimlet	0
Bronx	20.0
Harvey wallbanger	6.7
Moscow mule	13.3

(*Note:* The fractional drinks were put into smaller glasses.)

After the party, those who could remember commented to Lopez that they had never had so much to drink at the previous office parties. The president was also delighted, gave Lopez a raise, and put him in charge of all future parties. Ms. Jones, who has a Ph.D. in operations research, took great delight in telling Lopez that if he had used a variant of linear programming known as "integer programming," all of the values of the decision variables in the solution would have been integers, and he would not have had to make those few small drinks.

KEY CONCEPTS

- The graphic solution to a linear programming problem consists of graphing the feasible region (as defined by the system of constraints) and then shifting the objective function until an optimal solution is found at a corner of the feasible set.
- Solving a linear programming problem algebraically requires determining the values of the decision variables at each corner point of the feasible region and then evaluating the objective function for each set of the decision variables so determined.

Constrained Cost Minimization

Recall that linear programming is an optimization technique for finding the set of values for the decision variables that maximizes or minimizes an objective function subject to one or more constraints. In the preceding section, a profit function was maximized subject to resource constraints in the form of a limited number of available machine hours. In this section the solution to a minimization problem is outlined. The approach is analogous to that used in the maximization problem.

Structuring the Problem

The example used here comes from agribusiness, where linear programming models have been widely used. Consider a producer of milk whose objective is to feed the milk cows adequately but to do it at minimum cost. Suppose that an adequate daily feed ration consists of a minimum of 40 units of protein, 60 units of calcium, and 60 units of carbohydrates.

The manager must determine how much of two feeds, A and B, to use. One ton of feed A contains 1 unit of protein, 3 units of calcium, and 1 unit of carbohydrates. One ton of feed B contains 1 unit of protein, 1 unit of calcium, and 6 unit of carbohydrates. Let the price of feed A be $100 per ton and the price of feed B be $200 per ton. These basic data are summarized in Table 7-4.

The problem is to find the quantities of the two feeds, X_A and X_B (the decision variables), to be purchased so that the feed cost (C) will be minimized. Thus the problem is to minimize the objective function,

$$C = 100X_A + 200X_B$$

subject to the constraints on minimum nutrition requirements:

$$X_A + X_B \geq 40 \qquad \text{(protein constraint)}$$
$$3X_A + X_B \geq 60 \qquad \text{(calcium constraint)}$$
$$X_A + 6X_B \geq 60 \qquad \text{(carbohydrate constraint)}$$

and the usual nonnegativity requirements

$$X_A \geq 0 \quad X_B \geq 0$$

The constraints and the feasible region are shown in Figure 7-5. Note that the feasible region extends upward and to the right of the constraints, in contrast to the preceding problem, where the feasible region extended to the left and below the resource constraints. This is due to the nature of the resource constraints. In the first problem, the resource constraints were all of the form "less than or equal to" (i.e., ≤), thus restricting feasible combinations of the decision variables to points on or below those constraints when shown graphically. In

Table 7-4. Summary of Data for the Cost-Minimization Problems

	Feed	
	A	B
Price per ton	$100	$200

	Units of Nutrients per Ton of Feed		Minimum Units Required per Day
	A	B	
Protein	1	1	40
Calcium	3	1	60
Carbohydrates	1	6	60

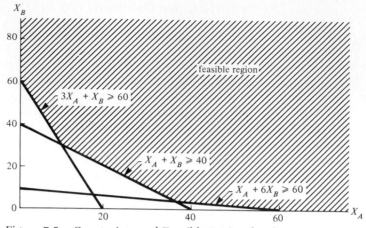

Figure 7-5. *Constraints and Feasible Region for the Cost Minimization Problem.*

this problem the resource constraints are of the form "greater than or equal to," which restricts feasible combinations of the decision variables to points on or above those constraints.

To find the combination of feed inputs (X_A, X_B) that meets the nutrition requirements at minimum cost, think in terms of starting at the origin and shifting the cost equation $C = 100X_A + 200X_B$ in a "northeasterly" direction until that cost function touches a point in the feasible region. The solution is shown in Figure 7-6. The cost function first touches the feasible set at point g, correspond-

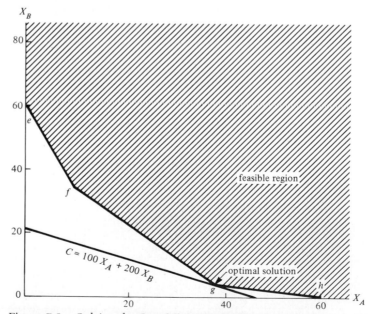

Figure 7-6. *Solving the Cost Minimization Problem.*

ing to 36 tons of A and 4 tons of B. This is the optimal solution. That is, it is the lowest-cost combination of the two feeds that meets the constraints. The cost of these feed inputs is \$4,400 [i.e., $C = 100(36) + 200(4)$]; there is no other (X_A, X_B) that satisfies the constraints and costs less than \$4,400.

Algebraic Solution

The algebraic approach is the same as that used for the profit-maximization problem. First, find the values of X_A and X_B at each of the corners (i.e., e, f, g, and h) by solving the two intersecting constraint equations simultaneously at that point. For example, consider point f in Figure 7.6, the intersection of the first two constraints. Writing these as equalities gives

$$X_A + X_B = 40$$

$$3X_A + X_B = 60$$

Subtracting the second from the first yields

$$-2X_A = -20$$

or

$$X_A = 10$$

Now, substituting $X_A = 10$ into the first constraint and solving for X_B yields

$$10 + X_B = 40$$

or

$$X_B = 30$$

Thus point f is ($Q_A = 10$, $Q_B = 30$). The next step is to evaluate the cost of that input combination by substituting X_A and X_B into the cost equation.

Repeating this process at points e, g, and h yields the values of the decision variables and cost at each corner point. These are summarized in Table 7-5.

Clearly, the optimal solution is at point g. The manager should use 36 tons of feed A and 4 tons of feed B. There is no other input combination that can satisfy the constraints at a cost less than \$4,400.

Table 7-5. Values of Decision Variables and Cost at Each Corner Point

Corner Point	Decision Variables		Cost
	X_A	X_B	
e	0	60	\$12,000
f	10	30	7,000
g	36	4	4,400
h	60	0	6,000

Whether the objective is minimizing or maximizing the objective function, the approach to solving the linear programming problem is essentially the same. That is, determine the values of the decision variables at each corner point of the feasible region, evaluate the objective function for each of those combinations, and select that combination that optimizes (i.e., minimizes or maximizes) that function. The only difference between the maximization and minimization problems is the direction of movement of the objective function in seeking the optimal solution.

CASE STUDY

THE TRANSPORTATION PROBLEM

One area where linear programming has been especially useful is determining optimal shipping patterns. A typical problem is to determine the minimum cost for shipping output from manufacturing plants to dealers. In general, the problem is to determine how much to ship from each source or supply point to each destination or demand point such that the total shipping costs are minimized. The constraints are the maximum production rates at each source and the demand that must be met at each demand point.

Consider the following hypothetical example. An automobile company with manufacturing plants in Detroit and Los Angeles must supply its dealers in Atlanta, Chicago, and Denver. Assign an index i to each plant (e.g., 1 for Detroit and 2 for Los Angeles) and an index j to each dealer (e.g., 1 for Atlanta, 2 for Chicago, and 3 for Denver). The data in the following table show the transportation cost per car from each plant to each dealer (i.e., C_{ij}), the maximum production per period at each plant, and the number of cars demanded at each dealership.

Plant	Transportation Cost per Car Dealer			Number of Cars Produced (Supply)
	Atlanta (1)	Chicago (2)	Denver (3)	
Detroit (1)	200 (C_{11})	100 (C_{12})	300 (C_{13})	3,000
Los Angeles (2)	400 (C_{21})	300 (C_{22})	200 (C_{23})	5,000
Number of cars demanded	3,000	4,000	1,000	

There are six decision variables, X_{ij} (where $i = 1, 2,$ and $j = 1, 2, 3$), representing the number of cars shipped from each plant to each dealer. For example, X_{23} would refer to shipments from Los Angeles to Denver. The objective is to minimize total shipping cost. That is, minimize

$$C = \sum_i \sum_j C_{ij} X_{ij}$$

The constraints are (1) that the total number of cars shipped from each plant (e.g., $X_{11} + X_{12} + X_{13}$ would be total shipments from Detroit) must be equal to or less than the maximum output rate; and (2) that shipments to each dealer (e.g., $X_{11} + X_{21}$ would be the number of cars shipped to Atlanta) must be at least as great as the quantity demanded.

Thus the linear program is to find those values of the decision variables X_{ij} that will minimize

$$C = 200X_{11} + 100X_{12} + 300X_{13} + 400X_{21} + 300X_{22} + 200X_{23}$$

subject to the production or supply constraints

$$X_{11} + X_{12} + X_{13} \leq 3,000$$
$$X_{21} + X_{22} + X_{23} \leq 5,000$$

the demand constraints

$$X_{11} + X_{21} \geq 3,000$$
$$X_{12} + X_{22} > 4,000$$
$$X_{13} + X_{23} \geq 1,000$$

and the nonnegativity constraints

$$X_{ij} \geq 0 \qquad i = 1, 2; \quad j = 1, 2, 3$$

Clearly, this problem cannot be solved graphically and the algebraic approach would be cumbersome. However, the problem can be solved easily using a microcomputer to yield the following optimal values of the decision variables:

From	Least-Cost Shipment Pattern to:			Total Production
	Atlanta	Chicago	Denver	
Detroit	$X_{11} = 3,000$	$X_{12} = 0$	$X_{13} = 0$	3,000
Los Angeles	$X_{21} = 0$	$X_{22} = 4,000$	$X_{23} = 1,000$	5,000
Total demand	3,000	4,000	1,000	

Note that supply (production) and demand constraints are met. For example, total production is 3,000 in Detroit and 5,000 in Los Angeles, which are the maximum output rates in those plants. Further, the dealers in each city receive exactly the number of cars necessary to meet demand. The total transportation cost is $2,000,000. No other set of values for the decision variables would meet the constraints and cost less than $2 million.

Special Problems in Linear Programming

There are several special situations that may be encountered in linear programming problems. Some do not pose a problem but generate rather curious results. In other cases, problems result in there being no solution to the problem.

Multiple Solutions

If the objective function has the same slope as one of the constraints, the result will be an infinite number of optimal combinations of the decision variables. Consider the following problem:

$$\text{maximize: } \pi = 10X_1 + 5X_2$$
$$\text{subject to: } X_1 + 2X_2 \leq 60 \quad \text{(constraint A)}$$
$$2X_1 + X_2 \leq 60 \quad \text{(constraint B)}$$
$$X_1 \leq 27 \quad \text{(constraint C)}$$
$$X_1 \geq 0, X_2 \geq 0$$

Note that the objective function and constraint B both have a slope equal to -2. These can be seen by rewriting each of those relations as a function of X_2. That is,

$$\text{Profit function: } X_2 = \frac{\pi}{5} - 2X_1$$
$$\text{Constraint } B: \quad X_2 \leq 60 - 2X_1$$

The problem is shown graphically in Figure 7-7(a).

The optimal level of the objective function is coincident with constraint B between points f and g. Thus all combinations of (X_1, X_2) in that interval yield the same profit, and therefore all are equally profitable. This situation does not pose a problem, and the approach to solving the problem is exactly as outlined earlier. The corner solutions are evaluated and both f and g yield the same profit. Thus either can be used as the optimal solution.

Redundant Constraints

Consider the following set of constraints

$$A: X_1 + 2X_2 \leq 50 \quad \text{(constraint A)}$$
$$B: X_1 + X_2 \leq 40 \quad \text{(constraint B)}$$
$$C: 5X_1 + 6X_2 \leq 300 \quad \text{(constraint C)}$$
$$X_1 \geq 0, X_2 \geq 0$$

The feasible region defined by these constraints is shown in Figure 7-7(b). Note that the feasible region is defined by constraints A, B, and the nonnegativity requirements. Constraint C is redundant because if either constraint A or B is satisfied, so is constraint C. This does not present a problem in solving the problem. It only means that the information contained in constraint C is irrelevant and therefore unnecessary. Obviously, constraint C is nonbinding and the resource associated with that constraint has a zero opportunity cost. The solution would proceed as before by evaluating profit corner points f, g, and h.

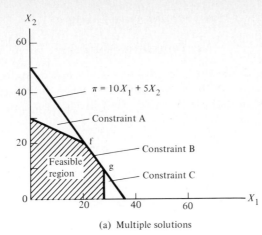

(a) Multiple solutions

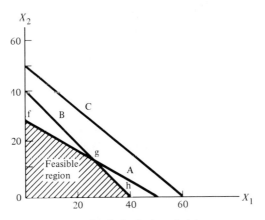

(b) Redundant constraint

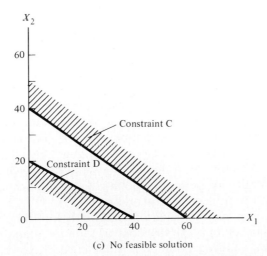

(c) No feasible solution

Figure 7-7. *Special Linear Programming Considerations.*

No Feasible Solution

A serious problem arises when the set of constraints is such that there are no values of the decision variables that simultaneously satisfy all the constraints. The following constraints have been graphed in Figure 7-7(c):

$$2X_1 + 3X_2 \geq 120 \qquad \text{(constraint } C)$$
$$X_1 + 2X_2 \leq 40 \qquad \text{(constraint } D)$$

Only points below $X_1 + 2X_2 = 40$ satisfy constraint D, and only points above $2X_1 + 3X_2 = 120$ satisfy constraint C. But there are no points that satisfy both these conditions simultaneously. Therefore, there is no feasible solution.

In a simple problem such as the example shown, the lack of a feasible solution is easily seen. However, in large linear programming problems with many constraints, there may be no way of knowing that there is no solution until the computer program is run. In such cases, obtaining a feasible solution means that one or more constraints must be modified. For example, additional hours of machine time may have to be acquired in order for any production to take place.

KEY CONCEPTS

- In some linear programming problems, multiple solutions and redundant constraints occur. Neither of these possibilities poses a problem for solving the linear program.
- Sometimes, the constraints are such that there is no feasible solution. In this case, obtaining a solution (i.e., finding nonzero values of the decision variables that meet all the constraints) will require that one or more constraints be changed by augmenting the resource(s) associated with those constraints.

The Dual Problem

It is known that when a resource constraint is binding, there is an opportunity cost associated with that resource. Consider a profit-maximization problem where the resource constraints are hours of time available on machines X, Y, and Z. Assume that the constraints or hours of time on machines Y and Z are binding. If one hour of time on either of those machines had to be given up, profit would fall. But if the constraint for hours of machine X is not binding, this means that there is a zero opportunity cost for this resource.

In terms of planning for expansion of facilities, it would be useful to have an estimate of the value or opportunity cost of time on machines Y and Z. For example, if the firm could hire one more hour of machine time, should it hire more of Y or Z? Suppose it was known that the opportunity costs of one hour of time on machines Y and Z are \$20 and \$10, respectively. This means that an additional hour on machine Y would add \$20 to profit in contrast to adding only \$10 to profit for an additional hour on machine Z. The dual linear program is a way to estimate the opportunity cost of the resource associated with each constraint.

For every linear programming problem (called the *primal problem*), there is an associated problem referred to as the *dual problem*. If the objective of the primal problem is maximization of an objective function, the objective of the dual problem is minimization of an associated objective function and vice versa. For example, if the objective of the primal problem is to maximize production subject to a set of machine-hour constraints, the objective of the dual problem would be to minimize the cost of the resources (i.e., the machine hours) subject to a constraint on production. The dual and primal problems are said to be *symmetric* because a solution to one is a solution to both. For example, in the production problem used at the beginning of the chapter, the objective was to find the values Q_A and Q_B that maximized profit. Determining this combination (Q_A, Q_B) also determined the hours of time used on each machine. The dual problem would find that set of hours on each machine that minimized the cost of the resources devoted to the production of the outputs Q_A and Q_B. The solution to the dual problem would allocate the same number of machine-hours to each product as did the primal problem.

Structuring the Dual Problem

The interpretation of the dual will be made clearer by setting up, solving, and interpreting a dual problem.

Recall the original or primal profit-maximization problem on page 236.

$$\text{maximize: } \pi = 3\,Q_A + 1\,Q_B$$

subject to:

$$1\,Q_A + 3\,Q_B \leq 90$$
$$2\,Q_A + 2\,Q_B \leq 80$$
$$2\,Q_A + 0\,Q_B \leq 60$$

The dual problem is constructed by using the columns of the coefficients of the primal problem as shown by the dashed lines above. Define three new variables C_x, C_y, and C_z that represent the opportunity cost of hours on machines X, Y, and Z, respectively. The objective function for the dual problem is to

$$\text{minimize: } C = 90C_x + 80C_y + 60C_z$$

That is, the objective is to minimize the opportunity cost of the firm's scarce resources (i.e., hours of machine time).

The first constraint in the dual problem is determined by the coefficients on Q_A from the first column of the primal problem. That is,

$$C_x + 2C_y + 2C_z \geq 3$$

meaning that the value of machine hours used to produce 1 unit of product A be at least as great as the profit on that unit of output. Thus 1 unit of output A

requires one hour of time on machine X, two hours on Y, and two hours on Z, and those hours are valued at C_x, C_y, and C_z, respectively.

The second constraint is based on the coefficients in the second column in the primal problem. Hence

$$3C_x + 2C_y \geq 1$$

Note that output B does not require processing on machine z, so that there is no cost associated with that machine.

As with the primal problem, there are nonnegativity requirements for the dual, that is,

$$C_x, C_y, C_z \geq 0$$

These requirements constrain opportunity costs from being negative. A negative opportunity cost would make no sense because it would mean that profit could be increased by giving up the resource.

Solving the Dual Problem

The solution to the dual problem follows exactly the same steps as before. That is, identify the values of the decision variables at each corner, evaluate the objective function using each set of values of the C_i, and select that set that yields the minimum value for the objective function.

Because there are three variables, a graphic solution would require three-dimensional analysis and would be extremely difficult to draw and interpret. An algebraic approach is more straightforward, but with three constraints and three decision variables, even this approach can be cumbersome. The solution to this particular problem is simplified because it is known that constraint X in the original problem is not binding, and therefore the opportunity cost of machine X hours is zero (i.e., $C_x = 0$). Thus the problem reduces to

$$\begin{aligned} \text{minimize:} \quad & C = 80C_y + 60C_z \\ \text{subject to:} \quad & 2C_y + 2C_z \geq 3 \\ & 2C_y \geq 1 \\ & C_y, C_z \geq 0 \end{aligned}$$

Further, it is known that both constraints Y and Z are binding so that both C_y and C_z must be positive. As this can only occur at the intersection of the two constraints, consider the constraints as equalities and solve them simultaneously. The solution is $C_y = 0.5$ and $C_z = 1$, which represent the opportunity cost per hour of time on machines Y and Z, respectively. That is, a one-hour reduction in time available on machine Y would reduce profit by $0.50 and on machine Z by $1.00.

Evaluating these costs using the objective function yields a cost of $100, that is,

$$C = 90(0) + 80(0.5) + 60(1) = \$100$$

This minimum cost is the same as the rate of profit for the primal problem. That is, at the point of optimal resource allocation, profit equals the value or the opportunity cost of the resources being used to generate that profit.

Thus the linear programming analysis has established the opportunity cost of an hour of time on each machine as $C_x = 0$, $C_y = 0.50$, and $C_z = 1$. The value of each C_i is the increase in profit associated with one additional hour of time on the ith machine.

The opportunity cost of any resource is its value to the firm. The term *shadow price* is often used in the context of dual programming problems to describe this opportunity price. That is, the C_i in the problem are the shadow prices of the machine hours. As the firm makes plans to add more machine capacity, it can compare the shadow price to the market or acquisition price of additional hours of machine time. If the shadow price exceeds the acquisition price, profit can be increased by acquiring more hours. Thus the dual problem provides direction to management when making decisions about expanding productive capacity.

Summary

Linear programming is a technique for solving constrained optimization problems where the objective function and the resource constraints are linear. Although the early applications of this tool were in the production area, linear programming has been successfully used in marketing, finance, transportation, and most other functional areas of management. To assume linear relationships in production is to assume that there are constant returns to scale in production and that output and input prices are constant. These relationships imply that cost and profit per unit are constant for all levels of output.

Conceptually, linear programming problems can be solved graphically or algebraically. The graphic approach consists of identifying the feasible region and then shifting the objective function until an optimal solution is found at a corner of that feasible set. In the algebraic approach, the corners of the feasible set are identified and the values of the decision variables determined at those corners. Then the objective function is evaluated for each set of decision variables so identified.

If the objective function has the same slope as one of the constraints, multiple solutions to the linear program will occur. This poses no problem, as the standard solution techniques still will result in finding one of these several optimal solutions. In other cases, there is no feasible solution because the constraint system is such that there are no values of the decision variables that simultaneously satisfy all of the constraints. A resolution of this problem requires that one or more constraints be relaxed.

For every primal linear programming problem, there is an associated linear program referred to as the dual problem. If the primal problem requires maximizing an objective function, the dual linear program will be a minimization problem. The dual problem is structured using the columns of the primal problem. The solution to the dual problem results in estimates of the opportunity cost or shadow price of the resources that constrain the primal problem. The optimal solutions to the primal and dual problem yield the same value for the objective functions.

Discussion Questions

7-1. What assumptions about production, cost, and profit functions are implied in linear programming analysis?

7-2. In Chapter Six, isoquant and isocost functions are used to demonstrate how to maximize output subject to a budget constraint. Describe the differences between that approach and the linear programming approach to solving a problem where the objective is to maximize output subject to one or more machine-time constraints.

7-3. Explain the relationship between the primal and dual linear programming problems. If the primal problem is to maximize production subject to machine-time constraints, how would the dual problem be stated?

7-4. Why is it that the resource associated with a binding constraint has a positive opportunity cost but the resource associated with a nonbinding constraint has a zero opportunity cost?

7-5. Why do only the corner points of the feasible region need to be evaluated in solving a linear program?

7-6. List two managerial problems (other than those described in the chapter) where linear programming tools could be used.

Problems

7-1. Graph the region that is defined by each set of inequalities listed below.

(a)
$$3x + 2y \le 150$$
$$x + 2y \le 80$$
$$x \ge 0$$
$$y \ge 0$$

(b)
$$2x + 2y \le 100$$
$$4x + 6y \le 240$$
$$2x + 5y \ge 100$$
$$x \ge 0$$
$$y \ge 0$$

(c)
$$10x + 5y \le 50$$
$$2y \le 15$$
$$3x \le 9$$
$$x \ge 0$$
$$y \ge 0$$

(d)
$$x + y \le 40$$
$$2x + y \le 60$$
$$3x + 3y \ge 60$$
$$x \ge 0$$
$$y \ge 0$$

7-2. Graph the feasible region defined by the following set of inequalities:

$$x + y \le 40$$
$$2x + 4y \le 100$$
$$3y \le 60$$
$$x \ge 0$$
$$y \ge 0$$

Using a graphical approach, determine that point in the feasible region (i.e., the values of x and y) that maximizes each of the following objective functions:

(a) $z = x + 3y$

(b) $z = 6x + 4y$

7-3. Given the following linear program,

$$\text{maximize } \pi = 4Q_A + 3Q_B$$

subject to the following machine-time constraints:

$$Q_A + 2Q_B \leq 100$$
$$2Q_A + Q_B \leq 80$$

and the nonnegativity constraints

$$Q_A, Q_B \geq 0$$

(a) Solve the program using both an algebraic and graphical approach. Check to be sure that the optimal values of the decision variables are the same for both solutions.

(b) Set up the associated dual problem and solve algebraically. Check to be sure that the value of the optimized objective function is the same for both the primal and dual problems.

(c) What is the opportunity cost of one hour of time on each of the machines?

7-4. The officer in charge of a military mess hall has been ordered to design a minimum cost survival type meal that could be used in the event of a serious emergency. The meal is to consist only of milk and ground beef but must provide the following nutrient-units: calories—300, protein—200, and vitamins—50. The nutrient content per ounce of each food is as follows:

	Milk	Ground Beef	Minimum Units
Calories	20	15	300
Protein	10	25	250
Vitamins	10	4	100

Milk can be purchased at $0.02 per ounce, and the price of ground beef is $0.04 per ounce.

(a) Use linear programming to determine the composition of the lowest cost meal (i.e., ounces of milk and beef) and the cost of that meal.

(b) Set up the associated dual problem and explain how the shadow price (i.e., the value) of calories, protein, and vitamins would be determined.

7-5. National Publishing produces textbooks in plants in Boston, Atlanta, St. Louis, Denver, and San Francisco that are then shipped to distribution centers in Newark, Chicago, Dallas, and Los Angeles. National is publishing a new managerial economics text and must supply its distribution facilities. The relevant data on demands from each distribution center, production capacity at each plant, and cost of shipping a book from each plant to each distribution center are shown below:

Manufacturing Plant	Distribution Centers				Production Capacity
	(1) Newark	(2) Chicago	(3) Dallas	(4) Los Angeles	
	Shipping Costs per Unit				
1. Boston	$0.20	$0.35	$0.40	$0.60	40,000
2. Atlanta	0.35	0.40	0.45	0.50	10,000
3. St. Louis	0.30	0.20	0.30	0.40	15,000
4. Denver	0.50	0.40	0.30	0.30	15,000
5. San Francisco	0.70	0.50	0.45	0.20	20,000
Demand	20,000	40,000	30,000	10,000	

The president of National wants to know how to supply each distribution center to minimize the total shipping costs of meeting the demands at each center. Set up the transportation linear program to solve this problem.

7-6. The Economics Department at Southern State University produces two products—teaching, measured in student credit hours taught (H), and research, measured in pages published in professional journals (P). In any academic term, the department has 8,250 faculty-hours to devote to teaching and research activities. Teaching output is valued at $40 per credit hour and research output at $1,000 per page published in journals. It is estimated that it takes 2.2 faculty-hours per quarter to produce one credit hour and about 24 faculty hours per page published in a good journal. In order to meet its mandate from the state legislature, the department must generate at least 1,800 student credit hours per quarter; to maintain credibility in the Economics profession, the department must publish at least 120 pages of research output each quarter.

(a) Set up the linear programming problem and draw a graph of the feasible region.

(b) Solve the problem algebraically to determine how the department chairman should decide the output mix between credit hours and pages in order to maximize the value of departmental output.

References

Dantzig, G. B. 1963. *Linear Programming and Extensions.* Princeton, N.J.: Princeton University Press.

Dorfman, R., Samuelson, P. A., and Solow, R. M. 1958. *Linear Programming and Economic Analysis.* New York: McGraw-Hill.

Hillier, F. S., and Lieberman, G. J. 1980. *Introduction to Operations Research,* 3rd ed. San Francisco: Holden-Day.

Loomba, N. P., and Turban, E. 1974. *Applied Programming for Management.* New York: Holt, Rinehart and Winston.

McNamara, J. R. 1976. "A Linear Programming Model for Long-Range Capacity Planning in an Electric Utility." *Journal of Economics and Business,* Spring–Summer, pp. 227–235.

Rau, N. 1981. *Matrices and Mathematical Programming: An Introduction for Economists.* New York: St. Martin's Press.

Summers, E. L. 1972. "The Audit Staff Assignment Problem: A Linear Programming Analysis." *The Accounting Review* 47(July): 443–449.

Cost Theory

8

Preview

The theory of cost, together with the principles of demand and production, constitute three of the basic areas of managerial economics. Few significant resource allocation decisions are made without a thorough analysis of costs. For the profit-maximizing firm, the decision to add a new product depends on a comparison of the additional revenues and costs associated with that new product. Similarly, decisions on capital investment (e.g., new machinery or a warehouse) are made by comparing the rate of return on the investment with the opportunity cost of the funds used to make the capital acquisitions. Costs are also important in the nonprofit sector. For example, to obtain funding for a new dam, a government agency must demonstrate that the value of the benefits of the dam, such as flood control and water supply, exceeds the cost of the project.

This chapter focuses on those principles of cost theory integral to decisions about optimal price and output rates. In contrast to the accountant's approach to costs, the economist focuses on the concept of opportunity cost. In the first section, this economic concept of cost is developed. Next, the link between production theory and the principles of cost is developed. It is shown that efficient resource combinations for producing specific rates of output can be translated into cost data. Cost functions are then developed for both the short-run and long-run cases. Finally, several special cost-related topics are discussed. These include profit contribution analysis, the principle of operating leverage, and the concept of social versus private costs.

The Economic Concept of Cost

The term "cost" has different meanings. Therefore, it is important that the term be defined precisely. As suggested in Chapter 1, the noneconomic definition tends to focus on the explicit and historical dimension of cost. In contrast, the economic approach to cost includes both explicit and implicit costs and emphasizes opportunity cost rather than historical cost.

Explicit and Implicit Costs

In general, *explicit costs* are those costs that involve an actual payment to other parties, while *implicit costs* represent the value of forgone opportunities but do not involve an actual cash payment. Implicit costs are just as important as explicit costs but are sometimes neglected in decision making because they are not as obvious. For example, a manager who runs his own business forgoes the salary that could have been earned working for someone else. This implicit cost may not be reflected in accounting statements, but rational decision making demands that it be considered.

Table 8-1. Accounting Versus Economic Approach to Determining Profit per Unit of Output for Buy Rite Bakery

	Accounting Approach	Economic Approach
Price of finished product	$5.00	$5.00
Less: Cost of wheat input	3.00	5.00
Less: Other costs	1.50	1.50
Net profit per unit	$0.50	− $1.50

The traditional accounting approach bases the dollar value of cost on an historical cost perspective. For example, a producer of refined cereal products may have an inventory of wheat that was purchased at $3 per bushel but that is now worth $5 per bushel. The traditional approach would value the wheat at the historical per bushel cost of $3, and could result in a poor decision being made. This problem is illustrated by the following example.

Buy Rite Bakery, a bread manufacturer, is considering using its inventory of wheat to make a new whole wheat bread that will be sold to stores for $5 per unit (six loaves). Suppose that 1 bushel of wheat is required to make each unit of this new type of bread, while $1.50 of labor, energy, and other costs per unit of output are also incurred.

The traditional approach to cost might value the wheat input at $3 per bushel and estimate profit on the finished product to be $0.50 per unit, as shown in Table 8-1. In contrast, the economic approach to cost would value the wheat at the current market price of $5 per bushel. Analyzing the decision from this approach would result in a loss of $1.50 for each bushel. Note that the only difference in the two approaches is the value placed on the inventory of wheat.

Consider this problem in another way. What will be the net revenue per bushel to the firm if the new bread is manufactured as opposed to simply selling the wheat inventory in the market without processing it? If the decision is made to manufacture the bread, the firm will have a net cash flow of $3.50 per bushel, that is, the $5 selling price less $1.50 of other costs. In contrast, if the wheat is simply sold rather than processed, the firm would receive a net cash flow of $5 per bushel. Clearly, selling the wheat rather than producing the bread is the better alternative because profits will be greater. The example demonstrates that the use of the correct cost concept is absolutely essential to sound decision making.

Normal Profit and Costs

In industries characterized by substantial competition, principles of managerial economics indicate a tendency for profit to be eliminated. This sounds inconsistent with the conventional idea that most firms report a profit each year. The apparent inconsistency disappears when the concepts of economic costs and economic profits are understood.

Because all opportunity costs must be accounted for, the proper concept of cost includes a normal payment to all inputs, including managerial and entrepreneurial skills and capital supplied by the owners of the firm. A normal return to management or capital is the minimum payment necessary to keep those resources from being transferred to some other firm or industry. Thus cost includes a normal rate of profit. The term *economic profit* refers to profit in excess of these normal returns. That is, economic profit is defined as revenue less all economic costs.

If only explicit costs are recognized, a firm earning zero economic profit could still show a positive accounting-type profit. That is, the normal return to entrepreneurial skill and capital and a return for taking risk are costs to the economist but profit to the accountant. Unless otherwise indicated, the term *cost* refers to all explicit and implicit costs, and the term *profit* refers to revenues after all economic costs, including the normal returns described above, have been subtracted.

Marginal, Incremental, and Sunk Costs

Clearly, cost is an important consideration in decision making. But it is essential that only those costs that matter be considered. Three types of cost need to be discussed: sunk costs, marginal costs, and incremental costs.

Sunk costs are expenditures that have been made in the past or that must be paid in the future as part of a contractual agreement. Future rental payments on a warehouse that must be paid as part of a long-term lease are an example. In general, sunk costs are irrelevant in making decisions. For instance, suppose that the monthly rental payment on the warehouse is $1,000 but the firm finds it no longer needs the space. The firm offers to sublease the space but finds that the best offer is for $800 per month. Clearly, the firm should take that offer; the additional revenue, $800 per month, is greater than the additional cost, which is zero. The $1,000 per month payment is irrelevant because it must be made regardless of the decision to rent the warehouse space. In retrospect, the decision to enter the long-term lease was a mistake, but the costs associated with that decision are sunk.

Marginal cost refers to the change in total cost associated with a 1-unit change in output. This concept is integral to short-run decisions about profit-maximizing levels of output. For example, in an automobile manufacturing plant, the marginal cost of making one additional car per production period would be the labor, materials, and energy costs directly associated with that extra car. In contrast, the term *incremental cost* refers to the total additional cost of implementing a management decision. The costs associated with adding a new product line, acquiring a major competitor, or developing an in-house legal staff fall into the broader class of incremental costs. In a sense, marginal cost is that subcategory of incremental cost that refers to the additional cost associated with the decision to make marginal variation in the rate of output.

In the warehouse rental example, the only incremental costs the firm faces when subleasing the property may be the cost of preparing and negotiating the details of the new rental agreement. Clearly, the $1,000 per month sunk cost is not a component of incremental cost. It is essential that incremental cost measurement be done carefully so that all possible additional costs are included, but costs that are sunk are not included.

The Cost of Long-Lived Assets

Another area where accounting and economic definition of cost diverge is for assets such as buildings, machinery, and other types of capital equipment that may last for a number of years. These are referred to as *long-lived assets*. The accounting approach is to combine historical cost and one of several depreciation methods to assign part of the historical cost to each year of the defined life of the asset so that the total expenses over that life will equal the historical cost. For example, using the straight-line depreciation method, an asset costing $1,000 and having a five-year life would be depreciated at the rate of $200 per year. Thus, the total historical cost will be exhausted entirely over this five-year period. The asset may have considerable value to the firm after this period, but this is not reflected in the accounting statements. Often, tax guidelines and considerations dictate the decision on the depreciation method used. The accounting approach to cost measurement is adequate if the objective is to have an arbitrary method for reporting on the flow of funds into and out of the business over some time interval. However, as a tool for managerial decision making, the approach is flawed.

In contrast, the economic approach determines the cost as the difference between the market value of the asset at the beginning and end of the period. This point can be illustrated by a simple example. If the market value of the machine was $1,000 at the beginning of the year and $600 at the end, the economic cost of using it for that period was $400.

KEY CONCEPTS

- All relevant costs, both explicit and implicit, must be considered in decision making. Opportunity cost, the value of the resource in its next best use, is the best way to measure cost.
- A normal profit is included in the concept of economic cost. Such a normal profit (or return to any factor of production) is the minimum payment necessary to keep that resource from moving to another firm or industry.
- In general, only incremental and marginal costs are relevant in decision making; sunk costs are of little or no importance.
- The economic cost of a long-lived asset during a period is the change in its market value from the beginning to the end of the period.

Production and Cost

A cost function relates cost to the rate of output. The basis for a cost function is the production function and the prices of inputs. Recall from Chapter 6 that the expansion path defines the efficient combination of capital and labor inputs rates for producing any rate of output. Thus the minimum cost of a specific level of output is found by multiplying the efficient rate of each input by the respective prices and summing the costs.

In Chapter 6 it was shown that the production function, $Q = 100\sqrt{KL}$, has an expansion path $K = (w/r)L$. Thus if the price of labor is 2 and the price of capital is 1, the expansion path would be $K = 2L$ and the firm would expand by adding inputs at the rate of 2 units of capital for each additional unit of labor. Table 8-2 shows a set of efficient labor–capital combinations, the rate of output associated with each combination, and the cost of those inputs. Columns (3) and (6) represent the long-run total cost schedule for this production function given that input prices are $w = 2$ and $r = 1$. This schedule shows the total cost of producing various rates of output. For example, the total cost of producing an output rate of 707 units per period is $20. That is, 10 units of capital at a price of $1 per unit and 5 units of labor at a price of $2 per unit would cost $20. In this example it is a long-run function because both inputs are variable—there is no fixed factor of production.

In the short run, at least one factor of production is fixed and the cost of that input is defined as *fixed cost*. Regardless of the rate of output, that cost does not change. That is, management has made a decision in the past that obligates the firm to pay certain costs that are independent of the rate of output. A long-term lease on a warehouse, an employment contract with an executive, and a collective bargaining agreement with a labor union are examples of commitments that may result in fixed costs.

As suggested in Chapter 6, the length of the short run varies with the nature of the business. A child's lemonade stand may be able to vary all inputs in a matter of minutes. Conversely, adding additional capacity to a nuclear generating facility would probably take years. The length of the short run depends on the degree of asset specialization, the economic life of the assets, the time necessary

Table 8-2. Production and Cost Data

(1)	(2)	(3)	(4)	(5) Cost	(6)
K	L	Q	Capital	Labor	Total
2	1	141	$ 2	$ 2	$ 4
4	2	283	4	4	8
6	3	424	6	6	12
8	4	565	8	8	16
10	5	707	10	10	20

to order and install new capital equipment, and the amount of training that labor requires.

Asset specialization refers to the number of uses of an asset. For example, a nuclear generator can only be used to generate electricity in a nuclear power plant and is a very specialized asset. Thus it might be difficult to sell that generator because only another nuclear power plant could use it. Conversely, many trucks can be used to haul a variety of products and are rather unspecialized assets. If a firm decides that one of its trucks is no longer needed, it could easily be sold in the market and its cost is eliminated. As a general rule, the more specialized a firm's assets, the longer the short run.

In general, the longer the life of the asset, the longer the period defined as the short run. Buildings and some types of machinery may have an economic life of many years. Once in place, their costs may be fixed for a long period of time. Also, it may take months or even years to order and install certain types of capital equipment and/or to develop a particular set of skills in labor. In such cases the firm may find that part of the cost of its productive capacity is fixed for that period.

KEY CONCEPTS

- The long-run total cost of any rate of output is determined by the expansion path of the firm and the prices of the inputs.
- If one input is fixed, the firm is operating in the short run, and the costs associated with that input are called fixed costs. The costs associated with the nonfixed inputs are called variable costs.

Short-Run Cost Functions

Managerial decision making is facilitated by information that shows the cost of each rate of output. Both short-run and long-run cost functions are considered in this section.

Total, Average and Marginal Cost Functions

Consider a production process that combines variable amounts of labor with a fixed capital stock, say, ten machines. In this process, the rate of production is changed by varying the rate of labor input. Assume that the firm can vary the labor input freely at a cost of $100 per unit of labor. Therefore, the expenditure for labor is the variable cost. If the ten machines are rented under a long-term lease at $100 per machine per production period, the fixed cost would be $1,000 per period. Table 8-3 summarizes the relevant production and cost data for this production process.

Table 8-3. Short-Run Production and Cost Data

Input Rate		Rate of Output	Total Fixed Cost	Total Variable Cost	Total Cost
Capital	Labor*				
10	0	0	$1,000	$ 0	$1,000
10	2.00	1	1,000	200	1,200
10	3.67	2	1,000	367	1,367
10	5.10	3	1,000	510	1,510
10	6.77	4	1,000	677	1,677
10	8.77	5	1,000	877	1,877
10	11.27	6	1,000	1,127	2,127
10	14.60	7	1,000	1,460	2,460
10	24.60	8	1,000	2,460	3,460

*The use of fractional units of labor is necessary to obtain integer values for output.

The total cost data from Table 8-3 are shown graphically in Figure 8-1a. Note that fixed cost is indicated by a horizontal line; that is, it is constant with respect to output. Total variable cost (TVC) begins at the origin, increases at a decreasing rate up to an output rate between 3 and 4, and then increases at an increasing rate. Total cost (TC) has the same shape as total variable cost but is shifted upward by $1,000, the amount of fixed cost.

Average or per unit cost functions often are more useful for decision making than are total cost functions. This is because managers must compare cost per unit of output to the market price of that output. Recall that market price is measured per unit of output. By dividing a total cost function by output, a corresponding per unit cost function is determined. That is,

$$\text{Average total cost: } ATC = \frac{TC}{Q} \tag{8-1}$$

$$\text{Average variable cost: } AVC = \frac{TVC}{Q} \tag{8-2}$$

$$\text{Average fixed cost: } AF = \frac{TFC}{Q} \tag{8-3}$$

The marginal cost per unit of output (MC) is the change in total cost associated with a 1-unit change in output, that is,

$$\text{Marginal cost: } MC = \frac{\Delta TC}{\Delta Q} \tag{8-4}$$

As is true of all associated total and marginal functions, marginal cost is the slope of the total cost function.

Using calculus, marginal cost is determined as the first derivative of the total cost function. That is, if the total cost function is

$$TC = f(Q)$$

marginal cost would be

$$MC = \frac{d(TC)}{dQ}$$

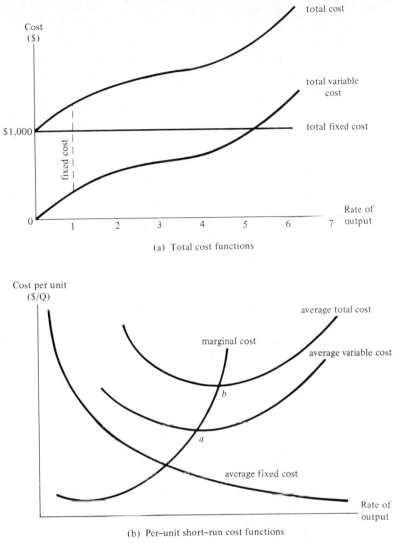

(a) Total cost functions

(b) Per–unit short–run cost functions

Figure 8-1. *Cost Functions.*

Based on the total cost functions in Table 8-3, data for each per unit cost function are reported in Table 8-4 and shown graphically in Figure 8-1b. The average total cost, average variable cost, and marginal cost functions are important in managerial decision making. In contrast, the average fixed cost function has little value for decision making. Further, the difference between average total cost and average variable cost is average fixed cost. Thus the *ATC* and *AVC* curves contain the information on fixed cost per unit in the unlikely event that such information is needed.

The per unit cost functions for many production systems have the U shape shown in Figure 8-1b. At low rates of production, there is too little of the variable input relative to the fixed input. As the variable input is increased, output rises

Table 8-4. Per Unit Cost Functions

Output	Average Fixed Cost (AFC)	Average Variable Cost (AVC)	Average Total Cost (ATC)	Marginal Cost (MC)
0	—	—	—	
1	$1,000	$200	$1,200	200
2	500	184	684	167
3	333	170	503	143
4	250	169	419	167
5	200	175	375	200
6	167	188	355	250
7	143	208	351	333
8	125	307	432	1,000

rapidly, and therefore the cost per unit falls. Initially, total cost increases but at a decreasing rate. This implies that marginal cost (the slope of total cost) is falling. Because of the law of diminishing marginal returns, additional units of the variable input result in smaller additions to output and thus marginal cost rises. When marginal cost exceeds average cost, then the average cost function begins to rise.

As is true of all marginal and average functions, as long as marginal cost is below the average cost curve, the average function will decline. When marginal is above average, the average cost curve will rise. This implies that marginal cost intersects both the average total cost and average variable cost functions at the minimum point of the average curves (points *a* and *b* in Figure 8-1b).

EXAMPLE
FINDING MINIMUM AVERAGE VARIABLE COST

Given the total cost function

$$TC = 1,000 + 10Q - 0.9Q^2 + 0.04Q^3$$

find the rate of output that results in minimum average variable cost.

Solution

Marginal cost is the first derivative of the total cost function

$$\frac{d(TC)}{dQ} = MC = 10 - 1.8Q + 0.12Q^2$$

Now, find the total variable cost function (TVC) by subtracting the fixed cost component ($1,000) from the total cost function. That is,

$$TVC = 10Q - 0.9Q^2 + 0.04Q^3$$

Then find average variable cost (AVC) by dividing TVC by output (Q). That is,

$$AVC = \frac{TVC}{Q} = \frac{10Q - 0.9Q^2 + 0.04Q^3}{Q}$$

$$= 10 - 0.9Q + 0.04Q^2$$

Now the minimum point of AVC occurs at its intersection with marginal cost, so equate the AVC and MC functions and solve for Q. That is,

$$AVC = MC$$

$$10 - 0.9Q + 0.04Q^2 = 10 - 1.8Q + 0.12Q^2$$

Rearranging terms yields the quadratic equation

$$-0.08Q^2 + 0.9Q = 0$$

or

$$Q(-0.08Q + 0.9) = 0$$

which has the roots

$$Q_1 = 0 \quad \text{and} \quad Q_2 = 11.25$$

Disregarding the root associated with a zero output rate, it is seen that the minimum AVC is achieved at an output rate of 11.25 units.

Average Cost Functions and Production Theory

There is a correspondence between the product functions developed in Chapter 6 and the per unit cost functions. Recall that average product is defined as output divided by the variable input. If labor is the variable input, the average product function is

$$AP_L = \frac{Q}{L}$$

or

$$\frac{1}{AP_L} = \frac{L}{Q}$$

Because labor is the only variable input, average variable cost is the expenditure on labor (wL) divided by output, or

$$AVC = \frac{wL}{Q}$$

but because

$$\frac{L}{Q} = \frac{1}{AP_L}$$

it follows that

$$AVC = w\frac{1}{AP_L} \tag{8-5}$$

Thus there is an inverse relationship between average product and average cost. If average product is increasing, average variable cost will be decreasing and vice versa.

The marginal product of labor is defined as the change in output divided by the change in labor, that is,

$$MP_L = \frac{\Delta Q}{\Delta L}$$

or

$$\frac{1}{MP_L} = \frac{\Delta L}{\Delta Q}$$

and marginal cost is the additional expenditure on labor $(w\ \Delta L)$ divided by output. Thus

$$MC = \frac{\Delta TC}{\Delta Q} = \frac{w \cdot \Delta L}{\Delta Q}$$

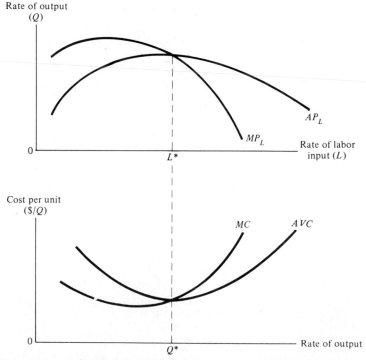

Figure 8-2.   *Relation Between Product Functions and Per Unit Cost Functions.*

but because

$$\frac{\Delta L}{\Delta Q} = \frac{1}{MP_L}$$

it follows that

$$MC = w\frac{1}{MP_L}$$

That is, marginal cost is the price of the input times the reciprocal of marginal product. As before, if marginal product is increasing, marginal cost will be decreasing, and vice versa. The law of diminishing marginal returns implies that as output increases due to the addition of more of a variable input to a fixed input, a point will be reached where marginal product will decrease. At that point, the marginal cost function will begin to increase.

These relationships between the product and per unit cost functions are depicted in Figure 8-2. As efficiencies in the production process are captured initially by using more variable input in combination with the fixed input, per unit marginal costs fall. When these efficiencies are exhausted, per unit marginal cost increases. Thus the concept of U-shaped average and marginal cost curves is based on the principles of marginal productivity developed in Chapter 6.

KEY CONCEPTS

- Per unit or average cost functions tend to be more useful than total cost functions in making some decisions. The average cost functions are found by dividing the relevant total cost functions by output, that is,

$$\text{Average cost: } ATC = \frac{TC}{Q}$$

$$\text{Average variable cost: } AVC = \frac{TVC}{Q}$$

$$\text{Average fixed cost: } AFC = \frac{TFC}{Q}$$

- Marginal cost per unit is the change in the total cost function associated with a 1-unit change in output, that is,

$$MC = \frac{\Delta TC}{\Delta Q}$$

- There is an important relation between the product functions and the per unit cost functions. When average or marginal product is increasing, average or marginal cost per unit will be decreasing, and vice versa.
- The law of diminishing marginal returns implies that as more of a variable input is combined with a fixed amount of another input, a point will be reached where marginal product will decrease, and therefore marginal cost will increase.

Long-Run Cost Functions

It is said that the firm operates in the short run but plans in the long run. At any point in time, the firm has one or more fixed factors of production. Therefore production decisions must be made based on short-run cost curves. However, most firms can plan to change the scale of their operation by varying all inputs in the long run and by doing so, move to a preferred short-run cost function.

Recall from Chapter 6 that returns to scale are increasing, decreasing, or constant depending on whether a proportional change in both inputs results in output increasing more than in proportion, less than in proportion, or in proportion to the increase in inputs. These three possibilities are shown in Figure 8-3.

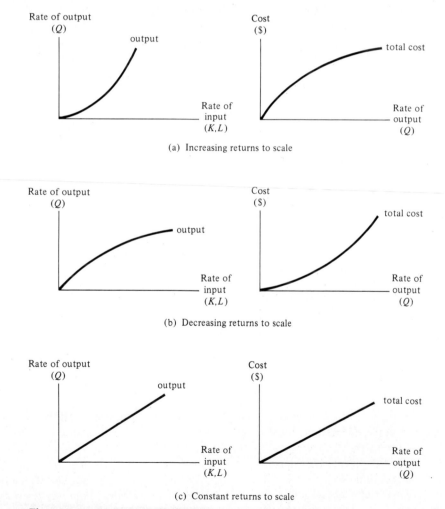

Figure 8-3. *Returns to Scale.*

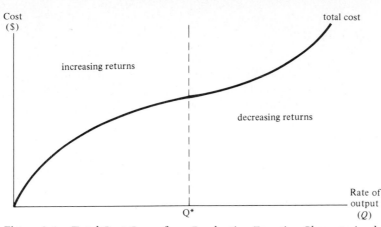

Figure 8-4. *Total Cost Curve for a Production Function Characterized by Increasing Returns, Then by Decreasing Returns.*

There is a direct correspondence between returns to scale in production and the long-run cost function for the firm. If returns to scale are increasing, inputs are increasing less than in proportion to increases in output. Because input prices are constant, it follows that total cost also must be increasing less than in proportion to output. This relationship is shown in Figure 8-3a. If decreasing returns to scale apply, the total cost function increases at an increasing rate. Constant returns to scale implies that total cost will change in proportion to changes in output. The latter two relationships are shown in parts (b) and (c) of Figure 8-3.

The production process of many firms is characterized first by increasing returns and then by decreasing returns. In this case, the long-run total cost function first would increase at a decreasing rate and then increase at an increasing rate as shown in Figure 8-4. Such a total cost function would be associated with a U-shaped long run average cost function.

Suppose that a firm can expand the scale of operation only in discrete units. For example, the generators for large electric power plants are made in only a few sizes. Often, these power plants are built in multiples of 750 megawatts (MW). That is, output capacity of alternative plants would be 750 MW, 1500 MW, 2250 MW, and so on. The short-run average cost functions in Figure 8-5 (labeled SAC_1 through SAC_4) are associated with each of four discrete scales of operation. The long-run average cost function for this firm is defined by the minimum average cost of each level of output. For example, output rate Q_1 could be produced by plant size 1 at an average cost of C_1 or by plant size 2 at a cost of C_2. Clearly, the cost is lower for plant size 1, and thus point a is one point on the long-run average cost curve. By repeating this process for various rates of output, the long-run average cost is determined. For output rates of zero to Q_2, plant 1 is the most efficient and that part of SAC_1 is part of the long-run cost function. For output rates Q_2 to Q_3, plant 2 is the most efficient, and for output rates Q_3 to Q_4, plant 3 is the most efficient. The scallop-shaped curve shown in boldface in

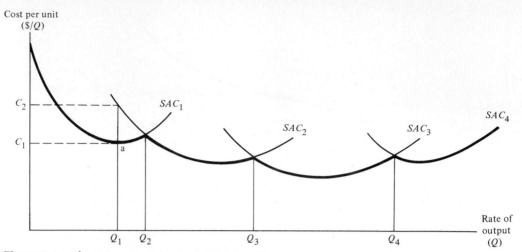

Figure 8-5. *Short-Run Average Cost Functions for Four Discrete Plant Sizes.*

Figure 8-5 is the long-run average cost curve for this firm. This boldfaced curve is called an *envelope curve.*

In general, a firm will have a great many alternative plant sizes to choose from. There is a short-run average cost curve corresponding to each. A few of the short-run average cost curves for these plants are shown in Figure 8-6. Only one point or a very small arc of each short-run cost curve will lie on the long-run average cost function. Thus long-run average cost can be shown as the smooth U-shaped curve labeled *LAC.* Corresponding to this long-run average cost function is a long-run marginal cost curve *LMC* which intersects *LAC* at its minimum point a, which is also the minimum point of short-run average cost curve 18.

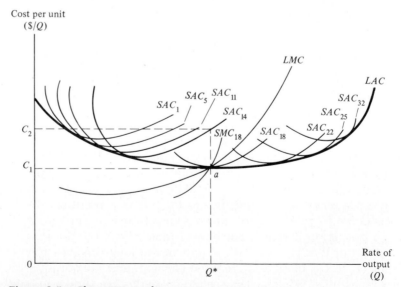

Figure 8-6. *Short-Run and Long Run Cost Curves.*

The short-run marginal cost curve (SMC_{18}) corresponding to SAC_{18} is also shown. But $SMC_{18} = SAC_{18}$ at the minimum point of SAC_{18}. Thus at point a and only at point a the following unique result occurs:

$$SAC = SMC = LAC = LMC \qquad (8\text{-}7)$$

The long-run cost curve serves as a long-run planning mechanism for the firm. For example, suppose that the firm is operating on short-run average cost curve SAC_{14} in Figure 8-6, and the firm is currently producing an output rate of Q^*. By using SAC_{14}, it is seen that the firm's cost per unit is C_2. Clearly, if projections of future demand indicated that the firm could expect to continue selling Q^* units per period at the market price, profit could be increased significantly by increasing the scale of plant to the size associated with short-run average curve SAC_{18}. With this plant, cost per unit for an output rate of Q^* would be C_1 and the firm's profit per unit would increase by $C_2 - C_1$. Thus total profit would increase by $(C_2 - C_1) \cdot Q^*$.

KEY CONCEPTS

- The firm's long-run average cost function will be:
  Decreasing where returns to scale in production are increasing.
  Constant where returns to scale are constant.
  Increasing where returns to scale are decreasing.
- The long-run average cost function is the envelope curve consisting of points or arcs on a number of short-run average cost curves.

Special Topics in Cost Theory

The cost functions developed thus far are essential to making managerial decisions about output and prices. At this point, several extensions of cost theory that have implications for managerial decisions will be discussed. These concepts include profit contribution analysis (including the special case of break-even analysis), operating leverage, and social and private costs.

Profit Contribution Analysis

The difference between price and average variable cost ($P - AVC$) is defined as *profit contribution.* That is, revenue on the sale of a unit of output after variable costs are covered represents a contribution toward profit. At low rates of output, the firm may be losing money because fixed costs have not yet been covered by the profit contribution. Thus, at these low rates of output, profit contribution is used to cover fixed costs. After fixed costs are covered, the profit contribution is a direct contributor to profit.

A manager may want to know the output rate necessary to cover all fixed costs and to earn a "required" profit of π_R. Assume that both price and variable cost per unit of output (AVC) are constant. Profit (π) is equal to total revenue (PQ) less the sum of total variable costs [($AVC(Q)$)] and fixed costs. Thus

$$\pi_R = PQ - AVC(Q) - FC$$

Solving this equation for Q yields a relation that can be used to determine the rate of output necessary to generate a specified rate of profit. That is,

$$Q = \frac{FC + \pi_R}{P - AVC} \tag{8-8}$$

For example, suppose that $FC = \$10,000$, $P = \$20$, $AVC = \$15$, and that the firm has set a required profit target of $\$20,000$. The required rate of output would be 6,000, that is,

$$Q_R = \frac{\$10,000 + \$20,000}{20 - 15} = 6,000$$

A special case of this equation is where the required economic profit is zero[2], that is, $\pi_R = 0$. This is called the breakeven point for the firm. The breakeven rate of output, Q_e, is given by the equation

$$Q_e = \frac{FC}{P - AVC} \tag{8-9}$$

Using the same data as above, it is seen that the breakeven rate of output is 2,000, that is,

$$Q_e = \frac{\$10,000}{20 - 15} = 2,000$$

This example of breakeven analysis is shown graphically in Figure 8-7. Fixed cost is shown as the horizontal line at $\$10,000$. Total cost is given by the equation

$$TC = FC + VC$$

Because $FC = 10,000$ and variable cost per unit is 15, the total cost function is

$$TC = 10,000 + 15Q$$

Since price is constant, the total revenue function is

$$TR = 20Q$$

which is shown as a straight line through the origin having a slope of 20. The breakeven point occurs at an output rate of 2,000, which is at the intersection of the total revenue and total cost functions. At this point, both total revenue and total cost are $\$40,000$.

This linear approach to profit contribution has been criticized because of the assumption that both price and average variable cost are constant. The price assumption is not unrealistic for many firms, as they are able to sell all they can produce at the going price. However, other firms, especially those where sales

---

[2] Recall that a zero economic profit means that normal returns are being earned by capital and other factors of production.

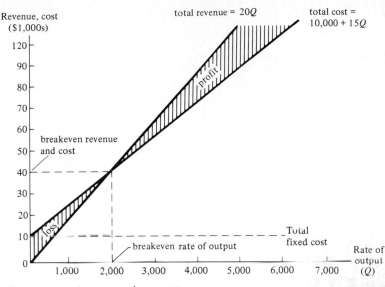

Figure 8-7. *Linear Breakeven Diagram.*

are large relative to the size of the market, may have to reduce price to sell more output. For some firms, the assumption of constant average variable cost may be unrealistic. However, if the price and average variable cost are roughly constant, at least over the limited range of output relevant to the problem, breakeven analysis is a useful tool for managerial decisions. However, care and judgment are required in its application.

EXAMPLE

BREAKING EVEN ON MICROCOMPUTER SOFTWARE

Microapplications Inc. is a small firm that specializes in the production and mail-order distribution of computer programs for microcomputers. The accounting department has gathered the following data on development and production costs for a typical program and the documentation (i.e., the manual) that must accompany the program.

Development costs (fixed):

Program development	$10,000	
Manual preparation and typesetting	3,000	
Advertising	10,000	
Total		$23,000

Variable costs per unit:

Blank disk	$ 2.00	
Loading cost	0.50	
Postage and handling	1.25	
Printing of manual	2.75	
Total		$ 6.50

A typical program including the manual sells for $40.

Based on this information:

1. Determine the breakeven number of programs and the total revenue associated with this volume.
2. Microapplications has a minimum profit target of $40,000 on each new program it develops. Determine the unit and dollar volume of sales required to meet this goal.
3. While this program is still in the development stage, market prices for software fall by 25 percent due to a significant increase in the number of programs being supplied to the market. Determine the new breakeven unit and dollar volume.

Solution

1. Based on fixed costs of $23,000 and variable costs per unit of $6.50, the unit volume required to breakeven is

$$Q_e = \frac{\text{fixed cost}}{P - AVC} = \frac{\$23,000}{\$40 - \$6.50} = 686.6$$

The dollar volume is determined by multiplying price times the breakeven quantity;

$$TR = PQ_e = 40(686.6) = \$27,464$$

2. The quantity necessary to meet the profit target is

$$Q_R = \frac{FC + \pi_R}{P - AVC} = \frac{23,000 + 40,000}{40 - 6.50} = 1,880.6$$

The associated dollar volume would be

$$TR = PQ_R = 40(1,880.6) = \$75,224$$

3. If the price declines by 25 percent to $30, the new breakeven quantity would be

$$Q_e = \frac{23,000}{30 - 6.50} = 978.7$$

The corresponding dollar volume is

$$TR = 30(978.7) = \$29,361$$

If the assumptions of constant price and average variable cost are relaxed, breakeven analysis can still be applied, although the key relationships (total revenue and total variable cost) will not be linear functions of output. Nonlinear total revenue and cost functions are shown in Figure 8-8. The cost function is conventional in the sense that at first, costs increase but less than in proportion to output as increasing returns to scale occur and then increase more than in

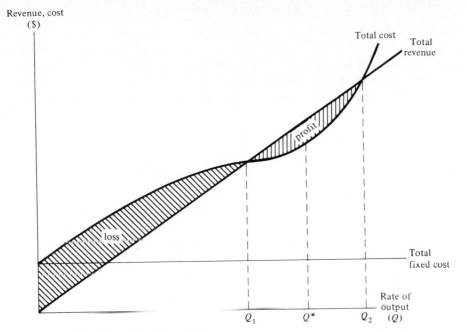

Figure 8-8. *Nonlinear Breakeven Diagram.*

proportion to output as decreasing returns to scale occur. There are two break-even points, Q_1 and Q_2. Note that profit, the vertical distance between the total revenue and total cost functions, is maximized at output rate Q^*.

Of the two breakeven points, only the first, corresponding to output rate Q_1, is relevant. When a firm begins production, management usually expects to incur losses. But it is important to know at what output rate the firm will go from a loss to a profit situation. In Figure 8-8, the firm would want to get to the break-even output rate Q_1 as soon as possible and then, of course, move to the profit-maximizing rate Q^*. However, the firm would not expand production beyond Q^*, because this would result in a reduction of profit. No rational manager would ever increase the rate of production to the second breakeven rate Q_2 and therefore that break-even point is irrelevant.

KEY CONCEPTS

- The output rate that yields a specified rate of economic profit is found by dividing required profit plus total fixed cost by profit contribution, that is,

$$Q_R = \frac{\pi_R + TFC}{P - AVC}$$

- Breakeven analysis is a special case of required profit analysis where the required or specified profit is zero.

Operating Leverage

A firm is said to be *highly leveraged* if fixed costs are large relative to variable costs. For example, relatively large fixed costs may result from the firm having large amounts of borrowed money with large fixed-interest obligations. Also, firms may have large investments in fixed assets, such as plant and equipment with heavy fixed expenses, including depreciation charges and/or lease payments that must be paid regardless of the rate of output.

A general characteristic of a highly leveraged firm is that it experiences more variation in profits for a given percentage change in output than does a less leveraged firm. This is because total cost for a highly leveraged firm will change less than in proportion to a change in output rate, and therefore profit will tend to change more than in proportion to output changes. Conversely, for a firm with little or no fixed cost, profit should change more nearly in proportion to output changes.

Leverage can be analyzed using the concept of *operating profit elasticity* (E_π), defined as the percentage change in profit associated with a 1 percent change in unit sales or rate of output. That is,

$$E_\pi = \frac{\% \text{ change in profit}}{\% \text{ change in unit sales}} \qquad (8\text{-}10)$$

or

$$E_\pi = \frac{\dfrac{\Delta\pi}{\pi}}{\dfrac{\Delta Q}{Q}} = \frac{\Delta\pi}{\Delta Q} \cdot \frac{Q}{\pi} \qquad (8\text{-}11)$$

For infinitesimally small changes in Q, the operating profit elasticity is

$$E_\pi = \frac{d\pi}{dQ} \cdot \frac{Q}{\pi}$$

If the price of output is assumed to be constant regardless of the rate of output, operating profit elasticity depends on three variables: the rate of output, the level of total fixed costs, and variable cost per unit of output. This can be seen by substituting the equations for profit

$$\pi = PQ - (AVC)(Q) - TFC$$

and change in profit

$$\Delta\pi = P(\Delta Q) - (AVC)(\Delta Q)$$

into equation (8-11). That is,

$$E_\pi = \frac{[P(\Delta Q) - (AVC)(\Delta Q)]/[PQ - (AVC)(Q) - TFC]}{\Delta Q/Q}$$

Simplifying this equation yields a computational formula for the operating profit elasticity:

$$E_\pi = \frac{Q(P - AVC)}{Q(P - AVC) - TFC} \tag{8-12}$$

Close inspection of this equation reveals that for two firms with equal prices, rates of output, and variable costs per unit, the firm having the greater total fixed cost will have the higher operating profit elasticity. This is because fixed cost has a minus sign in the denominator. Making the denominator smaller makes the elasticity greater.

Table 8-5 shows profit and operating profit elasticity data for two firms A and B with differing total fixed costs and average variable costs. Note the following characteristics. First, the elasticities are zero at a zero output rate and negative until a breakeven rate of output is reached because the denominator of equation (8-12) is negative. When the firm is incurring losses, the operating profit elasticity is not meaningful because it suggests that profit falls as output increases, which is not the case. However, when profits are being earned, a negative elasticity is meaningful. It means that output has increased beyond that rate that results in maximum profit. Thus any increase in output results in a decrease in profit.

The second important characteristic is that leverage is greatest for smaller output rates and declines as output increases. Finally, at the same rate of output, the elasticity is always higher for firm B than for firm A. This is because B has higher total fixed costs and lower variable costs per unit than does A. Therefore, if both firms are producing the same output rate, for any change in output the percentage change in profit will be greater for B than for A. For example, a 50 percent increase in output from $Q = 1,000$ to $Q = 1,500$ results in a 100 percent increase in profit for B compared to a 63 percent increase for A.

Over time, profits for firm B will vary considerably more than for A. In a sense, the management of B has structured the firm so that it takes more risk. When the rate of output is high, profits will be greater at B than A. However, if economic conditions become unfavorable and output falls, profit will decline more rapidly

Table 8-5. Operating Profit Elasticity for Two Firms

Firm A:		Firm B:	
Price = $10.00		Price = $10.00	
AVC = 5.00		AVC = 2.00	
TFC = 1,000		TFC = 4,000	

Rate of Output	Profit		Operating Profit Elasticity	
	Firm A	Firm B	Firm A	Firm B
0	$ -1,000	$ -4,000	0	0
200	0	-2,400	Undefined	-0.67
500	1,500	0	1.67	Undefined
1,000	4,000	4,000	1.25	2.00
1,500	6,500	8,000	1.15	1.50
2,000	9,000	12,000	1.11	1.33

for the highly leveraged firm *B*. If output continues to fall, firm *B* will incur losses before *A* will. In a prolonged period of low demand, the risk of bankruptcy is greater for *B*. Thus the operating profit elasticity can be used as an indicator of risk.

Recall from Chapter 3 that there usually is a trade-off between risk and return. That is, greater returns are usually associated with greater risk, and vice versa. A management decision to become more leveraged (e.g., by incurring significant debt or a large capital investment program) effectively is a decision to accept greater risk for the chance to earn higher profit.

Social and Private Costs

Sometimes the production of goods and services affects third parties. These effects can be positive or negative. For example, suppose that United Auto contracts with Coastal Metals to produce steel for which United Auto pays the going price per unit. Both firms benefit and willingly participate in the transaction. However, in the process of producing the steel, smoke pollutes the air that a nearby resident must breathe. Costs have been imposed on this person, but no compensation is paid. Thus there is an unwilling participant in the transaction.

Such third-party effects are called *externalities* or *spillovers*. They can be negative, as in the example, or positive. An example of a positive externality would be if an apple producer located an orchard adjacent to a honey producer's beehives. The bee raiser would reduce the production cost of the apple grower by providing pollination of the apple trees, and the apple producer would produce pollen for the beehives.

While both positive and negative third-party effects are important, it is usually the negative externalities that attract the most attention. Air and water pollution, congestion on urban streets, noise (i.e., "ear" pollution), and crime are examples of negative externalities. In economic terms, an externality can be measured as the difference between social and private costs. For the producer, private cost is the sum of all the costs both explicit and implicit borne by that producer. These private costs include explicit payments for labor, raw materials, and taxes and any implicit costs, such as the resources contributed to the business by owners. Social cost is the cost to society at large and includes all the private costs plus other costs, if any, involuntarily borne by third parties.

The private cost of production for the steel producer discussed above may be shown by the AC_p and MC_p curves in Figure 8-9. To the extent that this firm imposes external costs such as air and water pollution or noise on third parties, social cost will exceed private cost. The AC_s and MC_s curves in Figure 8-9 represent the social cost of producing steel. The vertical distance between the social and private curves represents the external cost per unit of output, that is, the cost per unit borne by third parties.

External costs usually arise because of a poorly defined property right. For example, if the firm needs iron ore, it buys that ore from a miner who owns a well-defined property right to the ore. That right will be transferred to the steel

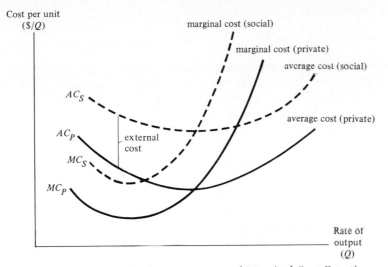

Figure 8-9. *Social and Private Average and Marginal Cost Functions.*

producer only upon payment of appropriate compensation. However, if the firm needs to dispose of certain waste products, it might choose to emit them into the atmosphere or dump them in a nearby river. The property rights to these air and water resources have not been well defined. Who owns the air or the water in the river? Who has the property right—those who want clean air or those who want to use the atmosphere as a waste receptacle? The market cannot operate effectively; thus, there may be a need for government action to define these property rights.

In recent years, managers have had to be much more cognizant of some of the possible third-party effects of their production decisions. State and federal antipollution laws have greatly reduced the problem of property rights to air and water, with the result that firms are more constrained in their actions that might have significant third-party effects.

KEY CONCEPTS

- A firm is said to be highly leveraged if fixed costs are high relative to variable costs. In general, the use of leverage implies higher risk (i.e., more variability in profit over time).
- Leverage can be measured by operating profit elasticity, defined as the percentage change in profit associated with a 1 percent change in output.
- Externalities result when the firm's production causes costs or benefits to be incurred by third parties. The most common externalities include air, water, and noise pollution and congestion.
- The net result of negative externalities is that the social costs (which include the externality costs) are higher than private costs.

Summary

The theory of cost is a fundamental area of managerial economics. The best measure of resource cost is the value of that resource in its highest-valued alternative use (i.e., its opportunity cost). Implied by an opportunity cost is the idea that both explicit and implicit costs are recognized. Examples of the latter include the value of labor and capital contributed to the firm by the manager/owner.

The cost of long-lived assets during the production period is the difference in the value of that asset between the beginning and end of the period. Because the opportunity cost concept is used, economic cost includes a normal return or profit to the firm. A normal return is defined as the minimum payment necessary to keep resources from moving to other firms or industries. Marginal and incremental costs are fundamental to decision making. Sunk costs generally are irrelevant.

The cost function relates cost to specific rates of output. The basis for the cost function is the production function and the prices of inputs. In the short run, the rate of input is fixed. The cost associated with that input is called fixed cost. The cost associated with the variable inputs is defined as variable cost. The total cost of any rate of output is equal to the total fixed cost plus the total variable cost of producing that output rate. Per unit cost functions include average total cost, average variable cost, average fixed cost, and marginal cost. Often, the per unit cost functions are more useful for decision making than are the total cost functions.

There is a correspondence between the per unit cost functions and the product functions. When the marginal or average product function is rising, the marginal or average cost function is falling. Conversely, when the marginal or average product function is decreasing, the associated per unit cost function will be increasing.

In the long run all costs are variable. The long-run average cost curve is the envelope of a series of short run average cost curves. If returns to scale are increasing, long-run average cost (LAC) will be decreasing. If returns to scale are decreasing, LAC will be increasing. The long-run cost functions are used for planning the optimal scale of plant size.

Profit contribution analysis is used to determine the output rate necessary to earn a specified profit rate. A special case of profit contribution theory is break-even analysis, wherein the rate of output necessary to generate a zero rate of economic profit is determined.

A firm is said to be highly leveraged if fixed costs are large relative to variable costs. Leverage is measured by the operating profit elasticity or the percentage change in profit associated with a 1 percent change in output. In general, increased leverage implies more variability in profit over time and therefore greater risk.

Private costs are those explicit and implicit costs paid by the firm. Social costs include private costs plus external costs incurred by third parties. External costs often arise because of poorly defined property rights and tend to cause inefficient resource allocations. Sometimes, government action is required to define these property rights.

Discussion Questions

8-1. Explain the relationship between the average product and average cost functions and between the marginal product and marginal cost functions.

8-2. The production manager of Interstate Insulation claims that breakeven analysis is of no value for her firm because cost per unit will vary with the rate of output. What is your reaction to this statement?

8-3. What is meant by each of the following terms: marginal cost, incremental cost, and sunk cost?

8-4. Why do increasing returns to scale imply a decreasing long-run average cost function and decreasing returns to scale imply an increasing long-run average cost function?

8-5. Why is the historical cost of inventory or capital equipment irrelevant for managerial decision-making?

8-6. If a firm found it could only operate at a breakeven output rate, would it stay in business?

8-7. The new president of United Motors has said, "We must reduce the operating profit elasticity for our company. We simply are too highly leveraged." What does this statement suggest about his attitude toward risk compared to that of the previous president? Explain.

8-8. Virtually all firms report the value of capital equipment and real estate based on historical cost less accounting depreciation. Do you think the reported value of these assets would approximate their market value? Explain. Would reporting the true market value of these assets provide investors with better information? Why?

8-9. A well-known consultant bills his clients $60 per hour for his services. His costs include rent on his office complex, two secretaries, subscriptions to professional journals, and depreciation on his car. These expenses are all fixed and total $4,250 per month or $25 per hour based on 170 hours per month.

During a slack period, he is offered a contract with a government agency but the maximum hourly rate the agency is allowed to pay is $22.50. He turns down the contract saying his hourly costs exceed $22.50 and he would lose money by taking the contract. Does this consultant need an evening course in managerial economics? Explain.

Problems

8-1. Use the cost and output data for each of five production periods below to determine equations for all of the relevant total and per-unit cost functions:

Production Period	Rate of Output (Q)	Total Cost (TC)
1	10	1,800
2	0	1,000
3	4	1,320
4	2	1,160
5	7	1,560

8-2. Based on a consulting economist's report, the total and marginal cost functions for Advance Electronics, Inc. are

$$TC = 200 + 5Q - 0.04Q^2 + 0.001Q^3$$
$$MC = 5 - 0.08Q + 0.003Q^2$$

P. R. Swensen, president of the company, determines that knowing only these equations is inadequate for decision-making. You have been directed to do the following:

(a) Determine the level of fixed cost (if any) and equations for average total cost, average variable cost, and average fixed cost.

(b) Determine the rate of output that results in minimum average variable cost.

(c) If fixed costs increase to $500, what output rate will result in minimum average variable cost?

8-3. President Cazier of Eastern State University has decided on a new budgeting system for all departments in the university. Historically, each department was provided with a fixed budget for the year. Being a trained economist, the president has decided to allow student demand for courses to determine how the university's budget is to be allocated to departments. Each quarter, every department will receive $40 for each student-credit-hour (SCH) taught. For example, a three-credit course for fall quarter might enroll thirty-five students, thus, generating 105 SCH. For offering that course, the department would receive $4,200 (i.e., $40 × 105 SCH).

The following table shows selected cost data for each of four university departments:

Department	Number of Faculty	Salary Cost (Fixed)	Variable Cost per SCH
Economics	10	$400,000	$2.00
English	15	410,000	1.50
Physics	8	280,000	6.00
Physical Education	7	175,000	3.50

(a) Determine the breakeven number of student-credit-hours for each department.

(b) What change in the type of course offerings and assignment of faculty to courses might result from such a budgeting system?

(c) Suppose that student-credit-hours have been declining steadily for several years in physical education while they have been growing rapidly in economics. What advantages and disadvantages would the new budgeting system offer given these trends?

8-4. Ruby Vazquez has invested $80,000 in a hardware store. Business has been good, and the store shows an accounting profit of $10,000 for the last year. This profit is after taxes and after payment of a $20,000 salary to Ms. Vazquez. This salary is less than the $40,000 she could make at another job. During the year, the interest rate was 10 percent. Considering the risk involved in the hardware business, she believes that a 15 percent after-tax rate of return is appropriate for this type of investment.

(a) Given this information, calculate the *economic* profit earned by Ms. Vazquez.

(b) What accounting profits would the firm have to earn in order for the firm to breakeven in terms of economic profits?

8-5. Universal Orthodontics, Inc. manufactures false teeth with a pliable base that allows one size to fit any mouth. A set of these dentures sells for $80. Fixed costs are $200,000 per production period and the profit contribution is 40 percent of price.

   (a) Determine the operating profit elasticity at output rates of 8,000, 10,000, and 12,000 units.

   (b) For the next production period, fixed costs will increase to $300,000 due to a major capital investment program, but the new and more efficient machinery will result in lower variable production costs so that variable cost per unit will be reduced by $8. If price is unchanged, recompute the operating profit elasticity at output rates of 8,000, 10,000, and 12,000 units.

   (c) What change in the risk-return trade-off has the company made?

8-6. Southern Airways, a small regional airline, has a daily late evening flight into Atlanta. The plane must be in Atlanta at 8:00 A.M. each morning for a flight to Richmond, Virginia. Unfortunately, the charge for a plane remaining overnight in Atlanta is $500. One alternative is to schedule a 9:00 P.M. flight to Gainesville, Florida (a one-hour trip) and a 6:00 A.M. flight back to Atlanta. There is no charge for the overnight stay at Gainesville. However, the flights to and from Gainesville will average only about ten passengers each at a one-way fare of $50. The operating cost of the plane is $600 per hour, and fixed costs are allocated to each flight at the rate of $300 per hour. Should the plane stay in Atlanta overnight, or should flights to and from Gainesville be scheduled? Explain your decision.

8-7. During the last period, the sum of profit and fixed costs totalled $100,000. Unit sales were 10,000. If variable cost per unit was $4, what was the selling price of a unit of output?

8-8. A firm that causes significant air pollution has the following private total cost function:

$$TC = 400 + 10Q - 0.08Q^2 + 0.002Q^3$$

If all of the social costs due to pollution are accounted for and added to the private costs incurred by the firm, the total cost function would be:

$$TC^* = 400 + 11Q - 0.07Q^2 + 0.003Q^3$$

Determine the total cost of pollution and the pollution cost per unit of output (i.e., social less private costs) at output rates of 25 and 50 units per period.

Problems Requiring Calculus

8-9. Given the total cost function for Randle Enterprises:

$$TC = 100Q - 3Q^2 + 0.1Q^3$$

   (a) Determine the average cost function and the rate of output that will minimize that function.

   (b) Determine the marginal cost function and rate of output that will minimize that function.

8-10. Logan Manufacturing produces ball point pens. Fixed costs in each production period are $25,000, and the total variable cost (TVC) is given by equation.

$$TVC = 0.15 + 0.1Q$$

where Q is the rate of output. What output rate would minimize average total cost?

References

Anthony, R. N. 1970. "What Should 'Cost' Mean?" *Harvard Business Review* 48(June):121–131.

Bassett, L. 1969. "Returns to Scale and Cost Curves." *The Southern Economic Journal* 36(October):189–190.

Henderson, J. M., and Quandt, R. E. 1980. *Microeconomic Theory: A Mathematical Approach*, 3rd ed. New York: McGraw-Hill.

Hirshleifer, J. 1962. "The Firm's Cost Function: A Successful Reconstruction." *Journal of Business* 35(July):235–255.

Koot, R. S., and Walker, D. A. 1970. "Short-Run Cost Functions of a Multiproduct Firm." *Journal of Industrial Economics* 18(April):118–128.

Miller, E. M. 1978. "The Extent of Economies of Scale: The Effect of Firm Size on Labor Productivity and Wage Rates." *Southern Economic Journal* 44(January):470–487.

Reinhardt, U. E. 1973. "Breakeven Analysis for Lockheed's Tri-Star: An Application of Financial Theory." *Journal of Finance* 28(4):821–838.

Shephard, A. R. 1971. "A Note on the Firm's Long-Run Average Cost Curve." *Quarterly Review of Economics and Business* 11(Spring):77–79.

Stigler, G. J. 1958. "The Economies of Scale." *Journal of Law and Economics* 1(October):54–71.

Appendix:
Calculus and Cost Theory

Calculus can be used to demonstrate important principles underlying the theory of economic cost. In this appendix, a hypothetical total cost function is used to demonstrate the derivation of the per unit cost functions and to show that for U-shaped per unit cost functions, the intersection of the marginal and average cost functions will occur at minimum average cost per unit.

Total cost (*TC*) is equal to the sum of the total variable cost (*TVC*) and total fixed cost, i.e.,

$$TC = TVC + TFC \qquad (8A\text{-}1)$$

The per unit cost functions [average total cost (*AC*), average variable cost (*AVC*), and average fixed cost (*AFC*)] are found by dividing the total cost function by output (*Q*). That is,

$$AC = \frac{TC}{Q} \qquad (8A\text{-}2)$$

$$AVC = \frac{TVC}{Q} \qquad (8A\text{-}3)$$

$$AFC = \frac{TFC}{Q} \qquad (8A\text{-}4)$$

The marginal cost function is found by taking the first derivative of the total cost function with respect to output,

$$MC = \frac{d(TC)}{dQ} \qquad \text{(8A-5)}$$

It can be shown easily that the MC and AC curves intersect at the minimum point of AC. The minimum point of AC occurs where the first derivative is zero, i.e.,

$$\frac{d(AC)}{dQ} = 0$$

Because

$$AC = \frac{TC}{Q}$$

it follows that

$$\frac{d(AC)}{dQ} = \frac{Q[d(TC)/dQ] - TC}{Q^2} = 0 \qquad \text{(8A-6)}$$

But the derivative $d(TC)/dQ$ is simply marginal cost, so (8A-6) can be rewritten as

$$\frac{d(AC)}{dQ} = \frac{Q \cdot MC - TC}{Q^2} = 0$$

or

$$\frac{MC}{Q} = \frac{TC}{Q^2}$$

Multiplying both sides of the equation by Q yields

$$MC = \frac{TC}{Q}$$

but TC/Q is average cost so it follows that

$$MC = AC$$

Thus, marginal cost equals average cost at the minimum point of the latter.

The following example will illustrate this principle. Given a total cost function of the form

$$TC = 40Q^3 - 900Q^2 + 10,000Q$$

By dividing the total cost function by Q, the average or per unit cost function is determined,

$$AC = \frac{TC}{Q} = 40Q^2 - 900Q + 10,000$$

The marginal cost function is

$$MC = \frac{d(TC)}{dQ} = 120Q^2 - 1{,}800Q + 10{,}000$$

It has been shown that marginal cost intersects average cost at the minimum point of the average cost functions. This will be demonstrated for the per unit average cost function used above, i.e.,

$$AC = 40Q^2 - 900Q + 10{,}000$$

The output corresponding to the minimum point of the average cost function is found by setting the first derivative of that function equal to zero and solving for Q.

$$\frac{d(AC)}{dQ} = 80Q - 900 = 0$$

$$Q = 11.25$$

That the function is a minimum and not a maximum at $Q = 11.25$ is seen by noting that the second derivative of the average cost function is positive, i.e.,

$$\frac{d^2(AVC)}{dQ^2} = 80 > 0$$

Thus, the second-order condition for a minimum is satisfied.

Now, it remains to be shown that the marginal cost and average cost functions will intersect at $Q = 11.25$. This is done by first equating MC and AC, i.e.,

$$MC = AC$$

$$120Q^2 - 1{,}800Q + 10{,}000 = 40Q^2 - 900Q + 10{,}000$$

Rearranging terms yields

$$80Q^2 - 900Q = 0$$

or

$$Q(80Q - 900) = 0$$

which yields two values of Q, specifically, $Q_1 = 0$ and $Q_2 = 11.25$. Disregarding the root $Q = 0$ (i.e., the zero output rate is not of interest), it is seen that at $Q = 11.25$, the minimum point AC, the two cost functions intersect.

Thus, it has been shown in general and for a specific cost function that marginal cost intersects average cost at the minimum point of average cost.

Estimation of Production and Cost Functions

9

Preview

The principles of production and cost theory developed in Chapters 6 and 8 are fundamental to an understanding of economics and provide an important conceptual framework for analyzing managerial problems. However, sometimes short-run price and output decisions and long-run planning require more than this conceptual framework. That is, quantitative estimates of the parameters of the cost and/or production functions are required for some decisions in both the short run and the long run.

The general approach to estimating production and cost functions is the same as that for most estimation problems. That is:

1. Use the principles of cost and production theory to specify the appropriate functional form, that is, the specific relationship among the relevant economic variables.
2. Collect the appropriate data.
3. Estimate the function using the data collected in step 2.
4. Evaluate and interpret the results.

Although this approach appears straightforward, each step can involve problems and special considerations. For example, there are a number of functional forms that can be used to describe a production process. Which of these is best suited to the problem being studied? Also, the data on inputs and costs sometimes are difficult to acquire. Necessarily, the process of specifying and estimating production and cost functions requires skill that comes only after considerable training and experience.

In this chapter four topics are developed. First, some general considerations relevant to the estimation of both production and cost functions are outlined. Of particular importance are the level of aggregation (i.e., firm, industry, or economy) and the choice of a cross-section or time-series approach. In the second and third sections, the general approaches to estimating production and cost functions are covered. In each case, data measurement problems, alternative functional forms, and interpretation problems are discussed. A final section is devoted to the principle of duality, the relationship between the production and cost functions. In that section it is shown that a knowledge of the production function and input prices is sufficient to derive all the relevant cost relationships.

General Considerations

Production and cost functions can be estimated for different levels of aggregation. For example, a plant manager may want to know the cost function for the plant. Management at the corporate level may be interested in a more aggregated production and cost function for the entire enterprise so that comparisons can be made with similar functions estimated for other firms in the industry. Finally, economists may be interested in estimating an aggregate production function for the economy.

Generally, as the level of aggregation increases, the problems of data collection and interpretation of results also increases. Consider a small plant that produces one homogeneous product using only one type of labor and one kind of capital equipment. Suppose that the production period is defined as one eight-hour shift. The measurement of output, labor, and capital is not especially difficult in this case. The measure of output is simply physical units produced each day. Labor could be measured in terms of total production worker hours and capital might be number of machine hours.[1]

At the corporate level the problem becomes more complex. Output may consist of a number of very different products produced in different plants using many different kinds of labor and capital equipment. Reducing these disparate data to some sort of composite measures of output, capital, and labor may be extremely difficult. Also, the interpretation of any resultant production or cost function may be equally difficult.

A production function for the economy could be estimated using gross national product (GNP) as an output measure, total hours of labor employed, and the aggregate capital stock data as reported in the U.S. Census of Manufacturers. However, the exact interpretation of the estimated equation would be difficult.

Clearly, the greater the level of aggregation, the greater the problem of data measurement and the more difficult it is to evaluate and interpret the estimated cost and production relations. As the level of aggregation increases, so does the disparity in types of outputs and inputs that must be added together. Also, the production process becomes more difficult to describe and to specify appropriately in a production function.

Another general problem is whether to use time-series or cross-section data to estimate the functions. This decision will depend on the type of data available and the purpose of the analysis. A time-series study uses data from one plant or industry over a number of different time periods to estimate the production or cost relationship. For example, cost and output data for a plant might be recorded weekly for a year and then these weekly observations used to estimate a cost function. In contrast, in a cross-section study, output and cost data from each of a number of plants might be collected for one week and those data used to estimate an average or composite cost function for the group of plants. Each approach has its advantages and disadvantages.

If the objective is a cost or production function for a particular plant, there is little choice but to use a time-series approach. One problem here is that important production characteristics tend to change over time. For example, production technology may change as new machinery and production methods are used. Also, changes in the prices of inputs may distort the cost function. Because

---

[1] Even in this simple case, there are some problems to consider. For example, how are the hours of nonproduction workers (e.g., secretaries, custodians, etc.) to be included? How will the building that houses the machines be included in the capital stock?

the cost function shows the cost of producing at different rates of output, it is assumed that technology and input prices are constant. If these prices have changed, some sort of price index must be used to deflate them to a common base. A similar problem can occur when output is measured in value terms. A price rise may increase the value of output even though there has been no change in the number of units produced.

The problem of prices changing over time is avoided in a cross-section study, but the analyst must be aware that input and output prices may differ among locations where production is taking place. Some adjustment will have to be made if such differences are significant. The fundamental problem with the cross-section study is that the estimated function is representative of the average cost or production function for the set of production facilities being studied. The function does not provide information about cost/production relationships in any one plant. However, such representative functions can provide useful information about returns to scale or differences in per unit costs in plants of different sizes. Also, a typical or representative function may provide an estimate of the cost or production relationships that could be expected if a new plant were built. Of course, that would be true only if the technology used in the new plant were comparable to that used in the facilities used to estimate the function.

This discussion should be a warning that estimation of cost and production functions can be a complicated process. Even when the aggregation and time-series versus cross-section issues have been resolved, there are other problems associated with measuring output and inputs. These problems will be discussed in the next two major sections.

KEY CONCEPTS

- Production and cost functions can be estimated at varying levels of aggregation, including the firm, industry, and economy-wide levels. The problems of data collection and interpretation of the estimated relationships increase with the level of aggregation.
- A cross-section study provides an estimate for the cost or production relationship for the typical or average firm in the group under study. Time-series data can be used to estimate a cost or production function for one firm, an industry, or the economy.

Estimating Production Functions

In general, estimation of production functions refers to making a quantitative estimate of the relationship between the rate of output and the rates of input of factors of production. It is assumed here that inputs can be combined into single measures of capital and labor so that the general production function to be estimated is

$$Q = f(K, L) \qquad (9\text{-}1)$$

The problems of measuring the inputs and output, specifying the functional form, and estimating the function are discussed below.

Data Requirements and Measurement Problems

Suppose that a decision is made to estimate the production function for a single plant based on time-series data. Measures of output and the capital and labor inputs are necessary. If the plant produces one relatively homogeneous product, measuring output should not be difficult. For example, tons of fertilizers, flour, or cement are relatively clear measures of output. But what about a plant that produces both compact and full-size cars and buses and trucks? How will those different products be combined into a composite measure of output? Even more difficult, what if the plant produces a number of altogether different products and the mix of those products changes from one production period to another? Obviously, considerable thought must be given to developing a composite output measure.[2] One alternative is to measure output in value terms by using market prices. But adjustments must be made for any price changes that may have occurred during the study period.

The labor input typically is measured in terms of total worker hours or days of labor, but other problems must be considered. For example, some adjustment might be made for workers of different skill levels. Suppose that a firm hired both journeyman and apprentice machinists and that the average journeyman produced 40 percent more output per hour than an apprentice. An adjustment for this difference in labor quality might be made by weighting each hour of journeyman time by some factor (e.g., 1.4) to reflect the higher productivity of these workers. Further, some labor at a corporate headquarters may be directly involved in production at other plants. How is this labor to be accounted for in the production function?

The capital input is usually the most difficult variable to measure. The capital stock includes the building, machinery, and other long-lived equipment that contributes to the production process. In any given production period, this capital stock contributes to production, but it is very difficult to measure that contribution. For example, not all machines are in use all the time. Some machines are newer and more productive than others. The typical approach is to estimate the market value of relevant capital stock in the plant and use that as a measure of the capital input. If new buildings, machinery, or other equipment are added (or withdrawn) during the production period, the capital input data are adjusted accordingly.

Although the data problems associated with estimating a production function are not inconsequential, they can be overcome. To focus on the other dimensions of the estimation problem, in the remainder of this section it is assumed that good measures of output, labor, and capital have been developed.

[2] Consider the problems associated with measuring output in a university. Teaching output might be measured by the number of student credit hours (SCH) taught. But one SCH in a graduate seminar in physics is not the same as one SCH in freshman English. University research output is even more difficult to measure. One approximation might be to use the number of pages of published results in books and professional journals. But a page in the most prestigious journal reflects greater output than a page in a much less prestigious journal.

Functional Forms

Although a variety of functional relationships have been used to describe production relationships, only the widely used Cobb–Douglas production function is discussed here. Recall that the general Cobb–Douglas function is of the form

$$Q = AK^a L^b \tag{9-2}$$

where A, a, and b are the parameters that, when estimated, describe the quantitative relationship between the inputs (K and L) and output (Q).

The marginal products of capital and labor are functions of the parameters A, a, and b and the rates of the capital and labor inputs. That is,

$$MP_K = \frac{\partial Q}{\partial L} = aAK^{a-1}L^b \tag{9-3}$$

$$MP_L = \frac{\partial Q}{\partial L} = bAK^a L^{b-1} \tag{9-4}$$

It can be shown that a and b are the production elasticities for capital and labor, respectively.[3] A production elasticity is the percentage change in output

---

[3] The production elasticity $\left(E_Q = \dfrac{\% \Delta Q}{\% \Delta \text{input}} \right)$ can be written

$$E_Q = \frac{\Delta Q/Q}{\Delta \text{input}/\text{input}}$$

For infinitesimally small changes in the input the elasticity can be written

$$E_Q = \frac{\partial Q/Q}{\partial(\text{input})/\text{input}}$$

or

$$E_Q = \frac{\partial Q}{\partial(\text{input}}\frac{\text{input}}{Q}$$

For the Cobb–Douglas production function ($Q = AK^a L^b$), the production elasticity of capital is

$$E_{Q,K} = \frac{\partial Q}{\partial K}\frac{K}{Q}$$

and the marginal product of capital is

$$\frac{\partial Q}{\partial K} = aAK^{a-1}L^b$$

Now substitute $AK^a L^b$ for Q in the denominator of the right-hand term of the elasticity formula, yielding

$$E_{Q,K} = (aAK^{a-1}L^b)\frac{K}{AK^a L^b}$$

which reduces to

$$E_{Q,K} = a$$

Similarly, the production elasticity for labor is derived as follows:

$$E_{Q,L} = \frac{\partial Q}{\partial L}\frac{L}{Q} = bAK^a L^{b-1}\frac{L}{AK^a L^b} = b$$

associated with a 1 percent change in input. Thus

$$a = \frac{\% \Delta Q}{\% \Delta K} \text{ or } \frac{\partial Q}{Q} \Big/ \frac{\partial K}{K} = \frac{\partial Q}{\partial K} \cdot \frac{K}{Q} \qquad (9\text{-}5)$$

and

$$b = \frac{\% \Delta Q}{\% \Delta L} \text{ or } \frac{\partial Q}{Q} \Big/ \frac{\partial L}{L} = \frac{\partial Q}{\partial L} \cdot \frac{L}{Q} \qquad (9\text{-}6)$$

Also, it was shown in Chapter 6 that the sum of these parameters $(a + b)$ can be used to determine returns to scale. That is, if

$(a + b) > 1 \Rightarrow$ increasing returns to scale
$(a + b) = 1 \Rightarrow$ constant returns to scale
$(a + b) < 1 \Rightarrow$ decreasing returns to scale

Having numerical estimates for the parameters of the production function provides a tremendous amount of information about the production system under study. The marginal product functions, production elasticities, and returns to scale can all be determined from the estimated production function. It is easily seen in Equations (9-3) and (9-4) that the condition for diminishing marginal productivity requires that the parameters a and b must be less than 1. Consider the marginal product function for capital

$$MP_K = aAK^{a-1}L^b$$

If $a > 1$, the marginal product will increase if K is increased. If $a < 1$, the marginal product will decrease if K is increased.

The Cobb–Douglas function does not lend itself directly to estimation by the regression methods described in Chapter 2 because it is a nonlinear relationship. Technically, an equation must be a linear function of the parameters in order to use the ordinary least-squares (OLS) regression method of estimation. Clearly, the Cobb–Douglas production function does not meet this criterion without some type of transformation. However, a linear equation can be derived by taking the logarithm of each term. That is,

$$\log Q = \log A + a \log K + b \log L \qquad (9\text{-}7)$$

That this is simply a linear relationship can be seen by setting

$$y = \log Q, \quad A^* = \log A, \quad X_1 = \log K, \quad X_2 = \log L$$

and rewriting the function as

$$y = A^* + aX_1 + bX_2 \qquad (9\text{-}8)$$

This function can be estimated directly by the least-squares regression technique and the estimated parameters used to determine all the important production relationships.

EXAMPLE
ESTIMATING A PRODUCTION FUNCTION

Given the following data on output and inputs for ten production periods:

Production Period	Output (Q)	Capital (K)	Labor (L)
1	225	10	20
2	240	12	22
3	278	10	26
4	212	14	18
5	199	12	16
6	297	16	24
7	242	16	20
8	155	10	14
9	215	8	20
10	160	8	14

1. Estimate the parameters (A, a, and b) of a Cobb–Douglas production function using the least-squares regression method.
2. Use the estimated parameters to determine:
   a. Returns to scale.
   b. The production elasticities for capital and labor.
   c. Whether the production function is characterized by diminishing marginal returns.
3. Determine the marginal products of capital and labor for the input combination $\{K = 20, L = 30\}$.

Solution

1. First, transform the production function by taking natural logarithms of each term in the function, that is,

$$\log Q = \log A + a \log K + b \log L$$

By transforming the output, capital, and labor data into logarithms, the least-squares regression method is used to estimate the parameters, yielding

$$\log Q = 2.322 \quad + 0.194 \log K + 0.878 \log L \qquad R^2 = 0.97$$
$$\qquad\;\; (12.66) \quad\;\; (3.74) \qquad\qquad (14.09)$$

The estimated parameters are $a = 0.194$, $b = 0.878$, and the value of A is determined by taking the antilogarithm of 2.322, which is 10.2. Thus the estimated production function in its original functional form is

$$Q = 10.2K^{0.194}L^{0.878}$$

The t-values are shown in parentheses below the estimated coefficients. All are greater than 2.365 (the tabled values of Student's t-distribution) meaning that the estimates of A, a, and b are all significantly different from zero at the

0.05 probability level. This means that one can be confident that there is a strong relationship between output and the two inputs, labor and capital.

2. a. Returns to scale are increasing because $a + b = 1.072$ is greater than 1.
    b. The production elasticities for capital and labor are 0.194 and 0.878, respectively. This means that a 1 percent change in capital or labor would increase output by 0.194 percent and 0.878 percent, respectively.
    c. Because both a and b are less than 1, the production function is characterized by diminishing marginal returns.

3. The marginal product functions for capital and labor are

$$MP_K = aAK^{a-1}L^b$$

and

$$MP_L = bAK^aL^{b-1}$$

Substituting the estimated values for the parameters A, a, and b and the values of capital and labor ($K = 20$ and $L = 30$) yields the following marginal products:

$$MP_K = (10.2)(0.19)(20^{-0.81})(30)^{0.87} = 3.50$$
$$MP_L = (10.2)(0.87)(20^{0.19})(30^{-0.13}) = 10.58$$

These estimates mean that a 1-unit change in capital would result in a 3.50-unit change in output, and a 1-unit change in labor would be associated with a 10.58-unit change in output.

KEY CONCEPTS

- The Cobb–Douglas production function $Q = AK^aL^b$ has been used to estimate production relationships in a number of industries.
- To estimate a Cobb–Douglas production function using the ordinary least-squares regression method, the function must be transformed into a linear relationship by taking the logarithm of each term [i.e., $\log Q = \log A + a \log K + b \log L$].
- The parameters a and b of a Cobb–Douglas production function are the production elasticities for capital and labor, respectively. The sum of these parameters can be used to determine returns to scale. If $(a + b) > 1$, returns to scale are increasing, if $(a + b) = 1$, returns to scale are constant, and if $(a + b) < 1$, returns to scale are decreasing.

Estimating Cost Functions

Many short-run and long-run decisions made by management require some knowledge of the firm's cost functions. For example, efficient short-run pricing decisions require that marginal revenue equal short-run marginal cost. Similarly, decisions on the optimal plant size may require information on long-run average and marginal cost relationships. Thus there often is a need for quantitative estimates of these key cost relationships. Obtaining the necessary data for estimating cost functions can be a challenge for the manager. In the following section some of the data measurement and collection problems are discussed. Also included is a discussion of estimating alternative forms of the cost function.

Data Requirements and Measurement Problems

As the cost function relates total or average cost to quantity produced, data on those two variables is the minimum information necessary for cost function estimation. However, other factors may also influence costs and they also should be considered. For example, firms that have more than one production shift may find significant differences in costs between or among shifts. These differences can arise because of the need to pay higher wage rates to those who work at night, lower electric power rates during off-peak hours, and/or differential intensity of use of capital equipment. Also, costs may vary during the year due to differences in heating and air-conditioning needs and other seasonal factors.

Once these problems have been considered and taken into account, another more fundamental set of problems must be addressed. Recall that opportunity costs are the most relevant for effective decision making and that costs based on traditional accounting methods may not accurately reflect the true opportunity costs. Yet, in most firms only accounting cost data will be available. These data should be examined closely to determine if they at least approximate the true opportunity costs. For example, is the raw materials inventory valued at the market price or at historic cost? If it is valued at its historic cost, some adjustment must be made so that the cost will reflect market value, which is the true opportunity cost. In the case of the owner-manager, are the opportunity costs of her time and capital investment being fully reflected in the cost data?

Matching up cost and output can also be a problem. In single-product firms, costs must be apportioned to each production period in accounting for total costs. Sometimes costs may be incurred in one period that are actually associated with output in a later period. In the multiproduct firm, relevant costs must be allocated to particular products and periods. Depreciation on plant and equipment must accurately reflect the change in the value of that capital during the production period and be allocated among products. The typical depreciation techniques, such as the straight-line or double-declining-balance methods, generally do not reflect the true opportunity cost of long-lived assets. Thus adjustments in accounting information will be necessary in many cases. As some accounting methods are quite arbitrary, such adjustments may be difficult.

Finally, the cost function may be estimated based on cross-section or time-series data. A cross-section study would draw data from a number of production facilities for the same production period. For example, data from each plant of a multiplant firm might be used or the data might be gathered from a number of similar plants of several firms. The cost function estimated using cross-section data represents the "typical" or "average" plant of the group under study. Because the objective is to measure cost differences at different output rates, the analyst must carefully check the production technology and input prices at each plant. If there are significant differences in prices or technology, some adjustment must be made. For example, what if a large plant had significantly higher input costs than did the others. The resultant cost function might show the average cost rising at high levels of output, not because of production technology but simply because input prices are higher in the large plant.

A time-series study uses data from one plant for a number of production periods. Thus a properly estimated cost function will describe the cost–output relationship in that plant. For most within-firm managerial decisions, such a cost function is more useful than one representative of a "typical" plant that has been estimated using cross-section data. But, there is a special set of problems associated with the use of time-series data. For example, the length of time covered by the data is very important. Recall that regression estimation requires a number of observations on the dependent and independent variables. The time interval must be long enough to include a minimum of ten to fifteen production periods. However, if the period of time is too long, inflation may have increased the price of one or more inputs or a change in production technology might have occurred. Because a cost function relates cost to output rate assuming that production technology and input prices are held constant, if such changes have occurred, the data must be adjusted to reflect their effect on cost. There may also be a problem associated with the timing of input costs and output. Sometimes costs incurred today are associated with output that may be produced at a later date. Care must be taken to associate costs and output accurately.

This discussion should illustrate the importance of maintaining a comprehensive and meaningful management information system. Not only is such a system required for the periodic financial reports and tax returns the firm must prepare, but a good information system is absolutely critical for sound decision making.

Short-Run Cost Functions

Recall that in the short run some costs are fixed. Although these fixed costs should be identified and measured, they typically are not used to estimate the short-run cost function. This is because their inclusion would obscure the relationship between output and variable cost. The usual procedure is to estimate the total or average variable cost function and then, if necessary, add the fixed cost component to obtain the total or average cost function.

Suppose that accurate data on variable cost and output have been collected. The remaining tasks are to specify the appropriate functional form (i.e., the hypothesized relationship between cost and output), statistically estimate the parameters of that functional form using the standard multiple-regression technique, and then interpret the results.

If the relationship between cost and output is approximately linear, the functional form

$$TVC = b_0 + b_1 Q \tag{9-9}$$

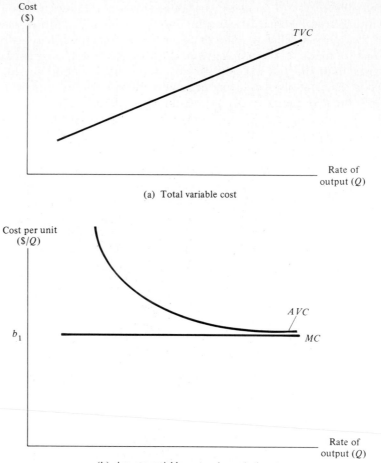

(a) Total variable cost

(b) Average variable cost and marginal cost

Figure 9-1.   *Cost Curves Based on a Linear Total Cost Function.*

may be used to estimate the cost function. If b_0 and b_1 are estimated, the average variable cost function would be given by

$$AVC = \frac{b_0}{Q} + b_1 \qquad (9\text{-}10)$$

and the marginal cost function by

$$MC = b_1 \qquad (9\text{-}11)$$

TVC, AVC, and MC curves that are consistent with this linear model are shown in Figure 9-1. These functions have the following properties: total variable cost is a linear function; average variable cost declines initially and then becomes quite flat approaching the value of b_1 as output increases; and marginal cost is constant at b_1.

Given that cost theory suggests a U-shaped average cost curve, the linear function used above will not capture that relationship between output and cost. Consequently, a quadratic total variable cost function of the form

$$TVC = c_0 + c_1 Q + c_2 Q^2 \qquad (9\text{-}12)$$

or a cubic cost function

$$TVC = d_0 + d_1 Q - d_2 Q^2 + d_3 Q^3 \qquad (9\text{-}13)$$

is often used because functions of this type can capture the hypothesized non-linear relationship. Clearly, the parameters of both (9-12) and (9-13) can be estimated using the least-squares regression method.

Although the shape of the quadratic and cubic functions will depend on the estimated parameters, conventional or typical estimated cost functions based on these functional forms are shown in Figures 9-2 and 9-3. The quadratic function

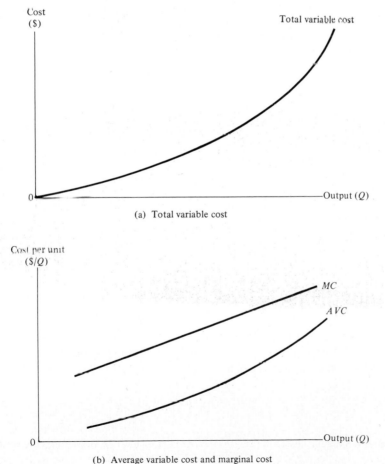

(a) Total variable cost

(b) Average variable cost and marginal cost

Figure 9-2. *Cost Curves Based on a Quadratic Total Cost Function.*

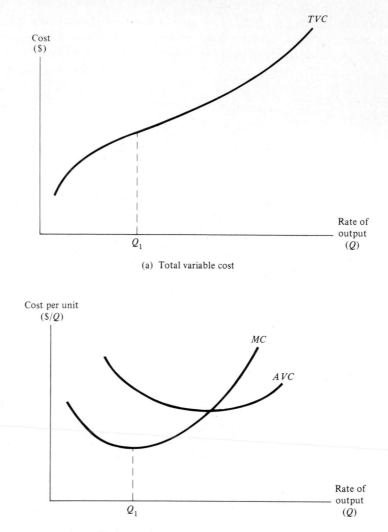

(a) Total variable cost

(b) Average variable cost and marginal cost

Figure 9-3. *Cost Curves Based on a Cubic Total Cost Function.*

(Figure 9-2) has the following properties: Total cost increases at an increasing rate; marginal cost is a linearly increasing function of output[4] (i.e., $MC = c_1 + 2c_2Q$); and average variable cost is a U-shaped function given by the equation

$$AVC = \frac{c_0}{Q} + c_1 + c_2Q \qquad (9\text{-}14)$$

---

[4] Recall that marginal cost is the first derivative of the total variable cost function, equation (9-12), that is,

$$\frac{d(TVC)}{dQ} = c_1 + 2C_2Q$$

Typical total variable cost, average cost, and marginal cost curves based on a cubic function are shown in Figure 9-3. The characteristics of these functions are: Total variable cost first increases at a decreasing rate (up to output rate Q_1 in the figure), then increases at an increasing rate; and both marginal cost

$$MC = d_1 - 2d_2Q + 3d_3Q^2 \qquad (9\text{-}15)$$

and average variable cost

$$AVC = \frac{d_0}{Q} + d_1 - d_2Q + d_3Q^2 \qquad (9\text{-}16)$$

are U-shaped functions.

In Figure 9-3, the conventional relationships among the cost functions are evident. For example, note the correspondence between the inflection point on TVC (i.e., at output rate Q_1, where the rate of increase goes from decreasing to increasing) and the minimum point on marginal cost. Of course, marginal cost intersects the average variable cost function at the minimum point of the AVC curve.

Although there is empirical evidence to support a variety of cost relationships, several studies of short-run cost functions have concluded that the marginal cost curve is approximately horizontal, that is, that marginal cost is constant over a fairly wide range of output rates. These empirical results would appear to be inconsistent with conventional cost theory, which suggests that average cost curves are U-shaped and that marginal cost functions are rising. One rationalization of this apparent inconsistency is that the "so-called" fixed inputs may not really be fixed. Recall from Chapter 6 that the marginal product function declines because increasing amounts of the variable input are being combined with fixed amounts of another input. Initially, returns to additional units of the variable factor may increase, but ultimately the law of diminishing marginal returns applies and the marginal product function declines and the marginal cost curve rises.

But if the "fixed" input is not really fixed, the fixed-variable input proportion may not change as output varies and the law of diminishing returns may not be observed. For example, a manufacturing firm may have a fixed stock of machines, but the number in use may vary as the rate of output changes. In that case, the ratio of labor to machines in use may be roughly constant even though the ratio of labor to the total stock of machines may vary considerably.

KEY CONCEPTS

- Data problems relating to estimating cost functions include the possibility that input prices and/or technology may have changed during the period under study, the need to adjust accounting data to reflect opportunity costs, and the difficulty of apportioning costs among products in the multiproduct firms.
- Linear, quadratic, and cubic functional forms are typically used to estimate the total variable cost functions.

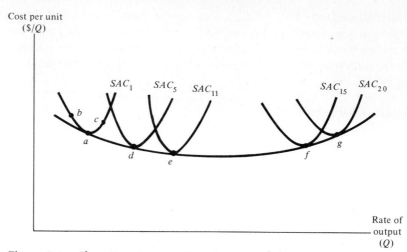

Figure 9-4. *Short-Run Average Cost Curves and the Associated Long-Run Average Cost Curve.*

Long-Run Cost Functions

Recall that the long-run average cost curve consists of points or small segments of each of a series of short-run average cost functions. A long-run cost function and associated short-run cost functions are shown in Figure 9-4. At any point in time, of course, a firm will be operating on one of these short-run functions. Estimating the long-run function requires: (1) obtaining data on each of a number of points on the long-run function (i.e., obtaining data on the relevant point on each of a number of short-run cost functions such as point *a, d, e, f,* and *g* on the short-run functions shown in Figure 9-4); (2) specifying the appropriate functional form; and (3) estimating parameters of the functions.

Either a time-series or a cross-section approach can be used, although most studies of long-run cost behavior have used cross-section data. One problem with time-series data on a single plant is that if the period is long enough for the scale to have changed, it is probably long enough for production technology and input prices to have changed as well. As suggested above, a cross-section study must assume that firms are operating at that point on the short-run function that lies on the long-run function. For example, in Figure 9-5, accurate estimation of the long-run cost function would require that the firm represented by SAC_1 would be operating at point *a*. If the firm was operating at some other point, say *b* or *c*, the estimate of the long-run average cost curve would be biased in an upward direction.

CASE STUDY
RETURNS TO SCALE IN HIGH SCHOOL EDUCATION

Studies of per student expenditures in the nation's schools have generally shown a tendency for these costs to increase as the size of school increases. Such studies have led to the conclusion that there are decreasing returns to scale in the production of education. One problem with this conclusion is that it has not taken account of differences in the quality of output among schools. If the larger schools are producing a higher-quality product (i.e., a better educated student), it is not legitimate to infer that higher cost per student in the larger schools is indicative of decreasing returns to scale.

Riew made a study of 102 accredited high schools in Wisconsin. He found that if adjustments are made for quality of education, there are significant economies of scale in producing high school education. Riew specified a general average cost function of the form

$$\text{average cost per student} = f(\text{number of students, quality.})$$

Average cost per student (AC) was measured by expenditure per student and number of students by average daily attendance. Although output quality generally is measured by reference to particular attributes of the good or service produced, in Riew's study quality was measured by the characteristics of the schools that were surveyed. The following measures were used: percentage of classrooms built within the last ten years; average teacher's salary; number of credit units offered; average number of courses taught per teacher; and change in enrollment.

The least-squares regression technique was used to estimate the parameters of a quadratic cost equation of the form

$$AC = C_0 + C_1 Q + C_2 Q^2 + \text{(quality variables)}$$

where AC is cost per student and Q is number of students. After adjusting for quality differences among schools, the following net relationship between cost and output was estimated:

$$AC = 10.3 - 0.402Q + 0.00012Q^2 \qquad R^2 = 0.56$$
$$(6.38) \qquad (5.22)$$

The values of the t-statistics are shown in parentheses and indicate that both coefficients are significantly different from zero at the 0.01 probability level. If graphed, this estimated function shows a U-shaped average cost curve having a minimum point at about 1,675 students, as shown in Figure 9-5.

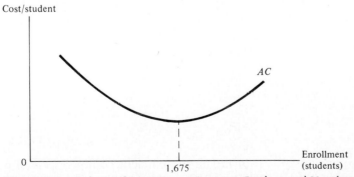

Figure 9-5. *Relationship Between Cost per Student and Number of Students.*

The slope of the average cost curve is given by

$$\frac{d(AC)}{dQ} = -0.402 + 0.00024Q$$

and is negative until a school size of 1,675 is reached and is positive thereafter.

Only the largest high schools in the state had enrollments of 1,675 or more. Thus, after adjusting for quality, it was found that there were significant economies of scale in high school education at least up to the largest schools in the state. As there were few schools larger than this threshold, it is possible that economies of scale might be achieved in even larger schools. The data simply were not adequate to test this possibility.

Source: Riew (1966).

Duality: The Correspondence Between Production and Cost

Associated with any production function is a corresponding total cost function. This total cost function can be derived from the production function using principles of production theory and information about the prices of the two inputs. This correspondence is referred to as *duality*. Not only is the duality principle important in understanding the relationship between production and cost, but the concept is also useful in that it implies that a cost function can be determined simply by knowing the estimated parameters of the production function and the prices of capital and labor.

A production function of the form

$$Q = AK^aL^b \tag{9-17}$$

will be used to show how the associated total cost function is derived. To aid the exposition, the value of A in the production function is assumed to be unity. Thus $Q = K^aL^b$ and the marginal products of capital and labor are

$$MP_K = \frac{\partial Q}{\partial K} = aK^{a-1}L^b \tag{9-18}$$

and

$$MP_L = \frac{\partial Q}{\partial L} = bK^aL^{b-1} \tag{9-19}$$

Next, the expansion path showing all the efficient combinations of capital and labor is determined by substituting the marginal product equations into the production efficiency condition,

$$\frac{MP_K}{r} = \frac{MP_L}{w} \tag{9-20}$$

where r and w represent the prices of capital and labor, respectively. Thus

$$\frac{aK^{a-1}L}{r} = \frac{bK^aL^{b-1}}{w}$$

Solving this equation for K yields the expansion path

$$K = \frac{waL}{rb} \tag{9-21}$$

If the input prices r and w are known, the expansion path and the production function comprise a system of two equations in three unknowns, Q, K, and L. Thus if the value of one of the variables is given, the values of the other two can be determined. For example, if the output rate is specified, the efficient combination of capital and labor is determined.

Now, the total cost function must be integrated into the analysis. That relationship is given by

$$TC = rK + wL \tag{9-22}$$

Substituting the expansion path equation (9-21) for K in the total cost function yields

$$TC = r\frac{waL}{br} + wL$$

which can be written as

$$TC = \left(\frac{a}{b} + 1\right)wL \tag{9-23}$$

Conventionally, total cost is expressed as a function of output. Thus L must be removed from equation (9-23). This is done by substituting the expansion path equation (9-21) into the original production function. That is,

$$Q = \left(\frac{waL}{br}\right)^a L^b$$

and solving for L, which yields

$$L = Q^{\frac{1}{a+b}}\left(\frac{aw}{br}\right)^{-\frac{a}{a+b}} \tag{9-24}$$

Next, substitute equation (9-24) for L in the cost function (9-23) to derive total cost as a function of output and the input prices:

$$TC = w\left(\frac{a}{b} + 1\right)\left[\left(\frac{aw}{br}\right)^{-a/(a+b)}\right]Q^{\frac{1}{a+b}} \tag{9-25}$$

Equation (9-25) looks complicated, but by letting

$$c = w\left(\frac{a}{b} + 1\right)\left[\left(\frac{aw}{br}\right)^{-a/(a+b)}\right]$$

equation (9-25) can be rewritten as

$$TC = cQ^{\frac{1}{a+b}} \tag{9-26}$$

Thus, equation (9-26) is the total cost function associated with the production function $Q = K^aL^b$. If the parameters of the production function have been estimated and if the prices of the inputs are known, the total cost function can be determined. That is, the estimated parameters a and b from the production function and the prices of the inputs, w and r, can be substituted directly into equation (9-25) and the total cost function is determined. Then all of the per unit cost functions can be derived from the total cost function.

Recall that if $a + b = 1$, there are constant returns to scale. In this case, equation (9-26) reduces to

$$TC = cQ$$

meaning that TC is a linear function of output and average cost is constant at c, that is,

$$AC = \frac{TC}{Q} = c$$

Thus the AC curve is a horizontal line. If $a + b > 1$, there are increasing returns to scale. The exponent $1/(a + b)$ in equation (9-26) will be less than 1, meaning that total cost will increase less than in proportion to output, implying a downward-sloping average cost curve. Finally, if $a + b < 1$, there are decreasing returns to scale. The exponent $1/(a + b)$ will be greater than 1, meaning that costs will increase more than in proportion to changes in output. Thus the average cost curve will be increasing as output increases.

Although the exact form of the cost equation will differ, this process can be used to derive the total cost function from any production function. Again, the power of a basic economics concept is demonstrated. That is, simply having only the information in the production function together with the prices of the inputs is sufficient to determine all of the relevant cost functions and important production relationships.

EXAMPLE
APPLYING THE DUALITY PRINCIPLE

Suppose that a firm's production function is estimated to be

$$Q = K^{0.5}L^{0.6}$$

and the input prices are $r = 1$ and $w = 2$. Determine the total cost function, average total cost, and marginal cost functions.

Solution

Using equation (9-25) and knowing that $a = 0.5$, $b = 0.6$, $r = 1$, and $w = 2$, the total cost function is

$$TC = 2\left(\frac{0.5}{0.6} + 1\right)\left[\frac{(0.5)(2)}{(0.6)(1)}\right]^{-[0.5/(0.5 + 0.6)]} Q^{\frac{1}{0.5 + 0.6}}$$

which reduces to

$$TC = 2.91Q^{0.909}$$

The average and marginal cost functions are determined in the conventional way:

$$AC = \frac{TC}{Q} = \frac{2.91Q^{0.909}}{Q} = \frac{2.91}{Q^{0.091}}$$

$$MC = \frac{d(TC)}{dQ} = \frac{2.645}{Q^{0.091}}$$

Note that total cost increases less than in proportion to output. For example, as shown in the following table, a doubling of the output rate from 1 to 2, 2 to 4, or 4 to 8 results in a less than doubling of total cost.

Q	Total Cost	Change in Quantity (%)	Change in Total Cost (%)
1	2.91	—	—
2	5.46	100	88
4	10.26	100	88
8	19.27	100	88

This means there are increasing returns to scale, which, of course, should already be known because the sum of the coefficients $a + b$ is greater than 1.

KEY CONCEPT

• The duality principle implies that knowing the production function and the input prices is sufficient to determine all of the relevant cost functions.

Summary

Decision making often requires a quantitative estimate of the parameters of production and cost functions. These functions can be estimated at varying levels of aggregation, including plant, firm, industry, and economy-wide levels. Time-series data on production or cost can be used to estimate functions for a particular plant. In contrast, cross-section data drawn from a number of production facilities are used to estimate a production or cost function for the average or typical plant.

Data problems associated with estimating production functions include combining diverse outputs into a single output measure and aggregating different types of labor and capital into aggregate measures of each input. Having quantitative estimates of the parameters of a production function allows determination of the marginal product of each input, production elasticities, and economies of scale.

The estimation of cost functions also involves several significant data collection problems. For example, accounting data maintained by the firm may not reflect the true opportunity cost of the resources used in production. Also, output produced in one production period may be associated with costs incurred in an earlier period. In the multiproduct firm there may be a problem associated with matching costs with each of several outputs. Further, the period of study must be long enough to generate enough observations to estimate the functions, but if it is too long, input prices and/or technology may change, thus distorting the cost–output relationship.

Linear, quadratic, and cubic functional forms are often used to estimate short-run cost functions. Both the quadratic and cubic functions can be used as functional forms if the cost data are consistent with the nonlinear cost curves suggested by economic theory. Long-run cost functions typically are estimated using cross-section data on costs in a number of plants. It must be assumed that the cost–output point observed on the short-run cost function of each plant is in fact a point on the firm's long-run cost functions.

The duality principle demonstrates the correspondence between production and cost functions. It shows that knowing the parameters of the production function and the input prices is sufficient to determine all of the relevant cost functions for the firm.

Discussion Questions

9-1. What are the four steps taken in estimating production and cost functions?

9-2. When estimating production functions, what are some of the problems of measuring output and input for each of the following:
(a) a multiproduct firm?
(b) a construction company?

9-3. What key assumption must be made in using data from actual company operations to estimate a long-run cost function?

9-4. What are the advantages and disadvantages of the cross-section and time-series approaches to estimating cost functions?

9-5. Explain how a non-linear production function of the form

$$Q = AK^aL^b$$

can be estimated by using the ordinary least squares regression technique that can only be used to estimate the parameters of a linear function.

9-6. Is there a problem using accounting data based on historical cost and standard depreciation techniques to estimate economic cost functions? Explain.

9-7. Many empirical studies have suggested that the marginal cost function is approximately horizontal, but conventional cost theory suggests that the marginal cost curve is U-shaped. Provide an explanation for this apparent inconsistency.

Problems

9-1. The production function for Everlight Flashlight Company is:

$$Q = K^{.6}L^{.5}$$

where Q is the rate of output and K and L are the input rates for capital and labor, respectively. The price of capital is $10 per unit (i.e., $r = \$10$) and the price of labor is $5 per unit (i.e., $w = \$5$). Determine the total and average cost functions for the firm.

9-2. The economics department of Western Drilling, a producer of natural gas, has estimated the long-run total cost function for natural gas distribution to be:

$$TC = 200Q - 0.004Q^3$$

where TC is total cost and Q is millions of cubic feet (MMCF) of natural gas per day.

(a) Determine an equation for the long-run average cost of distributing natural gas and plot it on a graph over the range $10 \leq Q \leq 150$.

(b) At present, Western produces but does not distribute natural gas. Interstate Pipeline is the only distributor of gas in the region and it carries about 100 MMCF per day. Management at Western estimates the regional market will grow from 100 to 150 MMCF per day and thinks it might be able to capture about 50 percent of the *increase* in the size of the market. Interstate has the capacity to deliver 200 MMCF per day. Will Western be able to compete against Interstate in the distribution of gas? Explain.

9-3. Keith Electronics produces transistors using a fixed capital stock valued at $10 million and labor, a variable input. The general form of the production function for the firm is thought to be

$$Q = AK^aL^b$$

where Q is output, A is a constant, K is the rate of capital input, and L is the rate of labor input. Production and labor input rates for the last six production periods are shown below:

Period	Production Q	Labor Input L
1	100	50
2	116	60
3	80	40
4	96	48
5	125	72
6	102	60

Use these data and the ordinary least-squares regression method discussed in Chapter Two to estimate the production elasticity for labor (b). (HINT: Because the capital stock is fixed, consider the term AK^a to be a constant. That is, estimate the function $Q = BL^b$ where $B = AK^a$.)

9-4. Consider the production function

$$Q = 10K^{.6}L_1^{.4}L_2^{.2}$$

where Q is the rate of output, K is the capital stock, L_1 is production labor, and L_2 is administrative workers. Determine the percentage change in output for each of the following:

(a) a 10 percent increase in capital;

(b) a 20 percent increase in production labor; and

(c) a 0.5 percent increase in administrative workers.

Problems Requiring Calculus

9-5. Economists at Jensen Enterprises used time-series data to estimate the following long-run total cost function for the firm

$$TC = 200 - 2Q + 0.05Q^2$$

where TC is total cost and Q is the output rate.

(a) Determine an equation for the long-run average cost function for Jensen Enterprises. Find the output rate that minimizes long-run average cost, and plot this function in a graph.

(b) Is the production process at Jensen characterized by decreasing, constant, or increasing returns to scale?

(c) If the market price of output is $4.32 per unit is there a scale of plant that would allow the firm to earn an economic profit or, at a minimum, to breakeven?

9-6. Given the production function

$$Q = K^{.3}L^{.6}$$

and input prices for labor and capital of $10 and $2 per unit, respectively (i.e., $w = 10$ and $r = 2$), determine the firm's expansion path and the total cost function.

9-7. For the production function

$$Q = AK^{0.3}L^{0.8}$$

prove that the production elasticities are 0.3 and 0.8 for capital and labor, respectively.

References

Christensen, L. R., and Greene, W. H. 1976. "Economies of Scale in U.S. Electric Power Generation." *Journal of Political Economy* 84(4):655–676.

Cobb, C. W., and Douglas, P. H. 1928. "An Approach to the Law of Production and Its Relation to Welfare." *American Economic Review* 38(March):139–165.

Dean, J. 1976. *Statistical Cost Estimation*. Bloomington, Ind.: Indiana University Press.

Douglas, P. H. 1976. "The Cobb–Douglas Production Once Again: Its History, Its Testing, and Some New Empirical Values." *Journal of Political Economy* 84(October):903–915.

Gold, B. 1981. "Changing Perspective on Size, Scale, and Returns: An Interpretive Survey." *Journal of Economic Literature* 19(March):5–33.

Haldi, J., and Whitcomb, D. 1967. "Economies of Scale in Industrial Plants." *Journal of Political Economy* 75(1):373–385.

Johnston, J. 1960. *Statistical Cost Analysis.* New York: McGraw-Hill.

Johnston, J. 1961. "An Econometric Study of the Production Decision." *Quarterly Journal of Economics* 75(May):234–261.

Keeler, T. E. 1974. "Railroad Costs, Returns to Scale and Excess Capacity." *Review of Economics and Statistics* 56(May):201–208.

Longbrake, W. A. 1973. "Statistical Cost Analysis." *Financial Management* 2(Spring):49–55.

Moore, F. T. 1959. "Economies of Scale: Some Statistical Evidence." *Quarterly Journal of Economics* 73(May):232–245.

Riew, J. 1966. "Economies of Scale in High School Operation." *Review of Economics and Statistics* 48(3):280–287.

Walters, A. A. 1963. "Production and Cost Functions: An Econometric Survey." *Econometrica* 31(January–April):1–66.

INTEGRATING CASE PROBLEM NO. III
BOND CONSTRUCTION COMPANY

Upon completing a bachelor's degree program in civil engineering in 1979, Allen Bond opened his own construction business that specializes in building garages for residential homes. By 1985, the firm had grown substantially and employed 20 carpenters who were paid $25,000 per year. This was the entire employment complement of the firm; all managerial, accounting, and clerical functions were provided by Mr. Bond. During 1985, the company built 400 garages. Excluding materials which are provided by the customer, each garage sells for $1,600.

The firm has a large stock of capital equipment including trucks, tools, and surveying instruments. Bond has developed a measure for a unit of capital that includes one truck and a specified amount of other equipment, including a ladder, several power tools, and an air compressor. Currently, the price to rent one of these units is $5,000 per year, and the firm used fifteen units during 1985. Costs of capital and labor are the only significant explicit expenses that the firm has. Both the capital and labor inputs can be varied daily.

Bond used a $100,000 inheritance to start the business and is quite pleased that he has received several offers in the past month to sell the firm for $300,000. The firm's accountant has prepared an income statement for 1985 that shows a profit of $40,000 after paying Bond a salary of $25,000 for the year. The market interest rate is 14 percent per year.

Bond has just completed a managerial economics course in the evening school program of the local community college. Although he is not sure he understood everything, the class did make him aware of many problems he had not considered before. For example, is Bond Construction really earning a profit? Is the current mix of capital and labor optimal?

The pressures of managing this business are beginning to bother Bond, and he is wondering if he would not be happier simply taking a job at Hectel, Inc., a very large civil engineering firm in the same area. Every year the personnel manager calls him with a job offer. In January of 1985, the salary offer was for $40,000 per year. Allen thinks he should have taken the job.

Bond decides to hire a consultant to make a thorough economic analysis of the firm's operation. Unfortunately, he has kept very few records that might be used for economic analysis, although records were maintained on output and inputs of capital and labor for each of the seven years of operation. These data are shown below.

Year	Output (Number of Garages)	Capital (Units)	Labor Input (Worker-Years)
1979	35	1	2
1980	49	1	3
1981	81	4	4
1982	156	4	9
1983	255	8	14
1984	277	12	14
1985	400	15	21

(Note: The labor input includes Allen Bond's time in addition to the other work-ers.)

Bond thinks that the Cobb-Douglas function,

$$Q = AK^aL^b$$

describes the production process and has used ordinary least-squares to obtain the following estimated function,

$$Q = 20K^{0.19}L^{0.81}$$

Assume that the firm has retained you as a consultant and that the information provided above is all that is available.

Requirements

a. Determine the true economic profit earned by the firm in 1985.
b. If the economic profit earned by the firm in 1985 was negative, determine the unit volume necessary to breakeven. Use the information developed to deter-mine all the relevant total and per unit cost functions.
c. Determine whether returns to scale are increasing, decreasing, or constant. Explain.
d. Determine the optimal mix of labor and capital that should be used to pro-duce 400 units of output. Compare this mix to the actual combination of labor and capital used in 1985. Note: For a Cobb-Douglas production function, the equations for the marginal products of labor and capital are:

$$MP_L = bAK^aL^{b-1}$$

and

$$MP_K = aAK^{a-1}L^b$$

MARKET STRUCTURE

Perfect Competition and Monopoly

10

Preview

One of the most important decisions made by managers is setting the price of the firm's product. If price is set too high, the firm will be unable to compete with other suppliers. But if the price is too low, the firm may not be able to earn a normal rate of profit.

Pricing decisions are affected by the economic environment in which the firm operates. An important dimension of this environment is the degree of competition faced by the firm. A firm in a very competitive market may have little or no control over price. In that case, managerial attention must be focused on the amount of output to be produced. Conversely, a firm that is the only seller of a product may have considerable freedom in making price and output decisions. In this chapter two market environments are considered: perfect competition and monopoly. These two cases can be thought of as opposite extremes of market structure. For each case, economic theory is used to analyze pricing and output decisions of managers.

The first section of this chapter suggests criteria for categorizing market structures. The second and third sections discuss pricing and output decisions in perfectly competitive and monopolistic market structures. The final section is a brief evaluation of the usefulness of the perfect competition and monopoly models. Other market structures are considered in Chapter 11.

Market Structure

Managers must tailor their decisions to the specific market environment in which their firms operate. For example, a manager of a business that is the patent holder and only supplier of a new wonder drug will behave differently than a manager of a firm trying to survive in the very competitive fast-food industry.

Because the decision-making environment depends on the structure of the market, it follows that no single theory of the firm can adequately describe all of the conditions in which firms operate. However, it does not follow that there must be a unique theory corresponding to every conceivable market structure. By categorizing markets in terms of their basic characteristics, it may be possible to identify a limited number of market structures that can be used to analyze decision making. Although there are many possible ways of categorizing market structures, four characteristics are frequently employed.

Number and Size Distribution of Sellers

The ability of an individual firm to affect the price and total amount of a product supplied to a market is related to the number of firms providing that product. If there are numerous sellers of nearly equal size, the influence of any one firm is likely to be small. In contrast, in a market consisting of only a few sellers, an individual firm can have considerable impact on price and total supply.

The size distribution of firms is also an important characteristic of market structure. When the market includes a dominant firm or a few large firms that provide a substantial proportion of total supply, those large businesses may be able to exert considerable influence over price and product attributes. For example, in the market for small business computers, IBM is the dominant firm. The products of many smaller manufacturers are designed to be IBM compatible and their prices are largely determined by the price of the IBM-PC. Conversely, in a market with firms of nearly equal size, individual sellers are likely to have less influence.

Number and Size Distribution of Buyers

Markets can also be characterized by the number and size distribution of buyers. Where there are many small purchasers of a product, all buyers are likely to pay about the same price. However, if there is only one purchaser, that buyer is in a position to obtain price concessions from sellers. Similarly, if a market consists of many small buyers and one or a few firms making volume purchases, the larger firms may be able to buy at lower prices. For example, because of its sales volume, IBM may be able to obtain electronic components at prices below those of competitors.

The market structures discussed in this chapter and in Chapter 11 assume that the market has a large number of small buyers. Situations where buyers can influence price are referred to as monopsonies or oligopsonies and are discussed in Chapter 14.

Product Differentiation

Product differentiation refers to the degree that the output of one firm differs from that of other firms in a market. Where products are undifferentiated, decisions to buy are made strictly on the basis of price. Sellers who attempt to charge a higher price are unable to sell their output. If there is no difference in price, the buyer has no preference as to sellers. Wheat is a good example of an undifferentiated product. Although there are several grades, all wheat of a given grade sells for the same price in a given market. Buyers are usually not told who produced the wheat, nor do they care. If properly graded, wheat from one supplier is considered as good as wheat from another.

At the other extreme, consider a product that is viewed by buyers as having unique characteristics. A new Rolls-Royce is an example. Even the most naive car buyer would be unlikely to mistake a Rolls for a Ford. A Rolls-Royce has come to represent the ultimate in automobile luxury. As such, it commands a price that may be ten to fifteen times that of a new Ford.

Product differentiation is an important market characteristic because it indicates a firm's ability to affect price. If a firm's product is perceived as having desirable features, it can command a premium price. However, products considered less desirable will be purchased only if the seller is willing to accept a lower price. For example, consumers will pay extra for fresh San Francisco sourdough bread, but will buy day-old Wonderbread bread only if the price is substantially reduced.

Conditions of Entry and Exit

Ease of entry and exit are crucial determinants of the nature of a market in the long run. When it is extremely difficult for new firms to enter, existing firms will have much greater freedom in making pricing and output decisions than if they must be concerned about new entrants who have been attracted by the lure of high profits. For example, consider a drug manufacturer that holds a patent which prohibits other firms from making the drug. If there are no close substitutes for the product, that firm will be essentially free from competition now and for the duration of the patent. Thus its managers can make pricing decisions without worrying about losing market share to new entrants. But if the drug can be easily copied, high prices may result in imitators competing for market share.

Ease of exit also affects managerial behavior. Suppose that certain firms in a market have been earning less than the normal rate of profit. If the resources used to produce the product can easily be transferred from one use to another, some of those resources will be shifted to other industries, where they can earn a higher rate of return. However, if the resources are highly specialized, they may have little value in another industry. For example, the track and terminals of an unprofitable railroad may have few alternative uses. Thus owners of these resources are faced with the choice of selling them for their salvage value or continuing operations at a loss.

KEY CONCEPTS

- In markets where there are a large number of small buyers and sellers, individual firms have little control over price.
- By differentiating its product, a firm can gain some control over price.
- If it is difficult for new firms to enter an industry, existing firms have more freedom in their pricing decisions.

Perfect Competition

The term "perfect competition" is something of a misnomer. In a perfectly competitive world there really is no competition between economic units. As buyers and sellers make business decisions, they do not have to take into account the effect of their actions on other participants in the market. The reason is that the individual economic units in perfect competition are so small relative to the total market that their actions have no perceptible impact on other buyers and sellers. Hence decisions can be made without considering the reactions of others. In perfect competition, market participants do not compete against one another. Rather, they make decisions in an economic environment that they perceive as being fixed or given.

Characteristics

The concept of perfect competition can be defined in terms of the market structure characteristics of the preceding section. First, there must be a large number of sellers in the market with no single seller able to exert significant influence over price. This criterion is sometimes described in terms of sellers being *price takers* who can sell all that they can produce at the market-determined price. Graphically, this situation is depicted as sellers facing a horizontal demand curve. Similarly, the second requirement for perfect competition is that there are a large number of small buyers, each buyer being unable to influence price. That is, all buyers are price takers.

Third, perfect competition assumes easy entry and exit from an industry. If there are above-normal profits, resources can be mobilized to create new firms or to expand the production capacity of firms already in the industry. If profits are below average, resources can easily be transferred from the industry and put to other uses where they are more productive. Finally, under perfect competition, it is assumed that the product is totally undifferentiated. One firm's output cannot be distinguished from that of other producers. As a result, purchasing decisions are based entirely on price. If the firm sets its price above the market-determined level, it will be unable to attract buyers. Price cutting is unnecessary because producers can sell their total output at the market price.[1] Characteristics of perfectly competitive markets are summarized in Table 10-1.

The Equilibrium Price

In the preceding section, reference was made to the market-determined price. Although no single entity in a perfectly competitive market can affect price, the aggregate effect of the participants in the market is important in price determination. Indeed, the interaction of supply and demand determines the equilibrium price and the quantity to be exchanged.

Table 10-1. Market Structure Characteristics of Perfect Competition

Number and size distribution of sellers	Many small sellers. No seller is able to exert a significant influence over price.
Number and size distribution of buyers	Many small buyers. No buyer is able to exert a significant influence over price.
Product differentiation	Product undifferentiated. Decisions to buy are made on the basis of price.
Conditions of entry and exit	Easy entry and exit. Resources are easily transferable among industries.

---

[1] Sometimes the assumption of perfect knowledge regarding prices and technology is included as a fourth characteristic of perfect competition. For ease of exposition, it is not included here.

Table 10-2. Market Supply Schedule

Price per Bushel	Quantity Supplied per Period				
	Firm 1	+ Firm 2	= Two-Firm Supply	× 10,000 =	Total Market Supply
$8	1,000	900	1,900		19.0 million
7	950	800	1,750		17.5 million
6	900	700	1,600		16.0 million
5	850	600	1,450		14.5 million
4	800	500	1,300		13.0 million
3	750	400	1,150		11.5 million

Consider the market for wheat. Each wheat producer has an individual supply schedule. Two such schedules are shown in Table 10-2. These schedules indicate the quantity of wheat that will be produced per period at different wheat prices. At each price the decision rule is the same. Additional wheat will be supplied only if the price is high enough to allow the supplier to earn at least a normal rate of profit on the incremental output. Table 10-2 shows that higher expected prices are necessary to induce the producers to supply more wheat.

For the moment, assume that the two supply schedules shown in Table 10-2 represent the only suppliers of wheat in the market. By adding the amount that each producer will provide at each price, the market supply schedule for wheat can be computed. This information appears in the fourth column of Table 10-2. For example, at a price of $6 per bushel, the first producer will supply 900 bushels of wheat per period and the second will supply 700 bushels per period. Thus the quantity supplied to the market at $6 is 1,600 bushels of wheat per period.

Now suppose that there are 10,000 wheat producers with supply schedules as shown in column 2, and another 10,000 with schedules like that of column 3. Thus the quantity of wheat supplied per period at each price will be 10,000 times the amounts shown in column 4 of Table 10-2, and the market supply schedule will be as shown in column 5 of the table.

The supply data can be plotted to form the supply curve shown in Figure 10-1. The market demand curve is also shown. As discussed in Chapter 4, the market demand is the horizontal sum of the demands of individual buyers. The equilibrium price of wheat is P_e and is determined by the point of intersection of the supply and demand curves. If price is greater than P_e, there is excess supply. Producers will respond by cutting prices in order to sell the excess wheat. As the price falls, quantity demanded increases and quantity supplied decreases. Alternatively, excess demand exists when the price is below P_e. This causes consumers to bid up the price of wheat. As the price increases, buyers reduce their purchases and suppliers increase production. These forces continue to operate until supply and demand come into balance at the equilibrium price, P_e.

Consider the impact of any of one seller on the market supply curve. Table 10-2 shows that at a price of $6, the amount supplied will be 16.0 million bushels of wheat per period. Suppose that one firm of type #1 decides not to produce. The effect would be to reduce supply, but only by 900 bushels or about six-

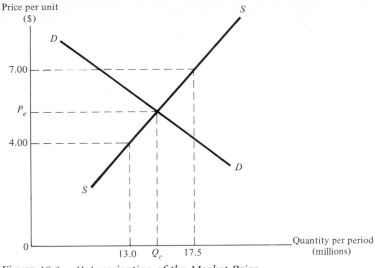

Figure 10-1. *Determination of the Market Price.*

thousandths of 1 percent of total supply. Thus the action of a single seller would have no real impact on the market. Although the supply function would shift to the left, the shift would be almost impossible to detect and would have essentially no impact on the equilibrum price, P_e.

Now consider the effect of individual consumer demands. Suppose that there are 20,000 buyers, each with the same demand schedule. Should one buyer drop out of the market, the demand curve would shift to the left. But the shift would be so small as to have no observable impact. Once again, the market price would be essentially unaffected. Thus it is seen that in markets with large numbers of buyers and sellers, individual firms and consumers are unable to affect price. That is, they are price takers in the market.

CASE STUDY
THE ECONOMICS OF MARIJUANA

The principles of supply and demand can be used to analyze many different problems. The question of legalizing marijuana is an interesting example. Under present law, the sale of marijuana is illegal in the United States. In many communities it is also a violation of the law even to possess the product. Despite this legal prohibition, a thriving market continues to exist. As with all products, there is a supply curve and a demand curve for marijuana. These interact to determine the equilibrium price. The supply and demand curves are depicted in Figure 10-2. The market price is P_e and the quantity exchanged is Q_e.

Now suppose that laws are changed such that marijuana suppliers and consumers are not subject to penalties if caught. How would this change in policy affect the market price and the equilibrium quantity of marijuana? First, consider the demand curve. For some, the thrill of pot smoking may be related to a desire to flout the law. But it is probable that most people are not motivated in this

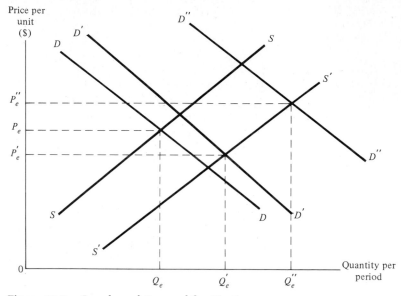

Figure 10-2. *Supply and Demand for Marijuana.*

manner. In most cases, the possibility of being caught is a deterrent to marijuana use. Thus legalization would probably cause demand to increase. This is shown in the figure as a shift of the demand curve to the right to $D'D'$.

Legalization would also affect the supply curve. The amount that producers are willing to supply at various prices is determined by marginal costs. Where the threat of apprehension forces growers to locate in remote areas, production costs will be high. Similarly, if the product must be transported in small boats and planes and marketed in a clandestine fashion, marijuana entrepreneurs will require substantial rewards to compensate them for the risk involved. In contrast, if sale of the substance does not carry the risk of legal penalties, modern, large-scale production techniques can be employed and more traditional methods of transportation and marketing used. These changes will cause the supply curve to shift to the right, meaning that sellers are willing to provide more at each price than they were before. The new supply curve is designated as $S'S'$.

The shifts in the demand and supply curves caused by legalization of marijuana result in a new equilibrium price and output. The price is now P'_e and the quantity is Q'_e. Note that the new quantity is greater than before. That is, more marijuana will be exchanged as a result of legalization. This is not a particularly surprising outcome. The effect on price is less clear. If shifts in the supply and demand curves are as shown by $D'D'$ and $S'S'$ in Figure 10-2, the new market price will be lower than the previous price. But what if legalization greatly increased the number of pot smokers as suggested by the demand curve $D''D''$? In this case the price would be P''_e, which is greater than the initial market price. This outcome is unlikely, but does illustrate that the price effect depends on the slopes and shifts of the supply and demand curves.

Profit-Maximizing Output in the Short Run

This section considers the profit-maximizing output of the competitive firm in the short run. As discussed in Chapter 6, the short run is defined as a period of time in which at least one input is fixed. Often, the firm's capital stock is viewed as the fixed input. Accordingly, this analysis assumes that the number of production facilities in the industry and the size of each facility do not change because the period being considered is too short to allow businesses to enter or leave the industry or to alter the basic nature of their operations. The period of time that can properly be designated as the short run depends on the characteristics of the industry. For production of electric power, it may take as much as ten years to bring a new generating plant on line. In contrast, above-normal profits in service industries may attract new entrants in a matter of weeks.

Demand. The firm in perfect competition faces a horizontal demand curve at the market price for its product. This can be seen by evaluating the effect of the firm's decisions on market demand. Using wheat as an example, let the market demand equation be given by

$$Q_D = 17,000,000 - 1,000,000P \tag{10-1}$$

The equation implies that quantity demanded per period is reduced by 1 million bushels per dollar increase in price. Suppose that the supply equation is given by

$$Q_S = 7,000,000 + 1,500,000P \tag{10-2}$$

Equation (10-2) corresponds to the market supply data from Table 10-2 and indicates that a $1 price increase results in 1.5 million extra bushels of wheat being supplied per period.

Equating these supply and demand functions and solving for P and Q yields the equilibrium values. Specifically, price equals $4 and quantity is 13,000,000 bushels per period. Now assume that one of the type 2 suppliers shown in Table 10-2 leaves the market. The table implies that the supply equation for that single supplier is given by the equation $Q^2_S = 100 + 100P$. Subtracting Q_S from equation (10-2) gives a new equation for market supply:

$$Q'_S = 6,999,900 + 1,499,900P \tag{10-3}$$

Solving equations (10-1) and (10-3) gives $P = \$4.0002$ and $Q = 12,999,800$. Note that the elimination of one producer increased the equilibrium price by $0.0002 and reduced quantity by 200 bushels.

Thus it is seen that the decisions of individual producers have no significant impact on the market price. If the one supplier remains in the market, the equilibrium price will be $4. But if the small producer leaves the market, the price is still very close to $4. Graphically, this is portrayed by a horizontal demand curve at the $4 equilibrium price, as shown in Figure 10-3. The curve indicates that an individual firm can sell as much as it can produce at the given price. However, if the firm attempts to set a price greater than $4, no sales will be made

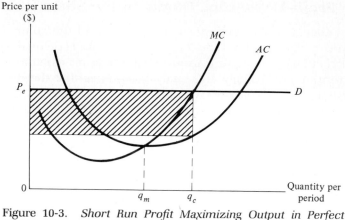

Figure 10-3.   *Short Run Profit Maximizing Output in Perfect Competition.*

because consumers will purchase from other suppliers. Conversely, there is no reason to sell below $4 because the firm's total output can be sold at $4 per bushel.

Costs.   It is assumed that the firm has U-shaped average and marginal cost curves, as shown in Figure 10-3. The figure shows that as quantity increases from 0 to q_m units, average cost declines and then increases beyond that point. It is important to remember that the cost curves of Figure 10-3 include a normal return to capital. Thus any time that the firm's average revenue (as given by price) is greater than average cost, it is earning economic profit.

Equilibrium Output.   Because price is determined in the market and the product is homogeneous, the only decision left to the manager of a firm in a perfectly competitive market is how much output to produce. The profit-maximizing output is determined where the extra revenue generated by selling the last unit (i.e., the market price) just equals the marginal cost of producing that unit. For a horizontal demand curve such as that of Figure 10-3, this condition is met by increasing the rate of production to q_c where price equals marginal cost. If the firm increases output beyond this point, the additional revenue, P_e, is less than the extra costs as shown by the marginal cost curve. In contrast, if production is reduced below q_c, the loss of revenues is greater than the reduction in costs and profits decrease. The output rate q_c represents the short-run equilibrium for the competitive firm in the sense that a profit-maximizing manager has no incentive to alter output as long as the demand and cost curves remain unchanged.

EXAMPLE

ECONOMIC PROFIT SELLING PIZZA

A new pizza place, Fredrico's, opens in New York City. The average price of a medium pizza in New York is $10 and, because of the large number of pizza sellers, this price will not be affected by the new entrant in the market. The owner of Fredrico's estimates that monthly total costs, including a normal profit, will be

$$TC = 1,000 + 2Q + 0.01Q^2$$

To maximize total profit, how many pizzas should be produced each month? In the short run, how much economic profit will the business earn each month?

Solution

Taking the derivative of the total cost equation with respect to Q gives the marginal cost equation

$$\frac{\partial TC}{\partial Q} = MC = 2 + 0.02Q$$

Profit is maximized by equating price and marginal cost. Thus the profit-maximizing output is given by the solution to

$$10 = 2 + 0.02Q$$

which is 400 pizzas per month.

Economic profit is total revenue minus total cost, or

$$TR - TC = 10(400) - [1,000 + 2(400) + 0.01(400^2)] = \$600$$

Thus, in the short run, economic profit will be $600 per month.

Profit-Maximizing Output in the Long Run

A key characteristic of the perfect competition model is ease of entry and exit. However, this assumption does not imply that such changes are instantaneous. It takes time for new firms to build facilities and for existing firms to increase output. Similarly, firms leaving an industry may experience delays in converting their resources to other uses. These problems of entry and exit are not considered in the short-run analysis.

In the long run all inputs are variable. Firms can enter or exit an industry and can also change the size of their production facilities. As a result, although the output rate Q_c represents the profit-maximizing decision in the short run, it may not be the optimal choice in the long run. Producing at Q_c, the firm is earning economic profit. This can be seen by looking at Figure 10-3. Per unit economic profits are given by the vertical distance between the average cost curve and the demand curve at the output rate Q_c. Total economic profit is shown by the shaded area. Because the average cost curve already includes a normal profit rate, the implication is that capital invested in the firm is earning substantially more than capital used in other sectors of the economy. Thus owners of capital have an incentive to withdraw their capital from those sectors yielding only a normal return and employ it in this industry where greater profits can be earned.

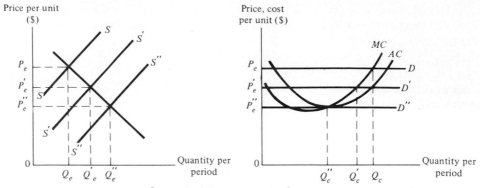

Figure 10-4. *Long Run Profit Maximizing Output in the Long Run.*

As additional capital flows into the industry, more output will be produced at each price. Thus the market supply curve, SS, shifts to the right to $S'S'$, as shown in Figure 10-4. This shift may be interpreted as more firms operating in the industry or the facilities of existing firms being expanded. It is useful to think of the supply shift as indicating that more of the product will be produced at any given price than before the inflow of capital. As the supply curve shifts to the right, the intersection of supply and demand causes a new equilibrium price, P_e'. This result is shown in Figure 10-4. At the lower price, the individual firm now faces a new horizontal demand curve, D'. But at the price, P_e', the output rate Q_c no longer maximizes profit. At Q_c marginal cost is greater than incremental revenue. Now the firm maximizes profits by reducing the rate of output to Q_c', where again price is equal to marginal cost.

Producing Q_c' units per period and selling at P_e', the firm is less profitable than before, but it is still earning economic profit. This can be seen by observing that the firm's average revenue, P_e', is greater than average cost at the output rate Q_c'. Thus there is an incentive for additional capital to flow into the industry. This additional capital expands capacity and causes further rightward shifts of the industry supply curve. The inflow of capital will continue until the supply curve is shifted to $S''S''$. With $S''S''$ as the industry supply curve, the equilibrium price is reduced to P_e''. Hence the demand curve faced by the individual firm is now shown by curve $P_e''D''$ in Figure 10-4. In this situation, profit is maximized by producing Q_c''. Notice that at Q_c'', price is equal to marginal cost, but price is also equal to average cost. Thus the firm's average revenue just equals average cost. Hence the firm is earning a normal rate of profit, but there is no economic profit.

Because the return to capital in the industry is no higher than the return earned in other segments of the economy, there is no further incentive for capital to flow into the industry. However, because capital earns at least a normal return, there is no reason for owners to withdraw capital from the industry. Hence the output rate Q_c'', where price equals average cost, is the long-run equilibrium for the representative firm in a perfectly competitive industry.

KEY CONCEPTS

- In the short run, the firm in perfect competition maximizes profit by producing where price equals marginal cost.
- In the long run, entry eliminates economic profit. The profit-maximizing point occurs where price equals both marginal and average cost.

Evaluation of Perfect Competition

Perfect competition occupies a unique position in the study of economics. Based on some fairly restrictive assumptions it is possible to derive conditions for allocating resources so as to maximize social welfare. It can then be demonstrated that markets that are perfectly competitive meet these criteria for optimal resource allocation. Formal proof of this proposition is beyond the scope of this book (see, e.g., Kohler, 1982, Chap. 14), but the basic ideas are presented here.

Prices play a central role in economic theory. The price a person is willing to pay for a good or service represents the value attached to having 1 more unit of that product. If a person is unwilling to buy the product at the offered price, it is because other goods and services can provide greater satisfaction for the same expenditure. Obviously, people differ in the value they attach to a particular product. Also, an individual's valuation of a good is affected by how much of the product the person already has.

Downward-sloping demand curves reflect consumer preferences for a product. When prices increase, consumers reduce their purchases. In contrast, as prices decline, previous consumers buy more and some new buyers are attracted. But all consumers usually are charged the same price. Thus those who purchase the product believe the item is worth at least the price they must pay to obtain it. Clearly, no one would buy a product if they did not believe it was worth the price. However, many individuals are willing to pay more than the purchase price to obtain the item. Essentially, these consumers receive more than they paid for. This extra benefit is often referred to as a *consumer surplus*.

The marginal cost curves in Figures 10-3 and 10-4 depict the opportunity cost of producing 1 more unit of the product. For example, to produce an additional automobile, fuel, labor, and capital must be diverted from other uses. The value of these inputs in those other uses is measured by their cost. The sum of these input costs is the marginal cost and represents the opportunity cost of producing an additional car. Note that the marginal cost curves are upward sloping in the region where they intersect the demand curve. This indicates that the opportunity cost of producing an additional unit of output is increasing.

The profit-maximizing firm in perfect competition will expand production until price equals marginal cost. Concurrently, buyers will purchase the firm's product until price exceeds the relative value that they attach to the product. Because the price paid by the consumer is identical to the additional revenue received by sellers, the equilibrium output has the following characteristic: The value that the last buyer attaches to the last unit of output produced is just equal to the opportunity cost of producing that unit of output.

It is often suggested that perfect competition results in the right amount of the product being produced. The preceding argument is the justification for that statement. If the value of the last unit of output is less than the cost of its production, social welfare would be improved by shifting the resources used in producing that last unit to production of some other good or service. Conversely, if there are potential customers who attach a value to the product greater than its marginal cost and who are not being served because of insufficient production, resource allocation could be improved by expanding output.

Another way of thinking about this result is in terms of voluntary exchange. Firms and consumers will exchange goods and services only as long as both parties benefit from the trade. Thus increased voluntary exchange implies improved resource allocation. Voluntary exchange is maximized under perfect competition because output is increased until there are no consumers willing to pay the opportunity cost of producing an additional unit of the good.

A second consequence of perfect competition is that resources are efficiently allocated among alternative uses. Consider the allocation of capital as depicted by the long-run equilibrium of the competitive firm shown in Figure 10-4. In the long run, individual firms earn no more than a normal rate of profit. If the rate of return on capital measures the productivity of capital in a given use, then whenever that capital is earning a higher rate of return in one use than in another, resource allocation could be improved by shifting resources to the higher-return use. This is exactly what occurs in the long-run model of perfect competition. Capital flows into the competitive industry (entry) until economic profit is eliminated. Conversely, if the return in the competitive sector is less than the normal rate of return, capital leaves the industry (exit) until the remaining capital is earning a normal rate of return.

A third characteristic of perfect competition in the long run is that production occurs at minimum cost. Notice that the profit-maximizing output in Figure 10-4 is at the minimum point on the average cost curve. This result does not mean that competitive firms necessarily are more efficient than firms in other types of market structure. However, it does imply that, given the technology available to the firm, producers in a perfectly competitive market minimize the per unit cost of production.

KEY CONCEPTS

- Consumers who would have been willing to pay more than the purchase price are said to receive a consumer surplus when they buy the product.
- In perfectly competitive markets, (1) the value of the last unit exchanged equals the opportunity cost of producing it, (2) capital moves to its highest valued use, and (3) production takes place at the minimum point on the average cost curve.

Monopoly

While conditions facing a monopolist are much different from those of firms in perfect competition, the firms have at least one thing in common—they do not have to compete with other individual participants in the market. Sellers in perfect competition are so small that they can ignore each other and consider the market environment as given. At the other extreme, the monopolist is the only seller in the market and has no competitors.

Characteristics

Monopoly can be thought of in terms of the market structure characteristics discussed earlier in the chapter. First, there is only one seller in the market. This means that the demand curve faced by the monopolist is the downward-sloping demand curve for the market. Second, for a firm to continue as a monopoly in the long run, there must be factors that prevent the entry of other firms. Such barriers to entry are discussed in Chapter 11. Finally, the product of the monopolist must be highly differentiated from other goods. That is, there must be no good substitutes. The market structure characteristics of a monopoly are listed in Table 10-3.

Consider a small, isolated community that has only one concrete company. Essentially, that firm has a monopoly position. When residents want concrete for foundations of new houses, they will have to buy from the monopolist. The high cost of transporting concrete makes it unlikely that concrete producers in other cities will be viable competitors. At the same time, there are few good substitutes for concrete foundations. Wood, stone, and cinder block are possibilities, but they are not as strong or as easy to use as concrete.

Profit-Maximizing Price and Quantity in the Short Run

Demand and cost curves for a monopolist are shown in Figure 10-5. As with the model of perfect competition, the cost curves depict first decreasing and then increasing average costs. There may be some products for which the cost curves are continually downward sloping, but the analysis of these cases is deferred to Chapter 19.

Table 10-3. Market Structure Characteristics of Monopoly

Number and size distribution of sellers	Single seller
Number and size distribution of buyers	Unspecified
Product differentiation	No close substitutes
Conditions of entry and exit	Entry prohibited or difficult

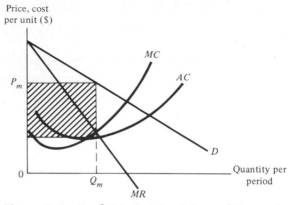

Figure 10-5.   *Profit Maximizing Price and Output for a Monopoly.*

Because they face a horizontal demand curve, managers of firms in a perfectly competitive world have no control over price. They simply choose the profit-maximizing output. However, because the monopolist has a downward-sloping demand curve, as shown in Figure 10-4, managers must recognize that their output decisions can influence price, and vice versa. Because price decreases with increased production, an increase in output will require that the firm sell at a lower price. The effect of output changes on total revenues depends on the marginal revenue curve shown in Figure 10-5. If marginal revenue is positive, increasing output increases the total revenue. If marginal revenue is negative, total revenue is reduced by the increased output.

The criterion for maximizing profits is the same for the monopolist as for firms in perfect competition—output should be increased until the additional revenue equals the marginal cost. For the competitive firm the price is unaffected by output, so the decision criterion is to produce until price equals marginal cost. For the monopolist, the equivalent criterion is to produce at Q_m in Figure 10-5, where marginal revenue equals the marginal cost. At this output the monopolist charges what the market will bear, as indicated by the demand curve. In Figure 10-5, this price is P_m.

Profit-Maximizing Price and Output in the Long Run

Notice that producing Q_m units of output, the monopolist is earning economic profit as indicated by the shaded area in Figure 10-5. If it were possible, other firms would enter the market to take advantage of the high rate of return. With other sellers in the market, the demand curve faced by the monopolist no longer would be the market demand curve. The firm's new demand curve would be relatively more elastic because the firm's output would represent a smaller share of total market sales and thus have a smaller effect on price. At the same time, part of the market and some of the economic profit earned by the monopolist would be captured by the new entrants. Ultimately, the market structure might evolve to an oligopoly (a small number of sellers) or even approach perfect competition. However, if the firm's monopoly position is the result of its control over scarce inputs such as mineral reserves, patents, unique managerial talent, or a choice location, entry by other firms may be impossible and the firm will maintain its monopoly position. In this case, economic profits may persist indefinitely.

KEY CONCEPTS

- As the only seller, a monopolist faces the market demand curve. The profit-maximizing output is determined by the point where marginal revenue equals marginal cost.
- If entry by other firms is difficult, the monopolist can earn economic profits even in the long run.

EXAMPLE
COMPUTING PROFIT-MAXIMIZING PRICE AND OUTPUT
FOR A MONOPOLIST

Suppose that the cost equation for a monopolist is given by

$$TC = 500 + 20Q^2$$

where TC is total cost. Let the demand equation be given by

$$P = 400 - 20Q.$$

Because total revenue is price times quantity, the total revenue equation is

$$TR = 400Q - 20Q^2$$

What are the profit-maximizing price and quantity?

Solution

Computation Approach. The equations can be used to compute total costs and revenues at various levels of output. In turn, these numbers yield the marginal cost and marginal revenue figures. The data for $0 < Q \leq 11$ are as follows:

Quantity	Total Cost	Total Revenue	Marginal Cost	Marginal Revenue
1	$ 520	$ 380	$ 60	$340
2	580	720	100	300
3	680	1,020	140	260
4	820	1,280	180	220
5	1,000	1,500	220	180
6	1,220	1,680	260	140
7	1,480	1,820	300	100
8	1,780	1,920	340	60
9	2,120	1,980	380	20
10	2,500	2,000	420	-20
11	2,920	1,980		

Note that marginal revenues exceed marginal costs for the first five units, but that the marginal cost of the sixth unit is greater than its marginal revenue. Hence profits will be maximized by producing 5 units of output. This result can be verified by computing total profit at various rates of output. For example, producing 4 units, total profit is $460, while total profit is $500 for 5 units. However, total profit is only $460 if the sixth unit is produced.

Algebraic Approach. The equation for marginal revenue is the derivative of the total revenue equation with respect to Q. Similarly, marginal cost is just the derivative of total cost with respect to quantity. That is:

$$\frac{dTR}{dQ} = MR = 400 - 40Q$$

and

$$\frac{dTC}{dQ} = MC = 40Q$$

Profits are maximized by choosing the quantity where marginal revenue equals marginal cost. Thus

$$400 - 40Q = 40Q$$

Solving for Q gives 5 units as the profit-maximizing quantity.

Evaluation of Monopoly

To simplify the discussion of the effects of monopoly, it is assumed that average costs and marginal costs are constant for all output levels, as shown in Figure 10-6. To maximize profit, the firm would produce Q_m and charge P_m. As an alternative, suppose that policymakers required the monopolist to use the competitive rule of equating price to marginal cost. In that case the price would be P_c. Those consumers who value the product in excess of P_c would be purchasers, resulting in total sales of Q_c. Because all consumers are charged the same price, most buyers would receive a consumer surplus as a result of their purchase. The dollar value of this surplus is the difference between their valuation of the product (as depicted by the demand curve) and the price, P_c. For example, in Figure 10-6, the person who values the product most highly receives a consumer surplus equal to the vertical distance AP_c. Marginal consumers, of course, have no surplus because they attach a value to the product just equal to the purchase price. Therefore, when output is determined based on the price equals marginal cost rule, the total consumer surplus is the area under the demand curve and above the price. In the figure this area is the triangle ADP_c.

Now consider output and price of the profit-maximizing monopolist. As indicated, the price will be P_m and the quantity will be Q_m. Although the price is higher than using the competitive pricing rule, there is still an area of consumer surplus created by those consumers who value the product above its price. The consumer surplus in the monopoly case is the area of the triangle ABP_m. This

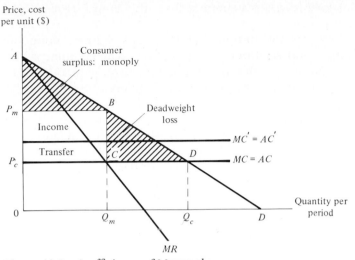

Figure 10-6.   *Inefficiency of Monopoly.*

triangle is part of the consumer surplus under competition, ADP_c. The rectangle P_mBCP_c was also a part of the consumer surplus under competition, but now is economic profit earned by the monopolist. This economic profit represents a redistribution of income from consumers to producers. Whether or not this change is considered an improvement requires an assumption about the appropriate distribution of income and cannot be evaluated using efficiency criteria.

Finally, the last component of the consumer surplus under competition is the triangle BDC. This area is referred to as the *deadweight loss* associated with monopoly. It represents the loss of consumer surplus stemming from monopoly pricing and is a net loss to society. No assumptions about the relative worth of different groups are required to assess this impact of monopoly. It is a loss suffered by consumers that is not captured by anyone.

The source of the deadweight loss can be identified using Figure 10-6. The monopolist produces until marginal revenue equals marginal cost. Expanding production beyond Q_m would result in reduced profit because the incremental revenues are less than the extra costs incurred. However, at the output rate, Q_m, the consumer is charged a price, P_m, which is greater than marginal cost. Thus only those consumers who value the product in excess of P_m will purchase if price is set at that level.

Note that the last person to buy values the product at exactly P_m, but the cost of producing is given by the marginal cost curve and equals P_c. Hence the value to the last buyer is greater than the opportunity cost of producing. Thus social welfare would be increased if more were produced. Specifically, expanding production by 1 unit would generate additional consumer surplus equal to the vertical distance between the demand curve and the marginal cost curve. Additional increases in output would create successively smaller consumer surplus gains until the output rate Q_c was reached. At that point there would be no additional consumer surplus. Thus the triangle BDC can be thought of as the loss of consumer surplus stemming from the output-restricting tendency of monopoly.

To summarize, relative to firms in perfect competition, monopolists produce too little output and set too high a price. Whereas competition results in the lowest price consistent with the survival of the firm, the monopolist charges the highest price consistent with profix maximization. From the perspective of society, resource allocation would be improved if more resources were used to produce the products provided by the monopolist. There is also an income distribution effect associated with monopoly, but an evaluation of this transfer depends on judgments regarding the relative needs of consumers and producers. Although economic analysis provides little assistance in judging this income transfer, its importance in public policymaking should not be underestimated. In political debate, a legislator's call to take action against the abuses of monopoly is not commonly based on esoteric notions of the deadweight loss as discussed in a textbook. Rather, it is more likely to focus on the alleged unfairness of the income redistribution from consumers to owners of the monopoly.

One other effect of monopoly should be mentioned. The cost curves shown for both monopoly and firms in perfect competition assume that firms are attempting to minimize costs at each level of output. For the competitive firm this is a reasonable assumption in that managers may have no choice. Firms that are inefficient simply will not to survive. The monopolist, however, may not be under the same constraint. When earning excess profits, a manager has some discretion with respect to minimizing costs. Rather than expending the effort to contain costs, managers may pursue a utility-maximizing strategy of sacrificing some excess profits in order to ease their work burden. This choice is depicted graphically in Figure 10-6 as an upward shift of the cost curves to $AC' = MC'$. That is, for each unit of output produced by the inefficient monopolist, an additional cost of $MC' - MC$ is incurred. This cost represents resources that cannot be used elsewhere and hence is an additional deadweight loss resulting from monopoly. Failure to minimize costs is called *technical inefficiency*.

KEY CONCEPTS

- Monopoly pricing results in a deadweight loss and a redistribution of income from consumers to producers.
- Technical inefficiency can also occur if monopolists fail to minimize costs.

CASE STUDY
THE NEW YORK TAXICAB MONOPOLY

To limit the number and regulate the operations of taxicab drivers, in 1937 the city of New York required that all cab operators purchase a license. These licenses were called medallions and were sold for $10 each. At that time, 11,787 medallions were issued and no additional licenses have been granted in the intervening years. Thus, those who own medallions are part of a business that others are legally prevented from entering—they have a monopoly over taxi service in New York.

Although the supply of licensed taxicabs has not changed, the demand for taxi service has increased dramatically since 1937. As a result, the medallions have become very valuable because ownership of a medallion confers the right to earn monopoly profit. Essentially, a medallion is worth the present value of the profit stream that it can provide. By the mid-1980s, New York City taxi medallions were selling for over $60,000. Not a bad return for an asset that originally cost $10.

Relevance of Perfect Competition and Monopoly

Over 60 years ago economist Frank Knight wrote: "In view of the fact that practically every business is a partial monopoly, it is remarkable that the theoretical treatment of economics has related so exclusively to complete monopoly and perfect competition" (Knight, 1921). Since that time important contributions have been made to the analysis of alternative market structures. However, classroom time typically is still heavily biased toward discussing the extremes of competition and monopoly. What is the rationale for such emphasis?

The assumptions of the model of perfect competition are very restrictive. Few markets would meet the requirements of many small sellers, easy entry and exit, and an undifferentiated product. Certain parts of the agricultural sector are the most likely candidates. For example, in the Midwest grain exchanges there are many buyers and sellers of wheat. Wheat of a given grade is relatively homogeneous. Compared to activities such as electricity production, resources can enter and leave agriculture without great difficulty. However, to claim that resources are perfectly mobile strains credibility. All in all, it is not easy to think of many circumstances where the requirements for perfect competition are closely approximated.

It is also difficult to think of examples of pure monopoly. In most communities the local electric and telephone utilities usually fit the definition of being single sellers of their product. However, there may be substitutes for their products that reduce the monopoly power of these firms. For example, with an electric utility, consumers usually have the option of heating their homes and water, cooking, and drying clothes with gas instead of electricity. Large industries may generate their own electricity if the rates of the local utility become too high. There are fewer substitutes for telephone service, although letters and telegrams are possibilities. Also, technological advances and pricing policies may make it advantageous for large firms to construct facilities that bypass the local telephone network.

If there are few, if any, examples of pure monopoly and perfect competition, why expend the time and effort required to discuss these extreme conditions?

John Kenneth Galbraith takes a cynical view and argues that the focus on competition by economists is an anachronism of bygone days when the profession was in its formative stages and the world could reasonably be characterized as competitive. He further contends that economists provide a valuable service to powerful business interests by convincing the public that the economy really is competitive and that market forces effectively constrain the activities of large corporations (Galbraith, 1973, Chap. 1).

Milton Friedman disagrees with the premise that the model of perfect competition is not relevant. He observes: "I have become increasingly impressed with how wide is the range of problems and industries for which it is appropriate to treat the economy as if it were competitive (Friedman, 1965, p. 120)." Friedman's view is not based on the belief that the criteria for perfect competition are frequently met, but rather that the results of actual market interaction are similar to those of the perfectly competitive model even if some of the assumptions are violated.

In many applications, it is useful to think of perfect competition and pure monopoly as extremes, with other market structures positioned in between. Although there may be few industries at either extreme, there are many that have most of the characteristics of perfect competition or monopoly. Hence the value of the extreme models is that they serve as benchmarks. Industries that approximate perfect competition are likely to function much like those in the perfectly competitive model. In contrast, those that have many of the characteristics of monopolies will generate monopoly-like results. In addition to providing information on the likely behavior and results of specific market structures, the extreme models of competition and monopoly provide guidance in making public policy. As a general rule, economists favor policies that move industries toward the competitive end of the spectrum.

KEY CONCEPT

- Perfect competition and monopoly can be considered as the extremes of market structure. As such, they serve as benchmarks and guides for public policy.

Summary

Market structures can be characterized on the basis of four characteristics: (1) number and size distribution of sellers, (2) number and size distribution of buyers, (3) product differentiation, and (4) ease of entry and exit. The model of perfect competition assumes a large number of small buyers and sellers, undifferentiated products, and ease of entry and exit. Firms in a perfectly competitive market face a demand curve that is horizontal at the equilibrium price. This price is determined by the interaction of the market supply and demand curves.

Because they have no control over price, the objective of managers is to determine the rate of output that maximizes profit.

The profit-maximizing output for the perfectly competitive firm occurs where price equals marginal cost. In the short run, firms in perfect competition may earn economic profit. However, in the long run, entry of new firms and/or plant expansion drive price down and eliminate the economic profit. Perfect competition results in efficient allocation of resources because production occurs at minimum average cost, voluntary exchange is maximized, and capital is employed in its highest value use.

The monopolist is a single seller of a differentiated product. Entry into the market is difficult or prohibited. Facing the market demand curve, the monopolist has power over price. The decision rule for maximizing profits is to produce until marginal revenue equals marginal cost and then charge the price that the demand curve will bear. Because entry is restricted, the monopolist may earn economic profits in both the short and the long run.

Consumer surplus is the difference between a consumer's valuation of a product and the price that must be paid to purchase it. The principle of consumer surplus can be used to demonstrate that monopoly pricing causes a deadweight loss because too little of the product is produced. If managers fail to minimize costs, technical inefficiency may also occur in monopolies. In addition, monopoly pricing causes an income redistribution from consumers to monopoly owners.

Few market structures meet the restrictive assumptions for perfect competition or monopoly. Still, the models are useful in that they represent extremes which bracket real-world outcomes. Also, the perfectly competitive model is often used as a benchmark for evaluating the performance of actual markets.

Discussion Questions

10-1. Why is concrete sold in local markets, while cement powder is sold in a national market?

10-2. Does product differentiation always refer to real differences between products? Use an example to explain your answer.

10-3. Does ownership of very specialized capital equipment affect ease of exit from an industry? Why or why not?

10-4. How would risk affect the normal rate of profit in an industry?

10-5. Suppose that firms in a perfectly competitive industry are earning less than a normal rate of profit. In the long run, what price adjustments will occur in this industry? What will cause these adjustments?

10-6. Basically, perfectly competitive firms and monopolists use the same rule to determine the profit-maximizing output. True or false? Explain.

10-7. Firms in a perfectly competitive market do not have to compete with the other individual firms in the market. True or false? Explain.

10-8. In the long run, firms in a perfectly competitive market produce at the minimum point on their average cost curves. However, the long-run profit-maximizing output for a monopolist will not be at the point of minimum average cost. Does this mean that competitive firms can produce at a lower average cost than the monopolist? Explain.

10-9. How is the deadweight loss from monopoly affected by the slope of the demand curve?

Problems

10-1. Suppose the market supply and demand equations for plywood are given by

$$Q_S = 20,000 + 30P$$

and

$$Q_D = 40,000 - 20P$$

(a) Graph the supply and demand equations and show the equilibrium price and quantity.

(b) Determine the equilibrium price and quantity algebraically.

(c) Suppose an increase in housing starts results in a new demand equation,

$$Q_D = 50,000 - 20P$$

What is the new equilibrium price and quantity?

10-2. The market supply and demand equations for plywood are the original equations used in Problem 10-1. The plywood industry is perfectly competitive, and the marginal cost equation for one firm, High Country Plywood, is given by

$$MC = 200 + 4Q$$

(a) What is the short-run profit-maximizing output rate for High Country Plywood?

(b) Average cost is given by

$$AC = \frac{1,000}{Q} + 200 + 2Q$$

In the short run, how much economic profit will the firm earn?

10-3. Tyson Brothers Manufacturing is currently earning economic profit. However, the market for the firm's product is perfectly competitive, so the economic profit is not expected to persist in the long run. Tyson's total and marginal cost functions are given by

$$TC = 500Q - 20Q^2 + Q^3$$

and

$$MC = 500 - 40Q + 3Q^2$$

(a) At what output rate will average costs be a minimum?

(b) If the cost curves for all other firms in the market are the same as Tyson's, determine the long-run equilibrium price.

10-4. The equilibrium price in a perfectly competitive market is $10. The marginal cost function is given by

$$MC = 4 + 0.2Q$$

The firm is presently producing 40 units of output per period. To maximize profit, should the output rate be increased or decreased? Explain.

10-5.   Lakeview Electric is the sole supplier of electricity to the community of Lakeview. Managers of the firm estimate that the demand for electricity is given by

$$P = 200 - 4Q$$

The firm's marginal cost equation is given by

$$MC = 4Q$$

(a) What is the profit-maximizing price and quantity?
(b) Can economic profit be determined from the information given? Why or why not?

10-6.   A consultant estimates that the demand for the output of Marston Chemical is given by the equation

$$Q = 2,000 - 50P$$

(a) If the managers of Marston decide to maximize total revenue instead of profit, at what output rate should the firm operate? What is the revenue-maximizing price?
(b) Will the revenue-maximizing output be greater than or less than the profit-maximizing output rate? Explain.

10-7.   The demand for a product is given by

$$Q = 50 - 5P$$

A price of $5 is charged for the product.
(a) Using this information, draw a graph that shows the consumer surplus.
(b) Compute the amount of consumer surplus generated by sale of the product.

10-8.   Lyon Concrete is a monopoly supplier of concrete in northern Arkansas. Demand for the firm's concrete is given by

$$P = 110 - 4Q$$

Marginal cost is constant and equal to 10.
(a) What is the profit-maximizing price and output?
(b) What is the deadweight loss resulting from Lyon's monopoly?
(c) Compared to pricing at marginal cost, how much income is redistributed from consumers to the owners of the monopoly?

10-9.   Show that the profit-maximizing quantity for a monopolist will always lie in the inelastic region of the demand curve.

Problems Requiring Calculus

10-10. The manager of Biswas Glass Company estimates that total revenue from the sale of her firm's product is given by the equation:

$$TR = 300Q - Q^2/2.$$

The total cost equation is estimated to be:

$$TC = 5,000 + 60Q + Q^2$$

(a) What is the profit maximizing price and output rate? What is the amount of economic profit?

(b) At what output rate is average cost a minimum? At this output rate, what is the amount of economic profit?

10-11. For a perfectly competitive firm, the market price is $16. The total cost equation is:

$$TC = Q^3/3 - 5Q^2 + 40Q$$

Use calculus to determine the profit *maximizing* and the profit *minimizing* rates of output. Explain.

References

Bain, J. S. 1956. *Barriers to New Competition.* Cambridge, Mass: Harvard University Press.

Cohen, K., and Cyert, R. 1975. *Theory of the Firm.* Englewood Cliffs, N.J.: Prentice-Hall.

Friedman, M. 1965. *Capitalism and Freedom.* Chicago: University of Chicago Press.

Galbraith, J. K. 1973. *Economics and the Public Purpose.* Boston: Houghton Mifflin.

Greer, D. F. 1980. *Industrial Organization and Prices.* New York: Macmillan.

Knight, F. 1921. *Risk, Uncertainty and Profit.* Boston: Houghton Mifflin, p. 193, note.

Kohler, H. 1982. *Intermediate Microeconomics: Theory and Applications.* Glenview, Ill.: Scott, Foresman.

Marris, R. 1968. *The Economic Theory of Managerial Capitalism.* New York: Basic Books.

Scherer, F. M. 1980. *Industrial Market Structure and Economic Performance.* Chicago: Rand McNally.

Appendix:
Profit Maximization
Using Calculus

In the chapter, graphic and algebraic techniques were used to identify profit-maximizing strategies for the firm. Frequently, such results can be derived more easily and in ways that provide greater insight by using calculus. In this appendix, calculus is employed to demonstrate the profit-maximizing output rate for the firm in perfect competition and also the profit-maximizing price and output rate for the monopolist.

Perfect Competition

Profit is the difference between total revenue and total cost. Because price is considered given, a manager of a perfectly competitive firm maximizes profit by the choice of output rate. Thus the problem in the short run becomes

$$\text{maximize profit} = PQ - TC(Q) \qquad \text{(10A-1)}$$

where PQ is total revenue and $TC(Q)$ is total cost. Total cost is shown as a function of quantity because the firm incurs extra costs as it increases production. The profit-maximizing output is determined by taking the derivative of equation (10A-1) with respect to Q and equating it to zero. But the derivative of PQ is price and the derivative of $TC(Q)$ is marginal cost. Thus

$$P - MC = 0 \qquad \text{(10A-2)}$$

which implies that profits are maximized by producing at the output level where price equals marginal cost.

However, to assure that equation (10A-2) represents the point of profit maximization, it is necessary to evaluate the second derivative of equation (10A-1). From the appendix to Chapter 2, it is known that this second derivative must be negative at the point where the first derivative is zero. That is, the requirement for profit maximization is

$$\frac{dP}{dQ} - \frac{d(MC)}{dQ} < 0$$

at the output rate where $P - MC = 0$. Because price is constant, it follows that $dP/dQ = 0$. Thus the sign of the second derivative depends on the sign of $-d(MC)/dQ$. This implies that profits are maximized if

$$\frac{d(MC)}{dQ} > 0$$

when $P - MC = 0$. But $d(MC)/dQ$ is the change in marginal cost. Hence equation (10A-1) identifies the profit-maximizing output rate if marginal costs are increasing at that point.

EXAMPLE

THE PROFIT-MAXIMIZING OUTPUT RATE

A firm in a perfectly competitive market faces a horizontal demand curve at a price of $55. The firm's total costs are given by the equation

$$TC = 100 - 5Q + Q^2$$

What is the profit-maximizing output? Demonstrate that the point really does maximize profits.

Solution

Profits are maximized where price equals marginal cost. The derivative of TC is $MC = -5 + 2Q$. Setting this expression equal to the $55 price yields

$$55 = -5 + 2Q$$

which has the solution $Q = 30$. To determine if a point of profit maximization has been found, the sign of $d(MC)/dQ$ must be computed. For this problem, $d(MC)/dQ = 2$ and hence $-d(MC)/dQ < 0$. Thus the second derivative test indicates that $Q = 30$ is a maximum.

Monopoly

The profit-maximizing price and output for the monopolist is determined in much the same way as for the perfectly competitive firm. The problem is

$$\text{maximize } TR - TC = [P(Q)]Q - TC(Q) \tag{10A-3}$$

where $P(Q)$ reflects that fact that the output rate chosen by the monopolist affects the price that can be charged.

Taking the first derivative of equation (10A-3) with respect to Q and equating this expression to zero gives

$$\left(\frac{dP}{dQ} Q + P\right) - MC = 0 \tag{10A-4}$$

But $[(dP/dQ) Q + P]$ is the derivative of the total revenue function, or marginal revenue. Hence applying the first derivative test, profits are maximized at the output level where marginal revenue equals marginal cost. That is,

$$MR - MC = 0 \tag{10A-5}$$

The second derivative test requires that

$$\frac{d(MR)}{dQ} - \frac{d(MC)}{dQ} < 0$$

Downward-sloping demand curves imply a declining marginal revenue curve. Thus $d(MR)/dQ < 0$. Hence if marginal costs are increasing, the second derivative is negative and profit is maximized at the output rate where marginal revenue equals marginal cost.

Monopolistic Competition, Oligopoly, and Advertising

11

Preview

Chapter 10 developed models of price and output determination for two important types of market structures: monopoly and perfect competition. But most markets have neither the single seller required to meet the definition of a monopolist nor the large number of small sellers and undifferentiated product necessary to qualify as perfectly competitive. Where the number of sellers is large and the product differentiated, the model of monopolistic competition may be a useful tool for analyzing price and output decisions. When there are only a few sellers, oligopoly theory can provide important insights for decision making.

The first section of this chapter develops the model of monopolistic competition. The second considers oligopoly theory in its various forms. In the third section, basic market structures are compared. The role of advertising in monopolistically competitive and oligopolistic markets is evaluated in the final section of the chapter.

Monopolistic Competition

The models of perfect competition and monopoly are useful as extreme cases, but there is a need to bridge the gap. An important contribution is the model of monopolistic competition developed by Edward Chamberlain (1933).[1] Chamberlain observed that even in markets with a large number of sellers, the products of individual firms are rarely homogeneous. For example, consider men's shoes. In a large community there may be hundreds of shoe stores. But men's shoes may be highly differentiated in the minds of consumers. This product differentiation may reflect materials and workmanship of the shoes sold in a particular store, or it may be the result of effective advertising. The manner in which the store displays the shoes can be another source of product differentiation. An establishment with thick carpet and soft music may have an advantage over a firm that stocks its merchandise on shelves like a warehouse. Location is another source of product differentiation. Sellers in a nearby mall will be more likely to get a consumer's business than stores on the other side of town.

Characteristics

The theory of monopolistic competition has elements of both monopoly and perfect competition. Like perfect competition it is assumed that there are a large number of small sellers. Thus the actions of any single seller do not have a significant effect on other sellers in the market. Also, like perfect competition, it is assumed that there are many buyers and that resources can easily be trans-

---

[1] Another important contributor in this area was Joan Robinson (see Robinson, 1969).

Table 11-1. Market Structure Characteristics of Monopolistic Competition

Number and size distribution of sellers	Many small sellers. Actions of individual sellers go unheeded by other firms.
Number and size distribution of buyers	Many small buyers.
Product differentiation	Slightly differentiated. Product of one firm is a fairly close substitute for that of other sellers.
Conditions of entry and exit	Easy entry and exit.

ferred into and out of the industry. However, the model of monopolistic competition resembles the monopoly models in that products of individual firms are considered to be slightly differentiated. That is, the product of one firm is assumed to be a close, but not a perfect substitute for that of other firms. The implication is that each firm faces a demand curve with a slight downward slope, implying that the individual firm has some control over price. Although increasing its price will cause the firm to lose some sales, because the product is slightly differentiated from that of competitors, some consumers will be willing to buy at the higher price. The characteristics of monopolistic competition are summarized in Table 11-1.

Profit-Maximizing Price and Output in the Short Run

Managers of firms in monopolistic competition determine the output, product attributes, and advertising expenditure that maximize profits. To simplify the discussion, it is assumed that advertising and product attributes have already been determined. Therefore, price is the remaining decision for managers. Chamberlain's monopolistic competition model also assumes that all firms have similar demand and cost curves. Thus it is possible to talk about a "representative" or "typical" firm. The demand and cost curves for such a firm are shown in Figure 11-1.

The results of monopolistic competition in the short run are similar to those of monopoly. The profit-maximizing output occurs at Q_c, where marginal revenue equals marginal cost. The corresponding price (as determined by the demand curve) is P_c. Like a monopolist, a firm in monopolistic competition may earn short-run economic profit. Recall that economic profit per unit is price minus average cost. Thus total economic profit is shown by the shaded area in Figure 11-1.

Profit-Maximizing Price and Output in the Long Run

In the long run, monopolistic competition generates results similar to those of perfect competition. Because entry into the industry is easy, economic profit induces other firms to enter the market. As this entry occurs, the market shares of existing firms decrease. Thus the demand curve faced by these firms shifts to the left, as shown in Figure 11-2. As long as there is economic profit, entry will continue to occur.

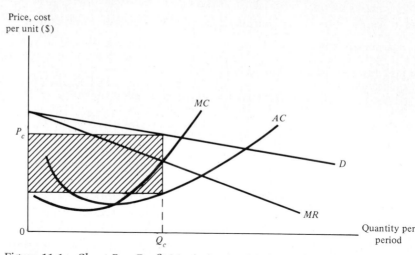

Figure 11-1.   *Short-Run Profit Maximization in Monopolistic Competition.*

As in the short run, the representative firm maximizes profit by equating marginal revenue and marginal cost. In Figure 11-2, profit maximization requires setting price at P_c and producing Q_c units of output per period. Note that the demand and average cost curves are tangent at this price–quantity combination. This implies that average revenue (i.e., price) and average cost are equal and so there is no economic profit. Thus there is no incentive for new firms to enter the market. Similarly, because the representative firm is earning a normal return, firms will not exit the market. Hence P_c and Q_c represent the long-run equilibrium for firms in monopolistic competition.

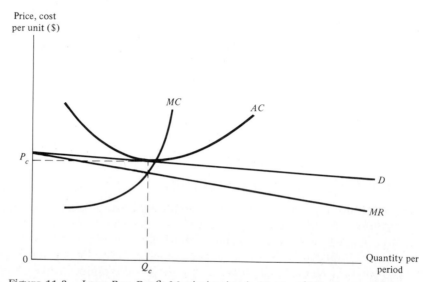

Figure 11-2.   *Long-Run Profit Maximization in Monopolistic Competition.*

KEY CONCEPTS

- Because of product differentiation, firms in monopolistic competition have some control over price.
- As with perfect competition, there are no long-run economic profits in monopolistic competition.

Evaluation of Monopolistic Competition

It is sometimes argued that firms in monopolistic competition are inefficient. Figure 11-2 shows that the profit-maximizing output does not occur at the minimum point on the firm's average cost curve. Thus it can be argued that the firm is operating at an inefficient output rate. In contrast, in Chapter 10 it was demonstrated that the long run equilibrium rate of output in perfect competition occurs at the point of minimum average cost.

The difference in the two outcomes is the result of the downward-sloping demand curve in monopolistic competition. Remember, the long-run equilibrium is the point of tangency of the demand and average cost curves. But because the demand curve is not horizontal, the tangency point cannot be at minimum average cost. However, this result does not necessarily denote inefficiency. The downward slope of the demand curve is the result of product differentiation in the market. Presumably, these differences are of value to consumers as they select goods that meet their particular needs. For example, although "name brand" canned goods are likely to cost more than generic brands, many buyers are willing to pay the extra price as a guarantee of quality. In general, the validity of the claim that monopolistic competition is inefficient depends on the benefits derived from product differentiation compared to the increased costs caused by differentiated products.

In addition to the efficiency question, two criticisms are levied at the theory of monopolistic competition. First, some scholars note that it is often extremely difficult to establish boundaries between markets. For example, at what point are products close enough substitutes to be considered as part of the same market, and when should they be viewed as in a different market? Similarly, if the products of firms have different attributes, is it reasonable to assume that those firms would have the same demand and cost curves?

A second criticism is that the assumptions of the model are rarely met. In markets with many small sellers, there is usually little product differentiation. Thus the theory of perfect competition probably is applicable. Conversely, markets with highly differentiated products usually have few sellers. Hence oligopoly models can be used to analyze price and output decisions.

When first introduced some fifty years ago, the theory of monopolistic competition was viewed as a major contribution to economic analysis. Over the years it has become apparent that the scope of its application is relatively limited. Still, the model provides valuable insight by emphasizing the role of product differentiation.

CASE STUDY

MONOPOLISTIC COMPETITION AND THE COMPUTER SOFTWARE INDUSTRY

The industry that supplies software for personal computers may meet the requirements for monopolistic competition. Even a casual scan of the dozens of computer magazines reveals that many firms are competing in the multibillion-dollar software market. Similarly, the number of magazines on the market is evidence of the vast numbers of potential software purchasers.

Introducing a sensible solution to the problems of dBASE II.

	dBASE II	The Sensible Solution
Records Per File	65,535	999,999
Maximum Record Size	1,024 bytes	1,536 bytes
Fields Per Record	32	384
Key Fields Per File	7	10
Number of Files Simultaneously Accessible	2	10
Number of Screens Per Program	Limited by system memory	Limited only by system storage
Data Dictionary	No	Yes

We don't mean to debase dBASE II, but if you're looking for a data base manager that's long on features, dBASE II can come up a little short.

For instance, a single dBASE II record can only contain 32 fields. And when you need to share information between one file and another, you can only access two at a time.

So, as good as dBASE II is, its limitations can quickly paint you into an electronic corner.

And that's why we created *The Sensible Solution.*

Finally. A sensational relational.

Along with all the usual things you expect from a data base manager, *The Sensible Solution* lets you handle the kind of tough assignments that dBASE II can't.

You can design data files with more than 300 variables. You can create reports using 10 different files at once. You can even set up file locking for multi-user computers.

Ready to get down to business.

A data base manager without ready-to-run application programs is hardly worth the disk it's copied on.

So, along with *The Sensible Solution,* you can also add *The Sensible Solution Bookkeeper*™ or *Sensible Management,*™ our complete one-entry accounting and management system.

They're both affordable. Business-tested. And supplied with source code so you can make your own modifications.

A sensible trial offer.

When you purchase *The Sensible Solution,* we'll send along a special trial disk that lets you create forms and enter a limited number of records. If, after 30 days, you're not satisfied, just return the unopened master system disk for a full refund.

So why not take us up on our trial offer? You've got nothing to lose.

Except the problems of dBASE II.

Figure 11-3. *Example of an Advertisement for Computer Software.*

The computer software industry is relatively easy to enter and exit. Indeed, if the magazine advertisements are a reliable guide, the participants in the market are constantly changing. Other than a computer, little capital equipment is necessary. Rather, the output of individual firms is dependent on the creativity and efficiency of their programmers. Although there are a few "stars" who command very high fees, most computer software is not closely identified with a particular person.

Perhaps the most striking aspect of the software industry is the extremely high degree of product differentiation. Although many different programs may perform similar tasks, the products of individual suppliers are sharply differentiated in the minds of computer devotees. Those who follow developments in the field typically have strong preferences for certain products. These preferences are carefully honed by advertisements that point out the salient features of each firm's product.

One of the best examples of product differentiation involves programs for data base management—software that allows manipulation of numbers and facts. Dozens of different data base management programs are currently marketed. Each has its own special features. Advertisements often compare software to demonstrate the superiority of the advertiser's product. Frequently, only those well-schooled in computer jargon are capable of deciphering the codes. For the informed, each phrase or number represents an important point. A sample advertisement is shown in Figure 11-3. Note the attempt to differentiate the product by comparing its special features to those of another supplier.

Oligopoly

The term *oligopoly* comes from the Greek words *oligos* and *polis* and means, literally, few sellers. Oligopoly is a common form of market structure in modern economic systems. The cereal, automobile, and steel industries in the United States would all qualify. However, oligopolies exist at the local as well as the national level. For example, although there are thousands of gas stations scattered throughout the nation, the typical consumer considers only a few nearby stations. More distant sellers may offer lower prices or better service, but close proximity is probably the dominant consideration. Hence the market for gasoline faced by the individual consumer is properly described as an oligopoly.

Characteristics

An oligopoly involves a large number of buyers but a small number of sellers. There is no precise limit on the number of sellers that a market can have and still be characterized as an oligopoly. The key issue is not numbers, but rather the reaction of sellers to one another. In the three forms of market structure described thus far, there was no need for sellers to be concerned about the actions of individual competitors. The monopolist has no rivals, while firms in perfect and monopolistic competitive markets are too small to have a significant impact on other firms. In contrast, the actions of each firm in an oligopoly do affect the other sellers in the market. Price cutting by one firm will reduce the market share of other firms. Similarly, clever advertising or a new product line can increase sales at the expense of other sellers.

For example, in the early 1980s, Pepsi mounted an aggressive advertising campaign against the industry leader in soft drinks, Coca-Cola. In grocery stores and shopping malls throughout the United States, shoppers were given unmarked samples of Pepsi-Cola and Coca-Cola and asked to indicate their preference. Millions of dollars were spent by Pepsi to tout the fact that its product was chosen by a majority of those who took the test. The consequence of this advertising campaign was an increased market share for Pepsi-Cola.

But the final effect of an oligopolist's decisions is heavily dependent on the response of other firms. In the soft-drink case, the Coca-Cola Company initiated an expensive advertising program of its own. Celebrities were hired to point out that even Pepsi admitted that Coke was the acknowledged standard for comparison. The objective of the Coca-Cola advertising campaign was to minimize the impact of Pepsi's advertising.

Figure 11-4 shows how the actions of rivals can affect the demand curve faced by oligopolists. If one firm reduces its price and the other firms in the market do not respond, the relatively elastic dd is the demand curve. For example, a price decrease from P_1 to P_2 will result in a movement along dd and increase sales from Q_1 to Q_2 as customers abandon other suppliers. However, if the price cut is matched by other firms, the increase in sales will be less. Since other firms are selling at the same price, any additional sales must result from increased total purchases of the product. Thus the effect of the price reduction is a move-

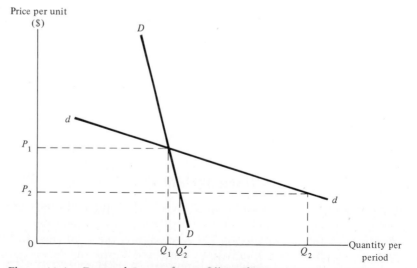

Figure 11-4. *Demand Curves for an Oligopolist.*

Table 11-2. Market Structure Characteristics of Oligopoly

Number and size distribution of sellers	Small number of sellers. Each firm must consider the effect of its actions on other firms.
Number and size distribution of buyers	Unspecified.
Product differentiation	Product may be either homogeneous or differentiated.
Conditions of entry and exit	Entry difficult.

ment down the relatively less elastic demand curve, *DD*. Now the price reduction from P_1 to P_2 will only increase sales to Q_2'.

Clearly, the responses of competitors can have a significant impact on the outcome of managerial decisions in an oligopoly market. Consequently, decision making in an oligopoly is much more difficult than in other market situations.

The other two characteristics that categorize market structure are product differentiation and condition of entry and exit. The product sold in an oligopoly can be homogeneous or differentiated. If the product is homogeneous, the market is said to be a pure oligopoly. The steel and copper markets in the United States would fit into this category. If the product is not homogeneous, the market is a differentiated oligopoly. The automobile and television industries are examples of differentiated oligopolies.

With respect to condition of entry, for an oligopolistic market structure to persist in the long run, there must be some factor that prevents new firms from entering the industry. For example, a drug manufacturer might hold a patent that provides legal protection against potential competitors who desire to produce the product covered by the patent. Market structure characteristics of oligopoly are summarized in Table 11-2.

Oligopoly Models

The most distinctive feature of an oligopolistic industry is that sellers must recognize their interdependence. But oligopolists are likely to deal with this interdependence in different ways, depending on the specific nature of the industry. In some cases, most actions of competitors will be ignored. In other situations, a price war may occur in response to a seemingly innocuous price change. Many factors, such as industry maturity, nature of the product, and methods of doing business, can affect the way firms respond to actions of rivals. The difficulty of formulating models of oligopoly stems from the many ways that firms interact. Consequently, there is no general model of oligopoly. There are, however, models that analyze oligopoly decisions on the basis of specific assumptions about the interaction between firms. Two such models are discussed here.

Kinked Demand Curve Model.   Early students of oligopoly noted that prices in such markets sometimes remained unchanged for long periods of time. For example, the price of steel rails was set at $28 per ton in 1901 and did not change for 15 years. Between 1922 and 1933, the price remained at $43. Similarly, sulfur prices hovered within a few cents of $18 per ton between 1926 and 1938. This

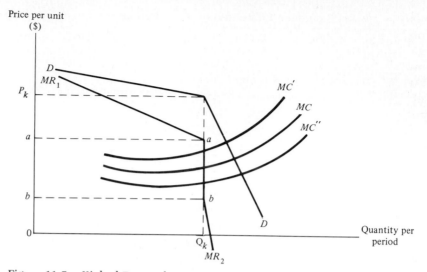

Figure 11-5.　*Kinked Demand Curve.*

apparent price rigidity led Paul Sweezy (1939) to suggest that oligopolists behave as if facing a kinked demand curve, such as the curve shown in Figure 11-5.

The kink in the demand curve stems from an asymmetry in the response of other firms to one firm's price change. Suppose that the price initially is at P_k, the point of the kink in the demand curve. Sweezy argued that if one firm raised its price, other sellers might not follow the increase. The result would be that the firm would lose a significant amount of sales. This is shown in Figure 11-5 as a relatively elastic demand curve above the existing price, P_k.

In contrast, if the firm reduces its price below P_k, it is likely that the other firms will follow suit in an attempt to maintain their market shares. As a result, the price cut by the original firm will not add much to its sales. Figure 11-5 depicts this outcome as a relatively inelastic demand curve below P_k.

Associated with the demand curve is a marginal revenue curve. For a linear demand curve, the absolute value of the slope of the corresponding marginal revenue is twice as great. Note that the kinked demand curve of Figure 11-5 consists of two linear curves joined at P_k. Marginal revenue for prices above the kink is given by MR_1. For those below the kink it is MR_2. At the point of the kink, the marginal revenue curve is a vertical line that connects the two segments.[2]

The model assumes that the firm has a U-shaped marginal cost curve, MC, as shown in Figure 11-5. As with previous models, the profit-maximizing output is determined by equating marginal cost and marginal revenue. Thus the output

---

[2] The marginal revenue function is the derivative of total revenue with respect to quantity. But if the total revenue function is discontinuous (i.e., not smooth), the derivative is not defined at the point of discontinuity. Because the demand curve of Figure 11-5 has a kink at Q_k, the total revenue curve is discontinuous at that output rate. Thus the marginal revenue curve is also discontinuous at Q_k.

rate is Q_k, and the price (as given by the demand curve at Q_k) is P_k. Note that the profit-maximizing solution occurs at the kink because it is in that region that marginal revenue and marginal cost intersect.

Now suppose that increases in input prices cause the marginal cost curve to shift upward to MC'. Profit maximization requires that marginal revenues again be set equal to marginal costs. But for the marginal cost curve MC', the optimal output is still Q_k, and the optimal price is still P_k. Although the marginal cost has increased, there is no change in the profit-maximizing price and quantity. The explanation is the vertical section of the marginal revenue curve found at the kink in the demand curve. Even though the marginal cost curve shifted upward, it still intersects marginal revenue in the region where that curve is vertical. Hence there is no change in the optimal output in response to the input price increase.

Similarly, assume that more efficient production techniques or lower input prices allowed the marginal revenue curve to shift downward, as shown by MC'' in Figure 11-5. As long as the new marginal cost curve intersects the vertical portion of the marginal revenue curve, there will be no change in the profit-maximizing price and quantity. The firm will continue to produce Q_k units and the price will remain at P_k. For price and quantity to change, the marginal cost curve must shift enough to cause it to intersect the marginal revenue either above point a or below point b.

The important implication of the kinked demand curve model is that firms in oligopolistic market structures may experience substantial shifts in marginal costs and still not vary their prices. This theoretical result is consistent with Sweezy's observation that oligopolists do not frequently change their prices, that is, that oligopoly is characterized by price rigidity.

CASE STUDY
SOMETHING'S RIGID IN DENMARK

One of the most interesting documented examples of price rigidity involved a leather tannery in Denmark. While interviewing the managers of 139 Danish firms about their pricing policies, Bjarke Fog came across a firm that charged a higher price for dyed shoe leather than it did for black leather. The price differential had existed since 1890, when dyed leather was more expensive to make. However, by the time of the interview, the dyed shoe leather had become less costly to produce. Queried as to why the pricing policy had not been changed, the firm's manager responded:*

> Perhaps we ought to raise the price of black leather somewhat and lower the price of dyed leather to a corresponding degree, but we dare not do so. The fact is that we shall then run the risk of being unable to sell black leather shoes, whereas our competitors will also reduce their prices for dyed shoes.

---

* B. Fog, *Industrial Pricing Policies* (Amsterdam: North-Holland, 1960), p. 130.

The kinked demand curve model can be criticized on at least two grounds. First, although it explains the reluctance of oligopolists to change prices, it provides no insight in understanding how the price was originally determined. Thus the model is incomplete at best. Second, empirical research has not verified the predictions of the model. George Stigler (1947) studied pricing in seven oligopolies. He found that firms in these industries were just as likely to match a price increase by a competitor as they were to follow a rival's cut in price.

When first proposed, Sweezy's kinked demand curve model was hailed as a general theory of oligopoly. Today, it is viewed in a more limited perspective as one of several descriptions of oligopoly behavior. In markets where the important firms are of nearly equal size, the product is homogeneous, and sellers are not yet certain how rivals will react, the kinked demand curve model can be a useful tool for understanding pricing practices. Where these conditions are not met, this approach is less useful.

Collusion Model.   By increasing production until marginal revenue equals marginal cost and then charging what the market will bear at that rate of output, a monopolist can earn the maximum profit consistent with the demand and cost conditions in the market. In contrast, in oligopolistic industries vigorous price competition between firms tends to drive prices down and reduce profits. Consequently, in such industries there is a strong incentive to collude and maintain prices as near the monopoly level as possible.

Although there may be difficulties in formulating an agreement or dividing the profit, successful collusion can result in substantial benefits to all of the firms involved. Thus, there is a tendency for collusion to occur in such industries. This tendency may take the form of explicit price-fixing agreements, price leadership, or other practices that reduce competitive pressures. The exact nature of collusion in an industry is determined by the specific characteristics of the industry and by the constraints imposed by government policy, especially antitrust enforcement. Still, a useful model of oligopolistic behavior can be based on the assumption that many managerial decisions are directed toward avoiding active competition and maintaining industry pricing discipline.

CASE STUDY

COLLUSION IN THE LEGAL PROFESSION

In 1971, Lewis H. Goldfarb and his wife contracted to buy a home in Fairfax County, Virginia. The lending agency required that a title search be made to assure that the property was not encumbered with legal claims of others. Under state law it was required that a member of the Virginia State Bar Association perform the title search.

The Goldfarbs contacted a lawyer who quoted them the price suggested in a minimum-fee schedule published by the Fairfax County Bar Association. The lawyer told them that it was his policy to keep his charges in line with this schedule, which indicated that the charge for a title search should be 1 percent of the value of the property. The Goldfarbs viewed the lawyer's fee as excessive because the home site was part of a larger development from a single parcel of land. Thus title searches had been done before and, essentially, the lawyer's job would be to copy this information.

The Goldfarbs then tried to find another lawyer who would perform the title search for a lower fee. Ultimately, they sent letters to 36 other lawyers in the county requesting their fees. Nineteen replied, but none indicated that they would charge less than the 1 percent rate proposed by the fee schedule. Several of the lawyers said that they knew of no other attorney who would charge less.

Although the minimum-fee schedule supposedly was voluntary, it was difficult to ignore. To practice law in Virginia, an attorney had to be a member of the Virginia State Bar Association. This body had consistently supported the fee schedules. In fact, at one point the association had stated that "evidence that an attorney habitually charges less than the suggested minimum fee schedule adopted by his local bar association raises a presumption that such lawyer is guilty of misconduct. . . ."

The Goldfarbs sued the Virginia State Bar for illegal collusion. The case finally went to the U.S. Supreme Court, which agreed with the Goldfarbs that the minimum-fee schedule was a violation of antitrust law.

Source: Goldfarb v. Virginia State Bar, 421 U.S. 773 (1975).

Although successful collusion can improve the profitability of all the firms in an industry, any one firm can still benefit more by cheating on the agreement. For example, if managers in an industry collude to raise prices, an individual firm will be able to increase its share of the market and its total profit by setting a price below that charged by the other firms. As long as the other firms adhere to the price-fixing agreement, the cheater will continue to earn additional profit. Eventually, however, other firms will become aware of the actions of the cheater and will reduce their prices. When this occurs the price-fixing agreement starts to fall apart. Unless there is a mechanism for restoring price discipline in the industry, the firms may revert to active price competition.

The success of collusive agreements depends on the costs of colluding and the ability of firms in the industry to detect and punish cheaters. If it is relatively easy to establish agreement among firms and if the actions of cheaters can be quickly identified and punished, collusion may be common behavior in the industry. However, if the number of firms in the market, government antitrust policy, or other factors make coordination more difficult, successful collusion is less likely. Similarly, if the actions of cheaters are difficult to detect, collusion will be more difficult. Factors affecting the success of collusive agreements are discussed in greater detail in Chapter 12.

KEY CONCEPTS

- The kinked demand curve model of oligopoly is based on the assumption that rivals will match price reductions but not price increases. It predicts that price changes will be infrequent in oligopolistic markets.
- Because profits can be increased, oligopolists have an incentive to collude. However, successful collusion requires that cheaters can be identified and punished.

Oligopoly and Barriers to Entry

Many factors can contribute to the existence of an oligopolistic market structure. However, in the long run, conditions of entry may be the most important determinant. Difficulties encountered in entering an industry are often referred to as *barriers to entry*.

What Constitutes a Barrier to Entry?   There is some disagreement among economists as to what constitutes a barrier to entry. Joe Bain (1956, pp. 3–5) argues that entry barriers should be defined in terms of any advantage that existing firms hold over potential competitors. In contrast, Stigler (1968, pp. 67–70) contends that for any given rate of output, only those costs that must be borne by new entrants but that are not borne by firms already in the industry should be considered in assessing entry barriers.

Two examples illustrate the difference in philosophy. Suppose that one firm had control over all the iron ore deposits in the United States. As a result, new entrants into the steel industry could get ore only by transporting it from Canada or another foreign supplier. Transportation costs would cause potential competitors to have higher costs of producing steel than those of the existing firm. This disadvantage could prevent the new firms from successfully entering the market. Both the Bain and the Stigler criteria for a barrier to entry are satisfied in this example. Alternatively, assume that iron ore deposits are equally available to the existing and the potential new firms, but that the existing firm is large enough to take advantage of highly efficient production technologies. If new entrants build plants of small scale, their costs may be so high that they cannot sell steel at a price competitive with the established firm. That is, successful entry requires construction of plants that are large enough to take advantage of economies of scale. Bain would consider this condition a barrier to entry because of the difficulties in coordinating and raising capital for large-scale entry. However, Stigler's definition would not recognize scale economies as an entry barrier, because the old and the new firms both face the same cost conditions. That is, for any given rate of output produced, the cost per unit would be the same for the new entrant as for an existing firm.

From a strictly conceptual point of view, the Stigler position that entry barriers should be confined to problems faced by new, but not existing firms has appeal. But the Bain definition is the more useful of the two approaches. By including all factors that impede entry into an industry, it provides a better framework for understanding the determinants of market structure.

Reasons for Barriers to Entry. Although there are many possible factors that impede entry, this discussion focuses on four of the most important. The first is product differentiation. A firm that has convinced consumers that its product is significantly better than the product of new entrants has an advantage. The new firm may be forced to sell its product at a lower price that may not generate an adequate profit. There is no requirement that the product really be superior, only that consumers perceive it as more desirable. For example, some aspirin manufacturers have extolled the virtues of their product for decades. The result is that the typical consumer has a subjective feeling that Bayer and other well-advertised aspirins are superior to other brands—despite their being chemically identical. The ability of firms such as Bayer to differentiate their product allows them to capture a larger share of the market, charge higher prices, and earn economic profit. Even if new firms were to spend as much on advertising each year as Bayer, it would be unlikely that they could ever catch up. Bayer's long tenure in the market has generated strong consumer loyalties that are difficult for new firms to overcome. Thus a barrier to entry exists.

A second restriction on entry is control of inputs by existing suppliers. If potential entrants cannot easily obtain the capital, raw materials, and labor needed to produce their product, entry may be difficult. Examples include scarcity of natural resources, locational advantages, and managerial talent.

Legal restrictions such as patent protection are a third source of entry barriers. In some industries, patents held by existing firms make it virtually impossible for other businesses to produce a comparable product. Exclusive franchises granted by government are another form of legal restriction. For example, an electric company may have a legal right to be the sole supplier of electricity in its service area.

Scale economics are a fourth source of barriers to entry. If the production process exhibits economies of scale, a large, existing firm will have lower costs than a new firm attempting to enter the industry on a small scale. As a result, the new entrant may not be able to operate profitably at a price that allows existing firms to earn substantial economic profit. At the same time, any effort to enter the industry on a larger scale may be frustrated by difficulties of obtaining capital and putting together the necessary organization. Thus the ability of existing firms to expand gradually as compared to the need for new entrants to start out with considerable production capacity can be a substantial advantage for existing firms. A good example is the automobile industry. Because of the economies of scale associated with the manufacture and sale of automobiles, no new domestic producer has successfully entered the industry in over fifty years.

KEY CONCEPT

- Sources of entry barriers include control of scarce inputs, product differentiation, legal factors, and scale economies.

EXAMPLE
BARRIERS TO ENTRY IN PENCIL MAKING

Johnson and Wyngate, a small manufacturing firm, is considering building a plant capable of producing 25 million wood pencils per year. Pencils are an undifferentiated product, the necessary raw materials are readily available, and patents are relatively unimportant in the industry. However, up to some output rate, economies of scale provide substantial cost savings for the large-scale producer. It is estimated that the average cost function is given by

$$AC = 100,000 - 1,000Q + 10.0Q^2$$

where Q is measured in millions of pencils per year.

The current wholesale price of pencils is $75,000 per million and this price will not be affected by the entry of Johnson and Wyngate into the industry. If it were to build this facility, would Johnson and Wyngate be able to earn at least a normal profit? What is the minimum output rate required to earn a normal profit?

Solution

The average cost equation includes a normal profit. Thus, to earn normal profit, price must be at least as great as average cost. But at 25 million pencils per year, average cost will be $81,250 per million, which is more than the $75,000 wholesale price.

The minimum output rate necessary to earn a normal profit is computed by setting price equal to average cost and solving for output. Thus

$$75,000 = 100,000 - 1,000Q + 10.0Q^2$$

The equation can be simplified to

$$Q^2 - 100Q + 2,500 = 0$$

In turn, this equation can be factored as

$$(Q - 50)(Q - 50) = 0$$

Thus the solution is $Q = 50$. Hence 50 million units of output per period is the minimum production rate necessary to earn a normal profit at a price of $75,000 per million pencils.

Spectrum of Market Structures

As discussed in Chapter 10, there are few markets that can properly be categorized as being either perfectly competitive or true monopolies. In the vast majority of cases, the characteristics of monopolistic competition or oligopoly seem

Table 11-3. Market Structures of Selected Industries

Perfect Competition	Monopolistic Competition	Oligopoly	Dominant Firm Oligopoly	Monopoly
Agriculture	Movie theaters	Automobiles	Computers (IBM)	Electric, gas, and
	Printing	Cereal	Aircraft (Boeing)	telephone
	Retailing	Cigarettes	Canned soup	utilities
	Restaurants	Beer	(Campbell)	
	Dresses	Oil refining	Film (Kodak)	
	Poultry	Steel	Detergents	
	Yarns	Newspapers	(Procter &	
	Sheet metal	Chewing Gum	Gamble)	

to be more accurate descriptors. Table 11-3 shows a spectrum of market structures. It also locates specific industries on the spectrum. Although agriculture is listed under perfect competition, it does not meet all the requirements for that designation. Rather, it is the industry that comes closest to being perfectly competitive. Similarly, electric, gas, and telephone companies may have legal monopolies in their service areas, but they still face some competition from substitute services. Thus even they are not true monopolies.

Note that two types of oligopolies are shown in Table 11-3. The first type (listed in the third column) consists of a small number of firms of nearly equal size. The second type (shown in the fourth column), has a dominant firm. These dominant firms are shown in parentheses with each industry and supply a large share of total industry output. For example, a relatively small number of firms manufacture most of the large computers sold in the United States. But IBM is clearly the dominant firm in that industry. In fact, during the late 1960s its market share was so large that it was accused of having an illegal monopoly. The IBM antitrust case is discussed in greater detail in Chapter 19.

Advertising

Of the market structures listed in Table 11-3, advertising is most important to firms in monopolistically competitive and oligopolistic markets. By definition, firms in perfect competition sell an undifferentiated product. Because they can sell all they produce at the market price, they have no need to advertise. At the other extreme, as a single seller, a monopolist does not need to advertise to maintain its market share. Rather, dollars spent on advertising by monopolists and near monopolists are intended to increase total demand for the firm's product. Thus advertising expenditures usually are a relatively small fraction of total revenues.

Monopolistic competition differs from perfect competition in that monopolistically competitive firms sell a slightly differentiated product. Advertising is one way of achieving product differentiation. Advertising is also important in oligopolistic markets where advertising is intended to increase a firm's market share. Competition through advertising may also serve as a partial substitute for active price competition in such industries. Consequently, firms in oligopolistic markets often spend a large proportion of total revenues on advertising.

The amount and type of advertising is an important managerial decision. The first part of this section presents the traditional view of advertising. Next is a revised view that focuses on advertising as a source of information. The section concludes by analyzing the optimal rate of advertising.

The Traditional View of Advertising

Over two thousand years ago the following poem was painted on the wall surrounding the Greek city of Athens:

> For eyes that are shining, for cheeks like the dawn,
> For beauty that lasts after girlhood is gone,
> For prices in reason, the woman who knows,
> Will buy her cosmetics of Aesclyptos.

The purpose of this "advertisement" was to convince the women of Athens that beauty aids purchased from Aesclyptos were preferable to those sold by others. Basically, Aesclyptos was trying to differentiate his (her?) product.

Many advertising practices have changed little in the intervening period. Advertising continues to be an important tool for product differentiation. In some cases advertising serves to make buyers aware of real differences between products. For example, advertisements in trade publications frequently provide detailed information regarding the attributes of products. A magazine read by dentists might contain ads that specify the speed of drills, the setting time and strength of adhesives, and the composition of materials used for fillings.

In other circumstances, advertising can persuade consumers that essentially identical products are quite different. Consider the case of aspirin. In terms of chemical composition, all brands of aspirin are very similar. But highly advertised brands such as Bayer have a commanding share of the market even though they sell at substantially higher prices than generic brands of aspirin. The explanation is that advertising has differentiated these brands in the minds of consumers.

CASE STUDY:

THE CASE OF SMIRNOFF VODKA

Vodka is an essentially colorless, odorless, and tasteless drink that is produced using a relatively simple production process. As such, if one brand of vodka is favored over others, the preference ought to reflect lower prices. Yet brand names are very important in purchasing vodka. By extensive advertising, some manufacturers have created a strong preference for their product. In particular, the Smirnoff Company has been highly successful in differentiating its vodka from that of other firms. Smirnoff advertisements have focused on the gaiety and excitement of their brand in the attempt to appeal to young, wealthy adults.

Rather than compete on the basis of price, the company priced its vodka above other brands to create an impression of quality. In fact, on one occasion Smirnoff responded to a price cut by a competitor by increasing the price of its brand. The strategy proved successful. For many years, Smirnoff's was the best-selling vodka and the second-best-selling brand among all hard liquors in the United States.

Historically, economists have been critical of advertising. The benefits of price advertising have been acknowledged, but other forms of advertising traditionally have been viewed as a cause of higher prices resulting from unnecessary product differentiation. Among the objections to nonprice advertising are that it reduces consumer sovereignty, creates barriers to entry, and results in wasted resources.

Reduced Consumer Sovereignty.   Fundamental to conventional economic theory is the concept of consumer sovereignty. Businesses are assumed to base their production decisions on the expressed preferences of consumers. As purchase patterns indicate a change in those preferences, firms respond by altering the attributes and amounts of the goods and services produced. In this view of the world, the role of the firm is assumed to be essentially passive. That is, managers make little attempt to alter preferences of consumers, but react rapidly to take advantage of changing conditions of demand.

But some economists argue that consumer sovereignty has been largely supplanted by producer sovereignty.[3] They contend that for many years, large corporations have effectively used advertising and other techniques of persuasion to manipulate consumer wants. For example, consider the experience of an advertising executive dealing with the tobacco industry in the 1920s (Bernays, 1971):

> George Washington Hill, a manic, boisterous, authoritarian salesman, president of the American Tobacco Company, was an exciting client for many years. Lucky Strikes were his dominating theme. Mr. Hill wanted more women to smoke Lucky Strikes, but research showed that sales to them were down because the green-packaged cigarettes clashed with their costumes. "Change the color of the package," I suggested. Mr. Hill was outraged. I then suggested we try to make green the dominant color of women's fashions. "What will it cost?" he asked. For want of a better figure, I said, "$25,000." He quickly rejoindered, "Spend it." For a year we worked . . . to hold a Green Ball, with tableaux of socialites dressed in green. . . . We worked with manufacturers of accessories for dresses and textiles to ensure that gloves, stockings, shoes, and other accessories would also be green. *Harper's Bazaar* and *Vogue* featured green covers of fashions on the date of the green ball. Green became fashion's color.

Although most advertising campaigns are not as ambitious nor successful as the "green campaign" of Lucky Strike, they probably do alter the preferences of buyers. The huge sums spent on advertising by McDonald's are intended to do more than tell customers that the firm sells hamburgers. Similarly, AT&T's fa-

---

[3] This concept is basic to the writings of John Kenneth Galbraith (see, e.g., Galbraith, 1973, Chap. 14).

mous "reach out and touch someone" slogan, while promoting closeness between family and friends, is designed primarily to touch the telephone customer
in the pocketbook.

If advertising can be used to manipulate demands of buyers, consumer sovereignty is reduced. However, the extent and effect of this manipulation is very
difficult to determine.

Barriers to Entry.   A second objection to advertising is that it may increase
barriers to entry into a market. This can happen in several ways. First, as product
differentiation becomes more pronounced, consumers become less sensitive to
price changes. Thus new firms find it more difficult to establish a position in the
market even if they sell their output at prices below those of the established
firms. Second, it is likely that there is a cumulative effect of advertising. That is,
the degree of differentiation of a firm's product depends not only on the amount
spent on advertising in a given year, but also on previous expenditures on advertising. For example, consumers' perceptions of Pepsi-Cola are based on their
experience with the product, on the advertisements they see each day, and also
on their recollections of previous advertising campaigns. To enter on an equal
basis, a new soft-drink manufacturer would be forced to spend millions more
on advertising than would Pepsi in order to offset the cumulative effects of the
Pepsi advertising. These extra dollars represent a barrier that restricts new entry
and tends to increase the market power of existing firms.

Sometimes it is alleged that advertising also creates entry barriers by allowing
existing firms to realize scale economies. The idea is that a successful advertising
campaign will increase the firm's sales. If the production process involves increasing returns to scale, average cost will decline as output is increased. This
will allow the firm to produce at lower average cost and may even result in a
price reduction. However, entry can be impeded in that new firms, with relatively
small production facilities, may be unable to compete with the larger, more
efficient existing firms. The new entrants could attempt to enter on a larger scale,
but this would require a larger investment and hence greater financial risk.

This argument is valid only if the industry is characterized by increasing returns to scale. Indeed, if the output expansion caused by advertising moves the
firm into a region of decreasing returns to scale, the average costs of existing
firms will increase. In this case, advertising might not cause greater barriers to
entry.

Wasted Resources.   Advertising may result in a waste of resources. Here the
point is not that advertising has no value, but rather that it may be self-canceling.
This is particularly true in an oligopolistic industry. Where the number of sellers
is few, firms may engage in advertising as a substitute for price competition. One
purpose of such advertising is to increase the firm's market share at the expense
of its competitors. But if all firms advertise, they cannot all succeed in this
attempt. What happens is that advertising of one firm counteracts that of others.
Yet no firm can afford to stop advertising while the others continue. Thus, con-

sidered from the perspective of the entire industry, the advertising dollars are wasted.

CASE STUDY

WHY DO OLIGOPOLISTS OVERADVERTISE?

The explanation for the resource waste from advertising in an oligopoly can be illustrated using the maximin decision strategy discussed in Chapter 3. Assume that an industry consists of only two sellers, that is, a duopoly. Further assume that managers of each firm can choose a high level of advertising or a low level.

Below is a table showing profit for each firm for each combination of advertising decisions. If both firms adopt the low level of advertising, the savings on advertising expenses will allow each firm to earn $30 million in profit. If both firms select the high advertising alternative, the efforts are largely offsetting and profits will be $20 million because of the substantial advertising expenditure. If the first firm advertises and the second does not, profits will be $40 million for the first firm and $10 million for the second. The profit figures are reversed if firm 2 advertises and firm 1 does not.

Now assume that the managers of both firms are risk averse and that their objective is to maximize the minimum profit earned by their company. That is, they use a maximin decision rule. Should they choose the low or high level of advertising? If firm 1 does not advertise, its profits will be $30 million if the second firm does not advertise and $10 million if it does. Thus the minimum profit from not advertising would be $10 million. In contrast, if firm 1 selects the high advertising strategy, it has guaranteed profits of at least $20 million regardless of what the other firm does. Hence the maximin strategy for firm 1 is to advertise. Similar logic suggests that firm 2 will also choose the high advertising option.

Firm 1	Firm 2	
	Low-Advertising	High-Advertising
Low-advertising	$30, $30	$10, $40
High-advertising	$40, $10	$20, $20

Thus both firms decide to make extensive advertising expenditures. The result is a profit of $20 million for each company. However, note that a joint decision not to advertise would have been more profitable because each firm would have earned a $30 million profit. But neither firm dares to opt for this choice because of the possibility that the other might select the high-advertising alternative. The result is that the firms earn less profit while wasting their resources on mutually offsetting advertising. Although much simplified, this simple analysis provides insight into the dilemma faced by oligopolists.

KEY CONCEPTS

- If advertising is effective in influencing consumer preferences, consumer sovereignty may be reduced.
- Advertising can create barriers that make new entry more difficult.
- Resources may be wasted if oligopolists engage in mutually offsetting advertising.

Advertising as Information

In 1961, George Stigler published a path-breaking article in which he criticized the traditional view that advertising usually results in higher prices as a consequence of product differentiation. Noting that different prices are often charged for products that are essentially the same, he argued that much of the variation in prices results from ignorance by consumers regarding the prices and qualities of products produced by different firms. One way that consumers reduce their ignorance is by search. That is, buyers spend time and money learning about potential purchases. For example, a consumer interested in new skis can inspect the equipment in a store, put demonstration skis to use, and talk with others about their experiences with various brands of skis.

But sometimes extensive search activities are not practical. This is particularly true when the cost of search is high relative to the price of the product. Clearly, the average person would not find it worthwhile to spend hours going from store to store in quest of the best brand of paper clips. The information obtained from advertising can be a substitute for search activity. To the extent that advertising reduces search costs, society benefits.

Obviously, advertising is not solely intended to supply factual information to consumers. Most advertising is also designed to persuade people that a product is needed, desirable, and should be purchased. Although almost all advertisements contain both informative and persuasive material, the relative proportions of the two depend on the type of good being advertised and also the characteristics of the perspective buyers.[4]

Buyer Characteristics.   Consider the perfect buyer. She should have extensive knowledge about the good to be purchased. Her preferences should be stable and well defined. She should also be aware of all substitute products on the market. Such a buyer probably would not be influenced by false or inflated claims on the part of sellers. Rather, she would be influenced by advertising only to the extent that it provided useful information that highlighted real differences between the various brands.

Where is this perfect buyer to be found? Probably no one meets all of the criteria, but some purchasing agents in business and government may come

---

[4] The discussion which follows is based on Greer (1980, pp. 62–75).

close. These are people who devote their work lives to buying specific types of products. They have access to other experts and may have funds that can be used in testing alternative brands. Basically, they can become extremely familiar with certain products because their employers purchase enough of the products to justify the cost of acquiring such detailed expertise. That is, search costs can be spread over a large volume of units. Let such buyers be designated as "professionals."

At the other extreme may be the typical consumer who buys an item infrequently and, as such, does not acquire much information about the attributes of different brands. That is, the search for information is costly relative to its value. With limited information coming from personal search, the consumer may rely on the advertising of sellers as a substitute source of knowledge. But such consumers are not well qualified to sort out factual information from exaggeration and puffery in these advertisements. As a result, they are prime candidates for persuasive advertising.

Product Types. Goods can be categorized as search goods or experience goods. Search goods are those having attributes that can be determined prior to their purchase. For example, a consumer should be able to make a good assessment of a copy of a famous painting before buying it. Fundamentally, the decision is based on whether the copy is attractive or not. If the buyer finds it aesthetically appealing in the store, there is a good chance that he will like it at home. Thus his search should provide adequate information.

In contrast, the desirability of experience goods is determined through their use. Generic brands of canned vegetables are an example. In a grocery store there really is no way to know how the vegetables will look or taste. These attributes can be determined only by consuming the product. However, once the product has been used, the shopper's experience is sufficient to decide if the product should be purchased again.

Content and Intensity of Advertising. The previous analysis of buyers and product types can be used to predict the content and intensity of advertising. Table 11-4 contains four cells based on the two categories of buyers and the two

Table 11-4. Advertising Content and Intensity

Type of Buyer	Type of Product	
	Search	Experience
Professionals	Content: objective Intensity: low Example: steel	Content: primarily objective Intensity: moderate Example: large computers
Consumers	Content: primarily objective Intensity: moderate Example: fresh fruit	Content: both objective and subjective Intensity: high Example: cosmetics

product types. At the top left are search goods purchased by professionals. Examples include raw materials (e.g., rubber and steel) and basic office supplies (such as pencils and paper). The cell at the top right represents professional experience goods. Sophisticated medical equipment or large computers might be included in this category.

Consumer search goods (the lower left-hand cell) include items that can carefully and easily be inspected, such as fresh fruits and vegetables, jewelry, and clothing. Finally, consumer experience goods would consist of products such as TV dinners, laxatives, and deodorants that can be evaluated only by use.

The table categorizes advertising in each cell by content and intensity. With respect to content, advertising can be considered objective or subjective. Objective advertising is primarily informational. It provides factual data about the product and makes little attempt to persuade customers on an emotional basis. In contrast, subjective advertising has a smaller informational content and relies heavily on the appeal to emotions. The three categories of intensity (low, moderate, and high) refer to the extent of advertising. They might be thought of in terms of advertising expenditure as a percent of total sales. Thus low intensity indicates a small percentage of sales dollars used for advertising, while high intensity suggests a substantial proportion.

For professional search goods, advertising expenditure represents a low percentage of sales and the advertisements are highly informational. The reason is that such goods can be carefully inspected by experienced buyers prior to purchase. As a result, purchase decisions are unlikely to be influenced by advertising and even less likely to be affected by appeals to emotion. The cell for professional experience goods indicates that advertising intensity will be moderate and primarily objective. Again, knowledgeable buyers are involved, but with experience goods the evaluation cannot be as precise as with search goods.

For consumer search goods advertising also is moderate and primarily objective. The explanation is that the buyers are less knowledgeable than the professionals, but exaggerated claims often can be detected by the consumer with relative ease. Finally, for consumer experience goods, advertising intensity is likely to be high and advertisements may be very subjective. Cosmetics are a good example. Some sellers of this product spend as much as 50 percent of total revenue on advertising. Rarely do such advertisements provide much factual information. Instead, they usually concentrate on beautiful women wearing expensive and provocative clothes being escorted to elegant places by handsome and charming men. The implication of such advertisements is that purchasers of the product should expect to find themselves in similar circumstances.

The classification scheme of Table 11-4 leads to two interrelated conclusions about advertising. The first is that advertising is likely to be most intensive where it is least informational. This is indicated by the consumer experience good cell of the table. The second is that needs for information are inversely related to the content of advertising. Of the four categories, it is consumers who purchase experience goods who are least able to evaluate the product. But Table 11-5 suggests that advertising is likely to have a relatively smaller informational content for the consumer experience goods than for the other three categories.

KEY CONCEPTS

- Advertising can be a substitute for search on the part of buyers. As such, it may result in lower prices as consumer ignorance is reduced.
- Search goods are those that can be carefully evaluated and inspected prior to purchase.
- As the name implies, experience goods cannot be fully evaluated prior to purchase.
- Advertising is likely to be most intense and least informational for experience goods purchased by consumers.

The Optimal Rate of Advertising

In analytical terms, the objective of advertising is to shift the demand curve to the right, as shown in Figure 11-6. Note that the figure implies that if advertising is effective, more of the product can be sold at each price.

But as with inputs in the production process, the marginal effectiveness of advertising diminishes as additional advertising dollars are spent. That is, advertising is subject to diminishing marginal returns. There may be several reasons why this occurs. First, to the extent that advertising conveys information to consumers, there may be a limit to the amount of information that a person wants to obtain or is able to process. If advertising proceeds beyond this limit, little additional benefit will be received. Second, consumers may become irritated if a product is advertised too often. If this happens, they may react by ignoring the information or by developing a distaste for the product. Finally, if one firm in an oligopoly increases its advertising rate, it may cause other firms to respond with extensive advertising campaigns of their own. Thus the advertising may be self-canceling and no single firm will benefit.

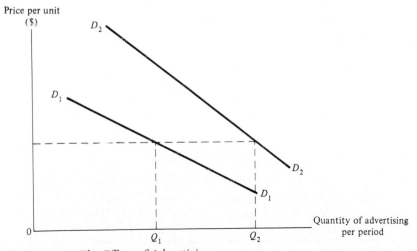

Figure 11-6. *The Effect of Advertising.*

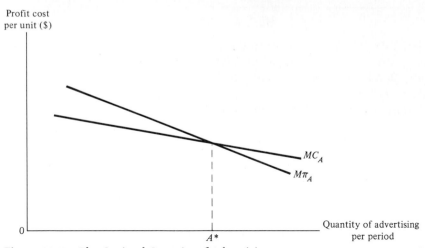

Figure 11-7. *The Optimal Quantity of Advertising.*

If advertising can increase demand but at the same time is subject to diminishing marginal returns, there is an optimal rate of advertising expenditure for the firm. This optimal rate is shown in Figure 11-7. The line $M\pi_A$ represents the marginal profitability of advertising. That is, it shows the extra dollars in profit earned on sales resulting from an additional unit of advertising (e.g., a 1-minute television commercial or a page in a magazine). Note that the line is downward sloping because of diminishing marginal returns to advertising. The line MC_A depicts the marginal cost of a unit of advertising. It is also shown as downward sloping because quantity discounts frequently are available to large advertisers. For example, Procter & Gamble spends nearly $1 billion on advertising each year. The firm's volume of advertising enables it to purchase time and space at a lower cost than that available to smaller firms.

The advertising decision is made like other resource allocation decisions—the activity is increased until marginal benefit equals marginal cost. In the example, this occurs at A^*, where the extra profit resulting from an additional unit of advertising just equals the cost of buying one more unit. Beyond that point, additional advertising costs more than it is worth to the firm.

KEY CONCEPTS

- Beyond some point, there are diminishing marginal returns to advertising.
- The objective of profit maximization requires that the rate of advertising be increased until the marginal profit generated by the last unit of advertising just equals its marginal cost.

Summary

Chamberlain's model of monopolistic competition assumes ease of entry and exit and a large number of small sellers. It differs from perfect competition by viewing sellers as providing products that are slightly differentiated. Thus firms have some control over price. In the short run, profits are maximized by equating marginal revenue and marginal cost and there are economic profits. In the long run, entry eliminates economic profits. The theory of monopolistic competition has been criticized as having a limited scope of application, but the model makes a useful contribution to economic analysis by calling attention to the importance of product differentiation.

Oligopolistic market structures have many buyers but only a small number of sellers. The product may be either differentiated or undifferentiated. Typically, entry into the industry is somewhat difficult. An important difference between oligopoly and other market structures is that oligopolists recognize their interdependence. Thus, in making decisions, managers must consider the effect on other firms and the probable response of those firms.

There is no single theory that describes all aspects of oligopoly behavior. However, specific models capture certain elements. One is the kinked demand curve model. It assumes that competitors will follow price cuts, but not price increases. The implication is that price changes will be infrequent in oligopolistic markets. Another theory of oligopoly is based on the observation that firms in an oligopolistic market can increase their profits if they avoid price competition. Thus there is a tendency for collusion. The success of collusion depends on the ability of firms to detect and punish cheaters.

Barriers to entry are perhaps the most important determinant of market structure. Bain argues that barriers to entry exist if an existing firm has an advantage over potential entrants. The most important sources of barriers to entry are (1) product differentiation, (2) control over vital inputs, (3) legal factors such as patents, and (4) economies of scale.

Advertising may be important in monopolistically competitive and oligopolistic markets. The traditional view is that advertising results in higher prices because of unnecessary product differentiation. In this view, problems associated with advertising include reduction of consumer sovereignty, increased barriers to entry, and wasted resources.

More recently, economists have focused on advertising as a substitute for consumer search. The argument is that by providing information, advertising may result in lower prices. However, the informational content of advertising depends on experience of the buyer and the nature of the product. In general, advertising is likely to be most intense and least informative for experience goods that are purchased infrequently by consumers. In contrast, advertising tends to be at lower levels and have a higher informational content for search goods that are purchased by professional buyers.

Advertising is intended to shift the firm's demand curve to the right. But beyond some point, there are diminishing returns to advertising. To maximize profit, the firm should increase its advertising expenditures until the marginal profit generated by advertising equals the cost of the last unit of advertising.

Discussion Questions

11-1. Is product differentiation important in the breakfast cereal industry? Explain.

11-2. Which of the following markets could be considered monopolistically competitive? Explain.
(a) Network television.   (b) Low-priced pens.
(c) Retail gasoline sales.   (d) Automobiles.

11-3. In monopolistically competitive markets, why is the firm's demand curve assumed to be relatively more elastic in the long run than in the short run?

11-4. Monopolistic competition assumes slightly differentiated products, but the average and marginal cost curves used in the analysis are those of a typical or representative firm. Is there an inconsistency in these assumptions? Explain.

11-5. Suppose that there are 5,000 firms selling candy by mail to people in the Pacific Northwest. Could this market be characterized as monopolistically competitive? If 5,000 firms are selling concrete in the same region, could that market be considered monopolistically competitive? Explain.

11-6. If there is no change in the cost of production, why might oligopolists be more likely to match a price cut than a price increase by a competitor?

11-7. Accumulated experience may allow firms that have been producing for many years to have lower costs than new entrants in a market. Would this "learning by doing" be a barrier to entry as defined by Bain? What about using Stigler's definition of entry barriers?

11-8. Are service industries more likely to be near the monopoly or the competitive end of the spectrum of market structures? Why?

11-9. For which of the following goods is advertising likely to be highly subjective? Explain.
(a) Lipstick.   (b) Fresh oranges.
(c) Rock concerts.   (d) Nuclear reactors.

11-10. More dollars are spent on television commercials than for all other forms of advertising combined. What are the advantages of television advertising compared to other media?

Problems

11-1. In Gotham City the movie market is monopolistically competitive. In the long run, the demand for movies at the Silver Screen theater is given by the equation

$$P = 5.00 - 0.002Q$$

where Q is the number of paid admissions per month. Average costs are given by

$$AC = 6.00 - 0.004Q + 0.000001Q^2$$

(a) To maximize profit, what price should the managers of Silver Screen charge? What will be the number of paid admissions per month?

(b) How much economic profit will the firm earn?

11-2. EnviroEast can produce recycled paper at a constant marginal cost of $0.50 per pound. Currently, the firm is selling 500,000 pounds each year at $0.60 per pound. Managers of EnviroEast are considering increasing the price to $0.90 per pound. Demand elasticity is constant and equals -0.6 if the price increase is matched by competitors and -4.0 if it is not matched. Management believes there is a 70 percent chance that other firms will follow EnviroEast's lead and increase their prices.

(a) If managers are risk neutral, should the proposed price change be implemented? Explain.

(b) Write an equation for the expected change in profit as a function of the probability that the price increase will be matched by the other firms. What probability would make a risk neutral manager indifferent to the change?

11-3. The price of steel is currently at $400 per ton. Pennsylvania Steel faces a kinked demand curve with a demand equation

$$P = 600 - 0.5Q$$

for prices above the present price of $400 and

$$P = 700 - 0.75Q$$

for prices below $400. The firm's marginal cost curve is given by an equation with the general form

$$MC = a + bQ$$

(a) If $a = 50$ and $b = 0.25$, graph the demand, marginal revenue, and marginal cost curves. Using the graph, determine the profit-maximizing quantity for Pennsylvania Steel?

(b) Starting from $a = 50$, how much can the constant term of the marginal cost equation increase before the profit-maximizing quantity decreases? How much can the coefficient decrease before the profit-maximizing quantity increases?

11-4. At present, the price of copper tubing is $1 per foot. Lyon Inc. is considering entering the industry by building a facility that will produce 40 million feet of tubing per year. It is estimated that the average cost curve for manufacturing copper tubing is given by the equation

$$AC = 1.21 - 0.010Q + 0.0001Q^2$$

where AC is average cost per foot (including a normal profit) and Q is millions of feet per year.

(a) If the price of copper tubing remains unchanged, should Lyon Inc. build the planned production facility? Why or why not?

(b) At a price of $1 per foot, what is the rate of output per year necessary to earn at least a normal profit?

(c) There is a possibility that Lyon's entry will cause the price of copper tubing to decline to $0.90 per pound. If managers of the firm are risk averse and use the minimax criteria as the basis for decision making, should they build the plant? Why or why not?

(d) Suppose the probability is 0.7 that the price will stay at $1 per pound and 0.3 that Lyon's entry will cause the price to drop to $0.90 per pound. If managers are risk neutral, should they build the production facility? Why or why not?

Problems Requiring Calculus

11-5. For Jensen Associates, profit as a function of advertising is given by the following equation:

$$\text{Total Profit} = 500 + 50A - A^2$$

where A is units of advertising and each advertising unit costs \$4.
(a) Graph the total profit from advertising function.
(b) Mathematically determine the optimal rate of advertising.
(c) Now suppose that quantity discounts are available for purchases of advertising and that the marginal cost of an additional unit of advertising is given by

$$MC_A = 60 - 3A$$

Determine the profit maximizing rate of advertising. Explain.

References

Bain, J. S. 1956. *Barriers to New Competition*. Cambridge, Mass.: Harvard University Press.

Bernays, E. L. 1971. "Emergence of the Public Relations Council: Principles and Recollections." *Business History Review* 45(3):296–316.

Chamberlin, E. 1933. *The Theory of Monopolistic Competition*. Cambridge, Mass.: Harvard University Press.

Galbraith, J. K. 1973. *Economics and the Public Purpose*. Boston: Houghton Mifflin.

Greer, D. F. 1980. *Industrial Organization and Prices*. New York: Macmillan, Chaps. 4, 5, 15.

Henderson, J. E., and Quandt, R. E. 1980. *Microeconomic Theory: A Mathematical Approach*. New York: McGraw-Hill.

Kohler, H. 1982. *Intermediate Microeconomics: Theory and Applications*. Glenview, Ill.: Scott, Foresman, Chap. 12.

Mansfield, E. 1982. *Microeconomics: Theory and Applications*. New York: Norton, Chaps. 11, 12.

Robinson, J. 1969. *The Economics of Imperfect Competition*. New York: St. Martin's Press.

Scherer, F. M. 1980. *Industrial Market Structure and Economic Performance*. Chicago: Rand McNally, Chaps. 5, 8, 14.

Stigler, G. J. 1947. "The Kinky Oligopoly Demand Curve and Rigid Prices." *Journal of Political Economy*, October, pp. 432–449.

Stigler, G. J. 1961. "The Economics of Information." *Journal of Political Economy*. 69(3):213–225.

Stigler, G. J. 1968. *The Organization of Industry*. Homewood, Ill.: Richard D. Irwin.

Sweezy, P. 1939. "Demand Conditions Under Oligopoly." *Journal of Political Economy*, August, pp. 568–573.

Industry Structure, Conduct, and Performance

12

Preview

Traditionally, industries are evaluated by examining their structure, conduct, and performance. The reason for this approach is that these three concepts are interrelated. Market structure is an important determinant of conduct which includes pricing, marketing, and product attribute decisions. In turn, market structure and conduct both affect performance as measured by factors such as profit and efficiency.

This chapter is organized using the structure–conduct–performance sequence. In the first section, methods used to measure market structure are discussed. The second section considers conduct and focuses on collusion, price leadership, and long-run pricing strategies in oligopolistic markets. The material in this section illustrates how conduct is affected by and, in turn, can affect market structure. The final section of the chapter illustrates how structure and conduct affect industry performance.

The Structure of U.S. Industry

To this point, the structure of markets has been considered as given in developing models that are used to analyze managerial decisions. But in this section, the market structure themselves are the focus of the discussion.

The Standard Industrial Classification (SIC)

To describe market structures, it is first necessary to have a method of differentiating one market from another. Thus far, the terms "market" and "industry" have been used essentially interchangeably. But technically, a *market* involves both buyers and sellers, whereas an *industry* includes only sellers. If the focus is on industries, the accepted method of classification is that of the *Standard Industrial Classification Manual* (SIC).[1]

The SIC method is by far the most common scheme for classifying industrial activity. It is used extensively by researchers in presenting and analyzing data. Its structure enables users to consider economic activity at the level of detail necessary for the particular project. The most general SIC category is the one-digit or division level, which includes 11 sectors: agriculture, forestry, and fishing; mining; construction; manufacturing; transportation, communications, electric, gas, and sanitary services; wholesale trade; retail trade; finance, insurance, and real estate; services; public administration; and nonclassifiable establishments. Industries are included in the one-digit category that best characterizes their activity.

To present or analyze data in greater industry detail, the two-, three-, or four-digit classifications of the SIC can be used. The two-digit scheme subdivides

---

[1] *Standard Industrial Classification Manual* (Washington, D.C.: U.S. Government Printing Office, (1972).

industries by major group within a division. The three-digit breakdown divides the major groups into more specialized groups, and the four-digit classification subdivides by individual industries. Table 12-1 is a sample page from the *Standard Industrial Classification Manual.*

Table 12-1. Sample Page from the *Standard Industrial Classification Manual*

Major Group 34.—FABRICATED METAL PRODUCTS, EXCEPT MACHINERY AND TRANSPORTATION EQUIPMENT

The Major Group as a Whole

This major group includes establishments engaged in fabricating ferrous and nonferrous metal products such as metal cans, tinware, hand tools, cutlery, general hardware, nonelectric heating apparatus, fabricated structural metal products, metal forgings, metal stampings, ordnance (except vehicles and guided missiles), and a variety of metal and wire products not elsewhere classified. Certain important segments of the metal fabricating industries are classified in other major groups, such as machinery in Major Groups 35 and 36; transportation equipment, including tanks, in Major Group 37; professional scientific and controlling instruments, watches and clocks in Major Group 38; and jewelry and silverware in Major Group 39. Establishments primarily engaged in producing ferrous and nonferrous metals and their alloys are classified in Major Group 33.

No. Group No. Industry

341 METAL CANS AND SHIPPING CONTAINERS

3411 Metal Cans

Establishments primarily engaged in manufacturing metal cans from purchased materials. Establishments primarily engaged in manufacturing foil containers are classified in 3497.

Beer cans, metal
Cans, aluminum
Cans, metal
Containers, metal: food, milk, oil, beer, general line
Food containers, metal
General line cans, metal
Ice cream cans, metal

Milk cans, metal
Oil cans, metal
Packers' cans, metal
Pails, except shipping and stamped: metal
Pans, tinned
Tin cans

3412 Metal Shipping Barrels, Drums, Kegs, and Pails

Establishments primarily engaged in manufacturing ferrous and nonferrous metal shipping barrels, drums, kegs, and pails.

Containers, shipping: barrels, kegs, drums, packages—liquid tight (metal)
Drums, shipping: steel and other metal

Fluid milk shipping containers, steel or other metal
Milk (fluid) shipping containers, steel or other metal
Pails, shipping: metal—except tinned

342 CUTLERY, HAND TOOLS, AND GENERAL HARDWARE

3421 Cutlery

Establishments primarily engaged in manufacturing cutlery. Establishments primarily engaged in manufacturing table cutlery made entirely of metal are classified in Industry 3914; those manufacturing electric razors in Industry 3634; and those manufacturing hair clippers for human use in Industry 3999, and for animal use in Industry 3523.

Barbers' scissors
Blades, knife and razor
Butchers' knives
Carving sets: except stainless, silver, silver plated, or other all metal
Cleavers
Clippers, fingernail and toenail
Cutlery, except all metal
Forks, table: except all metal
Hedge shears and trimmers, except power
Kitchen cutlery
Knife blades
Knife blanks

Knives: butchers', hunting, pocket, table, etc.—except all metal and electric
Potato peelers, hand
Razors: safety, straight
Safety razor blades
Shears, hand: barbers', manicure, pedicure, tailors', and household
Shears, metal cutting: hand
Snips, tinners'
Swords
Table cutlery, except all metal
Tailors' scissors

The industries shown in Table 12-1 are part of Manufacturing. In that division are 20 major groups, including Fabricated Metal Products, which is assigned the two-digit code, 34. Within Major Group 34 are nine groups or three-digit categories. Finally, under group 341, Metal Cans and Shipping Containers, two four-digit industries are shown. They are Metal Cans (3411) and Metal Shipping Barrels, Drums, Kegs, and Pails (3412). Under each industry classification are specific products that are produced. Although the four-digit breakdown is the most specific provided in the SIC manual, the products listed under a particular industry can be rather diverse. For example, industry 3421, Cutlery, includes swords, table forks, and hedge shears. Five-, six-, and seven-digit breakdown are available from other sources, but are not often used.

KEY CONCEPTS

- Industries commonly are classified using the *Standard Industrial Classification Manual.*
- The four-digit classification of the manual is the most detailed in common use and classifies firms by industry.

Measuring Market Structure

Once the classifications have been agreed on, the next step is to adopt a method of measurement. Although vague phrases such as "few sellers" may suffice in developing theoretical models of market structure, they are not precise enough to be of use in empirical work. Rather, it is necessary to have quantifiable descriptions of market structure. Two measures commonly employed are the concentration ratio and the Herfindahl Index.

Concentration Ratios.   *Concentration ratios* are the most commonly used measure of industrial structure and are computed as follows. Assume that the objective is to measure the concentration of sales in an industry. Let the fraction of total market sales accounted for by each firm be designated as X_i, where the firms have been ordered so that the largest market share is X_1, the next largest is X_2, and so on, until the smallest is X_m, where m is the number of firms in the industry. The n-firm concentration ratio is defined as the percentage of total industry sales made by the largest n firms and is calculated by summing the market shares of the n largest firms. Thus

$$CR_n = X_1 + X_2 + X_3 + \cdots + X_n \tag{12-1}$$

Industries are usually categorized according to their four-digit SIC code. The choice of n is arbitrary, but 4-, 8-, and 20-firm concentration ratios are the most common. However, in examining aggregate concentration, it would not be unusual to talk in terms of the proportion of sales of the largest 50, 100, or even 200 firms. In some cases, measures other than sales may be used. For example, concentration ratios can be computed based on assets, employment, or value

Table 12-2. Four- and Twenty-Firm Sales Concentration Ratios for Selected Industries

Industry	Number of Firms	1977 Sales Concentration Ratios	
		Top 4 Firms	Top 20 Firms
Motor vehicles and car bodies	254	0.93	0.99+
Aluminum production	12	0.96	1.00
Cereal	32	0.89	1.00
Soap and other detergents	554	0.59	0.82
Tires and inner tubes	121	0.70	0.97
Petroleum refining	192	0.30	0.81
Newspapers	7,821	0.19	0.45
Soft drinks	1,758	0.15	0.36

Source: U.S. Department of Commerce, *Concentration Ratios in Manufacturing: 1977 Census of Manufacturing* (Washington, D.C.: U.S. Government Printing Office), 1981, Table 7.

added. Although the results may differ, the method of computing the ratio is not affected by the choice of data. Whatever the variable, the n-firm concentration ratio measures the proportion of activity by the n largest firms in the industry.

To illustrate the computation and interpretation of concentration ratios, consider the following information. Suppose that there are ten firms in an industry with market shares of 20, 40, 15, 3, 10, 6, 1, 1, 2, and 2 percent, respectively. Thus the four largest firms make 85% of annual industry sales. Hence the four-firm concentration ratio is $CR_4 = 0.85$. Similarly, the eight-firm concentration ratio shows the market share of the eight largest firms and is $CR_8 = 0.98$. Concentration ratios for four-digit SIC industries in manufacturing are published by the Department of Commerce in *Concentration Ratios in Manufacturing.*[2] Examples are shown in Table 12.2.

Concentration ratios are a useful but incomplete measure of industry structure. One problem is the difficulty of correctly defining what constitutes an industry. Concentration ratios are usually based on somewhat arbitrary SIC classifications. Although the SIC is a helpful scheme for categorizing firms, it reveals little about conditions of entry or product differentiation in an industry. But these factors may be important determinants of the degree of market power exercised by the firms in an industry. For example, substantial barriers to entry may allow existing firms to charge high prices over a long period of time.

A second limitation of concentration ratios is their failure to reflect competition from foreign suppliers. For example, General Motors, Chrysler, Ford, and American Motors are the four largest manufacturers of automobiles in the United States. The four-firm concentration ratio for domestic production is greater than 0.90. But to evaluate the auto industry on this basis would not be meaningful. Firms such as Toyota, Honda, and Nissan have gained large shares of the U.S.

---

[2] U.S. Department of Commerce, *Concentration Ratios in Manufacturing: 1977 Census of Manufacturing* (Washington, D.C.: U.S. Government Printing Office), 1981.

automobile market. The industry, considered in a world market perspective, is much less concentrated than the domestic four-firm concentration would suggest.

A third difficulty with concentration ratios is that they may not reflect the size distribution of firms in an industry. Consider two industries each consisting of four firms. In the first industry each firm has a market share of 25 percent. In the second, the respective market shares are 80, 14, 3, and 3 percent. In each case the four-firm concentration ratio is 1.00, but the market structures really are much different. In the first industry the four firms are all the same size, but in the second, one firm has an overwhelming market share and may be able to impose its decisions on the other sellers. A simple examination of concentration ratios would not reveal this important difference.

The Herfindahl Index.   A second measure of industry structure is the Herfindahl index. This index is calculated by summing the squares of the market shares of all firms in the industry. That is,

$$H = \sum_{i=1}^{m} X_i^2 \qquad (12\text{-}2)$$

Where the industry consists of a large number of small firms, the index approaches zero. The reason is that each X_i is small and its impact is further reduced by squaring. For example, a market share of 1 percent contributes only 0.0001 to the Herfindahl index. At the other extreme, the Herfindahl index for a monopoly is 1.0.

The advantage of the Herfindahl index over the concentration ratio is that it takes into account the size distribution of firms. By squaring market shares, the Herfindahl index gives greater weight to large firms in an industry. Consider the two industries just discussed in the section on concentration ratios. It has already been noted that the concentration ratio for each would be 1.00. But the Herfindahl index for the first industry is 0.2500, whereas that of the second is 0.6614. Thus the Herfindahl index shows that concentration is greater in the second industry.

Until recently, the Herfindahl index was primarily of theoretical interest. But in 1982, the Justice Department announced new guidelines for evaluating proposed mergers. These guidelines (discussed in Chapter 19) are based on industrial concentration as measured by the Herfindahl index. As a result, the index now plays an important role in antitrust decisions.

KEY CONCEPTS

- Concentration ratios and the Herfindahl index are used to measure market structure.
- An n-firm concentration ratio shows the percentage of industry activity by the largest n firms in the industry.
- The Herfindahl index is computed by summing the squares of the market shares of all firms in the industry. It takes into account the size distribution of firms.

Industry Conduct

In the field of industrial organization, the topic of conduct considers actions of sellers as they compete for sales in markets. Dimensions of conduct that might be considered include pricing policy, decisions about product design and advertising, research and development activities, and other tactics, such as propensity to engage in litigation. This section focuses exclusively on pricing policies.

Collusion

Firms that collude and charge the monopoly price will have more profit to divide than if they continue to act independently. That is, if a mutually agreeable method of setting prices and sharing the profits can be developed, colluders can benefit by avoiding competition.

Collusive activities on the part of firms are seldom in the public interest. By coordinating their activities, firms are able to reduce competition that would otherwise exist. In the extreme, firms may be able to agree on pricing, advertising, quality, or other policies that are equivalent to those of a monopolist. Chapter 19 considers antitrust laws that are designed to prevent collusion. Basically, these laws attempt to make such behavior less attractive to oligopolists by increasing the costs and reducing the effectiveness of collusion. Antitrust policies are easier to understand if the factors that affect the likelihood and success of collusion are understood. Six such factors are considered here.

Number and Size Distribution of Sellers.   Usually, the difficulty in establishing and maintaining effective collusion increases with the number of sellers. One reason is problems with coordination. Successful collusion requires that all participants agree as to the proper policies to be implemented and the means of their administration. As the number of firms increases, there is greater diversity and an increased chance for misunderstanding and cheating.

A second reason is that, as the number of sellers increases, the market share and importance of any given seller decreases. Thus the actions of a single firm have a reduced impact on the activities of the other firms. As a result, firms become less concerned about their interdependence and tend to view their economic environment as fixed or given. Finally, the presence of more firms increases the probability that there will be at least one firm that chooses to cheat on the agreement in the attempt to increase its market share. If this firm succeeds in capturing a substantial share of the market, managers of other firms will be tempted to reduce their prices to maintain their market shares. As a result, industry coordination may eventually be destroyed and active competition may occur.

The size distribution of sellers also can be an important determinant of the success of collusion. Consider two industries of four firms each. In the first industry the firms are of equal size, while in the second there is a giant firm with 90 percent of the market and three smaller firms that divide the remaining 10 percent. In the first industry, any agreement to collude must be reached by persuasion and compromise. No firm is in a position to punish another that chooses to defect from the agreement. In contrast, in the second industry the large firm has the ability to use price reductions to discipline the smaller firms. As a result, pricing and other policies may overwhelmingly reflect the preferences of the industry leader.

Product Differentiation.   Industries in which products of individual firms are relatively homogeneous are usually better candidates for collusive behavior than are markets with products that are perceived as different by consumers. If the product is homogeneous, an agreement to collude can focus solely on the price. Determining this price should be a relatively simple task. In contrast, if the product is highly differentiated, any agreement may have multiple dimensions. Suppose, for example, that IBM purchases computer equipment from another manufacturer and then resells it as an IBM product. Also suppose that another, smaller firm also sells the equipment using its own brand name.

The two firms decide to collude on price. IBM proposes that because the product is identical, both companies should charge the same price. The other firm responds that IBM's reputation, advertising budget, and distribution system provide a tremendous advantage. That is, the IBM name on the product serves to differentiate it in the minds of consumers. The smaller firm's counter proposal is that IBM should charge 10 percent more for the equipment, that there be a specified ceiling on advertising expenditures, and that the locations where the product is sold also be limited.

It is likely that IBM would find some or all of these points unacceptable and respond with its own counter proposal. After a number of meetings, managers of the two firms may determine that they cannot reach a mutually satisfactory agreement. The result could be vigorous competition for sales of the product.

Size and Frequency of Orders.   Industries in which orders received by firms tend to be small and frequent are more likely to successfully collude than if firms receive very large orders for their product at infrequent intervals. Consider the case of a duopoly selling books or some other low-priced item by mail. The two firms agree to collude, set the monopoly price, and let profit be determined by the volume of orders received by each firm. In this circumstance there is little to be achieved by secretly offering lower prices to a few selected customers to obtain their business. The prospects for gain are outweighed by the possibility of causing retaliation from the other firm, which would destroy the cartel and result in a reduction in prices. Hence, in this case, the likelihood of successful collusion is relatively high.

Now consider the same two firms selling nuclear power plants. A single order may mean millions of dollars in profit for the firm. But given the uncertainties about nuclear reactors, orders may be very infrequent. Typically, an electric utility would put its reactor order out for bids, with the lowest bidder likely to receive the contract. Assume that the two firms have agreed to collude by alternating as the low bidder. Now suppose that a particularly large and profitable order comes to the attention of the managers of the firms and that it has been many months since either firm has signed a new reactor contract. Assume that firm 1 should be the low bidder because firm 2 got the last order. Unfortunately, the managers of firm 2 know that many months may pass before there is another comparable order. As a consequence, there is a strong incentive for firm 2 to defect from the cartel and submit a more competitive bid. The prospect of getting this lucrative contract may be considered more attractive than the uncertain benefits of dividing future sales. Once the actions of firm 2 become known, its rival will be extremely reluctant to enter into future deals. As a general proposition, the greater the stakes, the greater the incentive to cheat on a collusive agreement.

Selling Practices and Information Flows.   The ability to collude is a function of the ease of detecting and punishing cheaters. If there is little personal contact between buyers and sellers, the likelihood of cheating is much less than if the parties negotiate in private. This suggests that it would be easier for an industry that takes orders by mail to fix prices than for one that uses salespeople to make individual contacts with buyers. In a mail-order industry, it would be possible for each firm to make spot checks on the practices of its rivals. In contrast, a firm's sales staff can make secret price concessions without competitors being immediately aware of the practice.

The dissemination of information between firms can also be an important determinant of industry behavior. Collusion is much easier to police when firms publish price lists than when price information is not widely distributed. In industries where trade associations collect and publish detailed data on the operations of each firm, possibilities for collusion are further enhanced.

Industry Maturity.   Agreements to restrict competition are made by people, not by firms. Formulating these agreements requires that participants develop effective methods of communicating with one another. It also requires an understanding of the way in which people will react in given circumstances. This information does not come instantaneously but is the product of past social and business interactions. Usually, collusion will be more successful in industries where demand is stable, technology is not changing rapidly, and there is little turnover among top executives. In the latter, firms are rapidly entering and leaving the market, the state of the art is changing on an almost monthly basis, and the top executives may not be well acquainted with each other.

Cost Structure.   Industries where fixed costs are a high percentage of total costs may have special difficulties in maintaining price-fixing agreements during periods of weak demand. In such industries, declining sales reduce revenues of individual firms much more than costs because of the large fixed cost that must be paid irrespective of the volume of sales. By reducing its price, any single firm can increase its market share. Because variable costs associated with expanding production are a relatively small part of the selling price, the firm can make a substantial contribution to payment of its fixed costs by defecting from an agreement to fix prices. However, this strategy will not go unnoticed by other managers, who will also reduce prices. Because marginal costs are low, the breakdown in industry pricing discipline may result in a large reduction in prices that forces some firms out of the industry. The experience of the railroads during the late nineteenth century is a classic illustration of this tendency toward cutthroat competition in capital-intensive industries. Prior to the advent of government regulation, railroad fares oscillated wildly as cartels were established, broken apart by cheaters and new entrants, and then reestablished.

KEY CONCEPT

- The likelihood of successful collusion is increased by:
  1. A small number of sellers or a dominant firm in a market.
  2. Product homogeneity.
  3. Frequent orders of relatively small size.
  4. Easy access to information by the firms in the industry.
  5. Familiarity of industry managers with one another.
  6. Low fixed costs relative to variable costs.

CASE STUDY

SELECTIONS FROM THE PRICE-FIXING HALL OF FAME

The prediction that oligopolists will collude to fix prices is well supported by the evidence. Below is a partial list of industries in which firms and their man-

Market	Geographical Scope	Four-Firm Concentration in the Market* (%)	Number of Conspirators (and their percentage share of sales)*		Number of Firms in the Market*
Wrought steel wheels	National	85	5	(100)	5
Bed springs	National	<61	10		20
Metal library shelving	National	60	7	(78)	9
Self-locking nuts	National	97	4	(97)	6
Refuse collection	Local		86		102
Women's swimsuits	National	<69	9		
Steel products (wholesale)	Regional	66	5	(72)	
Gasoline	Regional	>49	12		
Milk	Local	>90	11	(>80)	13
Concrete pipe	Regional	100	4	(100)	4
Drill jig bushings	National	56	9	(82)	13
Linen supplies	Local	49	31	(90)	
Plumbing fixtures	National	76	7	(98)	15
Class rings	Regional	<100	3	(90)	5
Tickets	Regional	<78	9	(<91)	10
Baked goods (wholesale)	Regional	46	7		8
Athletic equipment	Local	>90	6	(100)	6
Dairy products	Regional	>95	3	(95)	13
Vending machines	Local	93	6	(100)	6
Ready-mix concrete	Local	86	9	(100)	9
Carbon steel sheets	National	59	10		
Liquid asphalt	Regional	56	20	(95)	

* The omitted figures are not available.

Source: George A. Hay and Daniel Kelly, "An Empirical Survey of Price Fixing Conspiracies," *Journal of Law and Economics* 17(April 1974).29–38.

agers have been successfully prosecuted for price fixing. Note the high four-firm concentration ratios in the market and the overwhelming market shares of the conspirators.

In most cases, fines were imposed on firms convicted of price fixing. Many of the managers responsible for the illegal actions were also fined and a few received prison sentences.

Price Leadership

U.S. antitrust laws make explicit collusion difficult and potentially costly. As a result, oligopolists sometimes use other methods to avoid active competition. One of the most prevalent is price leadership. Basically, price leadership occurs when one or more firms initiate changes in price and the other firms in the industry follow the lead of the first firm. Frequently, the practice of price leadership in an industry first occurred during a period when large price fluctuations and cutthroat pricing was the rule. As a result, price changes came to be made infrequently and in ways designed to maintain price discipline in the industry. Two forms of price leadership are considered here: dominant firm and barometric price leadership.

Dominant Firm Price Leadership. Consider an industry consisting of a single large firm and several smaller firms. The large firm may have achieved its position by being the first seller in the industry, because it has lower costs resulting from scale economies, or by virtue of superior management skill. Whatever the reason, assume that the firm is now able to dictate prices in the industry. Smaller firms that fail to conform may find themselves in a price war that they cannot survive. On a more positive note, because the price dictated by the dominant firm is likely to be higher than would result from active competition, the small firms probably will earn more profit by allowing the dominant firm to take the lead in price setting. From the perspective of the industry leader, a closely followed pattern of price leadership eliminates the cost of enforcing industry price discipline. Also, if a large firm is too aggressive in competing in a market, it may be prosecuted for illegal monopolization under antitrust statutes.

Figure 12-1 describes pricing and output decisions with dominant firm price leadership. Let $D_T D_T$ represent total demand. If the small firms in an industry look to the dominant firm to establish price, they can be viewed as price takers. As such, their behavior is similar to firms in perfect competition. If they can sell all they produce at the market price, they maximize profits by producing until price equals marginal cost. The implication of this assumption is that the marginal cost curve for each small firm shows the output that it will produce at various prices established by the dominant firm. Thus the total output supplied by all the small firms is the sum of their marginal cost curves. This curve is shown in Figure 12-1 as ΣMC_F.

If the dominant firm is content to set a price and let its small rivals supply as much as they want, the large firm can be thought of as supplying the residual demand. For example, if the price is set at P_o, the small firms will meet total

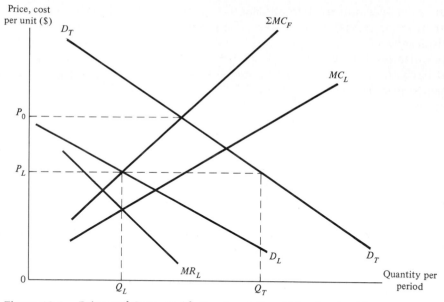

Figure 12-1.   *Price and Output with Dominant Firm Price Leadership.*

market demand and the dominant firm will have no sales because there is no residual demand. It is obvious, therefore, that price will be set below P_o. The demand curve faced by the industry leader can easily be determined for any price level. It is the horizontal distance between the total demand curve, D_T, and the ΣMC_F curve. The leader's demand curve is shown on Figure 12-1 as $D_L D_L$. The associated marginal revenue curve is MR_L.

The curve MC_L is the dominant firm's marginal cost curve. It is shown as being below the ΣMC_F curve to indicate a cost advantage of the price leader. Because the small firms follow the lead of the dominant seller, the managers of the dominant firm can act as monopolists. Taking $D_L D_L$ as their firm's demand curve, they maximize profits by choosing that rate of output where marginal revenue equals marginal cost. Thus output for the price leader will be Q_L. The profit-maximizing price, P_L, is determined by the price leader's demand curve. At this price, output of the small firms is determined from the $D_T D_T$ and $D_L D_L$ curves to be $Q_T - Q_L$ units.

Dominant firm price leadership is less common today than in years past. At one time, firms such as U.S. Steel, Firestone, Alcoa, and IBM were the acknowledged price setters in their markets. Over time, however, market growth, technological change, new U.S. producers, and foreign competition have reduced their dominance. Although still industry leaders, their relative importance has diminished.

Barometric Price Leadership.   Price leadership can occur even if there is no dominant firm in a market. Where price changes occur only in response to clear and widely understood changes in market conditions, a pattern of barometric price leadership may evolve. For example, suppose that a union wage settlement has increased labor costs in the industry or that fuel costs have risen. Either of these events will increase costs. One firm in the industry may take the lead in announcing that due to higher costs it is necessary to increase prices. Because the price hike reflects industry-wide cost changes, other firms are likely to follow suit and increase their prices.

Similarly, if stagnating sales are being experienced by all firms, one seller may announce a price cut to stimulate the demand for its product. If it is well understood that the price reduction is a response to changing market conditions and not an attempt to increase market share at the expense of competitors, the action is unlikely to precipitate a price war. Rather, other firms will match the first firm's price change in an orderly and nonthreatening manner.

With barometric price leadership, it is not necessary that the same firm always function as the price leader. The critical requirement for being a leader is the ability to interpret market conditions and propose price changes that other firms are willing to follow. Thus it may be somewhat misleading to define this pattern of behavior as price leadership. Rather, it represents an accepted and legal method of signaling a need for price changes.

CASE STUDY
REESTABLISHING PRICE DISCIPLINE IN THE STEEL INDUSTRY

Until the early 1960s, U.S. Steel was the leader in setting prices in the steel industry. However, in 1962, a price increase announced by U.S. Steel provoked such a costly confrontation with President John F. Kennedy that the firm became much less willing to act as the price leader and hence an object of criticism. As a result, the industry evolved from dominant firm to barometric price leadership. This new form involved one firm testing the waters by announcing a price change and then U.S. Steel either confirming or rejecting the change by its reaction.

In 1968, U.S. Steel found that its market share was declining. The company responded by secretly cutting prices to large customers. This action was soon detected by Bethlehem Steel, which cut its posted price of steel from $113.50 to $88.50 per ton. Within three weeks, all of the other major producers, U.S. Steel included, matched Bethlehem's new price.

The lower industry price was not profitable for the industry members. Consequently, U.S. Steel signaled its desire to end the price war by posting a higher price. Bethlehem waited nine days and responded with a slightly lower price than that of U.S. Steel. U.S. Steel quickly dropped its price to Bethlehem's level. Having been given notice that U.S. Steel was once again willing to play by industry rules, Bethlehem announced a price increase to $125 per ton. All of the other major producers quickly followed suit and industry discipline was restored. Note that the price of $125 per ton was higher than the original price of $113.50.

Long-Run Pricing Strategies

Based on the discussion in Chapter 1, it is assumed that long run profit maximization is the goal of managers. This objective is achieved by maximizing the
present value of profits over some planning horizon. To this point, however, the
analysis of managerial pricing decisions has focused on maximizing profit in a
single period. But the price that maximizes profits in one period may not be
consistent with long-run profit maximization. In this section, long-run pricing
strategies are considered.

Bain (1949) suggested that setting prices to limit entry describes the pricing
practice of many firms. His model assumes that monopolists or firms in an
oligopoly pursue a pricing strategy designed to prevent new firms from entering
the industry. The approach is illustrated by Figure 12-2. Consider a monopolist
facing the market demand curve, DD, and assume that increasing returns to scale
provide a cost advantage for large firms. This cost advantage is depicted in Figure
12-2 by an average cost curve that is downward sloping to the output rate Q_x
and upward sloping beyond that point.

To maximize profit in a single period, the monopolist should expand production until marginal revenue equals marginal cost. This implies an output rate of
Q_m and a price of P_m. At that price and output rate, the monopolist will earn
economic profit for the period. But unless there are substantial barriers to entry,
the lure of profit will cause new firms to enter the industry. A potential barrier
to entry is the cost advantage of the large firms. However, by setting the profit-
maximizing price, the monopolist makes it possible for new firms to enter on a
relatively small scale and still earn at least a normal profit. For example, suppose
a potential entrant believes that the monopolist will not reduce its price if a new
firm enters the market. Thus if the price is P_m, a new entrant could earn a normal
profit by producing at an output rate as low as Q_e. This can be seen by observing
that at the output rate Q_e, the price, P_m, equals average cost.

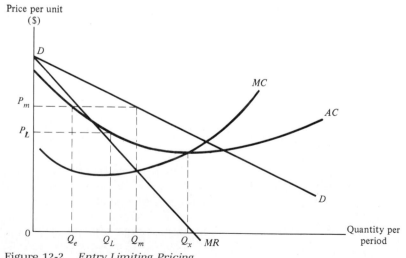

Figure 12-2. *Entry Limiting Pricing.*

Although a single new entrant may have little affect on the rate of profit earned by the monopolist, if the managers of the monopoly continue to use a pricing strategy that maximizes short-run profit, it is likely that additional firms will enter the market. Over time, the increased competition will force the firm to reduce its price and will also reduce the market share and economic profit of the firm.

Alternatively, the firm could utilize a pricing strategy designed to prevent entry. This approach would require that in each period, managers set a price below the level that maximizes short-run profit. For example, as shown in Figure 12-2, the price might be set at P_L. At this price, new firms entering the industry and producing at output rates less than Q_L could not earn a normal profit. Thus the pricing strategy establishes a barrier to small-scale entry. Although new firms still may enter the market, the size requirement makes entry more difficult and therefore less likely than if the short-run profit-maximizing price, P_m, had been set

Using *entry-limiting pricing*, managers alter the firm's profit stream as shown in Figure 12-3. Economic profit resulting from setting the profit maximizing price in each period is depicted by the profit stream labeled I. Note that economic profit is substantial in the initial period, but declines rapidly as new firms enter the market. In contrast, entry-limiting pricing generates a relatively constant profit stream over the planning horizon. In fact, if the market is growing, profit may actually increase over time. This is shown by the profit stream labeled II.

In contrast to the entry-limiting model is Stigler's (1952, Chap. 13) *open oligopoly model*. Stigler observed that the objective of managers is to maximize the present value of profit. In some cases this may be achieved by setting a price designed to deter entry. But in other circumstances, profits will be maximized in the long run by setting a high price that provides substantial economic profit in initial periods and then allowing profit to decline as new firms enter the market. In its extreme form, the open oligopoly model might involve setting the

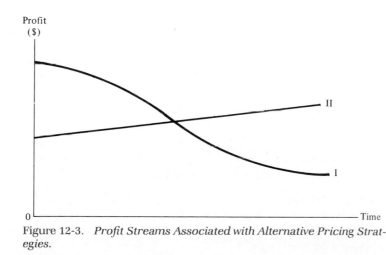

Figure 12-3.   *Profit Streams Associated with Alternative Pricing Strategies.*

Table 12-3. Alternative Profit Streams

Period	Profit Stream I (millions of dollars)	Profit Stream II (millions of dollars)
1	80	50
2	40	50
3	20	50

profit-maximizing price in each period. In this case, the profit stream would be as shown by I in Figure 12-3.

The optimal long-run pricing strategy is the one that maximizes the present value of profit. Examining the two profit streams in Figure 12-3, it is not obvious which should be chosen. Profit stream I has a high initial profit, but earnings decline rapidly over time. In contrast, profit stream II has less initial profit but shows a slight increase over time.

Basically, the optimal strategy depends on the discount rate used by managers to determine the present value of profit. A high discount rate gives less weight to profits in the future. Thus a high discount rate would cause the present value of profit stream I to be relatively greater. Conversely, a low discount rate would be more favorable to the entry-limiting approach associated with profit stream II.

The importance of the discount rate in selecting a pricing strategy can be illustrated by a simple example. Suppose that the two profit streams involve only three periods and the annual profit is as shown in Table 12-3. The first profit stream shows rapidly decreasing profit and is consistent with the open oligopoly model. Profit stream II has constant profit as might result from entry-limiting pricing.

Assume that the discount rate is 20 percent and profit is received at the end of the period. In this case the present value of profit stream I is $106 million, which is greater than the present value of II, which is $105 million. But if the discount rate is 10 percent, the result is reversed. Now the present value of II is $124 million, whereas that of I is only $121 million.

Clearly, the appropriate long-run strategy depends on how managers perceive future profits. Managers with a short planning horizon and those who view short-term profits as paramount would be more likely to behave in a manner consistent with the open oligopoly model. Conversely, those who have a longer time horizon and use a lower discount rate would be more likely to pursue entry-limiting pricing.

KEY CONCEPTS

- Dominant firm price leadership involves a single firm setting its profit-maximizing price and the other firms in the industry charging the same price.
- Barometric price leadership is a method of signaling that changes in costs or demand require a price change.

- Depending on the discount rate used by managers, a firm's long-run pricing strategy may involve setting a low price to deter entry or charging a higher price and letting new entrants gradually erode the firm's profits and market share.

Industry Performance

Market structure involves the conditions under which firms compete for sales. Conduct refers to the techniques employed in the competitive struggle. But performance is the bottom line in evaluating an industry. Are the firms earning economic profits? Do they produce efficiently? Is it possible for new firms to enter the industry successfully?

Economic theory predicts that there should be relationships between structure and conduct on one hand, and performance on the other. In this section, two such relationships are considered. They are (1) barriers to entry and profits and (2) market structure and profits.

Barriers to Entry and Profits

Bain has provided interesting and useful information on barriers to entry in different industries. His approach was to select twenty manufacturing industries and evaluate conditions of entry. Each industry was rated with respect to factors such as economies of scale and degree of product differentiation. The industries were then categorized as having (1) very high entry barriers, (2) substantial entry barriers, or (3) moderate to low entry barriers. Bain's classification of industries is shown in Table 12-4.

Note that automobiles and cigarettes were both included in the category of very high barriers to entry. The inclusion of automobile manufacturing is not surprising. The efficiencies of large-scale production and the advantage of a large system of distribution make entry by small firms extremely difficult. However, the rationale for categorizing cigarette manufacturing as having very high barriers to entry is less obvious because economies of scale are not significant in the production of cigarettes. The explanation is that product differentiation is important in the industry. Smokers often develop strong brand loyalties. As a result, new firms may have difficulty attracting enough buyers to be successful.

Bain and Michael Mann have investigated the relationship between barriers to entry and profit rates. Their research is based on Bain's classification scheme and is summarized in Table 12-5. Highly concentrated industries were defined as those with eight-firm concentration ratios greater than 0.70. Moderate concentration was taken to mean $CR_8 < 0.70$. Profit was measured as the average rate of return on stockholders' equity earned by firms in the industry over the period specified.

The findings of both researchers show a positive relationship between entry barriers and profit rates. For example, using Mann's data for the 1950s, the aver-

Table 12-4. Classification of Entry Barriers for Selected Industries

Industries with very high barriers to entry
  Automobiles
  Cigarettes
  Fountain pens ("quality" grade)
  Liquor
  Tractors
  Typewriters
Industries with substantial entry barriers
  Copper
  Farm machines (large, complex)
  Petroleum refining
  Shoes (high-priced men's and specialties)
  Soap
  Steel
Industries with moderate to low entry barriers
  Canned fruits and vegetables
  Cement
  Farm machinery (small, simple)
  Flour
  Fountain pens (low priced)
  Gypsum products
  Meat packing
  Metal containers
  Rayon
  Shoes (women's and low-priced men's)
  Tires and tubes

Source: Reprinted by permission of the publishers. From Joe S. Bain, *Barriers to New Competition* (Cambridge, Mass.: Harvard University Press). Copyright 1956 by the President and Fellows of Harvard College.

Table 12-5. Barriers to Entry and Rate of Return on Stockholder Equity

	Rate of Return on Stockholder Equity (%)		
Concentration	Very High Barriers	Substantial Barriers	Moderate to Low Barriers
1936–1940 (Bain)			
High	19.0	10.2	10.5
Moderate	*	7.0	5.3
1947–1951 (Bain)			
High	19.0	14.0	15.4
Moderate	*	12.5	10.1
1950–1960 (Mann)			
High	16.4	11.1	11.9
Moderate	*	12.2	8.6

* No industries in this category.

Source: Adapted from Bain (1956, pp. 192–200); and H. S. Mann, "Seller Concentration, Barriers to Entry and Rates of Return in Thirty Industries," *Review of Economics and Statistics*, August 1966, pp. 296–307.

age rate of profit for highly concentrated industries with very high entry barriers was 16.4 percent. In contrast, the rates for highly concentrated industries with substantial and moderate to low barriers were 11.1 percent and 11.9 percent, respectively. A similar relationship was found for industries with eight-firm concentration ratios less than 0.70. Those classified as having substantial entry barriers earned an average of 12.2 percent, while the rate for those with moderate to low barriers was only 8.6 percent. Although the data are not conclusive, they do suggest that conditions of entry can affect industry performance as measured by profit rates.

Market Structure and Profits

Economic theory suggests that there should be a general relationship between industry concentration and profits. Many studies have attempted to empirically estimate the market structure–profit rate relationship. In fact, a survey article by Weiss (1974, pp. 201–220), identified 54 such studies. With few exceptions, these studies have been consistent in concluding that there is a positive and statistically significant correlation between market structure (as measured by concentration) and profits. The robustness of this relationship is described by Greer (1980, pp. 454–455):

> Such positive effects have been found for all measures of profit, for many different measures of concentration (four-firm and eight-firm ratios plus the Herfindahl index), and for vastly different time periods (1936 to the present).... As if this were not enough, the positive relationship emerges from data gathered from every corner of the world—England, Canada, Japan, Pakistan, India, Mexico, Brazil, Kenya, and France.

A study by Kelly (1969, p. 7) illustrates the general approach to research in this area.[3] Kelly examined 97 firms producing food products. He used multiple-regression techniques to investigate how market concentration (as measured by the four-firm concentration ratio) is related to the rate of return on stockholders' equity. Kelly's results are shown in Table 12-6.

Table 12-6. Four-Firm Concentration Ratios and Profit Rates

Four-Firm Concentration Ratio	Profit Rate (%)
0.40	8.5
0.45	10.2
0.50	11.5
0.55	12.5
0.60	13.2
0.65	13.6
0.70	13.7

Source: W. H. Kelly, *On the Influence of Market Structure on the Profit Performance of Food Manufacturing Companies* (Washington, D.C.: Federal Trade Commission, 1969), p. 7.

[3] Kelly's analysis also considered the effect of varying the advertising/sales ratio. The results reported in Table 12-9 are for an advertising/sales ratio of 3.0%. The use of other ratios does not materially affect the results.

Table 12-6 shows that profit rates and the four-firm concentration ratio exhibit a close positive correlation. Note, however, that most of the increase in profit rates occurs as the concentration ratio goes from 0.40 to 0.60. Beyond $CR_4 = 0.60$ there is not much change. This result is consistent with the conclusions of other studies, which suggest that there is a threshold level of concentration somewhere between 0.40 and 0.60. Below this range, changes in concentration seem to have little effect on profits. When market concentration is above 0.60, the empirical research shows a gradual leveling off of profit rates.

KEY CONCEPTS

- Industries with high barriers to entry are likely to exhibit higher rates of profit than those with lower entry barriers.
- Many studies have considered the market structure–profit relationship. Most conclude that profit rates tend to be higher in industries that are more concentrated.
- A number of studies suggest that a positive profit–concentration relationship does not occur until four-firm concentration ratios are in the range 0.40 to 0.60.

Summary

The *Standard Industrial Classification Manual* (SIC) provides a method for categorizing firms in terms of their economic activities. The four-digit classification is the most commonly used and classifies firms by industry.

Concentration ratios are used to describe market structures. Based on sales, employment, assets, or value added, an *n*-firm concentration ratio indicates the proportion of industry activity generated by the *n* largest firms in the industry. The Herfindahl Index is another measure of market structure. Computed as the sum of squared market shares, it takes into account the size distribution of firms.

The success of collusive agreements is affected by several factors. A homogeneous product, limited number of sellers, well-established relationships between managers, and observable selling practices all facilitate collusion. In contrast, collusion is more difficult when firms are of near equal size, fixed costs are large in relation to variable costs, product orders are large and infrequent, and information is not readily available.

Where explicit collusion is not possible, firms in an oligopoly may be able to reduce price competition by practicing price leadership. This may take the form of dominant firm price leadership if one firm exerts a disproportionate influence in the market. In other cases, barometric price leadership is the rule, with firms announcing price changes in response to clearly understood fluctuations in cost or demand.

In some cases, the long-run pricing strategy of managers is to set a relatively low price as a means of preventing entry. In other firms, managers may set a higher price and allow entrants to gradually erode profit and market share. The optimal long-run pricing strategy depends on the discount rate used by managers to evaluate alternative profit streams.

In evaluating industries, the most important consideration is the relationship between structure and economic performance. One dimension of this topic is the effect of barriers to entry on the rate of profit. Studies by Bain and Mann suggest that very high barriers to entry are positively correlated with profits. A number of studies have considered the relationship between concentration ratios and profits. With few exceptions, the conclusion has been that profit rates are higher for firms in industries with high concentration ratios.

Discussion Questions

12-1. How could information about elasticities be used to identify products that are part of the same market?

12-2. Consider Industry 3411, Metal Cans, shown in Table 12-1. Obviously, both beer cans and oil cans would not be purchased by the same firm. Why, then, are these two products placed in the same category?

12-3. Would there always be a close relationship between a four-firm concentration ratio based on sales and a four-firm concentration ratio based on employment? Why or why not?

12-4. Which measure requires the most data, a concentration ratio or a Herfindahl Index? Explain.

12-5. The 1977 four-firm concentration ratio for Cereal is 0.89 and for Motor Vehicles and Car Bodies it is 0.93. Which of these ratios is the better measure of competitive conditions in the industry? Why?

12-6. Consider the factors affecting collusion as discussed in the chapter. In which of the following industries is collusion likely to be more successful? Why?
 (a) Steel manufacturing or liquor manufacturing.
 (b) Solar collector manufacturing or tire manufacturing.

12-7. Contracts for electric generating equipment are often awarded on the basis of sealed bids. As an employee of the U.S. Department of Justice, what would you look for as an indication of price fixing in the electric machinery industry?

12-8. Why would smaller firms be content to let a large firm practice dominant firm price leadership in an industry?

12-9. How does the optimal long-run pricing strategy depend on the rate used by managers to discount future profits?

12-10. How do barriers to entry affect the long-run pricing strategy of a firm?

12-11. Bain classified entry barriers as very high for quality-grade fountain pens, but barriers to entry were considered moderate to low for low-priced fountain pens. Provide a possible explanation.

Problems

12-1. Market shares for the firms in two industries are as follows:

Firm	Industry I	Industry II
1	0.05	0.05
2	0.05	0.05
3	0.20	0.05
4	0.05	0.60
5	0.05	0.02
6	0.20	0.03
7	0.20	0.05
8	0.20	0.15

(a) Compute the four-firm concentration ratio for each industry.
(b) Compute the eight-firm concentration ratio for each industry.
(c) Compute the Herfindahl Index for each industry.
(d) Which of the three measures (CR_4, CR_8, or the Herfindahl Index is the best indicator of relative market concentration in the two industries? Why?

12-2. An industry consists of four sellers of relatively equal size. One-fourth of total revenue is spent for advertising and one-tenth of revenue is used to pay fixed costs. Customers order goods from catalogs received by mail. Is it likely that managers of the firms in this industry will be able to collude successfully? Why or why not?

12-3. The market demand for televisions is given by

$$P = 1,000 - 10Q$$

The industry consists of one large firm and two much smaller firms. The marginal cost equations for the two smaller firms are

$$MC_1 = 8Q_1$$

and

$$MC_2 = 8Q_2$$

The large firm is the price leader and its marginal cost curve is

$$MC_L = 1Q_L$$

If the objective is to maximize profit:
(a) What price will the dominant firm charge?
(b) What price will the two smaller firms charge?
(c) What will be the market share of the large firm?

12-4. On a yearly basis, the total cost equation for Lebaron Carpet is given by

$$TC = 50,000 + 10Q$$

where Q is square yards of carpet. Without any competitors, the firm can sell 20,000 yards of carpet at $15 per yard. If Snyder Rugs, a potential competitor, enters the market, the price will decline to $12 per yard and Lebaron will sell 15,000 yards of carpet. If the price is maintained at $15, there is an 80 percent probability that Snyder Rugs will enter. If Lebaron drops its price to $13, sales will increase to 22,000 yards per year and there is a zero probability of Snyder's entry.

Assume the following: (1) the discount rate used by Lebaron's managers is 10 percent, (2) the planning horizon is three years, (3) profit is received at the end of each year, (4) if Snyder enters it will be at the beginning of the second year, and (5) Lebaron's managers are risk neutral. Should Lebaron immediately reduce the price of its carpet from $15 to $13 per yard? Explain.

References

Asch, P., and Seneca, J. J. 1976. "Is Collusion Profitable?" *Review of Economics and Statistics*, February, pp. 1–12.

Bain, J. S. 1949. "A Note on Pricing in Monopoly and Oligopoly." *American Economic Review*, March, pp. 448–464.

Bain, J. S. 1956. *Barriers to New Competition*. Cambridge, Mass.: Harvard University Press.

Demsetz, H. 1982. "Barriers to Entry." *American Economic Review*, March, pp. 47–57.

Greer, D. F. 1980. *Industrial Organization and Public Policy*. New York: Macmillan.

Kelly, W. H. 1969. *On the Influence of Market Structure on the Profit Performance of Food Manufacturing Companies*. Washington, D.C.: Federal Trade Commission.

Mann, H. S. 1966. "Seller Concentration, Barriers to Entry and Rates of Return in Thirty Industries." *Review of Economics and Statistics*, August, pp. 296–307.

Peltzman, S. 1977. "The Gains and Losses from Industrial Concentration." *Journal of Law and Economics*, October, pp. 229–263.

Scherer, F. M. 1980. *Industrial Market Structure and Economic Performance*. Chicago: Rand McNally.

Stigler, G. J. 1952. *The Theory of Price*. New York: Macmillan.

Weiss, L. 1974. "The Concentration–Profits Relationship and Antitrust." In H. J. Goldschmid, *Industrial Concentration: The New Learning*. Boston: Little, Brown.

INTEGRATING CASE PROBLEM IV
TAHITI COPPER

Tahiti Copper has been owned by the DuBois family for nearly 100 years. The firm's only product is copper that is purchased by other firms to make copper wiring, tubing, and sheets. The copper is produced in 1,000-pound ingots and is identifiable as having been produced by Tahiti Copper only by the firm's name stamped on each ingot.

Part I

Tahiti Copper operates the only copper mine and smelter in the South Pacific. Because imports are limited by high transportation costs, the firm is essentially a monopolist with respect to the sale of copper ingot. The only real source of competition comes from scrap copper that has been melted back into ingot form. However, this scrap copper is considered inferior by buyers and sells for a substantially lower price.

Tahiti Copper sells to approximately 200 firms in the South Pacific. Individual purchases are typically made by experienced buyers, but orders tend to be small and frequent to allow buyers to keep their inventory costs down. Although Tahiti maintains a published list of prices, it is not uncommon for preferred customers to be secretly quoted a lower price or better credit terms.

Management estimates that demand for the firm's product is given by the equation

$$P = 3,000 - 0.10Q$$

where P is the price per ton and Q is the number of tons sold per year. Regression analysis suggests that the firm's average and marginal cost equations are

$$AC = 2,400 - 0.10Q + 0.000002Q^2$$

and

$$MC = 2,400 - 0.20Q + 0.000006Q^2$$

where AC and MC are average and marginal costs per ton.

Periodically, Tahiti advertises in local business publications. Advertising costs $1,000 per unit and the marginal effect of additional units of advertising on profit per period is estimated to be

$$\frac{\Delta \pi}{\Delta A} = 5,000 - 1,000A$$

where A is units of advertising per period.

Part I Requirements

1. If the objective of Tahiti's management is short-run profit maximization, what will be the optimal price and rate of output? What will be the optimal rate of advertising?

2. What factors explain Tahiti's limited expenditures on advertising? Should the firm's advertising be primarily factual or should it have a substantial subjective component? Explain.

3. Suppose that copper ore deposits are discovered on nearby islands and various area entrepreneurs are considering the establishment of competing smelters to produce ingots. What factors should be considered by Tahiti's managers in adopting a long-run pricing strategy? Be specific.

Part II

Now assume that there are eight other firms in the market. At the present time, Tahiti has a 20 percent share of copper ingot sales and the rest of the market is shared equally by the eight new firms. During a recreational outing in Alaska, the managers of the nine copper producing firms decide to collude and set the price of ingot near the monopoly level.

Part II Requirements

1. Compute the four-firm concentration ratio and the Herfindahl Index for the industry. Is one index clearly superior as a measure of industry concentration? Why or why not?

2. Is the price-fixing plan likely to be successful? Why or why not? Be specific.

MANAGERIAL DECISIONS

Pricing of Goods and Services

13

Preview

Of the decisions made by a manager, none is more critical to the success of a firm than setting the price of output. The immediate and obvious effect of pricing choices is reflected in short-run profits. But prices set today also can have an important impact on future profits. Indeed, pricing decisions frequently are a major factor in determining a firm's long term success or failure.

The material presented in the previous chapters makes the pricing decision appear deceptively simple. If the firm has some control over price, the rule is to produce until marginal revenue equals marginal cost and charge the price indicated by the demand curve for that quantity. But, as always, theory involves simplifications of reality. A large corporation might produce several hundred products that are sold in many different markets. Often, the price set for one of these products can affect the demand for other products sold by the firm. Similarly, production decisions relating to one product may affect the manufacturing or marketing costs of other products.

This chapter provides a broader perspective for pricing decisions. The first section discusses firms with multiple products and considers both demand and production interdependencies. The second section examines price discrimination and peak-load pricing by firms selling in multiple markets. Finally, the third section introduces cost-plus pricing and demonstrates that this practice is consistent with profit maximization.

Pricing of Multiple Products

Procter & Gamble started in 1837 as a partnership selling soap to residents of Cincinnati, Ohio. Today, the firm has annual sales of over $12 billion and sells hundreds of products throughout the world. Procter & Gamble's most popular brands are shown in Table 13-1.

Table 13-1. Popular Brands Produced by Procter & Gamble

Laundry and Cleaning Products	Personal Care Products	Food Products
Cascade	Bounty	Crisco
Cheer	Camay	Crush
Comet	Charmin	Duncan Hines
Dash	Crest	Folgers
Downy	Head & Shoulders	Hires
Ivory Liquid	Ivory Soap	Jif
Mr. Clean	Luvs	Pringles
Spic and Span	Pampers	
Tide	Pepto-Bismol	
	Scope	
	Sure	

Some of these products are essentially unrelated. For example, the demand for Pringles Potato Chips is unlikely to be affected by the price of Tide. Similarly, production costs of Pringles are independent of the amount of Tide produced. However, demand and production of other Procter & Gamble's brands are interrelated. Clearly, Luvs and Pampers would be considered substitutes by consumers of disposable diapers. As such, the price of Luvs affects the demand for Pampers, and vice versa. Also, the two competing brands share the same production facilities. Thus if pricing decisions are based partially on costs, prices will be dependent on how costs are allocated between the two products.

When firms produce many products, managers must consider the interrelationships between those products. Four types of interdependency are considered in this section:

1. Products with interdependent demands.
2. Joint products.
3. Products with common costs.
4. Intermediate products.

Products With Interdependent Demands

Products with interdependent demands are either substitutes or complements. For substitutes, such as Luvs and Pampers, a price increase for one good tends to increase the demand for the other. However, the magnitude of the increase also depends on the number of substitutes available from other suppliers. For goods that are complements, a price increase tends to reduce the demand for the other good. Options that can be added to new cars are a good example of complements. Sales of diesel engines, power windows, and car stereo systems by an automobile manufacturer are dependent on the number of vehicles sold by the company. If the price of the basic automobile is increased, vehicle sales will decline and the demand for options will also decrease.

Correct pricing decisions require that demand interdependencies be taken into account. Instead of setting each price in isolation, the impact of each price on the demand for other products produced by the firm must be considered. The basic objective of the manager should be to determine prices that maximize total profit for the firm rather than profit earned by individual products.

When demands are interrelated, insight into managerial decisions can be gained by considering the marginal revenue equations for the products. Consider a firm that produces only two goods, X and Y. Assume that sales of X have an impact on the demand for Y, and vice versa. In terms of marginal revenues, this assumption can be stated mathematically as

$$MR_X = \frac{dTR_X}{dQ_X} + \frac{dTR_Y}{dQ_X} \qquad (13\text{-}1)$$

and

$$MR_Y = \frac{dTR_Y}{dQ_Y} + \frac{dTR_X}{dQ_Y} \qquad (13\text{-}2)$$

Equation (13-1) indicates that marginal revenue associated with changes in the quantity of X can be separated into two components. The first, dTR_X/dQ_X, represents the change in revenues for good X resulting from a 1-unit increase in sales of good X. The second, dTR_Y/dQ_X, reflects the demand interdependency. It indicates the change in revenue from the sale of good Y caused by a 1-unit increase in sales of good X. Equation (13-2) has a similar interpretation in terms of a 1-unit increase in sales of good Y.

The signs of the interdependency terms, dTR_Y/dQ_X and dTR_X/dQ_Y, depend on the nature of the relationship between X and Y. If the two goods are complements, both terms will be positive, indicating that increased sales of one good stimulate sales for the other. Conversely, if the two goods are substitutes, the two terms will be negative, because additional sales of one good reduce sales of the other.

Clearly, ignoring demand interdependencies can result in nonoptimal pricing and output decisions. Assume that goods X and Y are complements. In determining the profit maximizing rate of output for good X, if the effect of sales of X on the demand for Y is not considered, output of X would be increased only until dTR_X/dQ_X equals the marginal cost of producing X. But, as can be seen from Equation (13-1), dTR_X/dQ_X understates the actual incremental revenue generated by selling an additional unit of X. Specifically, revenue also is increased by dTR_Y/dQ_X, which is positive if the two goods are complements. Thus, when demand interdependence is taken into account, profit maximization requires a greater rate of output for good X. In fact, output of X should be increased until

$$dTR_X/dQ_X + dTR_Y/d_X = MC$$

where MC is the additional cost incurred by the firm in producing an additional unit of good X. Similarly, for goods that are substitutes, it can easily be shown that ignoring the demand interdependency will cause too many units of output to be produced.

KEY CONCEPTS

- If a firm produces complementary goods, the optimal rates of output for each should be greater than the rates that maximize profits if there is no demand interdependence.
- If a firm produces substitute goods, the optimal rates of output for each should be less than the rates that maximize profits if there is no demand interdependence.

CASE STUDY

TEXAS INSTRUMENTS INC. AND HOME COMPUTERS

In the early 1980s, Texas Instruments was a major manufacturer of home computers. Selling for about $400 with no printer or disk drives and a limited amount of memory, the firm's model 99/4a was one of the most popular machines on the market.

To increase sales, the firm reduced the price of the basic computer to about $100. However, prices of disk drives, printers, and other options were reduced very little. For example, the computer itself cost only $100, but a disk drive was over $300. Although the margin of profit on the computer was small or even negative, the margins on the peripheral devices were substantial.

The pricing scheme adopted by Texas Instruments recognized the complementary relationship between computers and peripheral equipment. Until the basic machine was sold, there was no opportunity to sell options that would increase the machine's capabilities. But by increasing the number of stripped-down 99/4a computers in people's homes, the firm hoped to create a market for the more profitable optional equipment.

Similar pricing practices have been used by other computer manufacturers. However, the success of such schemes has usually been limited because other vendors develop compatible equipment and sell it at lower prices. In the case of Texas Instruments, the firm's price cutting precipitated a rash of price reductions by other sellers, such as Atari and Commodore. Ultimately, Texas Instruments abandoned the market for low-priced home computers. The experience of Texas Instruments suggests that in addition to taking demand interdependencies into account, the reactions of competitors to a pricing policy must also be considered.

Joint Products

Products can be related in production as well as demand. One type of production interdependency exists when goods are jointly produced in fixed proportions. Beef and hides obtained from cattle by a slaughterhouse are a good example of fixed proportions in production. Each carcass provides a certain amount of meat and one hide. There is little that the slaughterhouse can do to alter the proportions of the two products.

When goods are produced in fixed proportions, they should be thought of as a "product package." Because there is no way to produce one part of this package without also producing the other part, there is no conceptual basis for allocating total production costs between the two goods. These costs have meaning only in terms of the product package. This idea is shown by Figure 13-1a. Note that the figure identifies two demand curves, one for hides and one for beef. Although the two goods are produced together, their demands are independent. However, there is a single marginal cost curve for both products. This reflects the fixed proportions of production. That is, the marginal cost is the cost of supplying one more unit of the product package.

Where goods are jointly produced, pricing decisions should take this interdependency into account. Figure 13-1a indicates how profit-maximizing prices and quantities are determined. MR_B and MR_H are the marginal revenue curves for beef and hides. But when an additional animal is processed at a slaughterhouse, both the beef and the hide become available for sale. Hence the marginal revenue associated with sale of a unit of the product package is the sum of the marginal revenues. This sum is represented by the line MR_T in Figure 13-1a. MR_T

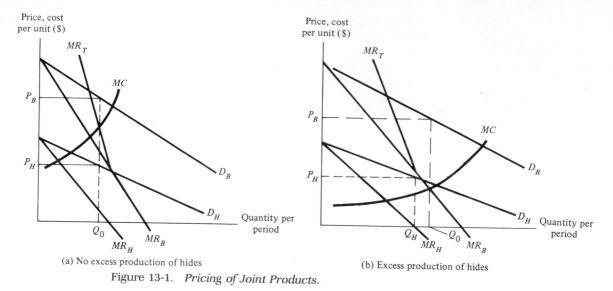

(a) No excess production of hides   (b) Excess production of hides

Figure 13-1.   *Pricing of Joint Products.*

is determined by adding MR_H and MR_B for each rate of output. Graphically, it is the vertical sum of the marginal revenue curves of the two products.

The profit-maximizing rate of output, Q_0, is determined by the intersection of MR_T and MC. The profit-maximizing prices, P_H and P_B, are specified by the demand curves for each good at output rate Q_0.

In Figure 13-1a, note that both MR_H and MR_B are positive at Q_0. In contrast, Figure 13-1b was drawn so that MR_H is negative at the profit-maximizing quantity. The implication is that sale of an extra hide reduces the revenues received from that product. Clearly, in this situation, Q_0 cannot be the optimal rate of output for hides. A firm should never produce at an output rate where marginal revenue is negative. But a problem arises because the products are jointly produced. Thus cutting back on production of hides would mean reduced supplies of beef for which marginal revenue is positive.

In cases such as that shown in Figure 13-1b, the profit-maximizing choice for beef is to sell Q_0 at a price of P_B. Although Q_0 hides will be produced, sales should not be made beyond the point where marginal revenue is negative. Thus only Q_H should be sold and the price set at P_H. Unless costs of disposal or storage are high, the excess hides should be withheld from the market.

EXAMPLE

CALCULATING THE PROFIT-MAXIMIZING PRICES
FOR JOINT PRODUCTS

A rancher sells hides and beef. The two goods are assumed to be jointly produced in fixed proportions. The marginal cost equation for the beef-hide product package is given by

$$MC = 30 + 5Q$$

The demand and marginal revenue equations for the two products are:

Beef	*Hides*
$P = 60 - 1Q$	$P = 80 - 2Q$
$MR = 60 - 2Q$	$MR = 80 - 4Q$

What prices should be charged for beef and hides? How many units of the product package should be produced?

Solution

Summing the two marginal revenue equations gives

$$MR_T = 140 - 6Q$$

The optimal quantity is determined by equating MR_T and MC and solving for Q. Thus

$$140 - 6Q = 30 + 5Q$$

and, hence, $Q = 10$.

Substituting $Q = 10$ into the demand curves yields a price of $50 for beef and $60 for hides. However, before concluding that those prices maximize profits, marginal revenues should first be examined. Substituting $Q = 10$ into the two marginal revenue equations gives $40 for each good. Because both marginal revenues are positive, the prices noted above maximize profits.

Products with Common Costs

Some costs are clearly related to the provision of a particular product or service. For example, meters on homes are there for the sole purpose of measuring the amount of electricity used in the house. No one could seriously challenge an accounting system that assigned the costs of those meters to residential electricity customers. However, other costs may not be clearly attributable to a particular product or service. High-voltage transmission lines fit into this category. Electricity for residential users is transmitted to urban areas over such lines. These facilities are also used to serve industrial and commercial customers. But if any two of the three classes of customers stopped using electricity, the same high-voltage transmission lines would still be required to continue serving the remaining customers.

For an electric utility, expenses associated with high-voltage transmission are referred to as *common costs*. Because the facilities are necessary to provide service to each class of customers, any allocation of these common costs is essentially arbitrary. In fact, the concept of allocating common costs really is a contradiction in terms. It involves allocating costs that already have been determined to be conceptually unassignable to any specific product or service.

Despite the problems, many businesses make extensive use of a practice called *fully distributed cost* pricing. This approach allocates a portion of the firm's common costs to each product or service. That is, all common costs are distributed among the products and services of the firm. Then the price of each is set so that it covers the designated portion of common costs plus costs that are directly related to the provision of the product or service.

As mentioned previously, any assignment of common costs must be arbitrary. But the real problem with this method of pricing is that the choice of allocation scheme may have an important effect on the price set and hence the quantity demanded of the goods and services provided by the firm. A scheme that allocates a small portion of common costs to a product will result in a lower price and greater quantity demanded for that product than will a method that apportions a larger fraction of such costs to the product.

Consider the following example. A firm provides two services, temporary secretarial help and data processing. Provision of the first service is very labor intensive, while the second is highly capital intensive. Assume that a significant portion of the company's costs are common costs.

The firm's management decides to base prices on fully distributed costs. Two allocation schemes are proposed. The first is to apportion common costs on the basis of labor costs resulting from each service. The second approach allocates common costs in proportion to the amount of capital investment that can be attributed directly to supplying each service.

Note how the alternative methods would affect the price set for each service. An allocation based on labor costs would result in a large fraction of common costs being assigned to temporary secretarial help. Thus the price set for this service would have to be relatively high to cover the common costs. But the data processing service with its relatively smaller labor expense would be priced lower because only a small proportion of common cost would be allocated to that service. Conversely, an apportionment based on investment would have the opposite effect. Because data processing is capital intensive, the price set for that service would be higher and that of temporary secretarial assistance lower than with the first allocation scheme.

Although a firm must recover its common costs, it is not necessary that the price of each product be high enough to cover an arbitrarily apportioned share of common costs. Proper pricing does require, however, that prices at least cover the incremental cost of producing each good. Incremental costs are additional costs that would not be incurred if the product were not produced. As long as the price of a product exceeds its incremental costs, the firm can increase total profit by supplying that product. Hence decisions should be based on an evaluation of incremental costs.

The contrast between fully distributed and incremental costs in pricing can be illustrated by considering railroad passenger service. Suppose a railroad has a route that carries passengers between San Francisco and San Diego. The managers are considering an intermediate stop in Los Angeles. The rails, locomotives, and passenger cars already exist, so the primary additional expense would be the energy cost of transporting extra passengers and the establishment of terminal facilities in Los Angeles.

Assume that competition from bus travel between San Francisco and Los Angeles limits the fare that can be charged by the railroad for the trip. Specifically, the managers of the railroad believe that the fare cannot be greater than $30. Should the new service be offered?

One member of the management team argues that the decision should be based on fully distributed costs and that the San Francisco–Los Angeles service should not be offered unless fares will cover direct costs plus a share of the common costs. For a railroad, the primary common costs would include the rails between the two cities and the engines and cars. Based on the common cost allocation method used by the railroad, it is determined that the fare would have to be at least $40. Thus with fully distributed costs as a standard for pricing, the service would not be offered because the fare would be higher than for bus transportation.

Incremental costs are advocated by another member of the management team. This person's analysis suggests that with the rail lines in place and trains already operating between San Francisco and San Diego, the additional expense of transporting a passenger from San Francisco to Los Angeles would be only $15. The implication is that the service should be offered and priced between $15 and $30 per trip.

Clearly, the decision regarding the service should be based on incremental analysis. Both the railroad and its patrons could benefit from adding the stop in Los Angeles. If the ticket price is set higher than $15, the total profits of the firm would increase. Travelers between San Francisco and Los Angeles would benefit because an alternative form of transportation becomes available. Even the customers going from San Francisco to San Diego could benefit. Although the San Francisco–Los Angeles fare would not be high enough to cover its full share of common costs, any price in excess of $15 could provide a contribution to common costs. Thus the price of traveling from San Francisco to San Diego could be reduced.

Obviously, where common costs are involved, all of a firm's products and services cannot be priced at their incremental cost. In aggregate, prices must be set high enough to allow the firm to cover its common costs. However, the example demonstrates that it is not necessary that each product cover an arbitrarily determined share of those costs. As long as price exceeds incremental costs, total profit can be increased by providing the product.[1]

The choice between incremental and fully distributed costs is far from academic. Frequently, poor choices are made by managers who insist that every price must cover fully distributed costs. But clearly, the proper approach by managers attempting to maximize profit is to make decisions based on incremental costs.

KEY CONCEPTS

- For products produced jointly in fixed proportions, output should be increased until the sum of the marginal revenues for each product equals the marginal cost of the product package.
- A firm's common costs are those that cannot be assigned to any single product or service.

---

[1] Ramsey pricing is often advocated as a way of pricing to cover common costs. This topic is discussed in Chapter 20.

- The use of fully distributed costs can lead to poor pricing decisions. A product can be profitably produced if its price exceeds incremental costs of supplying the product.

CASE STUDY
WHAT CONSTITUTES UNFAIR COMPETITION?

The Louisville and Nashville Railroad filed a petition with the Interstate Commerce Commission requesting permission to lower its freight rates for a particular route from $11.86 to $5.11 per ton. The firm's objective was to be able to meet competition from a company hauling freight by truck and barge. The railroad had substantial costs that could not be clearly allocated to specific routes. Fully distributed costs for the route in question were $7.59 per ton, but incremental costs were only $4.69. Because the truck–barge operation had few fixed costs, its fully distributed and incremental costs were nearly equal—about $5.19 per ton.

The railroad argued that a rate of $5.11 should be allowed because the $4.69 in incremental costs would be covered. The competing company contended that the proposed rail rates were unfair because they were less than the $7.59 per ton that represented the firm's fully distributed costs. In this case, the Interstate Commerce Commission based its decision on fully distributed costs and rejected the railroad's proposal for a rate reduction.* Historically, such decisions by the ICC made it difficult for railroads to compete with other modes of transportation.

* Ingot Molds, Pa. to Steelton, Ky., 326 ICC 77 (1965).

Intermediate Products

Vertical integration is common in modern economic systems. A firm is said to be vertically integrated when it operates at more than one stage of the production process. For example, some steel producers mine coal and iron, transport the ore on boats owned by the firm, use the coal as an energy source to transform the iron into steel ingots, shape the steel ingots into finished products, and distribute those finished products to consumers. The fabricated steel products received by the consumers are final goods. In contrast, the coal, iron ore, steel ingots, and undelivered steel products are referred to as *intermediate goods*. That is, they are goods or materials that will be needed as inputs at a later stage of the firm's operations.

By taking advantage of scale economies and bringing complementary aspects of the production process together, a vertically integrated company may be more efficient than several small firms each operating at a single stage of the production process. However, greater size resulting from vertical integration can cause control problems. Top management may find it difficult to become familiar with each stage of the operation or a cumbersome bureaucracy may develop that makes it difficult to implement decisions.

One method of dealing with such problems is to organize vertically integrated firms into semiautonomous divisions. Each of these divisions has its own function and its own management. Each management team is rewarded based on the performance of the division. In some cases, the evaluation is based on the profit earned by the unit. But in an integrated firm, determining the amount of profit that should be credited to a division producing an intermediate product is a difficult task. The problem is that if the unit's function is to provide an input for the next stage of the production process, revenue will depend on the price that is charged for the intermediate good. A high price will increase profits of the unit at the earlier stage of production, whereas a low price will make the later production stage appear more profitable.

A more serious problem is that an incorrect price set for an intermediate good can affect the total profit earned by the firm. Specifically, if the decision makers in each division attempt to maximize profits for their units, the total profit of the firm might be reduced. Thus it is important that prices of intermediate products be set so as to maximize overall profits rather than division profit. This objective may require that top-level management be involved in pricing intermediate goods.

The following discussion provides guidelines for the pricing of intermediate products. For simplicity, it is assumed that there are only two stages of production. In the first, rolls of paper are manufactured as an intermediate product. In the second, paper is cut into writing tablets and sold to final consumers. Two alternative situations are considered. The first occurs when an external market exists for the good. That is, the division making rolls of paper can sell its output to buyers outside the firm and the unit requiring the paper has alternative sources of supply. The second case is when there is no external market and paper can be bought and sold only between the two divisions of the firm. In this case, there is no market-determined price for the rolls of paper.

External Market.　Assume that the writing tablet division of the integrated firm has the option of obtaining paper from the paper manufacturing division or from independent suppliers. Similarly, the paper manufacturing unit can sell to the writing tablet division or to other buyers. Also assume that the external market is perfectly competitive. This implies that the two units can buy or sell as much as they want at the market-determined price.

With a perfectly competitive external market, there really is no price decision to be made. The paper manufacturing unit, like a competitive firm, faces a horizontal demand curve at the market-determined price. If the managers of that unit attempt to maximize profits, they will increase production until price equals marginal cost. If the paper manufacturing division tries to charge a price in excess of the market price, the writing tablet unit should buy paper from independent suppliers. But if the final product division is unwilling to pay the market price, the paper rolls can be sold on the open market.

Where an external market exists, it is not necessary that the output of the paper manufacturing division equal the input demand for the tablet unit. If there is an excess supply of paper rolls, it can be sold to other firms. Similarly, if the firm's internal supply of paper is insufficient, the tablet division can buy from other producers.

No External Market.   If no external market exists or if the divisions are not allowed to trade with other firms, a conflict may arise regarding the proper price to be charged for paper. The paper manufacturing unit may benefit from a higher price, while the division that makes tablets may benefit from a lower price. However, the goal of top management is to determine the price for paper that results in maximum profit for the combined firm.

The optimal price of both the intermediate and the final good can be determined using Figure 13-2. The demand and marginal revenue curves for writing tablets are D_w and MR_w, respectively. The marginal cost of producing the paper necessary to make a writing tablet is MC_p, while the marginal cost involved in transforming the paper into a tablet is MC_t. Hence from the perspective of the firm, the marginal cost of each additional tablet is the sum of MC_p and MC_t, which is designated as MC_w. Thus, for the combined firm, the profit-maximizing choice is to produce where $MR_w = MC_w$, or at an output rate of Q_w per period. The corresponding price would be P_w.

Because Q_w is the profit-maximizing output of writing tablets for the combined firm, the price set for the intermediate product (paper) must cause the managers of the writing tablet division to produce Q_w tablets, and managers of the paper division to supply an amount of paper consistent with producing Q_w tablets.

The solution is for top management to require the paper unit to set its price equal to the marginal cost of producing paper. This directive will cause the tablet division to view $MC_w = MC_p + MC_t$ as its marginal cost curve and select Q_w as the profit-maximizing quantity and P_w as the price. At the same time, by setting

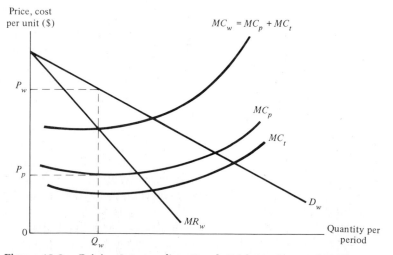

Figure 13-2.   *Pricing Intermediate Goods With No External Market.*

a price of P_p for paper, the paper division will supply the exact amount of product necessary to produce Q_w tablets.

KEY CONCEPTS

- If there is a perfectly competitive external market, the price of intermediate goods will be the marginal cost and no managerial decision will be necessary.
- In the absence of an external market, profit maximization will result if the price of intermediate goods is set equal to their marginal cost.

Pricing in Multiple Markets

In addition to producing dozens of products, many firms also sell those products in many different markets. Often, such firms can increase their total profits by setting prices that differ from market to market. For purposes of discussion, two situations involving multiple markets are identified. The first occurs when a firm is *simultaneously* selling a product in more than one market. For example, Coca-Cola is sold throughout the world. The second occasion for multiple market pricing involves products that use the same production facility at different times. Long-distance telephone calls are a good example. A call made at noon may use the same lines and switching facilities as a call made at midnight. However, because demand conditions differ, a lower price is charged for the midnight call.

Price Discrimination

Frequently, the same book is sold at a much lower price in South America and Europe than in the United States. This practice is an example of price discrimination and is designed to increase the total profit of the book publisher. From an economic perspective, price discrimination occurs when price differences between consumers or markets do not reflect variations in the cost of supplying the product.[2]

Sometimes price discrimination involves charging a uniform price when costs differ. Consider the firm that advertises an "all you can eat" buffet for $7.95. The first customer is a jockey who does little more than pick at the salads. The second is a defensive tackle for the Dallas Cowboys, who requires 10,000 calories a day just to maintain his body weight. The uniform price of $7.95 constitutes price discrimination because the cost of serving the two customers differs markedly.

More commonly, price discrimination occurs when prices differ even though costs are essentially the same. Physicians' services are an example. For a given

---

[2] The legal definition of price discrimination differs somewhat from the economist's definition. The legal status of price discrimination is discussed in Chapter 19.

treatment, there is no reason to believe that costs depend on the income of the recipient. Yet high-income patients are sometimes charged more than the poor for the same services.

Necessary Conditions for Price Discrimination.   Three conditions must be met before a firm can successfully practice price discrimination. First, the firm must have at least some control over price. Obviously, a price taker in a perfectly competitive market is not in a position to engage in price discrimination. Second, it must be possible to categorize different markets in terms of the price elasticity of demand in each. It will be shown later in the section that firms can increase total profit by charging relatively higher prices in markets where demand is less elastic.

Finally, the firm's markets must be separable, meaning that products cannot be purchased in one market and then resold in another. Suppose that a firm has identified two markets and charges a high price in the first and a lower price in the second. If the two markets are not separable, price discrimination cannot be successful. Either consumers will go to the low-priced market and make their purchases, or enterprising individuals will buy in the low-priced market and resell at prices below that established by the firm in the high-priced market. In either case, the price differential between the markets will disappear as prices decline in the first market and increase in the second.

Types of Price Discrimination.   There are many forms of price discrimination, but the standard method of classification identifies three types or degrees of discrimination. Their common characteristic is that they allow the firm to capture part of the consumer surplus that would have resulted from uniform pricing.

First-Degree Discrimination.   Figure 13-3a shows the demand curve faced by a monopolist. The curve indicates the maximum price that can be obtained for successive units of output. For example, the first unit, Q_1, could command a maximum price of P_1, the second could be sold for a maximum of P_2, and so on.

First-degree price discrimination involves charging the maximum price possible for each unit of output. Thus the consumer who attaches the greatest value to the product is identified and charged a price of P_1. Similarly, the consumers willing to pay P_2 for the second unit and P_3 for the third are identified and required to pay P_2 and P_3, respectively. With first-degree price discrimination the profit-maximizing output rate is where the marginal cost and demand curves intersect. In Figure 13-3a this occurs at Q_D. At this point, the maximum price that can be obtained for the product is just equal to the marginal cost of production. Any attempt to sell more than Q_D units would reduce profits because price would have to be less than marginal cost. Conversely, any rate of output less than Q_D would not maximize profits because the additional units could be sold (as shown by the demand curve) at prices greater than the marginal cost.

First-degree discrimination is the most extreme form of price discrimination. Because buyers are charged the maximum price for each unit of output, no

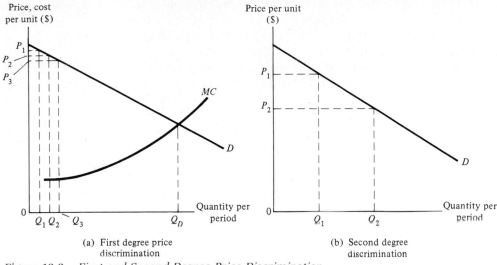

Figure 13-3.   *First and Second Degree Price Discrimination.*

consumer surplus remains. The total surplus that would have resulted from a uniform price has been captured by the producer as additional profit.

First-degree discrimination is not common because it requires that the seller have complete knowledge of the market demand curve and also of the willingness of individual consumers to pay for the product. In addition, the seller must be able to segment the market so that resale between consumers cannot take place. These requirements are seldom met in actual market situations. However, one possible case involves the sale of Treasury bonds by the federal government. In selling these bonds, the government requires each prospective buyer to submit a sealed bid. Those conducting the auction determine a minimum bid. All the bids that exceed the minimum are accepted and the bidders are obligated to buy at the price they indicated in their bid. Thus, through this process, the government attempts to extract the maximum price that each buyer is willing to pay.

Second-Degree Discrimination.   Second-degree price discrimination is an imperfect form of first-degree discrimination. Instead of setting different prices for each unit, it involves pricing based on the quantities of output purchased by individual consumers. This is illustrated by Figure 13-3b. For each buyer, the first Q_1 units purchased are priced at P_1 and additional units are priced at P_2. Thus for the demand curve shown by Figure 13-3b, Q_2 units would be purchased—Q_1 units at P_1 and $(Q_2 - Q_1)$ units at P_2.

Third-Degree Discrimination.   The most common type of price discrimination is third-degree discrimination. It involves separating consumers or markets in terms of their price elasticity of demand. This segmentation can be based on several factors. Often, third-degree price discrimination occurs in markets that are geographically separated. The practice of selling books at a lower price outside the United States is an example. Evidently, buyers in other countries have greater elasticities of demand than do U.S. buyers. At the same time, costs of collecting and shipping books makes it unprofitable for other firms to buy in foreign countries and resell in the United States.

Discrimination can also be based on the nature of use. Telephone customers are classified as either residential or business customers. The monthly charge for a phone located in a business usually is somewhat higher than for a telephone used in a home. The explanation is that business demand is less elastic than residential demand. An individual without a telephone may be able to use a pay phone or go to a neighbor's house to make a call, but for many businesses a telephone is an absolute necessity.

Finally, markets can be segmented based on personal characteristics of consumers. Age is a common basis for price discrimination. Most movie theaters charge a lower price for children than they do for adults. But there is no difference in the cost of providing service to the two groups—one seat is required for each patron regardless of age. The reduced price for children is based on differing demand elasticities. The assumption is that with less money to spend, a child's demand for movies is more price sensitive than an adult's.

Figure 13-4 is used to show how profit-maximizing prices and quantities are determined with third-degree price discrimination. Consider a firm selling in two markets, I and II. To simplify the discussion, it is assumed that marginal costs are equal and constant in both markets. Demand is assumed to be less elastic in market I than in market II. The marginal revenue curves for the individual markets are MR_I and MR_{II}, respectively.

The combined demand curve for the two markets is also shown in Figure 13-4. It represents the sum of the demands in each of the markets at each price.

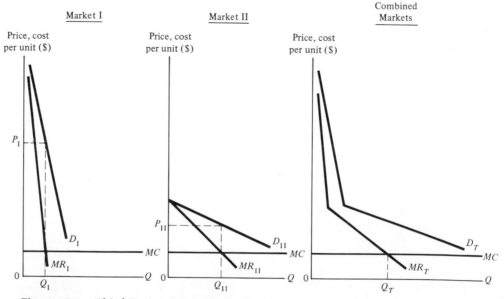

Figure 13-4.   *Third-Degree Price Discrimination.*

The combined marginal revenue curve is also shown and was computed as the sum of marginal revenues in each market. For the firm, the optimal total output is at Q_T, the point where $MR_T = MC$. Once the profit-maximizing total output has been determined, the next step is to determine the output rates and prices in each market.

Because marginal costs are constant, the decision rule for allocating output is that the marginal revenue should be equal in the two markets. That is, the extra revenue obtained from selling an additional unit in the first market should be the same as that received from selling one more unit in the second market. If the two are not equal, the firm could increase its revenue and profit by allocating additional output to the market with greater marginal revenue. In Figure 13-4, equating marginal revenue to marginal cost means that Q_I units of output should be sold at a price of P_I in market I and Q_{II} units at a price of P_{II} in market II.

Note that a higher price is charged in market I, where demand is relatively less elastic. This relationship is true in general and is easily explained. Where demand is less elastic, consumers are less sensitive to price, meaning that relatively high prices can be charged. Conversely, in markets where demand is more elastic, the quantity demanded is more sensitive to price. Hence the profit-maximizing price is lower.

EXAMPLE
THIRD-DEGREE PRICE DISCRIMINATION AND PROFITS

A firm sells in two markets and has constant marginal costs of production equal to $2 per unit. The demand and marginal revenue equations for the two markets are as follows:

Market I	Market II
$P_I = 14 - 2Q_I$	$P_{II} = 10 - Q_{II}$
$MR_I = 14 - 4Q_I$	$MR_{II} = 10 - 2Q_{II}$

Using third-degree price discrimination, what are the profit maximizing prices and quantities in each market? Show that greater profits result from price discrimination than would be obtained if a uniform price were used.

Solution

With price discrimination, the condition for profit maximization is

$$MR_I = MR_{II} = MC$$

Because marginal cost is equal to $2, the optimal quantities are the solutions to the equations:

$$MR_I = 14 - 4Q_I = 2 \quad \text{which implies that } Q_I = 3$$

and

$$MR_{II} = 10 - 2Q_{II} = 2 \quad \text{which implies that } Q_{II} = 4$$

Optimal prices are obtained by substituting the profit-maximizing quantities into the demand equations. Thus $P_I = 8$ and $P_{II} = 6$.

Profits in each market are equal to total revenue $(P \cdot Q)$ minus total costs $(MC \cdot Q)$. Hence

$$\text{profit}_I = \$24 - \$6 = \$18 \quad \text{and} \quad \text{profit}_{II} = \$24 - \$8 = \$16$$

Hence combined profit for the two markets is $34.

To compute profits in the absence of price discrimination, the combined demand and marginal revenue equations must be computed. The first step is to express the demand equations in terms of quantities. Thus

$$Q_I = 7 - \frac{P}{2} \quad \text{and} \quad Q_{II} = 10 - P$$

Note that the subscript has been dropped from price because the same price is to be charged in each market. Adding the two demand curves gives

$$Q_T = 17 - \frac{3}{2}P$$

The corresponding marginal revenue equation is calculated by solving for P and noting that the marginal revenue function for a linear demand curve has the same intercept and twice the slope. Thus

$$P = 11\frac{1}{3} - \frac{2}{3}Q_T$$

and

$$MR_T = 11\frac{1}{3} - \frac{4}{3}Q_T$$

Equating marginal revenue to marginal cost gives

$$11\frac{1}{3} - \frac{4}{3}Q_T = 2$$

which implies that $Q = 7$. Substituting $Q = 7$ into the combined demand equation yields $P = 6\frac{2}{3}$. Hence profit without price discrimination is

$$P \cdot Q - MC \cdot Q = \$46\frac{2}{3} - \$14 = \$32\frac{2}{3}$$

But price discrimination resulted in total profit of $34. Thus it has been demonstrated that profit can be increased by the use of price discrimination.

KEY CONCEPTS

- Price discrimination occurs when differences in price for a product do not reflect variations in costs.
- The three criteria for successful price discrimination are market power, separable markets, and variations in demand elasticity among markets.

- First-degree price discrimination consists of charging the maximum price for each unit. In second-degree discrimination, prices are based on the quantity purchased by consumers.
- Third-degree discrimination usually requires setting a higher price in markets with less elastic demand. Markets may be segmented on the basis of geography, use of the product, or personal characteristics of consumers of the product.

Peak-Load Pricing

A firm selling in many markets at the same time can increase its profit by practicing price discrimination. Similarly, a firm that uses the same facility to supply several markets at different points in time can increase total profits by use of peak-load pricing. Basically, peak-load pricing involves charging a higher price for consumers who require service during periods of peak demand and a lower price for those who consume during low- or off-peak periods.

Pricing of long-distance telephone calls is a good example. Most long-distance calls are for business purposes and are placed on weekday afternoons. As a result, the switching facilities and lines provided by telephone companies are designed to meet demand during this peak period. In contrast, fewer calls are made late at night and on weekends. But these off-peak calls use the same facilities necessary for peak-period calls. To induce consumers to shift their calling patterns to periods of low demand, phone companies offer substantial discounts for late-night and weekend long-distance calls. If successful, costly additions to capacity can be postponed and existing facilities used more efficiently. As a result, both the company and its customers can benefit. The firm will have reduced costs and increased profit. Off-peak customers will pay lower rates. Even peak-period customers may benefit in the long run if prices increase less rapidly because the firm's facilities are more efficiently utilized.

The fundamental principle of peak-load pricing is that those who impose the greatest demand on a firm for production capacity should be those who pay for most of that capacity. The traditional theory of peak-load pricing is discussed below.

Peak-load pricing may be appropriate if three conditions are met in producing a good or service. First, the product cannot be storable. For example, in the case of long-distance telephone calls, the service involves direct communication between two or more people. Calls cannot be stored for use at a later time. A busy executive in Portland would not consider a recorded message from an associate in New York to be an acceptable substitute for a telephone call received during business hours. Second, the same facilities must be used to provide the service during different periods of time. Again using long-distance telephone service as an example, this condition is met because calls placed at different times use the same lines and switching equipment. The third condition is that there must be variations in demand characteristics at different periods of time. Long-distance calls also meet this requirement. Demand is greater during business hours than at other times. In addition, demand for business calls at any given time is usually less elastic than is the demand for personal calls.

To illustrate the concept of peak-load pricing, assume that demand for telephone calls during a day can be divided into two periods of equal length.[3] Period 1 is a time of low demand and extends from 7 P.M. to 7 A.M. Period 2 is from 7 A.M. to 7 P.M. and is the time of peak demand. Let demand for telephone calls in period 2 be greater at all prices than demand in period 1. That is, at any given price the quantity demanded is greater in period 2 than in period 1.

Also assume that labor and capacity costs are the only costs involved in providing telephone service. Let b represent labor cost per unit of service where b is assumed not to vary by the period or by the demand for service. Similarly, let B represent the rental cost of a unit of capacity, with B assumed constant with respect to the amount of capacity purchased. That is, the first unit of capacity costs B, and all additional units cost the firm B.

Let the price paid for telephone service be the sum of the labor cost and the capacity cost (which includes a reasonable return on capital). Because the labor cost per unit of service is assumed to be constant, it can be subtracted from the price in each period without altering the results of the analysis. Figure 13-5 depicts the two demand curves, D_1 and D_2, after the labor cost has been subtracted. As a result, the vertical scale starts with b (the labor cost) instead of zero. Because labor costs have been netted out, Figure 13-5 can be considered a graph of the demand for telephone capacity. Hence each point on the two demand curves indicates the amount of capacity that the firm's customers demand at a given price of capacity.

The D_T curve in Figure 13-5 is the result of vertically summing the two individual demand curves (i.e., adding the vertical distances above the horizontal axis at each point along the horizontal axis). Remember that the demands are noncompeting and hence the same capacity is used to provide service in each of the two periods. The individual demand curves can be interpreted as indi-

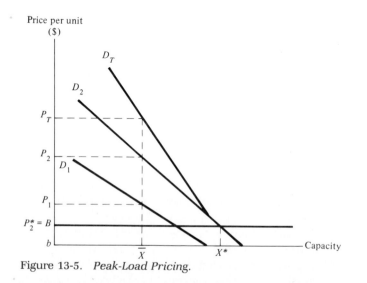

Figure 13-5.   *Peak-Load Pricing.*

[3] This discussion follows that of an article by Steiner (1957).

cating the willingness of consumers to pay for capacity during each period. For example, consumers in period 1 will pay P_1 per unit for $\overline{X}$ units of capacity and consumers in period 2 will pay P_2 for $\overline{X}$ units. Because the capacity is usable to serve consumers in each period, the total value or demand for $\overline{X}$ units of capacity is $P_T = P_1 + P_2$.

Efficient resource allocation suggests that capacity should be added until the value of the last unit is just equal to the cost of obtaining it. The cost of each unit of capacity is B. The total value of capacity is read from the D_T curve and indicates that at a cost of B, X^* units of capacity should be employed. The peak-load pricing problem is to determine who should pay for the X^* units of capacity. Notice that even if the cost of capacity were zero, less than X^* units of capacity would be required to meet the demand in period 1. Thus the selection of X^* units provides no benefits to consumers in period 1. The implication is that they should not be required to pay for capacity. Users in that period would properly be charged only the labor cost, b, per unit of telephone service consumed.

In contrast, because period 2 users attach a positive value to X^* units of capacity, they should be assessed the cost. Specifically, the value of capacity in period 2 is $P_2^* = B$. By assigning this cost to period 2 users, the marginal cost of capacity can be recovered. Thus the total price of telephone calls to period 2 users should be $P_2^* + b$ and to period 1 users, b.

Notice the basic principles involved in this scheme of peak-load pricing. Because the off-peak users place no value on the marginal units of capacity, they pay only the labor cost; the capacity charge is paid by the users who require the capacity. In general, peak-load pricing charges all or most capacity costs to peak-period users and charges off-peak users a price based on the noncapacity costs of serving them.

KEY CONCEPTS

- Peak-load pricing can be used to reduce costs and increase profits if:
  1. The same facilities are used to provide a product or service at different period of time.
  2. The product or service is not storable.
  3. Demand characteristics vary from period to period.
- The theory of peak-load pricing suggest that peak-period users should pay most capacity costs, while off-peak users may be required to pay only variable costs.

CASE STUDY
PEAK-LOAD PRICING OF COMPUTER TIME

The central processing unit (CPU) is the heart and brain of a computer. Input/output devices transmit information to and from the computer, and storage devices such as on-line disks maintain files of information, but it is the computer's CPU that manages the entire operation and processes the data.

The three criteria for successful peak-load pricing are met by CPU time at large computational facilities. First, usually a computer has only a single CPU, but this equipment is in use constantly. Thus the same facility is used to provide the service at different periods of time. Second, CPU time not used is lost forever— clearly, the service is not storable. Finally, although a computational center may be able to provide the same service at 3 A.M. as at 3 P.M., late-night service is often not as desirable to the customer. As a result, demand for CPU time is usually much greater during the day than it is at night.

To encourage the use of the computer during off-peak hours, many computational facilities have implemented peak-load pricing. Although the specifics differ among centers, these pricing policies specify relatively high prices during period of peak demand and much lower prices during off-peak early-morning hours. For example, at one university computer facility, CPU time is priced as follows:

Day	Time Period	Cost per Second
Monday–Friday	8 A.M.–1 P.M.	$0.03
Monday–Friday	1 P.M.–5 P.M.	0.06
Monday–Friday	5 P.M.–1 A.M.	0.01
Monday–Friday	1 A.M.–8 A.M.	0.002
Saturday–Sunday	8 A.M.–5 P.M.	0.01
Saturday–Sunday	5 P.M.–8 A.M.	0.002

The weekend rates also apply to holidays. Note that CPU time at peak hours (weekdays from 1 to 5 P.M.) is thirty times more costly than during off-peak hours (weekday evenings from 1 to 8 A.M. and weekends and holidays from 5 P.M. to 8 A.M.). As a result, computer usage has declined during peak periods and is much greater during the off-peak hours.

Cost-Plus Pricing

Thus far it has been assumed that firms attempt to maximize profits. It has also been assumed that this objective is accomplished by increasing production until marginal revenue equals marginal cost and then charging a price determined by the demand curve. But research findings cast doubt on these assumptions. An important study by Lanzillotti (1958) involved interviews with top executives from 20 large corporations. These managers were asked to indicate their objectives in setting prices. The most frequent response was that prices were set to achieve a target rate of return on investment. For example, the study reported that prices at General Motors, General Electric, and Alcoa were designed to yield an after-tax return of 20 percent. In contrast, the target rate of return at U.S. Steel was 8 percent. It is interesting to note that none of the managers explicitly mentioned profit maximization as their primary objective.

Research indicates that cost-plus pricing is the most widely used procedure for achieving the targeted rate of return. Basically, this approach involves setting prices that cover the cost of purchasing or producing a product plus enough profit to allow the firm to earn its target rate of return. A classic study by Hall and Hitch (1939) considered pricing behavior by 38 British firms. They determined that all but eight of those companies used some variant of cost-plus pricing. Results of subsequent research are consistent with the findings of Hall and Hitch.

The remainder of this section considers why cost-plus pricing is so popular and how it is implemented. The section also examines the apparent conflict between the cost-plus and marginal revenue equals marginal cost pricing rules.

Mechanics of Cost-Plus Pricing

Two steps are involved in cost-plus pricing. First, the cost of acquiring or producing the good or service must be determined. This total cost has a variable and a fixed component. In either case, costs are computed on an average basis. That is,

$$ATC = AVC + AFC \qquad (13\text{-}3)$$

where

$$AVC = \frac{TVC}{Q} \quad \text{and} \quad AFC = \frac{TFC}{Q}$$

and ATC is average total costs, AVC is average variable cost, TVC is total variable cost, AFC is average fixed cost, TFC is total fixed cost, and Q is the number of units produced. But there is a problem in making the computations. With cost-plus pricing, quantity is used to calculate the price, but quantity is determined by price. This problem is avoided by using an assumed quantity. Typically, this rate of output is based on some percentage of the firm's capacity. For example, for many years General Motors used cost-plus pricing and computed average costs on the assumption that sales would be 80 percent of capacity.

The second step in cost-plus pricing is to determine the markup over costs. As mentioned previously, the overall objective is to set prices that allow the firm to earn its targeted rate of return. Thus if that return requires $\$X$ of total profit, the markup over costs on each unit of output will be X/Q. Hence the price will be

$$P = AVC + AFC + \frac{X}{Q} \qquad (13\text{-}4)$$

EXAMPLE

COST-PLUS PRICING OF AUTOMOBILES

An automobile manufacturer has total variable costs of $500 million and total fixed costs of $1 billion. In setting prices it is assumed that sales will be 80 percent of the firm's 125,000 vehicle per year capacity, or 100,000 units. The target rate of return is 10 percent, which is to be earned on an investment of $2 billion. If prices are set on a cost-plus basis, what price should be charged for each automobile?

Solution

A target return of 10 percent on $2 billion requires that the firm earn a total profit of $200 million. Computations are based on assumed sales of 100,000 vehicles. Thus average fixed cost, average variable cost, and profit per unit are

$$AFC = \frac{\$1 \text{ billion}}{100,000} = \$10,000$$

$$AVC = \frac{\$500 \text{ million}}{100,000} = \$5,000$$

$$X/Q = \frac{\$200 \text{ million}}{100,000} = \$2,000$$

Hence if profit of $2,000 per vehicle is added to the $15,000 in average fixed and variable costs, the price will be $17,000 per car.

Evaluation of Cost-Plus Pricing

Cost-plus pricing has some important advantages that help explain its popularity. First, it usually results in relatively stable prices. This is a desirable result because price changes are expensive and may provoke undesirable reactions by competitors. Second, the formula used in cost-plus pricing is simple and easy to use. As will be discussed later, the necessary information is less than for marginal revenue equals marginal cost pricing. Finally, cost-plus pricing provides a clear justification for price changes. A firm desiring to increase its price can point to cost increases as the reason.

However, cost-plus pricing has been criticized on a number of points. One alleged problem is that it is based on costs and does not take demand conditions into account. This shortcoming is compounded by the fact that the cost data used may be the wrong costs. Instead of using incremental or opportunity costs, cost-plus prices rely on historical or accounting data. In addition, most applications of the procedure are based on fully distributing common costs to the various goods produced by the firm. Problems with prices based on fully distributed costs were discussed earlier in the chapter.

Cost-Plus Pricing and Economic Theory

At first glance, cost-plus pricing would appear to be totally inconsistent with economic theory that assumes profit maximization. Moreover, the wide use of cost-plus pricing seems to make analysis based on the marginal revenue equals marginal cost decision rule largely irrelevant. However, the conflict may be more apparent than real. There is reason to believe that use of cost-plus pricing is simply a tool used by businesses in pursuing the goal of long-run profit max-imization. As such, cost-plus prices can be shown to be related to, although not identical to, prices based on marginal revenues and marginal costs.

A comparison of the two approaches to pricing starts with a consideration of costs. Although it is true that cost-plus pricing is based on average rather than marginal costs, frequently long-run marginal and average costs are not greatly different. This is especially true in many retailing activities. Thus use of average costs as a basis for price determination may be considered a reasonable ap-proximation of marginal cost decision making.

The second step in the comparison involves the target rate of return and the resulting markup. How does a manager determine whether the target should be the 8 percent used by U.S. Steel or the 20 percent return used by firms such as General Motors, General Electric, and Alcoa? A study by Earley (1956) reported considerable variation in target returns and markups. Earley also determined that the variation could be explained by demand elasticities and competition. Lower markups were applied to products with relatively more elastic demand and where firms faced strong competitive pressures. An example would be gro-cery stores. The intense competition in these establishments holds down profits as a percent of sales. As a result, the typical markup for most food items is only about 12 percent over cost.

If the markup over cost is based on the manager's perception of demand conditions, cost-plus pricing may not be inconsistent with profit maximization. This can be shown mathematically. Profit maximization dictates that marginal revenue equal marginal cost. Marginal revenue is the derivative of total revenue with respect to quantity. Thus

$$MR = \frac{d(TR)}{dQ} = \frac{d(PQ)}{dQ} = P + \frac{dP}{dQ}Q$$

But the right-hand side of the equation can be rewritten as

$$MR = P\left(1 + \frac{dP}{dQ}\frac{Q}{P}\right)$$

But $(dP/dQ)(Q/P)$ is just $1/E_p$, where E_p is price elasticity of demand. Thus

$$MR = P\left(1 + \frac{1}{E_p}\right) \tag{13-5}$$

Assume that marginal and average costs are equal. Thus the profit-maximizing price is the solution to

$$P\left(1 + \frac{1}{E_p}\right) = AC$$

which can be written as

$$P\left(\frac{E_p + 1}{E_p}\right) = AC$$

Solving for P yields

$$P = AC\left(\frac{E_p}{E_p + 1}\right) \qquad (13\text{-}6)$$

But equation (13-6) can be interpreted as a cost-plus or markup pricing scheme. That is, the price is based on a markup over average costs. The markup, $E_p/(1 + E_p)$, is a function of the price elasticity of demand. As demand becomes more elastic, the markup becomes smaller.[4] For example, if $E_p = -1.5$, the markup is 3.0. But for $E_p = -4.0$, the markup is only 1.33 times average cost.

Thus cost-plus pricing may simply be the mechanism by which managers pursue profit maximization. Most managers have limited information on demand and costs. Obtaining the additional information necessary to generate accurate estimates of marginal costs and revenues may be prohibitively expensive. Hence cost-plus pricing may be the most feasible approach to maximizing profits.

KEY CONCEPTS

- Cost-plus pricing is widely used by managers and involves a markup over the average cost of acquiring or producing a product.
- Cost-plus pricing may stabilize prices and provide a justification for price changes.
- The markup used in cost-plus pricing is determined by demand elasticities and competition. Markups are lower where demand is more elastic and competition is intense.
- Cost-plus pricing may simply represent the decision rule used by managers in pursuit of profit maximization.

Summary

Frequently, modern corporations produce hundreds of different products. When the demand for products is interrelated, the firm should take this interdependence into account. When a firm produces complementary goods, the output rate of each good should be greater than if no demand interrelationship existed. For substitutes, output rates should be less than if the goods were independent.

Some goods are jointly produced in fixed proportions. Profit maximization requires that the two goods be considered as a product package. Thus the rate of output should be increased until marginal cost equals the sum of marginal revenues obtained from selling an additional unit of the product package.

Some costs are not clearly attributable to a particular good or service. Attempts

---

[4] If $E_p = -1.0$, the markup is undefined, and if $-1 < E_p < 0$, the markup becomes negative. However, these cases are irrelevant in that the profit-maximizing firm will never operate on the inelastic portion of its demand curve. The reason is clear. As long as marginal revenue is positive, demand is elastic. But the profit-maximizing firm produces where marginal revenue equals marginal cost. Because marginal cost is positive, marginal revenue is also positive and demand is elastic at the profit-maximizing rate of output.

to allocate such common costs are arbitrary. Decisions based on fully distributed costs can result in inefficient resource allocation; incremental costs are a better guide. A good or service can be profitably produced if its price exceeds the incremental cost of supplying it.

Vertical integration causes intermediate goods to be transferred from one division of a firm to another. However, profit maximization for the combined firm requires that those intermediate products be correctly priced. When a perfectly competitive external market exists, market forces will cause price to equal marginal cost. Hence the intermediate product will be appropriately priced. If there is no external market, management should set the price of the intermediate good at marginal cost.

Price discrimination occurs when variations in price do not correspond to differences in costs. The three conditions for successful price discrimination are market power, variation in the elasticity of demand, and separable markets. First-degree price discrimination involves charging each consumer the maximum amount that he or she is willing to pay. Second-degree discrimination occurs when prices vary depending on the amount purchased. Third-degree discrimination separates markets in terms of elasticity of demand. The segmentation may be based on location, use, or personal characteristics. Usually, higher prices are charged where demand is less elastic.

Peak-load pricing can reduce costs and increase profits. The practice is appropriate when three conditions are met. First, the same facilities must be used to provide a product or service at different times. Second, the product or service must not be storable. Third, demand characteristics of consumers must vary from period to period. With peak-load pricing, peak-period consumers will pay most of the capacity costs, while off-peak users will be charged a price based on variable costs.

Studies indicate that cost-plus pricing is widely used. This practice involves setting price as average cost plus a markup designed to provide a target rate of return. Advantages of cost-plus pricing include stable prices, a simple formula for pricing, and a clear justification for price changes. Problems include the use of historical and fully distributed costs rather than marginal costs and an apparent failure to take demand conditions into account in price setting.

On closer investigation, it can be shown that markups are related to demand elasticity and competition. Less elastic demand and lack of competition are associated with high markups over cost, while the reverse is true for markets characterized by more elastic demand and intense competition. Faced with a lack of information about demand and costs, it may be that cost-plus pricing is simply the method by which managers pursue profit maximization.

Discussion Questions

13-1. Macmillan Manufacturing produces razor blades and razors. Propose a pricing strategy that would allow the firm to maximize its profit on the two goods. Explain.

13-2. Why should goods produced in fixed proportions be regarded as a product package in developing production and pricing strategies?

13-3. Should a sheep-ranching operation consider lamb and wool as a product package? Why or why not?

13-4. What is meant by the statement that "the assignment of common costs must, by definition, be arbitrary"?

13-5. Generating equipment is used to provide electric power to both residential and industrial customers. On average the residential users require twice as much electricity as industrial consumers. In setting prices, would it be appropriate to assign two-thirds of the cost of the generating equipment to the residential users? Why or why not?

13-6. The managers of a firm are considering offering a new service. The proposed price of the new service would be greater than its incremental cost but would not cover fully distributed costs. As a user of services already provided by the firm, should you favor or oppose the new service? Explain.

13-7. How does the presence or absence of external markets affect the role played by top management in pricing intermediate products produced by a vertically integrated firm?

13-8. If an intermediate product is available from a perfectly competitive industry, why would a vertically integrated firm produce the product internally? That is, what is the advantage of vertical integration in this case?

13-9. Consider a store selling furniture in a single community. Is it likely that the store could successfully use price discrimination? Why or why not?

13-10. Are the three conditions necessary for peak-load pricing met in the case of movies shown in theaters? Explain.

13-11. How can peak-load pricing improve resource allocation?

13-12. The study by Lanzillotti discussed in the chapter found that General Electric had a target rate of return of 20 percent, whereas the rate for U.S. Steel was only 8 percent. Why was the target rate for General Electric so much higher?

13-13. How can cost-plus pricing be reconciled to the "marginal revenue equals marginal cost" rule of economic theory?

Problems

13-1. A small firm traps rabbits for their fur and feet. Each rabbit yields one pelt and two feet (only the hind feet are used to make good-luck charms). The demand for pelts is given by

$$P_P = 2.00 - 0.001Q_P$$

and the demand for rabbit's feet is given by

$$P_F = 1.60 - 0.001Q_F$$

The marginal cost of trapping and processing each rabbit is $0.60.
(a) What are the profit-maximizing prices and quantities of pelts and rabbit's feet?
(b) If the demand for rabbit's feet is $P_F = 1.00 - 0.001Q_F$, what are the profit maximizing prices and rates of output?

13-2. Mike's Shear Shop provides 4,000 hair cuts each month at an average price of $5.00 per haircut. The common costs of operating the store are $12,000 per month. The business is considering hiring a photographer who would take pictures of customers after they had their hair cut. The price of the photographs would be $2.50 and it is estimated that 2,000 customers would purchase the service each month. The total extra cost of the photographic service is $1,000 + 1Q$ per month, where Q is the number of photographs sold.

(a) If the decision is to be based on incremental revenue and incremental cost, should the service be offered? Explain.

(b) If the decision is to be made on the basis of fully distributed costs and if the $12,000 in monthly common costs are to be apportioned based on the revenues from haircuts and photos sold each month, should the new service be offered? Explain.

13-3. Write-Right, a vertically integrated firm, produces both paper and writing tablets. The demand for tablets is given by

$$P_T = 1.00 - 0.001Q$$

where Q is the quantity of tablets. The marginal cost of producing the paper necessary for each tablet is

$$MC_P = 0.20 + 0.001Q$$

It costs the firm $0.10 to make the paper into a writing tablet. If there is no external market for the paper, what transfer price should top management set for the paper?

13-4. A firm has found a way of using first-degree price discrimination. Demand for its product is given by

$$P = 20 - 2Q$$

Marginal cost is constant and equal to $6.

(a) With first-degree discrimination, what will be the profit-maximizing rate of output? How much economic profit will the firm earn?

(b) What will be the profit-maximizing rate of output if the firm does not discriminate and sets a uniform price? How much economic profit will the firm earn in this case?

13-5. Smith Distributing sells videocassettes in two separable markets. The marginal cost of each cassette is $2. For the first market, demand is given by

$$Q_1 = 20 \quad 5P_1$$

The demand equation for the second market is

$$Q_2 = 20 - 2P_2$$

(a) If the firm uses third-degree price discrimination, what will be the profit-maximizing price and quantity in each market? How much economic profit will the firm earn?

(b) If the firm charges the same price in both markets, what will be the profit-maximizing price and total quantity? How much economic profit will the firm earn?

13-6. The manager of a sporting goods store uses cost-plus pricing to determine the profit-maximizing price of bicycles. The cost of a bicycle to the store is $80. The manager estimates that the price elasticity of demand is -3.0. What is the profit-maximizing price?

13-7. Grasscutter Inc. makes a product used to trim lawns. The firm has fixed costs of $100,000 per year. Management expects to sell 2,000 units per year and at that rate of output, total variable costs will be $50,000. The firm uses cost-plus pricing to earn a target rate of return on an investment of $200,000. If the price is set at $100, what is the target rate of return?

Problems Requiring Calculus

13-8. The House of Music sells low cost turntables and speakers. The total revenue equation for sales of the two products is given by

$$TR = 200Q_T - 6Q_T^2 + 100Q_S - 4Q_S^2 + Q_T Q_S$$

where Q_T and Q_S are quantities of turntables and speakers, respectively. The marginal cost of turntables is \$20 and the marginal cost of speakers is \$10.
  (a) Are the two goods substitutes or complements?
  (b) What is the profit maximizing rate of output for each good?
  (c) What would be the profit maximizing rate of output if there was no demand interdependence between the two goods.

13-9. Culture Extravaganza produces ballets in Boston and New York. Monthly total revenues are given by

$$TR_B = 1,000Q_B^{0.5}$$

and

$$TR_N = 2,000Q_N^{0.5}$$

where Q_B is the monthly number of Boston patrons and Q_N is the monthly number of New York ballet attendees. The firm estimates that the marginal cost is \$10 per attendee in each city.
  (a) If Culture Extravaganza attempts to practice third degree price discrimination, what will be the profit maximizing prices and rates of output in each city?
  (b) Will the firm earn more profit using price discrimination than if a uniform price is set? Explain.

References

Earley, J. S. 1956. "Marginal Policies of Excellently Managed Companies." *American Economic Review* 46(March):44–70.

Friedman, L. E. 1984. *Microeconomic Policy Analysis.* New York: McGraw-Hill, pp. 300–316.

Greer, D. F. 1980. *Industrial Organization and Public Policy.* New York: Macmillan, pp. 335–344.

Hall, R. L., and Hitch, C. J. 1939. "Price Theory and Business Behavior." *Oxford Economic Papers* 2(May):12–45.

Hirshleifer, J. 1956. "On the Economics of Transfer Pricing." *Journal of Business*, July, pp. 172–184.

Hirshleifer, J. 1957. "Economics of the Divisionalized Firm." *Journal of Business* 30(April):96–108.

Lanzillotti, R. F. 1958. "Pricing Objectives in Large Companies." *American Economic Review*, December, pp. 921–1040.

Petersen, H. C. 1985. *Business and Government.* New York: Harper & Row, pp. 228–240.

Steiner, P. O. 1957. "Peak Loads and Efficient Pricing." *Quarterly Journal of Economics* 71(November):585–610.

Pricing and Employment of Inputs

14

Preview

Individuals earn income by selling resources to firms. The firm uses these resources to produce the goods and services demanded by consumers. Of critical importance to both the individual and the firm is the price of a unit of the resource. At any time, the distribution of resources among individuals is considered to be given. That is, the ownership of land, capital resources, and human resources has already been determined. Human resources refers to the education, training, and experience embodied in labor. Some individuals control a large amount of valuable resources, whereas others have few resources to sell. Given this initial distribution, the level and distribution of income is determined by the price of each resource unit, that is, the wage rate per hour of labor, the rent per acre of land, and the profit per unit of capital. Clearly, input prices are also important to the firm because they are a critical factor in determining the amount and mix of resources employed. This chapter focuses on the determination of those input prices.

The price of a productive input is determined by supply and demand just as is the price of output. However, the firm's demand for an input is a derived demand. That is, firms demand capital, labor, and land not because they have value as such, but because those resources can be used to produce goods and services that have value to consumers. Thus, the demand for inputs is dependent on the demand for the goods and services those inputs are used to produce, hence the use of the term "derived demand."

The first part of this chapter focuses on the determination of input prices and the amount of an input to be employed. Several different market structures are considered. In the second section, the correspondence between output and input decisions is outlined. The next two sections include an introduction to the concept of economic rent and a discussion of the reasons for significant income differentials among different types of workers. The role of labor unions in input markets is analyzed in the final section. Both the economics of collective bargaining and the objectives of labor unions are considered.

Input Pricing and Employment

The analytical framework for studying the demand for productive inputs has its basis in the theory of production developed in Chapter 6. Recall that efficient production requires that the ratio of marginal product to input price be equal for all inputs. For example, if capital and labor are the only inputs, the efficiency condition is

$$\frac{MP_K}{r} = \frac{MP_L}{w} \tag{14-1}$$

where MP_K and MP_L are the marginal products of capital and labor and r and w are the prices of those inputs. If one input, say capital, is held constant, it has been shown that the ratio of input price to marginal product is equal to marginal cost. Thus for labor

$$\frac{w}{MP_L} = MC \tag{14-2}$$

Recall that the profit-maximizing firm must increase output, and therefore the employment of inputs, to the point where marginal cost equals marginal revenue. Thus, in equilibrium, the ratio of input price to marginal product (i.e., marginal cost) must equal marginal revenue. That is,

$$\frac{w}{MP_L} = MR \tag{14-3}$$

Multiplying both sides of equation (14-3) by MP_L yields

$$w = MR \cdot MP_L \tag{14-4}$$

or

$$w = MRP_L \tag{14-5}$$

which indicates that the profit-maximizing firm should hire an input until the price of the input equals the marginal revenue product (MRP) of that input.

The MRP function is the firm's input demand function. Consider the MRP function shown in Figure 14-1. It can be used to determine the rate of labor input that will be hired at any wage rate. For example, if the wage is $10 per unit, 50 units of labor is employed; at $30 per unit, only 25 units will be employed.

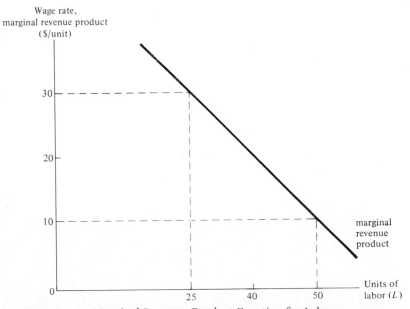

Figure 14-1.   *Marginal Revenue Product Function for Labor.*

The input demand function is determined by multiplying marginal product by marginal revenue. Because of the law of diminishing marginal returns, the marginal product function will be decreasing, at least in the range that is relevant for the firm. Further, the firm's marginal revenue function will either be horizontal, as in the case of the perfectly competitive firm, or downward sloping. Thus the input demand function will have a negative slope.

The firm sells goods and/or services in the product market and buys inputs in the factor market. The structure of both of these markets will influence the price of the input and the amount employed. The circumstance of the firm on the output side of the market (i.e., whether the firm is a perfect competitor, oligopolist, or monopolist) will affect the firm's input demand function, whereas the market structure on the supply side will influence the supply curve facing the firm. In this section, input pricing and employment decisions are considered for the following four different market structures:

Market Structure	Firm's Position in:	
	Output Market	Input Market
I	Perfect competition	Perfect competition
II	Monopolist	Perfect competition
III	Perfect competition	Monopsonist
IV	Monopolist	Monopsonist

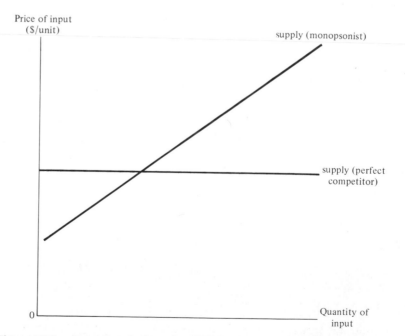

Figure 14-2.   *Input Supply Functions Facing a Perfect Competitor and a Monopsonist.*

The key difference in analyzing the effect of differing conditions in the output market is that price and marginal revenue are constant for the perfect competitor. In contrast, the demand curve facing the monopolist is downward sloping, which implies that the marginal revenue function also has a negative slope.

A perfect competitor in an input market is one of many buyers of the input. No one buyer has any influence on the price of the input. This implies that the input supply function is horizontal (i.e., perfectly elastic), meaning that any firm can buy as much of that input as desired without influencing the price. Thus the input price facing a perfect competitor in an input market is constant. In contrast, the input supply function facing the monopsonist or single buyer of an input is upward sloping. Additional inputs are obtainable only at higher prices. For example, a large firm in a small town may employ a substantial share of the local labor force. Thus, as a near-monopsonist, any significant increase in the firm's employment of labor would require an increase in the wage rate. Examples of these supply curves for a perfect competitor and a monopsonist are shown in Figure 14-2.

KEY CONCEPTS

- The demand for a productive input is derived from the demand for the goods and services that input is used to produce.
- The demand for an input is derived from the condition for efficient production. In general, an input should be employed until the input price equals the marginal revenue product of the input.
- Firms that are perfectly competitive in input markets face a horizontal input supply function. Monopsonists face an upward sloping input supply function.

Market Structure I: Perfect Competitor (Output Market)—Perfect Competitor (Input Market)

In this market structure, the input price has already been set in the market, and the firm's employment of that input has no effect on that price. The only input decision made by the firm is how much of the input to employ. This optimal input rate is determined by the intersection of the firm's input demand function with the input supply function. For the perfectly competitive firm, price equals marginal revenue, so that the general input demand function (14-4) can be written as[1]

$$MRP_L = P \cdot MP_L. \tag{14-6}$$

Table 14-1 shows hypothetical values for a firm's total product, marginal product, and marginal revenue product of labor. Note that the diminishing marginal product multiplied by a constant output price implies a decreasing MRP func-

---

[1] Sometimes $P \cdot MP$ is referred to as the value of the marginal product (VMP). To minimize any confusion that might arise from excessive terminology, the more general term marginal revenue product (MRP) is used here.

Table 14-1. Total Product, Marginal Product, and Marginal Revenue Product of Labor for a Firm in a Perfectly Competitive Output Market

(1) Rate of Labor Input	(2) Rate of Output	(3) Marginal Product	(4) Output Price	(5) = (3) × (4) Marginal Revenue Product
0	0		$5	
1	10	10	5	50
2	19	9	5	45
3	26	7	5	35
4	30	4	5	20
5	32	2	5	10
6	33	1	5	5

tion. The marginal revenue product function is the firm's demand function for labor and is shown graphically in Figure 14-3 together with the supply schedule, which is horizontal at an input price of $20 per unit. Recall that the perfect competitor in an input market can buy all the input needed at a constant price. The profit-maximizing firm will hire more labor as long as the value of the marginal product is greater than the wage rate. In this example, the firm will hire abut 3.5 units of labor because at that input rate the *MRP* of labor is equal to the wage rate. To use more or less labor would result in a lower profit. If the input price increased to $35 per unit, only about 2.3 units of labor would be employed.

Market Structure II: Monopolist—Perfect Competitor

If the firm is a monopolist, or at least has some degree of market power, it faces a downward-sloping demand function for its output. Thus the marginal revenue

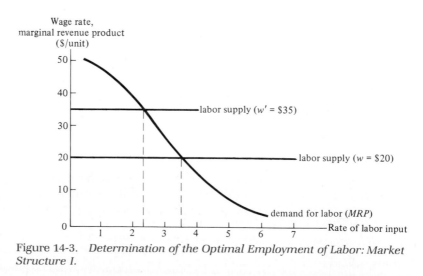

Figure 14-3.   *Determination of the Optimal Employment of Labor: Market Structure I.*

Table 14-2. Total Product, Marginal Product, and Marginal Revenue Product of Labor for a Monopolist

(1) Rate of Labor Input	(2) Rate of Output	(3) Marginal Product	(4) Output Price	(5) Total Revenue	(6) Marginal Revenue	(7) Marginal Revenue Product
0	0		--	--		
		10			$5.00	$50.00
1	10	9	$5.00	$ 50.00	3.94	35.50
2	19		4.50	85.50	2.64	18.50
		7				
3	26	4	4.00	104.00	2.13	8.50
4	30		3.75	112.50	1.35	2.70
		2				
5	32	1	3.60	115.20	0.30	0.30
6	33		3.50	115.50		

curve lies below the demand function. In this case, the firm's demand for labor, as shown by the marginal revenue product function, will decline more rapidly than if price equaled marginal revenue. Because the firm is a perfect competitor in the input market, the supply function is unchanged from the previous example.

Table 14-2 is based on the same production data as the previous example (Table 14-1), but the demand function slopes downward because output price falls as more output is sold and thus marginal revenue is less than price.

The resulting input demand function is shown in the right-hand column of Table 14-2. This demand is computed by multiplying each entry for marginal product by the corresponding marginal revenue per unit entry. As MRP_L is the net addition to the firm's total revenue associated with an additional unit of labor, MRP_L also could be determined as the change in total revenue [in column (5)] associated with a 1-unit change in labor.

In this example, the marginal product at each rate of output is the same as in the previous example. The difference here is that price falls as output increases and therefore the MRP function lies below the MRP function in the initial case. Both the input demand functions for market structures I and II are shown in Figure 14-4. If the market price of input is $20, the firm with power in the output market will employ about 2.5 units because at that input rate, the marginal revenue product is just equal to the wage rate. The monopolist restricts the level of output to maximize profit. Because less output is produced, fewer units of input are necessary. Thus not only is the monopoly market structure undesirable from a consumer's perspective because of lower output and higher price when compared to perfect competition, but monopoly may also be undesirable because it results in a lower rate of employment of inputs.

Market Structure III:
Perfect Competitor—Monopsonist

Now consider a firm that sells output in a perfectly competitive market but is the only buyer of labor. If the firm's output rate is to increase, it must hire more

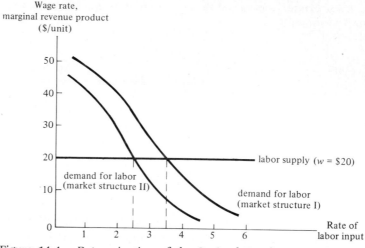

Figure 14-4.   *Determination of the Optimal Employment of Labor: Market Structure II.*

labor. Because the firm faces an upward-sloping supply curve, this will require that the wage rate be increased.

A labor supply schedule facing a monopsonist is shown in the first two columns of Table 14-3 and depicted graphically in Figure 14-5. Also shown is the firm's marginal expenditure on labor function. This function is defined as the change in total expenditure on labor associated with a 1-unit change in the rate of labor input. Note that to hire more input, the firm must offer a higher price for the input, and this higher price must be paid to all inputs hired. For example, if a firm must offer a higher wage rate to attract more workers, it generally must raise the wages of all workers, both new and old, to that new rate. Thus the marginal expenditure on input function lies above the supply curve, reflecting both the higher price necessary to attract new workers and the higher price that must be paid to those already working.

Table 14-3. Labor Supply, Total Expenditure, and Marginal Expenditure on Labor for a Monopsonist

Rate of Labor Input	Labor Price per Unit	Total Expenditure on Labor	Marginal Expenditure on Labor
0	$20	0	
1	20	$ 20	$20
2	21	42	22
3	23	69	27
4	26	104	35
5	30	150	46
6	35	210	60

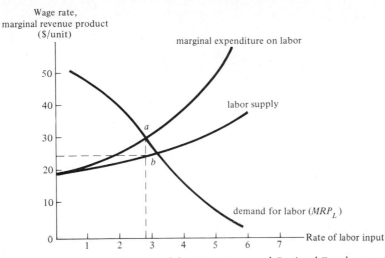

Figure 14-5. *Determination of the Wage Rate and Optimal Employment of Labor: Market Structure III.*

In this market structure, the firm should employ labor until the marginal revenue product is equal to the marginal expenditure on that input. That is, profits are maximized by using labor until the additional revenue generated by that input is equal to additional cost of the labor input. In the example shown in Figure 14-5, the same *MRP* function as used in market structure I is used. To maximize profit, the firm equates the marginal expenditure and marginal revenue product functions (point *a*) to determine the optimal rate of input. In the figure, this intersection indicates that slightly less than 3 units of labor would be employed. The price of labor would be determined by point *b* on the input supply schedule, or about $23 per unit. Note that wage rate is less than the input's contribution to the value of output (i.e., the *MRP*), which is about $30 per unit. This difference has led some analysts to conclude that firms with monopsony power exploit labor by paying them less than their marginal revenue product.

Market Structure IV: Monopolist—Monopsonist

The final case is where the firm is a monopolist in the product market and a monopsonist in the labor market. An example of such a firm might be an electric utility company with a large generating facility near a small community. The relevant functions are the marginal revenue product function (as shown in Table 14-2) and the marginal expenditure on labor function (Table 14-3). In this case, the firm will employ labor until the marginal revenue product equals the marginal expenditure on labor. As shown in Figure 14-6, the intersection of these two functions occurs at point *c*, defining an input quantity of about 2 units. The price of labor is determined by the corresponding point (*d*) on the labor supply function, about $21 per unit. Again, this wage rate is less than the input's marginal revenue product.

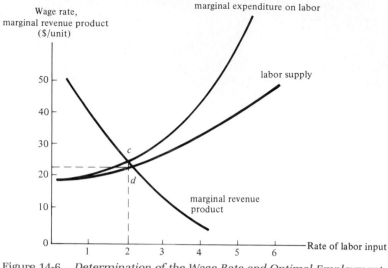

Figure 14-6.   *Determination of the Wage Rate and Optimal Employment of Labor: Market Structure IV.*

KEY CONCEPTS

- Firms that are perfect competitors in input markets face a constant input price. The amount of input employed in a perfectly competitive market for output will be greater than in an output market that is not characterized by perfect competition.
- A firm that has market power in input markets faces an upward-sloping input supply function. The determination of the profit-maximizing price–quantity combination for the input is made by equating the firm's marginal revenue product and marginal expenditure on input functions.

The Correspondence Between Output and Input Decisions

It should be obvious that the decision about how much to produce is not independent of the decision about how much input to employ. Suppose that the capital stock is fixed $(\overline{K})$ and the firm is jointly deciding the rate of output (Q) and the amount of labor to employ (L). Given the production function

$$Q = f(\overline{K}, L)$$

if either Q or L is specified, the other variable is determined. Thus in a technical sense, the firm has only one decision to make.

This can be shown in another way. Suppose that the firm is a perfect competitor in both the output and input markets. Profit maximization requires that the firm increase output until the price of output (P) equals marginal cost (MC), and efficient input resource utilization requires that labor be hired until the marginal revenue product (MRP) equals the unit price of labor (w). It can be shown that these two efficiency conditions,

$$P = MC \qquad\qquad (14\text{-}7)$$

and

$$MRP_L = w \qquad\qquad (14\text{-}8)$$

are equivalent; that is, if one is met, so is the other.

Recall that for the perfect competitor, the marginal revenue product is equal to marginal product multiplied by output price (P). Thus equation (14-8) can be rewritten as

$$MP_L \cdot P = w$$

Now divide both sides of this equation by the marginal product of labor (MP_L), yielding

$$P = \frac{w}{MP_L}$$

But the ratio is simply marginal cost which is the condition specified by equation (14-7). Thus the rule $P = MC$ implies that $MRP_L = w_L$, and vice versa. Although it is not demonstrated here, the profit maximization rules for a monopolist, $MR = MC$ and $MRP_L = w$, are also equivalent.

KEY CONCEPTS

- The decision to produce a given rate of output implies a decision to hire a certain rate of capital and labor, and vice versa.
- The condition for a profit-maximizing output rate (i.e., $MR = MC$) is equivalent to the condition for a profit-maximizing input rate (i.e., $MRP =$ input price).

Economic Rent

Rent is defined as a payment to any factor of production that has a relatively fixed supply. The term is often used to describe a return to land and reflects the notion that there is a fixed amount of land available.[2] As shown in Figure 14-7,

---

[2] Although in a strict sense the total amount of land in the world is fixed, from an economic perspective land is not fixed in supply. The relevant dimensions of the land input are the amount and quality of land in use. Both of these dimensions of the land input are variable. There is much land that is not used for any economic purpose. Periodically, some of this land is developed for agricultural or other uses.

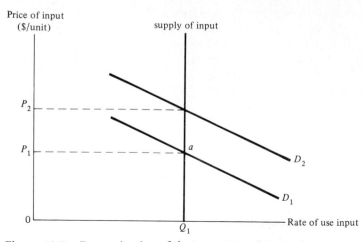

Figure 14-7. *Determination of the Input Price (Rent) When Supply is Perfectly Inelastic.*

when the supply of an input is fixed, the supply function is a vertical line. As a result, the price of that input or its rent is entirely determined by demand. If the demand curve is D_1, the price will be P_1. If the demand curve increases to D_2, the price will increase to P_2. Note that regardless of the change in price, the amount of the input supplied is unchanged.

Economic rent is defined as a payment to a factor of production in excess of the minimum amount necessary to induce that factor into employment. Suppose that Q_1 in Figure 14-7 represents the acres in a particular tract of urban land. Even at a near-zero price, the same amount of land would be supplied because the cost of supplying land is near zero. If the demand curve is D_1, the price per unit would be P_1 and the aggregate payment would be the area $0P_1aQ_1$. This payment is virtually all economic rent because it is in excess of the minimum necessary to bring that land into use. If the demand curve shifted to D_2, the price would increase to P_2, but no additional land would be supplied. However, the economic rent would be greater at price P_2.

CASE STUDY

ECONOMIC RENT IN PROFESSIONAL BASKETBALL

Suppose that a skilled basketball player's services are demanded by a professional team. The team's demand curve and the player's supply curve are shown in Figure 14-8. Note the slightly unusual shape of the supply function. For this athlete, the supply function is horizontal at a price of $30,000 and then rises vertically. This means that the athlete must have $30,000 per year to attract him to play basketball; otherwise, he would take another job. Thus $30,000 represents the opportunity cost to this athlete of playing basketball. That is, $30,000 is the forgone income from a job in another field, and any return above $30,000 is an economic rent. The intersection of demand and supply occurs at $300,000, and

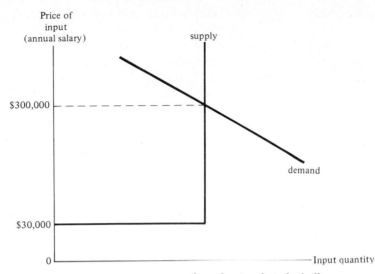

Figure 14-8.   *Economic Rent and Professional Basketball.*

the athlete is paid this wage. Of this amount, $270,000 is economic rent and $30,000 represents the payment necessary to attract this person away from some other job.

Salaries for most professional athletes are probably far in excess of the amounts necessary to keep them playing. For example, the average salary of a player in the National Basketball Association for the 1984–1985 season was over $300,000, and a number of players are paid in excess of $1 million per season. Based on a press release from the NBA Players' Association in January 1985, the highest salaries by position were as follows:

Position	Salary
Forwards	
Larry Bird, Boston Celtics	$1,800,000
Ralph Sampson, Houston Rockets	1,300,000
Mitch Kupchak, Los Angeles Lakers	1,150,000
Julius Erving, Philadelphia 76ers	1,050,000
Kevin McHale, Boston Celtics	1,000,000
Centers	
Moses Malone, Philadelphia 76ers	2,120,000
Kareem Abdul-Jabbar, Los Angeles Lakers	1,530,000
Bill Walton, Los Angeles Clippers	1,350,000
Jack Sikma, Seattle Supersonics	1,140,000
Pat Cummings, New York Knicks	800,000
Guards	
Magic Johnson, Los Angeles Lakers	2,500,000
Otis Birdsong, New Jersey Nets	1,070,000
Sidney Moncrief, Milwaukee Bucks	884,000
George Gervin, San Antonio	831,000
Isaiah Thomas, Detroit Pistons	750,000

If the average annual salary was reduced to $50,000 or even $30,000, probably few players would leave this industry for employment elsewhere. This means that the largest share of payments to these players is in the form of an economic rent. Thus the price of admission to basketball games, the value of television contracts, and the average salary level of players could be much lower without affecting the allocation of resources in this industry. However, this does not imply that there is anything wrong with the salaries paid to professional athletes or anyone else for that matter.

Wage and Income Differentials

It is obvious that there are large variations among the wage rates paid to different kinds of labor. Many unskilled workers are paid the federal minimum wage rate of $3.35 and others apparently have so little to offer employers that they are unable to find employment even at this low wage rate. In contrast, it is not unusual for senior lawyers to be paid $200 or more per hour, skilled surgeons may be paid several thousand dollars for an operation that may take less than an hour, and the salaries of some professional athletes are thousands of dollars per game. Why are there such large differentials in wage rates? Are they the result of market imperfections, such as a lack of information about prices and availability of competing services, or are there economic reasons that explain this phenomenon? Actually, there are important forces on both the demand and supply sides of the input market that explain most of the differences. These economic forces are considered in this section.

Demand-Side Considerations

All persons are not created equal. Differences in aptitude, intellectual ability, strength, and other individual attributes mean that some workers are more productive than others. The more productive workers add more to output and to the revenue of the firm. That is, their marginal revenue product is higher than for other workers. Therefore, they are able to command higher wage rates. Perhaps this is most obvious in the field of athletics. For example, basketball players whose output is twenty-five points and fifteen rebounds per game generally earn considerably more than players who score ten points and have five rebounds per game. Similarly, most firms in other industries pay higher salaries to the more productive managers and workers.

Of course, some firms have plant-wide or even industry-wide wage rate schedules which prescribe that all workers in a certain job category be paid the same rate. Thus one might find differences in productivity among workers who are paid the same wage rate. But even in these cases, it is expected that the more productive workers will earn more in the long run. These workers will be the first to be asked to work overtime at premium rates, and the better workers will tend to be promoted to higher-paying supervisory positions. Furthermore, the less-productive workers will be terminated if their contribution to output is significantly below that of their counterparts. Therefore, even in firms where there might be a fixed wage rate for all workers in a category, over time productive workers probably will earn significantly more than will their less productive associates.

Supply-Side Considerations

Adjustments in the supply of workers will also result in differential wage rates among jobs. Consider two jobs, *A* and *B*, where the skill and training requirements are much different. For example, job *A* may be a clerk in a retail clothing store that requires a high school education, whereas job *B* requires a college degree in electrical engineering. Clearly, it will be more costly for a person to prepare for job *B*. The cost of attending college for four or more years, including the opportunity cost of the lost income during that period, is substantial. That investment in education will not be made unless there is an expectation of higher earnings than can be earned in job *A*.

The wage adjustment for this required training is made on the supply side of the market. Considerably fewer high school graduates would attend college if they did not expect to increase their earning power. That is, fewer workers will make the necessary investment unless there is the prospect of higher earnings than can be earned in comparable jobs that do not require this training. Thus the supply function will be such that in any given wage, far fewer workers will offer their labor for sale for job *B* than for job *A*.

Other factors that result in supply-side adjustments in wage rates include risk of death or injury, working conditions, job content, and hours of work. Jobs that involve health risks, poor working conditions, unusual working hours, and/or tedious or strenuous work generally must pay a higher wage rate than jobs with more desirable characteristics. For example, holding constant other factors, a job that required heavy lifting in a very dirty place on the "graveyard" shift (midnight to 8 A.M.) would probably have to pay a premium to attract applicants. As in the example above, the wage adjustment for these job characteristics is made on the supply side of the market. At any given wage rate, more labor will be supplied to a firm offering a job with desirable characteristics than to a firm offering a less desirable job. Virtually all managers are aware of these factors and offer higher wages for less desirable jobs.

KEY CONCEPTS

- Economic rent is defined as the return to a factor of production in excess of the payment necessary to keep the factor in its current employment.
- Wage differentials among workers reflect demand-side considerations, such as greater productivity, and supply-side forces including training requirements, health risks, and working conditions.

CASE STUDY

THE PREMIUM FOR ACCEPTING RISK

The typical answer to the question "What value do you place on your life?" would be that it is of infinite value. Few people would offer to give up their life in return for a monetary gain except under the most extraordinary circumstances. Indeed, one of the arguments for a military draft is that military service is so risky that it is not possible to attract adequate volunteers by offering higher pay and benefits. However, the apparent success of the all-volunteer military in the United States has disproved that notion, at least in peacetime.

Reflection on individual behavior, particularly with respect to job selection, suggests that people will take all kinds of risk to obtain economic and other kinds of rewards. Some recreational thrills such as skydiving, hang-gliding, and skiing can only be obtained by assuming a rather significant risk of injury. Many drivers exceed the speed limit to conserve on time. In fact, even driving at the speed limit is risky. To eliminate deaths from vehicle accidents might require speed limits below 10 mph and vehicles built like Army tanks. For most people, the opportunity cost of eliminating traffic deaths is simply too high, and they are willing to take their chances at or above current speed limits.

Also, people regularly accept work in occupations that involve significant risk of injury. In fact, many of these occupations are more risky than being in military service during a war. During the Vietnam War, an average of about 7,000 U.S. servicemen were killed each year. At that time, there were some 3 million men and women in the military forces. Thus the death rate was about 2.33 per 1,000 employed in that field.

Thaler and Rosen studied death rates and income differentials for a number of high-risk jobs. Several of these jobs, including guards and lumberjacks, had annual death rates higher than that for a military force at war! Jobs such as firefighter and police officer, where risk is often publicized, are actually less risky than a number of other jobs. Annual death rates per 1,000 employees are shown below.

Occupation	Annual Death Rate per Thousand	Occupation	Annual Death Rate per Thousand
Firemen	0.44	Mine workers	1.76
Police officers	0.78	Lumberjacks	2.56
Electricians	0.93	Guards	2.67
Crane operators	1.47		

Source: Richard Thaler and Sherwin Rosen, "The Value of Saving a Life: Evidence from the Labor Market," in Nestor E. Terlecky, ed., *Household Production and Consumption* (New York: Columbia University Press—National Bureau of Economic Research, 1975), pp. 265–298.

Thaler and Rosen also analyzed the incremental annual wage associated with these jobs. This increment measures the trade-off people are willing to make between risk and income. On average, it was found that about $500 in additional annual wages are needed to offset the additional risk associated with the incidence of one more death per 1,000 workers per year. The difference in the death rate between lumberjacks (2.56) and electricians (0.93) is 1.63. This suggests that the average worker would have to be paid about $815 dollars in additional annual wages (i.e., 1.63 × $500) to accept the additional risk of being a lumberjack.

Labor Unions

About 25 percent of the nonagricultural labor force in the United States are members of labor unions. Where workers are organized, the nature of management–worker negotiations is different than for firms without labor unions. The union may act as a monopolist, that is, as a single seller of labor to the firm.

In this section two topics related to labor unions are considered. First, the economics of collective bargaining between firms and labor unions are discussed. The second section considers alternative objective functions that might influence labor union behavior.

Labor Unions and Collective Bargaining

Labor unions represent workers in negotiations with management concerning wage rates, fringe benefits, and working conditions. Where the workers of a firm are members of a union, wages are not set unilaterally by management in response to market conditions. Rather, they are determined by negotiations between management and union representatives. In many industries, collective bargaining is done on an industry-wide basis. Representatives from the major companies comprise an industry bargaining team and the labor union has a bargaining team that represents the workers. The result is similar to a bilateral monopoly situation where a single seller faces a single buyer in a market. The industry negotiating team acts as a monopsonist or the sole buyer of labor in the industry and the union acts as a monopolist or the sole seller of labor in the industry.

The relevant labor demand and supply functions for such a situation are shown in Figure 14.9. Industry demand for labor is shown by the demand curve DD, the marginal revenue product of labor, and MR is the marginal revenue curve associated with the labor demand curve. The supply function for labor is shown by line SS and the marginal expenditure for labor is shown by ME. If it could act without restraint, the industry bargaining team would maximize profit by equating the labor demand curve and the marginal expenditure curve at point a and would hire L_m units of labor. The price or wage rate is determined by the point on the supply curve corresponding to the quantity L_m, that is, W_m.

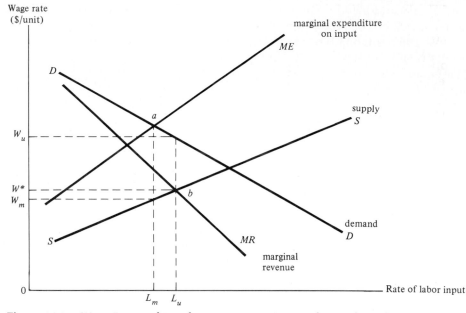

Figure 14-9. *Wage Rate and Employment Determination for a Bilateral Monopoly.*

In contrast, the labor union acting as a monopoly seller of labor will maximize the net surplus[3] paid to industry workers by equating the marginal revenue function and the supply curve at point b to determine the quantity hired of L_u. The wage rate W_u is that point on the industry labor demand curve corresponding to quantity L_u. Not surprisingly, the union approach results in a higher wage rate and more workers employed than occurs if the management objective is followed.

The exact result of the bargaining process is indeterminate. If management has much more bargaining power than the union, the wage rate may end up being close to W_m. Conversely, if the relative power lies with the labor union, the negotiations may result in a wage rate closer to W_u.

One factor determining the outcome is the negotiating skill of those at the bargaining table. However, other forces will also affect the outcome of the negotiations. For example, if the economy is in a recession and the firms have built up large inventories, management may be in a position to weather a prolonged strike. In such a period, labor's positions may be weak because of limited availability of alternative jobs for workers should there be a strike. In contrast, in a period of strong demand for industry output, a strike may mean the loss of otherwise large profits. This potential for large profits may also make it difficult for management to "plead poverty" at the bargaining table.

---

[3] In Figure 14-9, the area below the wage rate but above the supply curve can be thought of as a "surplus" paid to workers over and above the amount necessary to have them offer their labor for sale. In a sense, it is a form of economic rent. For example, workers would offer L_u units of labor for sale at a wage of W^*. That is, W^* corresponds to that point on the labor supply curve where L_u units of labor are offered for sale. If they are paid a wage above W^*, they are earning a surplus.

EXAMPLE

WAGE RATE DETERMINATION—THE BILATERAL MONOPOLY CASE

Suppose that teams representing the United Steelworkers of America and management of all major steel producers in the United States are negotiating a new labor contract. Assume that virtually all workers and all firms are represented by these teams. The industry demand for labor is $w = 200 - 2L$ and the associated marginal revenue function is

$$MR = 200 - 4L$$

The supply curve for labor and marginal expenditure or labor function are

$$w = 8 + 4L \quad \text{and} \quad ME = 8 + 8L$$

where w is the daily wage rate and L is the number of workers employed in thousands. Determine the wage rate and level of employment that will result from these negotiations.

Solution

Because virtually all firms and workers are represented by the two teams, this is a bilateral monopoly problem. As such, the solution will depend on the relative bargaining power of the two groups and their negotiating skills, and a unique solution does not exist. However, two extreme solutions can be determined.

First, assume that management is able to dominate the negotiations and dictate the terms of the contract. The amount of labor hired is determined by equating the labor demand and marginal expenditure functions

$$200 - 2L = 8 + 8L$$

and solving for L:

$$\boxed{L = 19.2}$$

The wage rate is found by substituting $L = 19.2$ into the labor supply function

$$w = 8 + 4(L) = 8 + 4(19.2)$$

or

$$\boxed{w = 84.80}$$

If the union is able to dictate terms of the negotiations, the quantity of labor hired would be found by equating the marginal revenue and labor supply functions and solving for L, that is,

$$200 - 4L = 8 + 4L$$

or

$$\boxed{L = 24}$$

The wage rate would be determined by substituting $L = 24$ into the labor demand function:

$$w = 200 - 2L = 200 - 2(24)$$

or

$$\boxed{w = 152}$$

The union "solution," of course, has both a higher wage rate and a greater employment than the management solution. In general, neither side would be able to dictate the terms of the agreement, and therefore the actual solution would lie somewhere between these two extremes.

Union Objectives

In the bilateral monopoly example, it was assumed that the goal of the union is to maximize the net surplus to its members. This surplus is maximized where the marginal revenue curve intersects the supply curve. Note that this approach is analogous to the monopolist maximizing profit by equating marginal revenue and marginal cost. In a sense, the labor union is a monopolist in this labor market and the supply function serves as the marginal cost curve.

Obviously, the union may have other objectives. For example, it may want to have all union members fully employed or it may want to maximize the aggregate income of the membership. To analyze the implications of these alternative goals, consider the demand for labor function and the associated marginal revenue function shown in Figure 14-10. Suppose that there are L_2 workers in the union.

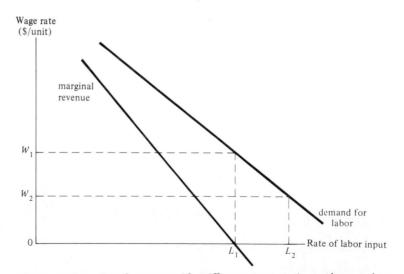

Figure 14-10.   *Employment with Different Assumptions About Labor Union Objectives.*

To keep all these workers employed requires that the firm bargain for a wage rate of W_2, the wage rate associated with L_2 on the demand curve.

Conversely, if the objective is maximizing aggregate wages, the union would want to move to L_1, the point where the MR curve intersects the horizontal axis. The wage rate associated with this point is W_1, again determined by the demand curve. In this case, however, there is an unemployment problem, as $L_2 - L_1$ members of the union will not be employed. Which members are to be unemployed? Will it be those with the least seniority or those with the fewest skills? These are difficult problems for union leaders to resolve, but it is clear that some union leaders have bargained for and obtained wage agreements that have led to unemployment for a significant number of the union members. For example, shortly after organizing as the United Mine Workers, coal miners bargained for and won much higher wage rates, but at the cost of a significantly higher unemployment rate for mine workers.

There are still other objectives the union leaders may have, such as maintaining their positions of leadership and power in the union. Usually, objectives of union leaders are stated in vague terms such as "higher wages," "better working conditions," or "more job security," and it is very difficult to identify the true objectives of the union. The final result of collective bargaining may reveal more about the true objectives than would any statement by union leaders.

KEY CONCEPTS

- Collective bargaining can be thought of as a bilateral monopoly situation where the firm acts as a monopsonist or the sole buyer of labor and the union acts as a monopolist or the sole seller of labor.
- The outcome of collective bargaining will depend not only on the relevant demand and supply functions but also on the relative bargaining skill and strength of management and union leaders.
- Alternative labor union objectives include full employment of all members of the union, maximization of the net surplus to workers, and maximization of aggregate wages paid to members.

Summary

Input prices are determined by the interaction of supply and demand. The demand for inputs is derived from the demand for the output that those inputs are used to produce. The marginal revenue product function, computed by multiplying marginal revenue and marginal product, is the firm's input demand function.

Determining input prices is important because these prices are used in deciding on the optimal mix of labor, capital, and natural resources to be employed by the firm. The approach to input price determination depends on the structure of both the input and output markets. A perfect competitor in an input market faces a constant input price. Thus the only decision made by the firm is the quantity of the input to be employed. A monopsonist has market power in the input market and, thus, faces an upward-sloping input supply function. The input price and quantity employed by the monopsonist is determined by the intersection of the input demand function with the firm's marginal expenditure on input function.

There is a unique correspondence between output and input decisions. A decision to produce a given rate of output implies a decision to hire certain rates of capital and labor input, and vice versa. The condition for a profit-maximizing output rate (i.e., marginal cost equals marginal revenue) is equivalent to the condition for a profit-maximizing input rate (i.e., marginal revenue product equals input price).

Economic rent is a return to a factor of production in excess of the minimum payment necessary to keep that factor in its present employment. Wage differentials among workers reflect both demand-side forces, such as differences in productivity, and supply-side factors, such as required training requirements, health risks, and working conditions.

Collective bargaining refers to the process of determining wage rates and other working conditions through negotiation between labor union representatives and management from one or several firms. In some cases, collective bargaining can be thought of as a bilateral monopoly situation where the firm acts as a monopsonist, the sole buyer of labor, and the union acts as a monopolist, the sole seller of labor. The outcome of collective bargaining will depend not only on the relevant demand and supply functions but also on the relative bargaining skill and strength of management and union leaders. Objectives of labor unions include full employment of all members of the union, maximization of aggregate wages paid to members, and maximization of the net surplus to workers.

Discussion Questions

14-1. What determines the mix of labor and capital used by the firm to produce output? Explain.

14-2. Explain why the term "derived demand" is used to describe the demand for factors of production.

14-3. Provide an intuitive explanation for the profit-maximizing rule that the firm should hire an input until the marginal revenue product of the input is equal to the additional cost of that input.

14-4. Why is the input supply function horizontal for a perfect competitor in the input market and upward-sloping for a monopsonist?

14-5. Why is it that there is no unique input price and quantity of input hired in the bilateral monopoly case? What factors will play a role in determining that price and quantity?

14-6. Given that a firm should always be producing efficiently, is it possible for management to separate the decisions about the rate of output to be produced and the rates of capital and labor to be employed?

14-7. In 1985, the average salary of a professional baseball player was more than $300,000. Is it "right" for these athletes to make many times more than the average American worker? If that average salary was reduced by one-half, how many baseball players do you think would leave the baseball industry for other occupations? Explain.

14-8. For many years the United States and other countries used a draft system to maintain required personnel levels in their military forces. During most of the period when the draft existed, earnings in military service, including such fringe benefits as housing and meals, were substantially less than in comparable civilian occupations. Supporters of the draft system argued that military service was sufficiently dangerous that regardless of the wage rate, there would not be adequate volunteers. Do you agree or disagree with this position? Explain.

14-9. The leader of a major labor union claims that the union's objective is full employment for all members. Despite an unemployment rate of 15 percent for workers in this union, labor negotiators are demanding a 15 percent increase in wage rates for each of the next three years. Workers in other industries have been receiving wage increase of 8 or 9 percent per year. Are the actions of the union negotiators consistent with the alleged objective of the union? Explain.

Problems

14-1. Suppose that the demand and supply functions for unskilled labor in the economy are

$$\text{demand: } L_d = 10 - 0.5w$$
$$\text{supply: } L_s = 6 + 0.9w$$

where L is millions of workers and w is the hourly wage rate.
(a) Determine the equilibrium wage rate and number of workers employed.
(b) If the U.S. Congress sets a minimum wage of $3.50 per hour, what will be the wage rate, the quantity of labor employed, the number of workers who will be unemployed, and the unemployment rate for unskilled workers?
(c) If the minimum wage rate is set at $3.15, what will be the wage rate, the number of workers employed, and the number unemployed? Compare these answers to those in part a.

14-2. Suppose the demand for power forwards on NBA basketball teams is given by the equation

$$L_d = 400,000 - 2w$$

while the supply of forwards is given by the following function

$$L_s = \begin{cases} 32 \text{ if } w \geq \$40,000 \\ 0 \text{ if } w < \$40,000 \end{cases}$$

where L is number of players and w is the annual salary.
(a) Graph the demand and supply functions.
(b) Determine the equilibrium wage rate for a power forward in the NBA.
(c) Suppose a sudden drop in attendance and number of television viewers shifted the demand function to

$$L_d^* = 300,000 - 3w$$

How would the annual salary change? Would the resulting resource allocation be any different than before the demand curve shifted?

(d) Based on the supply function shown above, what is your best estimate of the opportunity cost of playing power forward in the NBA?

14-3. Consider a firm in a perfectly competitive output market where the price of the product is $10 per unit. Given the following information on the total product of labor function, determine the firm's demand schedule for labor (i.e., MRP_L) by completing the table.

Quantity of Labor	Total Product	Marginal Product	Marginal Revenue Product
0	0		
1	21	_____	_____
2	30	_____	_____
3	38	_____	_____
4	42	_____	_____
5	43	_____	_____
6	40	_____	_____

Suppose this firm is a monopsonist that faces the following labor supply schedule. Use these data to determine the firm's total and marginal expenditure on labor schedules.

Wage Rate	Quantity of Labor Supplied	Total Expenditure on Labor	Marginal Expenditure on Labor
20	0	_____	
22	1	_____	_____
25	2	_____	_____
30	3	_____	_____
35	4	_____	_____
40	5	_____	_____
50	6	_____	_____

Use these data to determine how much labor the firm should employ? What will the wage rate be? Explain.

14-4. A team representing management of all firms in the automatic widget industry is currently negotiating a new three-year contract with the leaders of the United Widget Workers of America (UWW) labor union. The industry demand function for labor (i.e., the marginal revenue product of labor) is

$$MRP_L = 20 - 2L,$$

and the marginal revenue function associated with the demand curve is

$$MR = 20 - 4L,$$

and the labor supply and marginal expenditure on input functions facing the industry are

$$W = 5 + 2L$$
$$ME = 5 + 4W,$$

where L is the number of workers in thousands and W is the hourly wage rate.

(a) If the management team can dominate the negotiations and dictate the terms of the agreement, what wage rate and level of employment will be determined?

(b) If the labor union team can dominate the negotiations and dictate the terms of the agreement, what wage rate and level of employment will be determined?

Problem Requiring Calculus

14-5. The market demand and supply functions for Rhubarb Field Dolls are

$$Q_D = 2,000 - 250P$$

and

$$Q_S = 600 + 100P$$

where Q_D is quantity demanded, Q_S is quantity supplied, and P is the price.

Adamco Inc. manufactures these dolls using the following production function:

$$Q = K^{0.5}L^{0.5}$$

where Q is the rate of output, K is capital, and L is labor. Adamco is the largest employer in a small town and faces the following labor supply function

$$w = 0.5L_S$$

where w is the wage rate.

If the capital input is fixed at 225, determine the profit-maximizing labor input, rate of output, and wage rate.

References

Agarwal, N. C. 1981. "Determinants of Executive Compensation." *Industrial Relations* 20(1):36–46.

Ehrenberg, R. G., and Smith, R. S. 1982. *Modern Labor Economics: Theory of Public Policy.* Glenview, Ill.: Scott, Foresman.

Hill, J. R., and Spellman, W. 1983. "Professional Baseball: The Reserve Clause and Salary Structure." *Industrial Relations* 22(1):1–19.

Kwoka, J. E., Jr. 1983. "Monopoly, Plant, and Union Effects on Worker Wages." *Industrial and Labor Relations Review* 36(2):251–257.

Lewellen, W. G., and Huntsman, B. 1970. "Managerial Pay and Corporate Performance." *American Economic Review* 60(September):710–720.

Long, J. E., and Link, A. N. 1983. "The Impact of Market Structure on Wages, Fringe Benefits, and Turnover." *Industrial and Labor Relations Review* 36(2):239–250.

Mansfield, E. M. 1982. *Microeconomics: Theory and Applications.* New York: Norton.

Medoff, J. L., and Abraham, K. G. 1981. "Are Those Paid More Really More Productive? The Case of Experience." *Journal of Human Resources* 16(2):186–216.

Olson, C. A. 1981. "An Analysis of Wage Differentials Received by Workers on Dangerous Jobs." *Journal of Human Resources* 16(2):167–185.

Thaler, R., and Rosen, S. 1975. "The Value of Saving a Life: Evidence from the Labor Market." In Nestor E. Terleckyj, ed., *Household Production and Consumption.* New York: Columbia University Press—National Bureau of Economic Research.

Viscusi, W. K. 1983. *Risk by Choice.* Cambridge, Mass.: Harvard University Press.

Production Decisions

15

Preview

Managers maximize profits by increasing production until marginal revenue equals marginal cost. But not all firms are profitable. For some businesses, there is no rate of output that will allow the firm to earn a normal rate of profit. The first section of this chapter provides a decision rule for determining whether the managers of an unprofitable operation should continue to produce or shut down operations. The section also discusses the optimal mix of output for a multi-product firm; that is, the output rates for each product that will maximize total profit for the firm.

An important managerial task is to monitor costs of production. Indeed, minimum-cost production at the chosen rate of output is a necessary condition for profit maximization. Chapter 6 described how inputs should be combined to minimize costs. But in large corporations, producing efficiently can be much more complicated than is suggested by that simple model. In the second section of this chapter four problems relating to cost minimization are discussed. They are: (1) allocation of output between plants, (2) the optimal level of inventories to be maintained by the firm, (3) optimal queue lengths in the production process, and (4) the question of equipment replacement.

Production Rates

In some circumstances, a firm may be better off (i.e., lose less money) if it produces nothing. The decision to shut down or continue producing is analyzed in the first part of this section. If a firm produces more than one product, the amount to be produced of each must be determined. Optimal product mix is the focus of the second part of this section.

Produce or Shut Down?

Simply because profit maximization is the objective of managers is no guarantee that a firm will actually earn economic or even normal profits. Intense competition, inadequate demand, or high costs may prevent a firm from operating profitably at any rate of output. That is, maximum profit may actually be a loss.

The course of action adopted by managers of an unprofitable firm should be based on a consideration of the alternatives. One option would be to continue producing at the least unprofitable (i.e., smallest loss) rate of output. Another would be to shut down operations and produce nothing. The proper choice is the alternative that minimizes the firm's losses. In the short run, the consequences of shutting down versus continuing production are illustrated using the data in Table 15-1.

Table 15-1. Short-Run Output and Cost Data

(1) Quantity	(2) Total Fixed Cost	(3) Total Variable Cost	(4) Total Cost	(5) Marginal Cost	(6) Average Variable Cost	(7) Average Total Cost
0	$5	$ 0	$ 5		—	—
1	5	5	10	5	$5.00	$10.00
2	5	9	14	4	4.50	7.00
3	5	12	17	3	4.00	5.67
4	5	14	19	2	3.50	4.75
5	5	17	22	3	3.40	4.40
6	5	21	26	4	3.50	4.33
7	5	26	31	5	3.72	4.42
8	5	32	37	6	4.00	4.63
9	5	39	44	7	4.33	4.88

Column (1) shows various rates of output that could be produced, and Column (2) shows total fixed costs. By definition, these fixed costs are constant for all rates of output. In column (3) total variable costs are reported. The remaining data in the table have been computed from the information in the first three columns.

Recall that total costs are the sum of total variable costs and the constant total fixed cost. Marginal cost is the change in total cost (or total variable cost) resulting from a 1-unit change in output. Average variable cost is total variable cost divided by quantity. Similarly, average total cost is total cost divided by quantity. Note that marginal, average variable, and average total costs first decrease and then increase. This is consistent with the discussion of costs in Chapter 8.

Now consider the optimal rate of output for a profit-maximizing firm facing a horizontal demand curve. The optimal quantity depends on the market-determined price. The decision rule is that the firm should produce an additional unit of output if the selling price is at least as great as the marginal cost of production. The reason is that if price exceeds marginal cost, producing the extra unit increases total profit. If price equals marginal cost, the firm just covers the cost of the last unit.

For example, if the price is $5, the firm should produce 7 units because the marginal cost of the seventh unit is $5. If price increases to $6, the optimal quantity would be 8 units because the marginal cost of the eighth unit is $6. Similarly, at a price of $7, 9 units should be produced.

What if the price declines to $3? Applying the same logic, it would seem that the firm should produce 5 units. But note that average variable cost at 5 units is $3.40 and total variable cost is $17. This $17 is an expense that could be avoided if the firm did not produce the 5 units of output. Because the firm sells output for $3 per unit, its total revenue is $15. Hence, by producing the firm adds $15 to its total revenue but incurs additional (and avoidable) costs of $17. Adding the fixed cost of $5 results in a total loss of $7.

At a price of $3, producing at any other output rate would cause equal or greater losses. For example, cutting back to 4 units would also result in a total loss of $7, and expanding output to 6 units would increase the firm's loss to $8. However, the firm's managers do have one other option. They could shut down the firm's operations and produce nothing. In this case, there would be no revenue and no variable costs. The loss would be the $5 in fixed costs that must be paid whether or not the firm produces. Thus, by shutting down, the firm loses $5, compared to a minimum loss of $7 if any production takes place. In general, the decision rule is that a firm minimizes its losses by shutting down when price drops below average variable cost.

Now suppose that the firm can sell at a price of $4. Price equals marginal cost at a quantity of 6 units. Sale of 6 units will generate revenues of $24 and cause the firm to incur total costs of $26, for a net loss of $2. At any other rate of output, the losses are even greater. Is the optimal choice again to shut down, as it was at a price of $3?

If the firm shuts down, it must still pay the fixed costs of $5. However, by producing 6 units the loss is only $2. Clearly, the firm minimizes its losses by continuing to produce. The key to the decision is an examination of price in relation to average variable cost. As long as price exceeds average variable costs, the firm is better off if it continues to produce. The reason is that revenue will be sufficient to cover variable costs and make a contribution to payment of the firm's fixed costs. In contrast, shutting down means that losses are equal to fixed costs.

This concept is illustrated in Figure 15-1. That portion of the marginal cost curve that lies above average variable cost represents the firm's supply curve. That is, it shows the profit-maximizing output at each price. When price drops below average variable cost, the firm minimizes its losses by shutting down. If price is greater than average variable cost but less than average total cost, the firm loses money, but less than if its operations were shut down. Finally, for prices greater than or equal to average total cost, the firm is profitable.

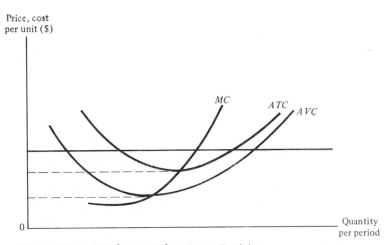

Figure 15-1. *Produce or Shut Down Decision.*

Two qualifications apply to the basic decision rule. First, the rule does not necessarily mean that managers should shut down operations every time price drops below average variable cost. In many cases, substantial costs are incurred when a production process is shut down and also when it is restarted. For example, in steel manufacturing several days may be required to bring a blast furnace up to operating temperature and there are costs involved in laying off and recalling workers. Also, a firm that shuts down and then reopens may find that its customers are buying from other suppliers. These costs must be taken into account. They suggest that a decision to shut down will be made only if it is expected that price will remain below average variable cost for an extended period of time.

The second qualification involves the distinction between the short run and the long run. Note that the decision to shut down depends on whether the firm can make a contribution to its fixed cost by continuing to produce. But in the long run there are no fixed costs. Buildings can be sold, equipment can be auctioned off, and purchase contracts will expire. Thus, in the long run, if price is expected to remain below average total cost, the firm will shut down and go out of business. Basically, the same decision rule applies to both the short and the long run—a firm should continue to produce as long as revenues exceed avoidable costs.

EXAMPLE
CALCULATING THE SHUT DOWN PRICE

A bicycle manufacturer faces a horizontal demand curve. The firm's total costs are given by the equation

$$TC = FC + 150Q - 20Q^2 + Q^3$$

where FC is fixed cost and Q is quantity.

Below what price should the firm shut down operations?

Solution

Marginal cost is the derivative of total cost with respect to quantity. Thus,

$$\frac{dTC}{dQ} = MC = 150 - 40Q + 3Q^2$$

The average variable cost equation is given by

$$AVC = \frac{150Q - 20Q^2 + 1Q^3}{Q} = 150 - 20Q + Q^2$$

The shut-down point is where price equals average variable cost. But profit maximization requires that price also equal marginal cost. Thus $MC = AVC$. Hence

$$150 - 40Q + 3Q^2 = 150 - 20Q + Q^2$$

Rearranging terms gives

$$-2Q^2 + 20Q = 0$$

which can be rewritten as

$$-2Q(Q - 10) = 0$$

Thus $Q = 0$ or $Q = 10$. Substituting $Q = 10$ into the marginal cost equation gives

$$P = MC = 150 - 40(10) + 3(100) = 50$$

A similar substitution for $Q = 0$ yields $P = 150$. The relevant solution is the lower of the two prices. Thus if the price falls below \$50 per unit the firm should not produce.

KEY CONCEPTS

- In the short run, managers of a firm should shut down the operation if price is below average variable cost.
- If price is greater than average variable cost but less than average total cost, the firm should continue to produce in the short run because a contribution can be made to fixed costs.
- In the long run all costs are variable. Thus the firm should shut down if price is less than average cost.

Optimal Product Mix for a Multiproduct Firm

In some multiproduct firms the facilities of the business are so specialized that there is little opportunity to vary the relative amounts of each good produced. However, in most multiproduct businesses, managers have considerable latitude in determining the product mix. In such cases, each product competes for inputs and use of the firm's productive capacity. Hence managers must choose the composition of output that maximizes total profit for the firm. Two steps are involved in this choice. First, the optimal bundle of outputs for each rate of input use must be determined. Second, the profit-maximizing rate of input use must be selected.

Consider a business that manufactures two goods: denim jackets and denim pants. The firm has a single plant that can be operated for either one or two shifts per day. Each shift lasts eight hours and requires 20 workers at \$10 per hour. Hence the labor cost is \$1,600 per shift. However, assume that the second shift also requires an extra \$200 per day in heating and lighting costs.

During each shift, the plant can be used to produce any proportion of jackets and pants desired. However, all the equipment is not equally suitable for producing jackets and pants. Thus, as more jackets are manufactured, an increasing

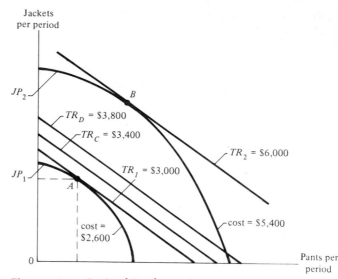

Figure 15-2. *Optimal Product Mix.*

number of pants must be forgone, and vice versa. The line JP_1 in Figure 15-2 shows all combinations of jackets and pants that can be manufactured each day by one shift of workers. That is, it depicts the production trade-off between the two goods. The bowed shape indicates an increasing opportunity cost of producing more of either good. At any point, the slope of JP_1 is the tangent to the line at that point and indicates the rate at which jackets can be substituted for pants during the first shift. This trade-off is referred to as the *marginal rate of transformation* (*MRT*).

Assume that the cost of denim is $1,000 per shift and is not affected by the product mix. Thus the total cost of operating the first shift is $2,600 ($1,600 in labor cost plus the $1,000 spent on denim). This information allows the line JP_1 to be interpreted as a product transformation curve. That is, it shows all combinations of jackets and pants that can be manufactured for a total cost of $2,600.

Next assume that the firm faces a horizontal demand curve for each good, and that each jacket can be sold for $30 and each pair of pants for $20. The lines TR_C and TR_D in Figure 15-2 are isorevenue lines. They show all combinations of jackets and pants that will generate given total revenue for the firm. The slope of each isorevenue line is the negative of the price of pants divided by the price of jackets, or $-\frac{20}{30}$.

For a given total cost, profit maximization requires that the managers of the firm select the product mix that maximizes total revenue. This occurs at the point where the highest isorevenue line is tangent to the product transformation curve. In Figure 15-2, for the first shift this occurs at point A, where TR_1 is tangent to JP_1. At this point, revenue is $3,000 and cost is $2,600. Thus profit is $400.

At the point of tangency, the slopes of the isocost and isorevenue lines are equal. But the slope of the isocost line is the marginal rate of transformation and the slope of the isorevenue line is the negative of the price ratio. Thus the profit-maximizing product mix is given by

$$MRT = -\frac{P_P}{P_J}$$

The intuitive explanation for this result is very simple. The MRT is the rate at which the two goods can be substituted in production. Thus it represents the opportunity cost of one good in terms of the other. The price ratio represents the relative value of the two goods to the firm in the marketplace. Therefore, the optimal product mix is where the relative cost equals the relative value. If one good makes a relatively greater contribution to revenue than it does to cost, more of that good should be produced.

The second step for the manager of the multiproduct firm is to decide whether to use one or two shifts. The profit-maximizing combination when both shifts are used is determined the same way as for the first shift. The curve JP_2 is the product transformation locus when operating with two shifts. In Figure 15-2, the optimal product mix is at point B where the isorevenue line TR_2 is tangent to the isocost curve JP_2. Because of the additional cost of operating the second shift, total cost associated with JP_2 is 2(2,600) + 200, or $5,400. All points on TR_2 generate a total revenue of $6,000. Thus total profit from the use of two shifts is $600. Because this profit is $200 greater than the profit associated with operating with a single shift, the firm should use two shifts of workers. The general principle is that additional inputs should be employed as long as the extra revenue received from the output they produce exceeds their additional cost.

CASE STUDY

FUEL OIL VERSUS GASOLINE

Crude oil can be used to produce either fuel oil for heating or gasoline for vehicles. Most oil refineries can vary the mix of the two products they produce from a given quantity of crude oil. This flexibility is required by seasonal fluctuations in demand for fuel oil and gasoline. Increased vacation travel causes demand for gasoline to increase during the summer. Refineries respond by using more of their crude oil to make gasoline. For example, in July 1984, oil companies were producing at the rate of 393 million gallons of gasoline and 203 million gallons of fuel oil per day. But during the winter, demand for gasoline decreases and refineries must meet the increased demand for fuel oil. Thus, in January 1985, the daily rate of gasoline production was down to 367 million gallons, while that of fuel oil was up to 275 million gallons.

KEY CONCEPT

- For any given rate of resource use, profit maximization requires that the product mix be adjusted until the marginal rate of transformation equals the negative of the ratio of output prices.

Production Methods

In previous chapters the discussion of profit maximization focused primarily on price and output determination. But maximizing profits also requires that managers pay careful attention to methods of production to assure that the firm is operating efficiently. This section considers four important problems relating to efficient production.

Multiplant Production

To this point it has been assumed that firms produce their output in only one plant. However, many large firms operate several separate production facilities. For example, General Motors manufactures Chevrolets in California, Michigan, Missouri, and several other locations in the United States. Where multiple plants are involved, managers must determine not only the total amount to be produced, but also how many units of output are to be produced at each facility.

Suppose that a firm sells only one product, but production takes place in two plants located in different regions of the country. Assume that differences in wages, transportation costs, and technology cause marginal costs to differ between the two facilities. The marginal cost for various rates of output for the two plants is shown in columns (2) and (3) of Table 15-2.

Minimizing the total cost of production requires that each additional unit be produced at minimum cost. Hence managers must compare marginal costs in each plant. Note that the marginal cost of the first unit is $4 in plant 1 and $5.50 in plant 2. Thus the first unit of output should be produced in plant 1. The next unit of output also should come from plant 1 because the marginal cost is $5, which is lower than the $5.50 for the initial unit from plant 2. However, the third unit should be produced in plant 2. The reason is that the $5.50 necessary to make the first unit there is less than the $6 marginal cost of the third unit from the plant 1. Similarly, the fourth unit should be produced in plant 1, the fifth in plant 2, and so on. This decision process results in the values shown in column

Table 15-2. Marginal Costs for the Multiplant Firm

(1)	(2)	(3)	(4)	(5)	(6)
		Marginal Cost			Marginal
Output	Plant 1	Plant 2	Firm	Price	Revenue
0	$ 4.00	$ 5.50	$4.00	$11.50	$10.00
1	5.00	6.50	5.00	11.00	10.00
2	6.00	7.50	5.50	10.50	9.00
3	7.00	8.50	6.00	10.00	8.00
4	8.00	9.50	6.50	9.50	7.00
5	9.00	10.50	7.00	9.00	6.00
6	10.00	11.50	7.50	8.50	5.00
7				8.00	

(4) of the table. These data show the minimum marginal costs to the firm of producing additional units of output.

Column (5) of Table 15-2 represents demand data showing the relationship between price and output. These data are used to compute the marginal revenue figures of column (6). To maximize profit, the firm should increase output as long as marginal revenue exceeds marginal cost, as shown in column (4). This decision rule implies that 5 units should be produced because the marginal revenue associated with the fifth unit is $7, while its marginal cost is only $6.50. The output should be allocated between the two plants so as to minimize total cost. In this case, 3 units should be produced in the first plant and 2 in the second, resulting in a total cost of $27. Note from Table 15-2 that any other allocation of the 5 units between the plants involves a greater total cost.

Profit maximization for the multiplant firm is shown graphically in Figure 15-3. The first panel shows demand and cost curves for the total firm. The marginal cost curve in that panel represents minimum cost production and is derived in the same way as the marginal cost data of column (4) of Table 15-2. The optimal output rate for the firm (Q_0) is shown in the panel as the point where marginal revenue equals marginal cost. The profit-maximizing price (P_0) is determined by the demand curve.

Just as $MR = MC$ is the decision rule for determining overall output of the firm, it is also the basis for allocation of output between plants. That is, each plant should be used until the marginal cost of producing 1 more unit in that plant equals marginal revenue received by the firm for its product. That is,

$$MR = MC_1$$

and

$$MR = MC_2$$

For an output rate of Q_0, marginal revenue is MR_0. Marginal cost curves for the two plants are shown in the second and third panels of Figure 15-3. Equating

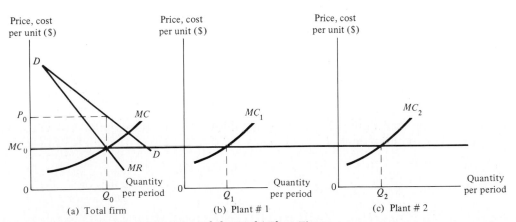

Figure 15-3. *Profit Maximization and the Multi-Plant Firm.*

marginal revenue to marginal cost, indicates that Q_1 units should be produced in the first plant and Q_2 in the second, Because the marginal revenue is the same in both cases, the condition for efficient production can also be stated as

$$MC_1 = MC_2 \tag{15-1}$$

That is, minimum-cost production for a multiplant firm requires that the marginal cost of producing 1 more unit in one plant be equal to the marginal cost of production in the other plant. If this condition is not met, output can be reallocated in such a way as to reduce costs. Specifically, additional output should be produced in the plant with the lower marginal cost.

EXAMPLE

OUTPUT ALLOCATION BY A MULTIPLANT FIRM

The marginal revenue equation for a product is

$$MR = 50 - 2Q_T$$

where Q_T is the total output of the firm. The product is produced in two separate plants with marginal cost equations

$$MC_1 = 2Q_1$$

and

$$MC_2 = 4Q_2$$

What is the profit-maximizing output, and how should it be allocated between the two plants?

Solution

The first step is to note that the cost-minimizing allocation between the two plants requires that the marginal costs be equal. Thus $MC_1 = MC_2$, or

$$2Q_1 = 4Q_2$$

and hence

$$Q_2 = Q_1/2$$

In that $Q_T = Q_1 + Q_2$, the firm's marginal revenue function can be written as

$$MR = 50 - 2(Q_1 + Q_2)$$

Profit maximization requires that marginal revenue equal marginal cost in each plant. For the first plant,

$$50 - 2(Q_1 + Q_2) = 2Q_1$$

Substituting $Q_1/2$ for Q_2 gives

$$50 - 2\left(Q_1 + \frac{Q_1}{2}\right) = 2Q_1$$

Solving this equation yields $Q_1 = 10$ and hence $Q_2 = 5$. Thus total output should be 15 units and $MR = 20$. Because $MC_1 = 20 = MC_2$, the requirements for efficient production and for profit maximization have been met.

KEY CONCEPT

• Production for the multiplant firm should be allocated such that the cost of producing an additional unit is the same in each plant and also equal to marginal revenue.

Inventories

Usually, firms maintain an inventory of materials necessary to produce their product. For example, automobile manufacturers keep stocks of steel, tires, paint, and other supplies on hand to meet the needs of production facilities. But managers must determine the optimal level of these inventories. There are costs involved in holding large inventories. One is the storage space required. Another is the forgone interest on the money spent to purchase inventories. But low inventories may result in shortages and the inability to meet the demand for the firm's product. In addition, there may be extra costs associated with making a large number of relatively small orders. Some of these costs represent extra work involved in making frequent orders. Other costs may be higher transportation costs or extra billing expenses charged by supplying firms.

The determination of optimal inventories can be a complex problem. However, considerable insight can be gained by considering a simplified version of the issue. Assume that the manager of a television store expects to sell a total of D sets during the year and that sales will be evenly distributed over the period.

Obviously, selling D sets to customers will require the purchase of D sets from a wholesaler. One alternative would be to place an order for all the sets at the beginning of the year. This approach would minimize the time and cost involved in reordering but would require a large initial outlay (resulting in lost interest earnings) and also a considerable amount of storage space. At the other extreme, the manager could place daily orders for $D/365$ sets. The result would be a low interest expense and little need for storage space, but a substantial expense associated with making the orders. Let the size of each order be X. What value of X will minimize the firm's inventory costs?

Suppose that the manager places orders such that new sets arrive immediately after the last set in the store is sold. Hence just before the shipment the firm's inventory will be zero, and just after it will be X sets. Because sales are assumed to be distributed evenly over time, the firm's average inventory over a year's period will be $X/2$. Now let $\$k$ be the interest and storage costs of holding one set in inventory for one year. Thus the total cost of inventories, TC_I, will be the average number of units in inventory times the annual cost per unit. That is,

$$TC_I = k\left(\frac{X}{2}\right)$$

If D sets are sold during the year and if each order is for X units, the manager of the store will have to place a total of D/X orders. But, as mentioned, there are costs associated with making an order. Part of this cost depends on the number of sets shipped. Let the cost of each set be b. Thus, if X sets are ordered, this variable cost of an order will total bX. There is also a fixed cost related to making an order. Part of this cost is the time spent by the store's manager in making the order. The other component is the expense to the supplier (passed on to the purchaser) of maintaining records and billing. These costs are incurred with each order and do not vary with the number of sets ordered. Let the fixed cost of each order be a. Thus the cost of each order will be $(a + bX)$. The total cost of orders is the number of orders times the cost per order, or

$$TC_O = \frac{D}{X}(a + bX) = \frac{aD}{X} + bD$$

Efficient production requires that the sum of inventory and ordering costs be minimized. Formally stated, the problem is to select an order size, X, such that

$$TC = TC_I + TC_O = \frac{kX}{2} + \frac{aD}{X} + bD$$

is minimized. Note that a large order size increases the inventory cost $(kX/2)$ but decreases the ordering cost $(aD/X + bD)$. The cost-minimizing value of X is where the increase in inventory costs associated with increasing the size of each shipment by 1 unit is equal to the decrease in ordering costs of shipments that are 1 unit larger (because of the reduced frequency of orders). That is, the minimum is where $dTC/dX = 0$.

$$\frac{dTC}{dX} = \frac{k}{2} - \frac{aD}{X^2} = 0$$

Solving for the optimal order size, X^*, gives

$$X^* = \sqrt{\frac{2aD}{k}} \qquad\qquad (15\text{-}1)$$

and

$$\frac{X^*}{2} = \frac{\sqrt{\dfrac{2aD}{k}}}{2} \qquad\qquad (15\text{-}2)$$

as the cost-minimizing level of inventories.[1]

---

[1] The second derivative test can be used to assure that a minimum has been found. The second derivative is

$$\frac{d^2TC}{dX^2} = \frac{-2X(-aD)}{X^4} = \frac{2aD}{X^3}$$

which is positive for $X > 0$. Thus the solution represents the point of minimum total cost.

Equations (15-1) and (15-2) provide useful insights regarding orders and inventories. Note that $X^*/2$ does not increase proportionately with sales. Rather, the optimal average level of inventories increases with the square root of sales—a less than proportionate increase. For example, equation (15-1) implies that if sales double, the new optimal order size is about 1.4 times the previous order size. Also note that order size and optimal inventories are positively related to the fixed cost of ordering, but inversely related to the cost of holding inventories. Finally, it should be observed that the cost per unit ordered (i.e., b) does not appear in equations (15-1) and (15-2). Thus the optimal order size and inventory level do not depend on this variable cost.

CASE STUDY

JAPANESE "JUST IN TIME" INPUT SCHEDULING

In recent years, Japanese firms have been viewed as models of production efficiency. One technique used by some Japanese manufacturers is "just in time" input scheduling. The basic concept is that the firm keeps almost no supplies on hand but schedules materials and parts to arrive as close as possible to the time they are needed. The Japanese automobile industry is an example. In ordering, firms such as Nissan and Toyota purchase only enough parts and materials to keep their assembly lines running for two or three days. The low level of inventories is made possible in part by the location of suppliers. It is not uncommon for a large Japanese manufacturing facility to be surrounded by many smaller firms. The geographic proximity of these firms makes it possible for the buyer to obtain supplies on short notice. Also, Japanese auto manufacturers have become very adept at managing production facilities. By closely monitoring their operations, they are able to reduce inventories with little risk of running short.

KEY CONCEPTS

- High inventory levels increase interest and storage costs. However, low inventories mean more frequent orders, which usually involve additional costs.
- The optimal average level of inventories increases with the square root of sales and the fixed cost of ordering. It is inversely related to the square root of the cost of holding inventories.

Queues

Related to the inventory question is the problem of the optimal length of queues in the production process. As an example, consider a manufacturing facility in which workers obtain certain tools from a specific location. The tools are handed out by clerks as workers request them. They are returned to the clerks when they are no longer needed.

If there was a clerk for every production worker, there would never be any delays in getting tools. A clerk always would be available to provide assistance. But there is a cost involved in having more clerks. Hence managers have an incentive to reduce costs by cutting back on clerks. However, fewer clerks mean more time spent waiting for tools. Even with a small number of clerks, workers may sometimes be able to obtain a tool without waiting. But at other times there may be a considerable delay while other workers are being served. In general, the average waiting time for service is inversely related to the number of clerks. Clearly, there is a cost involved in having production workers waiting for tools. During the waiting time, nothing will be produced. The longer the wait, the greater the loss of production.

Figure 15-4 illustrates the tool distribution problem. The horizontal axis shows the average time spent in a queue waiting in line for a tool. The vertical axis measures the costs associated with the average wait time. The line *PP* indicates the value of lost production while workers are in the queue. It is upward sloping because longer wait times mean more lost production. For simplicity, *PP* is shown as linear. This implies that the value of the lost output (i.e., the cost of waiting) increases proportionately with the average waiting time.

The line *CC* measures the cost of reducing average waiting time. It is negatively sloped because cutting the average time in a queue requires that more clerks must be hired. The slope of *CC* represents the change in cost per unit change in the average waiting time. Note that the slope changes. When average time in a queue is long, it can be reduced with a relatively small addition to cost. But when the waiting time is short, further reductions are costly. This can easily be explained. Suppose that there is only one clerk. Hence any time two workers come for tools at the same time, one will be required to wait. It is not unlikely that this could happen. But by hiring another clerk, the simultaneous arrival of two workers could be accommodated without any delay. Thus the average waiting time could be reduced significantly. In contrast, suppose that there are fifty

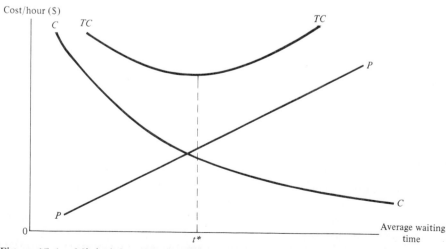

Figure 15-4.   *Minimizing Queuing Costs.*

clerks. In this circumstance, there would be no waiting unless fifty-one workers required tools at the same time. Clearly, this would be a very unlikely event. Hence hiring the fifty-first clerk would have very little impact on the average waiting time.

The total cost associated with the distribution of tools is the sum of the value of lost production and the cost of clerks. In Figure 15-4 total cost is shown as the line *TC*. Efficient production requires the minimization of total cost. Thus the optimal average time in queue is at the minimum of *TC*, which occurs at *t**. The decision rule for determining *t** is that average waiting time should be reduced until the marginal reduction in lost production equals the marginal cost of additional clerks. Although it may not be immediately obvious, this condition is met at *t** in Figure 15-4. As *t* is reduced, the value of increased production is equal to the slope of *PP*. Similarly, the additional cost of reducing wait time is measured by the slope of *CC*. At point *t**, the slope of *CC* equals the negative of the slope of *PP*

Note that the decision rule for optimal queues is very similar to that for optimal inventories. In both cases, the problem involves equating costs at the margin. For inventories, the optimal level is where the marginal cost of an additional unit of inventories equals the marginal cost caused by smaller, more frequent orders. For waiting times, the optimal average time is determined by equating marginal production savings and incremental clerking costs. The approach used in these two problems can be used in analyzing many other types of managerial decisions. Basically, the technique is to examine costs at the margin.

EXAMPLE

HOW MANY CLERKS TO HIRE?

Production workers obtain tools from clerks as described in the text. When the average waiting time in a queue is *t* hours, the value of lost production is given by

$$C_P = 1{,}000t$$

Average waiting time is given by $t = 0.1/Q$, where Q is the number of clerks. Expressing Q as a function of *t* gives

$$Q = \frac{0.1}{t}$$

Each clerk is paid $4 per hour. Hence the clerking cost associated with a given average wait time is

$$C_C = \frac{4(0.1)}{t} = \frac{0.4}{t}$$

How many clerks should be hired?

Solution

The marginal saving (which can be thought of as a cost reduction) from reducing average waiting time is $-dC_P/dT = -1{,}000$. The extra cost of clerks needed to reduce average waiting time is $dC_C/dt, = -0.4/t^2$. Hence the average time in queue should be reduced until

$$-1{,}000 = \frac{-0.4}{t^2}$$

Solving for the optimal average waiting time, t^*, gives

$$t^* = \sqrt{\frac{0.4}{1000}} = 0.02 \text{ hour}$$

which implies that the optimal number of clerks, Q^*, is

$$Q^* = \frac{0.1}{t^*} = \frac{0.1}{0.02} = 5$$

In general, the optimal number of clerks decreases as wages increase and increases as the value of lost production increases. But as with the inventory problem, the increases are not proportionate.

Replacement of Equipment

Periodically, managers are faced with decisions regarding the replacement of equipment. For example, a production facility may be using machines that still function but require expensive maintenance or that are inefficient compared to more modern equipment. How should managers decide when to replace the existing equipment?

With existing equipment, only operating costs are relevant for decision making. Consider an electric utility with generators that have been in service for many years. In this case, the total cost of generating electricity is the cost of fuel plus operation and maintenance expenses. In contrast, a decision to purchase new equipment involves both a purchase and an operating cost. Suppose that new generators become available that use fuel more efficiently and also have lower operation and maintenance expenses than the generators currently in use. By using the new equipment, the firm could reduce the variable costs of electricity generation. But there would be a substantial cost associated with the purchase of the generators. To make the new machines profitable, the savings in operating costs would have to more than offset the purchase price.

Assume that in deciding whether to purchase new generators, the utility's managers make their decision based on costs over the next T years. Also assume that there is no inflation and that the generating equipment will be used to produce Q kilowatt-hours of electricity each year. The operating cost per kilowatt-hour with the existing equipment is estimated to be OC_E and the operating cost using the new equipment is projected to be OC_N. Because the new generators are more efficient, $OC_E > OC_N$. However, in calculating the saving in operating cost, the time value of money must be considered. As discussed in Chapter 2, a dollar saved in ten years is less valuable than a dollar saved today. Thus the present value of the operating cost saving must be computed.

For the existing equipment, the present value of operating costs ($PVOC_E$) is given by

$$PVOC_E = Q \cdot \sum_{t=1}^{T} \left[\frac{OC_E}{(1 + r)^t} \right]$$

where r is the discount rate. The present value of operating costs for the new generating equipment ($PVOC_N$) is given by

$$PVOC_N = Q \cdot \sum_{t=1}^{T} \left[\frac{OC_N}{(1 + r)^t} \right]$$

Hence the present value of the operating cost saving ($PVOC_S$) is

$$PVOC_S = Q(OC_E - OC_N) \sum_{t=1}^{T} \frac{1}{(1 + r)^t} \tag{15-3}$$

Let the initial or purchase cost of the new generating equipment be PC. The replacement decision should be based on a comparison of the purchase cost versus the cost saving. If $PC < PVOC_S$, the firm should buy the new equipment. Otherwise, it should continue to use the old generators.

Clearly, this analysis of replacement economics has been simplified. For example, as the existing equipment becomes older, its operation and maintenance cost would probably increase. Also, in an inflationary environment the present value of the operating cost saving would become greater as fuel costs increased. Still, the basic approach used is valid. In deciding whether to purchase new equipment, managers should compare the present value of operating cost savings with the initial expenditure required to obtain the new equipment.

KEY CONCEPTS

- Optimal average waiting in queues is determined by equating the marginal cost of waiting and the marginal cost of reducing the wait time.
- Existing equipment should be replaced if the present value of operating cost savings associated with use of the new equipment exceeds the initial cost of that equipment.

Summary

Conditions of demand, cost, or competition may prevent a firm from earning even a normal profit. In the short run, the profit-maximizing firm should shut down operations if price drops below average variable cost. However, if price is less than average total cost but greater than average variable cost, the firm will lose less money by producing because a contribution can be made to its fixed costs. In the long run all costs are variable. Thus the firm should stop producing if prices decline below average cost.

In determining the composition of output, the profit-maximizing multiproduct firm should equate the marginal rate of transformation between goods to their price ratio. Once the optimal mix has been selected, the rate of input use is determined by a comparison of profits at different rates of input use.

Profit maximization dictates that the cost of producing the chosen rate of output be minimized. For a firm manufacturing a good in several different plants, this requires that production be allocated such that the cost of producing an additional unit of output is the same in all plants.

In determining optimal inventory levels, interest and storage costs must be compared to costs associated with making more frequent orders. A simple model suggests that inventories increase with the square root of demand and the fixed cost of ordering and decrease with the square root of interest and storage costs. The analysis of queue lengths is similar to that of inventories. The optimal waiting time occurs where the marginal cost of waiting is equal to the marginal cost of reducing the average waiting time.

An important decision facing managers is the replacement of existing equipment. Often, new equipment has a lower operating cost than older, existing equipment. Cost minimization dictates that the new equipment should be purchased if its initial cost is less than the present value of the savings associated with operating the new equipment rather than the older equipment.

Discussion Questions

15-1. The manager of a beauty salon is considering closing the shop because the market price is currently less than average variable cost. What other factors should be taken into account in making the decision?

15-2. The demand curve for a firm's product is downward sloping. How should the firm's manager decide whether to produce or shut down?

15-3. For the multiproduct firm, why is the product transformation curve bowed outward?

15-4. At present rates of output, the opportunity cost of producing an additional jacket is three pair of pants. The prices of pants and jackets are $20 and $40, respectively. Should the firm alter its product mix? Explain how and why.

15-5. Under what circumstances should a multiplant firm produce its product in only one plant?

15-6. Give an example of how transportation costs could affect the allocation of production between plants.

15-7. Consider an automobile dealership. In determining the optimal level of inventories, what factors might be considered in addition to those mentioned in the chapter?

15-8. For a risk-averse manager, how would uncertainty about demand affect the optimal level of inventories?

15-9. Why is the cost of reducing the average wait time not a linear function?

15-10. A grocery store is under construction. What factors should be considered in determining the number of checkout stands for the store?

15-11. How would the length of the planning horizon used by managers affect the decision to replace existing equipment with new equipment?

15-12. You are considering the purchase of a new car. If the decision is based strictly on economic considerations, how should you make the choice? What other factors might be relevant?

Problems

15-1. The market supply and demand curves for a product are given by

$$Q_S = 3,000 + 200P$$

and

$$Q_D = 13,500 - 500P$$

The industry supplying the product is perfectly competitive. An individual firm has fixed costs of $150 per period. Its marginal and average variable cost functions are

$$MC = 15 - 4Q + \frac{3Q^2}{10}$$

and

$$AVC = 15 - 2Q + \frac{Q^2}{10}$$

(a) What is the profit-maximizing rate of output for the firm?
(b) What is the maximum total profit for the firm?

15-2. Fashion Set Clothing can produce a maximum output of 1,000 skirts or 3,000 blouses per period. The opportunity cost of producing an additional skirt is constant and equal to three blouses. Skirts and blouses sell for the same price.

(a) What is the profit-maximizing product mix for the firm?
(b) How much would prices have to change to cause a change in the profit-maximizing mix? What would be the new product mix?

15-3. Pestkiller Manufacturing sells insecticides in a perfectly competitive industry and the market price is $2,000 per ton. The firm operates three plants with marginal costs as follows:

$$MC_1 = 1,000 + Q_1$$
$$MC_2 = 1,200 + 0.5Q_2$$
$$MC_3 = 800 + 1.2Q_3$$

where the output rates are in tons.

(a) How much output should be produced in each plant?
(b) How much output should be produced in each plant if the market price drops to $1,100 per ton?

15-4. Vista View Television expects to sell 1,000 television sets per year and sales are evenly distributed throughout the year. The fixed cost of ordering is $10 per order, the cost of shipping is $2 per set, and the inventory cost is $3 per set per year.

(a) What is the optimal order size and inventory level?
(b) If the cost of shipping increases to $3 per set, what will be the optimal order size and inventory level?

(c) If sales increase to 2,000 sets per year, what will be the optimal order size and inventory level?

(d) How does optimal order size and inventory level vary with the cost of holding inventories?

15-5. A homeowner is considering spending $1,000 to purchase a fuel-efficient furnace. In a typical year, the cost of heating using the home's existing furnace is $400. The new furnace is expected to cutting heating costs by 25 percent. The homeowner expects to remain in the house for five years and believes that the fuel-efficient furnace will increase the selling price of the house by $700 when she moves. The decision maker assumes that maintenance costs will be the same with either furnace. Based on a discount rate of 10 percent, should the new furnace be purchased?

Problems Requiring Calculus

15-6. Excluding its labor cost, an ice cream store makes a profit of $0.45 on each cone sold. If there was no waiting time to order, 10,000 cones could be sold each month. The probability that customers will leave if they have to wait in line to order is a function of the average waiting time. Specifically,

$$P = 0.2t$$

where P is the probability of leaving and t is average waiting time in minutes.

   Waiting time can be reduced by hiring more workers, but market conditions prevent the extra cost from being passed on to customers. The average waiting time is given by $t = 3/L$, where L is the average number of workers on duty. The monthly labor cost as a function of average number of workers on duty is $C = 1,200L$.

(a) From the perspective of the customer, what is the optimal average waiting time?

(b) From the firm's perspective, what is the optimal average waiting time?

(c) From the firm's perspective, on average, how many workers should be kept on duty?

15-7. A firm's total revenue equation is given by:

$$TR = 150Q - 2Q^2$$

Total fixed costs are $1,000 and total variable costs are given by:

$$TC = 30Q + 4Q^2$$

What is the profit maximizing rate of output for the firm? Should the firm shut down its operations? Explain.

References

Baumol, W. J. 1977. *Economic Theory and Operations Analysis.* Englewood Cliffs, N.J.: Prentice-Hall, Chap. 1.

Hillier, F. S., and Leiberman, G. J. 1980. *Introduction to Operations Research.* San Francisco: Holden-Day.

Kohler, H. 1982. *Intermediate Microeconomics.* Glenview, Ill.: Scott, Foresman, Chap 6.

Morse, P. M. 1958. *Queues, Inventories, and Maintenance.* New York: Wiley.

Investment Decisions

16

Preview

Most of the principles of managerial economics covered to this point have focused on short-run decisions. For example, determining the profit-maximizing price and output rate and deciding the optimal amount of labor to employ are important short-run decisions. Of at least equal importance are decisions about the nature of the firm in the long run. What new items should be added to or eliminated from the product line? Should old capital equipment be replaced? Should a competitor be acquired to broaden the product line and add retail outlets?

Decisions such as these are absolutely crucial to the long-run profitability of the firm. In order to maximize the value of the firm the assets of the firm must be continually deployed and redeployed to capture new profit opportunities. For example, the entrance of AT&T into the microcomputer business and Sears into the brokerage/financial services market represented a significant redeployment of part of the asset base of those firms.

In this chapter the firm's long-run decisions are considered. Two classes of investment decisions are discussed: capital budgeting, and mergers and acquisitions. In a sense, mergers and acquisitions could be considered a special case of capital budgeting, but there are special considerations that suggest that they be discussed separately.

Capital Budgeting

Capital projects are those that are expected to generate returns for more than one year. Capital budgeting refers to the process of planning capital projects, raising funds, and efficiently allocating resources to those capital projects. Examples of capital projects include new factories, machines, automobiles and trucks, and computers. Outlays for research and development and advertising programs are also capital expenditures if the returns on those projects will flow for more than one year.

It is useful to categorize capital projects in the following way:

1. *Cost reduction:* investments in training, machinery, or other capital assets that reduce the cost of producing output.
2. *Output expansion:* investments that accommodate increased output in response to actual or expected increases in demand.[1]
3. *Expansion into new products and/or markets:* expenditures for the develop-

---

[1] The same investments may result in both output expansion and cost reduction simultaneously. This certainly would be true if there are increasing returns to scale in production. In that case, an increase in output due to a capital expenditure necessarily would reduce the average cost of output.

ment and production of new products and/or the development of new markets by adding sales staff or by opening new outlets.

4. *Government regulation:* expenditures made to meet government safety and environmental rules.

Capital projects typically are very costly. Indeed, a firm often must seek external financing to implement a capital spending program. Furthermore, most capital spending projects are not easily reversed. For example, once a new manufacturing plant is built, it may have no other use than the one intended. Thus it would be difficult to sell if a change in market conditions rendered it unnecessary. For these reasons, capital planning decisions may determine the course for the firm for many years to come. A poor pricing decision or incorrect estimate for one production run can usually be rectified quickly. This is not the case for a major capital project. If capital spending decisions are poorly made, the firm's existence may be threatened.

Because of its long-run importance, the capital budgeting process is usually reviewed continually by the top management of a firm. Furthermore, capital budgeting requires information on sales, costs, advertising, and budgets, and therefore generally involves all areas of management.

General Approach to Capital Budgeting

In this section a summary approach to the capital budgeting process is outlined. Although this discussion is quite straightforward, it does gloss over some rather formidable problems in order to focus on the key elements. For example, to state that one investment has a rate of return of 14 percent is clear enough but fails to reveal the myriad of complications involved in making the sales, profit, and cost forecasts necessary to estimate that rate of return.

The principle underlying capital budgeting decisions is that expenditures are made until the marginal return on the last dollar invested equals the marginal cost of capital.[2] Suppose that management has identified and evaluated each of the capital expenditure items shown in Table 16-1. The projects are listed in decreasing order of rate of return. The schedule can be used to determine the quantity of capital demanded by the firm depending on the cost of capital. Thus these data represent the firm's demand for capital function which is shown in Figure 16-1.

Using the marginal revenue/marginal cost principle, the firm will invest as long as the return on an investment is equal to or greater than the cost of capital. For example, if the cost of capital is 20 percent, none of the investment projects would be implemented because the cost of capital (20 percent) exceeds the highest return (18 percent) available on a capital project. Thus if the firm borrowed $4.5 million at 20 percent interest to implement the first capital project, the annual interest of $900,000 would exceed the average annual return ($810,000)

---

[2] The cost of capital is the rate that must be paid on money raised externally by the firm (e.g., by borrowing or selling stock) or the opportunity cost (i.e., the foregone return) on funds the business has that it would have invested elsewhere.

Table 16-1. List of Hypothetical Capital Expenditures

Project Description	Type of Capital Expenditure	Cost (millions)	Rate of Return (%)
1. Replacement of obsolete equipment on an assembly line	Cost reduction	$4.5	18
2. Opening of three new stores on East Coast	Market expansion	6.2	17
3. Formal training programs for all production employees	Cost reduction	1.5	14
4. Replacement of outdated heating and air-conditioning system	Cost reduction	3.9	12
5. New production facility	Output expansion	5.1	10

on the project, and profit would be reduced. Clearly, the value of the firm would be reduced if the firm made a capital investment that returned less than the cost of capital. However, if the cost of capital was 15 percent, both projects 1 and 2 would be implemented because their rates of return are 18 and 17 percent, respectively. In this case, the firm would spend $10.7 million on these two capital items. If the cost of capital was lower, the firm would make even more capital outlays.

The marginal cost of capital function (MCC in Figure 16-1) shows the cost to the firm of obtaining various amounts of capital. Determining the firm's cost of capital is discussed later in the chapter. At this point the cost is shown as a gradually rising function to reflect the fact that the firm probably would be required to pay a higher cost in order to obtain increasing amounts of capital. Figure 16-1 indicates that the firm would make investments 1, 2, and 3 because the rate of return exceeds the cost of capital for these projects. Note that the rate of return on investment 3 is 14 percent, and the rate of return on investment 4 is 12 percent. However, because the firm's cost of capital for more than $12.2 million is more than 12 percent, investment 3 is made but 4 is not.

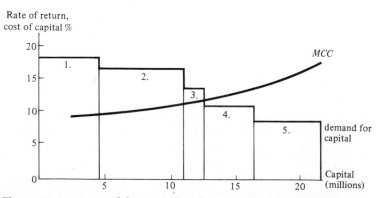

Figure 16-1.   *Demand for Capital and Cost of Capital Functions.*

KEY CONCEPTS

- Capital budgeting refers to the process of planning capital projects, raising funds, and efficiently allocating those funds to capital projects.
- Capital expenditures are made in order to reduce cost, increase output, expand into new products or markets, and/or meet government regulations.
- In general, capital expenditures are made until the rate of return on the last dollar invested equals the marginal cost of capital.

The Capital Budgeting Process

In most firms, capital budgeting is a continuous process, with proposals being made regularly in all areas of the organization. Typically, each level of the organization has authority to make capital expenditures up to some dollar limit. Proposals in excess of that limit must be screened and approved by higher levels of management to ensure that the projects are consistent with the overall plan for the firm. For example, the production line foreman may have authority to make capital expenditure decisions up to a level of $25,000. Proposals above that amount must be approved by the plant manager, who may be able to authorize expenditures up to $250,000 but must have approval from the division vice-president for projects that cost more than that amount. Thus the larger the dollar cost of the proposal, the more screening steps it must go through.

The first step in this evaluation is to determine the cost of the project. Next, the net cash flows associated with that capital project are estimated. Finally, evaluation techniques are used to compare cash inflows to the cost of the project. In the following example, it is assumed the cost of the project has been determined.

Project the Cash Flows.   Suppose that a firm is considering the addition of a new product line. It is estimated that the cost of new production machinery, reorganization of the production line, and additional working capital for inventory and accounts receivable will require an initial investment of $20 million. The breakdown of these costs is as follows:

Machinery	$15,000,000
Reorganization	2,000,000
Working capital	3,000,000
Total	$20,000,000

Sales revenues from this product are projected to be $12 million the first year, but because the new product is a substitute for one of the firm's existing products, the incremental sales revenue will be only $10 million. That is, the new product will add $12 million to sales, but sales of an existing product will fall by $2 million, yielding a net or incremental sales increase of $10 million. The marketing staff estimates that the life of the product is only five years but during that time incremental sales revenue will increase by 10 percent each year.

The production and engineering departments of the firm have developed the following incremental production cost estimates. Variable costs will be 40 percent of revenue and additional fixed costs will be $100,000 per year. The finance department reports that for depreciation purposes, the new machinery has a five-year life and that the straight-line depreciation method will be used. That is, the annual depreciation charge against income is one-fifth of the initial cost of the machinery, or $3 million per year:

$$\text{annual depreciation charge} = \frac{\text{cost}}{\text{years}} = \frac{\$15,000,000}{5} = \$3,000,000$$

The financial vice-president also indicates that the marginal income tax rate for the firm is expected to be 40 percent. Note that depreciation is a noncash expense that is included as an expense in computing income taxes but is then added back in to determine the net cash flow. The salvage value of the equipment at the end of the five years is estimated to be $4 million. Also, at the end of the five-year life of this project, the $3 million that was needed for additional working capital is recovered.

The detailed cash flow projection for each year is shown in Table 16-2. The problem now is to compare those cash flows to the initial $20 million investment that is required. As the cash flows extend over several years, time-value-of-money principles must be used. The two most commonly used evaluation tests are the net present value and internal rate of return. A capital project is said to be profitable if it passes the evaluation test used by management.

Net Present Value.   As outlined in Chapter 2, the net present value (*NPV*) method of evaluation consists of comparing the present value of all net cash flows (appropriately discounted using the firm's cost of capital as the interest

Table 16-2. Projected Incremental Cash Flow for Proposed Capital Investment

	Year				
	1	2	3	4	5
Sales	$10,000,000	$11,000,000	$12,100,000	$13,310,000	$14,641,000
Less: Variable costs	4,000,000	4,400,000	4,840,000	5,324,000	5,856,400
Fixed costs	100,000	100,000	100,000	100,000	100,000
Depreciation	3,000,000	3,000,000	3,000,000	3,000,000	3,000,000
Profit before tax	$ 2,900,000	$ 3,500,000	$ 4,160,000	$ 4,886,000	$ 5,684,600
Less: Income tax	1,160,000	1,400,000	1,664,000	1,954,400	2,273,840
Profit after tax	$ 1,740,000	$ 2,100,000	$ 2,496,000	$ 2,931,600	$ 3,410,760
Plus: Depreciation	3,000,000	3,000,000	3,000,000	3,000,000	3,000,000
Net cash flow	$ 4,740,000	$ 5,100,000	$ 5,496,000	$ 5,931,600	$ 6,410,760

Plus: Salvage value of machinery $4,000,000
     Recapture of working capital 3,000,000
Net cash flow (year 5) $13,410,760

rate) to the initial investment cost. If the present value of the cash flows exceeds the cost, the proposal meets the evaluation criterion; that is, the value of the firm will be increased by making the investment. Equivalently, the rate of return on the capital expenditure exceeds the firm's cost of capital, and thus future profits will be higher if the investment is made. Using the *NPV* method, the rate of return on the investment is not determined explicitly. Therefore, it is referred to as an *implicit rate of return*. If the net present value is negative, the implicit return is less than the cost of capital.

Define A_t as net cash flow in year t, r as the firm's cost of capital, n as the life of the project, and C as the initial cost. Formally, the *NPV* rule is that if

$$NPV = \sum_{t=1}^{n} \left[\frac{A_t}{(1 + r)^t} \right] - C > 0 \qquad (16\text{-}1)$$

the capital expenditure should be made.

For the example shown in Table 16-2, suppose that the firm's cost of capital is 12 percent. The annual net cash flows are given in Table 16-2. Note that at the end of the project's life (i.e., five years), the cash inflow from the salvage value of the machinery and the recapture of dollars tied up in inventory and accounts receivable is included. Based on a cost of $20,000,000, the *NPV* calculation would be

$$NPV = \left[\frac{4{,}740{,}000}{1.12} + \frac{5{,}100{,}000}{(1.12)^2} + \frac{5{,}496{,}000}{(1.12)^3} + \frac{5{,}931{,}600}{(1.12)^4} + \frac{13{,}410{,}760}{(1.12)^5} \right]$$
$$- 20{,}000{,}000$$
$$= 23{,}589{,}040 - 20{,}000{,}000 = 3{,}589{,}040$$

As the *NPV* > 0, the proposal passes the test. This means that the return on the new product line exceeds the firm's cost of capital, and the investment should be made because it will increase the value of the firm.

Internal Rate of Return.   The implicit rate of return on a capital expenditure can be measured using the internal rate of return (IRR) evaluation method. The internal rate of return is that discount rate that equates the present value of the cash flows with the initial investment cost. Conceptually, the *IRR* is determined by setting

$$\sum_{t=1}^{n} \left(\frac{A_t}{(1 + r^*)^t} \right) = C \qquad (16\text{-}2)$$

and solving this equation for r^*, the internal rate of return. If r^* is greater than the cost of capital, the investment should be made. That is, profits, and therefore the value of the firm, will be increased by making this investment because the firm is using capital that costs, say, 12 percent to earn a return greater than 12 percent.

However, solving equation (16-2) for r^* by hand is not a trivial problem when n is greater than 1. Fortunately, financial calculators and easily used computer programs are available that can solve IRR problems very quickly. In their absence, trial-and-error methods can also be used. To illustrate the trial-and-error approach, arbitrarily select a discount rate and evaluate the present value of the cash flows. If the present value is higher than the cost, increase the discount rate and repeat the process. If the present value is lower than the cost, reduce the discount rate. By gradually adjusting the discount rate, this iterative process will ultimately lead to the *IRR*.[3]

Again using the data from Table 16-2, the *IRR* method would require setting up the equation

$$\frac{4,740,000}{1 + r^*} + \frac{5,100,000}{(1 + r^*)^2} + \frac{5,496,000}{(1 + r^*)^3} + \frac{5,931,600}{(1 + r^*)^4} + \frac{13,410,760}{(1 + r^*)^5} = \$20,000,000$$

and solving for r^*, which yields $r^* = 0.179$, or 17.9 percent. Because this rate exceeds the cost of capital (12 percent), the investment should be made.

Comparison of NPV and IRR Evaluation Methods.   When evaluating a single project, the *IRR* and *NPV* methods always will yield consistent results. That is, if the net present value is positive, the internal rate of return will be greater than the firm's cost of capital, and vice versa. This is because for net present value to be positive, the implicit rate of return on the project must be greater than the discount rate. Therefore, for any single project, the two approaches will always give the same accept/reject signal.

However, in the case of two mutually exclusive projects (i.e., where only one of the investments will be made), the two evaluation techniques can result in contradictory signals about which investment will add more to the value of the firm. Consider the cash flow and evaluation criteria values for investments *A* and *B* in Table 16-3. Project *A* has a lower net present value but a higher internal rate of return. The reason for this inconsistency is that there is a difference in the implied reinvestment rate for the annual cash flows each year. That is, the cash returns that flow from the capital project each year are reinvested, but the rate earned on those reinvested dollars is not known. Therefore, an assumed rate must be used. In the *NPV* approach, it is implicitly and conservatively assumed that the cash flows are reinvested at an interest rate equal to the firm's cost of capital. Under the *IRR* method, the implicit reinvestment rate is the computed rate of return. This is a somewhat optimistic assumption because the rate of return on the firm's investment opportunities in future years may not be as high as the investment being considered. Because the reinvestment rate on other investments will usually be closer to the firm's cost of capital, the *NPV* method is generally considered to be the better evaluation technique.

---

[3] There are special cases where it is possible that two or more discount rates will equate the present value of the cash flows to the cost. That is, multiple values of the internal rate of return are obtained. This can occur only for unusual situations where cash flows vary from positive to negative from one period to another. Such cases are so special as not to be of concern in this text. The interested student is referred to Van Horne (1983), or Brigham, (1982).

Table 16-3. Cost, Cash Flow, and Evaluation Criteria Data for Two Hypothetical Capital Investments

	Project *A*	Project *B*
Initial cost	$1,000	$1,000
Net cash flows (year)		
1	450	−300
2	450	0
3	450	600
4	450	600
5	450	2,000
Evaluation criteria		
NPV (12% discount rate)	622	675
IRR	34.9	24.2

Capital Rationing and the Profitability Ratio

To this point it has been assumed that the firm would make all capital expenditures which meet the criteria that *NPV* > 0 or that *IRR* > cost of capital. However, for many firms, the total amount of money the firm has and that can be obtained externally is less than the total that would be spent if all projects were undertaken. In this case, choices must be made among those projects that meet the evaluation criteria. That is, available capital funds must be rationed among these competing projects.

There are several reasons why a business may be subject to capital rationing. First, the sheer number of capital proposals, if they all were implemented, may exceed management's ability to develop and manage them. Clearly, there is a limit to the scope and number of projects that can be effectively monitored at any given time. Second, internal funds are limited and management may prefer not to take the risk associated with additional borrowing and/or the possible reduction in control associated with the sale of additional shares of common stock. Finally, an operating unit of a larger firm may arbitrarily be assigned a maximum capital expenditure budget for the year.

Strict adherence to the *NPV* evaluation approach can lead to nonoptimal decisions if capital is rationed. Suppose that the firm's capital budget was limited to $20,000 and it was considering the three investments shown in Table 16-4. Further, assume that the firm's policy is to rank projects by their *NPV* and then implement projects beginning at the top of the list and continuing down until the available funds are exhausted. This approach would be suboptimal because only project *A* would be selected, thus adding $1,616 to the value of the firm. But if projects *B* and *C* were selected instead of *A*, the sum of the net present values would be $2,578. That is, the combination of investments *B* and *C* would add more to profit than would investment *A*. The problem here is that the *NPV* approach does not relate net present value to the initial cost of the project. In contrast, the *IRR* method does that implicitly. Thus, when capital rationing applies, the internal rate of return method may be the preferred approach to capital project evaluation.

Table 16-4. *NPV, IRR*, and Profitability Ratio Data on Three Capital Expenditure Projects

	Project *A*	Project *B*	Project *C*
Investment	$20,000	$10,000	$10,000
	Net cash flows (year)		
Period 1	9,000	4,700	4,700
Period 2	9,000	4,700	4,700
Period 3	9,000	4,700	4,700
NPV (12% discount rate)	1,616	1,289	1,289
IRR	16.6%	19.4%	19.4%
Profitability ratio (R_p)	1.081	1.129	1.129

By using the *IRR* method, both projects *B* and *C* would be ranked ahead of *A*. Clearly, this is a case where the *IRR* method is preferable. However, a method of adjusting the net present value also can be used. This adjustment involves constructing a profitability ratio (R_p) computed as one plus the present value of all future cash flows divided by the initial cost of the project; that is,

$$R_p = \frac{\text{cost} + NPV}{\text{cost}} \text{ or } R_p = 1 + \frac{NPV}{\text{cost}} \qquad (16\text{-}3)$$

If the firm ranked the three projects in Table 16-4 by the profitability measure (as shown in Table 16-4), projects *B* and *C* would rank ahead of *A* and would be adopted. Thus the profitability ratio provides a way to rank efficient projects to ensure that those with the highest return relative to their cost are implemented before those with lower relative rates of return.

Another approach is to add together the net present values of each combination of projects that could be "purchased" with the available budget. The combination that yielded the highest sum of the *NPV*'s would be selected. The only shortcoming of this approach is that it may be a very cumbersome process if there are many proposed investments. However, with the three projects outlined in Table 16-4, there are only two combinations (project *A* or projects *B* and *C*) that can be "purchased" for $20,000, and therefore the task is trivial.

Clearly, the manager must take a flexible approach to the capital budgeting process. Rather than use any one criterion or decision approach, rational executives should consider their investment options in light of all the relevant criteria (i.e., *NPV, IRR*, and profitability ratio). Further, it must be emphasized that the evaluation criteria are only as good as the underlying data. If the sales or cost estimates are not accurate, the computed values of the *IRR* or *NPV* will be of little value.

KEY CONCEPTS

- Using the net present value evaluation technique, if the present value of all future cash flows (discounted by the firm's cost of capital) exceeds the initial cost of the project, the investment should be made.

- The internal rate of return is that discount rate that equates the present value of all future net cash flows to the cost of an investment. If the internal rate of return on an investment exceeds the cost of capital, the investment will increase profits.
- For independent projects, the *NPV* and *IRR* techniques always give consistent accept/reject signals. However, when comparing two mutually exclusive projects, the relative rankings of the projects can be different using the two methods.
- The profitability ratio, computed as one plus the net present value divided by initial cost, can be used to rank alternative investments when the firm is subject to capital rationing.

The Cost of Capital

In general, the cost of capital is the return required by investors in the debt and equity securities of the firm. Basically, there are three sources of funds to the firm for capital spending: retained earnings, debt, and equity. In the following, the cost of debt financing and the cost of equity financing through the sale of common stock are considered. The cost of using retained earnings for capital spending is approximately the same as the cost of common stock, so the cost of retained earnings is not discussed explicitly.[4]

Cost of Capital: Debt. There is little controversy about the cost of capital raised by borrowing from banks or by selling bonds. That cost is the net or after-tax interest rate paid on that debt. Because interest, unlike dividends on stock, is deductible from income when computing income taxes, it is the after-tax cost that is important. For a given interest rate (i) and marginal tax rate (t), the after-tax cost of debt (r_d) is given by

$$r_d = i(1 - t) \qquad (16\text{-}4)$$

For example, if the firm borrows at a 15 percent interest rate and faces a 40 percent marginal tax rate, its after-tax cost of debt capital is

$$r_d = 15(1 - 0.40) = 9\%$$

Two important considerations should be mentioned. First, if the firm is not earning profits, the pretax and after-tax interest rates will be the same because the marginal tax rate is zero. Second, the concern is with the marginal cost of capital and not the average cost of capital for the firm. For example, that the average cost of debt in the firm's balance sheet is 9 percent is irrelevant. The only important consideration is the cost of raising new capital. This is because the investment decision requires comparing the rate of return on new projects (i.e., the marginal return) with the cost of acquiring additional capital (i.e., the marginal cost of capital).

---

[4] A naive manager might view the cost of retained earnings as being zero. This clearly is not the case, if for no other reason than that there is a significant opportunity cost to the owners of the business, who could use those funds for personal consumption or for investment in some other business.

Cost of Equity Capital.   In general, determining the cost of equity capital from retained earnings or sale of common stock[5] is more complicated and more controversial than determining the cost of debt. In the following, three approaches to estimating this cost are presented. However, no method is clearly the best, and the manager is well advised to think in terms of all three approaches when making cost-of-capital calculations. Also, note that dividends are not deductible from income when computing income taxes, so the firm's tax rate does not play a role in determining the cost of equity capital.

Method I: The Risk-Free Rate Plus Risk Premium.   Generally, investment in common stock is considered to be riskier than investment in bonds. The firm has a contractual obligation to make interest and principal payments to bondholders, and such payments must be made before dividends can be paid to stockholders. If profits rise and fall, it is likely that dividends will also fluctuate. However, except in the case of severe financial problems, bondholders will be paid. Thus it is thought that investors will demand a return on equity (r_e) composed of a risk-free return (r_f), usually considered to be the rate of return on long-term government bonds, plus a premium for accepting additional risk. This premium reflects the two sources of risk. First, there is the risk associated with investing in the securities of a private company as opposed to buying federal government securities. Second, there is the additional risk associated with buying stock rather than bonds of a business. The premiums associated with the two types of risk are labeled p_1 and p_2. Thus the cost of equity capital is

$$r_e = r_f + p_1 + p_2$$

One way to measure the first type of risk (p_1) is to use the difference between the rate of interest on the firm's bonds (r_d) and the rate of return on government bonds (r_f). This difference should increase as risk increases. A rule of thumb is used to approximate the risk of buying the common stock of a firm rather than bonds. It is assumed that the return on a firm's common stock should be about 3 to 5 percentage points greater than on its debt. Using the midpoint of this range (i.e., 4 percent) as an estimate of p_2, the total risk premium (p) would be calculated as

$$p = p_1 + p_2$$

or

$$p = (r_d - r_f) + 4$$

For example, suppose that the risk-free rate is 10 percent and the firm's bonds are yielding 12 percent. Therefore, the total risk premium would be 6 percentage points, that is,

$$p = (0.12 - 0.10) + 0.04 = 0.06$$

---

[5] Because there are costs associated with issuing stock, that alternative is somewhat more costly than is the use of retained earnings. That difference will not be considered to be significant here.

and therefore the firm's cost of equity capital would be

$$r_e = r_f + p = 0.10 + 0.06 = 0.16$$

or 16 percent.

Method II: Discounted Cash Flow.   Method I includes risk but fails to consider the possibility of growth in dividends and the value of common shares over time. An alternative approach is the discounted cash flow method. Theoretically, the value of a share of stock is the present value of all future dividends using the investor's required rate of return (r_e) as the discount rate. If the current dividend per share (D_0) is expected to be constant, the value (P) of a share will be

$$P = \sum_{t=1}^{\infty} \frac{D_0}{(1 + r_e)^t} \tag{16-5}$$

This equation can be reduced to

$$P = \frac{D_0}{r_e}$$

However, if the dividend is expected to increase over time at an annual rate of g, it can be shown that the price per share will be given by

$$P = \frac{D_0}{r_e - g} \tag{16-6}$$

Solving equation (16-6) for r_e yields an equation for the cost of equity capital:

$$r_e = \frac{D_0}{P} + g \tag{16-7}$$

That is, the return required by the investor is equal to the current dividend yield on the common stock (D_0/P) plus an expected growth rate for dividend payments. The estimate of that growth rate might be the historic rate of growth for the firm or, perhaps, the consensus growth rate being used by financial analysts who study the firm.[6]

For example, suppose that a firm is paying a dividend of $2 per share on common stock that sells for $20 per share and that there is agreement among financial analysts that the growth rate of dividends of this firm will be 6 percent per year. Using this approach, the firm's cost of equity capital is estimated to be 16 percent. That is,

$$r_e = \frac{2}{20} + 0.06 = 0.16 \quad \text{or} \quad 16\%$$

Obviously, variations in the price of the stock will change this cost. This is how the actions of investors influence the firm's cost of capital.

---

[6] Virtually every firm for which stock is traded in organized markets is followed by one or more security analysts in banks, brokerage companies, mutual funds, and other financial institutions. Their forecasts are readily available and managers usually make it a point to keep track of what these analysts are predicting for their firm. For some large firms, there are literally hundreds of analysts who follow each company.

Method III: Capital Asset Pricing model (CAPM).   The capital asset pricing model, widely used in the world of quantitative finance, emphasizes not only the risk differential between common stock and government bonds but also the risk differential among stocks. The risk differential between stocks and government bonds is estimated by $(r_m - r_f)$, where r_m is the return on the average common stock and r_f is the government bond rate.

Relative risk among stocks is measured using the beta coefficient, β, as a risk index. The beta coefficient is the ratio of variability in return on a given stock to variability in return for all stocks. Return on a stock for a period of time, typically one year, is the dividend plus the change in the value of the stock during the period. Using σ_s as a measure of the variability in returns for one stock over a number of periods and σ_m as the variability in returns for a large number of stocks, the beta coefficient is determined by estimating the parameters of the following regression equation:

$$\sigma_s = a + \beta\sigma_m$$

The estimated value of β is the beta coefficient.

A stock with average risk will have a beta value of 1.0, meaning that the returns on that stock vary in proportion to returns on all stocks. A higher-risk stock might have a beta of 2.0, meaning that the variation in returns on that stock is twice that of the average stock. For example, if $\beta = 2$, when the returns on an average stock increase 10 percent, the returns on this risky stock increase by 20 percent. Conversely, a beta of 0.5 would be associated with a low-risk stock where returns varied only one-half as much as for the average stock.

Using the capital asset pricing model, then, the cost of equity capital is the risk-free rate (r_f) plus a weighted risk component, that is,

$$r_e = r_f + \beta(r_m - r_f) \tag{16-8}$$

In this model, the overall risk premium for common stock is measured by $(r_m - r_f)$ and the beta weight (β) then adjusts for the risk associated with the specific firm in question.

For example, suppose that $r_f = 0.10$, $r_m = 0.13$, and the company's stock has a β value of 1.2. The cost of equity capital would be

$$r_e = 0.10 + 1.2(0.13 - 0.10) = 0.136 \text{ or } 13.6 \text{ percent}$$

The Composite Cost of Capital.   Many firms attempt to maintain a constant or target capital structure. For example, management of a manufacturing business may prefer a capital structure that is 30 percent debt and 70 percent equity. In contrast, managers of an electric utility company may prefer a 60 percent debt and 40 percent equity structure. In either case, capital would be raised periodically both by incurring debt and by selling stock. The differences in capital structure reflect the preference for risk on the part of owners and managers and the nature of the business. A capital structure heavily weighted toward debt implies greater risk because of the greater interest and principal payments that are required. Public utilities tend to have a higher percentage of debt than most other firms because they have a monopoly position and the product they sell is a necessity. This means that the firm will have a reasonably stable and dependable flow of revenue and profit, and this offsets part of the high risk associated with a large proportion of debt in their capital structure.

A firm with a target capital structure may maintain two separate ledgers—a list of capital projects and a list of financing plans (borrowing, stock sales, etc.). A particular financing option, say selling bonds having a cost of 12 percent, is not tied to one capital project. Rather, the firm uses an overall or composite cost of capital as the evaluation criterion for each capital project.

This composite cost of capital (r_c) is a weighted average of the cost of debt (r_d) and equity (r_e) capital. The weights are the proportions of debt (w_d) and equity (w_e) in the firm's capital structure. That is,

$$r_c = w_d r_d + w_e r_e \qquad (16\text{-}9)$$

For example, suppose that a firm's target capitalization structure is 40 percent debt and 60 percent equity. Over the next twelve months it plans to raise $100 million by selling $40 million in bonds at a cost of 11 percent and issuing 1 million shares of stock at $60 per share at a cost of 14.5 percent. Thus the firm's weighted or composite cost of capital would be 13.1 percent. That is,

$$r_c = (0.40)(11) + (0.60)(14.5)$$
$$= 13.1$$

This rate of 13.1 percent is used to evaluate all the proposed capital expenditure requests to ensure that they are profitable.

KEY CONCEPTS

- The cost of capital is the return required by investors in the debt and equity securities of the firm.
- The cost of debt capital is the after-tax interest rate on the firm's bonds or borrowing.
- Three methods of determining the cost of equity capital are:
  1. The risk-free rate plus a risk premium.
  2. Discounted cash flow.
  3. The capital asset pricing model.
- The composite cost of capital is a weighted average of the cost of debt and equity where the weights are the proportions of debt and equity in the firm's capital structure.

CASE STUDY

MEASURING THE COST OF EQUITY CAPITAL

Having several ways to determine the cost of equity capital can lead to different cost estimates, depending on the method used. The differences can be significant and may make the difference in a decision to make or not make a capital expenditure. Also, a public utility such as a gas or electric company generally has to offer evidence on the cost of capital in hearings about the rates the companies may charge. Obviously, in such cases, the company may want to document a high cost of capital to justify higher rates. In contrast, the staff of the regulatory body, who are supposed to represent the interests of the consumer, may use lower estimates of the cost to keep the rates down.

Although many cases could be cited, a good example is a 1978 application for a rate increase by South Central Bell Telephone Company before the Tennessee Public Service Commission. A financial expert hired by the telephone company used the discounted cash flow method to estimate the cost of equity capital at 14 percent. A member of the commission staff used the same technique to estimate the cost at about 11 percent. The explanation for the discrepancy was that the two experts differed in their opinions about the growth rate of dividends.

Clearly, the choice of a growth rate was important. The difference between an 11 percent and a 14 percent cost of equity capital translated into $20 million in annual profits for the firm. In its decision, the commission opted for a rate of just over 11 percent.*

* *Public Utilities Reports*, 4th Series, Vol. 22, pp. 257–280.

Mergers

The game of picking up companies is open to everybody. All you have to do is have indefatigable drive, a desire to perpetuate yourself or your family in control of an industry, or an unabsorbed appetite for corporate power.

> Meshulam Riklis, who turned an
> initial investment of $25,000
> into the $750 million Rapid-
> American Corporation

Corporate growth can come about either internally or externally. Internal growth occurs when a firm establishes new production or distribution facilities using the evaluation methods developed in the preceding section. For example, a newly constructed plant for producing Cadillacs would represent internal expansion by General Motors. External growth takes place when firms acquire facilities of existing firms. Frequently, this is accomplished by merger. Merger is defined as the joining of two or more firms under single ownership. If General Motors were to merge with Ford, that action would represent external growth through merger.

Types of Mergers

Mergers typically are divided into three categories: horizontal, vertical, and conglomerate. *Horizontal mergers* involve firms that directly compete for sales of similar products or services. The hypothetical General Motors–Ford merger just

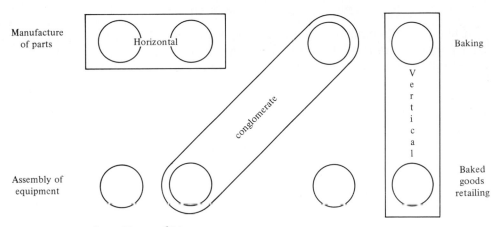

Figure 16-2. *Three Types of Mergers.*

mentioned would constitute a horizontal merger. *Vertical mergers* occur when firms that had been operating at different stages in the production and distribution of a product combine to form a single firm. Vertical mergers may consist of a firm acquiring a seller of its output, such as IBM purchasing a chain of computer stores that sell the firm's microcomputers. Often, this is referred to as "downstream" integration. Another type of vertical merger is the acquisition by a firm of a supplier of resources or components needed to make its product. An example would be if IBM purchased a manufacturer of computer chips or disk drives. Mergers with suppliers often are referred to as "upstream" integration. Finally, conglomerate mergers involve the joining of firms operating in unrelated product markets. An example would be the combination of Eastern Airlines and the Levi Strauss Corporation.

Figure 16-2 depicts the three basic categories of mergers. It shows two industries, construction equipment and bakery products. A horizontal merger is represented by the joining of two manufacturers of parts. The combination of a bakery and baked goods retailer would be a vertical merger. The merging of a firm that assembles equipment and a bakery would constitute a conglomerate merger.

KEY CONCEPTS

- Horizontal mergers involve firms competing for the sale of the same product or service.
- A vertical merger occurs when a firm acquires a seller of its product or a supplier of materials used to manufacture the product.
- Conglomerate mergers involve combinations of essentially unrelated firms.

CASE STUDY

THE POKER GAME FOR GULF OIL

In March 1984, Standard Oil of California (Socal) and Gulf Corporation signed an agreement proposing history's largest merger. The terms of the agreement were that Socal would pay $80 per share—a total of over $13 billion dollars for Gulf's stock. The result was a merger between the nation's ninth and tenth largest industrial corporations. Together, the two firms had 1983 assets of $45 billion and sales of nearly $60 billion.

The Socal-Gulf merger emerged as the product of a concerted effort by Gulf to avoid a hostile takeover by an investment group headed by T. Boone Pickens, Jr., the chairman of Mesa Petroleum. In late 1983, Pickens and his colleagues purchased 13 percent of Gulf's stock with the avowed purpose of restructuring the firm in order to increase profits. In response, Gulf's management convened a special shareholders' meeting to change corporate rules in order to make a takeover more difficult. About the same time, Gulf announced that it was considering the acquisition of Superior Oil Co. Although never completed, this merger would have increased Gulf's size and made a takeover less likely because of the higher cost.

In February 1984, the Pickens group announced that it would pay Gulf's stockholders $65 per share for 13.5 million shares of stock. If completed, this purchase would have raised the group's stock ownership to over 20 percent and might have enabled it to replace some of Gulf's directors at the firm's annual stockholder meeting in May.

Gulf's public reaction to the offer by the Pickens group was to label it as "unfair and inadequate." Privately, the company's management began to contact other firms that might be interested in acquiring Gulf. By March, the list of prospective suitors had been pared to three: Socal, Atlantic-Richfield, and an investment firm, Kohlberg, Kravis, Roberts and Co. Representatives of each of these firms were invited to come to Gulf's headquarters in Pittsburg and make a careful examination of the firm's records. Following this investigation, each firm was requested to submit a sealed offer for Gulf Oil.

Socal's bid of $80 per share was higher than Atlantic-Richfield's $72, but less than the $87.50 offered by Kohlberg, Kravis, Roberts, and Co. However, the Socal bid was accepted because the firm had access to the $13 billion necessary to complete the purchase, whereas the Kohlberg firm would have required several months to assemble its funds.

Lest one feel sorry for the unsuccessful effort of T. Boone Pickens and his associates, it should be noted that Socal's offer enabled them to earn a capital gain of $760 million on the Gulf stock that they owned.

Merger Incentives

Some acquisitions take place because managers embark on the creation of a vast empire over which they can preside. The experience of James Ling, former president of Ling-Temco-Vaught, is a case in point. In 1960, LTV ranked as the 335th largest firm in the United States on the basis of assets. After a flurry of acquisitions, the corporation had climbed to 22nd by 1968. Mr. Ling's merger efforts were well rewarded in the stock market. In 1963, the price of LTV common stock was $9 per share. In 1967 the price reached a high of $169.50 per share. Unfortunately, the bubble finally burst as cutbacks in defense spending after the Vietnam War and the prospect of legal actions against the firm caused the share price to plummet to about $7 in 1970.

Although ego and empire building sometimes play a role in merger activity, usually mergers take place because managers believe that the value of the combined firm is greater than that of its constituent parts. Among the possible sources of this synergy are the following.

Increased Market Power.   A merger between two competing firms can result in increased market power for the combined firm. In some cases, this increased market power stems from the elimination of an aggressive competitor. Consider an industry dominated by a few large firms. If one firm consistently reduces prices, the other firms may be forced to respond with price reductions of their own. The result of this price competition generally will be reduced profit levels. However, one firm may acquire the aggressive rival by merger. By eliminating the source of active competition, higher prices, and hence increased profit for all firms in the industry should result.

In other situations, a horizontal merger may increase market power by eliminating excess capacity in an industry. A case in point involves the tobacco industry at the turn of the century. In 1890, five cigarette manufacturers formed a trust to stabilize prices. In 1898, the trust expanded its activities into chewing tobacco by purchasing five other manufacturers. One year later, production facilities of thirty other chewing tobacco manufacturers were purchased and immediately closed. The result was a classic example of monopoly in action. By restricting output, the trust was able to increase prices and profits.

Technical Economies of Scale.   If technological conditions in an industry favor firms of large size, smaller entities may be able to produce more efficiently by merging. Such technical economies of scale may result from increased specialization of labor, greater use of automated production techniques, or sharing of overhead and management expenses.

Pecuniary Economies of Scale.   Pecuniary economies of scale are cost savings that result from increased monopsony power of large firms. Consider small farming operations seeking to ship fruits and vegetables. If the firms merge to form a single corporation, the resulting firm may require a significant proportion of total trucking capacity in its region. Because the single corporation has greater market power, it is in a better position to negotiate favorable rates with truckers than would many small firms acting independently. The same principle applies in capital and advertising markets. As a major borrower, firms such as AT&T may be able to obtain lower interest rates than those obtainable by smaller borrowers. Similarly, with aggregate expenditures approaching $1 billion, Procter & Gamble is able to obtain volume discounts for advertising time and space. Firms acquired by AT&T or Procter & Gamble would also be able to buy at lower prices.

Reduced Transaction Costs.   Vertical mergers reduce transaction costs for the acquiring firm. In the absence of vertical integration, purchasing inputs from suppliers or selling to distributors can involve substantial transaction costs. First, suitable trading partners must be located. Changing prices or needs may dictate periodic reassessment of the suitability of these partners. Next, the terms of transactions with these partners must be established. Because the interests of the trading partners may differ, skill and time may be required to reach agreement. When all parties are satisfied, there is still the problem of monitoring performance. Dissatisfaction by one party may result in a termination of the agreement or costly litigation.

The difficulty of negotiating and maintaining agreements with trading partners is compounded by the incomplete flow of information. Each firm will use caution to avoid disclosing facts that might allow competitors an advantage or permit the trading partner to better its relative position. Even the attempt to be completely open may be partially thwarted by differences in training and procedures of each firm.

Vertical integration reduces transaction costs by establishing permanent bonds among the different stages of production. Thus there is no need to search for trading partners, and the details of interaction between divisions can be dictated by the management of the firm. Similarly, a common set of procedures can be mandated for use throughout the firm. Being vertically integrated also reduces the risks associated with depending on only one or two firms for the supply of important inputs.

Risk Spreading.   Conglomerate mergers may be a means of spreading risk. By diversifying its product line, managers can reduce fluctuations in profit rates. Consider a hypothetical merger between Holiday Inn and the Twentieth-Century Fox Corporation. The hotel and resort business is adversely affected by gasoline shortages and increasing travel costs. In contrast, motion picture producers tend to benefit from conditions that keep people close to home, where they are likely to attend movies. Thus a merger between these two firms could produce a conglomerate with smaller fluctuations in profits than either of its constituent parts. Also, Holiday Inn may arrange to show Twentieth-Century Fox movies in its hotel rooms.

Valuation Discrepancies.   There may be a substantial discrepancy between the acquisition price of a firm and its value to a potential merger partner. In some cases, an acquiring firm may be able to purchase production capacity at a much lower cost than it could build comparable capacity. In other circumstances, resources may be available at a bargain price. The recent merger between Gulf and Socal is an excellent example. In early 1984, the exploration cost of crude oil was about $12 per barrel. But by acquiring Gulf, Socal increased its oil reserves by over 1.5 billion barrels at a cost of about $5 per barrel.

KEY CONCEPTS

- Horizontal mergers may result in increased market power by eliminating an aggressive competitor or by taking excess capacity from the market.
- Mergers may reduce costs as a result of:
  1. Technical economies of scale.
  2. Pecuniary economies of scale.
  3. Reduced transaction costs.
  4. Valuation discrepancies.
- A merger may be a way of reducing fluctuations in profits.

Merger Procedures

Typically, three basic steps are involved in a merger. First, a suitable acquisition candidate must be identified. Second, the value of the target firm to the acquiring company must be determined. Finally, the managers and/or stockholders of the target firm must be presented with and approve the offer.

Identification of a Merger Partner.   Several factors must be considered in selecting an acquisition target. One is the size of the prospective merger partner. Normally, a merger with a small firm is easier than with a larger firm because fewer dollars are involved. For example, the acqustion of Gulf cost Socal over $13 billion. To consummate the merger, Socal had to establish a multibillion dollar line of credit with banks around the country. A number of other firms were interested in Gulf but were unable to arrange the necessary financing. Possible antitrust problems also favor the acquisition of small firms. If the participants in a horizontal merger control a substantial share of the market, the combination may be prohibited by the courts. Antitrust law and its relationship to mergers is considered in Chapter 19.

The expected reaction of the owners and managers of the target firm is another factor to be considered in selecting a merger partner. Although hostile takeovers have become more frequent in recent years, this type of acquisition is more difficult than if both parties favor the action. Again, the Socal–Gulf merger is a good example. Gulf's management vehemently opposed a takeover by Mesa Petroleum. The firm issued public statements advising shareholders not to tender shares to Mesa. At one point, Gulf's managers went so far as to hold a meeting to change corporate rules to make a takeover more difficult. In contrast, when Socal expressed interest in a merger, Gulf opened its books and cooperated in every way. Thus time and dollar costs for an acquisition by Socal were much less than they would have been for Mesa Petroleum.

The extent to which the resources and facilities of a target firm complement those of the acquiring firm are a third factor in selecting a merger partner. A firm needing a stable cash flow to finance expansion or modernization of its facilities may seek out a "cash-rich" merger partner. A firm that perceives that it has an important gap in its product line will be attracted to a producer of that product. Similarly, firms requiring specific resources are likely to select the owners of those resources as targets for acquisition.

Finally, acquiring firms tend to select merger partners that appear to be the best bargain. It may be possible to purchase a firm at a price substantially below its actual value if its owner wants to retire or if the firm has encountered financial difficulties because of poor management or unfavorable economic conditions.

CASE STUDY

MERGERS AND THE INVESTMENT BANKER

Large corporations frequently engage the services of specialists to assist them in merger preparations. One source of help is merger and acquisition groups maintained by the major investment banking firms. These groups provide information on likely merger candidates and are also available to develop strategy for a takeover bid. Typically, their assistance is very expensive. For an acquiring firm, the investment banker's fee is based on the total amount paid for the target firm. At present, the standard rate is 5 percent of the first $1 million spent on the firm, 4 percent on the second million, 3 percent on the third million, 2 percent for the fourth million, and 1 percent for all dollars paid in excess of $4 million.

A large merger can generate huge fees for an investment banker. In early 1984, First Boston assisted in a merger between the Getty and Texaco oil companies. The firm's fee for 79 hours of work came to about $10 million. This total represented an hourly rate of $126,582.

Determination of the Value of the Target Firm.   Once the merger partner has been identified, the value of the firm to the acquiring company must be determined. Conventional analysis suggests that the value of an enterprise is equal to the present value of future profits. That is, annual profits over some planning horizon are estimated and then discounted back to the present. This estimated amount would represent the maximum price that should be paid for the firm.

But mergers take place because of an anticipated synergism between the two firms. Thus the value of the target firm to the acquiring firm may be considerably greater than the present value of its profits as an independent entity. Hence an acquiring firm may be willing to pay a premium price. Fundamentally, the maximum price should still be based on an analysis of the present value of profits. However, in this circumstance, it is incremental profits to the acquiring firm that are the relevant consideration. That is, management should estimate its profit over the planning horizon with and without the merger. The discounted value of the difference is the maximum price that should be paid. For example, if it is estimated that the discounted value of incremental future profit to the acquiring firm resulting from a merger would be $500 million and if the merger target has 5 million shares of stock outstanding, the maximum offer for the firm's stock would be $100 per share.

Theoretically, the value of the firm as an independent entity should be approximated by the value of its outstanding stock. If this is true, the likelihood of a merger will depend on the amount of synergism associated with the merger. If the merged firm is no more valuable than its constituent parts, there is no incentive for the acquiring firm to offer a premium price for the target. Thus owners and managers of the prospective merger partner will not benefit and the combination probably will not take place. In contrast, if there are substantial synergistic benefits to the merger, a larger premium over the market value of the target firm can be offered. Because the benefit to managers and owners of the target firm can be significant, it is more likely that a satisfactory price can be agreed upon.

Presentation of the Offer.   Once the maximum value of the target firm has been determined, the next step is to formulate a plan to facilitate the acquisition. If the management of the target firm is favorably disposed to the merger, the procedure should be relatively straightforward. Managers from both firms will meet to determine the details of the arrangement. Once an agreement has been reached, they will make a joint statement indicating the terms of the merger and urging acceptance by the acquired firm's stockholders.

The offer for the shares of stockholders may be in cash or it may be structured as an exchange of stock. A cash offer usually includes a premium over the current market price of the acquired firm's stock. Figure 16-3 shows the average premium for 1979–1983. The figure indicates that the typical premium was nearly 50 percent. In some cases, it is much more. For example, prior to merger discussions, the price of Getty Oil common stock was about $50 a share. But to acquire the

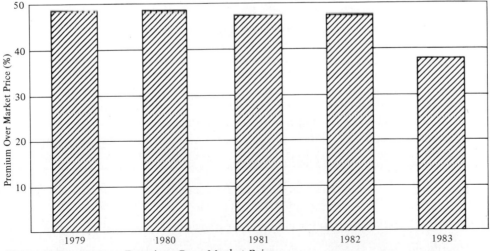

Figure 16-3.   *Average Premium Over Market Price.*

firm, Texaco ultimately paid $128 for each share of Getty stock—a premium of more than 150 percent.

Offers involving exchange of stock specify that shareholders of the target firm will receive a specified number of shares of the acquiring firm's stock for each share that they hold. The actual number of shares depends on the relative stock price of the two firms and the extent of synergistic benefits of the merger. Consider a hypothetical acquisition of Acme Inc. by Peabody and Co. Suppose that Acme's stock is currently selling for $10 per share, while that of Peabody is at $15 per share. If these market prices accurately reflect the values of the firms as independent corporations, two shares of Peabody stock would be worth the same as three Acme shares. But if combining the two firms increases their joint value, Peabody will be willing to offer a more favorable exchange rate. For example, Peabody may be willing to offer two and one-half shares of its stock for every three Acme shares. The greater the synergistic benefits, the more attractive the rate of exchange can be made to Acme stockholders.

If the management of the target firm opposes the merger, the endeavor is more complicated. In this case, the acquiring firm must make its appeal directly to the target firm's stockholders. This is often done with a tender offer. The tender offer typically indicates that a certain price will be paid for a specified number of shares of the acquiring firm's stock exchanged for that of the target firm. Frequently, the offer has a fixed termination date and is valid only if a minimum number of shares are submitted, or "tendered," to the acquiring firm. For example, suppose that Acme's management opposed the Peabody takeover. Peabody responds with a tender offer to purchase Acme's stock at $15 per share. However, the offer is to be valid for only sixty days and is conditional on at least 51 percent of Acme's stock being tendered to Peabody. If Peabody obtains the necessary 51 percent, the voting rights associated with this majority interest can be used to elect a new board of directors who will be favorably disposed to the merger. If sufficient shares are not received, the offer may be withdrawn and the shares returned to their original owners.

KEY CONCEPTS

- Prospective merger partners are evaluated in terms of size, anticipated reaction to a merger proposal, price relative to value, and extent of complementary resources.
- The maximum value of a target firm is the present value of the additional profits that would be earned by the acquiring firm after the merger.
- An acquiring firm may offer cash or an exchange of stock for the shares of a target firm.

CASE STUDY

THE WHITE KNIGHT AND OTHER ANTIMERGER STRATEGIES

Hostile takeovers can be extremely bitter and costly. As a means of thwarting such actions, several defenses can be used by managers of potential target firms.

One option is to identify a "white knight." The white knight is a firm that agrees to purchase the target firm to prevent its acquisition by a less favorable merger partner. A good example is Gulf, which used Socal and Atlantic Richfield as white knights to ward off unwelcome advances by Mesa Petroleum.

Another strategy is the sale of previously authorized but unissued shares to a sympathetic firm, financial institution, or group of investors. The additional shares outstanding make it more difficult to obtain the proportion of shares for a take-over. A related tactic is to initiate a merger with another firm. The advantage of this approach is that the resulting larger firm may be more difficult to acquire and perhaps less attractive with the new addition.

Then there is the "Pac-Man" strategy. It requires that the firm which is the target of a hostile takeover retaliate by using a tender offer of its own for the shares of the aggressor. That is, the target firm becomes the hunter instead of the hunted, as with the Pac-Man video game. Using the text example, if Peabody had offered to pay $15 for Acme shares, Acme might respond with an offer to buy Peabody shares for $20 or $25.

Finally, managers may protect themselves against the consequences of a hos-tile takeover by the inclusion of a "golden parachute" provision in their contract. Such provisions are simply short term employment contracts that become ef-fective when there is a change of corporate control. They provide displaced managers with compensation in the event that they are replaced as a result of a merger.

Summary

Capital projects are those investments that are expected to generate returns for more than one year. Capital expenditures are made to reduce costs, increase output, expand into new products or markets, and/or meet government regu-lations. Capital budgeting is the process of planning capital projects, raising funds, and efficiently allocating those funds to capital projects. In general, the firm continues to make capital expenditures until the rate of return on the last dollar invested equals the marginal cost of capital.

The capital budgeting process consists of two phases. First, the net cash flows are estimated, and second, the evaluation techniques are used to compare those cash flows to the initial cost of the project. The net present value (NPV) and internal rate of return (IRR) concepts are the two most commonly used evaluation methods. Using the NPV method, a capital project is determined to be profitable (i.e., would increase the value of the firm) if the present value of all future cash flows exceeds the initial cost of the project. In contrast, the internal rate of return is the discount rate that equates all future cash flows and the project's cost. An investment should be made if the IRR exceeds the firm's cost of capital.

A firm is said to be subject to capital rationing if the dollar amount of profitable capital projects exceeds the amount the firm has available for investment and the amount that can be obtained externally by borrowing or by selling stock. The profitability ratio is one plus the net present value divided by the project cost. This measure provides a way of ranking efficient projects based on their return relative to their cost.

The cost of capital is the return required by investors in the debt and equity securities of the firm. The cost of debt is the net (after-tax) interest rate paid on that debt. Alternative methods for estimating the cost of equity capital include (1) the risk-free rate plus a risk premium, (2) discounted cash flow, and (3) the capital asset pricing model. The last method uses the beta coefficient (a measure of the variability in return on a given stock relative to variability in return on the average stock) to measure relative risk among the common stock of different companies.

As firms often use both debt and equity financing sources, a weighted cost of capital measure is used. The composite cost of capital is a weighted average of the cost of debt and the cost of equity capital. The weights are the proportions of debt and equity in the firm's capital structure.

Merger is defined as the joining of two or more firms under single ownership. Usually, mergers take place because management believes that the value of the combined firm is greater than the sum of its individual parts. Horizontal mergers involve firms that compete directly for sales of similar goods or services. Vertical mergers occur when firms that had been operating at different stages in the production and distribution process combine to form a single firm. A conglomerate merger takes place when essentially unrelated firms are joined.

From the standpoint of the acquiring firm, a merger may be a means of increasing its market power by eliminating competitors. Other incentives to merge include cost reductions resulting from economies of scale, reduced transaction costs, and valuation discrepancies. A merger also may be a means of smoothing fluctuations in profits.

Several factors affect the choice of a target for acquisition. A merger with a very large firm may present financial problems and raise antitrust issues. If the management of the target firm is expected to oppose the merger, the acquisition is likely to be more costly and difficult than if the proposal is accepted by those managers. The best merger partners are those who have complementary resources and can be purchased at the lowest cost relative to their value to the acquiring firm.

The maximum price that one firm would be willing to pay for another is the present value of the additional profits that managers estimate would result from the merger. An acquiring firm may offer cash or it may propose an exchange of its stock for that of the target firm.

Discussion Questions

16-1.   What are the two phases of the capital budgeting process?

16-2.   What is the basic principle underlying the approach used by a profit-maximizing manager to capital budgeting decisions?

16-3.   Why is the marginal cost of capital schedule or function upward-sloping for most firms?

16-4. Contrast the net present value and internal rate of return approaches in the evaluation of capital projects. In general, if the *NPV* is greater than zero, what does this imply about the internal rate of return?

16-5. Why is it that the net present value and internal rate of return methods can yield contradictory results when evaluating two mutually exclusive investments?

16-6. What is the relationship between a firm's marginal income tax rate and the net cost of debt capital to the firm?

16-7. List two factors that influence the composition of a firm's capital structure.

16-8. The after-tax cost of debt capital is generally thought to be lower than the cost of equity capital. If this is the case, why don't firms rely exclusively on debt financing?

16-9. What is synergy as it applies to mergers?

16-10. Give an example (not used in the chapter) of each of the following types of mergers:
(a) horizontal.　　(c) conglomerate.
(b) vertical.

16-11. How could a conglomerate merger be used to reduce risk?

16-12. How could a vertical merger between an electric utility and a coal company reduce transaction costs for the combined firm?

16-13. What are three strategies a firm might use to avoid being acquired by another company?

16-14. Suppose that the capital market has correctly valued the price of a firm's stock. Why would an acquiring firm be willing to pay more than the market price? What would determine the premium over the market price that the firm would be willing to pay?

Problems

16-1. Staff members of the financial analysis department of Davis Electronics have determined the rate of return on each of the following capital projects.

Capital Projects	Required Investment (millions)	Internal Rate of Return (%)
A	5.2	12.9
B	8.6	15.2
C	3.4	10.0
D	5.1	14.8
E	11.2	19.0
F	6.5	7.9

The firm's marginal cost of capital is given by the function

$$r = 8 + 0.10C$$

where r is rate of return (in percent) and C is millions of dollars of capital raised for investment.
(a) Graph the firm's marginal cost of capital function and the firm's capital demand function.
(b) Which capital projects should be implemented? What should be the firm's total capital investment?

(c) If a general tightening in the financial markets shifts the firm's marginal cost of capital function to

$$r = 8 + 0.35C,$$

determine which projects should be implemented and the total amount spent on capital items.

16-2. Tarnutzer Construction Company must replace its front-end loader. The initial cost and annual net cash flows for the two models under consideration are shown in the table. Given the heavy use of the machines, they will be completely worn out at the end of five years and have no salvage value. The firm's cost of capital is 12 percent.

	Model	
	Heavyduty	Sure Shovel
Initial cost	$10,000	$10,000
Net cash flows (year)		
1	5,000	−4,000
2	5,000	−0−
3	5,000	6,600
4	5,000	6,600
5	5,000	20,000

Use both the *IRR* and *NPV* methods to evaluate these capital proposals. Which should be purchased? Explain. (Except for the initial costs, assume that all cash flows are received or paid at the end of each year.)

16-3. Top management at Transworld, Inc., a large conglomerate, uses the net present value method for evaluating capital expenditure proposals. The firm's cost of capital is 16 percent. Currently, the following eight proposals are under review:

Proposal	Initial Cost (millions)	Net Present Value (millions)
1	$11.6	$3.6
2	9.4	−1.3
3	8.7	2.2
4	13.2	2.4
5	14.0	2.0
6	7.5	1.4
7	6.5	1.7
8	9.5	−2.4

(a) If the corporation has a capital spending budget of $100 million for the coming year, which capital projects should be implemented? Explain.

(b) If the capital spending budget is limited to $47.5 million, which projects should be undertaken? Explain.

16-4. The board of directors of Alder Enterprises wants to maintain a capital structure that is 30 percent debt and 70 percent equity (i.e., retained earnings and common stock). For the current year, the firm expects to earn $2 million after taxes (the firm's marginal tax rate is 40 percent) on sales of $15 million. Company policy is to pay out 50 percent of net after-tax income in dividends to the holders of the firm's one million shares of common stock. Management and outside analysts project a growth rate of 8 percent for sales, profits, and dividends. The market value of the firm's common stock is $20 per share.

The average dividend yield on all common stocks is 14 percent, and the interest rate on U.S. government securities is 12 percent. Both management and the firm's investment advisors, Saunders & Wennergren, agree that Alder could sell bonds at an interest rate of about 14 percent. The estimated beta coefficient for Alder is about 1.5.

(a) Determine the cost of debt capital for Alder Enterprises.
(b) Determine the cost of equity capital using each of the three methods described in the chapter.
(c) Determine the composite cost of capital for the firm using the capital asset pricing model to compute the cost of equity capital.

16-5. Quickstor, Inc. builds and manages storage units that are rented to individuals and firms. Typically, the firm builds a number (usually 200 to 500) of these garage-like units at sites on the periphery of growing urban areas. Most of the time the storage units are demolished and the site cleared for housing and/or commercial development within five to ten years.

Management is deciding whether to build a 300-unit storage center between Oklahoma City and Norman, Oklahoma. Currently, similar units in the area are being rented for $85 per month. Each unit would contain 400 square feet and the construction cost per square foot, including site development costs, would be $8. The operating costs of the project (i.e., insurance, management, property taxes, electricity) are estimated at $0.125 per square feet per month. Both the rental rate and operating costs are expected to remain constant for the foreseeable future. Quickstor's cost of capital is 10 percent and its marginal income tax rate is 30 percent.

Because of the growth of the University of Oklahoma in Norman, it is likely that the storage units will be demolished after ten years to make room for student apartments. Demolition costs will be insignificant, and there would be no salvage value for any of the materials. The entire cost of the project will be depreciated in ten years, using the straight-line method. There is no alternative use for the land for the next ten years.

(a) Given that Quickstor's objective is profit-maximization, should this project be implemented? Use both the NPV and IRR evaluation criteria.
(b) If your answer to part (a) is that the project should not be implemented, determine the maximum initial investment that could be made such that the project would be profitable.

16-6. The common stock of Throckmorton Machinery is currently selling for $40 per share, while the price of McKnight Equipment stock is $10 per share. Top managers at McKnight are planning an offer for the shares of Throckmorton. They believe that by applying their considerable managerial talents, the value of Throckmorton could be increased 25 percent by a merger with McKnight.

(a) If a cash offer is to be made to owners of Throckmorton common stock, what is the maximum price that McKnight's managers should offer?
(b) If the acquisition is to be made by an exchange of stock, what are the most favorable terms that McKnight should offer?
(c) What will probably happen to the share price of Throckmorton's stock when the offer is announced? Explain.

References

Bierman, H., Jr., and Smidt, S. 1984. *The Capital Budgeting Decision*, 6th ed. New York: Macmillan.

Brigham, Eugene F. 1982. *Financial Management Theory and Practice*, 3rd ed. Hinsdale, Ill.: Dryden Press.

Clark, J. J., Hindelang, T. J., and Pritchard, R. D. 1984. *Capital Budgeting: Planning and Control of Capital Expenditures*, 2nd ed. Englewood Cliffs, N.J.: Prentice-Hall.

Hirschleifer, J. 1970. "Optimal Investment Decisions." In *Investment, Interest, and Capital.* Englewood Cliffs, N.J.: Prentice-Hall.

Keenan, M., and White, L., eds. 1982. *Mergers and Acquisitions.* Lexington, Mass.: Lexington Books.

Kim, S. H., and Farragher, E. J. 1981. "Current Capital Budgeting Practices." *Management Accounting* 62(12):26–30.

Magee, J. T. 1964. "How to Use Decision Trees in Capital Budgeting." *Harvard Business Review* 12(September–October):75–95.

Miller, M. H., and Modigliani, F. 1966. "Cost of Capital to Electric Utility Industry." *American Economic Review* 56(June):333–391.

Modigliani, F., and Miller, M. H. 1958. "The Cost of Capital, Corporation Finance and the Theory of Investment." *American Economic Review* 48(June):261–297.

Schall, L. D., Sudem, G. L., and Geijsbeek, W. R., Jr. 1978. "Survey and Analysis of Capital Budgeting Methods." *Journal of Finance* 33(March):281–287.

Steiner, P. O. 1975. *Mergers: Motives, Effects, Policies.* Ann Arbor, Mich.: University of Michigan Press.

Van Horne, J. C. 1983. *Financial Management and Policy*, 6th ed. Englewood Cliffs, N.J.: Prentice-Hall.

Weston, J. F., and Brigham, E. F. 1981. *Managerial Finance*, 7th ed. New York: Holt, Rinehart and Winston.

Location Decisions

17

Preview

The economic analysis developed thus far neglected an important factor—the effect of the spatial dimension and its implications for locating the firm. Locating a business in the right place is important because the cost of moving output and people across space is significant. For example, the best site for a retail store generally is one that is in close proximity to a large number of people who are the potential customers of the store. In contrast, a manufacturing firm may use raw materials from one or more sites and ship manufactured output to customers at one or more other sites. In this case, an important locational criterion is the relative cost of obtaining raw materials and shipping final output.

Another consideration is that all firms employ workers who must travel from their homes to the firm each working day. The firm must locate in close proximity to that labor supply or face the prospect of paying premium wages to compensate workers for traveling long distances and/or providing housing and other amenities for workers at the employment site. The latter are characteristic of installations located in remote locations such as offshore oil drilling platforms and some mining operations.

Clearly, some locations for the firm are better than others, and there are numerous examples of business failures that can be directly attributed to the selection of a poor location. In this chapter, four topics in location theory are discussed. First, some of the basic theoretical principles of industrial location are considered. Next is a discussion of the determination of the market area for a firm, that is, given the location of firms in a region, what share of the market will accrue to each. The third section covers the principle of "threshold" analysis, which explains why certain economic activities are found in some areas but not in others. Finally, the relative importance of a variety of location factors is discussed.

Basic Location Principles

In this section, the fundamental principles of industrial location are outlined.[1] Consider, for example, the problems that would be associated with locating a manufacturing firm that used several different raw materials, each of which could be obtained from suppliers in many parts of the country, and that sold several different products to many customers in a number of locations. Seeking the location that minimized the total transportation costs for raw material and output could become a very complicated problem.

The simple models discussed below, however, provide the flavor of location

---

[1] For an excellent summary of the basic principles of location theory, see Alonso (1975).

theory and illustrate some important location principles. One principle is that there is a tendency for firms and individuals to locate together in particular areas. Even the most casual observer of geography is struck by the concentration of economic and human activity in cities. There are a variety of reasons for this concentration, but one of the most important is economic in nature. By locating in close proximity, the costs associated with moving people, goods, and information are reduced. Furthermore, these concentration forces tend to be mutually reinforcing and can cause a cumulative buildup of population and economic activity in an area. For example, suppose that a shopping center locates near a concentration of people. As a result of the employment and shopping opportunities provided by this center, more residents are attracted to the area, which creates a demand for even more stores. This cumulative process is one explanation for the development of many urban areas.

In the following discussion, several alternative models are developed to demonstrate the optimal location for a firm under specified market conditions. In all these models, there is a tendency for the firm to locate at a central point, such as an urban area where output is sold or at the site of a supply of raw materials. Although the models are very basic, they illustrate many of the key principles of location theory.

Locating in a Linear Market

If demand for a firm's output does not vary with location, the problem of locating a plant or service center reduces to one of cost minimization. Suppose that the letters A through I in Figure 17-1 represent households located on a highway. Such a distribution of customers is referred to as a *linear market*. Assume that each customer must be served once each month by delivering one truckload of output (e.g., coal or fuel oil for heating) to each home. Where should a firm locate its distribution center to minimize the total transportation costs of servicing these consumers?

The cost-minimizing solution is to locate at the median point, where there are as many customers on either side of the distribution center. The median location is at the 5-mile mark, where there are four customers on either side of the firm. The total mileage required to serve all customers is 70 miles, computed as the sum of a 10-mile round-trip to A plus an eight-mile round-trip to B, and so on.

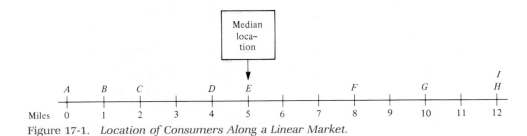

Figure 17-1. *Location of Consumers Along a Linear Market.*

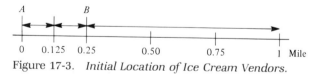

Figure 17-2.   *Number of Consumers at Each of Four Cities Along a Highway.*

No other location will allow each customer to be served and result in fewer than 70 miles driven.[2]

Consider another example of a linear market. Suppose that a firm is seeking a location to serve four cities *A, B, C,* and *D* along a highway. The number of customers in each city is shown in Figure 17-2. Using the principle of median location, the firm will minimize transportation costs by locating at *D*. Technically, the median location would be at some point on the west side of city *D*, where there are as many customers to the west as there are to the east.

Now, extend this analysis to another case where two firms are seeking locations along a linear market. Suppose that this market is one mile long with customers distributed uniformly along it. An example would be swimmers at a beach. Two vendors, *A* and *B*, sell ice cream to these swimmers using easily moved stands. Each consumer buys one ice cream bar each day, the price is the same at both stands, and consumers will patronize the closest vendor. Assume that the sellers initially set up their stands at the 0- and 0.25-mile marks along the beach, as shown in Figure 17-3.[3]

Because both sellers charge the same price and the swimmers go to the closest stand, initially *B* will have 87.5 percent of the market because all swimmers to the right of the 0.125-mile mark will buy from *B*. But this is not an equilibrium location pattern. As the stands are easily moved, *A* can capture most of *B*'s market by moving his stand just to the right of *B*, say, to the 0.26-mile mark. This would give *A* about 74 percent of the market. It is likely *B* would respond by moving to the right of *A*. Then *B* would move just to the right of *A*, capturing perhaps 73 percent of the market. Such continuous relocation would continue until both stands were located adjacent to one another at the 0.5-mile mark, as shown in Figure 17-4a. This is the equilibrium location pattern in this market because both

Figure 17-3.   *Initial Location of Ice Cream Vendors.*

[2] A logical, but incorrect answer might be to build the facility at the average or mean location. To find the mean location, start at point zero on the highway and find the average distance traveled if all customers are served. That is, customer *A* is zero miles away from the endpoint, *B* is 1 mile away, and so on. The total number of miles is $0 + 1 + 2 + 4 + \cdots + 12 = 54$, and thus the average distance is 6 miles (i.e., 54 miles divided by nine customers). Using this criterion, the firm would locate at the 6-mile mark and would make nine trips each period totaling 72 miles. That is, one 12-mile round trip would be made to *A*, one 10-mile round trip to *B*, and so on. But this solution requires two additional miles of driving compared to the median solution.

[3] This example was originally developed in a classic article by Harold Hotelling (1929).

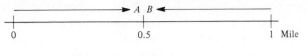

(a) Free market equilibrium location pattern

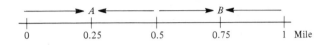

(b) Minimum transportation cost location pattern

Figure 17-4. *Alternative Locations for Ice Cream Vendors.*

sellers now have 50 percent of the market and neither seller can increase his market share by moving.

Although this example is somewhat simplified, one can think of many cases where a number of competing firms all locate in one part of an area. For example, some urban areas have a theater district where a number of stage and movie theaters are located together. Another example is the location of magazine shops, massage parlors, movie theaters, and related shops that cater to the "adults only" trade. These tend to locate in particular parts of urban areas.[4] Once again, principles of location economics suggest a concentration of economic activity.

Although the location of both vendors at the 0.5-mile mark is the free-market equilibrium, it is not socially optimal because total transportation costs for all swimmers walking to the ice cream stand are not minimized. With the swimmers evenly distributed along the beach, the average distance to the nearest ice cream stand will be 0.25 mile if both stands locate at the 0.5-mile mark. This distance can be reduced by one-half, to 0.125 mile, by a regulation requiring that the vendors locate at the 0.25- and 0.75-mile marks, as shown in Figure 17-4b. In a sense, the sellers are locating at the median locations of each half of the market. Note that both sellers still retain 50 percent of the market, but the average distance traveled by swimmers is reduced. Generally, free-market solutions to economic problems result in socially optimal outcomes. This is one case where that principle does not hold.

Thus far it has been assumed that the demand for ice cream by each swimmer is one per day and does not depend on the location of the stands. This is somewhat unrealistic because the quantity demanded would probably be inversely related to distance from a stand. A swimmer located near the stand might have three or four bars, whereas a swimmer located 0.5 mile away might decide that it is simply too far to walk. That is, the price, including transportation costs, is too high.

Assume that the maximum distance a buyer would walk is 0.25 mile. In this case, the vendors would each sell twice as many bars by locating at the 0.25-

---

[4] In some cases, this concentration is the result of zoning laws that restrict the location of such businesses.

and 0.75-mile marks (each having one-half the market) than by both locating at the center. In the latter case, each would have 50 percent of the entire market (i.e., one would have that part from the 0.00- to the 0.5-mile marks, while the other one would have that part of the market from the 0.5- to the 1.00-mile marks. Given these demand conditions, the profit-maximizing and the socially optimal solutions are the same.

In general, there is a tendency for firms to locate in the middle of market areas. In larger, urban areas, there typically is a central business district that serves the entire city with certain goods and services and a number of smaller business districts (e.g., shopping centers) that serve a submarket of the city. In any case, the principle of median location helps to explain the concentration of these businesses at particular points.

The principle of median location is one reason why the urban centers in the world have grown so much in the past fifty years; they are the median, or at least central, locations for many types of economic activity. For example, the downtown areas and suburban shopping centers of urban areas often have a number of the same type of store located very close together. All have sought the median location at the center of a market area. Obviously, one finds stores scattered at various points in urban and even rural areas. However, the growth of urban centers and the concentration of economic activity at points within those centers suggests a strong tendency to locate business at or near the median location within those markets.

CASE STUDY

LOCATION THEORY, PRODUCT ATTRIBUTES, AND
THE PERSONAL COMPUTER INDUSTRY

Firms producing similar goods or services tend to locate in close spatial proximity. Similarly, in many industries, there is little variation in the attributes of the products sold by the firms. That is, there is close proximity of attributes.

The microcomputer industry is a good example. In the early 1980s, IBM emerged as a leader in the personal computer industry. Attributes of the IBM-PC became the standard against which other computers were judged. As a result, other computer manufacturers began to advertise their computers in terms of their "IBM compatibility." This compatibility stressed the extent to which these computers would run software written for the IBM, but also involved features such as the ability to use expansion boards and peripheral devices designed for the IBM. Once basic compatibility was established, other features, such as lower price or greater memory, could be promoted in order to differentiate the product from the IBM-PC.

The task of these competing manufacturers was a difficult one. They had to position their product close enough to the IBM-PC to convince potential purchasers that it could do virtually anything that the IBM computer could do. But the product had to be differentiated enough to establish a reason for buying it instead of the IBM product.

The tendency for product attributes of different firms to be similar is not unique to the computer industry. Indeed, it is a characteristic of most mass-produced products. A television set must have most of the features of other makes. New automobile models seldom represent radical departures from competing models that are already on the market. Most new textbooks try to retain most of the features of texts that have been successful in the past. In each case, the explanation is the same as for the locational clustering of firms. If the product is too different, that is, too far from the "center" of the market, it is likely to attract fewer customers than if it has more traditional attributes.

KEY CONCEPTS

- Location of business is important because the cost of moving resources and output across space is significant.
- In general, principles of location theory suggest that firms and individuals benefit by locating close together and that these location forces tend to result in concentration of economic activity in urban areas.
- If demand does not vary with location, two firms serving a linear market will both tend to locate at the center of the market, resulting in maximum transportation costs for their customers.
- If demand is inversely related to distance from the seller, the two firms will tend to locate in the center of each half of the market.

Firm Location: One Market and One Raw Materials Source

In the previous examples, the focus was on minimizing only the transportation costs associated with sending final output to consumers. No consideration was given to the cost of shipping ice cream bars to the vendors. This section considers a more realistic but still simple case of location decision for a firm that obtains raw materials at one site (M), processes them, and distributes to customers in a city (C). As shown in Figure 17-5, the raw materials and market sites, M and C, respectively, are T miles apart.

Assume that production cost, the price of output, and the quantity sold are the same regardless of where the firm locates the plant. The only variables are the total costs of transporting raw materials and output. Let S_m be the cost per mile of shipping enough raw materials to make 1 unit of output (referred to below as 1 unit of raw material) and S_o be the cost per mile of shipping 1 unit of output. The cost function for shipping raw materials is $S_m t$, which determines the cost of shipping 1 unit of raw material from M to any location t miles to the right of M. If the plant is located at the raw materials site, then $t = 0$ and the cost of shipping raw materials is zero. The output shipping cost function is given by $S_o(T - t)$, which defines the cost of shipping 1 unit of final product from any location $(T - t)$ miles to the left of C to that city. If the plant is located at C, the value of $(T - t)$ is zero and the shipping costs for output are zero.

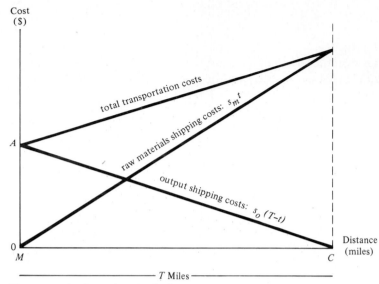

Figure 17-5. *Location Analysis.*

At any intermediate point between *M* and *C*, there are shipping costs for both raw materials and output. The sum of these two costs is defined as total transportation costs. As price and other production costs are assumed to be constant at all locations, the problem reduces to choosing that site with the lowest total transportation costs.[5] In the example shown in Figure 17-5, the per mile cost of shipping 1 unit of raw materials is greater than the cost of shipping 1 unit of output. Thus total transport costs are minimized at the raw materials site *M*. In contrast, had transportation cost per mile for raw material been lower than for 1 unit of output, the lower total transportation costs would be achieved by locating at *C*.

This principle can be demonstrated mathematically. The total transport cost (*TC*) of locating the plant at any site *t* miles to the right of *M* is the sum of shipping costs for raw material and output, that is,

$$TC = S_m t + S_o(T - t)$$

or

$$TC = (S_m - S_o)t + S_o T$$

Recall that the plant will be located at some point *t* where $0 \leq t \leq T$. As the objective of the plant location decision is to minimize *TC*, it should be clear that if $S_m > S_o$, the value of *t* should be made as small as possible. This is accomplished by locating the plant at *M*, where $t = 0$. Alternatively, if $S_m < S_o$, total

---

[5] Clearly, production costs and demand may vary among alternative locations, but this assumption simplifies the problem, allowing the analysis to focus on the transportation-related issues.

costs are minimized by making t as large as possible (i.e., $t = T$) and locating the plant at C.

If $S_m = S_o$, the total cost function would be horizontal and the firm would be indifferent about locating at any point between M and C. However, if there are costs associated with the loading and unloading of raw materials and/or output onto trucks, rail cars, or ships, then even if $S_m = S_o$, any intermediate location will have higher costs than at M or C because of the additional terminal costs incurred. For example, by locating at M, the loading of raw materials is avoided, and by locating at C, the loading of final output is avoided. If an intermediate location is selected, both of these costs will be incurred. Thus industrial location tends to take place either at a raw materials site or at the market. This phenomenon once again suggests the natural tendency for economic activities to be concentrated at certain sites.

In general, products that tend to be "weight losing" in the production process are associated with locations at the raw materials site. For example, the processing of gravel involves screening and washing large quantities of rock, dirt, and other debris to separate that part of the load that "qualifies" as gravel. The usable gravel may only be one-third of the material processed. Invariably, this process takes place at the raw materials site and then the finished product is taken to the marketplace, usually the site of a construction project. In contrast, "weight gaining" activities tend to locate at the marketplace. For example, soft-drink bottling plants add small quantities of concentrate to large volumes of water to manufacture soft drinks. As water is available in virtually all locations at a relatively low cost but is expensive to transport, the economics of location dictate that bottling plants be located in market areas. Indeed, bottling plants are found in virtually every area of the country. The market area of each plant is relatively small because it is too expensive to ship bottled soft drinks very far because they are more than 90 percent water.

CASE STUDY

LOCATING THE STEEL INDUSTRY

In the early part of the twentieth century, location decisions in the iron and steel industry were based primarily on minimizing the costs of the raw materials used in production, specifically coal and iron ore. At that time, it took approximately two tons of coal and one ton of iron ore to manufacture something less than one-half ton of steel. Clearly, this was a weight-losing process and the shipping costs of raw materials dominated the location decision. The steel industry also uses large quantities of water—about 65,000 gallons per ton of steel produced for cooling and processing. Although much of this water is continually reused, there must be large supplies available. Thus locations on rivers or lakes were definitely preferred. Because western Pennsylvania had abundant supplies of coal and water available at low prices, virtually the entire U.S. steel industry located there and Pittsburgh became the nation's steel capital.

Improvements in technology steadily reduced the amount of coal required to process a ton of iron ore, and by the mid-1970s less than one ton of coal was used per ton of ore. While the industry remained tied to raw materials sources, it became relatively more important to locate near the sources of iron ore, much of which was mined in the Upper Great Lakes area.

Taking advantage of low-cost water transportation for both coal and iron ore and large water supplies, major steel-producing complexes developed at Cleveland, Youngstown, Detroit, Buffalo, and Chicago—all cities located on the Great Lakes. Smaller complexes developed later at St. Louis, Birmingham, and Fontana, California.

More recently, the use of scrap metal as a raw material has become important. The existence of large supplies of scrap metal in Detroit and Chicago helped the steel industry to grow in those areas. In fact, relatively small steel mills that depend almost entirely on scrap metal have been developed in places never thought to have potential as steel industry locations.

The most recent development has been the growth of steel imports from Japan. Using more modern technology and lower-cost labor, Japanese producers have been able to sell finished steel in the United States at prices below those of domestic producers. Virtually all the raw material is imported to Japan, processed there, and shipped by water to markets all over the world. In Japan, lower-cost labor and more efficient production processes have more than offset the additional costs of transporting raw materials over long distances.

KEY CONCEPTS

- If other factors are held constant, a firm that uses raw materials from a site *A* and sells output in the market at *B* will locate at *A* if the cost of shipping raw materials is more than the cost of shipping final output. Otherwise, the firm will locate at the market, *B*.
- Even if the transportation costs are the same for raw materials and finished output, the lowest-cost location will be at either the raw materials site or the market, because additional loading and unloading costs would be incurred at any intermediate location.
- Production activities that are weight losing tend to locate at the source of raw materials, whereas production activities that are weight gaining tend to locate at the market.

Market Area Determination

The market area for any one seller will depend on relative production and transportation costs. In the following, market areas for two competing firms will be determined under different assumptions relative to those costs.

Case I: Equal Production and Transportation Costs

Suppose that two competing firms, A and B, have located production facilities in a region and that both have the same production and transportation costs. The price at the plant is set equal to production costs, and transport costs are paid by the consumer. Consumers will buy from that plant for which the delivered price (i.e., price at plant plus transport cost) is the lowest. Figure 17-6a

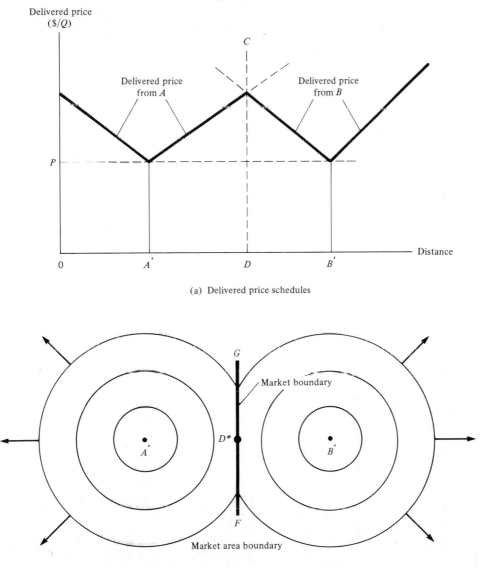

(a) Delivered price schedules

(b) Market areas corresponding to delivered price schedules in figure 17.6a

Figure 17-6. *Price Schedule and Market areas—Firms with Equal Production and Transportation Costs.*

shows delivered price functions for firms A and B located at points A' and B' along the distance or horizontal axis. Production cost is $0P$ at both plants. Any buyer located at point A' or B' pays $0P$, but more distant buyers must pay $0P$ plus the transportation cost from the plant. For example, if S is the per mile transportation cost per unit of output, a buyer located t miles from A must pay $0P + St$. Thus the delivered price functions shown in Figure 17-6a have a slope equal to S.

Because consumers seek the lowest price, all those located to the left of point D will buy from A and those to the right of D will buy from B. Looking down on this two-dimensional market area, as shown in Figure 17-6b, it is seen that the line FG separates the two market areas. Along this market boundary, the delivered price is the same for both plants. To the right of this line, the price is lower for B, and to the left, it is lower for A. Point D in Figure 17-6a corresponds to point D^* in Figure 17-6b.

Case II: Unequal Production Costs—
Equal Transportation Costs

Suppose that firm B's production cost per unit increases while the costs at firm A remain the same. Figure 17-7 depicts the market areas for the two firms where A is able to produce at a lower cost than is B. As a result, the price at the plant is lower for A than for B. Per mile transport costs are assumed to remain equal for both firms. Thus the slope of the delivered price functions is the same, but the function for firm B is shifted upward by the amount of the production cost differential between the two firms. This change results in A's market area increasing significantly. That is, now some customers who are geographically closer to B will buy from A because the lower production cost has more than offset the greater transportation cost. Also, the boundary between the markets, the curve $F'G'$ in Figure 17-7b, is now nonlinear. The point D' in Figure 17-7a corresponds to point D^* in Figure 17-7b.

The large share of the U.S. automobile market taken from American producers by Japanese producers located thousands of miles away is an example of this situation. Japanese automakers have lower production costs that enable them to more than offset the additional transportation costs of shipping their output to American buyers. Thus they have taken over a large share of the market for compact and subcompact cars in the United States.

Case III: Unequal Production
and Transportation Costs

Next suppose that both production and transportation costs are lower for A than for B. Transportation costs may be lower for A because it has developed access to lower-cost barge and/or rail service, whereas B may be restricted to using higher-cost truck service. Alternatively, B may simply have higher costs due to obsolete equipment and/or poor transportation management. The determina-

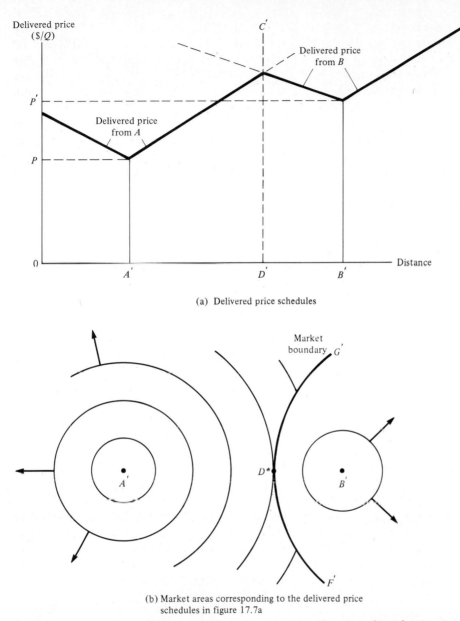

(a) Delivered price schedules

(b) Market areas corresponding to the delivered price
schedules in figure 17.7a

Figure 17-7. *Price Schedule and Market Areas—Firms with Unequal Production Costs but Equal Transportation Costs.*

tion of the market area for each firm is depicted in Figure 17-8. Note in Figure 17-8a that B's market area is restricted to the area between D'' and E'. Even though customers to the right of E' are closer to B' than to A', the delivered price from A actually is lower. A's lower production and transport costs have reduced B's market area to a small circular area. The two-dimensional perspective of this

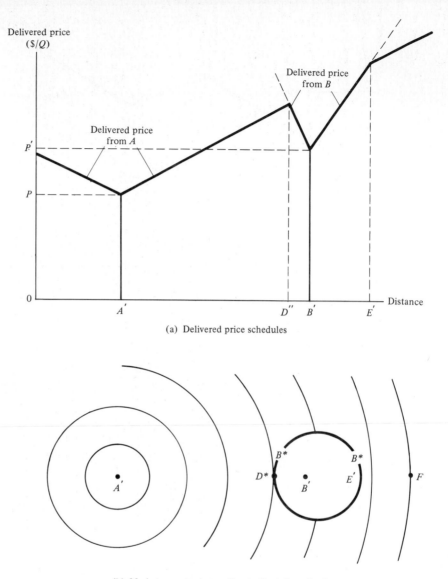

(a) Delivered price schedules

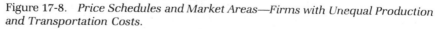

(b) Market areas corresponding to the delivered price
schedules in figure 17.8a

Figure 17-8.   *Price Schedules and Market Areas—Firms with Unequal Production
and Transportation Costs.*

market area analysis is shown in Figure 17-8b. The market area for firm B is the
small circular area B*B*. Firm A captures the remainder of the market areas.

   It is possible that further reduction in A's production and/or transportation
costs could occur to the point that the delivered price function for firm A would
intersect that for firm B below the level of B's production cost 0P'. In that event,
firm A would capture the entire market area and B would be out of business.

KEY CONCEPTS

- The market boundary for two firms is a function of relative production and transportation costs and is defined by that set of points where the delivered price is the same for each firm.
- If production and transport costs are equal for both firms, the market boundary will be a straight line midway between the two producers.
- If production costs are higher for one firm but transportation costs are equal, the market boundary will be a curved line around the higher-cost plant.
- If both production and transportation costs are higher for one plant, its market area will be reduced to a circular area around its plant site.

Threshold Analysis

There is a consistent hierarchical arrangement of businesses among cities of various sizes. For example, automobile service stations and convenience stores are generally found in even the smallest communities. Conversely, to find symphony orchestras and gourmet restaurants, one must usually go to large cities. The reason for this is a matter of economics. The demand for symphony orchestras in small cities simply is not great enough that revenue would cover costs. When that is the case, it is said that the threshold level for the activity has not been reached.

Figure 17-9 shows the demand curves for a gourmet restaurant in a small town (D_T) and in a city (D_C). The average cost curve for the restaurant is also shown.

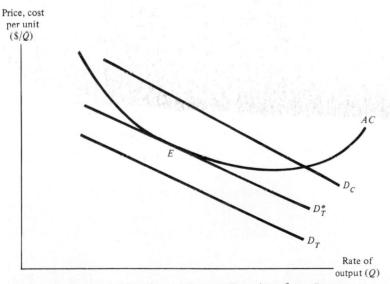

Figure 17-9. *Demand and Average Cost Functions for a Restaurant.*

It is assumed that the same cost conditions would prevail in both places. Note that average cost is above the "small town" demand curve at all points. Thus it is not possible for the restaurant to break even under these conditions. In contrast, part of the demand curve for the city is above the cost function and therefore there are output rates for which the restaurant is profitable.

If the small town increased in size, demand for restaurant services would probably increase. If demand increased to D_T^*, which is tangent to the average cost curve at point E, a threshold has been reached and it would be possible for the restaurant to breakeven. Of course, this threshold also could have been attained by a downward shift in the average cost curve. As population centers increase in size, not only do more businesses of the kind already there develop (i.e., another service station or drive-in restaurant), but new kinds of businesses appear. For example, banks or small department stores are often found in small cities but not in the smallest towns. As the latter grow, these activities appear when the threshold level is reached.

Selecting an Industrial Location

Obviously, the process used by managers to select a location for a store or plant is more involved than that suggested by the theoretical discussion above, but the process is consistent with that theory. Typically, the firm has a general idea about the set of possible locations for the facility. For example, a firm may find that a particular regional market such as the West Coast has grown so rapidly that a production facility can now be justified in that area. Often, a professional consultant with a particular expertise in facility location is brought in to make the evaluation. The firm provides that consultant with a rating of the importance of all location factors. For example, there may be specific requirements for rail service, large quantities of skilled labor or other input, or educational facilities that are found only in a few places.

In general, all significant factors that will influence the profitability of the proposed facility are evaluated at each location under consideration. Because both revenue and cost may differ at each location, the analysis must consider each location's attributes as they affect these two key variables. These locational factors are classified as primary and secondary.

Primary Location Factors

The locational attributes described here are fundamental in the decision to locate an industrial facility.[6] Although for particular firms some are more important

---

[6] For a detailed discussion of the industry location process and the importance of each locational attribute, see Miller (1977).

than others, a significant shortfall in an area's ability to provide even one of these may greatly reduce the attractiveness of that site.

Raw Materials Availability. Virtually all businesses depend on materials of various types, such as unprocessed raw materials for use in manufacturing and finished goods for inventory in wholesale and retail establishments. The availability and cost, including transportation costs, of these materials are critical location factors.

Labor. The availability, cost, and productivity of labor are also very important location determinants. Some think of a new business as attracting labor into an area rather than the business being attracted by existing labor supplies. This does happen. However, in most cases, a new facility is not built in a location unless management is convinced there is an adequate supply of labor available that has the training and experience needed for the planned operation. The cost of that labor is also important, although low labor cost is not necessarily an advantage if the workers are poorly educated and trained because that may mean that productivity is low. Labor availability, cost, and quality must all be taken into consideration.

Energy Resources. Some manufacturing processes use large quantities of energy per dollar of final output. For example, the processing of bauxite into aluminum requires large quantities of electricity. Thus it is not surprising that aluminum manufacturers have tended to locate in areas that offered low-cost electric power. The Pacific Northwest with its low-cost hydroelectric power plants and some areas in the South served with low-cost power from the Tennessee Valley Authority have been attractive locations for this industry. The availability of large supplies of low-cost coal for firing blast furnaces was a primary factor explaining the concentration of iron and steel manufacturing in western Pennsylvania.

Transportation. Transportation costs are also important factors in industrial location decisions. In the early history of the United States, locations near water and rail transportation were extremely important. This is evidenced by the rapid rate of growth of cities that offered good access to these transport modes. The relative growth of the service sector, which is not heavily dependent on transportation, and the emergence of truck transport have greatly expanded the range of good industrial locations. For example, the manufacturing activity that has developed in smaller communities and in suburban areas of large cities has depended largely on truck transport and the development of the interstate highway system.

Proximity to Markets for Output. In general, it is advantageous for firms to be able to serve their customers quickly and at low cost. Clearly, one way to do this is to locate close to these customers. Also, as indicated above, firms need to locate near their employees, and people need businesses as places of employment. These forces combine to ensure that many firms will locate in population centers. Except for firms that are tied to raw material sites (e.g., where the production process results in large weight losses during manufacturing), there are strong economic forces pushing firms toward locations in urban centers.

Government Regulation.   Federal, state, and local governments are assuming a more aggressive role in determining where industry can locate. Many local governments have used zoning laws to regulate the location of businesses within the city. More recently, air and water quality rules imposed by federal and state governments have been important in determining where polluting industries can locate.

Secondary Location Factors

There are other factors that influence location decisions but are of secondary importance. Two examples are the physical environment and government attitudes and policies.

Physical Environment.   The climate, scenery, and environmental quality of an area may affect a location decision, especially if the other more fundamental characteristics are approximately the same as in the other locations being considered. Although there have been reports of an industrial location being selected because the company president enjoyed the scenery of the area, such cases are probably few in number. The competitive pressures of the marketplace would drive out firms whose important decisions were based on whim rather than economics.

State and Local Government Attitudes and Policies.   Much has been written about the climate for business in the various states. Some states in the Northeast and Midwest are thought by some to be antibusiness, whereas others, especially in the South, are so pro-business that they offer subsidies to new firms to locate plants in their states. These subsidies may take the form of property tax reduction, free sites for factory construction, low-interest loans, and even the construction and lease of buildings at below-market rates. Despite the claim about the importance of these subsidies, most evidence suggests that they play a secondary role in the location decision. Sometimes, however, businesses are able to obtain such subsidies by threatening to go elsewhere even though they have already decided to locate in the area. Their objective is simply to achieve a further reduction of their costs. In other cases, a firm may have decided to locate in a region and then will go "shopping" among the communities in the region for the best set of subsidies.

It should be recognized that low taxes in an area are not an advantage to a business if they are associated with a low level of public services. Poor schools, inadequate water and sewer systems, and/or limited police and fire protection may be the product of low taxes. These are not the characteristics of a good industrial location and the firm may have to incur additional costs to offset these inadequate public services. For example, elementary and secondary schools are important to the business because they influence the quality of the local labor force and are an important consideration for managers and other workers who might have to be recruited by the firm. If the schools are poor, it may be very difficult to attract workers to the area. Thus, wage rates may have to be increased substantially to attract these workers, thus at least partially offsetting the advantage of low taxes.

KEY CONCEPTS

- The threshold level for an activity in an area occurs when the demand curve is tangent to the average cost function.
- Primary location factors include raw materials availability, cost and availability of labor and energy resources, transportation alternatives, and proximity to the markets of output.
- Location factors of secondary importance include the physical environment and the attitudes and policies of state and local governments.

CASE STUDY

RANKING INDUSTRIAL LOCATION DETERMINANTS

A number of surveys of managers responsible for industrial location decisions have attempted to determine the importance of various factors in choosing an industrial location. The relative importance of these factors as reported in one study is shown in the following table.

Location Factor	Number of Respondents Rating the Factor as Being:		
	Very Important	Important	Not Important
Proximity to markets	16	1	—
Labor quality and availability	10	7	—
Proximity to raw materials	10	6	—
Transportation cost and availability	7	10	—
State/local taxes	1	3	13
State/local subsidies	—	—	13

Source: W. Cris Lewis, "Tax Concessions and Industrial Location: A Review," *Reviews in Urban Economics* 1(2) (1968):29–50.

Proximity to markets was clearly the most important locational factor. Labor quality and availability and proximity to raw materials appeared to be the second and third most important, while transportation ranked fourth. Most respondents indicated that state and local taxes were not an important consideration.

Summary

Selecting the location for a business is important because the costs of moving output, workers, and customers across space are significant. To economize on these costs, people and firms tend to locate together. The urbanization process observed in the United States reflects the economic advantages of concentrating people and business.

A firm that serves a linear market should locate at the median location in that market, that is, where there are an equal number of customers on both sides of the firm. Such a location will minimize the total transport costs associated with serving those customers. If two firms serve a linear market where buyers are evenly dispersed along that market, and demand does not vary with the seller's location, both will tend to locate at the midpoint. If demand is inversely related to distance from the seller, the two vendors would tend to locate closer to the socially efficient points.

Firms that use raw material from one source and sell finished output at another site choose a cost-minimizing location that depends on the cost of shipping raw materials relative to the cost of shipping output. Because of additional terminal costs, firms tend not to locate at points intermediate between raw material sources and markets. Products that are weight losing in production tend to be produced at the raw materials site, whereas firms that produce weight-gaining products tend to locate at the market.

The market areas served by competing firms depend on their relative production and transportation costs. Firms with lower production and/or transportation costs have larger market areas than their competitors. The cost differentials can become so great that the higher-cost firm loses its entire market area to the lower-cost firm.

Firms do not locate facilities in an area until the threshold level of demand has been achieved. This threshold is defined as the tangency of the average cost function and the demand curve. At that point, price covers average cost and a normal profit is possible. Some activities have low threshold levels and are found in even the smallest towns. Conversely, other activities tend to be found only in larger urban areas.

Location factors can be classified as primary or secondary. Primary factors include availability of raw materials, labor cost and availability, the cost of energy resources, proximity to markets, transportation costs, and alternative modes of transport. Secondary factors influencing location include an area's physical environment and government attitudes and policy. In general, differences in state and local taxes are not significant in selecting an industrial location.

Discussion Questions

17-1. Why do businesses tend to locate together?

17-2. What location factors would be of primary importance and which would be of little significance to a firm in each of the following industries: retailing, oil refining, higher education, and lumber?

17-3. Is it wise for a local government to subsidize industries that locate in its city? What advantages and disadvantages are associated with such action?

17-4. In the 1970s and 1980s, technical and vocational education programs were expanded rapidly in states that were aggressively seeking new industry. What connection, if any, do you see between such education programs and the industrial location decision?

17-5. What is the market area for your university or college? That is, from what geographic area do most of the students come? Did the location of the school influence your enrollment decision? Explain.

17-6. What would you estimate to be the market area of each of the following firms?
(a) General Motors Corporation
(b) A soft-drink bottling plant
(c) Chase Manhattan Bank
(d) First National Bank of Manhattan, Kansas.

17-7. Consider your community and two others that you are familiar with—one half as large and one twice as large (if there is one). What goods and/or services are available in your city that are not available in the smaller one? What is not available in your city that is found in the larger city? What is the explanation for this distribution of economic activities?

17-8. In the chapter, microcomputers and automobiles are used as examples of products for which firms tend to produce a "median" product. What other goods and services have similar "median" characteristics? Explain.

Problems

17-1. Customers of a firm are located along a road as indicated by the letters A through J in the diagram below.

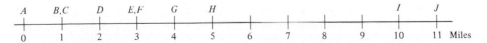

To service these customers, two truckloads of material must be delivered to each customer every week. The cost of making a delivery is $1.50 per mile.
(a) Determine the cost-minimizing location for the firm.
(b) Determine the total transportation cost each week assuming that: (1) the firm locates at the median location; and (2) the firm locates at the mean location.

17-2. United Express makes weekly deliveries to each of a number of customers located in cities along an interstate highway. The location of these cities, A, B, etc., and the number of customers in each is shown in the following figure:

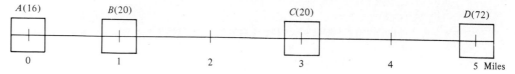

On one trip, four customers can be serviced. The transportation cost is $1 per mile.
(a) Determine the median location for locating the company's delivery center.
(b) Determine the total transportation costs at the median location.

17-3. Suppose that 500 swimmers are evenly distributed at intervals of two feet along a beach 1000 feet long (i.e., one at the two foot mark, one at the four foot mark, etc.). Initially assume that each will buy one hot dog during the day from the nearest vendor.

(a) If two hot dog vendors, A and B, locate at each of the following distances from the end of the beach, how many hot dogs will each sell during the day and what will be the total distance walked by the customers?

	Location of:	
Alternative	A	B
I	200′	400′
II	500′	500′
III	250′	250′

(b) Repeat the exercise of part (a) under the assumption that demand is inversely related to distance. Specifically, assume the following demand schedule for hot dogs:

Distance of Swimmers From Nearest Vendor	Number of Hot Dogs Purchased
Within 100′	3
101′ to 200′	2
201′ to 300′	1
More than 300′	0

17-4. U.S. Cement, Inc., uses 2 tons of raw material (i.e., limestone, clay, coal, and gypsum) to manufacture 1 ton of cement. All of the raw materials are available at site A and all final output is sold in a market (B) located twenty miles away. The transportation cost per ton of raw materials is $0.40 per mile, while the per ton cost of transporting cement is $0.60 per mile. Assume that rail is the only transportation alternative.
(a) Determine equations for the raw materials, output, and total transportation cost functions and plot these on a graph.
(b) Determine the location that minimizes total transportation costs (i.e., site A, B, or an intermediate location).

17-5. Consider two competing plants located at points A and B that are ten miles apart. Determine and sketch an equation for the market boundary separating these plants for each of the following cases:

(a) Product price is equal at both plants (i.e., $P_A = P_B = 20$) and per-mile transport costs per unit of output from each plant are the same (i.e., $s_A = s_B = 2$).

(b) $s_A = s_B = 2$ but $P_A = 25$ and $P_B = 20$.

(c) $s_A = 2$, $s_B = 3$, $P_A = 20$, and $P_B = 24$.

17-6. Mario's Fine Foods, a chain of ethnic restaurants, is considering locating a restaurant in Millville and Yorktown. The total cost and marginal cost functions of one of their restaurants are

$$TC = 1,000 + 2Q + 0.005Q^2$$

and

$$MC = 2 + 0.01Q,$$

where TC is total cost, MC is marginal cost, and Q is the number of meals served per week. The following demand and marginal revenue functions for each city have been estimated using data from market surveys:

Millville: $P = 10 - 0.005Q$, $MR = 10 - 0.01Q$
Yorktown: $P = 6 - 0.005Q$, $MR = 6 - 0.01Q$.

(a) Determine an equation for the average cost function. Sketch the average cost function and the two demand functions on the same graph. Use selected points from $Q = 0$ to $Q = 1,000$.

(b) What output rate in terms of meals per month would minimize the average cost per meal?

(c) Using the principles of threshold analysis, determine if a Mario's restaurant is feasible in Millville? Yorktown? Explain.

(d) For either or both cities where the restaurant is feasible, determine the profit-maximizing price-quantity combination, total revenue, total cost, and total profit.

References

Alonso, W. 1975. "Location Theory." In William Alonso and John Friedman, eds., *Regional Policy: Readings in Theory and Applications.* Cambridge, Mass.: The MIT Press.

Beckman, M. 1968. *Location Theory.* New York: Random House.

Dunn, E. A., Jr. 1983. *The Development of the U.S. Urban System, Vol. 2—Industrial Shifts, Implications.* Resources for the Future. Distributed by Johns Hopkins University Press.

Epping, G. M. 1982. "Important Factors in Plant Location in 1980." *Growth and Change* 13(2):47–51.

Fox, W. F. 1981. "Fiscal Differentials and Industrial Location: Some Empirical Evidence." *Urban Studies* 18(1):105–111.

Hotelling, H. 1929. "Stability in Competition." *Economic Journal* 39:41–57.

Kelton, C. M. L. 1983. *Trends in Relocation of U.S. Manufacturing.* Research in Business Economics and Public Policy, No. 6. Ann Arbor, Mich.: University of Michigan Research Press.

Lewis, W. C. 1968. "Tax Incentives and Industrial Location." *Reviews in Urban Economics* 1(2):29–50.

Miller, E. W. 1977. *Manufacturing: A Study of Industrial Location.* University Park, Pa.: The Pennsylvania State University Press.

Schmenner, R. W. 1982. *Making Business Location Decisions.* Englewood Cliffs, N.J.: Prentice-Hall.

INTEGRATING CASE PROBLEM V
GMG ENTERTAINMENT, INC.

GMG Entertainment, Inc., operates movie theaters in small cities throughout the United States. In many markets, the firm's theater is the only one in the area and typically serves several communities. GMG is considering the location of a theater in a regional market in Texas that consists of three communities along State Highway 84. The location of these cities and their population are shown below. In each city, 25 percent of the population are children under the age of 14.

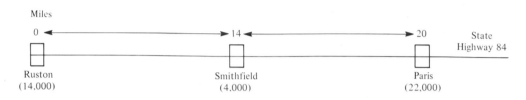

The number of movies demanded each month for each 100 persons in a city is given by the relationships

$$\text{Adults: } \overline{Q}_A = 100 - 10P_A - 1.5D$$
$$\text{Children: } \overline{Q}_C = 100 - 15P_C - 2D$$

where $\overline{Q}_A$ = the number of adult admissions per month per 100 population; $\overline{Q}_C$ = the number of children's admissions per month per 100 population; P_A and P_c are the prices of an adult and a child's admission; and D is distance from the customer to the theater in miles. Thus, if a_i and c_i represent the number of adults and children (in hundreds), respectively, in the ith city, the monthly demand functions for that city would be:

$$Q_A^i = a_i(100 - 10P_A - 1.5D)$$

and

$$Q_C^i = c_i(100 - 15P_C - 2D).$$

For Ruston, where there are 105 hundred adults, the demand function for adults would be

$$Q_A^R = 105(100 - 10P_A - 1.50).$$

The cost of building the theater is estimated to be $450,000, which includes the following:

Land: $50,000
Construction: $300,000
Equipment: $100,000

The board of directors of GMG insists that all capital investment projects be evaluated using 16 percent as the opportunity cost of capital. It is anticipated that the theater would have a fifteen-year life. GMG's marginal tax rate is 40 percent.

In addition to having overall responsibility, the manager also operates the projection equipment. She works seven nights per week. The jobs of ticket seller/taker and refreshment sales are filled by three workers whose schedules are varied so that two are on duty each night. It has been determined that janitorial service and utility expense (primarily for heating) vary with the number of customers and are estimated to total $0.15 per admission.

Estimated costs for operating the proposed theater include the following:

Movie rentals	$51,600 per month, plus $0.10 per admission
Property taxes	500 per month
Manager	1,800 per month
Employees	2,100 per month (total for all three employees)
Utilities, janitorial services, etc.	0.15 per admission

Thus, marginal cost is $0.25 per admission, and fixed costs each month are $56,000.

Requirement

Based on the information provided, prepare a report that determines the profit-maximizing location for the theater and the optimal prices for children and adults. Because the theater must have access to such urban services as police and fire protection, it must be located in one of the cities. Include in this report an evaluation of whether this capital investment should be made. Assume that there will be no change in demand or costs over the period, and, for simplicity, consider all revenues and costs as being collected or incurred at the end of each year.

LIFE IN A MIXED ECONOMY

SECTION VI

Taxes and Managerial Decisions

18

Preview

A large business may be required to pay dozens of different taxes and fees. At the federal level, there is the corporation income tax, the payroll tax, and various excise taxes. The state government is likely to utilize a sales tax, additional excise taxes, its own corporation income tax, and a payroll tax used to pay unemployment compensation. At the local level, firms may face property taxes, license fees, and other assessments.

In addition to providing revenue to finance the activities of government, the various taxes have something else in common—each can affect managerial decision making. Taxes affect managerial decisions in several ways. Sometimes tax considerations determine the legal form selected for a business enterprise. For example, a desire to avoid payment of the federal corporation income tax may cause a firm to continue to operate as a partnership rather than to incorporate. Taxes can affect methods of doing business. Effluent taxes provide incentives to reduce pollution, and property tax rates may affect locational decisions. Taxes can also be an important determinant of the demand for a product sold by a business. For example, an excise tax imposed on margarine made it difficult for that good to compete with butter. In contrast, a substantial income tax credit available to the purchasers of solar heating systems allowed such equipment to become more competitive with other methods of heating.

This chapter uses the tools of economic analysis developed in previous chapters to analyze ways by which taxes can affect managerial decisions. First, the impact of an excise tax on equilibrium prices and quantities is discussed. Next is a consideration of optimal strategies when a profits tax is imposed. The third section examines how taxes on inputs affect production decisions, and the fourth analyzes the effect of the property tax. The chapter concludes with an evaluation of preferential tax treatment, such as the income tax deduction for interest expenses, investment tax credits, and accelerated depreciation.

Excise Taxes

An *excise tax* is a sales tax levied on a particular good or service. For example, the federal government imposes excise taxes on gasoline, cigarettes, and liquor. Most states tax these three commodities, and many utilize excise taxes on other goods and services, such as soft drinks, hotel lodging, and theater tickets. In addition to providing revenues, excise taxes are sometimes used to decrease the quantity demanded for a product by increasing its effective price. Substantial excise taxes levied on cigarettes and liquor have always been justified as a means of reducing the quantity demanded of those products. Similarly, taxes on gasoline are used as a means of encouraging energy conservation. This approach is common in Europe, where excise taxes on motor fuel may cause retail prices to be double or triple the wholesale price of gasoline.

CASE STUDY
THE BEER TAX IN THAILAND

Using excise taxes to alter consumer behavior can be a tricky undertaking. Sometimes the results are not as intended. Recently, the government of Thailand imposed a heavy excise tax on beer. As a consequence of the tax, the price increased to $1.75 per pint and beer consumption dropped by 50 percent. But because the tax applied only to beer, other alcoholic beverages became relatively less expensive. For example, a pint of whiskey could be purchased for about the same amount of money as a pint of beer. The result was increased consumption of substitute beverages such as whiskey and other hard liquors. Thus by taxing beer, the government inadvertently encouraged people to switch to beverages with a higher alcohol content.

Typically, it is the ultimate responsibility of the seller to pay an excise tax. Consider a federal excise tax on cigarettes. Initially, assume that the rate is 6 cents per pack. Thus a store that sells cigarettes is obligated to remit 6 cents to the federal government for each pack sold. Now suppose that the tax is increased to 16 cents per pack. The store may raise the price of cigarettes by the amount of the tax increase, maintain the price at the pretax level, or increase the price by a portion of the tax increase. The pricing policy used by the store does not matter to the government as long as the seller pays 16 cents in tax for each pack of cigarettes sold.

How should the store determine the price to be charged for cigarettes? A first reaction might be that the choice is obvious; the price should be increased by the full amount of the tax. But that would not necessarily be a wise decision. In fact, it might be a very poor choice under certain conditions. Basically, proper pricing policy requires consideration of the demand and supply functions for the product being taxed.

Suppose that before the excise tax increase, the demand and supply schedules for cigarettes are as shown in Table 18-1. Note that supply equals demand at $0.50 per pack. Thus the equilibrium quantity is 16 billion packs and the equilibrium price is $0.50.

Table 18-1. Supply and Demand Schedules for Cigarettes

Price	Quantity Demanded*	Quantity Supplied* (Before Tax Increase)	Quantity Supplied* (After Tax Increase)
$0.65	10	22	18
0.60	12	20	16
0.55	14	18	14
0.50	16	16	12
0.45	18	14	10
0.40	20	12	8
0.35	22	10	6

*Billions of packs per year.

Now consider the 10-cent increase from 6 cents to 16 cents in the excise tax. Let the prices shown in Table 18-1 be those paid by the consumer. At each price level, the seller must pay an extra 10 cents in tax. Hence the net amount retained by the seller at any price level is 10 cents less than before. For example, if the consumer pays $0.50, from the perspective of the seller the price is the same as a price of $0.40 before the tax increase. But sellers' decisions are based on the amount of money actually received. Thus at a price to consumers of $0.50, only 12 billion packs per year will be supplied. Similarly, a price of $0.55 generates the same supply response as did a price of $0.45 before the tax increase. Thus the quantity supplied will be 14 billion. The other entries in the fourth column of Table 18-1 are determined in a similar manner.

The second and fourth columns of Table 18-1 can be used to determine the new equilibrium price. Note that supply and demand are equal at $0.55 per pack. This equilibrium price is 5 cents higher than the equilibrium before the 10-cent tax increase. The implication is that the tax increase is being shared by consumers and sellers. Consumers are paying 5 cents more for each pack of cigarettes and sellers are paying the other 5 cents. As expected, the new equilibrium quantity (14 billion packs per year) is less than the previous equilibrium amount (16 billion).

Figure 18-1 is a graphical representation of Table 18-1. The supply response to the tax increase is shown by shifting the supply curve upward by the amount of the tax (10 cents). This shift (shown in the figure as $S'S'$) reflects the increased cost to the firm of selling cigarettes. The new supply curve indicates that less is supplied at any price than before the tax increase. The new equilibrium price of $0.55 occurs at the intersection of DD and $S'S'$.

In general, an excise tax is not borne equally by consumers and sellers. The actual impact of the tax depends on the relative slopes of the supply and demand curves of the product being taxed. Consider Figure 18-2a. In this case the demand curve is vertical, indicating that demand is totally inelastic. Before the increase

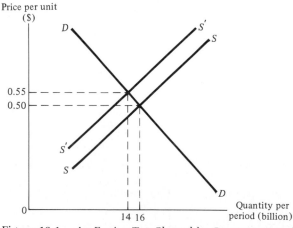

Figure 18-1.   *An Excise Tax Shared by Consumers and Sellers.*

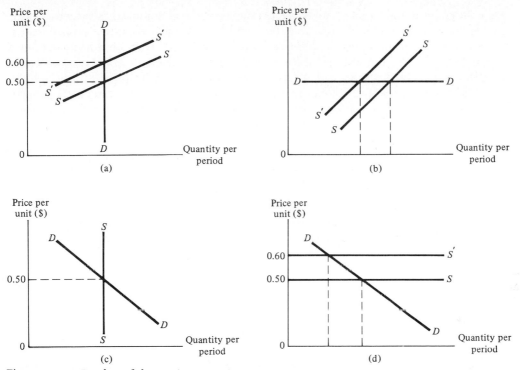

Figure 18-2. *Burden of the Excise Tax: Limiting Cases.*

in the excise tax the equilibrium price is $0.50. After the increase the new equilibrium price is $0.60, while the quantity remains unchanged. Note that the price has risen by the full amount of the tax increase. Thus there is no sharing of the tax increase. Consumers pay the entire 10 cents. The explanation is that quantity demanded is totally insensitive to price. Quantity demanded at a price of $0.50 per pack is the same as at $0.60 per pack. Thus the entire tax increase can be passed on to the consumer with no loss of sales to the producer.

Figure 18-2b depicts an upward-sloping supply curve and a horizontal (perfectly elastic) demand curve. As a result of the tax increase, the quantity decreases, but the equilibrium price does not change. Thus the seller pays all of the tax. The reason is that because demand is totally elastic, any price increase will cause quantity demanded to be zero. Hence no portion of the tax increase can be passed on to the consumer. The entire tax must be absorbed by the seller.

Figures 18-2c and d show vertical and horizontal supply curves. If supply is totally unresponsive to price (Figure 18-2c), there is no shifting of the supply curve in response to a tax increase. Equilibrium quantity remains unchanged and the entire tax is paid by the seller. In contrast, if the supply curve is horizontal (Figure 18-2d), consumers will bear the entire burden of the tax. This is because any decrease in the revenue per unit retained by the seller would cause quantity supplied to be zero. Thus the price increases by the full amount of the tax change.

In general, the effect of an excise tax on the price of a good or service depends on the elasticities of supply and demand. As demand becomes more elastic, a greater proportion of the tax must be paid by sellers. Similarly, as supply becomes more elastic, a larger share of the tax will be passed on to consumers. Thus if managers have information on elasticities of supply and demand, they will be able to anticipate the effects of changes in excise tax policies and plan accordingly. Although precise estimates of elasticities are not always available, even a rough guess can aid managers in making pricing decisions in response to changes in taxes.

KEY CONCEPTS

- As demand becomes less elastic, consumers pay a larger proportion of an excise tax.
- As supply becomes less elastic, sellers pay a larger proportion of an excise tax.

Taxes on Profit

In Chapter 10 it was shown that in the long run, firms in perfectly competitive markets earn no more than a normal rate of profit. In contrast, firms with market power may earn substantial economic profit. This economic profit represents a transfer of wealth from consumers to the shareholders of the firm. One means of redistributing this wealth is to impose a tax on profits. Ideally, such a tax would be paid only by firms that earn economic profits. As a practical matter, it is not possible to identify precisely the amount of economic profits being earned. Thus such taxes usually are structured as a percent of total accounting profit earned by a firm.

The purpose of this section is to analyze how a tax on profit affects pricing and output decisions of managers. It will be shown that the impact of such a tax depends on the objectives of managers. Specifically, it will be demonstrated that managers attempting to maximize total revenue respond to a profit tax differently than managers whose objective is profit maximization.

Profit Maximization and Profit Taxes

The profit-maximizing price and quantity for a monopoly are shown in Figure 18-3. Also shown is total profit earned at various output rates. Note that profit increases to output rate Q_m and declines for higher output rates.

Now assume that a proportional tax of t percent is levied on each dollar of profit. After-tax profit is also shown in Figure 18-3. Note that the effect of this tax is to reduce total profits by t percent at each output rate. However, it should also be observed that although less than before the tax, the output rate for

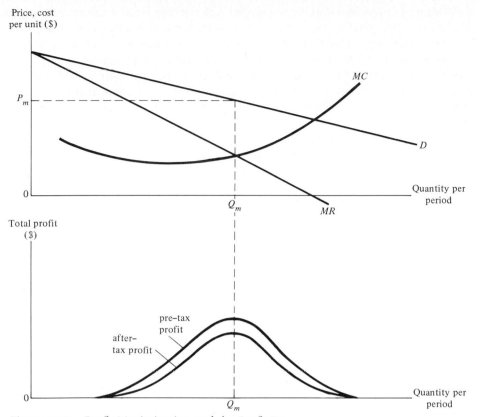

Figure 18-3. *Profit Maximization and the Profit Tax.*

maximum profit has not changed. The firm will maximize after-tax profit by producing Q_m units as before. Because the profit-maximizing quantity is the same, the price set by the firm for the product will not change either. The profit-maximizing price is still P_m. In the short run, the implication is that the entire tax is absorbed by the firm in the form of reduced profits. None of the tax is passed on to consumers in the form of higher prices.

However, a tax on profit can affect prices and output in the long run. Such a tax reduces the net return on investment. This means that less investment will take place and hence the amount of capital in an industry will be reduced. A result is that productive capacity will increase less rapidly than if the tax had not been imposed. Thus, because quantity supplied will be less, in the long run prices are likely to be higher because of the tax on profit.

Revenue Maximization and Profit Taxes

The models of firm behavior developed thus far have assumed that profit maximization is the goal of managers. However, profit maximization is not the only approach to developing models of the firm. Alternative assumptions regarding objectives of managers can be used. One alternative is revenue maximization, which presumes that a manager acts to maximize total revenues received by the firm. Use of the revenue-maximization assumption can result in conclusions that are quite different from those obtained by assuming profit maximization.

Figure 18-4 shows the revenue-maximizing rate of output. If profits are not a consideration, revenues are maximized at Q_1, where marginal revenue is zero. This result follows from the definition of marginal revenue—the extra revenue that results from producing 1 more unit of output. For any output rate less than Q_1, additional output increases total revenue because marginal revenue is positive. But beyond Q_1, marginal revenue is negative and hence total revenue declines.

The lower panel of Figure 18-4 shows profit at each rate of output. Let π_0 represent a target return set by management. Suppose that this target represents the minimum profit acceptable to the owners of the firm. Note, however, that profit is less than π_0 at Q_1. Thus managers must act to increase profit to at least the target return. In recognition of this constraint, a modified version of the

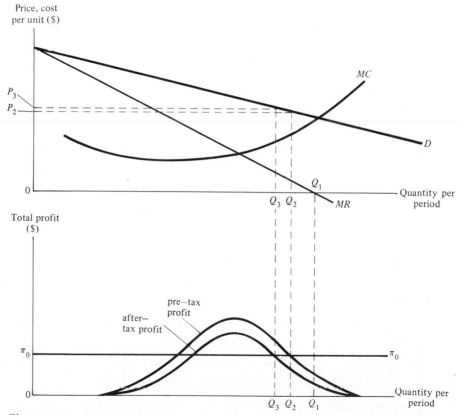

Figure 18-4.   *Revenue Maximization and the Profit Tax.*

revenue-maximizing hypothesis is often proposed. This variant assumes that the objective of managers is to maximize revenue subject to the constraint that the firm earn at least its target rate of profit. Output rate Q_2 in Figure 18-4 is the quantity that meets this objective. Any output greater than Q_2 yields less than the target profit. Because marginal revenue is positive, output rates less than Q_2 generate reduced total revenue. Corresponding to the output rate Q_2 is the price P_2.

Now suppose that a proportional profit tax is imposed. Figure 18-4 shows that after-tax profit at Q_2 is now less than π_0. Thus, to maximize revenue while satisfying the target profit constraint, output must be reduced to Q_3 and the price increased to P_3.

Note how the effect of the profit tax depends on the assumed objective of managers. For profit maximization, there is no short-run change in price or quantity as a result of the tax. In contrast, a revenue-maximizing manager subject to a target profit constraint will reduce output and increase price in the short run in response to a higher tax on profit.

KEY CONCEPTS

- If the firm's objective is profit maximization, the optimal price and quantity in the short run will remain unchanged if a profit tax is imposed.
- For revenue-maximizing managers subject to a target profit constraint, a profit tax will result in reduced output and higher prices.

Taxes on Inputs

A firm may be taxed or required to make other payments to government based on the amounts of certain inputs utilized in its production process. One example would be a state excise tax on energy use. Another is payments based on a firm's total wage bill to unemployment compensation or disability funds for those workers who lose their jobs or are injured while at work. Effluent taxes based on emission levels of certain pollutants are a third example of a tax on inputs. They can be thought of as taxes on the use of water and air as depositories for waste materials.

When a tax is levied on an input, a signal is provided to managers that relative prices of inputs have changed. Specifically, managers are signaled that the price of the taxed input is relatively higher than before the imposition of the tax. If managers are attempting to minimize costs, the tax may cause a change in the mix of inputs used for production.

Consider a firm that uses two inputs, capital and labor, to produce its product. Assume that the objective of managers is to minimize the cost of producing any

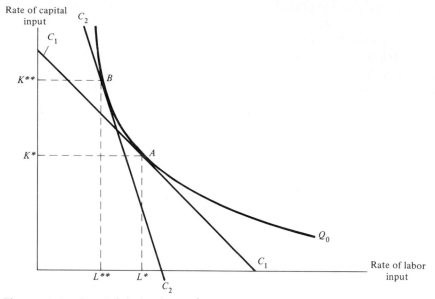

Figure 18-5. *Cost Minimization and Taxes on Inputs.*

given rate of output.[1] Figure 18-5 depicts an isoquant for Q_0 units of output. As discussed in Chapter 6, this isoquant shows all the efficient combinations of capital and labor that can be used to produce Q_0.

Let w be the cost of labor and r be the cost of capital. The isocost line C_1 shown in Figure 18-5 indicates the combinations of capital and labor that can be purchased for a given total expenditure, C_1. The slope of this isocost line is $-w/r$. For input prices w and r, the most efficient combination of capital and labor to produce Q_0 units is at point A, where the isocost line C_1 is tangent to the isoquant. Point A specifies use of L^* units of labor and K^* units of capital.

Now suppose that a tax of $\$t$ is imposed on each unit of labor used by the firm. What will be the least-cost combination to produce the given rate of output, Q_0? The tax raises the price of labor to $(w + t)$ and changes the slope of the isocost lines to $-(w + t)/r$. As before, the cost-minimizing rates of capital and labor are determined by the point where the lowest isocost line is tangent to the isoquant. The lowest isocost line is now C_2. Thus the optimal combination of inputs to produce Q_0 is at B, where C_2 is tangent to the isoquant. Point B indicates K^{**} units of capital and L^{**} units of labor. This combination includes more capital and less labor than before the tax. Thus the impact of a tax on labor is that managers substitute capital for labor in the production process.

This result is true in general. If technology allows substitution between inputs,

[1] The cost-minimization assumption is necessary for profit maximization because more efficient production results in increased profits. It is also a necessary condition for revenue maximization subject to a profit constraint as discussed in the preceding section. As costs decrease, the increased profit shifts the maximum output level at which a normal profit can be earned to the right. As long as marginal revenue is positive, the increased output level will generate greater total revenues. This point can be verified by referring to Figure 18-4.

a tax imposed on one input will cause greater use of the other inputs in the production process. One implication of this result is that input taxes can be used as a tool for public policy. For example, a tax levied on energy use would encourage energy conservation.

CASE STUDY

EFFLUENT TAXES

If private costs of production are less than the total costs imposed on society, too many resources may be allocated to an activity. The production of paper is a good example. A paper mill generates residuals in the form of chemicals, particulates, and odors that are discharged into the environment. The high level of pollution resulting from paper production occurs because the firm does not consider all the costs of its activities. The problem is that the prices of some of the inputs used by the firm do not reflect their true social cost. Specifically, the air and water used for waste discharge may be considered free goods by the managers of the firm.

High levels of pollution occur because of the lack of markets for air and water used in the production process. A business that uses energy or labor must pay for these inputs. But no one can exert an effective claim to ownership of the air, oceans, large lakes, and important rivers. Because there are no well-defined property rights, some individuals and firms can make free use of these resources. Further, there is no market mechanism to force them to take into account the social costs of their actions.

One approach to the problem of excess pollution is the use of effluent taxes. Under this approach, firms are allowed to select the level of emissions but are taxed for the privilege. A tax on pollution can be considered as a tax on the use of water and air as depositories for wastes. By raising the price of water and air in this use, policymakers encourage managers to substitute other inputs in the production process. For example, if a tax on emissions into the air is set high enough, a firm will find it can reduce costs by installing pollution control equipment that reduces the amount of emissions.

An advantage of effluent taxes is that they encourage the efficient allocation of resources. First, the divergence between private and social costs can be reduced or eliminated because the firm is forced to take into account the total social cost of its actions. Second, by allowing firms to select the optimal trade-off between polluting and paying taxes, variation in the cost of emission abatement can be taken into account. Firms with high control costs may find it profitable to make smaller reductions and pay larger amounts of effluent taxes. These funds can be used to compensate those who are affected by the firm's pollution. In contrast, firms that can easily reduce their polluting may find it less costly to make substantial reductions in discharges and thus avoid the tax.

Although they have promise, effluent taxes are not a panacea. It can be very difficult to determine the proper rate of the tax. Theoretically, the marginal tax rate should be equal to the marginal benefit of pollution abatement. Thus firms would devote resources to reducing emissions until the marginal cost exceeded the marginal benefit. In actual practice, marginal costs are very difficult to determine and any assessment of marginal benefits must be rather speculative. Effluent taxes have been used in Europe but have not found wide acceptance in the United States.

Property Taxes

Property taxes generate the bulk of revenues for local governments. Typically, the property tax is levied on land, structures, machines, and vehicles owned by a business. But there is considerable variability in property tax rates from one locality to the next. In one section of the United States the annual property tax assessment may represent about 1 percent of the market value of the property. In another location the property tax may be as high as 5 percent of market value. These variations in property tax rates can affect the value of the firm and also decisions of managers. Such effects are the focus of this section.

Fixed Property

Certain types of property are essentially fixed in location. Land is the best example, but large structures are much the same. Once constructed, it would be extremely costly and difficult to move a large manufacturing facility or an office building to a different location.

Assume that an economy has two taxing jurisdictions, A and B. Consider a parcel of land in A which has an exact counterpart in B. With no property taxes, suppose that both pieces of land have a market value of $1,000,000 and generate annual rents of $100,000. Thus the rate of return for each parcel is 10 percent.

A tax of 5 percent of total value is levied on property in jurisdiction A, but no property tax is assessed in jurisdiction B. As a result, the owner of the land in A must pay $50,000 in taxes every year. This means that net income for that property will be $50,000 and the after-tax rate of return will decline to 5 percent.

Now suppose that the two parcels of land are listed for sale at their pretax market values of $1,000,000. Clearly, the land in B would be preferred because of its higher rate of return. For the land in A to be competitive, its price would have to decline substantially. In fact, if the taxing policies of the two jurisdictions are not expected to change, the price would have to drop to $500,000. At this price the $50,000 in after-tax income of the property in A would provide the same 10 percent rate of return as the untaxed property in jurisdiction B.

When taxes are reflected in the value of property, the tax is said to be *capitalized*. The degree of capitalization of a tax is a function of the efficiency of capital markets in equalizing the rates of return on different assets. It is also dependent on the extent to which the tax is perceived as permanent. For example, if the 5 percent tax is expected to be eliminated after one year, the effect on property values would be much less than if the tax is expected to be maintained at the 5 percent rate indefinitely.

Basically, the effect of taxes on land and other property that cannot be moved is to cause a one-time reduction in the value of the property. Hence the full impact of the tax will fall on the owner of the property at the time the tax is imposed. Because any subsequent owner will acquire the property at a reduced price, only the original owner will experience a loss of wealth.

Mobile Property

Some property can be moved from one location to another. For example, a large firm can easily transfer its vehicles among different offices. It may also be possible to relocate machines and other capital equipment. If there is a significant variation in property tax rates between taxing jurisdictions, the firm may have an incentive to move capital from the high-tax to the low-tax area.

The effect of this reallocation of capital is shown by Figure 18-6. Suppose that there is a fixed amount of capital, as measured by the length of the horizontal line from O_A to O_B. The relocation of capital from jurisdiction B to jurisdiction A is shown as a movement to the right along the horizontal axis. Similarly, the relocation of capital from A to B is shown by a leftward movement. The curve D_A depicts the pretax rate of return earned by capital in location A. The curve is downward sloping from left to right in recognition of diminishing productivity as additional capital is employed in A. The pretax rate of return for capital in jurisdiction B is shown by D_B. This curve is read from right to left and is also downward sloping. If capital can move freely between the two jurisdictions, adjustments will be made until the rates of return are equalized. This equilibrium

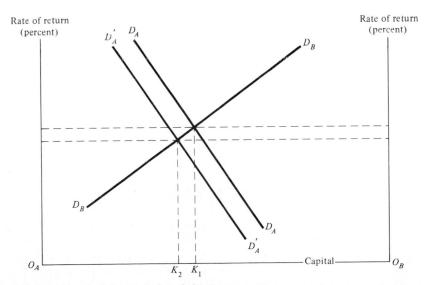

Figure 18-6. *Mobile Capital and the Property Tax.*

is shown by point K_1 in Figure 18-6. Thus the optimal amount of capital in A is $O_A K_1$, and the amount in B is $O_B K_1$.

Now consider the 5 percent property tax imposed on capital in jurisdiction A. This tax reduces the after-tax rate of return on capital. The new rate of return is shown by D_A. The impact of the tax is to cause capital to be moved from A to B until the rates of return are again equal. This occurs at K_2. Thus the tax causes $K_2 K_1$ units of capital to be shifted from A to B. Note that the rate of return earned in both areas is lower than before the imposition of the tax. Thus the property tax on mobile capital has caused a decline in wealth for the owners of capital in jurisdiction B as well as those in A.

In general, a property tax can be considered as a tax on certain inputs. As such, its effects are similar to those described in the preceding section. If substitution between inputs is possible, then, by increasing the prices of land and capital, the property tax tends to decrease the use of these inputs. But if the amounts of land and capital are fixed, production techniques remain unchanged and the property tax simply reduces the market value of the assets.

KEY CONCEPTS

- A tax imposed on one input causes a cost-minimizing manager to use more of other inputs and less of the taxed input.
- If property is fixed in location, a property tax will be capitalized. That is, the tax will reduce the market value of the asset and reduce its price.
- If capital is not fixed in location, it will tend to move from high-tax to low-tax jurisdictions until rates of return are equalized.

Tax Preferences

Although taxes extract a substantial share of the earnings of most firms, it is possible for managers to reduce tax payments by taking advantage of various tax preferences that have been incorporated into the tax system. As used here, tax preferences refer to business activities, decisions, or conditions that are given preferential treatment under tax laws. Three examples embodied in certain income tax laws are considered in this section. Discussed first is the provision that allows deduction of interest expenses. The second tax preference analyzed is the investment tax credit. Finally, the implications of using accelerated depreciation to compute tax liability are considered. In each case, the objective of the analysis is to show how these provisions affect managerial decisions.

Interest Deductions

As discussed in Chapter 16, firms obtain money for investment using a combination of debt and equity finance. But these sources of funds are treated differently with respect to tax laws. Interest payments on debt are considered as expenses and can be deducted in computing tax liability. In contrast, the dividends paid to stockholders and funds kept by the firm as retained earnings are not deductible.

The preferential treatment of debt under the corporation income tax affects the optimal capital structure used to finance the firm. Consider a corporation that needs to obtain X dollars to pay for a new production facility. The investment is to be financed using a combination of debt and equity. Thus

$$D + E = X$$

where D is the amount of debt and E is the amount of equity.

If the cost of \$1 of debt is r_d and the cost of \$1 of equity finance is r_e, the total cost of financing the investment is given by

$$(1 - t)r_d D + r_e E$$

where t is the rate of the corporation income tax. Note that the effective cost of debt is $(1 - t)r_d$ because deduction of the interest expense reduces the firm's tax liability by tr_d per dollar of debt.

Suppose that the objective of management is to minimize the total cost of financing the investment. One approach to the problem is to start with the assumption that only equity financing is to be used and then consider the effect on total cost of substituting dollars of debt for dollars of equity. Initially, it is assumed that r_d and r_e are not affected by the relative proportions of debt and equity.

Adding one more dollar of debt finance costs the firm $(1 - t)r_d$ while reducing equity generates a saving of r_e. Hence the net effect on total cost of financing the \$1 is

$$(1 - t)r_d - r_e \tag{18-1}$$

If $r_d = r_e$, then because of the tax deductibility of interest, the use of additional debt continually decreases the total cost. Generally, however, the cost of debt is less than the cost of equity because debt holders assume less risk than do those who have equity holdings. This is because interest on debt must be paid before any money can be paid to a firm's stockholders. As compensation for the greater risk they bear, shareholders demand higher rates of return. If it is assumed that $r_d < r_e$, the advantage of debt finance is even greater.

Equation (18-1) has a somewhat surprising implication. In that additional dollars of debt always decrease the total cost of financing the X of investment, costs will be minimized by using only debt finance. Clearly, this result is not consistent with actual practice. In fact, most firms have capital structures with more equity than debt. Relatively few large corporations have a capital structure with as much as 50 percent debt.

It should also be noted that the costs of debt and equity capital are probably not independent of the firm's capital structure. As relatively more debt is used, the level of risk also increases. This can be demonstrated by a simple example. Consider a corporation that earned \$1,000,000 after payment to all inputs except capital. Suppose that the firm has an interest expense of \$500,000. Thus the amount of income left for dividends and retained earnings is \$500,000. Note that earnings can decline substantially without impairing the firm's ability to meet its interest obligation. Of course, a decline in earnings would reduce the dollars left for dividends and retained earnings.

Now suppose that the firm's capital structure included more debt and that total interest expense was $950,000 instead of $500,000. If earnings are $1,000,000, the firm can still make its interest payments. But a relatively small decline in earnings can cause serious problems. If earnings drop by more than $50,000, the firm will be unable to meet its interest obligations. If this situation continues, the business may be forced into bankruptcy.

Investors require compensation for the increased risk associated with high debt/equity ratios. Thus, as more debt is used in the capital structure, the costs of both debt and equity finance increase. Let the higher costs of debt and equity (in comparison to the 100 percent equity case) be Δr_d and Δr_e, respectively. This increased cost is applied to the total dollars of debt (D) and the total dollars of equity (E). Thus the effect on total cost of using $1 more debt is given by

$$(1 - t)(r_d + \Delta r_d D) + (-r_e + \Delta r_e E)$$

which can be written as

$$[(1 - t)r_d - r_e] + [(1 - t)\Delta r_d D + \Delta r_e E] \qquad (18\text{-}2)$$

Equation (18-2) is easily interpreted. The first term in brackets is identical to equation (18-1) and represents the basic cost advantage of an additional dollar of debt finance. Note that for $r_d \leq r_e$, this term is always negative, indicating that total cost is reduced by using more debt. The second term in brackets is always positive and reflects the increased costs of capital associated with higher debt/equity ratios. As additional debt is utilized, $(1 - t) \Delta r_d D$ and $\Delta r_e E$ both become greater and thus the risk premium increases.

Equation (18-2) can be used to determine the optimal capital structure. Additional debt should be added until the basic cost advantage of debt is just offset

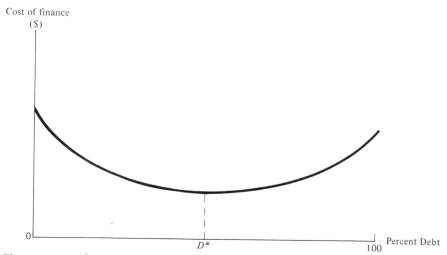

Figure 18-7.   *The Cost Minimizing Capital Structure.*

by the risk premium required for a higher debt/equity ratio. Initially, the risk premium will be small and total costs will be reduced by using more debt. But beyond some point, adding debt increases the total cost. This result is shown graphically in Figure 18-7, which indicates that financing costs are minimized when the capital structure includes D^* percent of debt.

Equation (18-2) shows how the tax preference for interest expenses affects the optimal capital structure. If $t = 0$, debt will be used only as long as the pretax cost advantage of debt $(r_d - r_e)$ exceeds the risk premium. By reducing the cost of debt relative to equity, the tax system provides an incentive for managers to use more debt. Hence, debt/equity ratios are likely to be higher than if the tax preference did not exist.

CASE STUDY
SALARIES VERSUS FRINGE BENEFITS

In hiring workers, a manager must consider the total cost of the compensation package being offered. This package includes a salary plus various fringe benefits. In evaluating a job offer, workers may be willing to trade salary for additional benefits. However, the terms of trade can be affected by the tax treatment of fringe benefits.

Certain fringe benefits are not subject to the personal income tax. For example, medical insurance and retirement contributions can be provided by an employer and not considered as taxable income to the worker. Thus the worker may be better off taking an additional dollar in fringe benefits rather than in salary. But the costs to the firm are the same. There is no tax advantage because both salary and fringe benefits can be deducted in computing the firm's income tax bill. Hence from the cost perspective of the firm, a dollar of salary is equivalent to a dollar of fringe benefits.

The preferential treatment of fringe benefits may alter the compensation package offered by the firm. Because the after-tax value to the worker of an additional dollar of fringe benefits is greater than an extra dollar of salary, the firm can provide the same total compensation to the worker at a reduced cost by offering relatively more fringe benefits than if the tax advantage was not available.

Investment Tax Credits

Business investment is crucial to a market economy. Without sufficient investment there will be little economic growth and existing facilities will soon become obsolete. Tax policy can be used to stimulate investment. One approach is the granting of tax preferences for investment. An investment tax credit is an example of such a preference. This credit allows businesses to reduce their corporation income tax liability by some fraction of the firm's investment spending during the year.

In Chapter 16 it was argued that firms should undertake only those investments that have positive net present value. Consider an investment that requires an initial outlay of $C dollars and has a useful life of T years. If the discount rate is r and the after-tax revenue resulting from the investment in a given year is $(1 - t)R_i$, the net present value of the investment is

$$NPV = \sum_{i=1}^{T} \left[\frac{(1 - t)R_i}{(1 + r)^i} \right] - C$$

If $NPV > 0$, the investment is profitable for the firm.

Now suppose that the provisions of the corporation income tax are changed to allow a 10 percent tax credit for investments made during the tax year. This credit would allow the firm to subtract $0.10C$ from its income tax payment, meaning that the actual cost to the firm of the investment would be only $0.90C$. Hence the net present value of the investment is now

$$NPV = \sum_{t=1}^{T} \left[\frac{(1 - t)R_i}{(1 + r)^i} \right] - 0.90C \qquad \text{(18-3)}$$

Because costs are reduced, the net present value increases. Thus one effect of the investment credit is to make profitable investment proposals more profitable. Another is to induce investment in projects for which net present value had been negative, but now are profitable because the net present value is positive. A third effect is to cause substitution of capital for other inputs in production. Because the effective after-tax cost of capital equipment is less than it would be without the credit, capital becomes relatively less expensive. Hence costs can be reduced by using more capital and less of other inputs.

CASE STUDY

SOLAR AND CONSERVATION CREDITS

Tax credits have also been used to alter consumer purchasing decisions. During the late 1970s, there was a strong sentiment in Congress to conserve energy and promote the use of alternative energy sources. Legislation was enacted that allowed taxpayers a credit against their income taxes of 15 percent of the cost of home energy conservation expenditures to a maximum tax saving of $300. A credit was also allowed for the purchase of solar, wind, and other alternative energy systems. This credit was set at 40 percent of the cost of the system, with a maximum tax saving of $4,000.

The effect of the conservation and alternative energy system tax credits was to reduce the cost of such investments. By making them less expensive relative to use of conventional fuels such as oil and gas, the intent was to induce consumers to increase their conservation and alternative energy system expenditures.

However, one concern about the consumer tax credits is whether they significantly change consumer purchasing patterns. Those consumers who would have invested in conservation or alternative energy systems even without the tax credits receive a windfall benefit. In evaluating the credits, this windfall must be compared to the benefits to society of the additional investment that was induced by the tax credits.

Although the evidence is not definitive, the case for conservation tax credits appears weak. Survey information collected by the authors suggests that almost all conservation expenditures would have been made even without the tax credits. In contrast, credits for alternative energy investments seem to have played an important role in stimulating investment in this area. Only a small proportion of the survey respondents said they would have bought solar or wind energy systems if the credits had not been available.

Accelerated Depreciation

In computing corporation income tax liability, depreciation expenses are deductible. Thus, when depreciation is taken into account, the net present value of an investment is given by the expression

$$NPV = \sum_{i=1}^{T} \frac{(1 - t)R_i + td_iC}{(1 + r)^i} - C$$

where d_i is the fraction of the total cost of the investment that can be depreciated in the ith year. Note that the depreciation allowance for any given year increases the net present value of the investment by $td_iC/(1 + r)^i$. The reason is that the present value of the firm's tax liability is reduced by that amount. The expression for net present value can also be written as

$$NPV = (1 - t) \sum_{i=1}^{T} \frac{R_i}{(1 + r)^i} + tC \sum_{i=1}^{T} \frac{d_i}{(1 + r)^i} - C \qquad (18\text{-}4)$$

For given C and t, note that the net present value increases as $\sum_{i=1}^{T} [d_i/(1 + r)^i]$ increases. But $\sum_{i=1}^{T} d_i = 1$. Thus the magnitude of $\sum_{i=1}^{T} [d_i/(1 + r)^i]$ depends on the size of the individual d_i. Because the depreciation benefit is discounted to the present, a method that allows larger write-offs in the early years of the depreciation period will result in greater net present value than one that specifies that the depreciation rate must be constant over the useful life of the investment. Thus if a firm is allowed to depreciate its assets more rapidly, otherwise unprofitable investment proposals may now show a positive net present value. The result is that additional investment may occur.

The straight-line method is the simplest technique for computing depreciation allowances. For a depreciation time of T years, this approach would specify $d_i = 1/T$ for all i. For example, if $T = 5$ and the cost of an investment is $100,000, the annual depreciation allowance is one-fifth of $100,000, or $20,000.

To stimulate additional investment, firms are sometimes allowed to use accelerated depreciation methods. The double-declining-balance technique is one example. Instead of deducting $1/T$ in the first year, the firm is allowed to deduct $2/T$ of the total amount in the first year and $2/T$ of the remaining balance in subsequent years. For the example given above, 40 percent of the $100,000 could be depreciated in the first year ($40,000), 40 percent of the remaining $60,000 in the second year ($24,000), 40 percent of $36,000 in the third year ($14,400), and 40 percent of the remaining $21,600 in the fourth year ($8,640). The final $12,960 of the original $100,000 would be written off in the last year of the depreciation period.

Although the total amount of depreciation is $100,000 under both schemes, the present value of the tax saving is greater with accelerated depreciation. If the tax rate is 50 percent and the discount rate is 10 percent, the present value of the tax saving for straight-line depreciation is

$$(0.50)\left[\frac{20{,}000}{(1.10)^1} + \frac{20{,}000}{(1.10)^2} + \frac{20{,}000}{(1.10)^3} + \frac{20{,}000}{(1.10)^4} + \frac{20{,}000}{(1.10)^5}\right] = \$37{,}900$$

while the amount using double declining balance is

$$(0.50)\left[\frac{40{,}000}{(1.10)^1} + \frac{24{,}000}{(1.10)^2} + \frac{14{,}400}{(1.10)^3} + \frac{8{,}640}{(1.10)^4} + \frac{12{,}960}{(1.10)^5}\right] = \$40{,}515$$

Note that the net present value of the investment increases by $2,615 under the double-declining-balance method. Thus the investment is more likely to have a positive net present value if accelerated depreciation is allowed for tax purposes.

KEY CONCEPTS

- Deductibility of interest payments on debt has the effect of increasing the amount of debt in a firm's optimal capital structure.
- Investment tax credits may stimulate investment by reducing the cost and hence increasing the net present value of an investment.
- By increasing the present value of tax savings, accelerated depreciation increases the net present value of an investment. Thus additional investment may be undertaken.

Summary

By increasing the effective price, an excise tax can be used to decrease the demand for a good or service. However, the effect of an excise tax on the profit-maximizing price charged by a firm depends on conditions of supply and demand. The proportion of the tax that can be passed on to consumers is inversely related to the elasticity of demand. If demand is totally elastic, an excise tax must be absorbed by sellers. Conversely, the price increase that is caused by an excise tax is directly related to the elasticity of supply. If the supply curve is horizontal, consumers will pay the entire tax.

The effect of a tax on profit depends on the objectives of managers. If the goal of managers is to maximize profit, a tax on profit will not affect the optimal price and quantity in the short run. However, if the objective is revenue maximization subject to a profit constraint, a profit tax will cause a reduction in output and an increase in price in the short run.

Excise taxes may be imposed on inputs used by a firm. Such taxes signal managers that the relative prices of the inputs have changed. If technology allows substitution, a tax on one input will cause other inputs to be substituted for the input that is taxed.

Property taxes reduce the rate of return earned on the taxed property. If the property is fixed in location, the property tax will be capitalized and the market value of the property will decline. But if the property can be moved from one location to another, firms will shift property from jurisdictions with high tax rates to those with lower rates. This adjustment will continue until the after-tax rates of return are equal in all jurisdictions.

Interest payments on debt can be deducted in computing income taxes. This preferential treatment of debt reduces its after-tax cost relative to equity. Hence the tax system causes relatively more debt to be used in the corporation's capital structure. But higher debt/equity ratios mean greater risk for those who provide funds to the firm. Thus the costs of debt and equity capital increase. The implication is that there is a cost-minimizing debt/equity ratio for the firm.

Investment tax credits are used to stimulate investment in capital goods. They allow the firm to reduce its income tax by some fraction of the cost of an investment. By increasing their net present value, some investments that would have been unprofitable without the credits may now be undertaken by the firm.

By treating depreciation as a deductible expense, the tax system increases the net present value of an investment by an amount equal to the present value of the tax saving. But methods of accelerated depreciation, such as the double-declining-balance approach, increase the present value of the tax saving. As a result, they stimulate investment demand and encourage the substitution of capital for other inputs.

Discussion Questions

18-1. An excise tax is imposed on a product for which there are few good substitutes. Who will pay the tax? Explain.

18-2. If there is no minimum profit constraint, how does the revenue-maximizing firm select the optimal rate of output?

18-3. Can a proportional tax on profit affect the long-run price and rate of output for a profit-maximizing firm? Explain.

18-4. A good is produced using capital and labor. Suppose that a tax is imposed on capital. What is the relationship between the convexity of the isoquant and the effect of the tax? Explain.

18-5. What does it mean to say that a tax has been "capitalized"?

18-6. A tax on capital used in jurisdiction A could reduce the rate of return on capital employed in jurisdiction B even though there is no tax on capital in B. Explain.

18-7. New legislation eliminates all taxes on profit. How would this change affect the optimal proportions of debt and equity in the capital structure of firms?

18-8. Why does the marginal cost of both debt and equity increase if relatively more debt is used in the firm's capital structure?

18-9. A firm operates in a country that imposes a highly progressive tax on profit. Interest paid on debt can be deducted from taxable income and there is an investment tax credit. How is the value of the interest deduction related to the profitability of the firm? How is the value of the investment tax credit related to the profitability of the firm?

18-10. For tax purposes, firms are allowed to use accelerated depreciation. In evaluating investment decisions, how is the effect of accelerated depreciation related to the discount rate used by the firm in decision making?

Problems

18-1. The market supply and demand functions for video tapes are given by:

$$Q_S = 100 + 20P$$
$$Q_D = 300 - 5P$$

where Q is quantity and P is the price of tapes.
(a) What is the equilibrium price and rate of output?
(b) If an excise tax of $2 per tape is imposed on the seller, what will be the new equilibrium price and rate of output? What proportion of the tax will be paid by purchasers of the tapes?

18-2. In a small, isolated college community there are 2,000 apartments. In the short run, the only use of these apartments is for rental to students. The college has a large summer school program that results in a 100% occupancy rate throughout the year. The demand for apartments by students is given by

$$Q_D = 4,000 - 2P$$

where Q_D is the number of apartments demanded and P is the average monthly rental rate.

Obscene graffiti painted on walls and sidewalks is a serious problem in the community. The mayor thinks that college students are responsible and that they should pay for the cleanup. Because students occupy all of the town's apartments, she proposes a monthly tax of $25 on each apartment rental.
(a) On an annual basis, how much revenue will the tax provide?
(b) Evaluate the tax as a means of forcing students to pay for cleanup of their obscene graffiti.

18-3. Fred Merkle and Co. is the monopoly supplier of old movies in a region. Over a year's time, the demand for movies is given by

$$P = 100 - Q$$

where P is the price of movies and Q is the quantity demanded per year. The firm's total (TC) and marginal cost (MC) functions are

$$TC = 800 + 20Q + Q^2$$

and

$$MC = 20 + 2Q$$

(a) What is the profit-maximizing price and rate of output?
(b) What is the revenue-maximizing price and rate of output?

(c) If the objective is to maximize revenue with a constraint that total revenue be greater than or equal to total cost, what is the revenue-maximizing price and rate of output?

(d) Repeat part (c) assuming that a 10 percent tax is imposed on profit, defined as the difference between total revenue and total cost. Is your answer consistent with the discussion of the profit tax in the chapter? Explain.

18-4. A firm manufactures a product using both capital and labor. A federal tax credit is available for capital expenditures. Use isoquant analysis (see Figure 18-5) to show how the optimal combination of inputs used to produce Q_0 units of output would be affected by the tax credit.

18-5. A parcel of land has a market value of $100,000 and is located in a county with no property tax. Assume that a permanent $500 per year property tax is imposed on the land. If the tax is fully capitalized, what will be the market value of the land after the imposition of the tax? Assume that investors use a discount rate of 10 percent.

18-6. Managers of Quick Foto of Fargo, North Dakota, are considering the purchase of a new device for processing film. The cost of the machine is $10,000, it has an expected useful life of ten years, and a salvage value of $1,000. The firm's managers believe that the machine will increase Quick Foto's revenues $2,000 per year. Operating expenditures are projected to be $500 per year. Assume that revenues and operating expenditures are incurred at the end of each year and that managers use a 14 percent discount rate in making investment decisions. The firm's marginal tax rate is 20%. What rate of investment tax credit would be necessary to cause managers to purchase the machine? Consider the credit to be received at the time of purchase.

18-7. A new cement truck would cost the Sure Stick Concrete Company $100,000. The law allows the firm to use either straight-line or double-declining-balance depreciation for tax purposes. The truck can be depreciated over five years and the discount rate used by managers is 12 percent. The firm's marginal tax rate is 30 percent. What effect does the choice of a depreciation method have on the net present value of the investment in the truck?

Problems Requiring Calculus

18-8. A property tax of T dollars per year is placed on a piece of urban property. If the tax is fully capitalized:

(a) Write a general equation showing the change in the market value of the property as the amount of the tax changes.

(b) Write a general equation showing the change in the market value of the property as the discount rate used to capitalize the tax changes.

18-9. Acme Manufacturing produces a product using labor and capital as inputs. The firm's production function is given by:

$$Q = 25K^{0.1}L^{0.9}$$

The price of labor is $10 and the price of capital is $20.

(a) If the product is to be manufactured at minimum cost, for any rate of output, how much labor should be used for each unit of capital employed?

(b) Suppose a 10 percent tax is imposed on capital. How much labor should be used for each unit of capital?

(c) Starting from the initial prices, if a 10 percent tax is placed on each input, how much labor should be used for each unit of capital employed?

References

Browning, E. K., and Browning, J. M. 1983. *Public Finance and the Price System*. New York: Macmillan.

Feldstein, M. 1978. "The Welfare Cost of Capital Income Taxation." *Journal of Political Economy 86*(April; Part 2):S29–S52.

Harris, J. 1980. "Taxing Tar and Nicotine." *American Economic Review*, June. pp 300–311.

Henderson, J. M., and Quandt, R. E. 1980. *Microeconomic Theory*. New York: McGraw-Hill.

Musgrave, R. A., and Musgrave, P. B. 1973. *Public Finance in Theory and Practice*. New York: McGraw-Hill, Chaps. 11–13, 17, 18.

Singer, N. M. 1976. *Public Microeconomics: An Introduction to Government Finance*. Boston: Little, Brown, Chaps. 10–12.

Appendix: Calculus and Tax Analysis

In the chapter it is demonstrated that the short run profit-maximizing price and quantity are not affected by a profit tax. It is also shown that a tax on one input results in greater use of the nontaxed input in the production process. Both of these propositions are easily demonstrated using calculus.

Profit Maximization and Profit Taxes

Assume that capital and labor are used in production and that their prices are r and w, respectively. Profit is defined as the difference between revenues and costs. Thus the objective of the profit-maximizing firm is to produce a rate of output such that the value of the profit function, $PQ - wL - rK$, is a maximum. This is done by taking the derivative with respect to Q and setting it equal to zero. Note that L and K are considered to be functions of Q. Thus

$$\frac{\partial \pi}{\partial Q} = \left(\frac{\partial P}{\partial Q}Q + P\right) - \left(w\frac{\partial L}{\partial Q} + r\frac{\partial K}{\partial Q}\right) = 0 \tag{18A-1}$$

But $(\partial P/\partial Q)\, Q + P$ is marginal revenue and $w(\partial L/\partial Q) + r(\partial K/\partial Q)$ is marginal cost. Hence the condition for profit maximization is that marginal revenue equal marginal cost.

Now assume that a tax of t percent is imposed on each dollar of profit. Thus the expression for after-tax profit is given by

$$(1 - t)(PQ - wL - rK)$$

and the first-order condition for maximum profit is given by

$$(1 - t) \left[\frac{\partial P}{\partial Q} Q + P - \left(w \frac{\partial L}{\partial Q} + r \frac{\partial K}{\partial Q} \right) \right] = 0 \qquad (18A\text{-}2)$$

But the value of Q that satisfies equation (18A-2) again occurs at the output rate where marginal revenue equals marginal cost. Thus it is seen that a profit tax has no effect on the profit-maximizing quantity. Because quantity is unaffected by the tax, it is also known that the profit-maximizing price does not change.

Cost Minimization and Taxes on Inputs

For any given rate of output, costs are minimized by minimizing the function $PQ - wL - rK$. This is done by taking partial derivatives with respect to K and L and equating them to zero. Thus

$$\frac{\partial \pi}{\partial L} = \left(\frac{\partial P}{\partial Q} Q + P \right) \frac{\partial Q}{\partial L} - w = 0 \qquad (18A\text{-}3)$$

and

$$\frac{\partial \pi}{\partial K} = \left(\frac{\partial P}{\partial Q} Q + P \right) \frac{\partial Q}{\partial K} - r = 0 \qquad (18A\text{-}4)$$

Dividing equation (18A-3) by (18A-4) and eliminating the term $\left(\frac{\partial P}{\partial Q} Q + P \right)$ yields

$$\frac{\partial Q}{\partial L} \Big/ \frac{\partial Q}{\partial K} = \frac{w}{r} \qquad (18A\text{-}5)$$

This is the same result as that obtained in Chapter 6 and specifies that minimum cost production occurs when the ratio of marginal products equals the ratio of prices.

Now suppose that a tax of $\$t$ per unit is imposed on labor. This causes the effective price of labor to be $w + t$. Hence equation (18A-3) becomes

$$\left(\frac{\partial P}{\partial Q} Q + P \right) \frac{\partial Q}{\partial L} = w + t \qquad (18A\text{-}3')$$

and the condition for cost minimization is now given by

$$\frac{\partial Q}{\partial L} \Big/ \frac{\partial Q}{\partial K} = \frac{w + t}{r} > \frac{w}{r} \qquad (18A\text{-}6)$$

Equation (18A-6) requires that the ratio of marginal products be greater than before the imposition of the tax. This can be achieved only by reducing the amount of labor used to produce the given output and/or increasing the amount of capital.

Antitrust, Regulation, and Price Controls

19

Preview

If competition benefits society, a top priority for government action should be the implementation of policies designed to enhance competition. In the United States, the primary public policy approach to increasing competition is through the use of antitrust laws. These statutes give enforcement agencies the power to alter existing or proposed market structures and to impose penalties for certain types of business conduct determined to be anticompetitive.

To avoid litigation, it is important that managers understand the scope and limits of antitrust law. Thus, the first section of this chapter considers antitrust activity in the United States. The objective is to make the reader aware of business activities that may violate antitrust statutes. The discussion begins with a review of basic U.S. antitrust laws and enforcement procedures. Next is a consideration of antitrust law as it applies to monopolization, mergers, collusion, and price discrimination. Finally, remedies and penalties used in antitrust enforcement are discussed.

Antitrust laws deal with industry structure and conduct. In contrast, the regulatory approach to public policy focuses on industry performance. It is based on the presumption that there may be circumstances where competition is not possible or is not desirable. Thus to prevent adverse consequences from the lack of competition, government may regulate firms so that they perform in a socially acceptable manner. Regulation may take the form of requiring approval for price changes, limiting entry or exit, or prescribing standards that a product or service must meet. The second major section of the chapter examines public utility regulation in the United States. The first topic considered is the need for public utility regulation. Following that is a brief overview of regulatory procedures.

Price controls are another tool that can be used by government to control business activity. Generally, they are used to combat inflationary pressures and expectations. The last section of this chapter evaluates the impact of price controls. Of particular importance is the differential effect of controls in competitive and concentrated industries.

Antitrust Policy

The highly restrictive assumptions of the model of perfect competition as discussed in Chapter 10 are rarely met in actual practice. Moreover, the complexities of markets and the politics of decision making make it unlikely that any reasonable set of public policies could generate the conditions for perfect competition. Thus public policy must be content with a more limited objective. J. M. Clark (1940) proposed that a realistic goal for policymakers is workable competition. He argued that it is not necessary that all the requirements for perfect competition be met to achieve results that approximate those of the competitive ideal.

Clark suggested that markets may fail to meet one or more of the criteria and still be "workably" competitive.

The achievement of workable competition is the goal of antitrust activity. The antitrust approach acknowledges that imperfections exist in many markets but is directed toward narrowing the gap between actual conditions and the competitive ideal. The philosophy underlying antitrust enforcement is that by modifying the structure of markets and conduct of participants in markets, performance can be improved without direct government involvement in the daily decision making of managers. Prevention of a merger between two large corporations is an example of a structural modification. A fine assessed for fixing prices illustrates antitrust policy intended to alter business conduct.

U.S. Antitrust Laws

The Sherman and the Clayton Act (as amended) represent the primary legal basis for antitrust activity in the United States. The most important provisions of these two statutes are discussed below.

Sherman Act. The Sherman Act was enacted in 1890 and has remained basically unchanged for over 90 years. It has two main sections:

Section 1. Every contract, combination in the form of a trust or otherwise, or conspiracy, in restraint of trade or commerce among the several states, or with foreign nations, is hereby declared to be illegal. Every person who shall make any such contract or engage in any such combination or conspiracy shall be deemed guilty. . . .

Section 2. Every person who shall monopolize, or attempt to monopolize, or combine or conspire with any other person or persons, to monopolize any part of the trade or commerce among the several states, or with foreign nations, shall be deemed guilty. . . .

These two sections focus on different types of undesirable business behavior. Section 1 is intended to prohibit firms from conspiring to initiate and maintain practices not in the public interest. For example, an agreement among managers to fix prices would violate Section 1. Section 2 of the Sherman Act is designed to reduce market dominance. Firms that aggressively act to gain control of their markets may be in violation of Section 2. For example, in 1911 Standard Oil of New Jersey was found guilty of illegal monopolization of the market for refined oil. As a result, the firm was split into 30 separate companies.

Clayton Act. The Clayton Act was enacted as a supplement to the Sherman Act. The intent of Congress was to provide legislation to prevent firms from obtaining monopoly power and also to specify specific business practices that are prohibited. The most important provisions of the act are contained in Sections 2 and 7.

Section 2. It shall be unlawful for any person engaged in commerce, to discriminate in price between different purchasers of commodities . . . where the effect of such discrimination may be to substantially lessen competition or tend to create a monopoly in any line of commerce. . . .

Section 7. No corporation engaged in commerce shall acquire, directly or indirectly, the whole or any part of the stock or other share capital of another corporation engaged also in commerce where the effect of such acquisition may be to substantially lessen competition between the corporation whose stock is so acquired and the corporation making the acquisition or to restrain such commerce in any section or community or tend to create a monopoly of any line of commerce.

These two sections each deal with a specific type of business practice. Section 2 is directed against certain types of price discrimination. Setting prices below cost to eliminate competition in a market is an example. Section 7 of the Clayton Act imposes restrictions on merger activity. For example, a merger between General Motors and Ford could (and probably would) be prevented based on Section 7. Notice that the language of the Clayton Act is not absolute. That is, price discrimination and mergers are prohibited only if they tend to "substantially lessen competition or create a monopoly in any line of commerce."

Two important amendments have modified the original Clayton Act. In 1936, the Robinson-Patman Act was passed to broaden the Section 2 provisions against price discrimination. The new act was aimed at large retailers who can undersell their smaller competitors because they can buy merchandise at lower prices from manufacturers and wholesalers.

In 1950 the Celler-Kefauver Amendment was enacted to supersede the provisions of Section 7 of the Clayton Act. The original Section 7 focused on competition "between the corporation . . . acquired and the corporation making the acquisition." This wording caused the courts to ignore the broader issue of a general lessening of competition. The result was that enforcement agencies found it difficult to prevent vertical and conglomerate mergers under the Clayton Act. Congress responded to this problem by passing the Celler-Kefauver Amendment, which amended Section 7 to read:

> That no corporation engaged in commerce shall acquire, directly or indirectly, the whole or any part of the stock or other share capital and no corporation subject to the jurisdiction of the Federal Trade Commission shall acquire the whole or any part of the assets of another corporation engaged also in commerce, where in any line of commerce in any section of the country, the effect of such acquisition may be substantially to lessen competition, or to tend to create a monopoly.

Note that the amendment reduced the emphasis on reduced competition between the merging firms and stressed the idea that the demonstration of a lessening of competition "in any line of commerce in any section of the country" could be used to prevent a merger. The effect of the change was to make vertical and conglomerate mergers subject to antitrust action.

Antitrust Enforcement

Antitrust proceedings are initiated in four ways. First the Antitrust Division of the Department of Justice may file a suit. If the suit is continued to the point of formal litigation, it is first heard in a federal district court. If either party wishes to contest the decision of the district court, the matter is taken to a circuit court of appeals and if the justices are willing to hear the case, to the Supreme Court.

The Antitrust Division's responsibility is limited to initiating and prosecuting a case. The courts must determine guilt and penalties.

The second path of antitrust enforcement is through the Federal Trade Commission. When the commission staff decides to issue a formal complaint and the matter is contested by the defendant, an initial hearing is held before an administrative law judge who is a part of the FTC. If the judge decides for the defendant, the matter is dropped. However, if the decision is to uphold the complaint, the defendant has the right to appeal to the five FTC commissioners. If their decision is again against the defendant, the matter can be appealed to the federal courts.

A third enforcement procedure involves state antitrust legislation. Most states have their own antitrust statutes. Typically, complaints are prosecuted by the state attorney general's office and decided by state courts. Appeals from decisions by the state supreme court can be taken to the federal court system.

The fourth method for dealing with alleged antitrust violations is litigation by private parties. Individuals or firms may file suits in the federal district courts. Appeals are heard by a circuit court of appeals and, ultimately, the U.S. Supreme Court. Currently, about 2,000 private antitrust suits are filed in the United States each year. Private suits represent over 90 percent of all antitrust actions.

Rule of Reason Versus Per Se Offenses

The standard of proof in antitrust prosecution differs with the nature of the alleged violation. Sometimes, although an apparent antitrust violation may have occurred, it is not clear that there has been a net injury to society. Such cases are decided under a *rule-of-reason standard.* In rule-of-reason proceedings, successful prosecution requires not only the demonstration that the act has been committed, but also that society is best served by prohibiting, modifying, or punishing the act. In contrast, certain activities are judged illegal without the requirement that the specific antisocial effects be shown. These acts are referred to as *per se offenses.*

The per se and rule-of-reason standards represent different points along a continuum. They differ in the volume and detail of evidence required for a successful prosecution. Rule-of-reason cases require extensive evidence proving that an act has been committed and demonstrating the damage that has been caused. Per se cases only require proof that the offense has been committed. In a sense, per se violations can be thought of as being judged as if the nature of the offense automatically dictates that the social costs of the act are clearly greater than any possible benefits. Thus there is no need to consider the issue on a case-by-case basis because the decision is inevitable.

Not all antitrust violations fit into the tidy categories of being per se or rule-of-reason offenses. Still, there are some examples that can be cited as illustrations of each. Generally, accepted as per se offenses are agreements to fix prices, divide markets between sellers, and to restrict or pool output. Activities evaluated under the rule-of-reason standard are mergers and monopolization of a market by a large firm or firms. As a rough guide, violations involving business conduct for which there is no strong justification are decided on a per se basis. In contrast, cases involving the structure of an industry usually are judged using the rule-of-reason approach.

KEY CONCEPTS

- Section 1 of the Sherman Act prohibits unfair business practices such as price fixing. Section 2 deals with monopolization.
- Section 2 of the Clayton Act (as amended by the Robinson-Patman Act) limits price discrimination.
- Section 7 of the Clayton Act (as amended by the Celler-Kefauver Act) is used to prohibit mergers that may result in a substantial lessening of competition.
- Antitrust actions can be initiated by the Department of Justice, the Federal Trade Commission, state officials, or private parties.
- Conviction of rule-of-reason offenses requires proof that the act has been committed and that social costs exceed benefits. Per se offenses require only a demonstration that the act has been committed.

Monopoly

Section 2 of the Sherman Act prohibits monopolizing, attempting to monopolize, and conspiring to monopolize. However, it is important to note that the economic and legal definitions of monopoly differ. In the study of economics, monopoly is defined as a single seller. The legal interpretation is much less restrictive. As used in antitrust proceedings, firms are viewed as having monopoly power if they have a high degree of control over the price of a good or service.

Since its enactment, the most controversial point with respect to Section 2 has been the standard of proof required for successful prosecution. The issue has been whether the Sherman Act made monopoly power in and of itself an offense or whether the showing of industry dominance had to be accompanied by evidence of illegal practices. During the past 90 years, the Supreme Court has positioned itself on both sides of this question. The position taken by the Court at any given time has had an overwhelming effect on the use of Section 2. When proof of illegal acts to achieve monopoly power has been required, there has been little Section 2 activity. When the Court has held that the government only had to show the existence of monopoly power, Section 2 cases have been more frequent and more successful. For example, between 1920 and 1945, the Court seemed to require some evidence of illegal activity. During that period there were very few successful Section 2 cases.

The current interpretation of Section 2 represents a compromise between the two extreme positions. The mere existence of monopoly power is not sufficient for successful prosecution under Section 2. However, the government no longer is required to show that a firm has engaged in acts that, considered by themselves, represent antitrust violations. Instead, prosecutors can focus on patterns of business behavior that have the net effect of allowing a firm to gain and maintain a monopoly position. Under this interpretation, practices that would be legal when considered in isolation or when used by smaller firms may be grounds for conviction if used by a firm judged to have dominance in an industry. That is, the standard used by the courts to judge large firms is more rigorous than that applied to smaller firms.

Most students of antitrust policy would agree that Section 2 of the Sherman Act has probably been a modest deterrent to high concentration in an industry. However, the main impact may come not from the results of litigation, but as firms modify their plans to take account of the costs and uncertainties of possible prosecution. It has sometimes been suggested that the ghost of Senator Sherman sits in every corporate boardroom.

CASE STUDY
THE GREAT ANTITRUST DOUBLEHEADER

In January 1969, the Justice Department brought suit against IBM under Section 2 of the Sherman Act for illegal monopolization of the general-purpose computer market. The government proposed that the firm be split into several competing companies. It took six years for the case to come to court. One reason for the delay was the discovery process whereby the government was required to make available over 25 million pages of documents to IBM and the firm provided over 60 million pages of documents to be used by the government in case preparation. The trial at the District Court level lasted six more years and generated 300,000 pages of testimony and exhibits.

In 1972, the Justice Department initiated litigation to force the American Telephone and Telegraph Company to sell off its manufacturing arm, Western Electric, and its local operating companies. The government charged that AT&T had used unfair practices to eliminate competition in the markets for telephone equipment and long-distance telephone service. The case has been referred to as the most important antitrust proceeding of all time because it sought the breakup of the largest privately owned enterprise that the world has ever known. At the time the suit was filed, AT&T employed several hundred thousand people and had revenues greater than the gross national product of all but 12 nations.

On January 8, 1982, the Justice Department announced resolution of both suits. The IBM suit was dropped because of changing conditions that had reduced the firm's market share and hence diminished the government's chances of obtaining a conviction. The AT&T suit was settled by a consent decree that required the firm to divest itself of all its local operating companies. These operating companies, such as Pacific Telephone and Telegraph, represented about two-thirds of AT&T's total assets. In return, the firm was allowed to keep Western Electric and to become an active competitor in marketing computers, an activity that had been prohibited by an earlier consent decree.

The settlement of the two cases on the same day probably was not a coincidence. While dropping one suit, the government could claim victory in another, thus avoiding political criticism. Also, although the IBM suit was terminated, a powerful new competitor, AT&T, was freed to compete with IBM in the computer industry.

Merger

The difficulty of constraining firms that already have market power suggests the need to halt monopolization in its formative stages. Because industry dominance has frequently been achieved by acquisition, merger policy is an important tool for antitrust action.

Evaluation of Mergers. Mergers between large firms create the potential for abuse of the market power obtained by the combined firm. This abuse may take the form of higher prices, actions to deter entry or to eliminate competitors, or exercise of monopsony power to obtain price reductions from suppliers.

The primary argument in support of mergers is the possibility of efficiency gains. These efficiency effects may result from several different factors. The merged firm may be able to reduce its cost of production and distribution by realizing economies of scale. Inefficient techniques may be abandoned as firms gain access to the patent rights and technical expertise of their new partners. Mergers may also concentrate assets under the direction of superior managers who have the ability to operate the firm more efficiently.

Although there may be other considerations, the basic decision to allow or prohibit a merger should rest on an evaluation of the costs of increased market power versus the social benefits of improved efficiency. Williamson (1968) has suggested a simple model for quantifying this trade-off. Consider the demand and cost curves shown in Figure 19-1. Suppose that a merger shifts the newly combined firm's cost curve down from AC_1 to AC_2, while providing market power that is exercised by increasing prices from P_1 to P_2. The welfare trade-off is shown in the figure. The crosshatched area A_1 represents the resource saving associated with producing Q_2 units at the reduced average cost, AC_2. The crosshatched area A_2 is the deadweight loss stemming from increasing the price from P_1 to P_2. It represents the loss in consumer surplus as the higher price reduces the quantity demanded from Q_1 to Q_2. The merger can be evaluated by comparing the cost saving and the deadweight loss.[1] If the deadweight loss is greater than the efficiency gain, the merger should not be allowed. But if the resource saving more than offsets the deadweight loss, there may be a net benefit to society from the merger.

However, income distribution effects may also be important in evaluating a merger. Prior to the merger, the rectangle B_1 was part of the surplus value re-

---

[1] Consumer surplus and deadweight loss are discussed on pages 338–339.

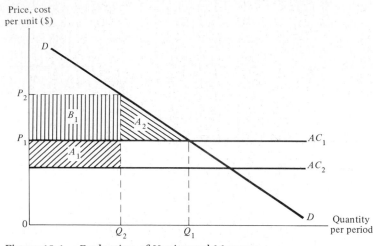

Figure 19-1. *Evaluation of Horizontal Mergers.*

ceived by consumers. After the merger, this area represents economic profit earned by the combined firm. This transfer of value from consumers to the owners of the firm may be viewed as a reason for prohibiting the combination.

Merger Guidelines.   Mergers between large corporations are a costly undertaking. Considerable expense is involved in finding a proper merger partner, structuring the merger proposal, communicating information to shareholders, and integrating the acquired firm. This cost can be greatly increased if the merger is challenged by the government. The actual expense of litigation can be substantial, but even more costly is the delay and uncertainty involved.

To aid firms in assessing the likelihood of government intervention, in 1982 the Justice Department announced guidelines to be used in deciding whether to challenge a merger. These guidelines are based on overall industry concentration as measured by the Herfindahl index. Described in Chapter 12, the Herfindahl index is usually computed by summing the squared market shares of all the firms in an industry. However, as used in the guidelines, the index is computed by squaring market share percentages, not fractions. Thus an industry with 10 firms each with a 10 percent market share would have a Herfindahl index of 1,000. The index for an industry that has a dominant firm with a 50 percent market share and five smaller firms each with 10 percent shares would be 3,000.

Under the new guidelines, any merger that leaves the industry with a Herfindahl index of less than 1,000 will not be challenged. Combinations resulting in a postmerger index greater than 1,800 will almost always be challenged. When the index falls between 1,000 and 1,800, the proposed merger will be carefully scrutinized to determine its competitive impact. In this case, other factors, such as efficiency impacts, trends in concentration, barriers to entry, and foreign competition are considered in deciding whether to challenge a merger.

EXAMPLE
TO CHALLENGE OR NOT TO CHALLENGE?

An industry consists of one firm with a market share of 30 percent and seven other firms with market shares of 10 percent each. The largest firm proposes a merger with one of the smaller firms. Would this merger be challenged by the Justice Department? Would a merger between two of the smaller firms be challenged?

Solution

After the merger, the industry would consist of one firm with a 40 percent market share and six with market shares of 10 percent each. Hence the post-merger Herfindahl index would be $40^2 + 6(10^2)$, or 2,200. Thus, because the index is greater than 1,800, the Justice Department is likely to challenge the merger.

If two of the smaller firms were to combine, the postmerger Herfindahl index would be $30^2 + 20^2 + 5(10^2) = 1,800$. In this case, the decision is less clear cut and would be determined by other factors, such as efficiency gains.

Present Merger Policy.   Horizontal mergers between large direct competitors are often challenged by the government. On most occasions, the courts have supported the government and prevented such mergers. The outcomes of proposed vertical and conglomerate mergers are less certain. During the 1960s and early 1970s, the government frequently was successful in challenging such mergers if they involved large firms. But during the late 1970s and early 1980s, antitrust enforcement agencies have shown less interest in preventing vertical and conglomerate mergers. At present, unless it appears that such mergers would increase horizontal market power, they are unlikely to be challenged.

Although the total number of mergers has not declined since passage of the Celler-Kefauver Act in 1950, there has been a dramatic change in the type of mergers. Government merger policy has been most effective in preventing horizontal acquisitions between large firms. But the outcomes of suits to prohibit vertical and conglomerate mergers have been less certain. The result is that merger activity is now biased toward vertical and conglomerate acquisitions.

KEY CONCEPTS

- Practices considered acceptable when practiced by small firms may represent antitrust violations if used by a large firm with considerable market power.
- One method of evaluating a merger is to compare efficiency gains with the social costs of increased market power. The income distribution effects may also be important.
- Mergers are likely to be challenged in industries where the postmerger Herfindahl index is greater than 1,800.
- The government has been very successful in preventing horizontal mergers between large direct competitors.

Collusion

Another important goal of antitrust activity is to prevent price fixing. Firms in oligopolistic markets have an incentive to collude. But the actual decision to collude is based on a benefit-cost calculation by the firms involved. The potential benefit of price fixing is obvious—increased profit. The costs fall into four inter-related categories. First, there is a cost associated with setting and changing industry price structures. Each firm in a cartel is in a different position, has different expectations, and varying economic power in the industry. Hence it may be difficult to reach agreement. A second cost of collusion is that imposed by the inevitable cheating that will occur. Although profits can be increased by collusion, a single firm can earn even greater profit by cutting its price slightly below the agreed level. Unless there is a mechanism for detecting and punishing cheaters, the cartel will soon fail as members cut prices to preserve their market shares.

A third cost of cartelization is that nonprice competition may replace price competition. For example, members of a cartel may engage in expensive advertising as a substitute for active price competition. Legal penalties imposed on convicted colluders are the fourth cost of price fixing. These may take the form of fines, prison sentences, damage awards to private parties, or court orders to alter certain business practices.

The objective of antitrust policy is to reduce the net benefits of collusive activities. As the likelihood of conviction and the magnitude of penalties increase, the expected cost of violating antitrust laws increases. Also, if firms perceive that they are being actively scrutinized by antitrust authorities and that penalties from conviction will be severe, they will tend to adopt less easily detectable and less effective methods of collusion.

The courts have consistently taken a hard line against collusion. The precedent-setting case [*U.S. v. Trenton Potteries Co. et al.*] involved 23 manufacturers of bathroom fixtures who had conspired to fix prices. Through their trade association the manufacturers published standardized price lists, met to consider prices, and pressured one another to sell only at list prices. When the association was brought to trial, it claimed that the agreement had not injured the public. The trial record supported this position, indicating that fixtures were often sold below the established prices. But the Supreme Court rejected the request for a rule-of-reason interpretation of price fixing. The justices argued that:[2]

> The reasonable price fixed today may through economic and business changes become the unreasonable price of tomorrow.... Agreements which create such potential power may well be held to be in themselves unreasonable or unlawful restraints, without the necessity of minute inquiry whether a particular price is reasonable or unreasonable.

The strong per se condemnation of price fixing has consistently been reaffirmed by the courts. Agreements to fix prices are a violation of the Sherman Act without regard to their effect. The prohibition applies not only to fixing

---

[2] *U.S. v. Trenton Potteries Co. et al.*, 273 U.S. 392 (1927).

minimum prices but also maximum prices and price differentials. Firms are simply not allowed to act in concert in determining prices.

Illegal price fixing costs billions of dollars each year in higher prices. Although explicit collusion has not been eliminated by antitrust efforts, the per se stand of the courts has had a significant impact in reducing the most effective forms of pricing fixing, group boycotts, and market allocation. Conspirators have been forced to abandon overt methods and to settle for less easily detectable and less efficient methods of collusion.

CASE STUDY

THE ELECTRIC MACHINERY CONSPIRACY

In the early 1960s, 29 corporations were successfully prosecuted for fixing prices of electrical equipment such as transformers, generators, and switchgear. The indictments alleged two primary types of conspiracies. For sales involving open bids, the firms simply met to fix the prices that would be charged for different types of equipment. It was the sealed bid sales to the government that made the case intriguing. The intent of the conspiracy was to inflate prices while allowing firms to maintain a predetermined market share. For example, GE was allocated 42 percent of the market for switchgear, Westinghouse 38 percent, Allis-Chalmers 11 percent, and ITE Circuit Breakers 9 percent. Market shares were maintained by rotating bids so that each firm became the low bidder the requisite percentage of the time. This was accomplished by changing the order of bids about every two weeks or "with the phases of the moon."

To avoid detection, the conspirators engaged in elaborate precautions. Only first names were used and mail was always sent in plain envelopes to the homes of the executives. Calls were made from pay phones. Each firm was referred to by a code number. Expense-account vouchers were disguised by making them out for cities that were approximately as far from the firm's offices as the actual location of the conspiratorial gathering. The meetings themselves were often held in out-of-the-way places—a favorite was Dirty Helen's Bar in Milwaukee. Above all, company lawyers were never told anything.

Luck played an important part in uncovering the conspiracy. As part of its investigation, the Justice Department subpoenaed the records of the ITE Circuit Breaker Company. Nye Spencer, an employee of ITE, served as the scribe for the switchgear conspiracy. Spencer had kept detailed records of the conspiracy meetings to assist him in training his assistant. Confronted with the request for information, he turned over all his files to the government. Larger cracks in the dike appeared as lower-level executives cooperated with the investigation rather than implicate themselves further. Thus the government was able to assemble a strong case that the conspirators decided not to contest. Following sessions of plea bargaining, an agreement was reached whereby the firms were allowed to enter reduced pleas to some of the indictments in return for pleading guilty to others.

In the penalty phase of the case, the judge sent seven defendants to jail for thirty days and granted suspended sentences to twenty others. Never before had business executives been sent to jail as a result of Sherman Act violations. The firms were also required to pay nearly $2 million in fines. However, the greatest cost to the corporations involved was 1,900 private suits resulting in damage awards of over $400 million.

Price Discrimination

Price discrimination can be used to discourage entry and weaken existing competitors. Predatory pricing is an important example. Consider the case of a large firm selling a single product in a number of distinct geographical markets. In some of the markets the firm has a monopoly, whereas in others it faces competition from smaller rivals operating in only a single area. The large firm can cut prices below cost in competitive markets and subsidize its losses from monopoly profits earned where the firm is the only seller. The smaller firms in the competitive markets may be forced from the market or into a merger if the dominant firm keeps its prices down. When the smaller firms have either gone out of business or been acquired, prices are then increased to the monopoly level.

Potential entrants into a market can also be deterred by the threat of predatory pricing. If the existing firm can create a credible threat that it will cut prices below cost if a new firm enters the market, all but the largest potential competitors may be discouraged. Used in this manner, predatory pricing may be a useful tactic to prevent entry in an industry where natural barriers are not effective.

The courts have not been entirely consistent in defining what constitutes predatory pricing. However, recent court decisions have defined predation as occurring if price is set below average variable cost. From the perspective of economic theory, this position is defensible. In the short run, average variable cost represents the threshold between continuing to produce and shutting down an operation. If a price is below average variable cost, entrepreneurs can cut their losses by ceasing to produce. However, if price exceeds average variable cost, it is better to continue producing even if price is below average total cost. The reason is that the excess can be used to pay a portion of the fixed costs. Thus a price that is above average variable cost but below the firm's average total cost can be justified in its own right. In contrast, a firm that sets its price below average variable cost and continues to produce can be logically viewed as having other motives, such as the exclusion of current or potential competitors.

Price discrimination suits may involve considerable disagreement as to whether a firm has practiced predatory pricing. But if the court determines that predation has occurred, the defendant will usually be found guilty of an antitrust violation.[3]

---

[3] Predatory pricing is not the only form of price discrimination that may violate U.S. antitrust laws. For a more extensive discussion of price discrimination and antitrust, see Petersen (1985, pp. 130–138).

KEY CONCEPTS

- The courts have consistently ruled that price fixing is a per se violation of the antitrust laws.
- Predatory pricing is a means of weakening competitors and deterring entry into an industry. Recent court decisions have defined predation as existing if price is set below average variable cost.

Remedies and Penalties

Alleged antitrust violations are resolved in a number of different ways. The most common remedies and penalties are discussed below.

Consent Decrees.   Most antitrust actions are resolved by consent decrees. These are agreements worked out between the government's attorneys and those of the defendant. Usually, they specify certain activities that the firm must or must not do. In return, the government agrees not to prosecute. In accepting a consent decree the firm, in essence, says: "We didn't do it, but we won't do it again." An important advantage of consent decrees is that they cannot be used as evidence of guilt in other proceedings, such as a private antitrust suit.

Dissolution and Divestiture.   In monopoly and merger actions, the court may use dissolution or divestiture as a remedy. In 1911 the Supreme Court split Standard Oil of New Jersey into 30 smaller firms. This was an example of dissolution, whereby the firm loses its identity. In contrast, a divestiture order requires the firm to sell certain of its assets, but the firm retains its identity. In approving a 1984 merger between Socal and Gulf Oil, the Department of Justice required Socal to sell off several thousand Gulf retail gas stations. This was an example of divestiture.

Injunctions.   In ruling against a defendent, the court may issue an injunction that prohibits or compels certain actions on the part of the firm. For example, as a result of a price-fixing suit, a trade association may be prohibited from the collection and dissemination of information that was used to fix prices.

Fines.   Firms convicted of Sherman Act violations may be fined up to $1,000,000 per violation. Officers of the firms may receive fines to a maximum of $100,000. For example, corporations in the electric machinery conspiracy paid fines of nearly $2 million.

Prison Sentences.   A 1974 amendment to the Sherman Act made criminal convictions under Section 1 felony offenses and set the maximum prison sentence at three years. However, actual periods of incarceration for Sherman Act violations are usually less than one year. Clayton and Federal Trade Commission

Act convictions are civil rather than criminal offenses and do not involve prison sentences.

Treble Damages.   Both the Sherman and the Clayton Acts include provision for award of treble (triple) damages. If a private party can demonstrate that the antitrust laws have been broken and can prove the amount of damages sustained, the offending firm may be required to pay the plaintiff three times the amount of damages. Suppose that Lewis Inc. and Petersen Manufacturing are convicted of price fixing by the government. Firms that purchased Lewis's (or Petersen's) product at inflated prices could sue for damages. The successful government suit is prima facie evidence that the firms had violated the law. Thus the task of the plaintiffs would be to show the amount of damages. Suppose that it is determined that a specific firm purchased $1,000,000 in supplies from Lewis Inc. during the price-fixing period and that the total price would have been $900,000 in the absence of collusion. Thus the plaintiff has been overcharged by $100,000 and would be entitled to claim three times that amount, or $300,000. The prospect of treble damage awards may be the most important deterrent to antitrust violations.

KEY CONCEPTS

- Most antitrust suits are settled by consent decrees.
- Cases that go to court may result in dissolution or divestiture, injunctions, fines, imprisonment, and/or the award of treble damages.

CASE STUDY
PRICE FIXING AND COLLEGE FOOTBALL

From 1951 to 1984, the National Collegiate Athletic Association (NCAA) negotiated with the television networks for broadcast rights to football games. These contracts gave an exclusive right to a network to televise a certain number of games and suggested the payment to each participating team. In addition, NCAA rules prohibited any team from appearing on television more than six times during a two-year period.

By increasing their national television exposure and their share of broadcast revenues, the NCAA–network pacts were probably beneficial to smaller colleges and universities. In contrast, the football powers, such as Notre Dame and Southern California, were limited both in terms of number of appearances and payment per game.

The NCAA's practice of negotiating exclusive broadcast packages for football was challenged by the University of Oklahoma and the University of Georgia. These institutions took the NCAA to court, charging that the agreements were anticompetitive. They asserted that the NCAA–network contracts violated the antitrust laws because they reduced that number of college football games broadcast on television and illegally fixed prices at a lower level than if the schools could negotiate individually.

The case went to the Supreme Court, where the justices ruled for the individual schools and voided the NCAA's agreements with the networks. As a result, each college or university (or their athletic conferences) now has the right to bargain for the broadcast of its own football games. The initial effect of this decision by the court has been a proliferation of televised football games. However, the long-term impact remains uncertain.

Public Utility Regulation

In contrast to antitrust, the regulatory approach to public policy directly alters industry performance by setting prices and establishing conditions of entry and exit. Although regulation extends to many industries, it is most common in dealing with public utilities. It is difficult to define precisely what makes a business a public utility. However, there seem to be two general characteristics. First, the industry provides a product or service of particular importance. Either the day-to-day livelihood or the future growth of a region depends on the continued and reasonable provision of the product or service. Second, the nature of the production process is such that competition is seen as yielding undesirable results. The public utility designation is usually applied to firms providing electric power; local water and sewage supply; telephone, telegraph, and cable communications; and urban passenger transportation.

The Need for Regulation

The traditional view of public utility regulation is that it serves the "public interest" by protecting consumers. The need for regulation exists when a supplier has a natural monopoly or to prevent undue price discrimination.

Natural Monopoly. Certain industries are sometimes referred to as *natural monopolies.* The term is used to describe production systems where technology results in continually declining average costs that provide a substantial cost advantage to larger firms. Because a firm can decrease its average cost by increasing its rate of output, the only stable market structure is that of a single firm serving the entire market. Smaller firms are either forced from the market or acquired by the dominant firm. Consumers in the market are then subject to the economic power of the resulting monopolist. Figure 19-2 depicts a natural monopoly. Note that the shape of the cost curves implies that a larger firm will be more efficient because it will have lower average costs.

The existence of a natural monopoly poses something of a dilemma for public policy. One alternative is to let the firm operate as a monopoly. If the firm faced the demand curve *DD* as shown in Figure 19-2, the monopoly price would be

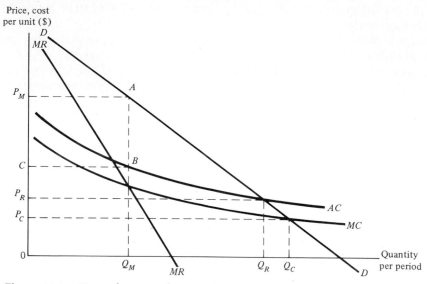

Figure 19-2. *Natural Monopoly.*

P_M and the quantity, Q_M. The firm would then earn economic profit as indicated by the area of the rectangle $P_M ABC$. Compared to marginal cost pricing (i.e., setting the price equal to marginal cost), the monopoly-pricing scheme would result in a deadweight loss and also a transfer of consumer surplus from consumers to producers.

If the firm is not allowed to act as an unconstrained monopolist, there are several alternatives available to the policymaker. One is to invoke antitrust laws and divide the firm into smaller competing firms. But it is not clear that the public interest would be served by this action. The inefficiency of these small firms (because of their higher average costs) requires that they charge a high price just to earn a normal return on capital. There is no guarantee that the price required by such firms to earn a normal return would not be higher than the price that the more efficient monopolist would charge to maximize profits. Thus, unless competition is desired for its own sake, the antitrust approach may not be a desirable solution.

A second alternative is to allow the firm to maintain its monopoly position but require it to price at marginal cost. For the demand and cost curves in Figure 19-2, this would result in a price of P_C and a quantity of Q_C. At this level of production there is no deadweight loss, because production is increased until the cost of producing the last unit is equated to the value of that unit. There is also no transfer of surplus from consumers to producers. In fact, the problem is quite the reverse. Because the monopolist is producing in a region of decreasing costs, its marginal cost is less than its average cost. Being required to price at marginal cost, the monopolist is unable to earn a normal return on capital. This is easily seen by observing that at the output rate Q_C, the average revenue as shown by the demand curve is less than the average cost.

If a policymaker requires a firm with decreasing costs to price at marginal cost over a long period of time, some provision must be made to compensate the investors in the firm for the losses that will be sustained. One way of doing this is to provide a subsidy. This approach is sometimes used with publicly owned bridges. The marginal cost of allowing another car over the bridge approaches zero. Thus cars are permitted to pass without charge or at nominal cost, and the cost of building and operating the bridge is paid from tax revenues. In the United States, providing explicit subsidies from public funds has never been very popular. There have been exceptions, such as subsidies for airlines, urban transportation, and telephone service to rural customers, but the general philosophy has been that public utility services should not be subsidized.

The most common method for pricing the products of a natural monopoly in the United States may best be thought of as a compromise solution. The nature of the compromise is depicted by Figure 19-2. A simple description of public utility price regulation is that price is set equal to average cost. That is, the firm is allowed to charge a price that allows it to earn no more than a normal return on its capital.[4] This is shown in Figure 19-2 by the price, P_R, and the quantity, Q_R. Regulation is a compromise because the price is less than the monopoly price but higher than marginal cost. There is some deadweight loss, because price is not equated to marginal cost, but the deadweight loss is far less than if the firm were allowed to act as a monopolist. Because the firm earns a normal profit, there is no need for the subsidy that would be required with marginal cost pricing. Thus this mechanism achieves some of the gains from marginal cost pricing without requiring a subsidy.

Undue Price Discrimination.   Price discrimination occurs when consumers are charged different prices for a product and the differences in price cannot be accounted for by cost differentials. As discussed in Chapter 13, the three requirements for successful price discrimination are that consumers have different demand elasticities, that markets be separable, and that the firm has some power over price.

The telephone industry provides an example of successful price discrimination policies by a public utility. Rates for basic telephone services are higher for business users than they are for residential users. There is no particular reason to assume that the cost of installing and maintaining a phone in an office is different than putting one in a kitchen. There are, however, possible differences in demand elasticity for business versus home phone customers. Consider the case of a stockbroker. The vast majority of orders for the purchase or sale of stock come to the broker by phone. There is no way the business could be conducted without a phone. In contrast, if there is a neighbor's phone that can be used in an emergency, it is quite possible to get along without a telephone in one's home. In economic terms, the stockbroker is said to have more inelastic demand for telephone service than does the residential customer.

---

[4] Recall that average cost includes a normal return to capital. Thus if price is set equal to average cost, the firm will be earning a normal return.

The other conditions for price discrimination are also met in the telephone industry. Because there is a physical connection between the customer and the phone company, there is no way that low-cost home telephone service can be resold to a business customer. Also, if the stockbroker does not interconnect with the local phone company, there is no practical way to have access to customers calling in orders.

When residential customers compare the price they pay for telephone service to that paid by the commercial user they are delighted. But commercial users are less pleased, and they frequently view the differential as being unfair. As the monopoly supplier, if the phone company were allowed to determine its rate structure without interference, a businessperson's only recourse would be to try to persuade the company to lower their rates. If the residential–commercial differential is not reduced, there is little else they can do except complain about the inequity of the matter.

The plight of the victim of price discrimination provides an argument for regulation. Perhaps government should intervene to protect the commercial user from an unfair situation. The issue is not one of efficiency, but of fairness. The presumption is that the monopolist should not be allowed to use its power to "unduly discriminate" against some consumers. Although some discrimination may be acceptable, government intervention may be necessary when that discrimination becomes excessive. But there is no clear definition of the distinction between due and undue discrimination. In the end, undue price discrimination is whatever the regulatory commissions or the courts determine it to be.

KEY CONCEPTS

- Public utilities are firms that provide an essential service and which have limited competition.
- The need for regulation exists to protect consumers from inequities created by natural monopolies and undue price discrimination.
- Public utility regulation as practiced in the United States is based on setting prices equal to average cost.

Regulatory Procedures

Public utility regulation occurs at both state and federal levels. Federal regulation focuses primarily on wholesale and interstate transactions, while state regulatory activities concentrate on the intrastate retail market. Commissions responsible for public utility regulation typically consist of two basic divisions: the commission staff and the commissioners.

The commission staff is an adversary of the regulated firm in hearings before the commissioners. The staff must evaluate the evidence presented by the firm and make its own recommendations. Although consumer groups are becoming increasingly important in regulatory proceedings, it is still the commission staff that has the major responsibility for presenting the public's case to the commissioners. In contrast, the commissioners consider evidence and recommendations of the staff, the regulated firms, and other groups and then formulate the commission's policies.

Probably the most visible function of the state and federal regulatory commissions is setting prices for the products and services of the industries they regulate. The procedure used for price determination is a quasijudicial exercise called the *rate case*. There are two basic objectives in the rate case. The first is to find a general level of rates or prices that will allow the firm to earn no more than a fair or normal return on its capital. This occurs in the revenue requirement phase of the proceeding. The second objective is considered during the rate structure phase and involves setting rates that do not unduly discriminate against any class of consumers.

The Revenue Requirement Phase of the Rate Case. The rate case is concerned primarily with equity or fairness. If prices are raised, stockholders of the firm benefit at the expense of consumers. If the firm is not allowed to raise prices or if the increase is small, the benefits to consumers from lower rates are obtained at the expense of lower returns to investors. If a general increase in profits to the firm is granted while keeping prices to some groups low, higher prices must be paid by other groups. The rate case is basically a zero-sum game in which one group can benefit only at the expense of others. Thus it becomes an adversary proceeding with each of the parties involved trying to get a bigger share of the pie.

The procedure for determining the general level of rates in a rate case is easily described in theory if not in practice. The firm is to be granted overall revenues sufficient to allow it to earn just a fair return on its capital. The procedure can be reduced to the following simple equation:

$$RR = E + s(RB - DEP)$$

where RR = revenue requirement

        E = expenses

        s = fair return on capital

      RB = capital, or the rate base

   DEP = depreciation

Equation (19-1) specifies that total revenue allowed by the regulatory commission should be sufficient to allow the firm to cover its expenses plus earn a fair return on the depreciated value of its capital base. Essentially, the public utility rate case is a cost-plus form of price setting. Revenues are set to cover the firm's costs of operating plus an add-on as a return to capital. In the rate case, each of the components of equation (19-1) is determined. The commission must decide on the firm's allowable expenses, a fair rate of return on capital, the depreciated capital or rate base to which the fair rate is to be applied, and finally, the revenue requirement necessary to cover the sum of expenses plus return to capital.

The Rate Structure Phase of the Rate Case.   The emphasis of the public-utility rate case has shifted over time. In the early days of regulation the major area of controversy was the valuation of the rate base. Later, attention shifted to the fair rate of return. Until recent years, commissions paid relatively little attention to the structure of rates. The need for increases in total revenue often was met simply by adjusting all rates on a nearly proportionate basis. Commissions considered the structure of rates primarily in response to complaints received from specific groups of consumers. Basically, it was the firm that took the lead in determining what the structure of rates should be.

In recent years, much more attention has been paid to the structure of rates. As commissions have become more involved in determining the rate structure they have required that firms provide additional information about the cost of serving individual categories of consumers. Often, the commission will request that the firm compute the rate of return being earned for each category of service or for each product that is provided. These data are then used by the commission in making rate adjustments. This is called *cost-of-service pricing.* For example, if a particular service or product is shown to be earning a very low rate of return under existing rates, the commission may approve a larger rate increase than for a service or product that is earning a higher rate of return. The commission's attempt to equalize rates of return is consistent with its mandate to prevent undue discrimination.

KEY CONCEPTS

- In a rate case the regulatory commission must determine prices that generate revenues sufficient to cover expenses and allow the firm to earn a fair return on its rate base.
- In determining the structure of rates, most regulatory commissions use cost-of-service pricing, which focuses on equating the rate of return earned by providing service to each customer class.

Price Controls

During periods of rapid inflation, price controls may be used to reduce the rate of price increases. In some cases, they are imposed on selected industries (such as rent controls or interest rate ceilings), while in other circumstances they have been used on virtually all industries.

Price Controls in Competitive Industries

Figure 19-3 depicts the supply and demand curves for a competitive industry. Each firm is considered to take as given the market price determined by the interaction of the supply and demand curves. The equilibrium price is P_e and

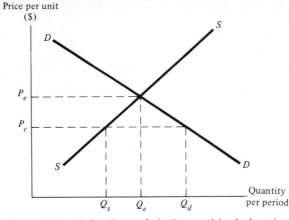

Figure 19-3. *Price Controls in Competitive Industries.*

the equilibrium quantity is Q_e. Suppose that public policy limits the price at which the product can be sold to P_c. The lower price reduces the amount that will be supplied to Q_s and induces additional consumers to enter the market so that the quantity demanded increases to Q_d. The amount that consumers want to purchase is now greater than the available supply, so there is a shortage of the price-controlled product.

In the free market, prices act as a rationing device to equilibrate supply and demand. Some consumers drop out of the market as prices increase. At the same time, quantity supplied will increase as production becomes more profitable. But when prices are set below the equilibrium level, another method of rationing must be found. Historically, alternative rationing schemes have taken many forms. The most common has been the black market. If products can be purchased at low prices by consumers who value them less than others who cannot obtain them, an opportunity to profit from exchange exists. The "low-valuation" consumers can sell the product to the "high-valuation" consumers, and both will be better off than if the black-market transaction had not occurred. The existence of black markets requires that there be people who are willing to break the law and risk incurring the penalties of running a black-market supply organization. It also requires that there be some consumers who are willing to purchase goods illegally. There has never been a documented case of effective price ceilings that were not accompanied by some sort of black market.

In many countries, the common manifestation of prices artificially kept below the market level is long queues of people waiting to purchase the limited supplies of goods. Such queues are common in poor nations and have periodically occurred at gas stations in the United States when price controls were in effect. Queues are a form of rationing in the sense that only those people willing and able to stand in line get the product. The inefficiency of this type of rationing is apparent when the value of time is considered. Suppose that the price of a product as determined by market forces would be $2 but the controlled price is set at $1. If the purchaser's time is valued at, say, $5 an hour, he has to stand in line only 12 minutes per unit purchased to lose the gain of being able to buy at a lower price.

Thus far, only the short-run implications of price controls of firms in competitive markets have been considered. The long-run impacts on investment may be far more important. One of the functions of prices is to signal needs for transferring resources from one sector of the economy to another. If prices are rising because of demand-induced pressures in one industry, capital tends to flow to that industry to increase supply. Rising prices also generate internal investment funds for expansion by firms within the industry. But if prices are kept at artificially low levels, the necessary signals are not provided to capital markets and sufficient internal funds are not generated. As a result, if controls are imposed for a long period of time, shortages become more acute because of the lack of expansion in the industry. When controls are lifted, pressures of excess demand may result in a significant price increase.

CASE STUDY
RENT CONTROLS IN PARIS

Rent controls have been imposed by many city governments. In almost every case, the result has been a shortage of rental units and a deterioration in the quality of rental housing. A dramatic example is Paris after World War II. Today, it is not uncommon for housing costs to take 30 percent of a family's gross income. In contrast, those lucky enough to have rent-controlled housing in Paris seldom had to pay more than 4 percent of their income for housing.

Unfortunately, quantity demanded far exceeded quantity supplied. For those who did not already have a low rent unit, there were none available. The death of existing tenants was about the only possibility. Search for an apartment sometimes took the form of young couples reading the obituaries or making agreements with undertakers for early notification of a death. Old people were often accosted by young wives wanting to make a "down payment" on future space. The rights to a rent-controlled apartment were sold for as much as $5,000 (in terms of 1985 dollars) per room. This high price is an indication of the misallocation of resources caused by the rent controls.

Another consequence of rent controls in Paris was the deterioration of the rental housing stock. With rents so low, it did not pay to build additional units, nor did it make sense to spend very much to maintain existing units. Between 1914 and 1948, the increase in rental rates was 6.8 times, while the cost of repairs increased by 120 times. As a result, repairs and other maintenance were neglected.

Price Controls and Firms with Market Power

On the basis of the theoretical discussions of the previous pages, the attempt to apply controls to competitive industries is not very promising. However, even casual observation of business in any developed nation reveals that many goods and services are not produced under conditions that satisfy or even approximate the competitive model. Rather, much of the economic activity in the United States involves firms with some power to set the price of their product. This power is not complete, because such firms have rivals, but it sometimes is enhanced by formal or informal price collusion among firms.

Where firms have power to affect prices, some of the traditional objections to price controls become less compelling. For economists who express concern about the loss of freedom resulting from price controls, a relevant question in this case is "Whose freedom?" For firms with market power, the invisible hand no longer functions as envisioned by Adam Smith. The loss of freedom caused by price controls is that of firms who have been exploiting the consumers of their product. For such firms, price controls might be viewed as limits on operations that markets do not effectively constrain.

Figure 19-4 depicts the application of price controls to a firm with market power. If left to maximize profits, the firm sets price at P_m and produces the quantity Q_m. By setting a price ceiling where the marginal cost curve crosses the demand schedule (point A), it is possible to constrain price without creating a shortage. The profit-maximizing firm chooses a quantity such that marginal revenues and marginal costs are equal. If the maximum price allowed is P_c, the firm has a new marginal revenue curve P_cA, out to quantity Q_c. Because P_c is below the demand curve for all quantities less than Q_c, the firm can increase production from zero to Q_c by selling additional units at the same price. That is, the marginal revenue curve is given by the horizontal straight line P_cA. The firm should continue to increase its production as long as marginal costs are less than P_c. Thus the profit-maximizing quantity is Q_c. If price is set at P_c, there is no shortage or excess. The firm maximizes profits by producing Q_c, which is the same amount as consumers want to purchase at the controlled price.

It should be noted, however, that analyzing price controls is much easier than their actual implementation. Regulators seldom have good information on demand and costs. Thus it would be unlikely that policymakers could consistently identify the precise level at which the demand and marginal cost curves intersect. If price is set below this level, shortages will result. A price above that level means that prices are higher than necessary.

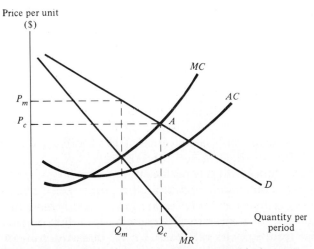

Figure 19-4. *Price Controls in Concentrated Industries.*

KEY CONCEPTS

- Price controls in competitive industries tend to result in shortages.
- In industries where firms have market power, if price is set equal to marginal cost, it may be possible to impose price controls without creating shortages.

Summary

The Sherman Act prohibits unfair business practices and the illegal monopolization of a market. Price discrimination and mergers are two important actions covered by the Clayton Act. The Robinson-Patman Act broadened Clayton Act provisions against illegal price discrimination, while the Celler-Kefauver Amendment put vertical and conglomerate mergers under the jurisdiction of the Clayton Act.

Antitrust suits may be initiated by the U.S. Department of Justice, the Federal Trade Commission, state government officials, or private parties. For successful prosecution, per se offenses require only showing that the act has been committed. In contrast, rule-of-reason offenses also require a demonstration that the social costs of the act are greater than the social benefits.

The current interpretation of Section 1 of the Sherman Act is that practices that are acceptable when used by small firms may constitute antitrust violations if used by firms with substantial market power. Mergers contested under the Clayton Act should be evaluated to determine if the effect of increased market power exceeds any efficiency gains that may result from the merger. Income distribution effects may also be a consideration.

In deciding to challenge a merger, the Justice Department relies on guidelines based on the Herfindahl index. A horizontal merger between large firms is likely to be prohibited, but vertical and conglomerate mergers will probably be allowed unless they increase horizontal market power.

Price fixing is usually considered a per se violation of the law. Predatory pricing can be used to weaken competitors and deter entry. Recent court opinions have defined predation as setting prices below average variable cost.

Most antitrust suits are settled by consent decrees before going to trial. Other remedies and penalties include dissolution or divestiture, injunctions, prison sentences, fines, and treble-damage awards.

Firms with continually declining average cost curves are referred to as natural monopolies because the only stable market structure is that of a single firm supplying the entire market. In the United States, the approach used to deal with natural monopolies is to give price-setting power to a regulatory body. Such bodies also protect consumers by prohibiting undue price discrimination.

In the revenue requirement phase of a rate case, a regulatory commission must determine the total revenue that will allow the firm to cover its expenses plus earn a fair return on its rate base. In the rate structure phase, a cost-of-service approach is often used whereby the commission adjusts rates to equalize the rate of return earned by each class of service.

Price controls in competitive industries tend to cause shortages and result in queues and black markets. In contrast, in industries where firms have market power, by setting the controlled price equal to marginal cost, it may be possible to impose price controls without creating shortages.

Discussion Questions

19-1. How could private antitrust suits be used as part of a firm's strategy in dealing with its competitors?

19-2. Why are some antitrust violations judged using a per se standard?

19-3. How could the definition of the relevant product market affect a court's decision in an antitrust case?

19-4. Consider an industry with a large, dominant firm and a number of smaller firms. Suppose that a merger of two of the small firms would result in a Herfindahl index greater than 1,800. Is there a basis for allowing the merger?

19-5. Trade associations are often involved in collusive agreements to fix prices. Why?

19-6. In the Trenton Potteries case, what did the Supreme Court mean by the statement, "the reasonable price fixed today may through economic and business changes become the unreasonable price of tomorrow?"

19-7. How would the value of a good relative to its transportation cost affect the success of a large, multimarket firm using predatory pricing? Explain.

19-8. Can a monopoly be maintained in an industry that does not have continually declining average costs? Explain.

19-9. In a public utility rate case, how could a commission use the structure of rates to redistribute income? Give an example.

19-10. How might price regulation affect the rate of innovation in an industry?

19-11. How should a regulatory commission determine what constitutes "undue price discrimination?"

19-12. In competitive industries, when prices are kept below the equilibrium level by price controls, incorrect signals may be provided to consumers and resource owners. Explain.

19-13. How do elasticities of supply and demand affect the magnitude of the shortages created by price controls imposed on competitive industries?

19-14. Would controls be more successful in keeping prices down during wartime than during a period of peace? Why or why not?

Problems

19-1. Bentley Manufacturing can produce desks at a constant average cost of $200 per unit including a normal profit. Because of intense competition, the company sells desks for $200 and is able to sell 100,000 units per year. Bentley's managers have initiated a merger with New Top, another desk manufacturer. The merger will allow the combined firm to produce at an average cost of $190 per unit. Additional market power increases the profit maximizing price to $250, but only 80,000 units will be sold at that price. The proposed merger is being evaluated by the Department of Justice.

(a) If the demand curve is linear between a price of $150 and $250, will the dead-weight loss exceed the efficiency gain resulting from the merger?

(b) What other factors should antitrust officials consider in deciding whether to challenge the merger?

19-2. An industry consists of eight firms of equal size. Two of the eight firms propose to merge. Based on the merger guidelines used by the Department of Justice, will the merger be challenged? What if the merger involved four of the eight firms in the industry? Explain.

19-3. A regulated telephone company utility has a depreciated rate base of $500 million. The utility's capital structure consists of 40 percent equity and 60 percent debt. The after-tax cost of debt is 8 percent, the firm's common stock is currently selling for $8 per share, the dividend is $1, and the expected dividend growth rate is 2.5 percent per year. The firm's total expenses are $400 million.

(a) If the regulatory body sets an allowed rate of return that is equal to the firm's cost of capital, what rate of return will the commission allow?

(b) Based on your answer to part (a), what is the revenue requirement of the firm?

19-4. Pilfur Oil has a monopoly on the sale of oil in Transylvania. Demand for the firm's product is given by

$$P = 100 - 20Q$$

where P is the price of a barrel of oil and Q is measured in thousands of barrels of oil per day. The marginal cost function for the firm is

$$MC = 10 + 5Q$$

(a) What is the profit-maximizing price and rate of output for Pilfur?

(b) The government of Transylvania decides that Pilfur's price is too high. Bureaucrats require the firm to set the lowest price that will not result in shortages. What will be the price and rate of output that meet these conditions?

References

Bork, R. H. 1978. *The Antitrust Paradox: A Policy at War with Itself.* New York: Basic Books.

Clark, J. M. 1940. "Toward a Concept of Workable Competition." *American Economic Review* 30(June):241–256.

Fuller, J. G. 1962. *The Gentlemen Conspirators.* New York: Grove Press.

Keenan, M., and White, L. 1982. *Mergers and Acquisitions.* Lexington, Mass.: Lexington Books.

Noll, R. G., and Owen, B. M., eds. 1983. *The Political Economy of Regulation: Interest Groups in the Regulatory Process.* Washington, D.C.: American Enterprise Institute.

Petersen, H. C. 1985. *Business and Government.* New York: Harper & Row.

Posner, R. A. 1976. *Antitrust Law.* Chicago: University of Chicago Press.

Schuettinger, R. L., and Butler, E. F. 1979. *Forty Centuries of Wage and Price Controls.* Washington, D.C.: The Heritage Foundation.

Stigler, G. J. 1971. "The Theory of Economic Regulation." *Bell Journal of Economics* 2(1):3–21.

Williamson, O. E. 1968. "Economies as an Antitrust Defense: The Welfare Tradeoffs." *American Economic Review* 58(March):18–36.

Management of the Nonprofit Enterprise

20

Preview

Chapters 1 through 19 focused primarily on decision making for managers of profit-maximizing firms. But the pursuit of profit is not the objective of every organization. In fact, certain organizations are specifically prohibited from earning more than a nominal profit. Furthermore, the profit cannot be distributed to those who control the organization. Such organizations are referred to as nonprofit enterprises.

Nonprofit enterprises can be grouped into two categories: public and private. Most goods or services provided by government come from public nonprofit enterprises. At the federal level, the U.S. Postal Service, Amtrak, and the Federal Reserve System are in this category. State-funded colleges and universities are examples at the state level. Municipally owned utilities, community swimming pools, and city garbage disposal departments typify nonprofit activities of local governments.

Private nonprofit enterprises include a wide variety of organizations, such as churches, hospitals, labor unions, charities, schools, research foundations, and music and dance groups. Such enterprises represent a significant fraction of total economic activity. In 1985, the private nonprofit sector employed about 5 percent of all workers and accounted for 3 to 5 percent of gross national product in the United States.

Many of the principles discussed in the previous chapters are directly applicable to both profit and nonprofit enterprises. For example, cost minimization should be a goal of every organization. In Chapter 6 it was demonstrated that minimizing the cost of producing any given rate of output requires that inputs be employed until the ratio of marginal products equals the ratio of input prices. This principle holds for a nonprofit enterprise as well as for a profit-maximizing firm. Costs will not be minimized unless this decision rule is followed.

Similarly, many of the other tools developed earlier can be extremely useful to the manager of a nonprofit enterprise. Linear programming techniques can be used to reduce production costs and to improve the efficiency of distribution networks. Econometric methods can be employed to forecast demand and quantify cost and production relationships in the enterprise.

Although there are many similarities between profit and nonprofit enterprises, there also are important differences that may require a modified approach to management. These differences and their implications for managers are the focus of this chapter. The first section considers how incentives differ in profit and nonprofit enterprises and the consequences of these differences. The next section examines pricing of goods and services provided by the nonprofit sector. The chapter concludes with a discussion of the use of benefit-cost analysis for making long-run decisions in nonprofit enterprises.

Evaluation of the Nonprofit Enterprise

A common perception is that nonprofit enterprises are inherently less efficient than are organizations whose objective is to maximize profit. But this judgment may be unfair unless the criteria for comparison are carefully specified. Frequently, economic analysis considers only profits and costs in evaluating performance. But nonprofit enterprises may be established with objectives other than profitability and efficiency. In some cases an organization may be a means of maintaining services that firms in the for-profit sector have abandoned as unprofitable. Amtrak is an example. This enterprise was formed in 1971 after investor-owned railroads announced plans to terminate their railroad passenger service operations. The government became involved because Congress decided that some form of passenger service should be maintained even though a subsidy is required.

Other nonprofit enterprises serve as vehicles for income redistribution. Consider the U.S. Postal Service, which has a legal monopoly for delivery of first-class mail. The fundamental purpose of this monopoly right is to assure that mail service will be available at reasonable rates in rural areas. Charges for delivering mail in urban areas generate surplus revenues that are used to subsidize delivery to rural locations. Thus income is redistributed from urban to rural areas. If competition were allowed, private firms would enter into the urban market and provide service at a lower price. This would force the postal service to reduce its rates for urban mail delivery. As a result, the available subsidy for rural service would be eliminated. Consequently, rates for rural delivery would have to be increased (thus eliminating the income redistribution function of the postal service) or else additional subsidies would be required.

When organizations are established to pursue different objectives, it is not appropriate to evaluate them using the same criteria. Indeed, such an approach may lead to incorrect or at least potentially misleading conclusions. Rather, it should be realized that managerial decisions in an enterprise reflect the standards used to judge the decision makers in the enterprise. Managers of investor-owned firms are evaluated primarily by the organization's profitability. Thus the managers of such firms would be expected to pursue strategies that increase revenues and reduce costs. In contrast, managers of nonprofit enterprises may be judged on the basis of criteria such as total volume of services provided or the quality of service. Thus the decisions made by these managers will reflect different concerns. Hence it is not surprising that nonprofit enterprises may not compare favorably when evaluated using criteria applied to profit-maximizing firms.

The effect of differences in managerial incentives on decision making and enterprise performance can be shown using traditional tools of economic analysis. Consider an investor-owned corporation and a public, nonprofit enterprise that provide the same service. Assume that managers of both organizations are motivated by the prospect of higher salaries and that their actions focus on activities that increase their salaries. Also assume that managerial salaries are determined by the perceived productivity of the manager. For the investor-owned firm, productivity is evaluated by the firm's top management and board of directors and is closely related to the profitability of the firm. For the public nonprofit enterprise, productivity is determined by a legislature or other governing body and involves a subjective evaluation of management's contribution to the achievement of the goals established for the enterprise.

The performance of the manager of an investor-owned firm can be evaluated based on the firm's success in the marketplace. Consumers indicate their acceptance of the firm's products by their purchase of its output. For a public nonprofit enterprise the standard of managerial success is not as well defined. If prices do not cover all the enterprise's costs (such as with Amtrak) or if the output of the firm is difficult to quantify (e.g., the Central Intelligence Agency), choices of consumers may not provide the information necessary to evaluate the contribution of management to the success of the enterprise. In such cases, those charged with evaluation must find other methods of judging performance. Frequently, this involves selecting certain aspects of the operation of the enterprise that are to be monitored.

Rational managers will respond by improving the performance of their enterprises in those areas that are most closely monitored. Conversely, if there are aspects of the operation that are not scrutinized, there will be a tendency to divert resources to more important (i.e., more closely monitored) activities. This tendency leads to a conclusion about the performance of profit versus nonprofit enterprises. When profit and nonprofit enterprises face the same demand conditions, variations in their performance may reflect differences in the standards by which their managers are evaluated. Criteria that are more important to those charged with evaluation in the private sector than to evaluators of nonprofit enterprises will be more strongly emphasized by the managers of investor-owned firms. Conversely, aspects of the nonprofit enterprise that are not or cannot be effectively monitored may tend to be neglected by the managers of those organizations.

Sometimes attributes of the performance of nonprofit firms are monitored on a threshold basis. That is, as long as an attribute does not drop below some minimum level, the managers of the enterprise will be evaluated favorably. The implications of this evaluation policy are illustrated by Figure 20-1. The axes represent two attributes of some service X that is sold to consumers. Let X_1 represent the number of hours each day that the service is provided and X_2 be the number of customers served each hour. The production possibilities curve $F(X)$ indicates different combinations of X_1 and X_2 that can be obtained for a given total expenditure. There is a trade-off between X_1 and X_2 because providing additional hours of service and assisting more customers per hour both require additional employees.

The $R^i(X)$ curves of Figure 20-1 are isorevenue lines. Each R^i represents all combinations of the attributes of X_1 and X_2 that produce equal total revenues. Because customers assisted per hour and the number of hours of service are both desirable attributes from the perspective of the buyer, greater demand and

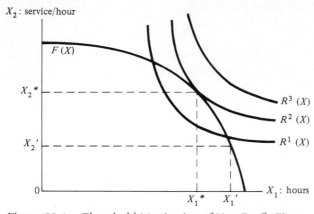

Figure 20-1. *Threshold Monitoring of Non-Profit Firms.*

hence increased revenue are indicated as the R^i curves shift to the right (i.e., $R^3 > R^2 > R^1$). For the investor-owned firm, profit maximization requires that maximum revenue be obtained from any given level of expenditure. Hence the point of maximum profit is at (X_1^*, X_2^*), where $R^2(X)$ is tangent to $F(X)$.

Now consider a nonprofit enterprise where customers served per hour, X_2, is monitored only on a threshold basis. That is, to avoid unfavorable evaluation, managers must be sure that the number does not fall below some rate, say, X_2'. However, there is no further reward for managerial efforts to increase the customers served per hour above that rate. Assume that total hours during which the service is available (i.e., X_1) are also monitored by those who evaluate the enterprise and that managerial compensation is positively correlated with this value. Thus the optimal combination of X_1 and X_2 from the perspective of the enterprise manager is (X_1', X_2') because this combination gives the maximum amount of X_1 while satisfying the customer service minimum of X_2'. Because $X_2' < X_2^*$, the nonprofit enterprise will serve fewer customers per hour than the investor-owned firm, but will be open more hours.

For the profit-maximizing firm, the preferences of consumers and the drive for profits determine the optimal combination of X_1 and X_2. For the nonprofit enterprise, the desires of consumers and revenues relative to costs are less important in directing the decisions of managers because they are not the basic criteria used for evaluation of managerial performance. As a general proposition, to the extent that the measures used to evaluate investor-owned firms differ from those used to judge nonprofit firms, the observed behavior of the two entities also will differ.

In general, how might the measures used to evaluate the nonprofit enterprise differ from those used in evaluating investor-owned firms? An important difference is that consumer behavior supplies information to profit-maximizing firms about the acceptability of their products and services. Poor-quality products or inferior service usually result in reduced sales and profits. In contrast, the nonprofit firm probably receives less information on the value of the goods and services it provides. Such enterprises may be monopoly suppliers, may not be required to cover their full costs, or may be required to pursue multiple goals. As a result, the information received from markets can be inadequate or misleading. Thus those responsible for evaluation are forced to devise other methods to assess performance. Frequently, these methods are somewhat arbitrary or mechanistic.

KEY CONCEPTS

- Managerial decisions in nonprofit and investor-owned enterprises will reflect the criteria by which the managers are evaluated.
- Aspects of the performance of an enterprise that are not important in the evaluation process may tend to be neglected by managers.

CASE STUDY

VETERANS ADMINISTRATION HOSPITALS

The performance of Veterans Administration Hospitals is evaluated based on patient-days of care provided and cost per patient-day. Note that both of these measures are easily quantifiable. However, assessment of patient comfort is much more difficult. Consequently, this factor carries less weight in the evaluation process. As long as a hospital does not receive an excessive number of complaints, patient comfort is unlikely to be an important issue in evaluating managerial performance. The result is that VA hospitals typically provide fewer patient amenities than do proprietary hospitals facing competitive pressures and attempting to maximize profits.

Pricing and the Nonprofit Enterprise

Pricing policies differ substantially among nonprofit enterprises. Some organizations must be financially self-sustaining. Thus prices set for the goods or services provided must generate sufficient revenues from sales to cover all costs. Other nonprofit enterprises receive subsidies from tax revenues or from charitable contributions. These subsidies allow the price to the buyer to be set below average total cost. Tuition at state-owned colleges and universities (often as little as 20 percent of total cost) is an example. Finally, certain nonprofit enterprises are completely supported by taxes and contributions. In these cases, there is no direct charge for the goods and services they supply. Police and fire protection provided by local governments are examples.

This section considers alternative ways of pricing the output of nonprofit enterprises. First, the concept of Ramsey pricing is introduced. This technique is used for efficiently allocating resources in enterprises where production is characterized by high fixed costs or where marginal cost pricing would result in high profits that are inconsistent with the nonprofit status of an enterprise. Next, a justification for using fees and licenses to meet revenue requirements is discussed.

Ramsey Pricing

In Chapter 10 it was argued that an efficient allocation of resources can be achieved if the prices of outputs are set equal to their marginal costs. However, this pricing scheme may not be feasible if average total costs are greater than marginal costs. This situation is depicted in Figure 20-2 and may occur if fixed costs are substantial and marginal costs are relatively low. Assume that an enterprise produces two goods, X and Y. If good X is priced at its marginal cost, the quantity sold will be Q_x and the price will be P_x. But because $P_x < ATC_x$, the enterprise will be unable to recover its fixed costs. Similarly, marginal cost pricing of good Y will result in a price of P_y and a loss on the Q_y units of good Y provided.

If the enterprise is required to cover its total costs, at least one of the two goods produced must be priced above marginal cost. But any deviation from marginal cost pricing will cause resources to be allocated less efficiently. Thus there is a need to develop a "second-best" pricing scheme that allows the enterprise to generate revenues equal to its total cost while minimizing the adverse affect on the allocation of resources. The Ramsey pricing technique meets these criteria.[1]

If an enterprise is providing several goods, Ramsey pricing suggests guidelines for the price that should be charged for each good. Because all prices cannot equal marginal costs, the question is how far to set the price of each good above

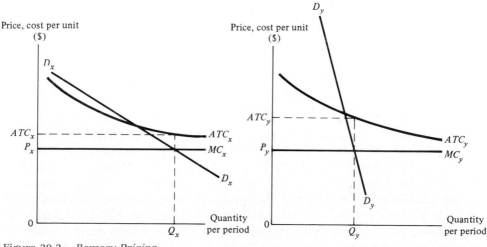

Figure 20-2. *Ramsey Pricing.*

[1] The name is in recognition of an early article by Ramsey (1927).

or below marginal cost for each good. In its most simple form, Ramsey pricing requires that price deviations from marginal costs be inversely related to the elasticity of demand. That is, for goods with very elastic demand the price should be set close to marginal cost. Conversely, for goods with relatively inelastic demand the price should deviate more from marginal cost. In terms of Figure 20-2, price elasticity for good X is relatively greater than for good Y. Thus the price of X should be closer to its marginal cost than the price of good Y.

The rationale for the Ramsey rule is easy to understand. If demand is elastic, increasing the price causes a substantial reduction in quantity demanded. But if demand is highly inelastic, large changes in price will result in little change in the quantity demanded. In the extreme, if the demand were totally inelastic (a vertical demand curve), there would be no change in quantity demanded as price increased. Hence if deviations from marginal cost pricing are greatest for those goods with inelastic demand, the resource misallocation will be minimized.

EXAMPLE

USING RAMSEY PRICING

Consider an enterprise that supplies two goods, X and Y. For ease of exposition, assume that the marginal cost of providing each is constant and equal to $10. However, also assume that the firm has fixed costs of $99 per period and that these fixed costs must be recovered. Further suppose that demand elasticities are -0.1 for Y and -1.0 for X, and that if prices are equated to marginal costs, 10 units of each product will be sold each period. However, note that if prices equal marginal costs, the firm will incur a loss of $99 per period. What prices for X and Y would allow the firm to recover its fixed and marginal costs while minimizing the adverse effect on resource allocation?

Solution

The pricing problem is how to increase prices to recover the $99 in fixed costs while minimizing the changes in consumption patterns in comparison to those with marginal cost pricing. The Ramsey principle suggests that since its demand is more inelastic, product Y should be priced higher in relation to marginal cost than should product X. One simple formulation of Ramsey pricing uses the inverse elasticity rule. This specifies that departures from marginal cost should be inversely proportional to elasticity of demand. In this example, since elasticity for Y is one-tenth that of X, the deviation of the price of Y from its marginal cost should be ten times the deviation of the price of X from its marginal cost.

Using the inverse elasticity rule, the solution can be shown to be pricing product Y at $20 and X at $11. Note that a 100 percent increase in the price of Y will decrease quantity demanded by only 10 percent (because the demand elasticity equals -0.1), to 9 units. The 10 percent increase in the price of X will decrease quantity demanded by 10 percent (because elasticity equals -1.0), also to 9 units. Now each unit of Y sold makes a $10 contribution to fixed costs for a total of $90. Each unit of X sold makes a $1 contribution for a total of $9. Together, this pricing approach allows the enterprise to recover its fixed costs of $99. This objective is achieved with minimal impact on the pattern of consumer demand. For both goods, the reduction in quantity demanded is only 1 unit as compared to marginal cost pricing.

Ramsey pricing is sometimes criticized because the largest deviations from marginal cost pricing are imposed on those with the fewest alternatives (i.e., least elastic demand). Although this is true, the more relevant point is that there really is no alternative to using some variant of Ramsey pricing. There is a limit to the contribution to fixed costs that can be obtained from the sale of goods with elastic demand. If large price increases are imposed on such goods, consumption will decline substantially as buyers shift to alternative goods. The net result is that the firm will obtain little contribution to fixed costs from goods with elastic demand.

Many nonprofit enterprises receive subsidies from tax revenues or charitable contributions. Where such subsidies are provided, revenues from sales do not have to cover the firm's total costs. However, the concept of Ramsey pricing may still be relevant for such enterprises. Even with a subsidy, prices set equal to marginal costs may not allow the enterprise to cover its total costs. However, by using the Ramsey principle, managers could set prices that would recover the necessary amount while minimizing the adverse effect on resource allocation.

In some situations, if prices are equated to marginal costs, the revenues of an enterprise (sales plus subsidies) might exceed its total costs. This could occur if the subsidy was very large or if decreasing returns to scale caused marginal costs to be greater than average total costs. In this case, the organization would be earning economic profit. But such an outcome is not generally consistent with the notion of a nonprofit enterprise. Thus there would be a need to reduce prices until total revenue just equals total cost. As before, this should be done in a manner that minimizes changes in consumption patterns in comparison to marginal cost pricing.

The Ramsey pricing rule can be used to achieve this result. The reductions of prices below marginal costs should be inversely proportional to the elasticity of demand. Thus prices of goods for which demand is elastic should be priced near their marginal cost. Conversely, where demand is inelastic, prices should be reduced in relation to marginal cost.

Although it is unlikely that managers would be familiar with the intricacies of Ramsey pricing, many decision-makers effectively use the principle in setting prices. If it is possible to segregate consumers by demand elasticity, higher prices are often charged to those with the more inelastic demand. For example, a minister may request larger contributions from faithful members than from those who are less committed, even though their incomes are the same. One explanation is that the demand for religion is assumed to be relatively less elastic for the first group than it is for the second. Thus requests are made such that a disproportionate share of the congregation's fixed costs are paid by its more faithful members.

Licenses and Fees

Certain goods and services provided by nonprofit enterprises are not priced on a per unit basis. Rather, users are assessed a fee or required to buy a license that allows them to consume unlimited quantities of the good or service. For example, a fishing license issued by a state allows its purchaser to fish as often as is desired (subject to daily catch limits). Similarly, in many cities, residents pay a flat monthly rate for usage of sewer facilities. This fee entitles them to make use of these facilities as often as they desire.

The use of fees and licenses has advantages and disadvantages when compared to pricing on a per unit basis. A disadvantage is that the rationing function of prices is eliminated. Because the consumer pays nothing for additional units, there is no incentive to conserve on the use of the good or service. As a result, consumption may proceed beyond the point where marginal benefits to the individual equal the marginal cost to society. However, the use of licenses and fees may be the preferred approach in some circumstances. Consider the case of fishing. In some states the number of fishing sites is so large that it would be impossible to monitor the number of fish caught by each individual. The only feasible alternative is to require a license for the privilege of fishing. Spot checks can then be made to identify those who have not purchased a license.

As a general proposition, licenses and fees may be preferable to per unit pricing when costs of collection on a per unit basis are high relative to the price that would be charged. When this condition exists, the benefits of rationing by unit pricing may be outweighed by the extra cost incurred.

KEY CONCEPTS

- Ramsey pricing is an alternative when marginal cost pricing is not feasible. One form of Ramsey pricing requires that that price deviations from marginal costs be inversely related to the elasticity of demand.
- If collection costs are substantial, the use of licenses and fees may be preferable to pricing on a per unit basis.

Benefit-Cost Analysis

The approach to investment decision making in profit-maximizing firms was discussed in Chapter 16. Like profit-oriented businesses, nonprofit enterprises also take actions that require a significant initial investment and result in a stream of monetary or nonmonetary returns for one or more years. For example, a religious organization may build a chapel for its members to use or a city health department may initiate a vaccination program to combat the outbreak of a disease. When a profit-maximizing business makes an investment, usually both the cost and the return are measured in dollars. For the nonprofit enterprise, the initial cost is typically measured in dollars, but the returns sometimes are nonmonetary, although in some cases a dollar value can be assigned for these returns. In the two examples above, the returns might be measured in terms of church attendance and reduced incidence of the disease.

For organizations that have goals other than profit maximization, the approach to evaluating a capital investment or a significant change in policy may be somewhat different than for the profit-oriented firm. One rather general evaluation technique is benefit-cost anaylsis, which is widely used by government agencies for evaluating water resource and highway investments, new defense systems, and the impact of proposed regulations.

Benefit-cost analysis is based on economic principles and is analogous to the capital budgeting process for the investor-owned firm. The objective of the profit-maximizing firm is to maximize profit, whereas the objective of the government is usually maximization of national income. Often, however, the government agency also considers social and environmental consequences of investment proposals that typically would not be considered by the firm. These might include the effect on some endangered species of animal or the income redistribution effects. Thus, in both the profit and nonprofit sectors, returns are compared to costs, but the nonprofit enterprise often takes a broader view of what those returns and costs are.

For a proposed investment or other action to be deemed efficient using benefit-cost analysis, the ratio of the present value of benefits to the present value of costs must exceed unity. It will be shown that this standard is equivalent to the net present value (*NPV*) criterion developed in Chapter 16. However, before discussing the benefit-cost procedure in detail, it will be useful to review the economic rationale and historical perspective underlying the benefit-cost approach.

Conceptual Basis of Benefit-Cost Analysis

If a resource reallocation makes one person better off without making anyone else worse off, that reallocation is said to be *Pareto efficient*.[2] Economists use the Pareto principle to evaluate various decisions and policy changes that result in a reallocation of resources.

Virtually all free-market transactions are Pareto-efficient because no one would voluntarily enter such transactions if their welfare or satisfaction would be reduced by doing so. For example, when individual *A* buys a product from individual *B* and both engage in the exchange voluntarily, it must be that *A* prefers having the product to having the money and *B* prefers the money to the product. Both are better off as a result of the exchange and hence the reallocation of resources is Pareto efficient.

Unfortunately, many transactions made in the public sector probably do not meet the Pareto criterion. Here resources are typically taken involuntarily through taxation from society at large and expended on a range of government programs.[3]

---

[2] Vilfredo Pareto was a nineteenth-century economist who first articulated this efficiency standard.

[3] An example of resource reallocation in the public sector would be levying a general income tax in order to pay for a new defense project, such as the construction and deployment of a new nuclear missile system.

Some may consider themselves better off as a result of such transactions, but others may be significantly worse off. This is evidenced by the complaints about some government programs being unnecessary, inappropriate, and inefficient.

Clearly, many government programs are essential. Examples include national defense, the court system, police and fire protection, and roads and highways. However, there probably is no way to implement even one of these programs and do it in a way that meets the Pareto criterion. That is, there probably is no way to levy a tax and implement a public program without making at least one person, and probably a great many more, worse off. The best evidence that this statement is true is found in the outcome of bond elections to finance state and local government activities such as schools and highway construction. Even where such programs are clearly necessary, and where the bond issues are passed by an overwhelming majority vote, there is almost always a significant number of voters who are opposed. Their negative votes indicate that they expect to be made worse off by the program and tax being voted on. Thus strict adherence to the Pareto criterion would mean that few, if any, government programs would be implemented.

A somewhat weaker but perhaps more reasonable efficiency standard for a social program is the compensation criterion that states that a resource reallocation is socially efficient if the gainers from that reallocation can compensate the losers and still be better off.[4] For example, a government program that conferred benefits of $100 each on ten people and losses of $50 each on ten other people is efficient because the gainers could compensate the losers by paying each of them $50 and the gainers would still be better off.[5]

Given that many government programs are essential, the compensation criterion does provide a theoretical basis for the evaluation of those programs. Benefit-cost analysis has been developed as an approach to decision making in the public sector based on this criterion.[6] That is, if benefits exceed costs this means that the gainers could pay the losers and still have something left over. This benefit-cost evaluation standard is used by many government agencies for evaluating investments, such as water resource projects, highway systems, schools, and medical research. Benefit-cost analysis is the public sector analogue of capital budgeting by profit-seeking firms. The basic question to be answered by a benefit-cost analysis of a government project or program is whether social wealth, the present value of national income in future years, will be increased by diverting resources to the project in question. Only if social wealth can be expected to increase should a project be implemented. This is analogous to the approach taken by the profit-maximizing firm, where no capital project is undertaken unless it is expected to increase the value of the firm. Benefit-cost analysis can also be used to choose the best of several mutually exclusive projects (i.e., those

---

[4] The compensation criterion is often referred to as the Kaldor-Hicks principle, in recognition of the economists responsible for its development.

[5] Economists have debated the issue of whether the compensation actually must be paid to meet this efficiency standard. As a practical matter, of course, such compensation usually is not paid.

[6] For a comprehensive review of benefit-cost analysis, see Snyder and Williams (1978), and Pearce and Nash (1981).

that are designed to meet the same goal) and to rank acceptable or efficient projects based on their rate of return. For example, suppose that a serious disease can be controlled either by a vaccination program or by an oral vaccine program. The option with the higher benefit-cost ratio should be implemented. Or if the cost of a set of acceptable projects exceeds the available budget, that is, if capital rationing applies, the projects can be ranked according to their benefit-cost ratios. Starting at the top of this ranking, projects are implemented in turn until the budget is exhausted. In this way, those projects with the highest ratio of benefits to costs are undertaken first.

Because many projects involve flows of benefits and/or costs over a period of more than one year, time-value-of-money principles must be used. Indeed, once the flows of benefits and costs have been estimated, the same basic present value principles apply that are used in capital budgeting decisions for the profit-maximizing firm. The main differences in approach used by, say, a government agency compared to a profit-maximizing firm are found in accounting for the benefits and costs and in determining the appropriate discount rate.

KEY CONCEPTS

- The Pareto criterion requires that at least one party be better off and no one be worse off as a result of a reallocation of resources.
- The compensation criterion states that a resource allocation is efficient if the gainers from that reallocation can compensate the losers and still be better off. This principle is the basis of benefit-cost analysis of social programs.
- Benefit-cost analysis is used to:
  Ensure that only projects that will increase national income are implemented.
  Choose the best (i.e., highest return) investment from a set of mutually exclusive projects.
  Rank acceptable projects by their rate of return.

Basic Techniques of Benefit-Cost Analysis

The benefit-cost approach to project evaluation consists of the following steps:

1. Estimate the construction, operation, and maintenance costs of the project.
2. Estimate the direct and indirect benefits of the project.
3. Determine the social discount rate to be used to reduce future benefits and costs to their present value.
4. Determine if the present value of all future benefits exceeds the present value of the costs. If so, the project meets the benefit-cost test and is socially efficient.

Estimating Costs. The direct costs for a typical government project fall into three categories: construction, operation, and maintenance. Usually, these costs are estimated by design engineers who project the timing and phasing of both the construction and operating phases of the project. There may also be significant indirect costs associated with the project. For example, the construction of a dam may innundate hundreds or possibly thousands of acres of land. The value of the farms, homes, and other property lost must be evaluated and the owners compensated. Such compensation must be included as part of the project cost.

In addition, there may be costs that are not directly associated with the project but which are indirectly borne by others. For example, a water project that creates a popular recreation site may cause traffic and law enforcement problems for nearby communities. Also, some endangered species of plant or animal life may be threatened by the project. Construction of the Tellico Dam in Tennessee was delayed for several years because of the presence of a small fish, the snail darter, that was on the list of endangered species. Although difficult to measure and typically not included as a cost item in the benefit-cost analysis, it may be useful at least to list such effects as nonquantifiable environmental costs that are to be considered by those making the decision.[7]

Estimating Benefits.   Benefits are also classified as being direct and indirect. Direct benefits are those that will result in an increase in national income. For example, an irrigation project should result in an increase in output of agricultural commodities. The value of that increased output is an addition to national income. A program to control disease will reduce the number of worker-days lost, so this, too, will increase national income.

Many projects have multiple purposes. For example, the nation's interstate highway system was justified on the basis of reduced transportation costs, increased national security, and increased safety. Clearly, accounting for all the diverse benefits of a multiple-purpose project is not a trivial matter. Furthermore, some benefits, such as those associated with recreation, are extremely difficult to measure.

Guidelines published by the U.S. Water Resources Council (1983) identify four benefit-cost categories that are to be included in water and water-related project evaluations. These categories are representative of the wide range of benefits that are often considered in benefit-cost analysis.

1. *National economic development benefits:* changes in the economic value of the national output of goods and services.
2. *Environmental quality benefits:* nonmonetary effects on significant natural and cultural resources.
3. *Regional development benefits:* changes in the distribution of economic activity among regions that may result from each alternative plan.
4. *Other social benefits:* benefits relevant to the planning process but not reflected in the other three categories.

---

[7] The National Environmental Policy Act of 1969 required that an environmental impact study (EIS) be prepared for any significant federal government action. These studies typically inventory potential negative (and positive) effects on air and water quality, traffic congestion, wildlife and plant life, and so on. Usually, no attempt is made to assign a dollar measure to these effects, but they are identified so that some consideration can be given to them.

The range of these benefits suggests that the government takes a very broad approach to the definition of benefits. To illustrate, the benefits of a multipurpose water resource project might include the following:

1. *The value of additional output of agricultural products:* The availability of irrigation water increases yields and may allow for multiple cropping (i.e., obtaining two or more crops instead of just one during the growing season). Also, having a relatively certain water supply may allow for a different mix of crops. That is, higher-valued crops that could not have been grown before because of lack of water may be substituted for low-value crops.
2. *The savings in life and property due to flood control:* An important primary purpose of many water projects is flood control, which is accomplished by building reservoirs to hold water during periods of heavy rain and then to release it at a controlled rate. Annual losses of life and property can be estimated based on historic flooding experience, and their reduction is counted as a direct benefit.
3. *Increased recreational opportunities:* The lakes and streams involved in the project may have enhanced recreation value (e.g., boating, swimming, and fishing). Surveys can be used to estimate the increased number of hours that people will spend recreating at these sites. By placing a value on each of these hours, estimates can be made of the increased recreation benefits.
4. *Reduced transportation costs:* The transport of freight by barge is significantly less costly than by truck, rail, or air. The difference in shipping costs on freight that is shifted to barge transportation is included as a benefit.

Indirect benefits are often associated with any significant government project. These can be classified as real or pecuniary. Real effects include savings in other government programs as a result of the project. For example, if the project increases the number of jobs in the area, the unemployment rate should fall. This will result in a reduction in the unemployment benefits that would have to be paid. This real indirect benefit should be included in the benefit-cost calculation.

Pecuniary effects are those that affect the prices of goods, services, labor, or natural resources. For example, construction of a new interstate highway can result in significant changes in land values and profits. Such effects are usually not included as benefits because they often represent a redistribution of income from one area to another. For example, the profit earned by a new motel located on the new highway may simply result from a redistribution of profits formerly earned by a motel on an old highway.

The Social Discount Rate.   Capital project evaluation in the private sector requires that all future benefits and costs be reduced to their present value using the firm's cost of capital as the discount rate. Similarly, future costs and benefits from government investment projects must be reduced to their present value by using a discount rate. As the projects use resources from and provide benefits to society at large, the discount rate is often referred to as the *social discount rate.* This rate should reflect the opportunity cost of resources transferred from the private sector to the public sector. For example, if funds are obtained by taxing away resources from business that would have been invested at a rate of return of, say, 18 percent, that opportunity cost is the social cost of capital and should be used as the discount rate.

Alternatively, if funds are raised by taxing individuals who would otherwise use those funds for consumption, the opportunity cost of that forgone consumption is used to measure the social cost of capital. For example, suppose that a variety of savings programs (e.g., money market accounts, certificates of deposit, and government bonds) offer the saver an annual return of 13 percent. This rate represents the minimum cost of forgone consumption. That is, an individual who chooses to consume rather than save when the interest rate is 13 percent has revealed that the implicit return to his or her consumption expenditure is at least 13 percent. Thus the interest rate available on the securities typically purchased by individuals represents a minimum estimate of the opportunity cost of consumption.

Evaluating the Project.   Once the benefits and costs have been estimated and an appropriate social rate of discount determined, the final step is to evaluate the present value of benefits and the present value of costs and compare the two.

The conventional benefit-cost evaluation standard is that the ratio of the present value of benefits (B) to the present value of costs (C) must be greater than 1. That is,

$$\frac{B}{C} > 1 \qquad\qquad (20\text{-}1)$$

This evaluation standard is equivalent to the net present value method of evaluating investments that was discussed in Chapter 16. For a profit-maximizing firm, an investment is profitable if the net present value, defined as the present value of net cash flows (A_t) less the cost of the investment (C) is greater than zero. That is,

$$NPV = \sum_{t=1}^{n} \frac{A_t}{(1 + r)^t} - C > 0 \qquad\qquad (20\text{-}2)$$

Define the present value of the net cash flows as B^* and rewrite equation (20-2) as

$$B^* - C > 0$$

Adding C to both sides of the inequality gives

$$B^* > C$$

Then divide both sides by C. This yields the conventional benefit-cost ratio test,

$$\frac{B^*}{C} > 1$$

Table 20-1. Estimated Costs and Benefits for a Hypothetical Government Project

| Year | Costs | | | Benefits | | |
	Construction	Operation and Maintenance	Total	Direct	Real Indirect	Total
1	$1,000	—	$1,000	$200	$200	$400
2	500	$100	600	200	200	400
3	—	200	200	200	200	400
4	—	200	200	200	200	400
5	—	200	200	200	200	400
6	—	200	200	200	200	400
7	—	200	200	200	200	400
8	—	200	200	200	200	400

| Discount Rate (%) | Present Value | | Benefit-Cost Ratio |
	Benefits	Costs	
5	$2,585	$2,417	1.070
10	2,134	2,125	1.004
15	1,795	1,896	0.947

The calculation of the benefit-cost ratio is demonstrated in the following example. Suppose that the flows of benefits and costs for a hypothetical project are as outlined in Table 20-1. For simplicity of calculation, assume that all the costs and benefits are paid or received at the end of each year shown. Note that a large part of the costs are associated with project construction in the first two years, but that benefits are expected to be the same each year during the eight-year life of the project. This concentration of costs early in the project is typical of most capital investments in either the public or private sector.

As mentioned earlier, the choice of discount rate can make the difference between a project being deemed socially efficient or inefficient. That is, the discount rate can determine whether the B-C ratio is greater than or less than unity. In the example shown in Table 20-1, three discount rates, 5, 10, and 15 percent, are used. The B-C ratio is 1.070 when using a rate of 5 percent and 1.004 for a 10 percent discount rate. But the B-C ratio is only 0.947 for a social discount rate of 15 percent. Thus whether this project should be implemented depends on the rate used to discount future costs and benefits.

The internal rate of return method (IRR) can also be used to evaluate a project. Recall that the internal rate of return (r^*) is that discount rate that equates the present value of all future benefits to costs. Thus

$$C = \sum_{t=1}^{n} \frac{B_t}{(1 + r^*)^t}$$

Suppose that a proposed project has an initial cost of $1,000 and annual benefits (B_t) of $150 for each of ten years. The equation then would be

$$1,000 = \sum_{t=1}^{10} \frac{150}{(1 + r^*)^t}$$

and the internal rate of return is calculated to be 8.14 percent. If this calculated internal rate of return exceeds the social discount rate, the project is efficient. That is, the return on the proposed project is higher than the social opportunity cost. As a result, national income will increase. If the internal rate of return is less than the opportunity cost, national income would decrease if the project is implemented.

The internal rate of return can also be computed for the cost and benefit data in Table 20-1. Note that the benefit-cost ratio is greater than 1 for a discount rate of 10 percent but less than 1 for a discount rate of 15 percent. Because the *B-C* ratio is only 1.004 for a 10 percent discount rate, this suggests that the internal rate of return is between 10 and 15 percent, but probably closer to 10 percent. Using a financial calculator, the *IRR* is determined to be 10.35 percent.

KEY CONCEPTS

- The general approach to benefit-cost analysis is to (1) determine the costs of the project, (2) estimate the direct and indirect benefits, (3) use a social discount rate to reduce these costs and benefits to their present value, and (4) determine if the present value of benefits exceeds the present value of costs.
- The social rate of discount should reflect the opportunity cost of reallocating resources from investment and consumption in the private sector.
- The benefit-cost test is equivalent to the net present value (*NPV*) evaluation standard used by the profit-maximizing firm to evaluate capital projects.
- A benefit-cost ratio in excess of 1 also implies that the internal rate of return on the project exceeds the social discount rate.

CASE STUDY
BENEFITS AND COSTS ON THE PORCUPINE

In 1961, construction began on the Porcupine Water Project in northern Utah. Federal, state, and local government departments all participated in the planning and evaluation of the proposed project.

There were three distinct parts of the project:

1. Construction of a dam and reservoir to store water for agricultural and municipal use.
2. Lining of canals with concrete to reduce erosion and water loss.
3. Construction of a water system for irrigating lawns and gardens in nearby cities.

Although the third part of the project was to deliver water for municipal use, the project was primarily designed to store and deliver water for agricultural production, and about 96 percent of project costs were accounted for by the agriculturally-oriented objectives of the project.

The benefits of the project included increased agricultural production, increased profits earned by firms that process the agricultural products, recreation on the reservoir created by the dam, and increased tax revenue. Preproject analysis given in the first part of the table below shows the present value of benefits and costs of each objective of the project and the associated benefit-cost ratio as estimated before the project was started. Although the B/C ratio for the city water system was less than 1, that part of the project was implemented anyway.

Curiously, different rates were used by the various government planners to discount future benefits and costs for each project phase. No explanation was provided for doing this, although it may be the result of different financing arrangements for each phase. Possibly, the opportunity cost of capital was different for each funding source.

Project Component	Discount Rate (%)	Present Value of Benefits (thousands)	Costs (thousands)	B-C Ratio	Life of Project (years)
		Preproject Analysis			
Dam and reservoir	$2\frac{1}{2}$	$3,058.20	$1,770.30	1.73	100
Canal	$5\frac{1}{4}$	840.00	204.50	4.11	15
City water system	6	150.10	158.20	0.95	50
		Postproject Analysis			
Dam and reservoir	$2\frac{1}{2}$	$4,153.30	$2,375.10	1.75	100
Canal	$5\frac{1}{4}$	937.00	318.70	2.90	15
City water system	6	250.60	174.00	1.44	50

In 1977, a postproject B-C analysis was made by a Utah state government department to test whether benefits had in fact exceeded costs. As shown in the second part of the table, initial estimates of both costs and benefits proved to be low, but the B-C ratio was greater than unity for all three project phases. Thus if the analysis is correct, the project increased national income.

Source: Utah Division of Water Resources, *Porcupine Project Economics Reevaluation,* (Salt Lake City, Utah: Department of Natural Resources, 1977).

Problems with Benefit-Cost Analysis

Although the principles of benefit-cost analysis are conceptually sound, there are several problems associated with their application. These include a potential bias in selecting the discount rate to be used and errors in forecasting future costs and benefits.

Bias in Determining the Discount Rate

The primary objective of a government agency or department may not be economic efficiency. Objectives such as maximizing size of budget and number of employees, increased personal power, or minimization of risk may be more important. Indeed, some government agencies are in the project-building business. Without projects to build, their perceived usefulness to society, and hence the employment tenure of their personnel, is reduced. As a result, there may be a tendency for benefit-cost analyses of proposed projects to err on the side of inflating projected benefits and reducing projected costs.

For most projects, the largest share of costs are incurred in the early years of the project. Often, there are few or no benefits in the early years, but benefits increase as the project is brought into full development. Thus the effect of discounting the costs will not be as great as the discounting of benefits, because the costs tend to occur early. Consequently, any group or organization with a real stake in promoting a project will want to use a low discount rate.

Libraries of government project reports are replete with examples where discount rates were used that were considerably below market rates. For example, in 1982 market interest rates on high-quality bonds were in excess of 16 percent. But during that year, some government agencies were using discount rates of less than 5 percent in benefit-cost studies. Clearly, the appropriate social discount rate would have been much closer to 16 percent. Furthermore, the rate used to discount future benefits and costs varies considerably among government departments. This means that agencies using a high discount rate might be rejecting projects that are more efficient than those being accepted by agencies using a low discount rate.

Errors in Forecasting Future Costs and Benefits

Any forecast of future conditions or events is subject to error. This is especially true when forecasting the effects of a proposed government policy. One factor that may result in errors in forecasting benefits is that a government action such as a change in a regulation may alter the relative costs of certain activities, causing individuals to change their behavior. Such changes may have a significant effect on the benefits associated with a government program. For example, one of the benefits of an irrigation project is greater output of crops and livestock, but it may be very difficult to predict how farmers will react to that new water supply. They may change the type of crops produced or shift to planting two crops during the growing season. Clearly, the benefits will differ depending on the farmers' reactions.

A good example of a change in behavior is found in the response of drivers to automobile safety regulations. Since 1968, the National Highway Traffic Safety Administration (NHTSA) has required special safety equipment for new automobiles such as seatbelts, dual-braking systems, and padded instrument panels. The objective of these regulations is to reduce fatalities and injuries for occupants of these automobiles. Field studies and accident data were used to show that the regulations would reduce the occupant death rate significantly. Unfortunately, these estimates were based solely on technological considerations. That is, it was assumed that driving behavior would not change and an assessment was then made of the effect of the safety equipment on death and injuries.

Such estimates might have been reasonably accurate if the regulations had no effect on the way people drive. But one study (Peltzman, 1975) suggests that the technological assessment greatly overestimated the benefits of the safety equipment because changes in driving behavior were not considered.

Changing the safety equipment in an automobile may change the way that

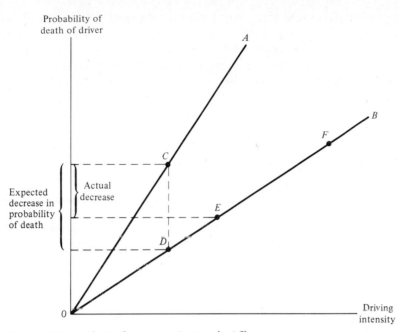

Figure 20-3.   *The Safety–Intensity Trade-Off.*

that automobile is driven. When driving, a person must balance the probability of death or injury against what might be referred to as "driving intensity," a measure of the speed, thrills, and excitement associated with driving a car in a particular manner. The driver who puts a premium on excitement will select a different safety–intensity mix than will the timid soul who drives only to church and back. This trade-off is depicted in Figure 20-3. The ray *0A* represents a possible trade-off between driving intensity and death. The positive slope implies that increased intensity (e.g., higher speed) is associated with a higher probability of death. Assume that with none of the newly-required safety equipment, an individual chooses the safety–intensity combination represented by point *C*.

Now, suppose the government requires that all automobiles have certain types of new safety equipment. This regulation changes the safety–intensity trade-off. With the new equipment, the probability of death is reduced for any given level of driving intensity. This new trade-off is shown by the ray *0B* in the figure. The vertical distance *CD* represents the effect of the safety requirements at the initially chosen level of driving intensity. It corresponds roughly to the technical esti-mates of increased safety previously mentioned. Notice, however, that the choice of *C* as the optimal safety–intensity trade-off was based on the driver's evaluation of the excitement of fast driving in comparison to the expected probability of death. With safer autos, the probability of death has been reduced, and hence driving with intensity becomes less costly.

With safer cars, it would be expected that the new safety–intensity choice made by the driver would involve more speed and thrills. Suppose that the new selec-tion is point *E*. The lifesaving effect of the safety regulations is now the vertical distance between *C* and *E*—a much smaller safety gain than predicted by the technological studies. Indeed, it is possible that the demand for driving intensity is such that the driver of the safer car will select point *F*. This choice would actually result in a higher probability of death than before the government regulation. In this case, the safety standards make no contribution to reducing driver deaths and impose a cost in the form of higher prices for the mandated equipment.

It is unlikely that government-mandated auto safety equipment would actually cause an increase in driver deaths, but there are other undesirable possibilities. Although the probability of driver death is likely to decrease, greater driving intensity may increase the total number of accidents. Thus there may be an increase in property damage and injuries. It is also possible that pedestrian deaths may increase as people increase their driving intensity.

The automobile safety example shows how behavioral changes can complicate benefit-cost analysis. Based solely on the technological forecasts, benefit-cost analysis might have justified the mandated safety equipment. However, the actual benefits of the regulation proved to be less than the estimated benefits. Had the actual benefits been known, it is possible that the benefit-cost ratio would have been less than 1 and thus the program would not have been implemented.

KEY CONCEPT

- Two problems associated with the use of benefit-cost analysis are (1) a bias toward using a social rate of discount that is too low; and (2) errors in forecasting future benefits and costs.

Summary

Nonprofit enterprises are found in both the private and the public sector. A common perception is that nonprofit enterprises are less efficient than their for-profit counterparts. But this judgment may simply reflect the fact that many nonprofit enterprises are charged with pursuing goals other than efficiency and profitability. As such, managers of these enterprises are evaluated on different criteria than are managers of profit-maximizing firms. In nonprofit enterprises, managerial decisions will be based on the aspects of performance that most influence the evaluation process.

In general, efficient resource allocation can be achieved by equating prices and marginal costs. However, there may be circumstances where marginal cost pricing is not feasible or desirable. In such cases, Ramsey pricing can be used as a second-best method for efficiently allocating resources. A simple form of the Ramsey pricing rule dictates that deviations between prices and marginal costs should be inversely related to price elasticity of demand. Using this approach, a disproportionate share of an enterprise's fixed costs and profit will be recovered from those goods or services for which demand is least elastic.

Fees and licenses are an alternative to pricing on a per unit basis. But because consumers pay nothing for additional units, there is no incentive to conserve on the use of the good or service. However, where collection costs are high relative to price, fees and licenses may be an efficient approach to pricing.

Benefit-cost analysis is based on the compensation criterion, which states that a reallocation of resources is socially efficient if those who gain from the investment could compensate the losers and still have some gains left over. The basic question to be answered by benefit-cost analysis is whether the present value of national income will be increased by the reallocation of resources.

The steps involved in a benefit-cost study are to: (1) estimate construction, operation, and maintenance costs; (2) estimate the relevant direct and indirect benefits; (3) use an appropriate social discount rate to compute the present value of benefits and costs; and (4) determine if the project is socially efficient.

The social discount rate selected for benefit-cost analysis should reflect the opportunity costs associated with reallocating resources from the private sector. These costs include the lost return on business investments and forgone consumption spending by individuals. The rates of return on business investments and the interest rates available in savings programs are measures of these opportunity costs.

The conventional social efficiency test is that the benefit-cost ratio be greater than 1. This is equivalent to requiring that the present value of benefits exceed the present value of costs. A benefit-cost ratio greater than unity also implies that the implicit rate of return on the project is greater than the social rate of discount.

Although benefit-cost analysis has a sound conceptual basis, problems can occur in its practical application. Sometimes, government agencies use unrealistically low discount rates to justify marginal projects. In other cases, price or behavioral changes cause actual benefits and costs to differ significantly from those used in the original analysis.

Discussion Questions

20-1. Suppose that a dam is built and operated by the federal government. List at least three services the dam could provide to the general population. Could increasing the rate of output of one of these services conflict with the provision of the other services? Explain. How might the manager of such a facility decide which service to emphasize?

20-2. Why is it often more difficult to value the outputs of a nonprofit enterprise than a "for-profit" enterprise?

20-3. Ramsey pricing is sometimes criticized as being unfair. What is the basis for this criticism? Is it valid?

20-4. Usually, a monthly charge is levied by municipalities for residential garbage pickup. Under what circumstances is this pricing scheme preferable to pricing based on the amount of garbage collected?

20-5. Explain why benefit-cost analysis for nonprofit enterprises is analogous to the capital budgeting process for a profit-maximizing firm.

20-6. What evidence is there that the Pareto criterion is not met for many public-sector policies and investments?

20-7. Benefit-cost analysis is based on the compensation criterion for resource reallocation. Explain.

20-8. Using benefit-cost analysis, how would the choice of a discount rate affect the evaluation of a government financed dam? Explain.

20-9. With benefit-cost analysis, which is usually more difficult, estimating benefits or estimating costs? Why?

20-10. "You cannot put a price on human life." Evaluate this statement as it relates to benefit-cost analysis.

Problems

20-1. The estimated costs and benefits over the ten-year life of a proposed government project are shown below. (For simplicity, assume that all costs and benefits occur at the end of each year.)

	Costs (thousands)			Benefits (thousands)		
Year	Construction	Operation and Maintenance	Total	Direct	Indirect	Total
0	$40,000	—	$40,000	$10,000	$5,000	$15,000
1	20,000	$5,000	25,000	10,000	5,000	15,000
2	—	5,000	5,000	10,000	5,000	15,000
3	—	5,000	5,000	10,000	5,000	15,000
4	—	5,000	5,000	10,000	5,000	15,000
5	—	5,000	5,000	10,000	5,000	15,000
6	—	5,000	5,000	10,000	5,000	15,000
7	—	5,000	5,000	10,000	5,000	15,000
8	—	5,000	5,000	10,000	5,000	15,000
9	—	5,000	5,000	10,000	5,000	15,000
10	—	5,000	5,000	10,000	5,000	15,000

The agency responsible for initiating the project wants to use an 8 percent discount rate to evaluate the proposal because that is the average interest rate on existing government securities. Economic consultants from a local university insist that the discount rate is 12 percent because that is the approximate cost of capital in the private sector.

(a) Evaluate the project using both discount rates.

(b) Which discount rate should be used? Explain.

20-2. The U.S. Department of Commerce has estimated the present value of lifetime earnings for the average person based on sex, age, and education. Some of those data are as follows:

	Present Value of Future Earnings for High School Graduates who:	
Education (Age)	Male	Female
Obtain no more education (18)	$1,087,000	$481,000
Obtain a bachelor's degree (22)	1,499,000	638,000
Obtain a master's degree (24)	1,615,000	862,000

Assume the following:
1. The cost of attending college is $15,000 per year (including all opportunity costs, such as forgone earnings) and that this cost is incurred on the first day of each year.
2. The future earnings are discounted back to the day of high school graduation.
3. It takes four years of college for a bachelor's degree and two additional years for a Master's degree.
4. The rate of return on all investments is 12 percent.

Analyzing men and women separately, use benefit-cost techniques to determine if it is worthwhile financially to (1) devote four years to obtaining a bachelor's degree, and (2) devote an additional two years to obtaining a Master's degree.

20-3. A federal agency responsible for safety is considering proposed legislation requiring that automobiles have much heavier bumpers that would protect the body of an automobile in a 10-mph crash into a concrete wall. Based on laboratory crash tests, it is estimated that having these bumpers on the average car would reduce expected repairs by $100 per year over the seven-year life of the average car. Assume that repair payments are made at the end of each year and that the appropriate social discount rate is 14 percent. (a) What is the maximum incremental cost per car that could be expended on these bumpers that would still meet the standard benefit-cost test? (b) Why might your answer to part (a) overstate the actual maximum cost that would provide net benefits?

References

Baumol, W. J. 1968. "On the Social Rate of Discount." *American Economic Review*, September, pp. 788–802.

Baumol, W. J., and Bradford, O. F. 1970. "Optimal Departures from Marginal Cost Pricing." *American Economic Review* 60(June):265–283.

Lindsay, C. 1976. "A Theory of Public Enterprise." *Journal of Political Economy* 84(October):1061–1077.

Pearce, D. W., and Nash, C. A. 1981. *The Social Appraisal of Projects: A Text in Cost-Benefit Analysis*. New York: Wiley.

Peltzman, S. 1975. "The Effects of Automobile Safety Regulation." *Journal of Political Economy* 83(July–August):667–725.

Ramsey, F. P. 1927. "A Contribution to the Theory of Taxation." *The Economic Journal* 37(March):27–61.

Snyder, R., and Williams, A. 1978. *The Principles of Cost-Benefit Analysis*. Oxford: Oxford University Press.

Turvey, R., ed. 1968. *Public Enterprise*. Baltimore: Penguin.

U.S. Water Resources Council. 1983. *Economic and Environmental Principles and Guidelines for Water and Related Land Resources Implementation Studies*. Washington, D.C.: U.S. Government Printing Office.

INTEGRATING CASE PROBLEM VI
AUTOEROTICA (UN)LTD.

Three years ago Hugo Matthews and Sloan Hefner developed a new method of renting adult videocassettes. Basically, the idea involves distribution through automated outlets in shopping centers. To use the service, customers must first obtain a membership which includes a customer identification number. There is no cost for the membership, but it is issued only after the company receives verification that the individual is of legal age. Once received, the ID number is used in the following way to obtain a cassette. The customer enters the ID number at a terminal in a rental outlet. If a valid number is entered, a list of available cassettes is displayed. To obtain a cassette, the customer simply enters the number of the cassette. This action causes the cassette to be given to the customer and a record to be made of the transaction. When a cassette is returned, the rental amount is recorded on the person's account. Each month the customer is sent a bill for rentals during that period.

Autoerotica was started in South Dakota and the company has a dominant share of the market for adult cassette rentals in that state. The firm's success is the result of being first to offer the service. Although there are nonautomated establishments that provide movies, they presently offer neither the convenience nor the range of choice of Autoerotica. In addition, the firm greatly benefited from publicity caused by vocal opposition from church groups and local politicians.

Rental prices are $5 per movie in South Dakota. During its last fiscal year, the firm's South Dakota operations earned total revenue of over $10,000,000 and a pretax profit of 50 percent on investment.

Fifteen months ago, AutoPorn began using Autoerotica's method in North Dakota. Matthews and Hefner immediately proposed a merger, but the offer was rejected by the management of Autoporn. A year ago, Autoerotica began opening rental outlets of their own in North Dakota. First year sales totaled $500,000 and the two firms currently each have half of the total market. In an effort to compete more vigorously, Autoerotica recently decreased its price in North Dakota to $2.50 per movie. After the price change, Autoerotica's North Dakota outlets averaged 100 rentals per day.

To facilitate better decision making, an accountant was hired to collect and analyze cost information. He determines that scale economies are unimportant and that daily costs for a typical outlet are as follows:

Lease payments: $40 per day. In each case, the lease contract is for two years and the property cannot be sublet to anyone else.

Movie inventory: $40 per day. Provisions of the purchase contract prevent resale to other firms or to the general public. Because of duplication of cassettes, an outlet's inventory cannot be used efficiently at other outlets.

Computer costs: $100 per day. The system is operated by use of a time-shared computer. The agreement with the system owner is based on actual days used and may be canceled at any time without penalty.

Rental costs: $1.00 per rental. The only cost that varies with the number of rentals is the billing cost and the replacement cost of cassettes. The more often a cassette is rented, the sooner it has to be replaced.

At a trade meeting, it is reported that the demand for adult movie rentals is very inelastic. After the meeting, Matthews and Hefner return to their office to find that:

1. In response to a complaint from AutoPorn, the North Dakota Attorney General's office is investigating alleged predatory pricing of cassettes by Autoerotica in the state.

2. A South Dakota state legislator appeared on a talk show to condemn the pernicous influence of Autoerotica. Noting the firm's 50 percent pretax profit in the state, the legislator proposed a flat-rate tax on profits earned from rental of adult cassettes. He believes the tax would cause firms such as Autoerotica to reduce the quantity of pornographic materials supplied.

3. At a news conference, the chairman of the tax commission in South Dakota proposes a $0.50 excise tax on the rental of adult cassettes. He argues that such a tax would be a good way to raise revenue while penalizing those who distribute unsavory materials.

4. In a Labor Day speech at Mt. Rushmore, a past governor of South Dakota decries the spread of pornography and announces that she supports the creation of a nonprofit enterprise to be given a monopoly right to sell and rent adult materials. This enterprise would be government-owned and similar to state-owned liquor stores that exist in many states. The main purpose of the enterprise would be to keep prices down and evaluate the suitability of available materials.

Requirements

a. As a law and economics professor in North Dakota, you are interested in the predatory pricing charge. Prepare a report that analyzes the strengths and weaknesses of this allegation.

b. The present governor of South Dakota must respond to the proposals for a profit tax, excise tax, and government ownership. You are the governor's administrative assistant. Prepare a report that analyzes the probable effects of each proposal.

Tables

Table I. Future Value of $1.00

$$FVIF_{i,n} = (1 + i)^n$$

Periods (n)	1%	2%	3%	4%	5%	6%	7%	8%	9%	10%
1	1.0100	1.0200	1.0300	1.0400	1.0500	1.0600	1.0700	1.0800	1.0900	1.1000
2	1.0201	1.0404	1.0609	1.0816	1.1025	1.1236	1.1449	1.1664	1.1881	1.2100
3	1.0303	1.0612	1.0927	1.1249	1.1576	1.1910	1.2250	1.2597	1.2950	1.3310
4	1.0406	1.0824	1.1255	1.1699	1.2155	1.2625	1.3108	1.3605	1.4116	1.4641
5	1.0510	1.1041	1.1593	1.2167	1.2763	1.3382	1.4026	1.4693	1.5386	1.6105
6	1.0615	1.1262	1.1941	1.2653	1.3401	1.4185	1.5007	1.5869	1.6771	1.7716
7	1.0721	1.1487	1.2299	1.3159	1.4071	1.5036	1.6058	1.7138	1.8280	1.9487
8	1.0829	1.1717	1.2668	1.3686	1.4775	1.5938	1.7182	1.8509	1.9926	2.1436
9	1.0937	1.1951	1.3048	1.4233	1.5513	1.6895	1.8385	1.9990	2.1719	2.3579
10	1.1046	1.2190	1.3439	1.4802	1.6289	1.7908	1.9672	2.1589	2.3674	2.5937
11	1.1157	1.2434	1.3842	1.5395	1.7103	1.8983	2.1049	2.3316	2.5804	2.8531
12	1.1268	1.2682	1.4258	1.6010	1.7959	2.0122	2.2522	2.5182	2.8127	3.1384
13	1.1381	1.2936	1.4685	1.6651	1.8856	2.1329	2.4098	2.7196	3.0658	3.4523
14	1.1495	1.3195	1.5126	1.7317	1.9799	2.2609	2.5785	2.9372	3.3417	3.7975
15	1.1610	1.3459	1.5580	1.8009	2.0789	2.3966	2.7590	3.1722	3.6425	4.1772
16	1.1726	1.3728	1.6047	1.8730	2.1829	2.5404	2.9522	3.4259	3.9703	4.5950
17	1.1843	1.4002	1.6528	1.9479	2.2920	2.6928	3.1588	3.7000	4.3276	5.0545
18	1.1961	1.4282	1.7024	2.0258	2.4066	2.8543	3.3799	3.9960	4.7171	5.5599
19	1.2081	1.4568	1.7535	2.1068	2.5270	3.0256	3.6165	4.3157	5.1417	6.1159
20	1.2202	1.4859	1.8061	2.1911	2.6533	3.2071	3.8697	4.6610	5.6044	6.7275
21	1.2324	1.5157	1.8603	2.2788	2.7860	3.3996	4.1406	5.0338	6.0188	7.4002
22	1.2447	1.5460	1.9161	2.3699	2.9253	3.6035	4.4304	5.4365	6.6586	8.1403
23	1.2572	1.5769	1.9736	2.4647	3.0715	3.8197	4.7405	5.8715	7.2579	8.9543
24	1.2697	1.6084	2.0328	2.5633	3.2251	4.0489	5.0724	6.3412	7.9111	9.8497
25	1.2824	1.6406	2.0938	2.6658	3.3864	4.2919	5.4274	6.8485	8.6231	10.834
26	1.2953	1.6734	2.1566	2.7725	3.5557	4.5494	5.8074	7.3964	9.3992	11.918
27	1.3082	1.7069	2.2213	2.8834	3.7335	4.8223	6.2139	7.9881	10.245	13.110
28	1.3213	1.7410	2.2879	2.9987	3.9201	5.1117	6.6488	8.6271	11.167	14.421
29	1.3345	1.7758	2.3566	3.1187	4.1161	5.4184	7.1143	9.3173	12.172	15.863
30	1.3478	1.8114	2.4273	3.2434	4.3219	5.7435	7.6123	10.062	13.267	17.449
40	1.4889	2.2080	3.2620	4.8010	7.0400	10.285	14.974	21.724	31.409	45.259
50	1.6446	2.6916	4.3839	7.1067	11.467	18.420	29.457	46.901	74.357	117.39
60	1.8167	3.2810	5.8916	10.519	18.679	32.987	57.946	101.25	176.03	304.48

Table I. (continued)

Periods (n)	Interest (Discount) Rate (i)									
	12%	14%	15%	16%	18%	20%	24%	28%	32%	36%
1	1.1200	1.1400	1.1500	1.1600	1.1800	1.2000	1.2400	1.2800	1.3200	1.3600
2	1.2544	1.2996	1.3225	1.3456	1.3924	1.4400	1.5376	1.6384	1.7424	1.8496
3	1.4049	1.4815	1.5209	1.5609	1.6430	1.7280	1.9066	2.0972	2.3000	2.5155
4	1.5735	1.6890	1.7490	1.8106	1.9388	2.0736	2.3642	2.6844	3.0360	3.4210
5	1.7623	1.9254	2.0114	2.1003	2.2878	2.4883	2.9316	3.4360	4.0075	4.6526
6	1.9738	2.1950	2.3131	2.4364	2.6996	2.9860	3.6352	4.3980	5.2899	6.3275
7	2.2107	2.5023	2.6600	2.8262	3.1855	3.5832	4.5077	5.6295	6.9826	8.6054
8	2.4760	2.8526	3.0590	3.2784	3.7589	4.2998	5.5895	7.2058	9.2170	11.703
9	2.7731	3.2519	3.5179	3.8030	4.4355	5.1598	6.9310	9.2234	12.166	15.916
10	3.1058	3.7072	4.0456	4.4114	5.2338	6.1917	8.5944	11.805	16.059	21.646
11	3.4785	4.2262	4.6524	5.1173	6.1759	7.4301	10.657	15.111	21.198	29.439
12	3.8960	4.8179	5.3502	5.9360	7.2876	8.9161	13.214	19.342	27.982	40.037
13	4.3635	5.4924	6.1528	6.8858	8.5994	10.699	16.386	24.758	36.937	54.451
14	4.8871	6.2613	7.0757	7.9875	10.147	12.839	20.319	31.691	48.756	74.053
15	5.4736	7.1379	8.1371	9.2655	11.973	15.407	25.195	40.564	64.358	100.71
16	6.1304	8.1372	9.3576	10.748	14.129	18.488	31.242	51.923	84.953	136.96
17	6.8660	9.2765	10.761	12.467	16.672	22.186	38.740	66.461	112.13	186.27
18	7.6900	10.575	12.375	14.462	19.673	26.623	48.038	85.070	148.02	253.33
19	8.6128	12.055	14.231	16.776	23.214	31.948	59.567	108.89	195.39	344.53
20	9.6463	13.743	16.366	19.460	27.393	38.337	73.864	139.37	257.91	468.57
21	10.803	15.667	18.821	22.574	32.323	46.005	91.591	178.40	340.44	637.26
22	12.100	17.861	21.644	26.186	38.142	55.206	113.57	228.35	449.39	866.67
23	13.552	20.361	24.891	30.367	45.007	66.247	140.83	292.30	593.19	1178.6
24	15.178	23.212	28.625	35.236	53.108	79.496	174.63	374.14	783.02	1602.9
25	17.000	26.461	32.918	40.874	62.688	95.396	216.54	478.90	1033.5	2180.0
26	19.040	30.166	37.856	47.414	73.948	114.47	268.51	612.99	1364.3	2964.9
27	21.324	34.389	43.535	55.000	87.259	137.37	332.95	784.63	1800.9	4032.2
28	23.883	39.204	50.065	63.800	102.96	164.84	412.86	1004.3	2377.2	5483.8
29	26.749	44.693	57.575	74.008	121.50	197.81	511.95	1285.5	3137.9	7458.0
30	29.959	50.950	66.211	85.849	143.37	237.37	634.81	1645.5	4142.0	10143.
40	93.050	188.88	267.86	378.72	750.37	1469.7	5455.9	19426.	66520.	*
50	289.00	700.23	1083.6	1670.7	3927.3	9100.4	46890.	*	*	*
60	897.59	2595.9	4383.9	7370.1	20555.	56347.	*	*	*	*

*FVIF > 99,999.

Table II. Present Value of $1.00

$$PVIF_{i,n} = \frac{1}{(1 + i)^n}$$

Periods (n)	Interest (Discount) Rate (i)									
	1%	2%	3%	4%	5%	6%	7%	8%	9%	10%
1	.9901	.9804	.9709	.9615	.9524	.9434	.9346	.9259	.9174	.9091
2	.9803	.9612	.9426	.9246	.9070	.8900	.8734	.8573	.8417	.8264
3	.9706	.9423	.9151	.8890	.8638	.8396	.8163	.7938	.7722	.7513
4	.9610	.9238	.8885	.8548	.8227	.7921	.7629	.7350	.7084	.6830
5	.9515	.9057	.8626	.8219	.7835	.7473	.7130	.6806	.6499	.6209
6	.9420	.8880	.8375	.7903	.7462	.7050	.6663	.6302	.5963	.5645
7	.9327	.8706	.8131	.7599	.7107	.6651	.6227	.5835	.5470	.5132
8	.9235	.8535	.7894	.7307	.6768	.6274	.5820	.5403	.5019	.4665
9	.9143	.8368	.7664	.7026	.6446	.5919	.5439	.5002	.4604	.4241
10	.9053	.8203	.7441	.6756	.6139	.5584	.5083	.4632	.4224	.3855
11	.8963	.8043	.7224	.6496	.5847	.5268	.4751	.4289	.3875	.3505
12	.8874	.7885	.7014	.6246	.5568	.4970	.4440	.3971	.3555	.3186
13	.8787	.7730	.6810	.6606	.5303	.4688	.4150	.3677	.3262	.2897
14	.8700	.7579	.6611	.5775	.5051	.4423	.3878	.3405	.2992	.2633
15	.8613	.7430	.6419	.5553	.4810	.4173	.3624	.3152	.2745	.2394
16	.8528	.7284	.6232	.5339	.4581	.3936	.3387	.2919	.2519	.2176
17	.8444	.7142	.6050	.5134	.4363	.3714	.3166	.2703	.2311	.1978
18	.8360	.7002	.5874	.4936	.4155	.3503	.2959	.2502	.2120	.1799
19	.8277	.6864	.5703	.4746	.3957	.3305	.2765	.2317	.1945	.1635
20	.8195	.6730	.5537	.4564	.3769	.3118	.2584	.2145	.1784	.1486
21	.8114	.6598	.5375	.4388	.3589	.2942	.2415	.1987	.1637	.1351
22	.8034	.6468	.5219	.4220	.3418	.2775	.2257	.1839	.1502	.1228
23	.7954	.6342	.5067	.4057	.3256	.2618	.2109	.1703	.1378	.1117
24	.7876	.6217	.4919	.3901	.3101	.2470	.1971	.1577	.1264	.1015
25	.7798	.6095	.4776	.3751	.2953	.2330	.1842	.1460	.1160	.0923
26	.7720	.5976	.4637	.3607	.2812	.2198	.1722	.1352	.1064	.0839
27	.7644	.5859	.4502	.3468	.2678	.2074	.1609	.1252	.0976	.0763
28	.7568	.5744	.4371	.3335	.2551	.1956	.1504	.1159	.0895	.0693
29	.7493	.5631	.4243	.3207	.2429	.1846	.1406	.1073	.0822	.0630
30	.7419	.5521	.4120	.3083	.2314	.1741	.1314	.0994	.0754	.0573
35	.7059	.5000	.3554	.2534	.1813	.1301	.0937	.0676	.0490	.0356
40	.6717	.4529	.3066	.2083	.1420	.0972	.0668	.0460	.0318	.0221
45	.6391	.4102	.2644	.1712	.1113	.0727	.0476	.0313	.0207	.0137
50	.6080	.3715	.2281	.1407	.0872	.0543	.0339	.0213	.0134	.0085
55	.5785	.3365	.1968	.1157	.0683	.0406	.0242	.0145	.0087	.0053

Table II. (continued)

Periods (n)	\multicolumn{10}{c}{Interest (Discount) Rate (i)}
	12%	14%	15%	16%	18%	20%	24%	28%	32%	36%
1	.8929	.8772	.8696	.8621	.8475	.8333	.8065	.7813	.7576	.7353
2	.7972	.7695	.7561	.7432	.7182	.6944	.6504	.6104	.5739	.5407
3	.7118	.6750	.6575	.6407	.6086	.5787	.5245	.4768	.4348	.3975
4	.6355	.5921	.5718	.5523	.5158	.4823	.4230	.3725	.3294	.2923
5	.5674	.5194	.4972	.4761	.4371	.4019	.3411	.2910	.2495	.2149
6	.5066	.4556	.4323	.4104	.3704	.3349	.2751	.2274	.1890	.1580
7	.4523	.3996	.3759	.3538	.3139	.2791	.2218	.1776	.1432	.1162
8	.4039	.3506	.3269	.3050	.2660	.2326	.1789	.1388	.1085	.0854
9	.3606	.3075	.2843	.2630	.2255	.1938	.1443	.1084	.0822	.0628
10	.3220	.2697	.2472	.2267	.1911	.1615	.1164	.0847	.0623	.0462
11	.2875	.2366	.2149	.1954	.1619	.1346	.0938	.0662	.0472	.0340
12	.2567	.2076	.1869	.1685	.1372	.1122	.0757	.0517	.0357	.0250
13	.2292	.1821	.1625	.1452	.1163	.0935	.0610	.0404	.0271	.0184
14	.2046	.1597	.1413	.1252	.0985	.0779	.0492	.0316	.0205	.0135
15	.1827	.1401	.1229	.1079	.0835	.0649	.0397	.0247	.0155	.0099
16	.1631	.1229	.1069	.0930	.0708	.0541	.0320	.0193	.0118	.0073
17	.1456	.1078	.0929	.0802	.0600	.0451	.0258	.0150	.0089	.0054
18	.1300	.0946	.0808	.0691	.0508	.0376	.0208	.0118	.0068	.0039
19	.1161	.0829	.0703	.0596	.0431	.0313	.0168	.0092	.0051	.0029
20	.1037	.0728	.0611	.0514	.0365	.0261	.0135	.0072	.0039	.0021
21	.0926	.0638	.0531	.0443	.0309	.0217	.0109	.0056	.0029	.0016
22	.0826	.0560	.0462	.0382	.0262	.0181	.0088	.0044	.0022	.0012
23	.0738	.0491	.0402	.0329	.0222	.0151	.0071	.0034	.0017	.0008
24	.0659	.0431	.0349	.0284	.0188	.0126	.0057	.0027	.0013	.0006
25	.0588	.0378	.0304	.0245	.0160	.0105	.0046	.0021	.0010	.0005
26	.0525	.0331	.0264	.0211	.0135	.0087	.0037	.0016	.0007	.0003
27	.0469	.0291	.0230	.0182	.0115	.0073	.0030	.0013	.0006	.0002
28	.0419	.0255	.0200	.0157	.0097	.0061	.0024	.0010	.0004	.0002
29	.0374	.0224	.0174	.0135	.0082	.0051	.0020	.0008	.0003	.0001
30	.0334	.00196	.0151	.0116	.0070	.0042	.0016	.0006	.0002	.0001
35	.0189	.0102	.0075	.0055	.0030	.0017	.0005	.0002	.0001	*
40	.0107	.0053	.0037	.0026	.0013	.0007	.0002	.0001	*	*
45	.0061	.0027	.0019	.0013	.0006	.0003	.0001	*	*	*
50	.0035	.0014	.0009	.0006	.0003	.0001	*	*	*	*
55	.0020	.0007	.0005	.0003	.0001	*	*	*	*	*

*PVIF < 0.0000.

Table III. Present Value of an Annuity of $1.00 per Period

$$PVAF_{i,n} = \sum_{t=1}^{n} \frac{1}{(1 + i)^t}$$

Periods (n)	_Interest (Discount) Rate (i)_								
	1%	2%	3%	4%	5%	6%	7%	8%	9%
1	0.9901	0.9804	0.9709	0.9615	0.9524	0.9434	0.9346	0.9259	0.9174
2	1.9704	1.9416	1.9135	1.8861	1.8594	1.8334	1.8080	1.7833	1.7591
3	2.9410	2.8839	2.8286	2.7751	2.7232	2.6730	2.6243	2.5771	2.5313
4	3.9020	3.8077	3.7171	3.6299	3.5460	3.4651	3.3872	3.3121	3.2397
5	4.8534	4.7135	4.5797	4.4518	4.3295	4.2124	4.1002	3.9927	3.8897
6	5.7955	5.6014	5.4172	5.2421	5.0757	4.9173	4.7665	4.6229	4.4859
7	6.7282	6.4720	6.2303	6.0021	5.7864	5.5824	5.3893	5.2064	5.0330
8	7.6517	7.3255	7.0197	6.7327	6.4632	6.2098	5.9713	5.7466	5.5348
9	8.5660	8.1622	7.7861	7.4353	7.1078	6.8017	6.5152	6.2469	5.9952
10	9.4713	8.9826	8.5302	8.1109	7.7217	7.3601	7.0236	6.7101	6.4177
11	10.3676	9.7868	9.2526	8.7605	8.3064	7.8869	7.4987	7.1390	6.8052
12	11.2551	10.5753	9.9540	9.3851	8.8633	8.3838	7.9427	7.5361	7.1607
13	12.1337	11.3484	10.6350	9.9856	9.3936	8.8527	8.3577	7.9038	7.4869
14	13.0037	12.1062	11.2961	10.5631	9.8986	9.2950	8.7455	8.2442	7.7862
15	13.8651	12.8493	11.9379	11.1184	10.3797	9.7122	9.1079	8.5595	8.0607
16	14.7179	13.5777	12.5611	11.6523	10.8378	10.1059	9.4466	8.8514	8.3126
17	15.5623	14.2919	13.1661	12.1657	11.2741	10.4773	9.7632	9.1216	8.5436
18	16.3983	14.9920	13.7535	12.6593	11.6896	10.8276	10.0591	9.3719	8.7556
19	17.2260	15.6785	14.3238	13.1339	12.0853	11.1581	10.3356	9.6036	8.9501
20	18.0456	16.3514	14.8775	13.5903	12.4622	11.4699	10.5940	9.8181	9.1285
21	18.8570	17.0112	15.4150	14.0292	12.8212	11.7641	10.8355	10.0168	9.2922
22	19.6604	17.6580	15.9369	14.4511	13.1630	12.0416	11.0612	10.2007	9.4424
23	20.4558	18.2922	16.4436	14.8568	13.4886	12.3034	11.2722	10.3711	9.5802
24	21.2434	18.9139	16.9355	15.2470	13.7986	12.5504	11.4693	10.5288	9.7066
25	20.0232	19.5235	17.4131	15.6221	14.0939	12.7834	11.6536	10.6748	9.8226
26	22.7952	20.1210	17.8768	15.9828	14.3752	13.0032	11.8258	10.8100	9.9290
27	23.5596	20.7069	18.3270	16.3296	14.6430	13.2105	11.9867	10.9352	10.0266
28	24.3164	21.2813	18.7641	16.6631	14.8981	13.4062	12.1371	11.0511	10.1161
29	25.0658	21.8444	19.1885	16.9837	15.1411	13.5907	12.2777	11.1584	10.1983
30	25.8077	22.3965	19.6004	17.2920	15.3725	13.7648	12.4090	11.2578	10.2737
35	29.4086	24.9986	21.4872	18.6646	16.3742	14.4982	12.9477	11.6546	10.5668
40	32.8347	27.3555	23.1148	19.7928	17.1591	15.0463	13.3317	11.9246	10.7574
45	36.0945	29.4902	24.5187	20.7200	17.7741	15.4558	13.6055	12.1084	10.8812
50	39.1961	31.4236	25.7298	21.4822	18.2559	15.7619	13.8007	12.2335	10.9617
55	42.1472	33.1748	26.7744	22.1086	18.6335	15.9905	13.9399	12.3186	11.0140

Table III. (continued)

Periods (n)	Interest (Discount) Rate (i)									
	10%	12%	14%	15%	16%	18%	20%	24%	28%	32%
1	0.9091	0.8929	0.8772	0.8696	0.8621	0.8475	0.8333	0.8065	0.7813	0.7576
2	1.7355	1.6901	1.6467	1.6257	1.6052	1.5656	1.5278	1.4568	1.3916	1.3315
3	2.4869	2.4018	2.3216	2.2832	2.2459	2.1743	2.1065	1.9813	1.8684	1.7663
4	3.1699	3.0373	2.9137	2.8550	2.7982	2.6901	2.5887	2.4043	2.2410	2.0957
5	3.7908	3.6048	3.4331	3.3522	3.2743	3.1272	2.9906	2.7454	2.5320	2.3452
6	4.3553	4.1114	3.8887	3.7845	3.6847	3.4976	3.3255	3.0205	2.7594	2.5342
7	4.8684	4.5638	4.2883	4.1604	4.0386	3.8115	3.6046	3.2423	2.9370	2.6775
8	5.3349	4.9676	4.6389	4.4873	4.3436	4.0776	3.8372	3.4212	3.0758	2.7860
9	5.7590	5.3282	4.9464	4.7716	4.6065	4.3030	4.0310	3.5655	3.1842	2.8681
10	6.1446	5.6502	5.2161	5.0188	4.8332	4.4941	4.1925	3.6819	3.2689	2.9304
11	6.4951	5.9377	5.4527	5.2337	5.0286	4.6560	4.3271	3.7757	3.3351	2.9776
12	6.8137	6.1944	5.6603	5.4206	5.1971	4.7932	4.4392	3.8514	3.3868	3.0133
13	7.1034	6.4235	5.8424	5.5831	5.3423	4.9095	4.5327	3.9124	3.4272	3.0404
14	7.3667	6.6282	6.0021	5.7245	5.4675	5.0081	4.6106	3.9616	3.4587	3.0609
15	7.6061	6.8109	6.1422	5.8474	5.5755	5.0916	4.6755	4.0013	3.4834	3.0764
16	7.8237	6.9740	6.2651	5.9542	5.6685	5.1624	4.7296	4.0333	3.5026	3.0882
17	8.0216	7.1196	6.3729	6.0472	5.7487	5.2223	4.7746	4.0591	3.5177	3.0971
18	8.2014	7.2497	6.4674	6.1280	5.8178	5.2732	4.8122	4.0799	3.5294	3.1039
19	8.3649	7.3658	6.5504	6.1982	5.8775	5.3162	4.8435	4.0967	3.5386	3.1090
20	8.5136	7.4694	6.6231	6.2593	5.9288	5.3527	4.8696	4.1103	3.5458	3.1129
21	8.6487	7.5620	6.6870	6.3125	5.9731	5.3837	4.8913	4.1212	3.5514	3.1158
22	8.7715	7.6446	6.7429	6.3587	6.0113	5.4099	4.9094	4.1300	3.5558	3.1180
23	8.8832	7.7184	6.7921	6.3988	6.0442	5.4321	4.9245	4.1371	3.5592	3.1197
24	8.9847	7.7843	6.8351	6.4338	6.0726	5.4510	4.9371	4.1428	3.5619	3.1210
25	9.0770	7.8431	6.8729	6.4642	6.0971	5.4669	4.9476	4.1474	3.5640	3.1220
26	9.1609	7.8957	6.9061	6.4906	6.1182	5.4804	4.9563	4.1511	3.5656	3.1227
27	9.2372	7.9426	6.9352	6.5135	6.1364	5.4919	4.9636	4.1542	3.5669	3.1233
28	9.3066	7.9844	6.9607	6.5335	6.1520	5.5016	4.9697	4.1566	3.5679	3.1237
29	9.3696	8.0218	6.9830	6.5509	6.1656	5.5098	4.9747	4.1585	3.5687	3.1240
30	9.4269	8.0552	7.0027	6.5660	6.1772	5.5168	4.9789	4.1601	3.5693	3.1242
35	9.6442	8.1755	7.0700	6.6166	6.2153	5.5386	4.9915	4.1644	3.5708	3.1248
40	9.7791	8.2438	7.1050	6.6418	6.2335	5.5482	4.9966	4.1659	3.5712	3.1250
45	9.8628	8.2825	7.1232	6.6543	6.2421	5.5523	4.9986	4.1664	3.5714	3.1250
50	9.9148	8.3045	7.1327	6.6605	6.2463	5.5541	4.9995	4.1666	3.5714	3.1250
55	9.9471	8.3170	7.1376	6.6636	6.2482	5.5549	4.9998	4.1666	3.5714	3.1250

Table IV. Future Value of an Annuity of $1.00 per Period

$$FVAF_{i,n} = \sum_{t=1}^{n} (1 + i)^{t-1}$$

Periods (n)	\multicolumn{10}{c}{Interest (Discount) Rate (i)}
	1%	2%	3%	4%	5%	6%	7%	8%	9%	10%
1	1.0000	1.0000	1.0000	1.0000	1.0000	1.0000	1.0000	1.0000	1.0000	1.0000
2	2.0100	2.0200	2.0300	2.0400	2.0500	2.0600	2.0700	2.0800	2.0900	2.1000
3	3.0301	3.0604	3.0909	3.1216	3.1525	3.1836	3.2149	3.2464	3.2781	3.3100
4	4.0604	4.1216	4.1836	4.2465	4.3101	4.3746	4.4399	4.5061	4.5731	4.6410
5	5.1010	5.2040	5.3091	5.4163	5.5256	5.6371	5.7507	5.8666	5.9847	6.1051
6	6.1520	6.3081	6.4684	6.6330	6.8019	6.9753	7.1533	7.3359	7.5233	7.7156
7	7.2135	7.4343	7.6625	7.8983	8.1420	8.3938	8.6540	8.9228	9.2004	9.4872
8	8.2857	8.5830	8.8923	9.2142	9.5491	9.8975	10.259	10.636	11.028	11.435
9	9.3685	9.7546	10.159	10.582	11.026	11.491	11.978	12.487	13.021	13.579
10	10.462	10.949	11.463	12.006	12.577	13.180	13.816	14.486	15.192	15.937
11	11.566	12.168	12.807	13.486	14.206	14.971	15.783	16.645	17.560	18.531
12	12.682	13.412	14.192	15.025	15.917	16.869	17.888	18.977	20.140	21.384
13	13.809	14.680	15.617	16.626	17.713	18.882	20.140	21.495	22.953	24.522
14	14.947	15.973	17.086	18.291	19.598	21.015	22.550	24.214	26.019	27.975
15	16.096	17.293	18.598	20.023	21.578	23.276	25.129	27.152	29.360	31.772
16	17.257	18.639	20.156	21.824	23.657	25.672	27.888	30.324	33.003	35.949
17	18.430	20.012	21.761	23.697	25.840	28.212	30.840	33.750	36.973	40.544
18	19.614	21.412	23.414	25.645	28.132	30.905	33.999	37.450	41.301	45.599
19	20.810	22.840	25.116	27.671	30.539	33.760	37.379	41.446	46.018	51.159
20	22.019	24.297	26.870	29.778	33.066	36.785	40.995	45.762	51.160	57.275
21	23.239	25.783	28.676	31.969	35.719	39.992	44.865	50.422	56.764	64.002
22	24.471	27.299	30.536	34.248	38.505	43.392	49.005	55.456	62.873	71.402
23	25.716	28.845	32.452	36.617	41.430	46.995	53.436	60.893	69.531	79.543
24	26.973	30.421	34.426	39.082	44.502	50.815	58.176	66.764	76.789	88.497
25	28.243	32.030	36.459	41.645	47.727	54.864	63.249	73.105	84.700	98.347
26	29.525	33.670	38.553	44.311	51.113	59.156	68.676	79.954	93.323	109.18
27	30.820	35.344	40.709	47.084	54.669	63.705	74.483	87.350	102.72	121.09
28	32.129	37.051	42.930	49.967	58.402	68.528	80.697	95.338	112.96	134.20
29	33.450	38.792	45.218	52.966	62.322	73.639	87.346	103.96	124.13	148.63
30	34.784	40.568	47.575	56.084	66.438	79.058	94.460	113.28	136.30	164.49
40	48.886	60.402	75.401	95.025	120.79	154.76	199.63	259.05	337.88	442.59
50	64.463	84.579	112.79	152.66	209.34	290.33	406.52	573.76	815.08	1163.9
60	81.669	114.05	163.05	237.99	353.58	533.12	813.52	1253.2	1944.7	3034.8

Table IV. (continued)

Periods (n)	Interest (Discount) Rate (i)									
	12%	14%	15%	16%	18%	20%	24%	28%	32%	36%
1	1.0000	1.0000	1.0000	1.0000	1.0000	1.0000	1.0000	1.0000	1.0000	1.0000
2	2.1200	2.1400	2.1500	2.1600	2.1800	2.2000	2.2400	2.2800	2.3200	2.3600
3	3.3744	3.4396	3.4725	3.5056	3.5724	3.6400	3.7776	3.9184	4.0624	4.2096
4	4.7793	4.9211	4.9934	5.0665	5.2154	5.3680	5.6842	6.0156	6.3624	6.7251
5	6.3528	6.6101	6.7424	6.8771	7.1542	7.4416	8.0484	8.6999	9.3983	10.146
6	8.1152	8.5355	8.7537	8.9775	9.4420	9.9299	10.980	12.135	13.405	14.798
7	10.089	10.730	11.066	11.413	12.141	12.915	14.615	16.533	18.695	21.126
8	12.299	13.232	13.726	14.240	15.327	16.499	19.122	22.163	25.678	29.731
9	14.775	16.085	16.785	17.518	19.085	20.798	24.712	29.369	34.895	41.435
10	17.548	19.337	20.303	21.321	23.521	25.958	31.643	38.592	47.061	57.351
11	20.654	23.044	24.349	25.732	28.755	32.150	40.237	50.398	63.121	78.998
12	24.133	27.270	29.001	30.850	34.931	39.580	50.894	65.510	84.320	108.43
13	28.029	32.088	34.351	36.786	42.218	48.496	64.109	84.852	112.30	148.47
14	32.392	37.581	40.504	43.672	50.818	59.195	80.496	109.61	149.23	202.92
15	37.279	43.842	47.580	51.659	60.965	72.035	100.81	141.30	197.99	276.97
16	42.753	50.980	55.717	60.925	72.939	87.442	126.01	181.86	262.35	377.69
17	48.883	59.117	65.075	71.673	87.068	105.93	157.25	233.79	347.30	514.66
18	55.749	68.394	75.836	84.140	103.74	128.11	195.99	300.25	459.44	700.93
19	63.439	78.969	88.211	98.603	123.41	154.74	244.03	385.32	607.47	954.27
20	72.052	91.024	102.44	115.37	146.62	186.68	303.60	494.21	802.86	1298.8
21	81.698	104.76	118.81	134.84	174.02	225.02	377.46	633.59	1060.7	1767.3
22	92.502	120.43	137.63	157.41	206.34	271.03	469.05	811.99	1401.2	2404.6
23	104.60	138.29	159.27	183.60	244.48	326.23	582.62	1040.3	1850.6	3271.3
24	118.15	158.65	184.16	213.97	289.49	392.48	723.46	1332.6	2443.8	4449.9
25	133.33	181.87	212.79	249.21	342.60	471.98	898.09	1706.8	3226.8	6052.9
26	150.33	208.33	245.71	290.08	405.27	567.37	1114.6	2185.7	4260.4	8233.0
27	169.37	238.49	283.56	337.50	479.22	681.85	1383.1	2798.7	5624.7	11197.9
28	190.69	272.88	327.10	392.50	566.48	819.22	1716.0	3583.3	7425.6	15230.2
29	214.58	312.09	377.16	456.30	669.44	984.06	2128.9	4587.6	9802.9	20714.1
30	241.33	356.78	434.74	530.31	790.94	1181.8	2640.9	5873.2	12940.	28172.2
40	767.09	1342.0	1779.0	2360.7	4163.2	7343.8	22728.	69377.	*	*
50	2400.0	4994.5	7217.7	10435.	21813.	45497.	*	*	*	*
60	7471.6	18535.	29219.	46057.	*	*	*	*	*	*

*FVAF > 99,999.

Table V. Critical Values for Student's t Distribution

Degrees of Freedom	$\alpha = 0.10$	$\alpha = 0.05$	$\alpha = 0.025$	$\alpha = 0.01$	$\alpha = 0.005$
1	3.078	6.314	12.706	31.821	63.657
2	1.886	2.920	4.303	6.965	9.925
3	1.638	2.353	3.182	4.541	5.841
4	1.533	2.132	2.776	3.747	4.604
5	1.476	2.015	2.571	3.365	4.032
6	1.440	1.943	2.447	3.143	3.707
7	1.415	1.895	2.365	2.998	3.499
8	1.397	1.860	2.306	2.896	3.355
9	1.383	1.833	2.262	2.821	3.250
10	1.372	1.812	2.228	2.764	3.169
11	1.363	1.796	2.201	2.718	3.106
12	1.356	1.782	2.179	2.681	3.055
13	1.350	1.771	2.160	2.650	3.012
14	1.345	1.761	2.145	2.624	2.977
15	1.341	1.753	2.131	2.602	2.947
16	1.337	1.746	2.120	2.583	2.921
17	1.333	1.740	2.110	2.567	2.898
18	1.330	1.734	2.101	2.552	2.878
19	1.328	1.729	2.093	2.539	2.861
20	1.325	1.725	2.086	2.528	2.845
21	1.323	1.721	2.080	2.518	2.831
22	1.321	1.717	2.074	2.508	2.819
23	1.319	1.714	2.069	2.500	2.807
24	1.318	1.711	2.064	2.492	2.797
25	1.316	1.708	2.060	2.485	2.787
26	1.315	1.706	2.056	2.479	2.779
27	1.314	1.703	2.052	2.473	2.771
28	1.313	1.701	2.048	2.467	2.763
29	1.311	1.699	2.045	2.462	2.756
inf.	1.282	1.645	1.960	2.326	2.576

Source: Statistical Methods for Research Workers, 14th edition, by R. A. Fisher. Reprinted with permission of Macmillan Publishing Company. Copyright © 1970 University of Adelaide.

Index